S9C

SHIPPING IN INTERNATIONAL TRADE RELATIONS

Dedication

To the memory of my father

Shipping in International Trade Relations

ADEMUNI-ODEKE

Maritime Consultant, Southampton

Avebury

Aldershot · Brookfield USA · Hong Kong · Singapore · Sydney

Published by
Avebury
Gower Publishing Company Limited
Gower House
Croft Road
Aldershot
Hants GU11 3HR
England

Gower Publishing Company
Old Post Road
Brookfield
Vermont 05036
USA

British Library Cataloguing in Publication Data

Ademuni-Odeke, Dr.
    Shipping in international trade relations.
    1. Commerce 2. Shipping 3. International
    economic relations
    I. Title
    382   HE582

Library of Congress Cataloging-in-Publication Data

Ademuni-Odeke, Dr.
    Shipping in international trade relations.

    Bibliography: p.
    Includes index.
    1. Shipping. 2. Commerce. 3. Maritime law.
  I. Title.
  HE571.A34 1988   387.5   87-8770

ISBN 0 566 05371 3

Printed and bound in Great Britain by
Athenaeum Press Limited, Newcastle upon Tyne

Contents

PART VI   CONCLUSIONS

ANNEXES

Tables

Foreword

In this book Dr Ademuni-Odeke has introduced a fascinating and revolutionary approach to the study and research in maritime literature in general and maritime law and policy in international relations in particular. Under one roof the author has skilfully encompassed maritime law, politics, economics, finance, and policy. Arguing that shipping has a dual character as a servant of, and itself an item of, international trade, Dr Ademuni-Odeke prepares the background by outlining the role of merchant shipping in the development and sustaining of international trade as well as its role, as a means of transportation, in the national economic development. The main body of Chapter 1 is devoted to the treatment of the liner conference system including the Code of Conduct for Liners as well as the effect of the Brussels Package in the TMNs–DMNs conflict and its bearing on the transatlantic shipping relationships. The appendix and notes add to the richness of this opening chapter, while Chapter 2 treats the open registry in a way never before attempted; the debate over this is brought up-to-date with the inclusion of discussion on the UN's newest Convention on Conditions for the Registration of Ships.

This book has perhaps no equal among the literature available in its area. The author has used his academic ability, practical experience and legal training to the best advantage. Take for instance Part II wherein he documents the implementation of shipping policies via the mechanism of protectionism, maritime subsidy and state regulations in all their multiplicity of forms as principally discriminations and preferences in international shipping. The consequences of such measures could lead to the interaction between shipping policies and international trade, especially bilateralism, CIF, and FOB operations. Should governments participate in equity and control of the shipping industry? If so, why and how? If not, why not and what is the alternative? The author does not only ask these questions, and many more, but also provides the rationale for either course of action in Part III of this book, with Chapter 5 handling 'State Control' while Chapter 6 is devoted to 'State Ownership' of the industry.

In that respect it can be said that this book partly records and discusses the main rationale for state involvement in maritime transport. It also discusses the origins, evolution and efficacy of supportive measures adopted in the developing and developed countries to augment their national fleets. The underlying theme is the pivotal role of shipping in national development and international trade relations. It is in the interdisciplinary presentation that that role can be better appreciated. This is the approach the author adopts. I have had the benefit of looking through his earlier book *Protectionism and the Future of International Shipping*: it is the same novel approach he continues here.

Having said that, of course, I do not agree with everything that Dr Ademuni-Odeke says in this book, neither do I expect other readers to. Nevertheless, I could not but agree with the persuasive arguments which he generally uses and the main thrust of his exposition in relation to the following aspects:

1   The role of merchant marines as a factor in national or regional economic development and, in particular, in the diversification of the economic structure of developing countries;
2   The relative priority of investment in shipping as compared with investment in other sectors;
3   The net effect of shipping operations on the balance of payments, especially of the developing countries;
4   National merchant marines as a factor in securing employment within a country; and
5   National merchant marines as an instrument for the promotion of exports from, especially, developing countries.

It is the deep analysis of these and many other contrasting issues which makes the book a truly important study of a very complex problem. The author does not, I am sure, expect all of us to agree with everything he says; not even I hope the writer of the Foreword.

Whether one agrees with him or not, all who are concerned with the problem of international shipping and trade relations will be grateful to him for his profound study of the efficacy of the international system. He establishes, I think, that shipping is a global process or mechanism which does result in inequality between richer and poorer nations. Having got that far, he has no difficulty in demonstrating that it is a practice which, when scrutinized, will be seen in some instances to offend everyone's sense of equality. He makes full use of notes, tables, annexes and statistics to aid his case.

The author lectures in maritime law and international trade; is a UN consultant; and Visiting Professor, in his specialization, at the prestigious (UN/IMO) World Maritime University. He is widely travelled, having been born in the DMNs and now lives in the TMNs, and has an impressive background of technical, professional and academic qualifications. Dr Ademuni-Odeke has written a formidable book encompassing different trends in world shipping: the shipping policies of individual nations and of major groupings of nations specifically the traditional maritime nations (TMNs) and the developing maritime nations (DMNs); and the implementation of shipping policies via the mechanism of protectionism, regulations, controls and the manipulation of foreign exchange quotas.

Nagendra Singh
President, International Court of Justice
Peace Palace, The Hague, The Netherlands

Winter 1987

Preface

This book examines the function of shipping in the economic, financial, legal, political and commercial relations between the trading nations of the world community. Starting with the role of transport in the economic development of a nation, it extends to the function of maritime transport in the development of international ocean-borne commerce and, therefore, in international trade relations. The book adopts an interdisciplinary approach in its treatment of all possible contributions of this key industry which is both a servant of commerce and a factor of production in its own right. Further background to these issues and themes forms the subject matter of my earlier publication *Protectionism and the Future of International Shipping*, 1984. The rationales often given for state involvement in the industry are economics, employment, balance of payments, politics and geopolitics. These issues are examined and analysed in their historical, present and future context. The strategic aspects are further covered in detail in my forthcoming book *The Role of Merchant Shipping in National Defence and Global Security*. The economic and geopolitical issues are elaborately treated in my other forthcoming book *The Political Economy of International Shipping*. A quick perusal of these sister-books would be useful. Otherwise, the present book is a comparative survey of varying state shipping practices and an analysis of their ocean-borne commercial interests within the context of different and opposing global ideologies. The module adopted is to place the traditional maritime nations (TMNs) and the developing maritime nations (DMNs) at the opposing ends of national interests with the state trading nations (STNs) in the middle ground.

The book is divided into five major parts, each comprising two chapters. Part I, 'Shipping in International Relations' describes the industry's contributions in world diplomacy. Chapter 1 opens with a revolutionary treatment of the Liner Conference System and includes discussions on the Liner Code in the light of the Brussels Package. An extensive appendix to the chapter tables all conceivable criticisms of the system. Texts of the Code and the Package come at the end of the book. Chapter 2 handles Flags of Convenience (FOCs) in a way never attempted before and includes discussions on the 'genuine link' and the new UN Convention on Conditions for Registration of Ships, 1986. A text of the Convention is annexed. Part II, 'Shipping in International Trade Relations, is in effect a consideration of the topical protectionism in international shipping. Chapter 3 covers the milder shipping preferences, while Chapter 4 is about the almost-penal shipping discriminations: including their whens, whys and hows. Part III, 'Shipping in International Politics' moves on to the interactions between state interests and international obligations. Chapter 5 evaluates political interventions in shipping, while Chapter 6 questions state participation and ownership of shipping. These are backed by statistics and tables. Part IV, 'Shipping in International Economics' is self-explanatory, with Chapter 7 sceptical about the industry's provision and defence of employment, while Chapter 8 doubts the rationale for state employment of financial and other resources into the industry: maritime subsidies. Part V concerns the all-important 'Shipping in International Finance', with Chapter 9 considering foreign exchange issues, while Chapter 10 sums it up with the balance of payments considerations. Part VI comprises the customary bibliographical details, i.e. Conclusion, Glossary, About the Author, Annexes, Author Index and Subject Index.

Never before has this style and approach to the treatment of the industry been attempted. It is humbly submitted that only this interdisciplinary stance leads to the clear understanding of the industry's history and problems, as well as to an appreciation of its future prospects. The book is a product of my practical experience of the industry, maritime consultancy and academic experiences, and took several years of preparation which included extensive travels and consultations with varying nations, individuals and organizations worldwide. I have also had to call on my legal, international relations and academic trainings. In this book I have considered conflicting interests, opposing national aspirations and differing prevailing political, economic, and other ideologies. It is a realization that the world system survives only on the basis of compromises of polarizations. Ample notes and bibliographies are provided in addition to statistics, tables, glossary, annexes, appendices, indices, a lengthy introduction and abbreviations. I believe that this work will be useful to all — researchers, diplomats, individuals, professionals, students, practitioners, executives, libraries, governments, institutions and organizations with even the most marginal of interests in any of the issues (except scientific) that are covered herein.

Ademuni-Odeke
Buckingham/Southampton

Winter 1987/88

Acknowledgements

General

The help of many people, from all corners of the globe, contributed towards this book over the last five years. To thank all organizations and individuals involved, both directly and indirectly, would need another whole book. I would like to thank all in this brief statement and would like to draw the reader's attention to the list of some of these individuals and organizations. However, my special gratitudes go to: His Excellency, the Honourable Justice Nagendra Singh, President of the International Court of Justice, The Hague, for writing the Foreword; Professor John Wilson, Institute of Maritime Law, Southampton University, for reading through and commenting on the first draft; Jacqueline Betteridge (Whitenap), Amanda Nicholls, Susan Kilpatrick and Maureen Mercer (Aberdeen) for their patient secretarial assistance over the years; and above all to Helmy and Zinzi for their encouragement, support and understanding. However, the final responsibility for any shortcomings, or errors, and for the views herein expressed, remains with the author.

Individuals

Honourable Justice Nagendra Singh, ICJ, The Hague
Professor John Wilson, Maritime Institute, Southampton

Helmy M. Duyvesteyn, Southampton
Zinzile Anke Ademuni-Odeke, Southampton
Jacqueline Betteridge, Whitenap, Hampshire
Susan Kilpatrick, Aberdeen University, Scotland
Amanda Nicholls, Aberdeen University, Scotland
Maureen Mercer, Aberdeen University, Scotland
Jeff Fanning, Nautical College, Warshash
Margaret Woodford, Nautical College, Warshash
Paula Noble, Nautical College, Warshash
Jacqueline Larmer, Aberdeen, Scotland
Dr Rosalind Shaw, Aberdeen University, Scotland
Dr Auni Benham, UNCTAD Secretariat, Geneva
Dr Rainer Vogel, UNCTAD Secretariat, Geneva
Joan Hoyle, Library, University of Southampton
Diana Marshallsay, Library, University of Southampton
Professor Stanley Sturmey, Piraus, Greece
Frederick Korswagen, Lima, Peru
Dr Omar Franco, Caracas, Venezuela
Dr Anil Vitharana, Safat, Kuwait
Richard Gage, MARAD, Miami, USA
Dr Mark Camilleri, Valetta, Malta
Stephen Orosz, MARAD, London
Dr Ralph Beddard, Law Faculty, Southampton University
Professor Robert Grime, Law Faculty, Southampton University
Dr David Petropoulos, Transport Commission, EEC, Brussels
David Ross, Library, London School of Economic and Political Science
Mrs Ann Cox, National Library of Scotland, Edinburgh

Institutions

Aberdeen University
African Exenterprises, London
African Educational Trust, London
Bremen Institute of Shipping Economics, Bremen
Canadian Marine Transport Centre, Dalhousie
Canadian Transport Commission, Ottawa
College of Nautical Studies, Warshash, Southampton
Dalhousie Ocean Development Programme, Halifax
European Economic Community, Brussels
Federal Maritime Commission, Washington DC
General Council of British Shipping, London
Inter-Library Loan Services, Southampton University
Inter-Library Loan Services, Aberdeen University

International Chamber of Commerce, Paris
International Chamber of Shipping, London
International Labour Organization, Geneva
International Maritime Organization (IMO), London
International Monetary Fund, Washington DC
International University Exchange Fund, Geneva
Institute of Maritime Law, Law Faculty, Southampton University
Lloyds List, London
Lloyds Register of Shipping, London
Maritime Administration, Washington DC
National Library of Economic and Political Science, London
National Library of Scotland, Edinburgh
Nautical Institute, London
Netherlands Maritime Research Institute, Rotterdam
Organization for Economic Cooperation and Development, Paris
Seatrade, Academy, Cambridge
Seatrade, Colchester
University of Aberdeen, Old Aberdeen, Scotland
United Nations Conference on Trade and Development, Geneva
United Nations Economic and Social Commission for Asia and Pacific–Bangkok–Thailand
University of Southampton, Southampton
University of Wales, Institute of Science and Technology, Cardiff
World Bank (IBRD), Washington DC
World Maritime University, Malmo
World University Service (UK), London

Abbreviations

ABP	Associated British Ports
AID	Agency for International Development (USA)
AMPTC	Arab Maritime Petroleum Transport Company
ANCAP	National Fuels, Alcohol and Portland Cement Administration (Uruguay)
ASEAN	Association of South East Asian Nations
ATDAA	Agricultural Trade Development and Assistance Act (USA)
BIMCO	Baltic and International Maritime Conference
BISPCO	British and Irish Steam Packet Company Limited (Irish)
BMLA	British Maritime Law Association
BP	British Petroleum
BR	British Rail
BSC	British Shipbuilders' Corporation
BSF	British Shippers' Federation (Association)
BSRA	British Ship Research Association
BTBD	British Transport Docks Board
CAACE	Comité des Associations d'Armateurs des Communautés Européenes
CALTRAM	Compagnie Algéria-Libyenne de Transport Maritime
CAVN	Compania Anonima Venezuelana de Navigacion (Venezuela)
CCF	Capital Construction Fund (USA)

CEN(J)SA	Council of European and Japanese National Ship-owners' Association
CENSA	Committee of European Shipowners' Association (see CES)
CES	Committee of European Shipowners (see CENSA)
CEWAL	Conferences of the Associated Central and West African Lines
CGM	Compagnie Generale Maritime (French)
CIF	'Cost insurance freight'
CIPE	Comitato Interministeriale per la Programmazione Economica (Italian)
CMEA	Council for Mutual Economic Assistance (see COMECON)
CMI	Comité Maritime Internationale
CMZ	Compagnie Maritime Zaïroise
CNAN	Compagnie Nationale Algérienne de Navigation
CNAP	Consorcio Naviera Peruoma SA (Peru)
COMANAV	Compagnie Marocain de Navigation
COMECON	Commission for Economic Cooperation (see CMEA)
COMPSA	Compania Arrendataria Monopolis de Petroleons SA (Colombia)
CPP	Corporacion Peruana Peruoma (Peru)
CPSA	Corporacion Naviera Peruana Sudamericana (Peru)
CPV	Compania Panana de Vapores (Chile)
CRF	Construction Reserve Fund (USA)
CSAV	Compania Sudamericana de Vapores (Chile)
CSG	Consultative Shipping Group
DBP	Development Bank of the Philippines
DHSS	Department of Health and Social Security (UK)
DMNs	Developing maritime nations
DOA	Department of Agriculture (USA)
DOC	Department of Commerce (USA)
DOCENAVE	Vale de Rio Doce Navegaco SS (Brazil)
DOJ	Department of Justice (USA) (The Judiciary)
DOT	Department of Trade (USA)
dwt	Deadweight tons (see grt)
EAC	East African Community (former)
ECA	Economic Commission for Africa (UN)
ECAFE	Economic Commission for Asia and the Far East (UN)
ECE	Economic Commission for Europe (UN)
ECLA	Economic Commission for Latin America (UN)
ECOSOC	Economic and Social Council (of the UN)
ECOWAS	Economic Organization of West African States

EEC	European Economic Community
EEZ	Exclusive Economic Zone
EFTA	European Free Trade Area
ELMA	Empressa Lineas Maritimas Argentinas
EMPREMAR	Empressa Maritimas del Estado (Brazil)
EPU	European Payments Union
ERP	European Recovery Programme (under Marshall Plan)
EUSC	Effective United States Control
EXIMBANK	Export-Import Bank (USA, Japan)
FAMCO	Federal Arab Maritime Company
FAO	Food and Agricultural Programme (UN) (Rome)
FINCANTIERI	Finanziaria Cantieri Navali (Italian)
FINMARE	Financia Maritima
FMB	Federal Maritime Board (USA; see FMC)
FMC	Federal Maritime Commission (USA; successor of FMB)
FMG	Federal Maritime Grancolombiana (Colombia)
FOA	Foreign Operations Administration (USA)
FOB	Free on board
FOC	Flag of Convenience
FRG	Federal Republic of Germany (West Germany)
FRONAPE	Flota Nacionale de Petroleiros (Brazil)
GATT	General Agreements on Tariffs and Trade
GAZOCEAN	Moroccan-French Gas Company
GCBS	General Council of British Shipping
GDP	Gross Domestic Product (see GNP)
GDR	German Democratic Republic (DDR; East Germany)
GMTC	General Maritime Transport Company (Libya)
GNP	Gross National Product (see GDP)
grt	Gross registered tons (see dwt)
IAC	International Admiralty Court (Appellate) (see IDC)
IBRD	International Bank for Reconstruction and Development (World Bank)
ICA	International Cooperation Administration (USA)
ICFTU	International Confederation of Free Trade Unions
ICJ	International Court of Justice
IDA	International Development Association
IDC	International Admiralty Court (see IAC)
IFC	International Finance Corporation
ILC	International Law Commission
ILO	International Labour Organization

IMF	International Monetary Fund
IMO	International Maritime Organization (successor of IMCO)
IMS	International Monetary System
INI	Industriale Nacionale Italia
INTERTANKO	International Association of Independent Tanker Owners
IRI	Instituto per la Ricostruziane Industriale (Italian)
ISC	Irish Shipping Company
ISF	International Shipping Federation
ITO	International Trade Organization (forerunner of GATT)
ITWF	International Transport Workers' Federation
LAFTA	Latin American Free Trade Area
LAMCO	Liberian Mining Corporation
LASH	Lighters Aboard Ship
LDCs	Less Developed Countries
LNG	Liquefied natural gas (carriers)
Lo–lo	Lift on, lift off
LSC	Liberian Shipping Corporation
LSE	London School of Economics and Political Science
MARAD	Maritime Administration (USA)
MARINA	Maritime Industry Authority (Philippines)
MARPHOCEAN	Marocain Phosphate Ocean
MFN(C)	Most Favoured Nation (Clause)
MISC	Malaysian International Shipping Corporation
MIT	Massachusetts Institute of Technology
MNCs	Multinational corporations
MSE	Multinational shipping enterprise
NATO	North Atlantic Treaty Organization
NDRF	National Defence Reserve Fleets
NEDCO	National Development Council
NIC	National Industry Commission (Peru)
NICs	Newly industrialized countries
NIEO	New International Economic Order
NIMO	New International Maritime Order
NNSL	Nigerian National Shipping Line
NUS	National Union of Seamen
NY	New York
OAS	Organization of American States
OAU	Organization for African Unity
OBO	Oil–bulk–ore (combine carriers)
OCP	L'Office Chirifione de Phosphate (Moroccan)
ODS	Operating-differential subsidy

OECD	Organization for Economic Cooperation and Development (successor of OEEC)
OEEC	Organization for European Economic Cooperation (see OECD)
OPEC	Organization of Petroleum Exporting Countries
OUP	Oxford University Press
Panlibho	Panamanian, Liberian and Honduras (see FOC)
PCL	Polytechnic of Central London
PEMEX	Petroleos Mexicanos
PERNI	Indonesian National Shipping Line
PSC	Provident Shipping Company (Liberia)
RBPCs	Restrictive Business Practices
R & D	Research and Design (Department of British Ship Research Association)
RDF	Rapid Deployment Force
RNSA	Royal Netherlands Shipowners' Association
ROC	Republic of China (Nationalist) (Taiwan, Formosa)
RORO(s)	Roll-on, roll-off(s)
SAFMARINE	South African Marine
SAS	Scandinavian Airline Services
SCINDIA	Shipping Corporation of India
SCs	Socialist Countries
SDR	Special Drawing Rights
SEA	South East Asia
SEATO	South East Asian Treaty Organization (see ASEAN)
SIMA	Peruvian national shipyards
SONATRACH	Société Nationale pour la Recherche, la Production, le Transport, la Transformation, et la Commercialisation des Hydrocarbones (Algeria)
STNs	State trading nations (Planned Economics)
SUNAMAM	Superintendency of the National Merchant Marine (Brazil)
TCM	Export Development Corporation (Portugal)
TDB	Trade and Development Board (of UNCTAD)
TISC	Total Investment Shipping Company (Liberia)
TMM	Transportacion Maritima Mexicano (Mexico)
TMN(s)	Traditional maritime nation(s)
TW	Third World
UAE	United Arab Emirates
UAR	United Arab Republic (Egypt)
UDI	Unilateral Declaration of Independence
UK	United Kingdom (England, Ulster, Wales, Scotland, Isle of Man, Channel Isles)
UN(O)	United Nations (Organization)

UNCLOS	United Nations Conference on the Law of the Sea
UNCTAD	United Nations Conference on Trade and Development
UNDP	United Nations Development Programme
UNESCO	United Nations Educational Scientific and Cultural Organization
UNIDO	United Nations Industrial Development Organization
USC	United States Codes
USC	Universal Shipping Company (Libya)
US CONG	United States Congress
US SEN	United States Senate
VAT	Value Added Tax
VCD	Verolme Cork Dockyard (Irish)
WHO	World Health Organization
WMU	World Maritime University
YPF	Yacimientos Petroliteros Fiscales (Argentine oil company)
ZIM Lines	Israeli National Shipping Line

Flag abbreviations

Ag	Algeria	Co	Colombia
Al	Albania	CR	Costa Rica
Am	USA	Cu	Cuba
An	Angola	CV	Cape Verde
Ar	Argentina	Cy	Cyprus
As	Austria	Cz	Czechoslovakia
Au	Australia	Da	Denmark
Ba	Bahrain	DD	East Germany (Democratic Republic)
Bd	Barbados		
Be	Belgium	Do	Dominican Republic
Bh	Bangladesh	Du	Netherlands
Bm	Burma	Ec	Ecuador
Bn	Benin	Eg	Egypt
Bo	Bolivia	ES	El Salvador
Br	United Kingdom and Colonies	Et	Ethiopia
		Fa	Faroes
Bs	Bahamas	Fi	Finland
Bu	Bulgaria	Fj	Fiji
Bz	Brazil	Fr	France
Ca	Canada	Ga	Gabon
Ce	Sri Lanka (Ceylon)	Ge	West Germany (Federal Republic)
Ch	Chile		
Cm	Comoros	Gh	Ghana
Cn	Cameroun	Gm	Gambia

Gn	Guinea	Ph	Poland
Gr	Greece	Pk	Pakistan
Gu	Guatemala	Po	Portugal
Ha	Haiti	Pp	Philippines
Ho	Honduras	Pv	Peru
Hu	Hungary	Py	Paraguay
Ia	Indonesia	RC	Peoples Republic of China
Ic	Iceland		
Ih	Irish Republic	RK	North Korea
In	India	Rm	Romania
Iq	Iraq	Ru	USSR
Ir	Iran	SA	South Africa
Is	Israel	Sc	Seychelles
It	Italy	Se	Senegal
Iv	Ivory Coast	Sg	Singapore
Ja	Japan	Si	Saudi Arabia
Jm	Jamaica	SL	Sierra Leone
Jo	Jordan	Sn	Suriname
Ke	Kenya	So	Somalia
Ko	South Korea	Sp	Spain
Ku	Kuwait	Ss	Switzerland
Le	Lebanon	Su	Sudan
Li	Liberia	SV	St Vincent and Grenadines
Ly	Libya	Sw	Sweden
Ma	Malta	Sy	Syria
Mb	Mozambique	Ta	Tanzania
Me	Mexico	Tg	Togo
Mg	Madagascar	Th	Thailand
Mn	Monaco	Tn	Tunisia
Mo	Morocco	To	Tongo
Ms	Mauritius	Tr	Trinidad and Tobago
Mt	Mauritania	Tu	Turkey
Mv	Maldives	Tw	Taiwan
My	Malaysia	UA	United Arab Emirates
NA	Netherlands Antilles	Ug	Uganda
Ne	Nepal	Ur	Uruguay
Ng	Nigeria	Va	Vanautu
Ni	Nicaragua	Ve	Venezuela
No	Norway	Vn	Vietnam
Nu	Nauru	WS	Western Samoa
NZ	New Zealand	Ye	Yemen (Democratic Republic)
Om	Oman	Ys	Yugoslavia
Pa	Panama	Za	Zambia
PG	Papua New Guinea	Zr	Zaire

Introduction

Shipping in International Trade Relations explores the role of merchant marines in the political, economic, financial and trade development of the national economy and in the international trade relations between states and individuals of the world community. In its analysis of these crucial factors this book adopts a multidisciplinary approach to the subject of international–ocean-borne commerce, encompassing law, economics, finance, politics, trade, geopolitics, transportation, statistics, and their related aspects. The treatment of these issues throughout bears in mind the five factors that come into the interplay:

1 The role of merchant marines as a factor in national or regional economic development and, in particular, in the diversification of the economic structure of developing countries;
2 The relative priority of investment in shipping as compared with investment in other sectors;
3 The net effect of shipping operations on the balance of payments, especially of the developing countries;
4 National merchant marines as a factor in securing employment within a country; and
5 National merchant marines as an instrument for the promotion of exports from, especially, developing countries.

These, it is submitted, are within the spirit of the aspirations of

1

many a nation to establish and or develop own national fleets for which rationales are normally given as economic, political, employ- ment and geopolitical (i.e. national security and defence). These are also sometimes summarized as the seven sister reasons:

1 Prevention of disruptions of services during hostilities: the availability of shipping in times of war as an important factor for countries that are not themselves directly involved in the hostilities;
2 Reduction of economic dependence: a number of countries have considered that the economic dependence implied by com- plete reliance on foreign shipping is a permanent source of difficulty for a non-maritime nation;
3 Influencing conference decisions: many countries have mis- givings about the operation of liner conferences whose rate agreements, control of sailings, loyalty ties and so forth involve a considerable departure from free competition;
4 Economic integration: in countries with a long coastline in re- lation to their area, or with difficult terrain, or which consist of a number of separate land areas such as island archipelagoes, a shipping fleet linking the various parts of the nation may be essential;
5 Promotion of exports: trade cannot occur between nations unless means of communication are developed; the provision of shipping services is generally one of the most important prerequisites of the development of international trade;
6 Provision of employment, including the diversification of that employment; needed because the economics of, especially, developing countries are often heavily influenced by conditions in comparatively few product markets; and above all
7 Earnings and/or savings of foreign exchange: the establishment of a national shipping industry is widely regarded by, especially, the developing countries as a means of earning or saving foreign currency.

Shipping in International Relations

The first theme of this book is that shipping has been (and will remain) an important tool of international relations: the practice of conducting relations between states. Shipping seems to be involved in the entire foreign relations process, policy formulations as well as executions — at least in the case of the major TMNs. Shipping assists in the means and mechanisms towards the achievements of ends and objectives in foreign relations. In this more restricted role the function of shipping includes the operational techniques whereby a state pursues its interests beyond its jurisdiction. The extraterritoriality of the shipping industry makes it suitable as a vital tool of foreign, as well as domestic, policy. Increasing interdependence of states has steadily expanded the number of international meetings and the instances of multilateral conference and parliamentary diplomacy. These were made possible by shipping, first by creating and then expanding international trade. Before air services, shipping was the only method of international travel. In terms of the use of force, gunboat diplomacy comes readily to mind. Although this book is dedicated to merchant shipping, nevertheless it cannot be divorced from the naval aspects of shipping. States deal with one another on such a great number of occasions and topics, however, that the bulk of international relations activity remains bilateral and is conducted through the normal diplomatic channels of the foreign ministry and the resident diplomatic mission.

Critical issues are sometimes negotiated at the highest level, involving heads of government in summit diplomacy. Nevertheless annexes, such as the International Maritime Organization (IMO), International Labour Organization (ILO), United Nations Conference on Trade and Development (UNCTAD) and the Third United Nations Conference on the Law of the Sea (UNCLOS III), where shipping issues dominate, have become as important if not more important channels of settling international relations. In this respect one aspect of shipping has been the promotion of exports. Trade cannot occur between countries unless means of communication are developed. The provision of shipping services is generally one of the most important prerequisites for the development of international trade. It is often argued that the existence of national flag carriers on a trading route will promote the national export trade. There are two aspects to this issue which must be clearly separated. First, in historical terms, there is the provision of shipping services between a metropolitan country and a colony for the purpose of expanding the export trade of one or both. Secondly, there is the provision of a fleet to trade between two nations. More and better trade means better relations, although the reverse is not necessarily true. The first case is a special one since, even without cabotage restrictions which reserved the trade to national ships, the shipping of the metropolitan country was generally preferred to foreign ships. The result was that a position of dominance was built up in the trade which, in many cases, has survived the change of status of the countries. The second aspect of the question embraces two separate issues, namely whether the use of national flag ships is in some way more likely to increase national trade than is the use of foreign ships, and whether national ships may be needed because foreign ships, for whatever reasons, are not operating in the trade.

In general it appears that if a potentially viable trade exists, then trade will take place no matter who provides the ships. But this does not answer the question of whether foreign lines will, in fact, provide the ships since the provision of tonnage for new trades is not in any sense automatic, but requires a conscious innovating decision which may not be forthcoming. Be that as it may, the other crucial function of national merchant marines in international economics is to be found in the reduction of economic dependence. A number of countries have considered that the economic dependence implied by complete reliance on foreign shipping is a permanent source of difficulty for both the DMNs and the non-maritime nations. For such countries, the dominance of foreign shipping enterprises in the seaborne trade appears to leave vital questions of freight rates and services in hands over which the nation concerned may have some influence but over which it has no direct control. The problem of defence is partly related to conferences and partly related to FOC fleets, but is wider than this. There is the fear that tonnage may be withdrawn from the trade when more profitable alternative opportunities occur, and also the very real problem that a trade which is too small to support rival services in competition may be served by old or unsuitable ships. How real are these fears of dependence on foreign shipping depends largely on the extent of competition in the provision of services. These issues (liner conferences and the FOC operations) are analysed in Part I (Chapters 1–2) of this book.

Shipping in International Trade

Secondly, shipping is considered vital in international trade. One aspect of this relates to economic integration. Transport and communication are a vital prerequisite for any form of economic and political integration of states. As mentioned later in Chapter 9, developments in shipping contribute decisively to the integration of, especially, the developing countries into the world economy. While this integration could theoretically be achieved no matter who provides the services, only the existence of a national fleet — and consequently of effective control of shipping services — can ensure that the transport links needed to maintain the integration process are not duly interrupted. Unfortunately the traditional pattern of shipping services has linked the DMNs only to the TMNs.

4

Lack of linkage among the DMNs has created an economic distance, inhibiting trade flows among them. In other words, the emphasis of the North–South pattern has been to the detriment (and expense) of the South–South linkage.

Another aspect of economic integration through an engagement in shipping relates to the provision of services itself. Although this has not been dealt with adequately in this book, suffice it to say that shipping development for most DMNs is a matter of finance and manpower. These resources are not equally distributed among the DMNs. While some DMNs have a large pool of trained labour but lack finance, others lacking the necessary labour of sufficient quality and quantity have an abundance of finance.

It is not only these differences in factor endowments that cause shipping to be a particularly suitable area of cooperation in international trade. The inherent internationality of the industry as well as the mobility of assets are equal, if not more important, factors. As has just been noted above, in countries with a long coastal line in relation to their area, or with difficult terrain or which consist of a number of separate land areas such as island archipelagoes, a shipping fleet linking the various parts of the nation may be essential. Norway, for example, has assisted its coastal shipping for this reason. The DMNs examples are the Philippines and Indonesia. The type of ships required may be quite different from those used in international trading so that local shipping and international shipping exist as separate enterprises with no interchange or interaction. On the other hand, the type of ship used in the coastal trade may be so similar to those used in international trades that they can easily be switched between the two types of trades, although the growth in the use of roll-on, roll-off (RORO) ships in coastal services makes this increasingly difficult. In the case of switching in the physical sense, however, it does not necessarily mean that it is economic to combine local or regional shipping activities with international shipping. Indeed even in such countries as Australia and the US, where the ships used in coastal trades could be used in international trades, it is usual to keep the two activities separate.

In the particular case of coastal trade, most nations are unwilling to permit any dependence upon foreign shipping. This type of trade is then reserved to their own flag by cabotage restrictions. By such measures the nation achieves considerable control over a means of transport which may be an important factor in maintaining national economic unification. Chile, Australia and the US are examples of countries with an important reserved coastal trade. The latter, in fact, includes transport between Hawaii and the US mainland by means of ocean-going ships working within the concept of the coastal trade.

5

This contrasts with the coastal trade of the UK to which no cabotage restrictions are applied. In the past many countries with colonial interests felt that only nationally owned ships could provide the essential links between the metropolitan and colonial territories. In recent years, countries embarking upon schemes of regional economic integration have similarly felt that shipping services and rates between the participating countries are important aspects of the international process which should be under regional control. This was the case, for example, with LAFTA (Latin American Free Trade Area), the EAC (East African Community) and now with ECOWAS (Economic Organization of West African States). Thus integration relates to the domestic as well as the foreign trade, just as shipping contributes to both the national and international development and trade. These are some of the issues covered in Part II of this book with Chapter 3 dealing with preferences and Chapter 4 with discriminations in international trade.

Shipping and International Politics

Thirdly, shipping is an essential element in international politics. The creation of a national fleet is an important element in attaining and maintaining national independence, and national independence rather than autarchy is a prerequisite for political integration on the basis of equality. Consequently, striving for independence is not contrary to integration but is a condition for its attainment. Another element of independence is the safeguarding of supplies for the national economy and population in times of political crisis. This supply function of shipping is generally recognized and is one reason why most countries, whether TMNs or DMNs, maintain a minimum level of maritime engagement. The necessary engagement would not go so far as to ensure autarchy in times of absolute non-availability of shipping services but would rather be kept at a level either preventing a complete breakdown of national economic activities or maintaining the functioning of the economy at times of exceptional scarcity of tonnage caused by external factors. This is linked with the geopolitical functions of national fleets: prevention of disruptions of services during wars and/or hostilities. The availability of shipping in wartime is an important factor for countries that are not themselves directly involved in the hostilities. In both World Wars leading DMNs requisitioned parts of their own merchant fleets and this affected both the freight rates charged and the services that were available to other countries heavily dependent upon these foreign-owned vessels.

In major wars in the past, services were disrupted and freight rates rose owing to the difficulties and dangers of operation. Even conflicts on a smaller scale — for example the Korean hostilities, the Vietnam war and now the Iran–Iraq war — can lead to disrupted services and sharply rising freight rates, but this would not adversely affect the balance of payments. Domestic industries could be partly or wholly compensated for any adverse effects of the higher freight rates — for example, by means of revenue collected from a special tax imposed on the higher profits of the national shipping line. Between August 1950 and November 1961, as a result of the Korean hostilities, for example, the tramp trip charter rates more than doubled, tanker voyage charter rates more than trebled and the limited sample of liner rates covered by the index published in the Federal Republic of Germany rose by nearly 50 per cent. Such rises are extremely serious for countries which have to pay a larger part of their freight bills in foreign currency and may also cause the exports of such countries to be priced out of markets where they are competing with home-produced goods or those from less distant sources. One of the DMNs badly affected by this kind of problem during the Second World War was Argentina, whose foreign trade declined by 60 per cent between 1939 and 1943. This decline in foreign trade stimulated Argentina's interests in industrialization generally, and the establishment of a national merchant marine was an important part of its post-war industrialization programme, which was designed to raise the level of national income.

The experience of Chile at the same time was similar — the withdrawal of foreign tankers had widespread adverse effects on the national economy. In recent times the threatened withdrawal of Aramco tankers, as a result of the Saudi King's proclamations and similar threats from President Tolbert of Liberia have been documented in Chapter 2. Briefly, these occurred during the 1967 and 1973 Arab–Israeli Wars: the Saudis were angered by American support for Israel while the Liberians reacted on Israeli occupation of Sinai — an African territory. Both times the aim was, *inter alia*, to deny the use of these tankers to the American forces in Europe. The US response in 1974 was the enactment of the Security Transportation Act and the reappraisal of both the EUSC (Effective United States Control) and the NDRF (National Defence Reserve Fleets) principles. So it can happen not only to the DMNs but to a leading TMN as well. Geopolitical reasons are also behind the establishment of the system of essential trade routes as enunciated by the US, and documented in Chapter 5 of this book. More recently the role of the merchant marines in geopolitics was more than illustrated in their participation in the Falklands war, the details of which are to be found in the forthcoming sister book to this: *The Role of Merchant*

Shipping in National Defence and Global Security. One should also mention the role of merchant marines in the proposed Rapid Deployment Force (RDF). These, *inter alia*, are the issues covered in Part III (Chapters 5 and 6) of this book.

Shipping in International Economics

The foregone discussions lead to (and are interrelated to) the fourth theme of this book: the role of merchant shipping in international economics. Contrary to what the subtitle suggests, the issues discussed are mainly the provision and diversification of employment. It is often claimed that, as a capital-intensive industry, shipping is not an appropriate area of investment for, especially, the DMNs in view of their scarcity of capital and abundance of labour. While the capital intensity of shipping is not disputed, a number of factors have to be taken into account to put the issue into the right perspective. First, a differentiation must be made among the various types of shipping since their employment effects vary considerably. At one extreme there are forms of specialized shipping that are highly capital-intensive and these will generally not be provided by independent owners. However, even with regard to shipping services provided independently, employment effects vary considerably both quantitatively and qualitatively. Capital requirements per job directly or indirectly linked to liner shipping are much lower than those for bulk shipping, due to much higher labour requirements for shore-based administrative and support services. Similarly, the quality of labour requirements differs greatly. While such differences do not exist with regard to ship-based personnel, these employment considerations have led the DMNs to concentrate their activities on liner shipping in the early stage of fleet establishment and expansion and only later to diversify into bulk shipping.

The actual level of capital required per job in shipping cannot be generally determined. However, it can be positively stated that investment in shipping creates employment of a relatively high quality in the shipping companies themselves as well as in the numerous support activities. The DMNs have been quite capable of providing the adequate manpower at all levels to fulfil these tasks, a fact which is underlined by the growing tendency of shipowners in the TMNs to resort to employment of shipboard personnel from the DMNs generally and the FOC in particular. The fact that labour costs are the only cost item that varies considerably from country to country is indicative of the shift of comparative advantages in favour of the DMNs. The second facet to this theme is the diversification of

8

employment. Diversification of employment is needed because the economics of the DMNs in particular are often heavily influenced by conditions in a comparatively few product markets, with the result that unfavourable developments in them can have widespread consequences throughout the economies concerned. Direct employment in shipping is a distinctive type of economic activity and the fluctuations in shipping are not closely related to the fluctuations in other single markets, but to the world trading situation in general. It may be noted here that the diversification of employment does not necessarily entail the establishment of a national merchant marine. To some extent, the employment market for seamen is international in nature, particularly in the FOC fleets.

To say that the market is *completely* international can be rather misleading. For some reasons of national security or in response to trade union pressure, many countries have rules concerning the nationality of crews. Such rules may require wholly national manning or may require that all the officers and a certain percentage of other crew members be nationals. The existence of language difficulties further limits the international nature of the labour market for seamen. Otherwise, opportunities for employment as seamen are not completely restricted to the nationals of countries with shipping fleets. If national seamen can be employed in foreign ships, the effects of employment diversification are the same as if they had been employed in national fleets. If they are then repatriated to work in national ships, their employment has no further favourable effects on the diversification of employment in the home economy. An important feature of such employment (that is, in foreign ships), is that it provides training for seamen. The extensive employment of Indian personnel in British ships provided a reservoir of trained labour on which the Indian shipping industry was able to draw. Any country now contemplating the establishment of a national fleet might well note that encouragement to nationals to seek employment in foreign ships simplifies the task of establishing its own national fleet. This has also been cited as an advantage of the FOC fleets. One valuable form of assistance which the TMNs can give to the DMNs is in the training of officers, crew members and other personnel needed in their own shipping industry. These issues, *inter alia*, are the subject of discussion in Part IV (Chapters 7 and 8).

Shipping in International Finance

The fifth, and final, theme of this book concerns the function of merchant marines in international finance: the earning and/or saving of foreign exchange and the consequent improvement of a country's balance of payments position. The establishment of a national shipping industry is widely regarded by the DMNs especially, as a means of earning or saving foreign exchange. This may arise from actual balance-of-payments difficulties in which case the establishment of a national merchant marine is seen as possibly contributing to the solution of those difficulties. Consideration of the balance of payments is not limited to countries which are actually experiencing difficulties since the maintenance of a balance-of-payments equilibrium is desirable for all countries engaged in international trade. The DMNs, especially, as a group have an unfavourable balance on the maritime transport account of the balance of payments, this being implicit in their relatively small share of world tonnage. As specialization is the basis of trade, there is no reason why any particular country or group of countries should necessarily expect its international receipts and payments for any one type of economic activity to balance. But it is natural that each country, in attempting to create or maintain equilibrium in its international payments, should consider how deficit items may be reduced as well as how credit items may be increased (see also Chapter 10).

Each country will naturally be seeking the most economic use of its resources. But as special difficulties may arise from existing forms of protection in world trade (see Chapters 3-5) — for example, tariffs, import quotas and other non-tariff measures), the combination of resources which would be most economically desirable in a free trade situation may yield a product which, because of trade restrictions and barriers, in practice cannot be sold in world markets at a price which is economic to the producer. In such a situation, which is likely to be particularly relevant for the DMNs, it is not surprising that they should resort to measures which, under a regime of completely free and undistorted international trade, would be considered an uneconomic use of resources. Classical economists, beginning with John Locke and Adam Smith, have claimed that the artificial protection of certain domestic industries whose products could be bought cheaper abroad and the artificial limitation of the most efficient foreign producer's market results in a misallocation of resources that impedes the nation's and the world's economic welfare. This view has been disputed on political, military and ethical grounds by the DMNs who sought to subsidize and protect their newly established national fleets. And they are not the only ones who dispute these classical arguments. The rationales for departure given by the DMNs are true also of the TMNs, to an extent that, in international trade relations, protectionism is now more of a general rule than an exception.

10

The DMNs' economic argument against it is generally based on one of these grounds:

1 that a judicious tariff structure (the optimum tariff) can (if other countries do not retaliate by levying a tariff of their own) improve a country's commodity terms of trade, on balance of payments;
2 that the concentrated injury to an important industry (such as shipping) which loses its tariff protection outweighs the broadly scattered benefits of tariff reduction to the rest of the economy; and
3 that a new or infant industry (such as their new national fleets) requires tariff protection while it is growing to the size and efficiency that will subsequently assure its success in a world of free trade.

Recourse to such measures by individual countries in the real world of trade restrictions may be a rational method of attempting to increase national income, in the sense that they lead to the attainment of a solution which is optional within the existing constraints, although it would be sub-optional if the conditions could be changed, for instance, by removing trade barriers. These are among the issues discussed in Part V of this book; with Chapter 9 dealing with shipping and foreign exchange and Chapter 10, shipping and the balance of payments.

PART I
SHIPPING IN
INTERNATIONAL RELATIONS

1 Liner conferences

Introduction

After the Second World War, there was mounting pressure, notably from Third World Countries, for a worldwide regime for liner shipping. Developing countries (who were at the time understandably conscious of their new national identities) thought their vital commercial and industrial interests were too much in the hands of shipowners from the developed world. They felt they were being squeezed and wanted a bigger say in the operation and profits of the shipping services which affected them. The matter was raised in the middle and late 1960s in UNCTAD where developed countries made a number of concessions. As these did not, however, extend to the crucial issue of the determination of freight rates, there was increased pressure for worldwide rules.[1]

Progress was made both in the developed world and in UNCTAD. In the United Kingdom a Committee of Enquiry under Viscount Rochdale was appointed in July 1967 to look into shipping policy generally. When it reported in May 1970, the Committee 'concluded that as a condition of shipowners whether United Kingdom or foreign, continuing to benefit from the operation of restrictive agreements relating to trade to and from the United Kingdom, members of conferences should collectively accept a published Code of Conference Practice'. Thereafter the Ministers of the Consultative Shipping Group (CSG), meeting in Tokyo in February 1971, enjoined shippers and shipowners to establish a Code of Practice before 31 December 1971. The Code which emerged (generally known as the CENSA/CES Code) was subsequently accepted by Ministers of CSG countries, but did not prove to be so popular outside the developed world. Meanwhile, within UNCTAD, it had been decided to include the Code in the provisional agenda for UNCTAD III (April–May 1972). After long negotiations the Final Act of the UN Conference of Plenipotentiaries on a Code of Conduct for Liner Conferences emerged at Geneva on 6 April 1974.[2]

The UN Code attracted much support in the developing world, but received a mixed reception in the developed world. Some Western countries, such as France, Belgium and the Federal Republic of Germany, voted in its favour; others, notably the United Kingdom, USA and Denmark, were opposed. The desire of several member states to join the UN Code presented the EEC with a dilemma. Adoption of the Code by some Member States and not others would have resulted in wide divergence between national shipping practices in the Community. Eventually a common position on the Code was achieved in 1979 in the form of Regulation 954/79, the 'Brussels Package'. That regulation required Member States to adopt the Code subject to certain modifications, the most important of which are that in conference trade between Member States the cargo-allocation provisions of the Code (the '40–40–20 provision') are not to apply and that the mechanism for resolving disputes is to be replaced by other adjudication procedures more suited to the Community. Where suitable reciprocal arrangements can be negotiated with other OECD (Organization for Economic Cooperation and Development) countries the Code is to be applied with similar modifications in conference trade between the Community and those third countries. In the United Kingdom both the Code and the 1979 Regulation have now been implemented by means of the Merchant Shipping (Liner Conferences) Act 1982. The Code will come into force six months from the date when 24 states, controlling 25 per cent of the world liner tonnage have ratified or acceded to the convention. Ratification, on 6 April 1983, by the Federal Republic of Germany and the Netherlands meant that both conditions have been met. So the Code came into force on 6 October 1983.[3]

The Liner Conference System

UN Code of Conduct for Liners

For some time after its passage in 1974 little was heard of the UN

Convention on a Code of Conduct for Liner Conferences.[4] At one point there seemed some likelihood that it might not get the necessary ratifications to enable it to come into effect. Much of the delay and uncertainty was due to the opposition or indecision from the traditional maritime nations (TMNs), mainly the Member States of the EEC and OECD.[5] However, the Code's prospects were revived and brought back into the limelight. The Code came into effect in October 1983[6] following ratifications by the Federal Republic of Germany (FRG) and Denmark.[7] No doubt there will continue to be debate, and it is the intention of this chapter to participate in that debate. The study comprises an introduction and a brief introduction to the Code and the EEC requirements for a Common Policy (under the Treaty of Rome) on the basis of which the Brussels Package was devised. This is followed by the Package itself and its implications, including the UK Merchant Shipping (Liner Conferences) Act 1982 and the House of Lords' Report on the EEC competition Rules. The conclusion is followed by a summary of abuses of the Liner Conferences as viewed by the DMNs. Annexes at the end of the book give the text of the Code, its signatories, and the text of the Brussels Package.

The UN Convention on the Code of Conduct for Liner Conferences, signed at Geneva on 6 April 1974, was a compromise reached between those countries — mostly TMNs — which did not want a convention at all,[8] or if pressed, one which would be largely voluntary, and those — mostly DMNs and Socialist countries (SCs) — which wanted specific regulatory rules and procedures based on a balanced rather than unilaterally imposed (conference-biased) considerations. They are known as 'self-policing' methods.[9] The Code would come into effect six months after accession or ratification by not less than 24 countries, provided that in July 1973 they owned at least 25 per cent of world general cargo tonnage, i.e. on 6 October 1983.[10] It is not our intention to go into details of the Code; this has been done ably elsewhere.[11] The genesis of the Code is to be found in the general desire by recently independent nations (DMNs) to establish and develop their own merchant fleets, and it represents only one aspect of this drive.[12] The attitude of the British shipping community and the UK government is that regulation of liner conferences is, in principle, undesirable and that restrictions on competition are liable to increase prices.[13] The principal objection is the cargo-sharing provisions of Article 2 of the Code which essentially seek to ensure first that cargo carried by a liner conference trading between two countries is divided equally between the member lines of these countries.[14] Article 2 does, however, leave the member lines of third countries the right to acquire a significant part, such as 20 per cent in the trade — the notorious and often quoted '40–40–20' formula.[15] Over 40 per cent of the earnings of British liner shipping comes from the cross-trades, i.e. from trading between overseas countries, including cross-trades to and from continental European ports. Clearly then the United Kingdom, the EEC and OECD opposed the Code from the beginning because of the effect it would have on this trade, and for other reasons.[16] The EEC countries are required by the Treaty of Rome to adopt a common transport policy.

The EEC and the Code

The EEC–OECD opposition to the Code is basically that it is discriminatory. The Treaty of Rome requires by Title IV (on Transport), especially Article 74, that matters governed by this Title be within the framework of a common transport policy.[17] Article 75 calls upon the Council, by unanimous decision – on a proposal from the Commission, and after consulting the *Economic and Social Committee* and the *Assembly* – to lay down common rules applicable to international transport from or to the territory of one or more member states.[18] Article 79 provides that, in the case of traffic within the EEC, discrimination which takes the form of carriers charging different rates and imposing different conditions for transporting the same goods on the same routes, because of the country of origin or destination of the goods in question, be abolished before the end of the second stage at the latest.[19] The kind of practices envisaged by Article 2 of the Code would therefore be contrary to the EEC Rules of Competition,[20] which prohibit flag discrimination, cargo-sharing, and other related restrictive practices. All that remained was for the Council to act, since it has power to decide by unanimous decision, whether, to what extent, and by what procedure appropriate provisions could be made in respect of sea and air transport.[21]

Having failed to kill it at infancy, the UK, the EEC and the OECD did not know how to react to the Code; the situation was analogous to the dilemma facing the parents in the film *Omen III*. Opinion on how best to respond to the Code varied, ranging from some support, on the part of France, the FRG and the Scandinavian countries, to total opposition or neutrality on the part of the others.[22] The former were in favour of ratifying the Code, while the UK led the opposing camp. When it became clear that the latter course of action would be futile, the whole club decided to formulate a common approach, or at least to appear united, in line with the EEC Treaty[23] which calls upon member states to approach transport policies within the framework of a common transport policy. Hence, the birth of the so-called Brussels Package.

The decision of a number of continental countries to accede to the

Code threatened the imposition of serious restrictions on British shipping lines' trading opportunities, and thus on job opportunities in the cross-traders to and from European ports. To avoid this the EEC developed a common policy embodied in Council Regulation. [24] The Regulation is directed to securing that there is no discrimination between shipping lines of EEC member states or of other member countries of the OECD which do not themselves practise discrimination, such as Australia and the USA. [25] It creates directly applicable law in the UK, and accession to the Code by EEC member states is subjected to the reservations required by it. The Package therefore permits member states to ratify or accede to the Code subject to regulation. [26]

There are two issues worth noting. First, the Package was a formal admission by the EEC that the questions covered by the Code are of importance not only to member states, but also to the EEC, in particular from the shipping and trading viewpoints, and it was therefore important that a common position should be adopted in relation to the Code. [27] Second, that besides the common position respecting the principles and objectives of the Treaty of Rome, the ratification or accession would make major contributions to meeting the aspirations of the DMNs in the field of shipping while at the same time pursuing the objective of the continuing application in this field of the commercial principles applied by shipping lines of the OECD countries and in trades between these countries. [28] Finally, it is an admission that, although they held dear the stabilizing role of the liner conferences in ensuring reliable services, it was nonetheless necessary to avoid possible breaches by liner conferences of the rules of competition. [29]

The United Kingdom and the Code

After the EEC Council Resolution establishing the Brussels Package, as is the practice with international conventions of this type, it was left to each member state to put the Code Convention into effect in the way it saw fit. [30] In parliamentary democracies, this is normally done through the legislature. When it comes into effect, the Merchant Shipping (Liner Conferences) Act 1982 will implement the Code in the UK. [31] The Act empowers the Secretary of State to make regulations creating rights and duties in domestic law to enable the UK to implement the Convention. [32] The Secretary of State is also specified as the appropriate authority in the UK to perform the function ascribed to the appropriate authority by the Code. [33]

The general scheme of the regulations is laid down by s.2(2), which outlines the Conference to which Chapters I to V of the Code shall apply. But the Secretary of State has power to exclude or restrict the operation of the Code for lack of reciprocity.[34] Parties to the Convention can make such reservations as they see fit. Bulk cargoes are not covered by the Code. Section 3 prescribes the matters which may be provided for by regulations and s.13(1) requires the Secretary of State to consult such persons in the UK as he considers will be affected by the proposed regulations, although this does not give a right to be heard to every affected person who believes he has this right.[35]

Section 13 also lays down the means by which the regulations are to become effective, and Article 49 of the Code, the means by which the Convention itself is to enter into force. Of course, the Code confers rights and duties on shippers, shipping conferences and their members, as between themselves.[36] Disputes arising out of it are to be settled in accordance with Chapter VI of the Code and sections 5–9 of the Act. Article 5 of the Code places conferences under a general obligation to police themselves and under a special obligation to provide the Secretary of State with reports on action taken against malpractices; Article 6 creates a similar obligation in respect of conference agreements and related documents.[37]

Section 10(2) of the Act restricts the disclosure of information obtained by the Secretary of State. Article 52 of the Code provides a procedure for reviewing the operation of the Code five years from the Convention's coming into force — which will be not later than 5 October 1988.[38] Section 11 attempts to remove potential conflict between the Act and domestic competition law by excluding statutory restrictive business practice[39] and the common law doctrine of restraint of trade. The Merchant Shipping (Liner Conferences) Act 1982 is therefore a compromise enabling the UK to protect its international interest by acceding to the Code, so as to help forestall more drastic measures being taken by UNCTAD or the DMNs, but simultaneously availing itself of the Brussels Package.[40] It has been estimated that the Code's cargo-sharing will apply in practice to only about a quarter of the world's liner conference trades.[41]

The Brussels Package

What it is

It cannot be said that the UK, EEC and OECD accepted the Code willingly; it was an acceptance based on a realization that any continued opposition would be futile, if not too late. But, above all, it seems to have been made to maintain the badly needed unity that had begun to crack in both the EEC and OECD.[42] Although Belgium, France and the FRG have always supported the Code — probably after assessing the situation — it appears that the others may be ratifying collectively for the wrong reasons. It seems that two major factors caused the UK and others in the EEC to reappraise the Code:[43]

1   a realization that in the absence of the Code, an increasing number of the DMNs would seek to take even more damaging unilateral action to reserve cargoes to their own ships;[44] and
2   certain EEC members were adamant that they intended to ratify the Convention, whatever the view of their partners.[45]

It is also likely that the EEC, in accepting the Code, was more conscious of its value in assisting to combat the incursion of Soviet tonnage into Common Market trades,[46] often operating outside the conferences, than of contributing to the realization of the legitimate aspirations of the DMNs. It is also probable that, to the Soviets, the Code is seen as a tool to tame — and weaken — Western imperialist shipping. To the EEC and OECD, however, there seems to be no difference between the Soviets and the DMNs' encroachments.[47] On this point, one speaker in the House of Lords commented:

> There are many people who think that these poor developing countries . . . ought to be allowed to carry cargoes in their own ships . . . . But, of course, they are not their own ships. In many cases they are ships chartered from the Russians and chartered at very special rates for very special purposes.[48]

This explains why the Act in question, and others before it,[49] are rigid and protective.

The sum total of the Package and the Act is that the objectionable Parts (I–V) of the Code, especially Article 2(4)(a) and (b) will fall under reservations and will operate as between the DMNs–SCs on the one hand and the EEC–OECD and others on the other — but not between the EEC and OECD member states themselves.[50] The instrument of ratification or accession by the EEC–OECD will be accompanied by these reservations set out in Annex 1 of the Council Regulations.[51] According to the EEC–OECD therefore, the purpose of the Brussels Package is to reduce to a minimum the damage to international trade caused by the Code's cargo-sharing provisions.[52] This is done by implementing them only in so far as it is necessary to meet the rights which the Code gives the DMNs who conceived the idea.[53]

The idea is that, assuming all the EEC–OECD countries continue to renounce cargo-sharing favouring their own lines, government-imposed cargo reservation will be avoided in all intra-OECD conference trades.[54] In trades between the OECD signatories to the Code and Codist-DMNs, the latter will receive allocations to them under the Code rules, but the share that would otherwise fall to the EEC–OECD lines will be aggregated and redistributed by them on a commercial basis.[55] It is hoped, by this, that this pattern of DMN protectionism, together with renewed commitment on the part of the EEC–OECD, to commercial trading principles, will be the way forward for the development of the world's liner trades.[56]

Implications of the Code to the TMNs

The British shipowners and shippers, and successive British governments have remained united in finding the Code's government-imposed cargo-sharing obnoxious and voted against it in 1974.[57] The government has only been forced to go along this time for fear of being left behind by the others. The most serious problem facing the UK was that a number of continental European countries had signed the original Code Convention,[58] and there was, therefore, the clear prospect that the Code might eventually apply generally on the continent, imposing serious restriction on the UK's shipping lines, its trading opportunities and thus its job opportunities in the cross-trades to and from European ports.[59] Britain faced this possibility whether or not she acceded to the Code, by virtue of the continental countries' intention to do so. It was therefore essential to agree on a common position in the EEC to enable her to avoid this danger.[60]

Another effect of the Brussels Package was to save the British cross-trades by displacing cargo-sharing from among the TMNs. Were this not to be the case, it would have placed British shipping in an invidious situation and effectively cut it out of much of the European cross-trades.[61] It was with this situation in mind, and largely on the initiative of the British government, that the Brussels Package was negotiated, providing a regime for the disapplication of the Code's cargo-sharing provision in the intra-OECD trades. The result of the Package is that, as long as all OECD countries acceding to the Code disapply its cargo-sharing provisions, then 75 per cent of the world's liner conference trades will remain free of cargo reservation.[62] This means that, on a route between the EEC–OECD, other countries' conference liners from all member states will compete on the same footing except where the third country is a developing one.

This move effectively disarms much of the Code and deprives it of its most important provision. As a result of this fundamental modification of the Code's provisions, calculations suggest that the

Code's cargo-sharing will apply in practice to only about 25 per cent of the world's liner conference trades.[63] The other 75 per cent will be free of the Code's cargo reservation (the 40–20–20) provisions because they will either not be applicable in intra-OECD trades, and will be substantially modified in trades between the OECD and the DMNs, or because of the intention of the other OECD countries, such as the US and Australia, not to accede to it at all.[64] If liner conference trade is about 20 per cent of the world shipping, it follows that only (25 x 20/100) or 5 per cent of world shipping will be subject to the Code's cargo-sharing provisions.[65]

The combined effect of the Act and the Package has enabled the UK to forestall potential threats to her cross-trading supremacy from the other EEC–OECD countries who would have taken advantage of the Code's potential weakening of her shipping position.[66] The UK was faced with the situation that some EEC countries with less extensive cross-trading interests did not share her view of the Code. The Germans, the French and the Belgians voted in favour of the Code in 1974 and showed every sign of ratifying, possibly taking others with them.[67] Thus, it became increasingly necessary to have an EEC view on the issue and in the end the so-called Brussels Package was negotiated, first initiated between the major European shipping lines, and subsequently taken over by governments and enshrined in the EEC Regulation No. 954/79.[68]

This effectively brought the doubting Thomases back to the fold, and this new-found EEC unity is thought essential for the battle that looms ahead. Nevertheless, the early years following the entry into force of the Liner Code will be critical. In many ways there will be no immediate, dramatic changes.[69] Conferences have seen the Code coming for some years now and may have already accommodated themselves substantially to the new regime. In recent years, the national lines of the DMNs have found difficulty in gaining membership of the conferences that serve their direct trades. Similarly, in many of the major trades, the DMNs' national lines already have carryings — or the right to carry — in the region of 40 per cent.[70]

Implications of the Package to the DMNs

The Brussels Package is meant to send a warning signal to adversaries that the EEC–OECD will not tolerate cargo-sharing in the proposed Code of Conduct in the Bulk Trades.[71] The French and the Germans were mentioned at that time as the EEC member states who had gone along with the idea. This worried the UK who threatened to use her EEC membership to get a solid Community view against the proposed sharing in bulk trades.[72] Maybe that is the sort of thing that Britain ought to do; a little more toughness at the negotiating table, rather than assuming that the problem will go away simply because she was once a powerful maritime nation. A realistic approach to the changed circumstances might best serve the country's interests.

The other objective of the Package was to reverse the regulatory aspect.[73] The interests of the EEC–OECD countries would seem to coincide in opposing these further manifestations of protectionism, regardless of whether they intend to accede to the Liner Code or not. It is inevitably a complex problem to regulate world shipping, as it is to regulate world aviation.[74] It is interesting to note that, in the field of aviation, the British governments have fairly and squarely nailed their flag to the mast of deregulation, though not much has been heard of this since the effects of deregulation have shown up in the operations of a number of airlines. It is therefore noteworthy, that in the field of merchant shipping, by bringing forward the Act for British accession to the Code,[75] the government was firmly nailing the flag to the mast of regulation. Indeed, this will be the first time that British liner conferences have been subject to any form of regulation in UK law. The fear of the British shipping community is that when governments begin to tamper with and intrude into commercial arrangements, profitability goes out through the window.[76] However, only experience will demonstrate the results of turning a commercial understanding into a legal provision. It is very much hoped that the shipping lines of the countries involved will be able to work together satisfactorily. It is also hoped and believed that British shipowners will continue to play the very prominent and constructive role that they have hitherto played over many years of conference arrangements.[77]

The general free-trade position of the UK is similar to its position generally. France and Germany on the other hand have long traditions of protectionisms followed with equal consistency in this context.

The Brussels Package and the UK legislation aim to restore the principle of *laissez-faire* in liner conference system. The British government has always recognized that the legal privileges under which liner conferences trade operates require the discipline of exposure to competition if they are to remain acceptable.[78] If, therefore, the UK finds competition eliminated from its trade routes by another government, whether or not that government cites the Code in its aid, she will continue to make clear to the government concerned that this is unacceptable and that the British government stands ready to use the very considerable powers which Parliament has provided to counteract such damage to British shipping and trading interests.[79]

The Packaged Code in International Shipping

The Transatlantic Implications

Finally, the effect of the Brussels Package and the Merchant Shipping (Liner Conferences) Act 1982 was to allay the fears of the USA and repair the strained transatlantic shipping relationship.[80] There was a corollary, however, among the Europeans, that national status and cargo generation have become increasingly important factors in commercial negotiations within many conferences,[81] and there was a danger — which had to be resisted — that this could undermine the effects of the Brussels Package. Already, certain voices have been heard on the continent reasserting an EEC shipping lines' *prima facie* 'right' to a Code-style market share if any proposed commercial redistribution proved not to be to its advantage.[82]

Such assertions might misinterpret the Package. Moreover, they might be dangerous due to their potential effects, particularly in the USA. The USA has always been wary about the Code (seeing it as protectionist) and the intentions of the Brussels Package might widely be misunderstood.[83] In such circumstances, those who would gain from a resurgence of American protectionism are likely to seize upon any incautious European statements about the effects of the EEC reservation as evidence that the EEC has abandoned its adherence to commercial principles.[84]

Unfortunately, it appears that the threat that the USA might respond to the Code by following a protectionist path in shipping, and entering into bilateral cargo-sharing arrangements with any country that proposed them can no longer be dismissed as fanciful.[85] If the USA were to be made to believe, however erroneously, that the EEC and most other OECD nations were introducing a protectionist regime by the back door, she might feel bound to take countermeasures. The UK view is that such a development would be a serious blow to world trade.[86] Not only would it be damaging in itself, but it would encourage the worst excesses of cargo reservation in the DMNs and SCs. The losers would be not only extensive cross-traders, such as the UK, but also shipowners and consumers everywhere. The EEC's Code/Package exercise would then have failed.[87]

These gloomy developments can be avoided. The Member States of the EEC, together with other OECD members who accede to the Code, will have to continue doing their utmost to convince the USA, by their deeds as well as their words, that the Brussels Package will neither operate as a protective measure in their favour nor discriminate against US interests.[88] Similarly the USA must make a renewed effort to understand the outlook of the EEC and her OECD colleagues and to respect their political judgement that the cargo shares granted to the DMNs by the Code are a minimum response to the clamour by these countries for greater participation in the world's liner trades.[89]

The European Dimension

With the coming into force of the UN Code of Conduct for Liner Conferences and the Brussels Package the regulation of maritime transport within the EEC has become even more confusing.[90] The Brussels Package might have bought a temporary intra-EEC truce and forged unity in the EEC–OECD response to the DMNs–SCs challenge. But it has left more problems unresolved as well as created new ones. Altogether, the EEC now has to contend with how to achieve a common transport policy;[91] implement, monitor and assess the progress of the Brussels Package; deal with the challenge of the UN Code; implement the UN Code through respective national legislations; and/or revive the fortunes of the CENSA Code where necessary.[92]

However, there is another problem that has a direct bearing on all these factors. This is the proposed Council Regulation applying Articles 85 and 86 of the EEC Treaty on maritime transport. These will affect both liner shipping and — therefore indirectly — the UN Code as well as the Brussels Package.[93] The said Council Regulations were recently the subject of the House of Lords' Third Report in this country: namely, the *House Select Committee Report on the European Communities Competition Policy: Shipping*,[94] which was published at the same time that the UN Code came into force and as the (UK) Merchant Shipping (Liner Conferences) Act 1982 received Royal Assent.[95]

Briefly then, the problem is this: liner conference monopoly and loyalty agreements are prohibited by Articles 85 and 86 of the EEC Treaty.[96] However, according to the Lords' Report, until 1974 it was widely believed that Articles 85 and 86 did not apply to maritime transport,[97] the premises for this stand being that the EEC Treaty contemplates specific provisions to be made for such regulations.[98] Unfortunately no such rules had or have been made.

It was not until 1974 when the Commission brought a case against France in the European Court of Justice that the position was clarified.[99] In that case the court ruled that the general rules of the EEC Treaty, as well as those concerned exclusively with transport, applied to shipping.[100] It is worth noting that, although the case concerned labour relations, it is now accepted by the Commission and most Member States (the UK included)[101] that the competition rules apply to maritime transport. For the last decade the state of ambiguity existed and persisted unchallenged.[102] However, with the coming into force of the UN Code, and the Brussels Package giving a green light for its implementation in the EEC, there is now an urgent need for the competition rules to be implemented.[103] The entry into force of the UN Code and the Brussels Package has changed the situation dramatically as is exemplified by the Lords' Report.[104]

Until such times as the competition rules are made, the operation of Articles 85 and 86 is such that shipping is exempted[105] from the general regulations made to enable proceedings to be brought against restrictive agreements.[106] According to the Lords' Report:

> It is implicit in the Code that parties to it accept the legitimacy of liner conferences and loyalty agreements which comply with its provisions.[107] Community acceptance of the Code took the form of the *Brussels Package* which imposed on liner conferences in the Community certain additional restraints.[108] So to claim legitimacy a liner conference or loyalty agreement has to comply with the UN Code as modified by the *Brussels Package*,[109] but, as the community countries are parties to the Code, liner conferences and loyalty agreements can no longer be treated as inherently illegal restrictive agreements.[110]

Thus, the anomaly that existed before has persisted beyond the Brussels Package.[111] Its elimination would require the competition rules to either expressly exempt or prohibit the restrictive practices of the liner conferences and loyalty agreements.[112] This could not be achieved by — neither was it the intention of — the Brussels Package. The main conclusion of the Lords' Report is for the Commission to wait and monitor the effects of the Code[113] before acting. If anything else that would be probably playing it safe.

Concluding Remarks on the System

There was a case for compromise and, in 1979, all EEC governments agreed on a number of major reservations (the Brussels Package) that would enable them all to accede to the Code. Sweden, Norway and Finland have indicated that they will follow suit.[114] Others, such as Japan, may yet do so. For various reasons, some OECD countries, notably the US and Australia, will probably not accede, or if so, much later. Thus, the stage is set for the UK to accede to the Code, probably together with a number of EEC and OECD countries that have not done so already, sometime this or next year. The Code came into force that autumn, some nine years after it was adopted by the votes of the DMNs, the SCs and a handful of (EEC-OECD) TMNs.[115]

The bulk of the Code is uncontroversial, if not cosmetic and ineffective. It contains a series of provisions concerning relations between lines and their customers, the shippers, which are based upon a voluntary code agreed in 1974.[116] There is no objection to the DMNs' lines playing a full role in liner conferences serving their countries and, indeed, as cross-traders, if they are commercially competitive. Indeed, no one would deny the national fleets, of whichever country, the rights to participate in the carriage of cargoes generated by their international trade.[117] Some of the advantages of the Code, which have been acknowledged by even the sceptical British government, are:

1 That by laying down an internationally agreed trading regime, it is less likely to lead to international friction than a variety of conflicting unilateral, national and protectionist measures.
2 The Package would safeguard the position of that large proportion of UK fleets which operate as cross-traders, and would permit developments which would be of considerable benefit to the country's national interests.
3 It acknowledges that granting the DMNs the 40 per cent share of their liner trades as of right has to be regarded as a safeguard against extreme unilateral measures[118] by some of these countries.
4 This must be seen against a background of increasing protectionism by many foreign governments in respect of liner shipping.[119]
5 The Package will give legal sanctions to protect shippers' rights and acknowledge, to a limited extent, the aspirations of the DMNs to have a greater share in liner shipping.

We should not, however, assume that the Brussels Package has provided solutions to all the EEC–OECD problems relating to the Code. There are still several worrying features to what is happening,[120] some of which are noted in the Lords' Report above. Secondly the Code, which entered into force after the Brussels Package had done its work, was to be virtually stripped of its most important visionary elements. Thirdly, a further threat that the EEC–OECD countries will have to face is the possibility that some countries will attempt to continue or expand existing protectionist measures[121] even when the Code has come into force. If the DMNs, or any others for that matter, were to be allowed to succeed with unilateral measures more restrictive than the Package envisages, whether in Code or non-Code trades, the Code itself will soon become irrelevant.[122]

Some countries are already inclining towards extending Codist (cargo-sharing) principles to non-conference operators, bulk traders, or to trades involving a non-Codist trading partner.[123] Finally, critics of the Code would argue that the continued rise of government-controlled mechanisms has led many to believe that they would be used to give unfair preference to the indigenous national line.[124]

Notes

1 Para. 14, p. xi of the *House of Lords Select Committee on the European Communities*, HMSO, London, 12 July 1983, hereinafter referred to as the Lords' Report.
2 Para. 14 of the Lords' Report on p. xi, Session 1983–4, 3rd Report also known as the *Report on Competition Policy: Shipping*.
3 Para. 16, p. xi of the Lords' Report. The Report was on 'Proposed Council Regulations Applying Articles 85 and 86 of the Treaty to Maritime Transport'.
4 For the text of the UNCTAD Code of Conduct for Liner Conferences see *Report of the Conference of Plenipotentiaries*, vol. II, UNCTAD Document no. TD/Code/13/Add. 1.
5 See, for instance, David Mott, 'UNCTAD Code will lead to trade war' in *Lloyd's List*, no. 52373, Wednesday 25 May 1983, p. 3.
6 'UNCTAD Code — October 6 is tomorrow', *Norwegian Shipping News*, vol. 39, no. 7, 24 June 1983, pp. 26–8.
7 For details see an article by James Brewer, 'West Germany in dramatic move over the Liner Code' in *Lloyd's List*, no. 52318, Friday 18 March 1983, front page.
8 This division was reflected in the voting pattern at Geneva with the DMNs, supported by the SCs, overwhelmingly for and the TMNs basically against.
9 For details on 'self-policing' see also 'Conference self-policing plans enrage shipping agents' in *Fairplay International Shipping Weekly*, pf 27, January 1983, p. 7.
10 Article 48 of the Code; see also 'Liner Code to be activated this year' in *Fairplay International Shipping Weekly*, vol. 286, no. 5199, 28 April 1983, p. 7.
11 For detailed analysis of the Code see B. Larsen and Valerie Vetterrick, 'The UNCTAD Code of Conduct for Liner Conferences — reservations, reactions and U.S. alternatives' in *Law and Policy in International Business*, vol. 13, 1981, pp. 223–80.
12 See also UN–ECOSOC, 'Main issues in transport for developing countries during the 3rd UN development decade 1981–1990', UN Document no. ST/ESA/177, New York; Elis Moses, 'The UNCTAD 40:40:20 Convention should Israel join or not', *Sapanut*, vol. 13, no. 1, Summer 1983, pp. 1–5.
13 See 'Sproat warning on pitfalls in Liner Code talks' in *Lloyd's List*, no. 52385, Thursday 9 June 1983, p. 3. (Mr Sproat was the Minister responsible for shipping in the previous British government.)
14 For a quick reference to this article see the Code Text in *Lloyd's List*, no. 52403, Thursday 30 June 1983, p. 10.

15 For further text see, again, *Lloyd's List*, no. 52404, Friday 1 July 1983, p. 6.

16 'European Shippers Council worrying over the UN Code', *Lloyd's List*, no. 52342, Monday 18 April 1983, front page; 'Indian owners press for UNCTAD Code', *Fairplay International Shipping Weekly*, vol. 289, no. 5240, 16 February 1984, p. 9.

17 Cf. 'The case for the defence — failure of the EEC's Council of Ministers to formulate a common transport policy' in *Cargo Systems International*, vol. 10, no. 5, May 1983, pp. 73-5.

18 See also an article by Howard Smith, 'New Call for EEC Shipping Policy' in *Lloyd's List*, no. 52383, Tuesday 7 June 1983, p. 2.

19 And Howard Williams, 'EEC lashed over transport policy failure', *Lloyd's List*, no. 52312, Friday 11 March 1983, front page.

20 Section 1 — Rules applicable to undertakings, Articles 85-94 of the Treaty of Rome.

21 Article 84(2), ibid.

22 'West German ratification of the Liner Code may fuel talks', an article by Bridget Hogan in *Lloyd's List*, no. 52334, Saturday 11 April 1983, front page.

23 Howard Smith, infra 'EEC moves to protect independent operators', *Lloyd's List*, no. 52383, Tuesday 24 May 1983, front page.

24 EEC Regulations No. 954/79.

25 The Brussels Package, Regulation, DJ 1979 L 121/1.

26 The Regulations were made on 15 May 1979.

27 Preamble to the Package. Ibid.

28 Ibid.

29 Articles 82-94 of the Treaty of Rome.

30 Subject to the reservations in Annex 1 to the Regulations.

31 Chapter 37/82; for general note, see Francis D. Rose in *Current Statutes Annotated*.

32 S.7c(1) of the Act.

33 S.10, ibid.

34 S.4, ibid.

35 S.3(8), ibid.

36 See also, Françoise Odier, 'La Code de Conduite des Conferences Maritimes' in *Françoise de Droit International*, 1979, pp. 686-92.

37 For a short commentary see *Current Law*, vol. 7, 1982, p. 342.

38 Or any such time five years after the coming into effect of the Code.

39 E.g. The Restrictive Trade Practices Act 1976.

40 See, for instance, 'Impasse over UNCTAD Cargo Code checks trade for expanding fleet' in *Lloyd's List*, no. 52292, Wednesday 16 February 1983, p. 7; 'The UN Convention on a Code of Conduct for liner conferences in a changing maritime environment', *Proceedings of the Second Symposium*, Montreux, Switzerland, 15-16 October 1980, CS Publications, Worcester Park, Surrey, 1981, pp. 7-20.

41 Because 75 per cent of world liner trade is carried between developed countries.

42   See, also generally, Anne E. Breedmans, 'The Common Shipping Policy of the EEC', *Common Market Law Review*, vol. 18, 1981, pp. 9–32.

43   See also, R. Goy, 'Shipping and the European Community' in M.B.F. Ranken (ed.), *Greenwich Forum VI: World Shipping in the 1990s*, Guildford, 1981.

44   See *Hansard* (House of Commons), vol. 23, col. 726.

45   'UK under Pressure on Liner Code' in *Lloyd's List*, no. 52403, Thursday 30 June 1983, front page.

46   *Hansard* (House of Lords) 29 June 1982, cols 163–6; 'Turning the other cheek', 'Just watch it', 'Bearded in Brussels', 'Liberal Eclipse?', 'No contest — A call for retaliation', 'Tough talking from Free Traders', 'Even tougher talking from the US and USSR', *Fairplay International Shipping Weekly*, vol. 288, no. 5227, 10 November 1983, pp. 3–6.

47   *Hansard* (House of Commons) vol. 21, col. 708.

48   Ibid.; Lisa Buckingham, 'Wrangles open Soviet–British shipping talks', *Lloyd's List*, no. 52540, Thursday 8 December 1983, headlines.

49   Such as the Shipping Contracts and Commercial Documents Act 1964 (1964 C.87) repealed and replaced by the Protection of Trading Interests Act 1980 (1980 C.11); Merchant Shipping Act 1974 (1974 C.43); and the Merchant Shipping Act 1979 (1979 C.39).

50   Article 4(1) of the Regulations. Cf. 'Cargo preference decision splits the Indian government', *Fairplay International Shipping Weekly*, vol. 228, no. 5230, 1 December 1983, p. 9.

51   Annex 1 of the Council Regulations, i.e. the Reservations, reproduced (at the end) as annex to this article.

52   Article 4(2), ibid.

53   Article 4(3), ibid.

54   Article 4(a), ibid.

55   Article 9(5), ibid.

56   See also Benford Harvey, 'A simple approach to fleet development' in *Maritime Policy and Management*, vol. 8, 1981, pp. 223–8; Juan Oribe-Stemmer, 'Cargo preference in Latin America', *Journal of Maritime Law and Commerce*, vol. 10, October 1978, p. 123.

57   Steven Taylor, 'UK shipping crisis. Self-help is no longer sufficient', *International Freighting Manager*, April 1983, p. 7.

58   These were presumably West Germany, France, Belgium, The Netherlands, and the Scandinavians; see also 'West German pledge to end flag discrimination', *Lloyd's List*, no. 52607, Tuesday 28 February 1984, p. 3.

59   James Brewer, 'Labour pressured on Liner Code' in *Lloyd's List*, no. 52369, Friday 23 May 1983, front page; G.J. Benwick, 'Who can find the way to stop decline in British shipping', *Lloyd's List*, no. 52584, Wednesday 1 February 1984, p. 6.

60   And Bridget Hogan, 'Industry views are canvassed on Liner Code' (UK) in *Lloyd's List*, no. 52352, Friday 29 April 1983, front page; 'Decline of UK merchant fleet', *Sea Breezes*, vol. 57, no. 448, April 1983, pp. 243–5.

61   See 'Sproat attacked over cuts in merchant fleets', *Lloyd's List*, no. 52330, Monday 14 April 1983, p. 5; Thomas Brewer, 'UK flag share of trade with EEC falls', *Lloyd's List*, no. 52604, Friday 24 August 1984, front page.

62 The TMNs (i.e. EEC–OECD) between them own about 75 per cent of world liner shipping; Stephen Taylor, 'UK shipping crisis. Self-help is no longer sufficient', *International Freight Management*, April 1983, p. 7.

63 See, for instance, 'Liner shipping and the developing countries' in *Norwegian Shipping News*, vol. 39, no. 7, 3 June 1983, p. 7.

64 Vanya Walker-Leigh, 'US negotiations under pressure on Liner Code', *Lloyd's List*, no. 52398, Friday 24 June 1983, front page.

65 James Brewer, 'Third World operator's interests buoying prices', *Lloyd's List*, no. 52366, Tuesday 17 May 1983, p. 2.

66 See also Lisa Buckingham (ed.), 'Zaire shipping curbs threaten European unity', *Lloyd's List*, no. 52393, Saturday 18 June 1983, front page.

67 See again, Lisa Buckingham (ed.), 'British owners fear Zaire's demands', ibid., p. 3.

68 'UNCTAD assailing source of livelihood', *Lloyd's List*, no. 52390, Wednesday 15 June 1983, p. 2.

69 See, for instance, 'Third World drops finance demands at UNCTAD', *Lloyd's List*, no. 32395, 21 June 1983, front page.

70 James Brewer, 'Hong Kong to sign UN Code of Liner Ethics', *Lloyd's List*, no. 52369, 19 June 1983, front page.

71 For details on the bulk-sharing, see 'Talks begin on Liner Code regulations', *Lloyd's List*, no. 52308, Monday 7 March 1983, front page.

72 Howard Smith, op. cit.

73 Bridget Hogan, 'The GCBS Report backs freedom to flag out', *Lloyd's List*, no. 52372, Tuesday 24 May 1983, front page.

74 Howard Williams, 'Controlled fleet seems in trouble once more', *Lloyd's List*, no. 52351, Thursday 28 April 1983, front page; 'India sorting out cargo-sharing and UNCTAD', *Fairplay International Shipping Weekly*, vol. 288, no. 5226, 3 November 1983, p. 6.

75 Merchant Shipping (Liner Conferences) Act 1982 (chapter 37).

76 'FMC warns on protectionism', *Lloyd's List*, no. 52322, Monday 23 March 1983, p. 3; 'Nationalism battles with common sense over Lykes Lines', *Fairplay International Shipping Weekly*, vol. 289, no. 5237, 26 January 1984, p. 3.

77 'The UNCTAD Code, what is it?', *Norwegian Shipping News*, vol. 39, no. 7, 3 June 1983, p. 7; 'UN Code of Liner Conduct — impressions from a conference', *Norwegian Shipping News*, vol. 39, no. 14, 4 November 1983, p. 53.

78 Tony Gray, 'A table of two viewpoints over merchant fleets', *Lloyd's List*, no. 52266, Monday 17 January 1983, p. 5.

79 Bridget Hogan, 'GCBS Report highlights dramatic fall in UK fleet', *Lloyd's List*, no. 52372, Tuesday 24 May 1983, p. 3.

80 'US — wheat deal may revive trade war with the EEC', *Lloyd's List*, no. 52272, Monday 24 January 1983, back page; Bridget Hogan, 'US claims on cargo-sharing are undermined', *Lloyd's List*, no. 52607, Tuesday 28 February 1984, headlines.

81 James Brewer, 'Senators back liberalism of conferences', *Lloyd's List*, no. 5299, Thursday 24 February 1983, front page.

82 James Brewer, 'Europeans set to fight US shipping clamp', *Lloyd's List*, no. 52301, Saturday 26 February 1983, front page.

83 Ademuni-Odeke, 'Differences which set the US apart', *Lloyd's List*, no. 52434, Friday 5 August 1983, p. 4; 'US–Europe liner trades in disarray, open conference system faulters as carriers chase shares of declining cargo', *Fairplay International Shipping Weekly*, vol. 288, no. 5188, 10 February 1983, p. 12.

84 Bridget Hogan, 'US–European deadlock over liner trades', *Lloyd's List*, no. 52328, Wednesday 30 March 1983, front page.

85 Bridget Hogan, 'Protectionism talks break-up', *Lloyd's List*, no. 52326, Monday 28 March 1983, front page; 'US Shipping Policy. The meritocracy in action', *Lloyd's Shipping Economist*, vol. 4, no. 12, December 1982, pp. 8–13.

86 Howard Williams, 'Owners in US plea on UNCTAD position', *Lloyd's List*, no. 25310, Wednesday 9 March 1983, p. 3.

87 Cf. Howard Williams, 'US prepares to adopt Northern Shipping Rules', *Lloyd's List*, no. 52324, Friday 24 March 1983, p. 3.

88 Bridget Hogan, 'FMC planning review of bilateral accords', note 80 (supra); 'Pocket book for patriotism in the US', *Fairplay International Shipping Weekly*, vol. 28, no. 5234, 5 January 1984, p. 5.

89 Bridget Hogan, 'MARAD warns of Liner Code repercussions', *Lloyd's List*, no. 52322, Saturday 6 April 1983, front page.

90 With the member states still undecided about what to do regarding competition rules, see for instance, 'The case for the defence (failure of the EEC's Council of Ministers to formulate a Common Transport Policy)', *Cargo Systems International*, vol. 10, no. 5, May 1983, pp. 73–5.

91 Ibid; see also Francisco Santoro, 'The EEC and the transportation market', *International Journal of Transport Economics*, vol. 10, nos. 1–2, April–August 1983, pp. 67–79.

92 Although the CENSA Code seems beyond redemption it is just possible, were they dissatisfied with the operations of the UN Code, the EEC may threaten to revive the former, at least as a bargaining counter.

93 As exemplified by the Lords' Report 10150/81 + Add 1, Com (81) 423 final. For various reactions see 'UK rejects attempts to defer Competition Policy', *Fairplay International Shipping Weekly*, vol. 288, no. 5230, 1 December 1983, p. 7.

94 The Lords' Report; see also 'The General Council of British Shipping welcomes report on EEC rules', *Fairplay International Shipping Weekly*, vol. 288, no. 5226, 3 November 1983, p. 6.

95 Ademuni-Odeke, 'Implementing the UNCTAD Code of Conduct – the UK Merchant Shipping (Liner Conferences) Act 1982', *Marine Policy*, vol. 6, no. 1, January 1984, pp. 56–64.

96 Paras 7–9 of the Lords' Report; see also Dennis Thompson, 'The competition policy of the European Community', *Journal of World Trade Law*, vol. 12, no. 3, May–June 1978, p. 249.

97 Para. 10 of the Lords' Report; see also Ademuni-Odeke, 'How the Brussels Package will effectively undermine Liner Code', *Lloyd's List*, no. 52434, Friday 5 August 1983, p. 4.

98 Para. 1 of the Lords' Report notes: 'Although the provisions are quite

detailed, further implementing regulations are needed before the rules can be applied effectively.'

99 In the case of *Commission v. French Republic*, Case 167/73, 1974, ECR 359.

100 A view corroborated by the Lords' Report (para. 1): 'most sectors of the business are now subject to such regulation'; see also Lisa Buckingham, 'Owners view EEC competition moves as threat to conferences', *Lloyd's List*, no. 52535, Friday 2 December 1983, p. 4.

101 On a note on a recent case involving the Commission and the UK, see John A. Usher, 'Injunction to prevent breach of EEC Competition Rules', *Journal of Business Law*, November 1983, pp. 494–5.

102 The decade from 1974 when the French case (note 99, supra) was decided to 1984 when the Lords' Report came out; see also Ademuni-Odeke, 'Joint ventures could become more attractive', *Lloyd's List*, no. 52434, Friday 5 August 1983, p. 4.

103 The delay, according to the Lords' Report (para. 1) was due to the fact that '. . . Shipping (like air transport) has special features which make it particularly difficult to draw up detailed rules'.

104 That the liner conferences or loyalty agreements in the EEC would have to comply with the UN Code as modified by the Brussels Package (para. 13).

105 As an agreement which improves production or distribution or promotes technical or economic progress with resulting benefits to the consumer. Maritime transport would only marginally gain that exemption.

106 Council Regulations 17/62, 141/62, and 1017/68. In the case of the UK, see the Restrictive Trade Practices Act 1976.

107 Para. 13 of the Lords' Report. In the case of the UK, cf. the type of business concerns that would be subject to review by the Monopolies and Mergers Commission.

108 See also the Restrictive Trade Practices (Services) Order (SI 98/76) Schedule, para. 2, made under s.107 and 110 of the Fair Trading Act 1973.

109 Ibid; now re-enacted in s.11 of the Restrictive Trade Practices Act 1976; see also M.J. Shah, 'The implementation of the UN Convention on a Code of Conduct for Liner Conferences', *Journal of Maritime Law and Commerce*, vol. 9, October 1977, p. 79.

110 Peter Green, 'Shippers' Council raps report on liner conferences', *Lloyd's List*, no. 52542, Saturday 14 December 1983, p. 2.

111 David Tinsley, 'Like-for-like response to growing protectionism', *Fairplay International Shipping Weekly*, vol. 288, no. 5237, 26 January 1984, pp. 41–3.

112 Mark Andrews, 'Protectionism and its adverse effects', *WW/World Ports*, vol. 46, no. 6, October–November 1983, p. 28; cf. Howard Williams, 'State intervention policy attacked', *Lloyd's List*, no. 52587, Saturday 4 February 1984, headlines.

113 'Liner Code: a vision blurred?' (UNCTAD liner code), *Cargo Systems International*, vol. 10, no. 11, November 1983, p. 69; 'UNCTAD Code of Conduct for Liner Conferences', *Journal of World Trade Law*, vol. 8, no. 5, September–October 1974, pp. 536–74.

114 'UNCTAD Code. The poor countries' shipping charter – but will it work?',

Transport Management, December 1983, p. 24; cf. Ademuni-Odeke, 'Differences which set the US apart', *Lloyd's List*, no. 52434, Friday 5 August 1983, p. 4.

115 Bridget Hogan, 'Three months to zero in liner trade deadlock', *Lloyd's List*, no. 52331, Tuesday 5 May 1983, front page. See also 'The case against bilateralism' in *Norwegian Shipping News*, vol. 38, no. 9, 27 August 1982, p. 2.

116 Cf. Howard Williams, 'CENSA protests at plan for US flag preference', *Lloyd's List*, no. 52386, Friday 10 June 1983, p. 2.

117 David Mott, 'Owners seek UK protectionist move', *Lloyd's List*, no. 52350, Wednesday 27 April 1983, p. 3; Alan M. Smith, 'Two faces of nationalism under the Philippines flag (cargo reservation formula effects)', *Containerisation International*, vol. 18, no. 1, January 1984, pp. 33–5.

118 See also, David Mott, 'GCBS plea on state help and protection', *Lloyd's List*, no. 52324, Friday 25 March 1983, p. 3; Werner Fante, 'Damages of governmental intervention and subsidies for the world ship builders market – part 2', *Hansa*, vol. 120, no. 23, December 1983, p. 2662.

119 But cf. 'No protectionism pledge by Norwegian Minister', *Lloyd's List*, no. 52322, Monday 23 March 1983, front page; V. Drychenko, 'Against Protectionism in Shipping', *Motor Ship*, vol. 64, no. 759, October 1983, p. 154.

120 See Ademuni-Odeke, 'How the Brussels Package will effectively undermine the Liner Code', *Lloyd's List*, no. 52434, Friday 5 August 1983, p. 4.

121 Cf. David Mott, 'No state intervention in cruise ship dispute', *Lloyd's List*, no. 52352, Friday 29 April 1983, front page.

122 See also, David Mott, 'UNCTAD Code will lead to trade war', ibid.

123 And 'European Shippers Council warning over the UN Code', ibid.

124 This is despite 'Optimism over competition agreement' as in *Lloyd's List*, no. 52286, Wednesday 9 February 1983, front page.

Appendix 1 Conference malpractices

Conferences serving Africa

Conference	Admission requirements	Malpractices		Rates		Conference administrative expenses
		Definition	Policing	General	Contract	
American West African Freight	must provide regular service to trade route	payment of agency fees in excess of 5% and 2½% at loading and discharge port respectively	neutral body reviews all complaints	reserve the right to declare rates on certain commodities open	the spread between the contract and non-contract rate is 15% of the contract rate	each segment (inbound, outbound) of the conference shall bear 50% of all expenses and each member shall be charged equally for expenses
Exports Imports	admission fee is US $5,000	employment of more than one agent at either port	complaints referred to screening committee by the Chairman of the neutral body	establishment of agreed minimum rate	in the Westbound group the contract rate is offered for only specific commodities	
East Coast	Security deposit is US $25,000	payment of *unreasonable* agent/husbanding fees, entertainment, souvenirs, and/or holiday gifts	screening committee consists of 3 member lines elected on rotating basis for 1 year			
Canada/United States			neutral body investigates upon decision of Screening Committee			
			1st offence (a) max. US $10,000 or (b) equivalent to freight money, whichever is the greatest sum			
			2nd offence (a) max. US $15,000 or (b) same as above			
			3rd offence (a) max. US $20,000 or (b) same as above			
			4th offence (a) max. US $25,000 or (b) same as above			
			damages liquidated on pro-rata basis with members			

Conferences serving Africa (cont.)

Conference	Admission requirements	Malpractices		Rates		Conference administrative expenses
		Definition	Policing	General	Contract	
Canada–South Africa Rate Association Exports East Coast Canada	requires a letter to the conference outlining the corporate and trade name, the service contemplated and such *other* information as the conference may request	absorption by lines of wharfage storage or other charges accrued against cargo	Chairman/Chief Executive shall refer complaints to a committee of 3, one of whom shall be himself acting as Chairman with the other 2 appointed by him from representative lines; Committee investigate the allegations in a way they deem appropriate; 1st offence max. Cdn. $2,500; 2nd offence max. Cdn. $3,000; 3rd offence max. Cdn. $25,000	reserve the right to declare rates on specific commodities to be open provided there exists *unanimous* consent of members; establishment of agreed minimum rates	No contract rate	50% of the total operating expenses shall be shared equally, remaining 50% shall be pro-rated between the members on the basis of the number of sailings made by their respective ships
	acceptance based on at least ¾ majority of existing members; admission fee is Cdn. $10,000; security deposit is Cdn. $5,000					

Association	Membership requirements	Definitions	Penalties	Rates	Contract	Cost sharing
Canada East Africa Rate Association / Exports / East Coast Canada	must provide regular service to trade route; acceptance based on at least ¾ majority of existing members; admission fee is Cdn. $10,000; security deposit is Cdn. $5,000	a member permitting any vessel owned, chartered, controlled, or operated by him to be used in this trade which does not fully adhere to all rates, charges and practices; an agent of the signatories to this agreement performing the ship's husbanding of tramp vessels carrying full unpacked homogeneous cargoes in bulk, where the Agent is connected with the fixing of the vessel control of the cargo or is in any manner interested in the vessel or cargo	Chairman needs unanimous vote of conference members to determine what action should be taken; for the violation of tariff — sum equal to 10 times the freight and other monies which said member would have received had applicable tariff been assessed; for the violation of agreement; 1st offence max. Cdn. $2,500; 2nd offence max. Cdn. $5,000	reserve the right to declare rates open; establishment of agreed minimum rates	No contract rate	50% of the total operating expenses shall be shared equally by all members, remaining 50% shall be pro-rated between the members on the basis of the number of sailings made by respective ships during the whole calendar year
South Africa Canada Rate Association / Imports / East Coast Canada	must provide regular service to trade route; acceptance based on at least 2/3 majority of existing members; admission fee is Cdn. $10,000; security deposit is Cdn. $5,000	member engaging either directly or indirectly in the transportation of cargoes at rates other than what was agreed upon; all vessels owned or operated by a member not adhering to all rates and regulations; an agent of the signatories to the agreement performing the ship's husbandry of tramp vessels carrying full unpacked homogeneous cargoes in bulk, where the agent is interested in the vessel or cargo	Secretary has the authority to investigate any allegations as he/she deems necessary; 1st offence max. Cdn. $2,500; 2nd offence max. Cdn. $5,000; 3rd offence max. Cdn. $25,000; the above fines for non-observance of Agreement; for non-observance of Tariffs sum equal to 10 times the freight which said member would have received had the applicable tariff been assessed	reserve the right to declare rates on particular commodities to be open; establishment of agreed minimum rates	No contract rate	50% of the total operating expenses shared equally, the remaining 50% shall be pro-rated among the members on the basis of the number of sailings made by their respective vessels during the whole calendar year

Conferences serving Africa (concluded)

Conference	Admission requirements	Malpractices		Rates		Conference administrative expenses
		Definition	Policing	General	Contract	
East Africa Canada Rate Association	same as above (South Africa Canada Rate Association)	same as above	same as above	same as above	same as above	same as above
Imports						
East Coast						
Canada						
United States Great Lakes & St Lawrence Ports/West African Agreement	must provide regular service to trade route / all applications for membership will be acted upon immediately	no information	neutral body which has complete authority to conduct an investigation as warranted / penalty for damages max. US $10,000 for each violation	reserve the right to declare rates on specific commodities to be open / establishment of agreed minimum rates	the spread between the contract and non-contract rate is 15% of the contract rate	no information
Exports Imports						
East Coast						
Canada United States						

Conferences serving Americas (excluding United States)

Conference	Admission requirements	Malpractices			Rates	Conference administrative expenses
		Definition	Policing	General	Contract	
Inter-American Freight Section A –	must provide regular service to trade route admission fee is US $25,000	no information	neutral body agreement stipulates that the neutral body shall have no financial interest in any member line	reserve the right to declare rates on specific commodities to be open	no contract rate	expenses shared equally
Exports				establishment of agreed minimum rates		
East Coast			1st violation (a) max. fine US $10,000 or (b) amount of freight money in US dollars or (a) or (b) whichever is the greater sum			
Canada						
Section B –			2nd violation (a) max. fine US $15,000 or (b) amount of freight money or (a) or (b) whichever is the greater sum			
Imports						
East Coast			3rd violation (a) max. fine US $20,000 or (b) amount of freight money or (a) or (b) whichever is the greater sum			
Canada						
Section C –			4th violation (a) max. fine US $25,000 or (b) amount of freight money or (a) or (b) whichever is the greater sum			
Imports						
East Coast			damages liquidated on pro-rata basis			
Canada						

Conferences serving Americas (excluding United States) (cont.)

Conference	Admission requirements	Malpractices		Rates			Conference administrative expenses
		Definition	Policing	General	Contract		
Association of West Coast Steamship	must provide regular service to trade area	employment of more than one agent at each port	Chairman has complete authority to conduct an investigation	establishment of agreed minimum rates	no contract rate		the expenses of maintaining the Association will be paid pro-rated by all the members whether active or non-active
Imports	admission fee is US $100	the pre or post dating of bills of lading	if damage cannot be determined then a sum equal to 4 times the ocean freight charges which cannot be less than US $500 or exceed US $2,000				
East Coast West Coast		bill of lading which fails to show the name of the port at which the cargo is received					
Canada United States	security deposit is US $2,000						
Pacific Coast River Plate Brazil Section A –	must provide regular service to trade area	no information	Executive Administrator of each Section under the direction of the applicable Board of Directors shall have overall responsibility for the investigation	establishment of agreed minimum rates	the spread between the contract and non-contract rate is 15% of the contract rate		expense shall be borne as determined by the members
Exports West Coast	admission fee is US $1,000		for violation of tariff must pay sum of full amount of the freight charges involved				
Canada United States			for violation of rules and regulations the max. fine is US $5,000 for each violation				
Section B –			damages liquidated on pro-rata basis				
Imports West Coast							

Canada United States Section C – Imports West Coast					
Latin America Pacific Coast Steamship (Canada United States, Exports Imports, West Coast, Canada United States)	must provide regular service to trade route; admission fee is US $1,000	no information	Chairman and any special committee appointed by him has complete authority to investigate all allegations; for violation of the tariff, the fine will be the full amount of freight charges which should have been assessed; for violation of rules and regulations the fine is max. US $5,000 in addition to all other charges due; damages liquidated on pro-rata basis	establishment of agreed minimum rates	the spread between the contract and non-contract rate is 15% of the contract rate	expenses shall be borne as determined by the members
Cavn/ Saguenay Joint Venezuelan Service (Exports, East Coast, Canada)	no information	no information	no information	outlines rates for automobile parts	no contract rate	no information

Conferences serving Asia

Conference	Admission requirements	Malpractices		Rates		Conference administrative expenses
		Definition	Policing	General	Contract	
Deli East Imports East Coast Canada	must provide regular service acceptance based on at least 2/3 majority of existing members	employing more than one agent at any port or place the payment of agency fees or more than 5% commission at loading and 2½% at disloading port	three arbitrators, one appointed by accused, one by the other members, then the two appoint a third fine depends on gravity of breach damages liquidated on a pro-rata basis	establishment of agreed minimum rates	no contract rate	no information
Deli Pacific Rate Agreement Imports West Coast Canada United States	must provide regular service admission fee is US $6,500	no information	Secretary has the authority to investigate and determine whether or not a malpractice has occurred each case is considered individually but in no case shall the damages to be paid be less than US $650 for violation of rules and regulations for violation of tariffs guilty members must pay sum equal to 4 times the freight and other monies which the member would have received had the proper tariff been assessed	establishment of agreed minimum rates	no contract rate	no information
East/ Canada Japan Freight Exports East Coast Canada	any common carrier may apply in writing to the Chairman admission fee is US $2,000	no information	conference members fines of a sum not less than US $5,000 nor more than US $10,000 for each violation damages liquidated on a pro-rata basis	establishment of agreed minimum rates	the spread between the contract and non-contract rate is 15% of the contract rate	no information

Pacific–India Rate Agreement No. 9247 Exports West Coast Canada United States	must provide regular service	no information	Secretary conducts the investigation breach results in a max. fine of US $5,000	establishment of agreed minimum rates	no contract rate	all expenses shared equally
Japan/Korea East Canada Freight Imports East Coast Canada	provide evidence of good faith and abide by all the terms and conditions of agreement admission fee is US $2,000	the payment of rebates, commissions or brokerage of any nature to any person, partnership, corporation, association or organization in direct or indirect manner	Executive Committee investigates all allegations fines: 1st offence max. US $20,000 2nd offence max. US $60,000 3rd offence max. US $80,000 4th and subsequent offence max. US $120,000	set up Rate Committee establishment of agreed minimum rates reserve the right to declare the rates on specific commodities open	the spread between the contract and non-contract rate is 15% of the contract rate	the expenses of the conference shall be pro-rated among the parties as they shall from time to time determine
Japan/Korea West Canada Freight Imports West Coast Canada	same as above (Japan/Korea East Canada Freight)	same as above	same as above	same as above	same as above	same as above

Conferences serving Asia (cont.)

Conference	Admission requirements	Malpractices			Rates		Conference administrative expenses
		Definition	Policing	General	General	Contract	
West Canada Freight	must provide regular service	freight or other charges, for the carriage of cargo either directly or indirectly being refunded in any manner to the shipper or any person whatsoever connected with him	Chairman has complete authority to conduct the investigation	establishment of agreed minimum rates		the spread between the contract and non-contract rate is 15% of the contract rate	expenses of the conference are shared among Full and Associated members with each Associate member's share being ¼ of the share of each Full member
Imports	acceptance based on at	accepting cargo at less than its weight or measurement	1st offence max. fine US $3,000				
West Coast	least ¾ majority of existing members	absorption of loading or discharging ports charges	2nd offence max. fine US $5,000				
Canada	security deposit is US $10,000	granting of free storage at ports of shipment or ports of destination or places of delivery	3rd and subsequent offence max. fine US $10,000				
		post-dating or predating of freight documents					
		the members agreed that any act of their own commission or that of their parent companies, agents, etc., which in the opinion of ¾ of the membership constitutes a malpractice					

Agreement					
Hong Kong–Taiwan/East Canada Freight Agreement, Imports East Coast Canada	no information	no information	no information	no contract rate	no information
West Coast of United States, Canada/India Pakistan, Ceylon & Burma Rate Agreement, Exports West Coast, Canada United States	must provide regular service	no information	Secretary appointed by unanimous consent with power to conduct an investigation	establishment of agreed minimum rates	no contract rate	shared equally
Malaysia–Pacific Rate Agreement, Imports West Coast, Canada United States	must provide regular services	no information	Secretary appointed by unanimous consent with the authority to conduct an investigation; max. fine for breach is US $5,000	establishment of agreed minimum rates	no contract rate	shared equally

Conferences serving Asia (cont.)

| Conference | Admission requirements | Malpractices | | Rates | | Conference administrative expenses |
		Definition	Policing	General	Contract	
Canada India Exports East Coast Canada	agreement between three lines and the government of India	no information	no information	increase in rates written notice not less than 90 days in advance government of India reserves the right to invite special freight quotation for certain commodities (75% of the cargo controlled by the government of India will be allocated to the lines)	no contract rate	no information
Java East Canada Imports East Coast Canada	applicants must satisfy members that they are operating a liner service within the scope of the conference trade acceptance based on at least 2/3 majority of existing members	employment of more than one agent at any port or place the payment of agency fee of a sum greater than 5% commission for loading any cargo the payment of brokerage fees or any refunds made directly or indirectly of freight or any other charges collected	Arbitration (3-member board) has complete authority to investigate the accused line fine determined by gravity of breach	establishment of agreed minimum rates	no contract rate	no information

	Service / admission	Absorption of rebates	Investigation / fines	Minimum rates	Contract spread	Expenses
Pacific Indonesian Exports — West Coast Canada United States	must provide regular service; admission fee is US $500	absorption of rebates of any kind; freight brokerage paid in excess of 1¼% on the amount of freight earned by initial carrier lines but not including trans-shipment freight unless authorized by 2/3 of members; the absorption of wharfage or tolls, storage, trucks or handling charge or any charge against cargo except if 2/3 of the members approve	Executive Administrator has complete authority to investigate any allegations; fines: for violation of a tariff, a sum not to exceed the full amount of the freight charges involved; for any other violation, a sum not in excess of US $5,000 in addition to all other sums due	establishment of agreed minimum rates	the spread between the contract and non-contract rate is 15% of the contract rate	expenses shall be pro-rated among the members
Pacific Straits Exports — West Coast Canada United States	must provide regular service; acceptance based on at least 2/3 majority of existing members; admission fee is US $500	no information	Secretary investigates, forms an arbitration hearing — if the secretary deems necessary; fines: (a) violation of tariff amount not exceeding full amount of the freight charges which should have been assessed (b) rules and regulations — max. US $5,000 in addition to all other charges due for each violation; damages liquidated on pro-rata basis with members	establishment of agreed minimum rates	the spread between the contract and non-contract rate is 15% of the contract rate	expenses shall be pro-rated among the members

Conferences serving Asia (cont.)

Conference	Admission requirements	Malpractices		Rates		Conference administrative expenses
		Definition	Policing	General	Contract	
Pacific Westbound Exports	must provide regular service to trade routes	employment of more than one agent at any port or place	neutral body set up with complete authority to investigate all information they deem necessary	establishment of agreed minimum rates	the spread between the contract and non-contract rate is 15% of the contract rate	the payment of fees (Secretary, clerical, staff, etc.) and the necessary expenses of the neutral body incurred in the performance of its duties shall be borne by the conference as follows:
West Coast Canada United States	admission fee is US $1,000	payment of any kind directly or indirectly to any officer, agent or employee of a shipper, etc.	1st offence max. fine US $20,000			1) 60% divided equally
	security deposit is US $60,000	issuance of bills of lading which bear false information	2nd offence max. fine US $60,000			2) 40% divided among the parties in proportion to the carryings of general cargo by each
		the payment of any unsubstantiated claim for cargo loss	3rd offence max. fine US $80,000			
		any act, failure or omission which if done, committed or suffered by a party would constitute a malpractice	4th and subsequent offence brings a max. fine US $120,000			

Philippines North America **Imports** East Coast West Coast **Canada United States** must provide regular service to trade area admission fee is US $10,000 security deposit is US $25,000	any part of the rates that are directly or indirectly refunded or remitted payment of illegitimate claims of any nature to any party(ies) either directly or indirectly manipulation of any mercantile business transactions so that any shipper(s) may obtain commissions, extra profits etc. carrying commodities at less than the rates agreed upon use of more than one agency or sub-agency for any one trade route at any port granting of free or reduced passage allowance except for what is allowed in Passenger Conference Agreements	Conference Chairman and 2/3 majority of members decide how to handle the case, whether to (1) form arbitration board (2) Secretary investigates and passes judgement or (3) members decide on the basis of ¾ majority for violation of tariff – sum equal to 4 times the amount of freight, other monies which the member would have received had the proper tariff been assessed for violation of rules and regulations: max. fine Cdn. $25,000 for each violation damages are liquidated on pro-rata basis with members	establishment of agreed minimum rates effective rate need 2/3 majority separate rates may be charged for cargo destined for overland common point and for cargo destined for local territory	the spread between the contract and non-contract rate is 15% of the contract rate	assessments may be adjusted from time to time to meet the expenses of maintaining a satisfactory organization
Straits-East Canada **Imports** East Coast Canada must provide regular service acceptance based on at least 2/3 majority of existing members	no information	no information	establishment of agreed minimum rates	contract rate is $5.00 less than non-contract rate regardless of the type of cargo for example: *Contract Non-Contract* Beer 137.25 142.25 32ft Yacht 4,741.00 4,746.00	no information

Conferences serving Asia (concluded)

Conference	Admission requirements	Malpractices		Rates		Conference administrative expenses
		Definition	Policing	General	Contract	
Java Pacific Rate Agreement Imports West Coast Canada United States	must provide regular service acceptance based on unanimous consent if membership is 3 or less, however, greater than 3 unanimous consent less one of existing members	breach of any provision of the agreement or tariffs	Secretary has the authority to investigate any allegations; for violation of tariff: fine not to exceed twice the amount of freight or US $10,000 whichever is less	establishment of agreed minimum rates	the spread between the contract and non-contract rate is 15% of the contract rate	no information
East Canada Freight Imports East Coast Canada	must provide regular service to trade area acceptance based on unanimous consent of existing members admission fee is US $1,000 security deposit is US $5,000	to engage either directly or indirectly in the transportation of cargoes at rates contrary to this agreement; employment of more than 1 agent at any port or place commission exceeding 5% on net freight, however, at Hong Kong only, each party may in addition, appoint 1 Chinese freight agent and commission may be paid within a max. 4% of net freight members entering into an agreement of any nature which would affect the integrity of this agreement	conference members members may if they unanimously decide, collect from the member so charged, a penalty of not more than US $5,000 for each breach	establishment of agreed minimum rates	the spread between the contract and non-contract rate is 15% of the contract rate	shared equally

Conferences serving Europe

Conference	Admission requirements	Malpractices		Rates		Conference administrative expenses
		Definition	Policing	General	Contract	
Canada Mediterranean Freight Exports East Coast Canada	requires a letter to the conference outlining the corporate and trade name, the service contemplated and such other information as the conference may require acceptance based on at least ¾ majority of existing members admission fee is Cdn. $10,000	any refund of any type payment of any of the following: insurance, differentials, port equalization or absorption of rail, storage or other charges against cargo, etc. the employment of more than one agent at any port or place	Secretary investigates complaints of malpractices 1st offence max. Cdn. $2,500 2nd offence max. Cdn. $5,000 3rd offence and subsequent max. Cdn. $25,000 ¾ majority to determine whether accused is expelled or pays a fine	reserve the right to declare rates on specified commodities open, provided there exists unanimous consent of members establishment of agreed minimum rates	the spread between the contract and non-contract rate is 15% of the contract rate	50% of total operating expenses shared equally, other 50% shared in proportion to amount of trade carried by each member

Conferences serving Europe (cont.)

Conference	Admission requirements	Malpractices		Rates		Conference administrative expenses
		Definition	Policing	General	Contract	
Canada UK Freight	must provide regular service	breach of any provision of the agreement or tariffs	Shipping Inspectors Limited will have complete authority to investigate any malpractice or breach of the agreement	establishment of agreed minimum rates	the spread between the contract and non-contract rate is 15% of the contract rate	borne by the members as may be mutually agreed
Exports	acceptance based on unanimous consent of existing members		liquidate damages on a pro-rata basis with members			
East Coast			for non-cooperation during investigation a member is subject to a fine up to Cdn. $5,000 per week for non-cooperation and max. fine of Cdn. $50,000 for each such violation			
Canada	contingent on admittance to corresponding Canadian North Atlantic Westbound conference		every violation is subject to a fine not exceeding Cdn. $50,000			
	admission fee is Cdn. $7,500		fine is determined on the basis of the nature of and gravity of the violation			
	conference has option of requesting information as they deem appropriate					

Canadian Continental Eastbound Freight Exports East Coast Canada					
must provide regular service (i.e. provide service to the indicated ports not more than 4 weeks apart)	unless *agreed otherwise* the following is *prohibited*: payment, refund or absorption of rail or coastal steamer or barging or trucking freights or of any other charges or any concession of any nature	appointed Shipping Inspectors Limited have complete authority to conduct any investigation they deem necessary	reserve the right to declare rates on commodities open, provided there exists unanimous consent of members	the spread between the contract and non-contract rate is 15% of the contract rate	borne by the members as may be mutually agreed
acceptance based on unanimous consent of existing members		every violation shall be subject to a fine not exceeding Cdn. $50,000 for each violation but such fine shall be fixed with due regard to the nature and gravity of violation involved	establishment of agreed minimum rates		
contingent on admittance to Continental Canadian Westbound conference		fines liquidated on pro-rata basis with members			
admission fee is Cdn. $7,500					

Conferences serving Europe (cont.)

Conference	Admission requirements	Malpractices		Rates		Conference administrative expenses
		Definition	Policing	General	Contract	
Canadian North Atlantic Westbound Freight	must provide regular service; acceptance based on unanimous approval of existing members	breach of any provision of the agreement or tariffs	Associated Conferences (independent authority) has complete authority to inspect all information they deem important	establishment of agreed minimum rates	contract and non-contract rate is 15% of the contract rate	borne by members as may be mutually agreed
Imports			1st offence max. £1,000			
East Coast			2nd offence and subsequent max. £2,000			
Canada	contingent on admittance to the corresponding Canada–UK Eastbound conference; admission fee is £3,000		fines liquidated on pro-rata basis with member			
Continental Canadian Westbound Freight	must provide regular service; acceptance based on unanimous consent of existing members	breach of any provision of the agreement of tariffs	Associated Conferences (independent authority) has complete authority to inspect all information they deem necessary	establishment of agreed minimum rates	no contract rate	borne by members as may be mutually agreed
Imports			fine depends on gravity of breach			
East Coast			penalty not to exceed Cdn. $20,000 for each violation			
Canada	contingent on admittance to Canadian Continental					

	Admission / Requirements	Absorption / Other provisions	Arbitration / Fines	Minimum rates	Rate system	Expenses
Eastbound conference	admission fee is Cdn. $7,500			establishment of agreed minimum rates	yes, triple rate system: non-contract, regular and tariff; shipper contract 6.25% reduction; shipper and receiver contract 12.5% reduction	borne by the members equally
Mediterranean Canada Westbound Freight	must provide regular service	absorption by lines of wharfage, storage or other charges against cargo	conference members select arbitration with at least ¾ majority			
Imports	acceptance based on at least 2/3 majority of existing members	absorption by lines of charges of delivering or non-carrying connecting carriers, port equalization or absorption of rail or other differentials	3 arbitrators, one appointed by members, one by accused and a third jointly			
East Coast			fines for each violation are assessed by members			
Canada	admission fee is Cdn. $10,000	absorption or equalization of insurance differential as between vessels of the Member Lines or of other carriers	damages liquidated on a pro-rata basis with members			
Mediterranean North Pacific Coast Freight	must provide regular service; admission fee is US $4,500	no information	Controlling Committee appointed has complete authority	establishment of agreed minimum rates	the spread between the contract and non-contract rate is 15% of the contract rate	the expenses incurred by the conference shall be divided according to agreements to be purposely reached among the members
Imports	security deposit is US $7,500		1st offence: a fine not less than US $1,000 nor greater than US $3,000			
West Coast	US $7,500		2nd offence: a fine not less than US $3,000 nor greater than US $5,000			
			3rd offence: a fine not less than US $5,000 nor greater than US $7,500			
Canada United States			liquidated damages on pro-rata basis			

Conferences serving Europe (cont.)

| Conference | Admission requirements | Malpractices | | Rates | | Conference administrative expenses |
		Definition	Policing	General	Contract	
Western Canada Europe Exports West Coast Canada	must provide regular service acceptance based on at least ¾ majority of existing members admission fee is Cdn. $25,000	prohibition of return of commission fees, compensation, concession, free or reduced storage, free or reduced passenger fares, any bribe, gratuity, gift of substantial value or other payment or remuneration through any device whatsoever the payment of brokerage fee of more than ¾% for grain, grain products and oil seeds in bulk	Controller polices the conference 3 arbitrators, one appointed by accused and a third jointly fine for non-observance of this agreement or any of the rules, regulations or tariffs of the conference shall be not less than Cdn. $500 nor more than Cdn. $25,000 for any single offence	establishment of agreed minimum rates the members may from time to time open rates on certain commodities	the spread between the contract and non-contract rate is 15% of the contract rate	regulations adopted from time to time which shall include provisions in respect to meeting payment of expenses incurred in the maintenance of the conference
North Europe Canada Pacific Freight Imports West Coast Canada	must provide regular service acceptance based on unanimous consent of existing members	no information	Secretary has the authority to investigate any member to determine whether or not an infraction had occurred penalty for any breach max. US $10,000	establishment of agreed minimum rates	no contract rate	expenses will be divided between the members on an equal basis, unless later on it becomes advisable or necessary to divide some in agreed proportions

Canada European Eastbound Mail Committee Exports East Coast Canada	must provide regular service and approval by Canadian Post Office	no information	Secretary has authority to investigate	establishment of agreed minimum rates Canadian Post Office representatives shall have the right to appear before the membership of the agreement in support of their requests	no contract rate	no information
Outbound Asbestos Agreement Exports East Coast Canada	no information	no information	Secretary has authority to investigate ocean carriers try to resolve the matter but if unable to do so it is referred to the Associated Conferences	establishment of agreed minimum rates	the spread between the contract and non-contract rate is 15% of the contract rate	no information
Polaric Joint Service Exports Imports East Coast Canada	no information	no information	dispute first submitted to General Director if dispute is not unanimously resolved then referred to arbitration in the country of the accused party	establishment of agreed minimum rates	no contract rate	no information

Conferences serving Oceania

| Conference | Admission requirements | Malpractices | | Rates | | Conference administrative expenses |
		Definition	Policing	General	Contract	
Australia East Coast St Lawrence & Great Lakes Imports East Coast Canada	must provide regular service acceptance is based on unanimous consent of existing members	no information	no information	reserve the right to declare rates on specified commodities open and/or closed as the conference deems necessary provided there exists unanimous consent establishment of agreed minimum rates	the spread between the contract and non-contract rate is 10% of the contract rate	each member is charged 50% and the other 50% shall be shared on the basis of the proportion that a member's sailings in the trade bears to total sailings of all members
Eastern Canada Australia–New Zealand Exports East Coast Canada	must provide regular service acceptance based on unanimous consent of existing members admission fee is Cdn. $5,000	no information	Secretary has the authority to investigate and determine whether or not an infraction took place fine is determined by breach in accordance with contract law, if uncertain of amount then will be equal to freight charges damages liquidated on pro-rata basis with members	establishment of agreed minimum rates rates on any commodity or commodities may be declared open	the spread between the contract and non-contract rate is 15% of the contract rate	all expenses shared equally

Australia/ Eastern Canada Shipping	no information no information	no information	establishment of agreed minimum rates	the spread between the contract and non-contract rate is 10% of the contract rate	no information
Imports					
East Coast Canada					
Pacific Coast Australian Tariff Bureau	must provide regular service; admission fee is US $5,000	no information	Secretary has the authority to conduct the investigation; in case of a violation one of the following courses of action will be taken: 1) fine *not to exceed* US $10,000 for each violation; 2) suspension of voting rights not to exceed 6 months; 3) expulsion from conference	reserve the right to declare rates on certain commodities to be open; establishment of agreed minimum rates	the spread between the contract and non-contract rate is 15% of the contract rate	expenses shall be borne as may be determined from time to time by the members
Exports					
West Coast					
Canada United States					

Source: Conference agreements filed with the Canadian Transport Commission, December 1977.

2 Flags of convenience

Introduction

After the liner conferences, the second most important issue in international maritime trade relations during this last half of a century has been open registry. The development of open registry (or 'flag of convenience' (FOC) as it is more frequently, but less meaningfully, called) was one of the most notable features of the 1960s and early 1970s. In 1963, 11 per cent of the world fleet was operating under such flags. By 1976 it had risen to 27 per cent and the tonnage involved had grown more than six times to about 100 gross registered tons (grt). Since then, however, their share of the world fleet has more or less stagnated and, by mid-1981, the total fleet of the six leading countries traditionally regarded as FOC registries had started to decline in absolute terms with a drop of one and a quarter million grt from the mid-1980 level. But the debate over them, at international fora, did not abate.

The concept of the FOC registry is the complete antithesis of the completely state-controlled transporter (of the State trading nations (STNs) or semi-controlled of the DMNs) of nationally generated cargo and, as such, is philosophically acceptable and encouraged by the basic approach of the TMNs. Unfortunately, the idea of the 'free flag' was for a considerable period associated with an abdication of the obligation that:

a state must effectively exercise its jurisdiction and control in administrative, technical and social matters over ships flying its flag.

This principle has also been endorsed in the Convention on the Law of the Sea of 1982. As a result, these fleets have come under attack from both those countries (particularly DMNs) who saw the existence of such fleets as economic colonialism and a bar to their own national development, and by those countries and organizations such as the International Transport Workers' Federation (ITWF) who have sought to improve substandard ships and restrict the undercutting of wage levels, particularly in North-West Europe.

What could have been expected to happen to the FOC registry fleets during the 1980s and 1990s? If left to the action of pure economic forces, there was little doubt that those fleets would have probably maintained their steady growth, as the various competitive pressures forced increasing concentration on cost minimization, as they had done throughout the period of the shipping depressions of the late 1970s and the early 1980s. However, the future of open registry did, and will, depend far more on social and political forces than upon the question of pure economics and/or market forces. In essence the decision lay with the authorities of the FOC registry states themselves as to whether they considered that the provision of open registry facilities gave them advantages outweighing the opprobium to which they were exposed in the international community.

What became apparent was that the world community was becoming impatient and progressively less willing to accept the operation of substandard ships under whatever flag, and the FOC registry countries themselves were all working towards this end under the aegis of the IMO and ILO, although there was still a long way to go. Singapore led the way in this direction, first by legislation to eliminate the oldest ships on its register and to establish clearly the ownership of ships under its flag, and then to limit its register to genuinely resident companies: this entailed its removal from the list of the FOC registers from the beginning of 1982. There seemed every reason to expect that in this sense the genuine link between ship and country of registry, as defined in the Geneva Convention on the High Seas and later by the Third United Nations Convention on the Law of the Sea (UNCLOS III) 1982, would become progressively more real as the FOC registry countries acquired mechanisms to ensure that the international obligations that they had accepted — particularly under IMO- and ILO-sponsored Conventions — could be honoured and policed.

Were that to materialize, the issue of 'genuine link' might have been settled once and for all. But it was not to be. Instead, the debate was elevated from the legalism of genuine links to the socio-politico-economics of genuine *economic* link. The forum was transferred from the labour (ILO) and the technical (IMO) to the economic (UNCTAD). Thus, UNCLOS III had not qualitatively changed the position as it pertained in 1958 at Geneva.

This study examines the genuine link within the context of past, present and future. It traces the development, nature and future of the new United Nations Convention on Registration of Ships and points out its shortcomings. In addition, the advantages and disadvantages of FOC operations (to the owners, registry states, beneficial states and the international community) are outlined.

The Flag, Shipping and Nationalism

Flags and Shipping Nationalism

There is something about the flag, *per se*, which is not easily appreciated. Although it is true that a flag can be a mere piece of coloured or plain paper or fabric, over the centuries this paper or fabric has played crucial roles in many circumstances to an extent that, at the other extreme, men and women have been willing to fight and defend and even die for it.[1] Why? A clearer appreciation of the deeper functions of flags, and their linkage to the policies of the countries that fly them, might provide an insight into the current controversy surrounding international shipping generally and the flags of convenience (FOCs) particularly.

Flags have practical uses, but their primary function has always been social communication.[2] This role is enhanced in relation to nationalism where they stimulate the viewer to feel and act in a particular way. In that aspect they represent or identify the existence, presence, origin, authority, possession, loyalty, glory, beliefs, objectives, and status of an entire nation.[3]

Thus football clubs, ships, airlines, companies and army regiments have all symbolized their greatness with flags. It is not uncommon to see victorious athletes shedding tears when their national anthems are played and national flags raised simultaneously at international competitions. In these examples, *inter alia*, flags are employed to honour and dishonour, warn and encourage, threaten and promise, exalt and condemn, commemorate and deny.[4] They remind, incite and defy the schoolchild, the soldier, the voter, the enemy, the ally, and the stranger. Furthermore flags authenticate claims, dramatize political demands, establish a common framework within which like-minded nations[5] are willing to work out mutually agreeable solutions — or postulate and maintain irreconcilable differences that prevent agreements from being reached. It is for this reason that the first thing explorers did was to plant their flags on arrival at the North and South Poles just as astronauts did on the moon.[6]

It is scarcely possible to conceive of the world — of human society — without the flag. This is particularly true of shipping and airlines in this era of political and economic nationalism in which the world is organized into a definite number of nation-states. In fact, in a classical sense, a ship flying a national flag is treated as a floating island: part of that nation.[7] Thus, international shipping, as ideologies, religion, and social and class distinctions, have all resorted to the flag to symbolize their importance in the everyday life of individuals and in great political movements, yet none of these have slowed down the growth of nationalism and many have reinforced the nation-state.[8] Because flags constitute explicit self-analysis by nation-states, vexillology, the study of flag history and symbolism, may justly claim to be an auxiliary to international maritime law and policy. Although that general study is beyond the scope of this chapter since we are here more concerned with the flag in relation to shipping, it provides a useful start.[9]

UNCLOS I and II and the Flag State

The important thing to note from the foregone discussion is that there had always been a genuine link between a state and a particular flag before the invention of the FOC system. This, however, has been lacking in the FOC; hence the present controversy. The Geneva Convention on the Law of the Sea 1958 or the United Nations Conference and Convention on the Law of the Sea (UNCLOS I as it is now popularly known)[10] was probably the first modern international instrument to link the flag to the state and to a national ship. Nations had, of course, flown flags on ships for centuries and on airlines for decades. The Geneva Convention on the High Seas (part of UNCLOS I) introduced five major provisions relating to flags and shipping in international maritime law.[11] This is first that:

> Every state, whether coastal or not, has the right to sail ships under its flags on the high seas.[12]

In so providing, the Convention merely codified the customary position in international law that had hitherto prevailed.

The second provision was that:

> Each state shall fix the conditions for the grant of its nationality to ships, for the registration of ships in its territory, and for the right to fly its flag. Ships have the nationality of the state whose flag they are entitled to fly . . . .[13]

Unfortunately the Convention did not prescribe these conditions for the grant of registration. In so doing UNCLOS I left it to different states to impose varying standards or, as in some cases, none at all. The exercise of that option meant that some states had higher standards than others. It is submitted that it is the attraction of flags from high to low (or no) standard requirements that gave birth to FOC registry especially when economics entered into the equation. Otherwise there is no problem with the third requirement that:

> Each state shall issue to ships which it has granted the right to fly its flag document to that effect.[14]

The fourth provision is thus:

> Ships shall sail under the flag of one state only and, save in exceptional cases expressly provided for in international treaties or in these Articles, shall be subject to its exclusive jurisdiction on the high seas. A ship may not change its flag during voyage or while in a port of call, save in the case of a real transfer of ownership or change of registry.[15]

This provision was probably intended to catch pirates, slave-trading ships and others abusing the grant of a particular flag such as smugglers and drug-traffickers. However, the provision does not eliminate the possibility of dual nationalities or the use of a different nationality for every voyage. In this day and age satellite transfers and changes can be made almost instantly. In fact there is evidence to suggest such instant changes are fast becoming common practice, and they are proper within the provision.[16]

It is the fifth requirement which relates, for the first time, to the expression *convenience*. It provides that:

> A ship which sails under the flags of two or more states, using them according to *convenience*, may not claim any of the nationalities in question with respect to any other state, and may be assimilated to a ship without nationality.[17] (Emphasis supplied.)

This provision reappears in 1982, but surprisingly not in 1986. We shall return to a fuller discussion of 'convenience' later. Suffice to mention, however, that the above provision prohibits only the contemporaneous use of dual nationality but not the incidence of instant or frequent changes according to *convenience*. Unsatisfactory as the above provisions are, they remain in force until the new 1982 Convention, which repeals and replaces it, comes into force.[18] The Second Geneva Conference on the Law of the Sea 1960 (UNCLOS II) was aborted and, even if it had materialized, it would probably have made very little difference to the issue in question since all the United Nations Conferences on the Law of the Sea tend to ignore completely, or treat only in passing, economic issues relating to international maritime transport. That leads us to the Third United Nations Conference (and Convention) on the Law of the Sea (UNCLOS III) 1982.[19]

UNCLOS III and the Duties of the Flag State

With regard to the five provisions described above, the 1982 Convention merely endorsed the 1958 position, and it would be unproductive to repeat them here. However, due to the advent of the coastal state as a power in international ocean-use policy-making, the Convention did reflect the move to external enforcements as a means of avoiding infringement upon state sovereignty while meeting world environmental concerns.[20] This advent was marked by the extension of coastal state jurisdiction from 3 to 12 miles and the creation of the Exclusive Economic Zone (EEZ). Thus, a tripartite system was set up in the Convention under which the flag state has increased responsibility for ensuring vessel compliance with international standards. This is complemented by a limited coastal and port state enforcement of international standards to vessels sailing in their waters or on the high seas. Much of the Convention was directed towards balancing flag state sovereignty and freedom of navigation with coastal state resources management and environmental concerns.[21]

The actual regimes set up to deal with passage through territorial waters are topics of interest in themselves but are beyond the scope of this study and have nothing to do with the issue of *genuine link*. Suffice to say, they exist and are a tangle of overlapping jurisdictions and evident compromises at the negotiating table.[22] However, although the 1982 Convention evidences some cosmetic changes from the 1958 High Seas Convention, many of the provisions were imported with very little alteration. Article 91 duplicates Article 5 of 1958 with the dropping of the phrase 'in particular'. Article 94 replicates Article 10 of 1958, except that it is an expanded version.[23] In addition Article 94(6) provides for supervision of flag state enforcement by other states while Article 94(7) obliges flag states to hold an inquiry in the event of a marine casualty or navigational accident on the high seas. Article 217 requires compliance with international standards set out for pollution control. Finally, Article 235 renders states liable for ensuring that recourse is available for environmental compensation damages.[24]

But the question of attribution of nationality and genuine link is neither attempted nor clarified to any extent by the 1982 Convention. Although it was a great pity that this opportunity was missed at the largest, longest and most international gathering ever to codify sea law, it is not, however, surprising that it ignored the economic aspects of maritime transport,[25] for the Convention was more concerned with the economics of the exploitation and distribution of deep sea-bed resources which formed its central theme. Under organized and orchestrated pressure from the pro-FOC lobby the Convention again ducked the real issue of *economic link* in favour of the amorphous *legal link*. Indeed, it was never the intention of the Convention to add the requirement of an economic link, a view supported by an eminent academic:[26]

> To my knowledge, there was no intention by the Conference to change existing international law on the question of flags of convenience or open registries in general and there was no intention to add any requirement of economic link. In fact, I would say that the general intention of the conference in dealing with these issues was to avoid opening yet another controversial problem and from what I understand the separation sentences in Articles 91 and 94 was merely a drafting matter . . . .[27]

This thesis was backed by subsequent events. It is not a coincidence that most of the states offering FOC registry facilities had signed the Convention by December 1982, indicating, perhaps, substantial agreement with the document on the issue. It is doubtful that this would have occurred if it had been believed that the Convention contained a clause similar in effect to the 1958 non-recognition clause.[28] As they say in Africa: one can hardly expect a monkey to pass judgement on a forest. However, for quite different reasons, the beneficiaries of FOC registry in the TMNs declined to sign in opposition to the seabed clauses. Thus, the problem that plagued the non-recognition clause concerning infringement on the economic sovereignty of a state or interference in international law- and policy-making are still very much alive for international law-makers.[29] For the progressive development of open registry between 1939 and 1982, see Table 2.1.

Table 2.1   Flag of convenience fleets (vessels of 100 grt and over — as at mid-year)

Year	Liberia Ships	Liberia mil grt	Panama Ships	Panama mil grt	Honduras Ships	Honduras mil grt	Costa Rica Ships	Costa Rica mil grt	Lebanon Ships	Lebanon mil grt	Cyprus Ships	Cyprus mil grt	Somalia Ships	Somalia mil grt	Singapore Ships	Singapore mil grt	Bahamas Ships	Bahamas mil grt	Bermuda Ships	Bermuda mil grt	FOC total mil grt	World total mil grt	FOC as % of World tonnage
1939	—	—	159	0.72	32	0.06															0.80	69.44	1.2
1949	5	0.05	536	3.02	123	0.41															3.47	82.57	4.2
1951	69	0.59	607	3.61	152	0.51															4.71	87.24	5.4
1952	105	0.90	606	3.74	145	0.47															5.11	90.18	5.7
1953	158	1.43	593	3.91	146	0.47	50	0.15													5.96	93.35	6.4
1954	245	2.38	595		130	0.44	70	0.20													7.11	97.42	7.3
1955	436	4.00	555	3.92	117	0.43	114	0.34													8.69	100.57	8.6
1956	582	5.58	556	4.09	106	0.39	142	0.51													10.40	105.20	9.9
1957	743	7.47	580	4.13	94	0.37	152	0.52													12.49	110.27	11.3
1958	975	10.08	602	4.26	89	0.34	144	0.51													15.27	118.03	12.9
1959	1085	11.94	639	4.58	78	0.20	91	0.29													17.01	124.94	13.6
1960	977	11.28	607	4.23	59	0.15	44	0.09	74	0.26											16.01	129.77	12.4
1961	903	10.93	601	4.05	58	0.12			131	0.55											15.65	135.96	11.5
1962	853	10.57	592	3.85	54	0.11			164	0.75											15.28	139.98	10.9
1963	893	11.39	619	3.89	49	0.10			190	0.91											16.29	145.86	11.2
1964	1117	14.55	691	4.27	46	0.09			174	0.85											19.76	153.00	12.9
1965	1287	17.54	692	4.46	47	0.08			157	0.78											22.86	160.39	14.3
1966	1436	20.60	702	4.54	43	0.07			149	0.74	35	0.18									26.13	171.13	15.3
1967	1513	22.60	757	4.76	45	0.07			139	0.60	60	0.36									28.39	182.10	15.6
1968	1613	25.72	798	5.10	45	0.07			122	0.44	109	0.65	15	0.06	73	0.13					32.17	195.15	16.5
1969	1731	29.22	823	5.37	51	0.07			95	0.30	134	0.77	58	0.20	112	0.23					36.25	211.66	17.1
1970	1869	33.30	886	5.64	52	0.06			79	0.18	207	1.14	79	0.37	153	0.42	144	0.28	48	0.68	42.07	227.49	18.5
1971	2060	38.55	1031	6.26	54	0.07			65	0.13	277	1.50	109	0.59	185	0.58	145	0.36	47	0.81	48.85	247.20	19.8
1972	2234	44.44	1337	7.79	58	0.07			70	0.12	394	2.01	148	0.87	281	0.87	144	0.21	48	0.81	57.19	268.34	21.3
1973	2289	49.90	1692	9.57	57	0.07			81	0.12	589	2.94	239	1.69	387	2.00	143	0.18	52	0.86	67.33	289.93	23.2
1974	2332	55.32	1962	11.00	56	0.07			88	0.12	722	3.39	276	1.92	511	2.88	129	0.15	59	1.53	76.38	311.32	24.5
1975	2520	65.82	2418	13.67	60	0.07			123	0.17	735	3.22	273	1.81	610	3.89	119	0.19	59	1.45	90.29	342.16	26.4
1976	2600	73.48	2680	15.63	57	0.07			136	0.21	765	3.11	255	1.79	722	5.48	119	0.15	69	1.56	101.48	372.00	27.3
1977	2617	79.98	3267	19.46	63	0.10			163	0.23	800	2.79	31	0.16	872	6.79	109	0.11	88	1.75	111.37	393.68	28.3
1978	2523	80.19	3640	20.75	70	0.13			189	0.28	793	2.60			954	7.49	93	0.08	99	1.81	111.33	406.00	27.9
1979	2466	81.53	3803	22.32	99	0.19			185	0.26	762	2.36			1031	7.87	91	0.12	112	1.73	116.38	413.02	28.2
1980	2401	80.29	4090	24.19	124	0.21			203	0.27	688	2.09			988	7.66	91	0.09	114	1.72	116.52	419.91	27.7
1981	2281	74.91	4461	27.66	143	0.20			230	0.32	588	1.82			828	6.89	106	0.20	75	0.50	112.50	420.83	26.7
1982	2189	70.72	5032	32.60	172	0.23			240	0.37	587	2.15			849	(7.18)	96	0.43	68	0.47	114.15 or 106.97	424.74	26.9 or 25.2

Source: Lloyd's Register of Shipping Statistical Tables.

71

Economic Link and Open Registry Phenomena

Genuine Link: the Legal Regime

Part of the problem is that nowhere are the precise details and contents of *genuine link* provided. The Geneva Convention on the High Seas simply provided that:

> There *must* exist a *genuine link* between the State and the ship; in particular the State must effectively exercise its jurisdiction and control in administrative, technical and social matters over ships flying its flag.[30] (Emphasis added.)

In normal circumstances the use of such words as 'must' implies a mandate or precedent and 'effective' would imply real or material. But practice since 1958 implies that their use here is only superficial and tantamount to the words 'may' and 'optional' respectively. It is also interesting to note that flag state control only relates to legal, administrative, technical and social matters but not to *economic* control which is at the very heart of the controversy.[31] Even if we were to read the provision in accordance with the *ejusdem generis* rule there would still be very little guidance obtainable. Would *genuine link* be found in the state's ability to effectively exercise those powers or in something more, and would that something more include *economic link*? It is accordingly submitted that for *genuine economic link* to exist between a ship and its state of registry, it would mean ownership of the vessel by nationals, residents, indigenous companies and other persons, naturalized or not, wholly subject to the jurisdiction and control of the flag state.[32] That would include citizens, permanent residents and people who have allegiance to and/or have interest of the state of registry at heart. It would, in other words, exclude foreigners, proxy owners and other ownerships for the mere purposes of convenience. As things stand at the moment beneficial ownership and true management of the FOC is held by persons and entities who are wholly unconcerned about the interests of the flag state and are free to come and go as it suits their more or less mercenary interests.[33]

The phrase 'genuine link' first emerged in a context quite un-related to shipping, but was nevertheless a legal aspect, a factor which further clouded the issue. It came to the attention of the international legal community in a judgement rendered by the International Court of Justice (ICJ) in 1955 — the *Nottebohm* case. In 1933 Nottebohm, a German national, obtained naturalization from the tiny principality of Liechtenstein.[34] From 1905 to 1939 he had been resident in

Guatemala, but had resided in Liechtenstein for only three weeks prior to naturalization. During the Second World War he was interned and his property in Guatemala seized. In 1945 he returned to Liechtenstein where he remained until his death,[35] whereupon his adopted country sponsored a claim for compensation on his behalf in 1951. The ICJ decided that, although Liechtenstein as a sovereign state had the right to grant nationality on whatever basis it chose, its so doing did not create obligations beyond its boundaries.[36] Perhaps the same principle should be applicable to FOC registry.

It can of course be argued that the Nottebohm case was decided on issues and principles quite unrelated to shipping. Nevertheless the principle enunciated there helps to illuminate the inadequacy of the genuine link requirement in international maritime law. Just to remind ourselves the material holding was that:

> . . . nationality is a legal bond having as its basis a social fact of attachment, a genuine connection of existence, interests and sentiments, together with the existence of reciprocal rights and duties.[37]

In all honesty, it cannot be argued that the relationship between the FOC vessel and the registry states resembles, even minimally, the principle of this case. In 1958 the delegates at Geneva had the benefit of the Nottebohm case before them, but chose to turn a blind eye. It is submitted that that kind of interpretation would have been in line with the natural meaning of the word 'genuine': viz. natural; native; real; pure; direct; and sincere; not spurious.[38]

It will be remembered that only about 80 countries attended the 1958 Geneva Conference. Most TMNs were mindful of beneficial interests of the FOC, which had already existed for some time. In the end, the Convention merely codified customary law, created by these same countries for themselves, and confirmed what had in practice been a status quo.[39] It could hardly be expected to be radical and/or creative. The real opportunity for change first occurred in 1982 but went begging. Given that the reasons for moving to an FOC registry will vary from each owner, it is still possible to point to a common element: the desire for freedom from burdensome regulation and allowance of maximum operating flexibility.[40] This enables the shipowner to operate his vessel in the most profitable manner possible, and also presupposes a free market economy. The owners and beneficiaries were horrified at threats of international regulation replacing the very (national) regulation they had run away from. That marked the limit of legal solution to the question of genuine link.[41]

*Economic Link: the Nature of Free Flags
and the Economic Regime*

The shift in the strategy of organized labour and those TMNs who had opposed FOC registry from direct regulation of registration in the 1950s, which proved politically and legally unacceptable, to indirect regulation through international standards, succeeded in its object of emphasizing the legal over the economic as far as genuine link is concerned.[42] It is important, however, to realize that, in the interim period from 1950 to 1982, the world economic and political structure changed greatly as many more states became participants in the international decision-making process. This, in turn, led to shifting allegiances and changed perceptions on the part of many opponents of FOC registry shipping, as different economic costs were foreseen.[43] It is as if the world was agreeing with the Chinese saying that in politics there are no permanent friends.

Concern about the existence and commercial impact of FOC registries (especially Panama and Liberia) had grown commensurate with the increase in tonnage registered under them. From the late 1940s to the early 1960s the TMNs and other international maritime unions reacted strongly to FOC registry fleets.[44] Their historical monopoly in shipping was ironically broken as several DMNs emerged through the FOC registry system to become major flag states. Reaction to this commercial threat took the form of politico-legal action at the 1958 Geneva Conference. This was followed by an attempt to block the Liberian and Panamanian claims (based on registered tonnage) to positions on the Maritime Safety Committee of IMCO (now IMO).[45] During this period pressure was exerted on the international community by adversely affected interests to restrict FOC registry practice through registration requirements. As is now well known, this tactic ran into trouble at the Conference, where the obvious legal problem of infringement on state sovereignty and the accepted right to grant nationality came to the fore.[46]

Because both the Geneva and 1982 Conventions avoided the central issues, it was left to the academics, *inter alia*, to make an educated guess at what constituted the definition of FOC registry. The FOC have been called all sorts of names: flag of necessity, free flags; flags of refuge; mercenary flags; fly-by-nights; 'ship with its body in Famagusta, its money in Monaco, and its sail entrusted to a group of mercenaries';[47] 'Sovereignty for Sale'; etc. Doganis and Metaxas looked at it from the viewpoint of the firm which resorts to using open registry:

> Flags of Convenience are the national flags of those states with whom shipowners register their vessels in order to avoid (a) the fiscal obligations and (b) the conditions and terms of employment of factors of production that would have been applicable if their ships were registered in their own countries.[48]

Thus, they see it in terms of financial advantages, made possible by lack of uniformity in conditions for registry, and manning costs. But perhaps the most satisfactory of all definitions is the one developed at the Polytechnic of Central London and based on the function of the registry:

> A flag of Convenience is the flag of a state whose government sees registration not as a procedure necessary in order to impose sovereignty and hence control over its shipping but as a service which can be sold to foreign shipowners wishing to escape fiscal and other consequences of registration under their own flag.[49]

It takes two to tango, as it were. FOC registry has nothing to do with sovereignty as its supporters would have us believe, but rather with hard economics. It is as if some countries have suddenly discovered that sovereignty is something which can be bought and sold hence 'Sovereignty for Sale'.[50] In short it is providing refuge for outlaws, i.e. operators evading legal requirements in their own jurisdictions: hence 'flags of refuge'.

Characteristics of Open Registry

In addition to the provisions of the 1958 and 1982 Conventions and the definitions above, further insights into the understanding of the nature, characteristics, working and root-causes of FOC registry can be gathered from samples of the descriptions below.[51] To start, my own definition would be thus:

> Flags of convenience are national flags flown by mercenary ships that have been registered in countries other than those of their owners in order to escape high domestic wages and taxation, and stringent regulations on safety, manning, employment and related requirements. Shipowners argue that they must engage in this practice because they cannot fulfil all these domestic requirements and then be able to compete with foreign shipowners. Labour unions contend that these flags constitute unfair violation of collective bargaining. Environmentalists point out that flags of convenience are largely responsible for most of the world's sea-based pollution. And non-open registry developing countries fear that the system exploits their cheap labour and comparative advantage; is an abuse of sovereignty and obstacle to the development of their own genuine fleets.[52]

This definition-cum-description summarizes the arguments of all interested and concerned parties and elevates the argument squarely to the level of economics. Economic problems can only be solved by a requirement for an economic link. So long as that is not the case (and it has not been) then the controversy over the genuine link in FOC registry will ramble on.[53] Be that as it may, the authors of the *Rochdale Report* admitted that it was not easy to provide a simple definition of flags of convenience or open registries as they are sometimes called. They instead identified a number of common features which have been repeated ever since by almost everybody writing and researching on FOC registry (myself being no exception) and these are:[54]

1. The country of registry allows ownership and/or control of its merchant vessels by non-citizens;
2. Access to registry is easy;
3. Taxes on the income from the ships are not levied locally or are low;
4. The country of registry is a small power with no national requirements under any foreseeable circumstances for all the shipping registered, but receipts from very small charges on a large tonnage may produce a substantial effect on its national income and balance of payments;
5. Manning of ships by non-nationals is freely permitted; and
6. The country of registry has neither the power nor the administrative machinery to impose any governmental or international regulations; nor has the country the wish or the power to control the companies themselves.[55]

The above definitions, descriptions and comments are not conclusive. The *Rochdale Report* for instance, was only up-to-date as of 1967 when it was produced in 1970. The point to be made, however, is that, on the basis of the *Rochdale Report* at least, the FOC registry countries are clearly unable (nor wish) to fulfil their national and international obligations[56] under both the 1958 Geneva Convention and the new 1982 Convention. Of more significance is the pro-FOC registry argument that to require these countries' adherence to their obligations under international law would be an infringement on their national sovereignty[57] and, in addition, that to do so would infringe on the freedom of navigation and, therefore, of the high seas. So the ploy continues. Hiding behind all these legalistic shams is an escape from the real rationale, i.e. economics and politics, which were deliberately avoided by both the Geneva and the 1982 Conventions.[58]

As will be apparent in the next paragraph, the developments and rationale for FOC registry can only be found in the antagonistic contradictions inherent in capitalism and the system's failure to resolve those contradictions. In short, the contradiction lies in the capitalist shipowners' desire for truly free enterprise[59] in a system that, by its very nature, thrives on monopolies and the deridal of the very competition on which it was supposed to have been founded. In order to drive this point home, take for example the case of shipping in the USA, the supposed protector of capitalism. One of the principal advantages for owners using FOC registries lies in the field of crew costs, and applies particularly to ships beneficially owned by US companies or individuals.[60] Ships flying the US flag should, as a rule, be manned by US citizens paid at US agreed wage rates. In many cases too they must be built in US yards and, except in emergencies, carry out repairs and dry docking in US ports. These regulations would seem to price many US flag ships out of the international market and directs us towards the history and the reasons for the development of FOC registry.[61]

Why Open Registry? Development and Rationale

The Emergence of Open Registry

From the foregone discussion the natural consequence of the contradictions is that a US operator was faced with two choices: extinction or *flag out*. But the same choice probably faced his ancestors, although nobody really knows exactly how far back the FOC goes. They are probably as old as the invention of the flag itself and the emergence of seafaring.[62] The precise details lie in the domain of maritime historians. What is relevant is that it was probably created by Europeans and perfected by Americans. The three major phases in its recent history are: the pre-First World War era (formative years); between the Wars to the 1960s (active and systematic); and post-1960s to late 1970s (golden era).[63] Otherwise, the origins of the modern FOC are generally to be found in the ancient (and relatively modern) wars and the need to dispose of the surplus builds following these engagements, as well as the inevitable recessions that ensued.

First, there were the European Wars, including both pre- and post-Napoleonic, during which certain European powers registered elsewhere in neutral parts of Europe or even abroad to avoid capture and seizure. Then came both the American War of Independence and the American Civil War during which Panamanian registry[64] was created to avoid capture first by the British, and later by either the federates or the confederates respectively. By the First World War, the practice had been perfected. The then-allied TMNs registered in neutral territories to avoid German torpedoes and capture. The same thing was repeated in the Second World War to evade destruction by German U-boats and battleships as well as capture by the Axis powers of Hitler, Hirohito and Mussolini.[65]

The second rationale for FOC development is to be found in the romantic and adventurous nature of seafaring and the quest for the freedom to engage in illicit trade. It is this aspect which is universally abhorrent and is also the classical type that would run foul of the Geneva and now the 1982 Conventions.[66] Under this heading would fall pirates and other plunderers. But a notable practice concerned slave-trading ships, resulting from the fact that abolition did not take place simultaneously between Britain on the one hand and the rest of Europe and the USA on the other.[67] In addition, those involved in narcotics smuggling are also known to have found foreign registry appealing on their trade routes between North and South America. Also in the USA, during the Prohibition of the 1920s the so-called rum-runners and bootleggers flourished by resorting to the use of foreign flags. Down the list, under this heading, one would add gun-runners and the arms trade;[68] fugitives and others who use tax havens; and the use of such flags to evade embargoes, blockades and sanctions. That does not necessarily mean the FOC was used mainly by criminal and other such elements. Far from it. The majority of the operators were probably honest businessmen whose sole motives were (and are still) only profitmaking.[69]

The third rationale presupposes a few assumptions: that shipping is the most international of all multinational ventures; that it is both a service industry and an industry in its own right; and finally, that it is also the most politicized of all industries. In the midst of all these is the paradox that this industry had once always been run as a private venture.[70] However, the ravages of the Second World War necessitated some form of state intervention, even within the predominantly free enterprise TMNs. In return for this assistance, shipowners had to subject themselves to a certain amount of state regulation or even outright nationalizations in a few incidences.[71] There were, however, a few private operators who loathed any form of state control and would have none of it but nevertheless faced extinction without some form of state aid. The only way out for these cavalier capitalists was to register abroad. These neo-classical capitalists wanted to pursue *laissez-faire* to its natural or logical (but absurd) conclusions.[72] In the era of imperialism and the export of capital, the era of the spread of shipping multinationals such as the liner conferences, these adventurers were aided by the discovery of willingness, cheapness and the co-liberalism of certain DMNs. Thus, the need to survive recession, competition and to escape state control was the principal rationale for the development of the

78

FOC.[73] Once again, capitalism had found a way out of its own contradictions.

Fourth, and finally, geopolitical reasons provided the modern context of free flags. In this respect the FOCs date back to the cold wars of the 1950s and 1960s when the USA sought to expand its fleets in readiness against perceived Soviet threats. It was assumed that if and when the Soviet Union attacked there would be sufficient US and Western Alliance flags registered abroad to be called upon.[74] So, just as in the first rationale above, war and hostilities did not only lead to the creation of the FOC but has also continued its maintenance. I refer, of course, to the National Defence Reserve Fleets (NDRF) of the USA and the 'Preparedness for War' mania, a system and principle whereby she registered some of her flags overseas, paid their war insurance and other benefits on condition that the owners would make them available to the US Navy in the event of war and/or hostilities.[75] Hence the concept of Effective United States Control (EUSC). One added impetus to this build-up was the supposed threat of the so-called rapid and large expansion of the Soviet merchant and naval fleets; the other being the lessons learnt in the Arab–Israeli wars of 1967 and 1973; the oil crisis of the 1970s and 1980s; and the unstable situations in the world generally.[76] It must also be pointed out that the Panamanian and Honduran flags were there for the taking whereas the Liberian registry was deliberately created by the USA due to their historical links. It is probably true to say that to understand US maritime policy and history in the last century is to understand the history, rationale and fundamentals of the FOC.[77]

Perceived Advantages of Open Registry

To the Shipowner and Operator

There are several advantages that made FOC registry attractive to shipowners. The first is low or non-existent taxation, with the ability to carry forwards which improved their liquidity problems. All FOC registry nations offer extremely low taxation levels. Normally the only payments are the initial registration fee and annual renewal fee with certain dues for official certifications; no income or corporation taxes are levied on maritime operations.[78] The scales of payment for the major FOCs were of very little significance to the shipowner. For example one of the largest ships then afloat, the *Universe Iran*, and her sister ships under the Liberian flag, paid about US $10,000 p.a. But it was perhaps misleading to say all was fine: as the *Rochdale Report* pointed out, a company operating ships under FOC:[79]

> ... may not be free from tax. Shipping companies, wherever their place of residence, are often liable to tax in a foreign country or on any profits they derived from international traffic originating in that country. A flag of convenience company is liable for any such tax without means of relief, because the countries offering these facilities cannot have double taxation agreements. It is not, therefore, true to say that flags of convenience operators are necessarily free from taxation.[80]

It is possible that, in cautioning, the *Report* had other factors in mind. For example, from the taxation viewpoint there might be very little to choose between the FOC countries and tax havens. The establishment of subsidiary residence in Bermuda by UK owners and in the Netherlands Antilles by Dutch owners were cases on point,[81] with the further advantages that their ships flew the British or Dutch flag respectively: i.e. dual registrations or open flags within FOC flags. The other factor was that, until recently, in many TMNs shipping enjoyed considerable tax facilities and/or direct financial assistance up to a point where the tax advantages offered by the FOC were only of secondary importance.[82] For instance, there was no strong fiscal inducement for UK owners to operate under the FOC since, for a long time, most operators were unlikely to pay corporation tax as a result of relatively low profitability in the past and allowances on levy. When it was decided in 1970 that investment grants would be discontinued, UK owners then transferred to the facility of free depreciation on 100 per cent of the capital cost of the ship rather than 80 per cent as previously.[83]

Thus, so long as the UK owners, and those elsewhere in the TMNs, were not paying corporation tax, they were in this respect in a similar fiscal position to the operators of vessels under FOC, and there was no strong inducement for them to operate under such flag. However, the position soon changed in the UK and other TMNs, giving FOC operations the edge.[84] But, above all, the then equivalent tax haven and subsidy advantages within the TMNs did not take account of the different positions of some of the FOC operators as regards distributed profits. Many FOC operators are also resident in tax havens. Freedom from the need to account for tax on distributed profits gave these operators an advantage over all those whose personal profits suffer tax in one form or another.[85] In this respect, companies resident in the FOC states and which have no need to remit distributed profits to countries where these are liable to tax clearly have an advantage over companies with public equity shareholding in the TMNs. An essential point to bear in mind is that not only do FOC countries not impose heavy taxes but they do not even require the submission of tax returns.[86] What more can you hope for?

To True Managers and Beneficial Owning States

We have already commenced discussions on the principal advantages of the FOC especially in relation to the USA. As a further example, a 47,000 ton tanker on a ten-year charter might be expected to give an annual revenue of about US $1,050,000 in the late 1960s and early 1970s. Estimated operating costs together with depreciation for the same vessel was about US $1,664,000, and even on bare operating costs[87] the owner would only just break even. Labour costs for US-manned ships were more than two and a half times the cost of an Italian-manned ship, in themselves 30–50 per cent higher than certain other countries' crew costs. Thus, particularly from the point of view of crew costs, the use of the FOC by the USA is indeed a necessity in many cases, if they are to compete internationally without subsidies.[88] The crew cost element, however, is also significant for operators of other nationalities since, even when the crew of an FOC ship are paid direct wages comparable to, or even higher than those of the TMNs, there may still be significant savings on social security contributions, pension benefits and other indirect wage elements. In Italy, for example, sickness insurance alone is considered to add 25 per cent to direct wages, of which half could be saved by access to the international insurance market.[89] See Table 2.2 for the shares of beneficial ownership and true management of open registry fleets.

The use of the FOC also enables the owner to operate his ships on lower manning scales than those imposed by many governments of the TMNs or established by unions in those countries. This was another handicap to operation under first the USA and then in the European TMNs.[90] The *Deutsche Afrika-Linien*, for instance, estimated that they would have been able to operate one of their ships with only 27 men or less, compared to the 38 then required for operation under the German flag, with possible daily savings of some DM 1,000. As the manning scales imposed by the TMNs do not necessarily constitute a minima required for the safe operation of ships,[91] it is not therefore surprising that the manning practices of the FOC operators, led in several instances to circumstances which endangered the safety of both the vessel and the personnel on board as well as to the adjacent coastal state. The *Torrey Canyon* and the *Amoco Cadiz*, are only two of the many examples in point.[92]

As far as other operating costs are concerned, there seems no

Table 2.2 True managers and beneficial owners of open-registry fleets, 1983 (Number of vessels and thousands of dwt)

Home country or territory	True Managers			Beneficial Owners		
	Number	Dwt (000)	% of total dwt	Number	Dwt (000)	% of total dwt
United States of America	724	49,439	24.5	748	52,138	25.8
Hong Kong	1,172	45,129	22.3	916	39,595	19.6
Greece	797	18,438	9.1	978	30,835	15.2
Japan	946	20,379	10.3	997	21,556	10.7
Norway	150	5,359	2.6	183	7,152	3.5
Unspecified	233	5,123	2.5	267	6,652	3.3
Germany, Fed. Rep. of	359	6,171	3.1	366	6,237	3.1
Switzerland	152	4,778	2.4	157	5,483	2.7
United Kingdom	292	10,706	5.3	192	3,998	2.0
China	10	124	—	138	3,365	1.7
Republic of Korea	88	2,489	1.2	85	2,456	1.2
Italy	61	1,529	0.8	72	1,753	0.9
Netherlands	101	1,581	0.8	100	1,604	0.8
Canada	25	1,408	0.7	39	1,593	0.8
Israel	25	1,019	0.5	34	1,346	0.7
Denmark	60	1,210	0.6	61	1,219	0.6
Indonesia	80	1,126	0.6	85	1,199	0.6
Monaco	75	6,899	3.4	23	1,138	0.6
Pakistan	7	37	—	53	1,075	0.5
France	40	783	0.4	40	1,041	0.5
Countries, entities or territories, each beneficially owning less than 0.5 per cent	713	14,731*	7.3	576	7,383	3.6
Unidentified	293	3,229	1.6	293	3,229	1.6
Total open-registry fleets	6,403	202,047	100.0	6,403	202,047	100.0

*This figure is mainly attributable to the UK-based Greek shipowners (7.6 million tons) and the US-based Greek shipowners (1.8 million tons).

Source: UNCTAD Document No. TD/B/C.4/261, Table 1, p. 3.

reason why a Liberian or Panamanian ship should have lower operating costs than a similar ship under the flag of a TMN provided that nation does not impose regulations which insist on the use of particular national facilities, as was very evident in the US example.[93] This certainly applies to repairs, bunkers, port charges and, for similar manning scales, victualling. Insurance, however, can be a special case. Where a particular FOC has a bad loss record the premiums paid may well be higher than they would be under a national flag, although the assessment of premiums will take into account the owner's personal standing and record more than that of the flag of registry.[94] That is why, *inter alia*, the US pays the war insurance of these FOCs scheduled to the NDRF. This may also be counteracted by the fact that certain nations which have significant insurance industries, such as France, require that their ships must be insured on the national market, which, regardless of the owners' records, may be more expensive than on the international market.[95]

This disregard for the owners' poor loss records probably means the FOC true managers and beneficial owning states compromise safety standards and lead to the threats to the environment now firmly associated with the FOC. The payment of insurance or national requirements thereof emphasizes that these TMNs never really let go of these vessels and are, therefore, merely using them for economic, political and strategic convenience.[96] The other criticism is that the FOC, being part of the export of capital, has become part of the sinister operations of finance capital. The fact that profits made by FOC ships can be retained without any formality for further investments and without taxation makes finance houses more willing to provide credit facilities, particularly against the security of firm period charters, since the threat of changes in tax levels is removed.[97] Furthermore, in the view of many finance houses, the stability of the government and the currency, particularly of Liberia, then, combined with, until recently, its unwillingness to interfere in the internal operation of the ship, significantly reduce the financial risks. In at least one instance it was a condition of obtaining funds on the US market to finance bareboat charters to a major oil company that the ships should be under the Liberian flag.[98]

To the DMNs — States of Registry

Although recent events in Liberia have probably knocked the confidence of international capital in the FOC in general and in that country in particular the fact remains that, on the above monetary criteria, it is harder for the TMNs' (and almost impossible for the DMNs') national fleet to secure a loan from international financiers than for the FOC.[99] The ease with which FOC operations attract capital and labour contrasts vividly with the difficulties of the DMNs and some TMNs. One explanation of this contrast is the special relationship that some FOC operators have had with US commodity-owning concerns. Professor Sturmey has shown how large Liberian and Panamanian fleets were built up, with long-term charters being contracted by the commodity owners, allowing the shipowners to obtain up to 95 per cent mortgages for new tonnage.[100] However, for the DMN operators sailing under normal registry flags, such finance is not forthcoming. It is not surprising, therefore, that UNCTAD's calls for phasing out, or even more reforms, was met with scepticisms by the TMNs' financiers.[101]

This scepticism was followed by threats from some quarters in the international finance and commodity market. Leading ship finance expert, Paul Slater, had warned that UNCTAD proposals would lead to an exodus by international bankers from the ship finance market. This is further proof of the obstacles facing maritime expansion in the DMNs, reinforcing dependency on the TMNs, FOCs and international finance capital.[102] There are further advantages to the FOC beneficial states and their nationals. The FOC registration can be useful if owners are reluctant to be identified with a particular country. For this reason both Israel and South Africa have made extensive use of the FOC to avoid embargoes and sanctions. This could not be more opportune to South Africa than now when the international community is demonstrating its abhorrence of their racist regime.[103] Similarly the Greek independents in the 1950s, preferred to register their ships abroad, although special efforts by the Greek authorities, coupled with liberal tax policies and revised maritime regulations, induced a large amount of Greek-owned tonnage to return to the Greek flag.[104] For the shares of the registry states' holdings of open registry fleets, see Table 2.3.

It is important not to underestimate the special independence from state intervention in the decision of many owners to use the FOC. Various allowances and grants may often make operation under national flags as economical as under the FOCs. However, a strong tradition of secrecy, self-reliance and opposition to government regulation makes certain owners prefer the flags of even certain socialist ports.[105] A particular aspect is the way in which many countries limit, by import restrictions or other means, the ship-owner's choice of shipyards on the international market and his opportunities to purchase second-hand tonnage.[106] Swiss maritime law, for instance, imposes stringent requirements on the domicile and nationality of owners as well as on the source of financial investment in their ships, this last requirement being linked to the fact that

Table 2.3 True management* of open-registry fleets, 1983 (number of vessels and thousands of dwt)

Country or territory of true managers	Liberia Number	Liberia dwt (000)	Panama Number	Panama dwt (000)	Cyprus Number	Cyprus dwt (000)	Bermuda Number	Bermuda dwt (000)	Bahamas Number	Bahamas dwt (000)	Total Number	Total dwt (000)
United States of America	437	44,035	273	5,065	2	5	4	10	8	324	724	49,439
Hong Kong	491	30,785	675	14,284	4	56	2	4	–	–	1,172	45,129
Japan	204	10,236	741	10,139	1	4	–	–	–	–	946	20,379
Greece	127	9,759	418	6,162	251	2,500	–	–	1	17	797	18,438
United Kingdom	114	7,588	116	1,657	20	131	34	1,143	8	187	292	10,706
United Kingdom-based Greek shipowners	66	4,815	37	1,744	27	1,065	1	29	–	–	131	7,653
Monaco	42	4,259	32	2,611	–	–	1	29	1	29	75	6,899
Germany, Federal Republic of	79	1,905	194	3,266	84	987	1	7	1	6	359	6,171
Norway	108	4,413	36	838	–	–	1	13	5	95	150	5,359
Unspecified	65	2,473	168	2,650	–	–	–	–	–	–	233	5,123
Switzerland	61	3,540	84	1,165	3	26	–	–	4	47	152	4,778
Republic of Korea	10	1,053	78	1,436	–	–	–	–	–	–	88	2,489
United States-based Greek shipowners	24	1,649	9	75	2	101	1	6	–	–	35	1,825
Netherlands	17	1,018	80	551	1	3	3	9	2	3	101	1,581
Italy	14	1,008	38	390	6	122	–	–	–	–	61	1,529
Singapore	12	467	140	954	2	9	–	–	–	–	154	1,430
Canada	11	1,017	8	378	–	–	2	5	4	8	25	1,408
Denmark	24	892	16	60	3	7	–	–	17	251	60	1,210
Indonesia	19	345	61	781	–	–	–	–	–	–	80	1,126
Israel	17	837	7	180	–	–	1	2	–	–	25	1,019
62 countries, entities or territories, each managing less than 1 million dwt	66	2,627	344	2,257	29	136	6	72	5	35	450	5,127
Unidentified	13	533	231	1,728	42	947	4	6	3	15	293	3,229
Total	2,021	135,254	3,786	58,371	477	6,099	60	1,306	59	1,017	6,403	202,047

*The 'true manager' is the person, company or organization responsible for day-to-day husbandry of the ship concerned (as distinct from the manager of the company nominally owning the vessel). The country of management has been assumed to be the country of domicile of the true manager.

Source: UNCTAD Document No. TD/B/C.4/261, Table 2, p. 4.

85

Switzerland has an abundance of secret international finance, confirming further the secrecy of the FOC operations and its strong links with finance capital and commodity markets.[107]

A final advantage to the owner of operating under the FOC is that, in the event of war or emergency, his ship will be less liable to control by the government of the beneficial ownership. This is not a contradiction in terms for although the NDRF principle would then come into operation, it would only affect FOC ships registered under it.[108] The majority of the FOC fleets outside the NDRF might continue enjoyment of their freedom both in war and peace. The bad news for these non-NDRF FOCs is that the USA has attempted to combat even this apparent freedom by establishing formal contracts with owners, either by surety bonds or by arrangements to be associated with the war-risk insurance; other ships being covered by letters of commitment.[109] The US Maritime Administration considered that in 1968 (at the peak of FOC) some 45 per cent of the tonnage under the Panamanian and Liberian flags alone, as well as a further 44,000 grt flying the Honduran flag were under the NDRF and, therefore, the EUSC. Hence, yet another strong link between the FOC and political, defence and other strategic matters.[110]

To the International Shipping Community

After what has been said there appears to be almost no advantages, to either the registry states or the international community, of operating FOCs. To the beneficial owning states the ability to operate in cross-trades and obtain business that would not otherwise have been available is a major consideration.[111] This explains why the majority of FOC operations are in cross-trades, which normally result in the TMNs' foreign currency earnings being repatriated back home by the shipowners, officers, crews etc. Foreign currency earnings are in turn linked to the savings of foreign exchange that would have been expended in the absence of these and/or the national flag. Consequent upon these are the improvements in the already well-off TMNs' balance of payments situations.[112] In addition, sight should not be lost of the dispensation of the need to (and therefore the cost of) administering and regulating these vessels in the domestic registry. The provision of employment for nationals, mainly officers, that might have otherwise been unemployed, leads to a reduction and/or part solution to the problem of unemployment not only in the merchant marine but to the national economy as a whole.[113] For the beneficial ownership of open registry fleets as of 1983, see Table 2.4.

Factors related to national defence in the event of war or hostilities, such as the ability to disguise the true nationalities of the vessels and

Table 2.4 Beneficial ownership* of open-registry fleets, 1983
(Number of vessels and thousands of dwt)

Country or territory of beneficial ownership	Liberia Number	Liberia dwt (000)	Panama Number	Panama dwt (000)	Cyprus Number	Cyprus dwt (000)	Bermuda Number	Bermuda dwt (000)	Bahamas Number	Bahamas dwt (000)	Total Number	Total dwt (000)
United States of America	429	44,558	293	7,166	2	5	16	85	8	324	748	52,138
Hong Kong	452	29,427	460	10,112	4	56	–	–	–	–	916	39,595
Greece	237	18,730	462	8,441	278	3,647	–	–	1	17	978	30,835
Japan	204	10,736	792	10,816	1	4	–	–	–	–	997	21,556
Norway	138	6,113	39	931	–	–	1	13	5	95	183	7,152
Unspecified	95	3,943	172	2,709	–	–	–	–	–	–	267	6,652
German, Federal Republic of	81	1,923	196	3,302	87	999	1	7	1	6	366	6,237
Switzerland	69	4,008	81	1,401	3	26	–	–	4	48	157	5,483
United Kingdom	35	2,106	120	1,164	16	100	14	442	7	186	192	3,998
China	4	140	134	3,225	–	–	–	–	–	–	138	3,365
Republic of Korea	10	1,053	75	1,403	–	–	–	–	–	–	85	2,456
Italy	18	1,175	45	447	6	122	3	9	–	–	72	1,753
Netherlands	18	1,050	78	547	1	3	–	–	3	4	100	1,604
Canada	13	855	7	53	–	–	15	677	4	8	39	1,593
Israel	25	1,148	7	180	1	16	1	2	–	–	34	1,346
Denmark	24	892	16	60	4	16	–	–	17	251	61	1,219
Indonesia	23	401	62	798	–	–	–	–	–	–	85	1,199
Monaco	16	1,023	6	86	–	–	–	–	1	29	23	1,138
Pakistan	31	849	22	226	–	–	–	–	–	–	53	1,075
France	9	879	30	144	–	–	–	–	1	18	40	1,041
64 countries, entities or territories, each beneficially owning less than 0.5 per cent	77	3,712	458	3,432	32	158	5	65	4	16	576	7,383
Unidentified	13	533	231	1,728	42	947	4	6	3	15	293	3,229
Total	2,021	135,254	3,786	58,371	477	6,099	60	1,306	59	1,017	6,403	202,047
Share in total open-registry fleets	31.6	67.0	59.2	28.9	7.4	3.0	0.9	0.6	0.9	0.5	100.0	100.0

*The beneficial owner is the person, company or organization which gains the pecuniary benefits from the shipping operations.

Source: UNCTAD Document No. TD/B/C.4/261, Table 3, p. 5.

therefore benefit from neutrality has been mentioned in part. This is coupled with the availability of these vessels for national defence as and when required at no maintenance cost when the alternative would be either to spend a fortune putting idle and perhaps rusted ships instantly back into service or to spend taxpayers' money keeping them in service and ready at all times.[114] In addition, in a world full of restrictive practices and nationalism, the FOC's freedom to evade and benefit from protective measures afforded to national lines of the registry state should not be underestimated. There are also spin-off opportunities to sell spare parts, services, etc., overseas that might not have been available but for the FOC.[115] There are said to be benefits to the countries of registry too, although these should not be over-estimated. These include the provision of employment for nationals in shipping, crewing, officers (limited) and maritime-related services such as transport and the infrastructure, hotels and catering, banking and insurance, as well as brokerage and/or agencies.[116]

There is also the possibility of revenue earnings from direct taxation, fees, etc., coupled with the possible earnings of foreign exchange and the attraction of foreign investments in shipping, ports, as well as in the economic and social infrastructure mentioned above. Earnings of foreign exchange, however little, can make a lot of difference in the case of the DMNs, where they are badly needed.[117] It has also been suggested that FOC operations constitute the easiest way of transferring technology and skills from the TMNs to the DMNs, something that has proved difficult to achieve by the normal channels. Some mention should also be made of the possible diversification of the national economy from such spin-offs and other indirect benefits to the provisions of services nationally and invisible exports externally.[118] To the list should therefore be added the possible mushrooming of tourism, repair and salvage services and bunkering. It is therefore not surprising that, in defence of the system, the Liberian Bureau of Maritime Affairs has cited the flexibility of their vessels, which are unhindered by any political restraints on routes, and are thus able to minimize empty back-hauls.[119]

Then there are the psychological considerations such as the (false) satisfaction of the national ego in seeing vessels flying the national flag abroad, calling in home ports and displaying the state symbol in the high seas and foreign ports. It is argued that publicity given the nation this way far outweighs damage done to national prestige by those who despise the system and its operators.[120] However, the greatest advantages are perhaps only incidental and are to be found in the possible acquisition of the leverage to negotiate for foreign aid and other favourable treatments from the (richer) beneficial owning states.[121] It is thought that Sergeant Doe obtained large concessions from the USA in response to his threats to dismantle FOC operations in Liberia. It is also no accident that the largest registry nation[122] and the largest beneficial owning nation in the world happen to have not only strong historical and political links but also do actually use what amounts to the same internationally convertible currency.[123]

However, few people share the view that FOC operations ever benefit the international community apart from the FOC registries and the beneficial owners to a limited extent. These pro-FOC groups argue that together they add up to the most important constituency of the international maritime community and, therefore, that what is good for them is necessarily beneficial to the rest. They cite in their favour the contention that the existence of the FOC led to efficient international maritime transport[124] and therefore stability, not only in the maritime industry but also in international trade. They argue further that low wages paid to the DMNs' nationals and the ensuing low running costs have resulted in stable and low freight rates and thus cheaper exports and imports which is good news to consumers. They also contend that the operation of the FOC has helped the industry avoid and/or minimize the effects of recessions[125] and consequently resulted in the maintenance of a stable and flexible shipping industry for the last century. (This is more or less identical to the nuclear powers' argument that these weapons have served to maintain world peace since 1945.) And, finally, these countries point to the promotion of joint ventures and the fostering of international trade relations being a direct product of the existence and operations of the FOC.[126]

The Problems of Flags of Convenience

To the Operators and True Owners

Considering the emotional debate that has raged over the FOC especially in the last decade and regardless of the above persuasive arguments, it is not clear to the onlooker that the advantages of the FOC outweigh their problems. It is obvious that an owner under an FOC cannot take advantage of the fiscal and financial benefits which particular governments grant to vessels flying their flag.[127] Fiscal benefits such as accelerated depreciation, investment allowances, etc. cannot generally put national owners in a better position than an FOC owner except where the annual registration fee charged by the FOC country is appreciable; but positive grants or the provision of loans at lower than market rates (unless similarly favourable rates are obtainable elsewhere) can offer actual incentives to the operator to remain under the respective flag.[128] Although it was admitted above that the FOC may evade national restrictions, this relates only to export trade. Generally the FOC ships will also, of course, be excluded from cabotage trades where these are reserved to ships of particular flags[129] — emphasizing further that they can only be *national* for limited purposes and that, otherwise, they are treated as foreign and for *convenience* by even their host nations some of the time.[130]

There has been very little participation by FOC ships in liner shipping or in liner conferences, which have traditionally been dominated by lines with direct national trade interests or by traditional cross-traders. What further revelation does that provide? That the FOCs are neither liners nor genuine cross-traders, which limits them to bulk trade and oil tankers.[131] Another handicap is that in comparison to the TMNs (and to DMNs to a limited extent), the FOC registry countries are extremely limited in their provision of worldwide diplomatic and particularly consular protections for the reasons already outlined in the *Rochdale Report*. This lack of consular support or adequate diplomatic protection has several consequences.[132] It can lead to reluctance by financiers to invest in the system because of high insurance premiums and therefore high running costs. Partly as a result of this, it is natural for the charter parties for Liberian and Panamanian ships, *inter alia*, to exclude, for instance, certain socialist ports. Non-admission in certain national ports could lead to hardships in the event of emergency, general commercial uncertainty and, of course, to loss of business opportunities.[133]

Coupled with this is the inability or non-availability of normal protection in the high seas in the event of war and hostilities. Two factors tend to strengthen this argument. First, it appears that where there are pirate operations, they tend to board and harass vessels of non-naval powers — mainly the FOC of Liberia, Panama, etc. — since chances of retaliation are apparently non-existent.[134] Second, although in the Gulf war even the TMNs' flag vessels suffer casualties, these have been few and far between, and it is probably no co-incidence that the largest brunt of the attacks have been borne by FOC tankers. There is a clear contrast in the fact that the major TMNs such as the USA, the UK and France have had the resources to station naval patrol fleets at the mouth of the Gulf of Hormuz and thereby flex their muscles as it were,[135] whereas Liberia and Panama are unable to do that even if they wanted to. The naval forces of the *true* owners could come to the aid of the FOC fleets but that could pose a few problems in international law not to mention the criticism that would follow such open admission of any links between the FOCs and their true owners.[136]

The assurances of political stability given by the Liberian Bureau of Maritime Affairs have not been borne out by recent history. In the first instance, both the coup in Liberia in 1982 and its consequent threat to the FOC, and political instability in the Caribbean and Latin American countries have served to shatter that myth.[137] The wrangle between the USA and Panama over the new treaty that returned control of the Canal to Panama did not help the situation either. Second, even before the coup, the late President Tolbert of Liberia interfered with FOC tankers, preventing them from servicing American forces in Europe in retaliation against US support for Israel during the 1973 Arab–Israeli War[138] when Israel invaded Egypt, an African country and member of the Organization of African Unity (OAU) of which Liberia is part and parcel. That incident shocked US military and foreign policy advisors, and resulted in the hasty passage of the Military Transport Security Act 1975 as well as the re-examination of the effectiveness of the NDRF and the EUSC which are both dependent on FOC operations. These few incidents have given rise to further doubts in the minds of the FOC operators: the uncertainty of not knowing how long to be (and remain) on a particular registry, as if the FOC operations were not more than enough risks and gambles in them-selves.[139]

To the operators, the risks of political instability in the country of registry are now more than real; hence the inability to plan and the need to live from hand-to-mouth, as it were. In the trade, this state of limbo is sometimes described as the inability to look far ahead and plan resulting from having to deal with foreign and sometimes unfamiliar regimes and/or jurisdictions.[140] This revelation came as a great blow to a system that is hypersensitive and that had always thrived on the political and economic stability of the registry countries. In the changed material conditions, the thriving FOC operations have generated envy and anger among the opposition and the nationalistic elements within the FOC countries. With the growing influence of nationalists resenting what they call exploitation and abuse of their sovereignty by the FOC, anything can happen. Thus, always looming on the horizon are the dangers[141] of nationalization, or even confiscation in the event of coups and/or changes from hitherto docile and cooperative to nationalistic regimes. It happened in Egypt in 1956; it nearly happened in Liberia in 1982; it can therefore happen anywhere anytime.[142]

In most ways, in the international context, the problems of the operators are the same as those facing their (beneficial owning) nations, although ironically the intervention of the FOC was meant to sever links with own countries. It will be noted that, of the total world tanker tonnage vessels over 10,000 dwt, about 29 per cent were registered under the FOCs at the beginning of the 1970s,[143] thus forming together with the cross-trading tanker tonnage of the TMNs a world pattern with a relatively weak correlation between oil trading countries and the flags flown by tankers. For the breakdown of these fleets together with types and countries, see Table 2.5. It may thus be noted in passing that, at the time of the Suez Crisis and the boycott of several TMNs' flags by the Arab states, the presence of block tanker tonnage of politically uncommitted nationalities contributed greatly to the oil companies' freedom of action.[144] In future there could be national directives or individual political commitments by the crew. One could easily foresee that looming over the horizon in the event of the final showdown over South Africa. So continued political non-commitment by the operators and crews cannot be banked on. Things change and 'fall apart when the centre can no longer hold', to borrow from Chinua Achebe.[145]

Besides, from a purely national point of view, registration under FOCs may mean the withdrawal of a productive element and source of employment and of income and tax revenue from the national economy. It may also affect the balance of payments through additional freight and charter payments in foreign currency.[146] This is already happening in some TMNs such as the UK where flagging out, *inter alia*, has led to massive unemployment among seamen and the concurrent collapse of the maritime-related industries and infrastructure. Surely the FOC–TMNs should learn from the DMNs about the drain on foreign currency due to freight payments in foreign exchange as a result of a lack of own fleets?[147] Maybe, if all were equal, flagging out in the TMNs would have meant net gains in the DMNs. To the TMNs the net outflow of foreign currency due to FOC operation could have been more than compensated for by similar repatriation home, but that is not necessarily the case where the FOC is resident in some tax haven and therefore unwilling to do so.[148]

Furthermore, to the true managing and beneficial owning state, flagging out might have the added disadvantage of leading to unfairly low-cost competition for the national shipowners and thus limit their productive capacity. Thus, certain operators might be punished for remaining loyal to the mother flag.[149] We noted that often those who

Table 2.5   Flags of convenience and world fleet: 1982 analysis by principal types

Type	World %	Liberia 000 tons gross	Liberia %	Panama 000 tons gross	Panama %	Cyprus 000 tons gross	Cyprus %
Oil tankers	39.3	41,223	58.4	8,723	26.8	560	26.0
Liquefied gas carriers	2.1	1,728	2.4	436	1.3	2	0.1
Chemical tankers	0.7	604	0.9	122	0.4	6	0.3
Misc. tankers	0.1	24	–	13	–	–	–
Bulk/oil carriers	6.1	7,346	10.4	1,506	4.6	–	–
Ore and bulk carriers	22.0	15,576	22.0	9,303	28.5	298	13.9
General cargo	18.7	3,156	4.5	9,946	30.5	1,173	54.6
Passenger/cargo	0.2	–	–	134	0.4	6	0.3
Container ships	3.0	362	0.5	750	2.3	9	0.4
Lighter carriers	0.2	71	0.1	–	–	–	–
Vehicle carriers	0.6	371	0.5	342	1.0	–	–
Fish factories and carriers	0.9	–	–	28	0.1	–	–
Fishing	2.2	–	–	154	0.5	5	0.2
Ferries/passenger	1.8	117	0.2	306	1.0	80	3.7
Misc.	2.1	140	0.1	837	2.5	11	0.5
Total	100	70,718	100	32,600	100	2,150	100

Source: Lloyd's Register of Shipping Statistical Tables 1982.

remain loyal are not duly concerned by state regulation and, indeed, may be rewarded by subsidies. However, we also saw that all these inducements may not offset the freedom, unfair competition and other enormous advantages enjoyed by the unpatriotic FOC operator. From the point of view of owners operating under the TMNs or national flags, the financial and other advantages enjoyed by the FOC owners/operators can thus be legitimately regarded as constituting a handicap in competition;[150] hence the earlier assertion that in the FOC, *inter alia*, capitalism has found itself in a mess of antagonistic contradictions: a system created supposedly for free competition has boomeranged on the creator by seeking to destroy the very competition it is supposed to be based on. This seems to be particularly relevant for the stayees (the loyal owners) in the TMNs which offer no subsidies or incentives which might counterbalance the competitive advantage of the FOC.[151]

In addition there are the legal problems in international law arising from foreseen or attempted extraterritorial jurisdiction, such as the operation of the EUSC, relating to the NDRF. Apart from a few minor incidents that were solved diplomatically a case has not yet arisen where the theory of the EUSC has been tested in a national jurisdiction or international case. The chances are that it could be messy. I have amply dealt with this problem in a separate article.[152] Quite apart from that, there are just the logistical problems of having to control these vessels in a particular location at a given time. True, the availability of satellites might have solved the technical problem of locating the vessels but locating a ship is only part of a larger problem. Secondly, the beneficial owning states have had to address themselves to hitherto unforeseen problems such as those posed by the ARAMCO incident arising from the 1967 Arab–Israeli War when, for obvious reasons, the Saudi King ordered the company not to supply American forces in Europe[153] or the identical problems such as those of the actions of the late President Tolbert during the later 1973 Arab–Israeli War. On the other hand, the uncertainties of having to maintain expensive commercial intelligence to predict and respond to coups and changes of regimes as happened in Liberia in 1982 can be both unsettling and nerve-racking — not to mention the possible weakening of the domestic fleet and its consequent inability to cope in the event of war should the EUSC and NDRF systems fail to go according to plans.[154] For the shares of the true managers and beneficial owners of the open registry tankers, see Table 2.6.

To the DMNs' Country of Registry

It is, however, with regard to the DMNs that the FOC operations have attracted the widest criticisms and therefore received the heaviest battering. Although FOC vessels are registered in the DMNs and are therefore legally owned by them, this ownership is only nominal. Both UNCTAD and other independent researchers have demonstrated that they tend to be owned by the TMNs and their related interests.[155] In 1980, for instance, the USA beneficially owned some 64.5m dwt, or 29.7 per cent of the total FOC fleet, whilst Japan beneficially owned 23.4m dwt or some 10.7 per cent. On the other hand, Knudsen has shown how the TMNs' dominance, not only in international shipping and FOC fleets but also in the DMNs' maritime trades, has imperialist connotations for many Third World nationals.[156] In the aspiring DMNs, therefore, the FOC can be seen as a symbol of the dependency that was inherited from colonial days. Third World nations have suffered, and continue to suffer, from this dependency when attempting to establish and develop national fleets of their own.[157]

It is precisely for these reasons, *inter alia*, that during the First World War the black nationalist, Marcus Garvey, set up the Black Star Line to try to provide an alternative to US and UK lines for black peoples. Although the project was fairly unsuccessful, suffering from

94

Table 2.6 True management of tankers of open-registry fleets, 1983 (Number of vessels and thousands of dwt)

Country or territory of registration → / Country or territory of true management ↓	Liberia Number	Liberia dwt (000)	Panama Number	Panama dwt (000)	Cyprus Number	Cyprus dwt (000)	Bermuda Number	Bermuda dwt (000)	Bahamas Number	Bahamas dwt (000)	Total Number	Total dwt (000)
United States of America	205	33,681	43	3,160	–	–	–	–	2	177	250	37,018
Hong Kong	104	15,935	44	2,671	–	–	–	–	–	–	148	18,606
Greece	39	5,720	34	1,470	12	673	–	–	–	–	85	7,863
Japan	53	5,538	58	1,838	–	–	–	–	–	–	111	7,376
Monaco	19	3,352	11	2,264	–	–	–	–	1	29	31	5,645
United Kingdom-based Greek shipowners	27	3,091	15	1,343	11	785	1	29	–	–	54	5,248
United Kingdom	20	4,160	8	384	1	59	2	281	2	175	33	5,059
Norway	15	1,617	5	418	–	–	1	13	1	89	22	2,137
Republic of Korea	6	920	5	531	–	–	–	–	–	–	11	1,451
Germany, Federal Republic of	5	573	4	276	3	399	–	–	–	–	12	1,248
United States-based Greek shipowners	9	1,051	–	–	1	100	–	–	–	–	10	1,151
26 countries, entities or territories each managing less than 1 million dwt	64	5,391	92	1,583	4	109	1	3	4	39	165	7,125
Unidentified	3	221	22	172	5	623	2	2	–	–	32	1,018
Total	569	81,250	341	16,110	37	2,748	7	328	10	509	964	100,945

Source: UNCTAD Document No. TD/B/C.4/261, Table 4, p. 6.

95

insufficient capital and a shortage of skilled officers and crew, the point had nevertheless been made.[158] It is equally not surprising that Kwame Nkrumah took up the mantle and named the Ghananian National Line the Black Star Line. Such problems still face the DMNs. Even the relatively industrialized developed Latin American DMNs or the newly industrialized DMNs (NICs) of the Far East have suffered from both capital and skilled crew shortages.[159] African countries, especially the black African ones, are of course in a far worse situation. Labour aspects have always come first when analyzing the master/servant relationship between the FOCs and the DMNs and, in this respect, it must be pointed out that there are two independent issues here: those DMNs that provide registry and those that provide only cheap labour.[160] There are of course those who provide both, including, sometimes, tax haven status.

The personnel of FOC vessels have in various instances been provided with lower than average standards, especially during periods of shipping depressions and abundant labour supply. For instance, the Greek government, assisted by the Panhellenic Maritime Federation, did organize a considerable number of foreign Greek-owned ships, and its effect was gauged by the fact that the personnel on 1,242 such ships were included in the Greek Seamen's Pension Fund Coverage.[161] The development of unionization on FOC vessels has contributed considerably to the reduction of pressure by the International Trade Union movement since the 1958 boycott.

The seafarers on FOC ships also suffer from the fact that legal disputes — e.g. in the case of breach of a seaman's contract — will normally have to be pursued in the country of registration which may be different from that of the pursuer,[162] thereby exposing the powerless seamen to all the rigours of the law generally and of the conflicts of law in particular. But in the first instance the seaman in question will have been extremely lucky to have had a definite contract. It is not uncommon for the seaman in dispute to be starved to death locked up; abandoned at a distant port of call; or even thrown overboard to be eaten by sharks![163]

Furthermore, critics point out that the FOC-DMNs have had to suffer the indignity, abuse, and even surrender of their national sovereignty in return for mere 'pieces of shackles'. Their position has also been likened to surrogate motherhood; hence the description 'Sovereignty for Sale'. It has already been pointed out that these countries' inability to establish, develop and have their own genuine national fleets has in part been due to the false security some have found in owning the FOC fleets in proxy.[164] This has meant continued reliance on former colonial masters and other foreigners for vital services instead of self-help in this crucial area of international trade relations. Indeed, it is rather ironic to continue reliance on the very people one wishes to break away from![165] The system has allowed foreign interests to evade, take advantage of and benefit from privileges and protective measures operated by the DMNs and intended for their infant national fleets. Additionally, it has led to the DMNs surrendering the comparative advantages they had to the already-advanced fleets of the TMNs.[166]

Coupled with these disadvantages is the exploitation of the DMNs' nationals and other endowments. It is not unknown for the FOC companies and the beneficial states — just like other multinationals — to meddle in the FOC-DMNs' internal politics or affairs or even influence change of governments. Yet the amount of revenue collected by these nations is minimal and not commensurate with the damage to national prestige caused by these flags.[167] To small, poor and power-less nations the attempt to offer the necessary naval, consular and diplomatic protection to these vessels might lead to a diversion of their meagre resources and efforts from national priorities to the sole benefit of the very foreigners who can, after all, take care of them-selves.[168] This is all happening at the very time when the DMNs' call, backed by the international community, is for the very opposite: the transfer of real resources, technology and skills from the advanced nations of the North to the underdeveloped countries of the South. It would only be logical to link the plight of the DMNs to the concern of the international community.[169] See Table 2.7 for the distribution of bulk and combined carriers in open registry markets, and Table 2.8 for tanker fleets.

To the International Shipping Community

One way or another the international shipping community has had to pay for the consequences of FOC operations. As should be apparent by now, one of the problems of FOC registrations is that the host countries are normally unable or unwilling to provide enforcement mechanisms for safety and social regulations.[170] With all fairness to the FOC countries this assertion needs qualifications. Generally speak-ing this does not apply to hull and machinery certification, since the major FOC countries have transferred responsibility by requiring certification by international classification societies. In other respects, international safety certificates are required by vessels flying the flag of any state which is a signatory to the appropriate conventions in-cluding the countries.[171] Liberia, Panama, Lebanon, Cyprus, Somalia and Singapore have all accepted the International Convention for the Safety of Life at Sea 1960 and the International Convention on Load Lines 1966.[172] Liberia also requires that ships under its flag should

Table 2.7 True management of bulk and combined carriers of open-registry fleets, 1983 (Number of vessels and thousands of dwt)

Country or territory of true management / Country or territory of registration	Liberia Number	Liberia dwt (000)	Panama Number	Panama dwt (000)	Cyprus Number	Cyprus dwt (000)	Bermuda Number	Bermuda dwt (000)	Bahamas Number	Bahamas dwt (000)	Total Number	Total dwt (000)
Hong Kong	243	12,779	223	7,916	1	38	—	—	—	—	467	20,733
United States of America	127	6,932	18	573	—	—	—	—	3	139	148	7,644
Japan	78	3,557	151	4,007	—	—	—	—	—	—	229	7,564
Greece	54	3,420	67	2,011	20	638	—	—	—	—	141	6,069
United Kingdom	51	2,882	13	576	—	—	11	664	—	—	75	4,122
Switzerland	46	2,993	19	431	—	—	—	—	—	—	65	3,424
Unspecified	40	1,671	44	1,454	—	—	—	—	—	—	84	3,125
Germany, Federal Republic of	15	880	27	1,660	4	163	—	—	—	—	46	2,703
Norway	38	2,125	6	156	—	—	—	—	—	—	44	2,281
United Kingdom-based Greek shipowners	30	1,597	3	254	8	234	—	—	—	—	41	2,085
Monaco	20	835	5	132	—	—	—	—	—	—	25	967
Republic of Korea	4	133	16	565	—	—	—	—	—	—	20	698
Denmark	10	451	1	18	—	—	—	—	3	115	14	584
Brazil	4	573	—	—	—	—	—	—	—	—	4	573
United States-based Greek shipowners	14	543	—	—	—	—	—	—	—	—	14	543
Italy	9	515	—	—	1	22	—	—	—	—	10	537
26 countries, entities or territories each managing less than 500,000 dwt	34	1,568	30	1,133	1	44	1	35	—	—	66	2,780
Unidentified	5	237	20	730	6	152	—	—	1	14	32	1,133
Total	822	43,691	643	21,616	41	1,291	12	699	7	268	1,525	67,565

Source: UNCTAD Document No. TD/B/C.4/261, Table 5, p. 7.

Table 2.8 Beneficial ownership of tankers of open-registry fleets, 1983
(Number of vessels and thousands of dwt)

Country or territory of beneficial ownership	Liberia		Panama		Cyprus		Bermuda		Bahamas		Total	
	Number	dwt (000)	Number	dwt (000)	Number	dwt (000)	Number	dwt (000)	Number	dwt (000)	Number	dwt (000)
United States of America	200	34,287	52	5,076	–	–	–	–	2	177	254	39,540
Hong Kong	101	15,366	31	2,284	–	–	–	–	–	–	132	17,650
Greece	88	12,342	45	2,983	24	1,558	–	–	–	–	157	16,883
Japan	53	5,942	60	1,943	–	–	–	–	–	–	113	7,885
Norway	20	2,334	6	497	–	–	1	13	1	89	28	2,933
United Kingdom	10	1,651	8	135	1	59	3	310	2	175	24	2,330
Republic of Korea	6	920	5	531	–	–	–	–	–	–	11	1,451
Switzerland	6	851	12	524	–	–	–	–	1	32	19	1,407
Germany, Federal Republic of	5	573	4	276	3	399	–	–	–	–	12	1,248
Unspecified	16	1,112	–	–	–	–	–	–	–	–	16	1,112
28 countries, entities or territories each beneficially owning less than 1 million dwt	61	5,651	96	1,689	4	109	1	3	4	36	166	7,488
Unidentified	3	221	22	172	5	623	2	2	–	–	32	1,018
Total	569	81,250	341	16,110	37	2,748	7	328	10	509	964	100,945
Share in the total for tankers of open-registry fleets	59.0	80.5	35.4	16.0	3.9	2.7	0.7	0.3	1.0	0.5	100.0	100.0

Source: UNCTAD Document No. TD/B/C.4/261, Table 6, p. 8.

conform with, *inter alia*, the stipulations of the International Telecommunications Conference 1966; the ILO Conventions Nos. 53, 55 and 58; the International Regulations for Preventing Collisions at Sea 1960; and the International Convention for the Prevention of Pollution of the Sea by Oil 1962.[173]

Liberia also lays down requirements in detail for the Certification of Officers. These are, however, formal requirements which can be effective only if the administration retains direct or indirect control of their fulfilment. These controls are, however, frequently lacking in the case of the FOC countries (as well as for certain other flags) and, under such circumstances, the ships involved may and do endanger the safety both of other ships and of the countries whose shores they pass.[174] A particularly blatant case of such neglect of control over the required rules occurred in October 1970 when the *Allegro*, a 95,445 dwt vessel, and the *Pacific Glory*, a 77,648 dwt vessel (both laden tankers flying the Liberian flag) collided with the loss of 14 lives. In the subsequent Liberian inquiry, it transpired that three officers on the *Pacific Glory* and four on the *Allegro* did not in fact possess the required Liberian certification and that the third officer of the *Allegro*, who was on watch at the time of the collision, held no certificate whatsoever.[175] An accident is an accident and it can happen to anybody, with or without a certificate. Neither is it suggested that this was the sole cause of these accidents, but when it happens so often with the FOCs and it transpires that the officers involved had no certification of competence, it provides circumstantial evidence and, therefore, further ammunition to the system's opponents.[176]

When these are considered within the context of the fact that most of the FOC vessels (at least earlier ones) also happen to be sub-standard with higher average age, it becomes further circumstantial evidence and stops being mere accidents and/or coincidences. Be that as it may, it appears that, partly as a result of the public reaction to this accident, Liberia announced in April 1971 that it was to establish an inspection and enforcement system, by positioning qualified inspectors at major ports.[177] A comprehensive evaluation of the licensing regulations and procedures was also envisaged. These were welcome developments and in the right direction but they were too little too late: the damage had already been done, associating FOC operations with uncertified officers, old and substandard vessels, and therefore, with accidents and pollution.[178] It does not necessarily matter whatever length one goes to repair a damage; it is the first impression which normally counts and it takes a lot of time and effort to erase it. It is that negative connotation that has been, and will probably remain, in the mind of FOC opponents and the international community for a long time to come.[179]

It did not help their already hopeless case when information received from the ITWF — a report compiled in October 1971 by the Liberian Services Incorporated — revealed that almost half of the then 1,600 officers serving in Liberian ships that year did not hold Liberian licences at all. Worse still, the report referred to cases when even forged licences had been accepted and Liberian licences issued on the strength of them. In the case of the larger and more reputable owners[180] it may be a matter of enlightened self-interest to ensure that international regulations are observed, but it is certainly true that, particularly under the then Lebanese flag, smaller and less reliable owners often offended against international maritime regulations. The Rochdale Committee also referred to a case of a certificate of competence as engineer being issued by the consul of an FOC country to a man with no previous engineering experience or qualification whatsoever.[181] There are now of course FOC operations with brand new vessels and with clean casualty records who would dissociate themselves from the 'bad guys'. It remains true, however, that compliance with the safety conventions is always far better assured under the control and responsibility of governmental administrations than when left to the conscience or self-interest of owners.[182]

UNCTAD and the Flags of Convenience

Repercussions of Phasing Out

It is by now apparent from the foregone discussion on the advantages and disadvantages of the FOC that the debate over genuine link had become one of economic link and the forum had been elevated to the highest order: the UN, championed by UNCTAD. The issue had crystallized from the legal to the economic. It can be seen, then, that there are credible motives in the anti-FOC campaign.[183] The debate at the UN generally and UNCTAD in particular aimed at some international instrument. It would be futile to attempt the narration of the 10-year debate within these few pages. That has been dealt with ably elsewhere and it will also be touched on further on. Its summary, however, forms the substance of this part of the discussions. First, at the top of the agenda were two alternatives at Geneva: to completely eradicate (or phase out as it was popularly known) the FOC or simply reform but retain it.[184] Identical choices had faced the international community when pondering what to do with the liner conferences. Would the same compromise prevail again or would the-mainly-DMNs have their way this time and go for radical measures to abolish the FOC altogether?[185]

The protagonists were not too slow to reach for their 'big guns'. The first to fire were the pro-FOC lobby who were quick to point out the supposed advantages of free competition over regulations and, of course, what they perceived as worldwide existence of the continued operation of the system. First, they pointed out the flexibility of investments which the FOC owners enjoy through their tax status and the other advantages already mentioned.[186] They claimed that these have resulted in efficient development and modernization of some of these fleets considerably above those of the TMNs. They further emphasized that this had been particularly noticeable since the middle of the 1960s. It will be remembered that between 1963 and 1971 Liberian tonnage increased by 238 per cent compared with 45 per cent for the European members of the OECD and faster even than Japan and the Soviet Union.[187] Secondly, they claimed that the FOC owners had been at the forefront of tanker and large bulk carrier development with the first 100,000 and 300,000 tonners both under Liberian flag and that the same was true for combination carriers, though not for more specialized fields such as gas transportation or container ships. Of the 209 container ships on order as of 1 February 1972, for instance, only five were for the Liberian and none were for Panamanian registry.[188]

If the phasing out approach were adopted, to the operators and beneficial states this would have meant a repatriation of the tonnage to where the link lies: i.e. back to the home flag. This would have further resulted in the owners having to face the realities of high running (and manning) costs as well as stringent safety and other costly regulations.[189] It would on the other hand have re-established the real legal genuine link and therefore the economic link between the flag and the registry state: ownership, loyalty and accountability by citizens or permanent residents. The economic consequence of this would have called for subsidy from the *natural* state or bankruptcy and probably the end of the FOCs as we know them today. In the alternative to this grim reality, the FOCs would have faced three further choices.[190]

The first choice would have been to transfer to other TMNs with reasonably low wages such as the UK, Spain, Italy and Portugal. There are indications that this is already happening with the Spanish fishing trawlers registering in Britain to benefit from national fishing rights; and the Norwegian supply vessels operating in the North Sea registering in Britain to qualify for business and possibly benefit from marginally lower running costs.[191] This new brand of FOC registries would be less profitable than the classical ones due to union activities and in some cases the minimum conditions of the welfare state requirements. Nor would they be typical FOCs since, in the case of the EEC, there is a requirement for the free mobility of capital, personnel and skills.[192]

Secondly, there might have been transfers to DMNs (for beginners in FOC registry) or other liberal DMNs (for those already existing FOC registries). This could have been achieved by way of disguised FOC such as nominal joint ventures with either equally shared benefits or more benefits accruing to one party. They would, however, be less profitable to the FOC operator than the original or classical FOC.[193]

Third, and finally, failing all these, our FOC operation would have to face the reality: either return home and surrender to state regulations or cease to invest in/or operate shipping business and sell up — especially in the likely event of bankruptcy due to the inability to continue trading.[194]

Repercussions of Reforms

To the current FOC countries it is claimed that there would follow loss of revenue and consequential effects on employment, balance of payments problems and general disruption to the national economy. For world trade there would follow rising freight rates and, therefore, both the slowing down of international trade as well as expensive exports and imports.[195] Looked at from the viewpoint of the non-FOC-DMNs, however, it might have been a good thing.

1 For firms in home countries there would be a declaration of earnings; and a reduction in crew costs from the ITWF levels to the levels in labour-supplying countries would have exactly the reverse effect to those predicted by the pro-FOC lobby: the economic collapse of the current FOC beneficial owning countries.[196]

2 Contrary to it having an adverse effect on international trade, world freight would in fact fall (or not be increased) because the DMNs and low-cost TMNs (that would occupy the vacuum vacated by the classical FOCs) can offer crew rates below ITWF levels which, in turn, would lead to cost-saving and therefore to competitive shipping and cheaper and efficient world trade: the comparative advantage argument.[197]

3 It might have benefited the DMNs by affording an inflow of capital (presumably through joint-venture investment and increasing earning capacity), increased employment, industrial diversification and improvements in the balance of payments.[198]

4 For world shipping, it would contribute to the implementation

of the New International Maritime Order — through consequent establishment of both the legal genuine link as well as the economic link; establishment and development of national fleets by the DMNs; equal participation in international maritime transport; and equitable distribution of world tonnage.[199]

5   It would have improved accountability, safety and the environment. An end would be brought to the situation where much of the world's fleets (30 per cent) is operating outside governmental jursidiction: an economic link would have been established at last![200]

It can be seen then that there are credible motives in the anti-FOC campaign. The FOC operation has obstructed the establishment and/or development of national merchant marine in the DMNs, with investment being denied by the TMNs-controlled finance institutions. The international division of labour in maritime transport sponsored by the FOC-beneficial owning and user TMNs is very much on their terms.[201] The labour-supplying DMNs have very little jurisdiction or protection over their nationals sailing under the FOCs. The vulnerability of such crews has been illustrated above and was further demonstrated only too well when the Filipino crew of the *Globtik Venus* were violently removed from their vessel following a labour dispute in the French port of Le Havre. Furthermore, and to underline the real argument that genuine link is economic rather than legal, the TMNs' perception of bulk shipping as a market-oriented industry may need some adjustment, given the dominance of its organization.[202] Somehow, the image of open market tramping has superimposed itself on the reality of an often closed market, with the TMNs' commodity-owning concerns exercising their economic power in an aligopsonic manner. This results in FOC tonnage being preferred to any possible genuine link or competition; and it is this reality that needs to be measured against pro-FOC-TMNs' opinions.[203]

Faced with the threats of bankruptcy and extinction of the FOC, the above interests managed to marshall enough support at the UNCTAD debate to defeat the threats of 'phase out' cries from the radical non-FOC-DMNs. The power of the lobby and the pressure from the operators managed to swing opinions from even the formerly critical TMNs, such as France and the UK, to support the alternative: the reform of the FOC.[204] This change of position was very crucial to these TMNs: the economic threats from the anti-FOC interests was more important than anything else. Increasingly since 1974 the states which in 1958 were vociferous in their demands for a clearly defined link between flag state and vessel had found themselves supporting the continued existence of FOC registries barely a decade later.[205]

When general Western economic interests were at risk, the minor differences between the TMNs were put aside to ensure resources were not transferred to the development and expansion of the DMNs' fleets. These, and these alone, were the real issues at UNCTAD. Any legal jargons in support of the legal genuine link such as the pretentious 'respect for national sovereignty' were mere camouflage.[206]

The TMNs which had been uncharacteristically outspoken on this issue, were not anxious (as they put it) to subsidize development and/or expansion of national fleets in the DMNs through possibly higher shipping costs to themselves. The fact is that the FOCs would have been replaced by the genuine national fleets of the DMNs.[207] It is probably apparent by now that a shift in ownership of vessels to the DMNs was not in the strategic interest of many of the TMNs whose nationals are the beneficial owners of much of the tonnage registered in the FOCs. In short, the DMNs had mounted a brave fight against international finance capital, commodity interests and the international division of labour in bulk shipping, but had failed.[208]

The DMNs' growing opposition to FOC operations has highlighted important differences in the North–South perceptions of bulk shipping. Whereas there is now a strong body of opinion in the TMNs supportive of the FOCs; maritime opinion in the DMNs view such vessels as a threat. Thus, once again, abolition gave way to reforms because the still-powerful TMNs' forces in international maritime transport can cope with reforms but not revolutionary changes.[209]

Compromise at UNCTAD

The phasing out of the FOCs by the countries concerned would have introduced economic links (as opposed to the vague genuine link) concerning manning, local management and shareholding, and incorporation into the economic structure of the host DMNs as proposed in the UNCTAD context.[210] It was always doubtful whether it would succeed. Earlier in this discussion it was pointed out that the phrase genuine link entered the international legal scene in 1955 in a context quite unrelated to shipping. What was omitted was the fact that between 1950 and 1955 the International Law Commission (ILC) had been preparing provisions for submission to the 1958 Geneva Conference.[211] During this period attempts had been made, reflecting the concerns of the members, to draft provisions regulating conditions for the grant of nationality to vessels. The act of registration traditionally constituted a grant of nationality, the flag being *prima facie* or visible evidence of registry. Prior to 1956 the draft had emphasized *economic* considerations as opposed to merely *legal* considerations.[212]

Three decades later, in 1986, UNCTAD tried to reinforce economic link and/or consideration. The legal genuine link had been inserted by the drafters because they neither agreed nor wanted to introduce economic link. It had led one to wonder:

> The concept of genuine link has always puzzled me and it seems to me it is one of those concepts, as legal realists in our jurisprudence have taught us, that we came up with when we really are not sure whether there ought to be a requirement or not.[213]

Thirty years earlier — a point of some interest in the light of the 1986 UNCTAD proposals — the Commission had suggested that:

> Article 2. Right to a flag: each state may fix the conditions for the registration of ships in its territory and the right to fly its flag.
>
> Nevertheless for purposes of recognition of its national character by other states a ship must either:
>
> (1) Be the property of the State concerned; or
> (2) Be more than one-half owned by:
>   (a) Nationals or persons legally domiciled in the territory of the state concerned and actually resident there; or
>   (b) A partnership in which the majority of partners with personal liability are nationals or persons legally domiciled in the territory of the state concerned and actually residents there; or
>   (c) A joint stock company formed under the laws of the state concerned and having its registered office in the territory of that state.[214]

The Commission had run into problems trying to reconcile the various national interests and/or requirements in order to determine what were internationally accepted standards. Thirty years later UNCTAD met a similar fate trying to trace the ILC path.[215]

Thus, although the first steps towards a convention on terms of registry had been taken at Geneva, it was extremely hard to see how these aspects could be defined in such a way as not to restrict severely the existing systems of the non-FOC-TMNs (e.g. the UK) which placed no restrictions on foreign shareholding or non-FOC-DMNs (e.g. Libya) which were unable to find sufficient nationals to man the greater part of their tanker fleets.[216] It became apparent that even if a convention was introduced, its application to countries which might not be contracting parties would be extremely difficult. There seemed little evidence that any of the TMNs or DMNs, who provide much of the vessels and personnel respectively on board these fleets, felt sufficiently strongly about the FOC phenomenon to be able to introduce discriminatory legislation against it.[217] Without such legislation it was hard to see sufficient pressure upon the FOC registers to remove the facilities they offer. Faced with imminent threats of failure the only option open to UNCTAD, if it wanted to salvage the convention, was to compromise. The compromise was once again to drop the requirements for economic link and/or consideration in favour of the wishy-washy genuine link or mere legal requirements.[218]

The Need for and Development of a New Convention

The Road to Geneva 1974-1984

The demand for the convention had begun in earnest at Geneva even before the ink that had signed the Code Convention had dried.

Its rationale is therefore to be found in the DMNs' desire to build own fleets, the implementation of the New Order and the fulfilment of the Development Strategy for the UN Development Decade. With the Liner Code behind them, the DMNs started work on the FOCs and bulk trade.[219] Under the guise of adherence to the genuine link concept, the TMNs had managed to walk a tightrope, deploring the existence and evils resulting from the FOC registry, while at the same time providing indirect sanction by continued emphasis on a vague standard such as the legal genuine link. The response of the TMNs to demands for a clearly defined genuine link — i.e. economic link — had been to adopt the very argument put to them in 1958 — the national sovereignty concept.[220] In 1974 a decision was made at UNCTAD forum to examine the consequences of a lack of genuine link between vessel and flag state. That position was reaffirmed by the UN General Assembly and by UNCTAD V at Manila in 1979. Between 1974 and 1984 there were numerous studies, action papers, resolutions and finally a realignment of forces.[221]

At some point the FOC registries supported the TMNs. There were accusations and counter-allegations. While there has been much criticism of the political views and bias taken in the UNCTAD studies it has been mainly directed at the implementation of these UNCTAD proposals. The basic thrust of the argument in the studies has not been refuted. The FOC system is perceived by the DMNs as a mechanism for continued economic colonialism by the TMNs.[222] The practice is seen as a convenient method for the TMNs to make use of the DMNs' resources while retaining the control and benefit of the wealth generated. In accordance with the requirement of the New Order, the DMNs wanted a major alteration in the world's economic system so that benefits were more equitably shared, and also full involvement in the making of economic and political decisions affecting their wellbeing.[223] The basis of the DMNs' interest in the FOC system and the genuine link requirement was therefore economic. The FOC system had adversely affected the development and competitiveness of their fleets. In developing fleets, the DMNs want to earn foreign currency, broaden their industrial bases, provide employment, and exercise greater control over the transport of cargo generated by their foreign trade.[224]

In all these efforts the FOC and liners stood in their way. UNCTAD had recently been instrumental in producing a Code of Conduct which would assist the DMNs to participate in the liner trade, which until now had been dominated by cartels. The Code involves a concept of cargo reservation which basically allocates certain percentage (40-40-20) of shipping business to the cargo-generating country.[225] The DMNs' attention had now turned from anticipation in liner trade to the bulk cargo trade, of which they generate a substantial proportion (30 per cent). The FOC operates mainly in the bulk trade areas — i.e. oil tankers and bulk carriers.[226] Thus, the concern about FOC practice is intimately connected with the desire to achieve greater control over the wealth generated in the form of bulk cargo carriage.

> The linkage between cargo allocation and fleet financing, as in the case of liner vessels, is strongly emphasised by the UNCTAD and developing states, for the best way of securing needed financing is to demonstrate conclusively that the financed vessel is assured of regular employment. A system of cargo allocation, assuming reasonable prices is thus a key element in plans for an expanded merchant marine.[227]

It was noted earlier that the FOC used cargo guarantees from commodity traders to attract investment from finance capital. Equally, in order to even begin asserting a system of cargo reservations and financing the DMNs need some measure of control over the shipping trade.[228] It is at this point — commercial interest and regulation of competition — that once again law, economics and policy interest and the concept of genuine link is revived as a slogan for the battle:

> The genuine link debate has now taken a different character. Allegation of the need for a genuine link — and the assertion that open registry fleets do not meet the required criteria — has become the mechanism for implementing the bulk rights proposal of the UNCTAD Secretariat.[229]

The main theme of UNCTAD–DMNs proposals has been the redefinition and identification of new elements of the acceptable requirements of genuine link. These new elements essentially consist of economic preconditions for registration, i.e. *economic link*. The newly identified economic elements necessary for valid registration of vessels are integrated into the accepted *effective jurisdiction and control* aspects of *genuine link*.[230] This is done by using the argument that effective control is only possible if there is economic link between vessel and state. The argument made for the definition of genuine link in economic terms seeks also to address the needs of the DMNs in terms of world community concerns:

> The open registry issue calls for international agreement on the need for economic links between a vessel and its flag state so that the flag state can control owners and/or managers and key shipboard personnel. Such linkage is essential not only to encourage the expansion of the merchant fleets of the developing countries but also in the interests of a more orderly development of the world fleets in general.[231]

The Final Phase at Geneva 1984–1986

Thus, the veil had been lifted: the issue was economic rather than legal. Since 1958 the problem of conflict with sovereignty had meant that genuine link had been left undefined as a prerequisite for attribution of nationality. This vagueness, originally decried by the TMNs, was now proving a convenient loophole to legally and politically justify lack of any action against the FOC registries which would result in economic loss to them.[232] In the final two years at UNCTAD it was not surprising, therefore, that essentially the disagreement remained and/or boiled down to the question of economic interests. For this reason it was equally not surprising that a representative of the leading beneficiary — i.e. the USA — was quite open about the real concerns and motives involved:

> My delegation does not see the issue of substandard ships to be the major issue that separates us at this negotiation. The real issue as we see it is the potential economic trade effects of the conditions which have been proposed here for limiting the use of open registries. Let us call these proposals openly what they are: a call for protected shipping.[233]

To call a spade a spade: it is not that the DMNs–UNCTAD had hit the TMNs below the belt but rather that they had, for the first time, managed to accurately pinpoint the sensitive points — the nerve centre of the TMNs' control of international maritime transport. To put it another way, the DMNs–UNCTAD alliance had exposed the myths of the legal genuine link: they had lifted the veil and exposed the conspiracy between the TMNs and the FOC owners on the one hand, and international finance capital and commodity interests on the other. UNCTAD was particularly concerned at the involvement of multinational corporations in the DMNs' commodity exports.[234] The use of FOC vessels in a vertically integrated sense was seen as an extension of the economic hegemony inherent — in the eyes of the DMNs — in the North–South trade. FOC operations allow the TMNs' multinationals to keep control of important commodity movements, whilst at the same time circumventing the penalties of high-cost TMNs' labour.[235] UNCTAD's study of the iron ore, phosphate rock and bauxite/alumina trades, for instance, had shown that the terms of shipment of these important South–North commodity flows are invariably FOC and under the control of the TMNs' concerns. A substantial amount of the shipment contracts are long-term; for example, 67 per cent of the bauxite trade is made under contracts of ten years or longer, making it attractive to investment from finance capital.[236]

Furthermore, the 'closed market' character of these trades is enforced by the largest number of shipping arrangements made outside the open market fixture-setting mechanism. The use of FOC vessels on these commodity routes represent very real problems for the DMNs' exporting interests. Vertically integrated FOC operations can then be used by the multinational corporations in order to practise transfer pricing far beyond the reaches of the commodity-producing DMNs.[237] The actual FOC nations are not aware of the profits made by operators using their registries; and UNCTAD has identified a practice of income being shifted between multinational subsidiaries in high-tax countries to those in low-tax countries, or, indeed to tax havens and secret bank accounts.[238] This procedure would increase the non-taxed revenue of the ship operator (sailing under the FOC), and decrease taxable revenue in the home country of the multinational. It is precisely this sort of activity which earns the wrath of the DMNs who feel (and rightly so) that the income generated by their commodity exports, their registries and abundantly low-cost factors of production is instead distributed inequitably, with the TMNs and their interests taking either the lion's share[239] or everything. The DMNs find themselves in a no-win situation.

The 1986 Convention Comes into Being

Thus, while there are still valid concerns about the use or abuse of the FOC system to avoid fishing and whaling conventions or nuclear obligations, the needs of the TMNs had largely been met through provisions in the 1958 and 1982 Conventions.[240] Although some of the economic advantages of the FOC registry, at least in terms of commercial flexibility, had been decreased by international standards and inspections enforceable by states other than the flag state, nevertheless the benefits and actual control of the FOC registry fleets have been retained by the TMNs by continuing to proclaim the legal genuine link requirement because they found the ambiguity of the phrase anything but beneficial.[241] Any attempt to introduce real economic link is met with a national sovereignty argument. As pointed out by Professor Juda, economic arguments about the overall costs of world shipping do not address the fundamental concepts underlying the philosophy of the New Order — the equitable distribution of world resources:

> Equity is not a concept of economics but rather of politics as it involves notions of fundamental fairness and justice. It is the legitimacy of the distribution of influence, control and benefits in world shipping that is currently at the heart of the matter of the developing states.[242]

At the dawn of the new Convention the question, then, was whether the shipping world which spawned the FOC registry system — a world rooted in commercially influenced policy-making — remained or would remain in the face of the demands for a new structure in which free enterprise was no longer the mainspring.[243] At Geneva, states responded according to national economic interests as they inevitably do. Economic self-interest has yet to be overcome if the concept of economic link is to succeed in international shipping generally and the FOC operations in particular.[244] A comment made by a leading authority perhaps best summed up the story of the genuine link requirements at Geneva:

> When, with the benefit of hindsight one considers what the fight was all about, the conclusion is that the campaign had different objectives and emphasis in different countries all depending on the extent of their interest for one reason or another in flags of necessity vessels versus the extent to which they considered themselves harmed by the existence of this new development in international shipping.[245]

With that background the events leading to the Convention itself were very straightforward. The General Assembly of the UN, by resolution 37/209 of 20 December 1982, decided that a conference of plenipotentiaries should be convened in order to consider the adoption of an international agreement concerning the conditions under which vessels should be accepted on national shipping registers.[246] The UN conference on Conditions for Registration of Ships, convened under the auspices of UNCTAD, held its first part from 16 July to 3 August 1984.[247] The conference resumed its work at its second part from 28 January to 15 February 1985 in accordance with the General Assembly resolution 39/213A of 18 December 1984; its third part from 8 to 19 July 1985 in accordance with General Assembly resolution 39/213B of 12 April 1985; and its fourth part from 20 January to 7 February 1986 in accordance with General Assembly resolution 40/187 of 17 December 1985. All four parts of the conference were held at the Palais des Nations, Geneva.[248]

The UN Convention on Conditions for Registration of Ships, 1986

Introduction

It was in this light that, after several years of wrangling, negotiations and compromises, the United Nations Convention on Conditions for Registration of Ships (hereinafter known as The Registry Convention) was adopted on 7 February 1986 in the presence of some 110 states and an equal number of liberation movements, specialized agencies, intergovernmental and non-intergovernmental agencies as well as observers.[249] That number has been exceeded only once — by UNCLOS III — as the largest gathering of representatives of peoples and states ever in the world history of conferences. The aims of the Convention were to introduce new standards of responsibility and accountability for world shipping generally and FOC operations in particular.[250] Amidst the euphoria that accompanies the conclusions of these types of international instruments, it was claimed that for the first time an international instrument now existed which defined the elements of the genuine link that should exist between a ship and the state whose flag it flies.[251]

There are of course problems with this type of generalization. First, it remains to be seen whether such assertions have foundations and, even if they do, whether they would be proved right with time and practice. But, second, and above all, contrary to earlier claims by the TMNs that the issue had been solved by the 1958 and 1982 Conventions, this is a clear admission that it had not. It may be added that neither did this Convention resolve the issue.[252] Mr Lamine Fadika, the Marine Minister of the Côte d'Ivoire, who presided over all four sessions of the Conference in which the agreement was negotiated, told a press conference prior to the final plenary that the Convention filled a major gap in international maritime jurisprudence. Mr Fadika, arguably the influential and instrumental President of the Conference, went on to emphasize the admission[253] that, although the concept of the genuine link had been embodied in other instruments such as the 1958 Geneva Convention on the High Seas and in the 1982 Third United Nations Convention on the Law of the

Sea, its components had never been identified. If this admission is to be taken seriously (and it should be) why had the FOC-TMNs maintained all along that the 1958 and 1982 Conventions had dealt with the matter once and for all? And if they had done so, why yet another Convention on the issue? If it succeeded in identifying those elements (and it is arguable whether it did) it remains to be seen whether, in fact, the new Convention went further than that.[254]

The heart of the UN/UNCTAD's newest Convention is supposed to be Articles 8, 9 and 10 which, *inter alia*, provide for participation by nationals of the flag state in the ownership, manning and management of ships, thus supposedly establishing the key economic links between a ship and the flag state which have constituted the missing link in the hitherto legally-oriented current practice of genuine link.[255] A distinctive feature is that states have an option between the two mandatory articles on *ownership* and *manning* and herein we find the first major loophole in the Convention: the continuation of legalism and vagueness that was to prove the downfall of the two earlier Conventions.[256] Continuing that tradition, Article 7 of the Convention on participation by nationals in the ownership and/or manning of ship states:

> With respect to the provisions concerning manning and ownership of ships as contained in paragraphs 1 and 2 of Article 8 and paragraphs 1 and 3 of Article 9, respectively, and without prejudice to the application of any other provisions of this Convention, a state of registration has to comply *either* with the provisions of paragraphs 1 and 2 of Article 8 *or* with the provisions of paragraphs 1 and 3 of Article 9, but may comply with both.[257] (Emphasis added.)

The allowing of that option tore through the heart of the Convention, all its claims and what it would have stood for. Only if both Articles 8 and 9 were mandatory could the idea of genuine link have survived. As things stand, the concept has again eluded a major world convention. Mr Fadika tried to repair the damage by explaining that his element of flexibility[258] was introduced to take account of the different conditions prevailing in flag states: that some might lack sufficient manpower among their nationals or 'persons domiciled or lawfully in permanent residence' within their territory to provide for significant participation by nationals in the crews of ships flying their flag; while others might not have sufficient capital to participate effectively in ship ownership.[259] That is all well and good but it ignores the fact that unless the genuine link requirement is tightened these disadvantages will persist. It is like the argument of a surgeon who simply papered over (and allowed the cancer to spread) instead of operating, for fear of causing pain to his patient. The same argument was used in 1958 and 1982: namely to allow for recognition and respect for national sovereignty.[260] It is like looking at different sides of the same coin 30 years later and saying it is not the same coin.

Manning and Ownership

The provision for options in Article 7 rendered the operations of Article 8 on ownership and Article 9 on manning ineffective. As though to emphasize that the economic link requirement stood or fell on this, it was only when the DMNs gave in on it that the conclusion of the Convention was ever possible.[261] Mr Luis Amado Castro of Mexico, speaking on behalf of the Group of 77, admitted that:

> Within the conference itself, successive phases could also be identified, in particular the breakthrough made a year ago by the Group of 77 in allowing states to opt either for manning or ownership articles. The success of the July 1985 session in settling these two issues, as well as management, had cleared the way for the present meeting . . . .[262]

That contention was backed by Mr Anatoly Kolodkine of the Soviet Union speaking on behalf of Group D:

> Group D considered that giving governments an option on two elements served to weaken the instrument . . . .[263]

Article 8 on ownership is rather vague and nowhere does it provide for elements of ownership. It is submitted that it marked no departure from either the 1958 Geneva Convention or the UNCLOS 1982 in supposedly upholding national sovereignty by leaving it up to the flag state. Hence the use of such vague phrases as 'appropriate' and/or that: 'These laws and regulations should be sufficient to permit the flag state to exercise effectively its jurisdiction and control over ships flying its flag'.[264] Otherwise, what are these regulations and would leaving it up to the flag state not rob the regulations of international uniformity and hence provide an escape route to the very conditions in which the FOC thrive? At the negotiations the Group of 77 had offered a draft which included 'adequate', 'appropriate', 'satisfactory' and 'sufficient', but 'sufficient' was preferred because of its vagueness.[265] Otherwise, even from the elementary requirements of good legislative drafting, Article 7 should have followed Article 9. Putting it before Article 8 is so out of context. One explanation is that it was a late addition, an afterthought, a compromise won by the TMNs' insistence. The other explanation being that the TMNs had foreseen a platform where factors of production (labour, skill, finance and technology) could be brought together in a joint venture.[266] As Mr Fadika was to explain later that compromise and/or vagueness envisaged joint-venture operations (reform rather than phasing out), to save the FOC from extinction: hence Article 13. Only if read in that context can Article 7 make any sense, coming before Articles 8 and 9.[267]

Among the provisions also considered important is Article 9 on manning which states that the state of registration shall ensure that the manning of its ships is of such level and competence as to ensure compliance with applicable international rules and standards, in particular those regarding safety at sea. It will be remembered that another part of that Article stipulates that the state of registration shall ensure that the terms and conditions of employment are in conformity with applicable international rules and standards.[268] Bearing in mind that Article 7 eliminated any chances of economic elements from both Articles 8 and 9, all that was left for Article 9 was to dwell on the technical and safety issues — and even then not to any significant level, for Article 94 of the 1982 Convention had sufficiently expanded and strengthened the registration and coastal states' powers on safety regulations. So, like the 1982 Convention, the 1986 Convention merely served to emphasize the jurisdictional aspects of the 1958 Convention.[269] Although technical and safety issues are equally important, it was nevertheless generally agreed that by the 1980s the safety standards of the FOC fleets had improved and were no longer the major obstacles. Rather the argument had by now shifted to economic matters. At Geneva the TMNs wanted to discuss only social issues; the DMNs wanted economic issues on the agenda upgraded: once again the TMNs won the day.[270]

Maritime Management and Administration

Article 10 with respect to *management* is also considered significant, being part of the heart of the Convention. In brief, this article makes the state of registration responsible for ensuring that persons accountable for the management and operations of ships are in a position to meet the financial obligations that may arise from the operation of such ships[271] and to cover risks which are normally insured in international maritime transportation in respect of damages to third parties. Although Article 10 is somehow out of the shadow of Article 7, nevertheless, like Article 9, it deals with only issues peripheral to genuine link such as the regulatory and technical aspects. It clearly accepts the continued existence of FOC operations, except for cosmetic changes here and there.[272] These changes, dealt with at length, are nonetheless only quantitative rather than qualitative. It was only after the DMNs had caved in on the key issues the previous July that the way was paved for the Convention. At first sight Article 10 looks like the kind of provision appropriate to deal with the abuses by the liner conferences rather than those of the FOCs.[273]

There are also one or two provisions outside the heart of the Convention which merit mention. One of such is Article 5 of the instrument which provides for the establishment by a flag state of a *competent and adequate national maritime administration* which is charged with a number of specific tasks such as ensuring that a ship flying its flag complies with the states' laws and regulations concerning registration of ships[274] and with applicable international rules and standards concerning, in particular, the safety of ships and persons on board and the prevention of pollution of the marine environment. In the first instance, and as Mr Fadika correctly pointed out, at present a number of (especially) DMN states had no such maritime administration hence their inability to give shipping the due priority it deserves.[275] Speaking to a cross-section of representatives from the DMNs one discovers that shipping is either synonymous to ports administration or relegated to one of the following ministries: trade, commerce, transport or communications. In this respect perhaps these countries would learn from, say, the USA which has not only the Maritime Administration but also the Federal Maritime Commission, with residual maritime issues also falling to the Judiciary, the State Department and the Department of Commerce.[276]

Returning to the Convention, it should be mentioned that Article 5 is not one of the substantive — i.e. economic — provisions but rather one of the procedural or secondary requirements. Like Article 9 it only covers the administrative and technical aspects. It supplements Articles 9 and 10 both of which were, of course, no departures from either the 1958 or the 1982 Conventions.[277] The aim of Article 5 is to require that these administrations be based in the state of registry. It was probably aimed at countries like Sweden which has no such requirements and, above all, Liberia which has always had its registration office in New York. But the requirement for what might turn out to be only a kiosk office would be of no consequence so long as the control or nerve centre remains outside. There is nothing in the Convention to discourage that.[278] However, all in all, the issues raised by Article 5 had long ceased to be of major consequence to the operations or criticism of the FOC registry. Nevertheless, taken on its own merits, effective measures to ensure that those responsible for the operation and management of vessels can be readily identifiable and accountable will be a good thing.[279]

If the economic link, and therefore full powers, had been vested in

116

the flag state as Articles 8 and 9 had provided (were it not for Article 7) it would have been unnecessary to provide for Article 5. But even the most liberally minded do not find Article 5 of any consequence.[280] Mr Kristian Fuglesang, speaking for Intertanko, although welcoming the provisions of the Convention that the flag state shall have a competent maritime administration, nevertheless retorted:

> Safety at Sea and protection of the marine environment is dependent on the existence of efficient maritime administrations capable of enforcing internationally recognised safety standards.[281]

He stated, warning that:

> Such administrations will not magically appear simply because an international convention says they should. This is an area where there is scope for further co-operation between developed and developing nations.[282]

Finally, similar warning should be heeded when considering Article 6 on *identification and accountability* which provides that a state shall have the necessary measures to ensure that owners and operators on a ship on its register are adequately identifiable for the purposes of ensuring their full accountability.[283] Regarding the history and abuses of FOC operations, this provision would be of particular importance in identifying and punishing perpetrators of maritime fraud, who might have used the FOC registries to aid their crimes. For the first time information will be required on owners and operators including (also for the first time) stipulations on log books.[284] But like the fate awaiting Article 5, Article 6 is both procedural, i.e. peripheral, and too little too late.

Shortcomings of the Registry Convention

On the Genuine Economic Link Issue

It is probably apparent by now where I stand on this issue. Unfortunately I do not share the Conference President's interpretation that:

> For the first time an international instrument now exists which defines the elements of the *genuine link* that should exist between a ship and the state whose flag it flies.[285] (Own emphasis.)

nor, the optimism of the spokesman for the DMNs at Geneva that it is

> a clear and unequivocal statement of the elements that constitute the *genuine link* or that the success that had been achieved constituted an indispensable link in the chain of international efforts that will facilitate a claim of international efforts that will facilitate a larger participation on the part of developing countries in world shipping.[286] (Emphasis added.)

nor with approving noises coming from the Soviet spokesman for Group D that:

> The fact that it defined the criteria for the *genuine link* was very important. (Emphasis added.)

and the French spokesman that it:

> . . . inspired at the outset an irrepressible will to fight against abuses of all kinds and to create for the first time an international rule setting out new and binding standards in an essential sector of the economy.[287]

These sentiments are characteristic of international gatherings but do not mean much. The same thing was said about the 1958 Geneva Conference, the 1974 Liner Code Convention and the 1982 UNCLOS. What difference did they make?

Rather these issues should be looked at coolly and sceptically much later, with the benefit of hindsight and away from the heated atmosphere of international gatherings. One way or another, I tend to agree with the contention, disputed by the President at the plenary session, that the Convention legitimized the present state of affairs in world shipping, including the FOC registry system.[288] One would like to borrow from the French spokesman's statement that: 'The compromise that had been achieved was expressed in subtle and complex rules which mirrored the shipping world itself'.[289] It is submitted this is the exact manner in which the compromise had been couched both in the 1958 Geneva Convention and the 1982 UN Convention with the sole purpose of using legal niceties to disguise and deny genuine economic link. The speed with which the FOC interests signed the 1982 Convention and welcomed the 1986 Convention is clear evidence that, on both occasions, they were very relieved: both times their interests in the FOC operations in particular and international shipping in general emerged unscathed.[290]

In this particular instance 'economic link' slipped through the DMNs' fingers because they compromised on the key word 'options' just as they had compromised on 'recognition of territorial sovereignty' both in 1958 and 1982. Yet this time they were so near yet so far. It was not surprising that Mr Michael Fielder (UK) speaking for Group B could not hide his delight when he admitted that the speed[291] with which the issues of 'bareboat charter', 'identification' and 'accountability' had been satisfactorily settled in the first week of the final session had made it possible for Group B to agree that the instrument should be a full international convention of a binding character. Equally Group B was also pleased that the preamble had made it clear that the agreement recognized the competence of specialized agencies, such as the ILO and the IMO.[292] The TMNs prefer to deal with these specialized agencies to which only technical and procedural issues are relegated, but not with UNCTAD where fundamental economic and political issues are raised. More crucial, the optional possibility first proposed by the Group of 77 was highly satisfactory to Group B, and in general Group B was pleased to be associated with the outcome. Mr Fielder considered that the turning point had been the consultations held by the President (Mr Lamine Fadika) with government officials and shipping industry interests between the first and second sessions.[293]

On the Encouragement of Mere Book Transfers
and Exonoration of the Status Quo

By maintaining the status quo the 1986 Convention has in effect exonorated the operations of the FOC system. Take, for instance, its stipulations in Article 4 on General Provisions:

1. Every state, whether coastal or land-locked, has the right to sail ships flying its flag on the high seas.
2. Ships have the nationality of the States whose flag they are entitled to fly.
3. Ships shall sail under the flag of one state only.
4. No ships shall be entered in the registers of ships of two or more states at a time, subject to the provisions of paragraphs 4 and 5 of Article 11 and Article 12.
5. A ship may not change its flag during a voyage or while in a port of call, save in the case of a real transfer of ownership or change of registry.[294]

With all due respect these are identical word-by-word to Articles 4–6 of the 1958 Geneva Convention on the High Seas and Articles 90–92 of the 1982 Law of the Sea Convention. So nothing has changed. It is interesting to note, however, that 1986 not only omits any reference to 'convenience' but also leaves out the equivalent to Article 6(2) of Geneva which was in fact reproduced in Article 92(2) of 1982.[295] From that point of view it could, in relation to the 1958 and 1982 Conventions, be regarded as a retrogressive development with regard to the *genuine link* issue. It is possible that the distribution of the fleets (bulk, combined and tankers) will remain roughly as indicated in Table 2.9.

In addition, Article 94 of the 1982 Convention probably more than compensates for the lack of adequate provisions in the 1986 Convention on safety and jurisdictional requirements: especially Articles 8–11. From the foregone it is difficult to comprehend or agree with the 1986 Convention's claims that it is:

> For the purpose of ensuring or, as the case may be, strengthening the *genuine link* between a state and ships flying its flag, and in order to exercise effectively its jurisdiction and control over such ships with regard to identification and accountability of shipowners and operators as well as with regard to administrative, technical, economic and social matters . . . .[296] (Emphasis added.)

Nothing could be further from the truth than the above provision. It probably does so with other matters, but not with economic issues let alone the *genuine economic link*. It is therefore not surprising that the DMNs and other critics are already unhappy about UNCTAD's newest-born baby. The main criticism is that an instrument originally intended to curb the FOC registry had been turned on its head in Geneva and had ended up legitimizing its continued existence.[297] That was the charge the ITWF laid before the final plenary session (and rightly so) approving the new registration treaty. The ITWF, it will be remembered, was one of its original backers when the process began. That they ended up unconvinced that the genuine economic link had been achieved at Geneva should be taken very seriously[298] on account of their long experience.

The discontent with the ineffectiveness of the registry convention is not confined to the DMNs and organized labour. Although the ITWF has been a solitary voice of complaint from within the TMNs' ranks, that does not mean others disagree with their analysis. Quite the opposite.[299] Although most of the Group B representatives would avoid admitting it publicly, there is a clear sense of satisfaction that an attack on what they see as a crucial part of the structure of international shipping has effectively been seen off. According to the TMNs, nobody likes the Convention, but what matters to them is that the early threat has been eliminated, so they can return to their respective capitals congratulating themselves[300] and more than willing to pay the meagre sacrifice of having to implement the cosmetic changes the convention introduced. The DMNs had, of course, wanted

Table 2.9 Beneficial ownership of bulk and combined carriers of open-registry fleets, 1983
(Number of vessels and thousands of dwt)

Country or territory of registration / Country or territory of beneficial ownership	Liberia Number	Liberia dwt (000)	Panama Number	Panama dwt (000)	Cyprus Number	Cyprus dwt (000)	Bermuda Number	Bermuda dwt (000)	Bahamas Number	Bahamas dwt (000)	Total Number	Total dwt (000)
Hong Kong	232	12,248	148	5,210	1	38	—	—	—	—	381	17,496
Greece	107	5,589	74	2,562	28	872	—	—	—	—	209	9,023
United States of America	134	8,014	19	624	—	—	—	—	3	139	156	8,777
Japan	74	3,600	161	4,271	—	—	—	—	—	—	235	7,871
Unspecified	55	2,341	45	1,478	—	—	—	—	—	—	100	3,819
Switzerland	46	2,993	18	461	—	—	—	—	—	—	64	3,454
Germany, Federal Republic of	15	880	28	1,686	4	163	—	—	—	—	47	2,729
China	4	140	57	2,260	—	—	—	—	—	—	61	2,400
Norway	38	2,022	6	156	—	—	—	—	—	—	44	2,178
Canada	12	841	—	—	—	—	10	635	—	—	22	1,476
Israel	12	601	4	150	—	—	—	—	—	—	16	751
Monaco	13	644	3	77	—	—	—	—	—	—	16	721
Pakistan	18	656	2	40	—	—	—	—	—	—	20	696
Republic of Korea	4	133	15	547	—	—	—	—	—	—	19	680
United Kingdom	7	172	9	408	—	—	1	30	—	—	17	610
Denmark	10	452	1	18	—	—	—	—	3	115	14	585
Brazil	4	573	—	—	—	—	—	—	—	—	4	573
Italy	9	515	2	32	1	22	—	—	—	—	12	569
25 countries, entities or territories each beneficially owning less than 500,000 dwt	23	1,040	31	906	1	44	1	34	—	—	56	2,024
Unidentified	5	237	20	730	6	152	—	—	1	14	32	1,133
Total	822	43,691	643	21,616	41	1,291	12	699	7	268	1,525	67,565
Share in the total for bulk and combined carriers	53.9	64.7	42.2	32.0	2.7	1.9	0.8	1.0	0.4	0.4	100.0	100.0

Source: UNCTAD Document No. TD/B/C.4/261, Table 7, p. 9.

121

nothing less than the total phasing out of FOC operations. But they were forced, against overwhelming odds from the TMNs–FOC pressure, to compromise on the single most crucial element: *option* between Articles 8 and 9 introduced by Article 7.[301]

So how was this complete *volte face* achieved? UNCTAD veterans are putting it down to three factors. First, a change of heart by the Latin American DMNs, many of whom have big FOC registry fleets themselves. Second, a change in the people running the Shipping Secretariat of UNCTAD, and in particular the departure of the hitherto uncompromising Dr Al Jadir.[302] Third, the tireless effort of Ivory Coast Shipping Minister and President of the Conference, Lamine Fadika, who stuck his neck out a long way in search of compromise: hence the tribute paid him by the spokesman for Group B, who considered that the turning point in the Conference had been the consultations held by the President between the first and second sessions with government officials and shipping industry interests. The TMNs' jubilation implied that the Convention falls far short of what the DMNs and the international labour federations had expected.[303] Sight should not be lost of the final and equally crucial factor: the change of heart by those TMNs who had once loathed the FOC system but performed a U-turn on lobby from their shipping operators and on prompting from the USA that UNCTAD was a dangerous instrument bent on something more than simply phasing out the FOC system. This was not the first nor will be the last time that ranks are closed in the face of a common enemy.[304]

The President maintained his optimism to the end that the Convention would bring about changes in the shipping industry 'gradually and progressively' and that it would eventually lead to the abolition of certain abusive practices stemming from inadequate links between a ship and its flag. Although he is probably right about the existence of abuses, it cannot be certain that the Convention will bring about their abolition. In excusing his search for a compromise he claims to have read it in the mandate for the Conference formulated by the General Assembly in 1982 to the effect that the views of all interested parties had to be taken into account in drawing up the Agreement. Only in that light can one appreciate (though not support) the options. The answer to that bitter pill is to be found in the consoling realization that the Convention represented a unique compromise between contradictory and divergent interests.

Encouragement of Flagging Out:
The New Flags of Convenience and Dual Registry

The failure of the registry convention implies that the international community has shied away from its responsibility to introduce genuine economic link on no less than three occasions over three decades (1958, 1982 and 1986). Ake Selander, of the International Confederation of Free Trade Unions (ICFTU) speaking for the ITWF,[305] while considering that the recommendations on identification and accountability and joint ventures (Article 13) were particularly useful, pointed to what he considered further shortcomings in the Convention. He viewed the measures in Article 14 on labour-supplying countries as 'completely out of the context of the genuine link principles'[306] and charged that Article 5 providing for a national maritime administration 'will ensure the continued existence of flag of convenience shipping since there is no obligation on the flag state to ensure that its national maritime administration is located within its territory'.[307] Moreover, he added that Article 10, dealing with the role of flag states in respect of the management of shipowning companies and ships, 'in no way guarantees the owner's solvency'.

Thus, with all these many unsatisfactory attempts to solve the problems of international shipping in general, and those raised by FOC operations in particular, it will not be surprising if the DMNs feel frustrated and let down and possibly resort to restrictive shipping practices. The final blow was probably the watering down of the Registry Convention, which was signed in haste, despite remaining differences of opinion between the negotiating groups.[308] Besides, the opposing views of the interested parties will lead to a long delay in the treaty becoming law. Furthermore, although the tonnage requirements are the same as for the Liner Code, the country requirement is substantially higher resulting in longer than the ten years it took for the former's ratification. The Convention will enter into force, in accordance with Articles 16–19, when ratified by 40 states representing 25 per cent of relevant gross registered tonnage (ships used in international seaborne trade of 500 grt and above.[309] Mr Fadika estimated that this might be achieved in five years but, once again, he is probably too optimistic. A longer period would suit the TMNs–FOC alliance, for by the time it is operative they will have safeguarded their interests to almost render the Convention redundant: it happened with the Liner Code and there is no guarantee that it will not happen again.[310]

The Group of 77, representing the DMNs, stressed that it was particularly unhappy that more had not been done to halt FOC operations — one of their main aims. Criticisms of the treaty have also continued to emanate from the international labour unions, especially the ITWF and the ICFTU,[311] the main thrust of these being that the treaty favours the TMNs, the FOC operators and its beneficiaries. It is not therefore surprising that the TMNs' group, Group B, was much happier at the outcome, seeing it as a vindication for its stand as a pro-FOC group. All in all, the conclusion of the registry treaty has wider consequences than its negotiators thought. It has probably hardened the resolve of the DMNs to pressure extra-economic measures such as protectionism, in pursuit of national fleets and equitable distribution of international shipping.[312] The DMNs are now looking towards Liner Code-like cargo reservation in the bulk trades and the internationalization of marine insurance. It was frustratingly painful to them that, faced with the DMNs' demands, some of the TMNs who once loathed the FOC system had no problem in making U-turns when the crunch came. At Geneva the DMNs and labour unions were suddenly and unexpectedly abandoned, exposed and made to look fools. To the FOC operators and the DMNs proxy owners, it may have provided only a temporary reprieve.[313]

To the beneficial owners and true managers the treaty has legitimatized their ability to exploit the glaring inequality that has for long existed in international shipping. It will be remembered that one of these, the USA, sees the FOC operations as a way out to provide for the EUSC or the NDRF: its national defence and international security machinery. Furthermore, the treaty has given a boost to the recent TMNs' policy of flagging out. FOC operations are no longer anything to be ashamed of: it is now an official international shipping policy.[314] Ironically this process has given rise to new FOC registries even within the TMNs, such as the UK where higher labour cost TMNs register in the lower-cost ones. It has already been noted how, in this way, both Norwegian supply vessels and the Spanish fishing fleets have taken advantage of the UK in the North Sea operations. New registries have also mushroomed in the DMNs themselves. Two other issues need to be mentioned about the FOC in relation to the future prospects for the development of national and international shipping. First, not only has the treaty rehabilitated[315] the once despised FOC to respectability, but neither can it be said that it will solve pollution, safety and other problems that have always accompanied it. Second, it may give a boost to joint ventures between the TMNs and DMNs and intra-DMNs, as the actual transfer machinery is ironed out, but these will not be the genuine joint ventures anticipated in Article 13: it will mean mere book transfers as the DMNs continue to act as custodians, proxies, and dumping grounds for sometimes obsolete and rejected or inappropriate technology.[316] As pointed out by Professor Lawrence Juda in a recent analysis of the original UNCTAD proposals:

> The desire for a New International Economic Order (NIEO) provides a general context in which to understand the demands being made by the developing states. The call by these states for an NIEO encompasses at least two general and inter-related themes. The first is the need for a major alteration in the world's economic system so that benefits are, from their point of view, more equitably shared — that is, with more benefits accruing to the developing countries. The second is that Third World States should be fully involved in the making of economic and political decisions that will affect their well being.[317]

Concluding Remarks

It is hoped that this study has contributed first to the appreciation of the history, development, rationale and future of the FOC operations. Second, as to the *ratio decidendi* of the real nature and function of the concept of genuine link, the inescapable conclusion is that that function is economic (rather than legal) and its solution can only therefore be found within the realms of political economy in international trade relations. The search for genuine link has been elusive only because the resort to legality casts 'darkening confusion upon darkening confusion'. It is for this reason that we have ended up with no less than three International Instruments (1958, 1982 and 1986) all covering various aspects of FOC operations and the search for genuine link. Yet none really confronts the issue at its roots. The quest for genuine link will probably continue to haunt international shipping for years to come, because every time an attempt is made the solution is sought in the wrong place: in the legal rather than in the economic adjustments and political reality. Yet these three spheres are inseparable.

The issue is simply this. The TMNs have dominated the international political and economic system (which includes international shipping) for years. In shipping, this control was exercised through the liner conferences, FOC operations and bulk trade, *inter alia*. In relation to FOC registry the TMNs have always evaded discussing economic and political issues that might have led to genuine economic links since they could delay the inevitable by hiding behind the legal genuine link as embodied in the three conventions. As a colleague put it recently:

The evolution of open registry shipping is a colourful story, replete with debate, stratagem, strife and disaster. It provides a vivid illustration of the interface between law, commerce, politics and economic philosophy. The availability and use of open registry facilities is an important fact of international commercial and political life.[318]

The DMNs now seek to end that TMNs' domination of the international political and economic system through participation and equitable distribution of the world's resources. In international shipping that would only be possible if they established and developed their own national fleets. But in that effort they find that the FOC registry liner conferences, the organization of the bulk trade and other unfair systems are ranged against them.

In their desperate attempt to retain their domination of international shipping the TMNs are no doubt aided by commodity interests and finance capital. It is therefore not surprising that the basis of the TMNs' defence of FOC operations stems from *economic efficiency* criteria: namely that there are strong arguments for the coordination of the TMNs' capital and technology with the cheap DMNs' labour and other factors of production in FOC operations. However, in order to understand the DMNs' position, it is necessary not only to lift the veil of the *legal genuine link* but to go beyond a strict market methodology to arrive at *genuine economic link*. A failure of the market-oriented approach to deal with such non-quantifiable objectives as reducing economic dependence upon the TMNs leads to the DMNs campaigning all UNCTAD to being dismissed as 'too political' or 'merely ideological'. It is of course in the interests of the TMNs to maintain that separation between the legal and economic, the market and the political: it suits them to maintain that confusion by using the *legal link* smokescreen.

Turning specifically to the 1986 Convention and the future of FOC operations there will probably be a number of changes. First, it seems probable that the share of the traditional FOC countries' fleets in world shipping will decline: Liberia is already losing out to Panama for the reasons already outlined above. It has also been noted that, now the FOC operations have been made acceptable by no less than an International Instrument, some TMNs are now also bidding for the system. One reason for this would undoubtedly be the increased administrative and verification control just introduced by the new Convention which, if effective, will undoubtedly deter the unscrupulous operator who cannot, or will not, meet the necessary standards. Although these constitute a relatively limited part of any fleet, their influence is out of proportion to their size and their elimination by the new Convention through both flag and port state control, would be highly desirable.

Second, there appears some strong indications that traditional division between open and closed registries will probably become less clear, with the decisions of the Philippines, Sri Lanka, Nigeria, as well as the other DMNs and TMNs to open their registries to foreign operators, subject to commitments on the use of a substantial proportion of nationals on board and under fairly stringent conditions of transparency and accountability in line with Articles 6 and 7 of the new Convention. There are differing schools of thought on this: one argues that this is in effect an end to FOC operations as we know them; the other holds the contrary view that the new developments are only new brands of FOC operations. Be that as it may, such a direction, which Singapore has already taken, may well prove attractive to the other FOC registries as a means of trying to head off direct attack although, once gained, the FOC registry label might be very difficult to lose. Presumably, also, there will continue to be countries like Vanuatu (formerly the New Hebrides) who see the FOC register as a convenient source of national income, without in any way being in a position to maintain effective control over ships flying their flag.

Third, and probably the most important element in the longer run, however, will be the inevitable decline of the role of the cross-trader in world shipping. This would be regretted by the TMNs just as it would be welcomed by the DMNs. The reason for this is simple. Almost by definition, ships on FOC registries are essentially operating as cross-traders, since, like the TMNs of Norway and Greece (and indeed Hong Kong), the flag states are without substantial volumes of trade to and from their countries. Admittedly, Liberia's iron ore trade is sufficient to give full employment to some 2 million dwt of dry bulk carriers, but its present fleet of such ships is about 22 times as much, standing at 44 million. It is not surprising that to the DMNs the 1986 Convention was meant to be only the second in a series of measures designed to handicap the TMNs' monopoly and therefore pave the way for the DMNs' entry. Had the Liner Code not dealt a blow to cross-traders by requiring cargo reservation to cargoes generated by a country's foreign trade? To follow the Registry Convention will be another one on cargo-sharing in the bulk trade along similar lines as the 1974 Code. The proposed bulk trade Convention will probably be followed by one on the internationalization of marine insurance, etc.

Fourth, and finally, it seems quite certain that the TMNs' ship-owners during the late 1980s and 1990s will have to recognize, as mentioned above, that more and more cargo will not be available for cross-trade and that new mechanisms — in particular the use of joint ventures and other types of partnerships between countries which can produce either the expertise, the personnel, the capital or the cargo — have to be created. This was emphasized by Mr Lamine Fadika, the President of the 1986 Conference. It is also for this reason that Articles 7–10, 13 and Annex 1 were inserted in the 1986 Convention on the insistence of the TMNs. It is pressures from the DMNs that are now forcing the TMNs to accept that, without economic links, genuine links are unobtainable. One now hears conciliatory signals from the TMNs that the FOC system which was originally utilized not to provide such a partnership but for quite other reasons, established a most unequal association, and that it should be the aim of an international organization such as UNCTAD to seek ways whereby partnership between these countries which can contribute can be facilitated, rather than to pursue a somewhat sterile attack upon a system, which, if a suitable economic climate could be developed, might well wither away. And wither away indeed!

Notes

1   Whitney Smith, *Flags and Arms Across the World*, Cassell Ltd, London, 1980, pp. 5–8; see also S. Bergstrand and R. Doganis, 'The impact of flags of convenience (open registries)' in W.E. Butler (ed.), *The Law of the Sea and International Shipping: Anglo-Soviet Post UNCLOS Perspective*, New York, 1985.

2   See also generally Gordon Campbell and I.O. Evans, *The Book of Flags*, 7th ed., Oxford University Press, 1975; see also generally M. Thomas, *Hawaiian Interisland Vessels and Hawaiian Registered Vessels*, Seacoast Press, Santa Barbara, 1982, 81pp.

3   But see generally R.N. Barraclough and W.G. Crampton, *Flags of the World*, Frederick Warne, New York, 1978; cf. N. Singh, 'Maritime flags and state responsibility' in J. Makarczyk (ed.), *Essays in International Law in Honour of Judge Manfred Lachs*, The Hague, 1984, pp. 657–69.

4   Ibid. See especially chapter 13, pp. 227–33, 'On flags worn by merchant ships'; M.L. McCarnell, '. . . "Darkening confusion mounted upon darkening confusion"': The search for the elusive genuine link', *Journal of Maritime Law and Commerce*, vol. 16, 1985, pp. 365–96.

5   For details see various issues of *Flag Bulletin* published by the Flag Research Centre, Winchester, Mass. 01890 US; see also M. Rowlinson, 'Flags of convenience: The UNCTAD case', *Maritime Policy and Management*, vol. 12, 1985, pp. 241–4.

6   See also Christian Pedersen, *The International Flag Book in Colour*, Morrow, New York, 1971; 'Conditions for Registration of Ships' and *Ocean Yearbook*, 1983, pp. 492–514. Note: Report by the United Nations Conference on Trade and Development Secretariat TD/B/AC 34/2 (2 January 22/982).

7 Cf. Ottfried Neubecker and Wilhelm Rantzmann Wappenbilder, *Lexikon*, Battenberg, Munich, 1974; cf. S. Farrell, 'The use of flags of convenience by Latin American shipping', *Maritime Policy and Management*, vol. 11, 1984, pp. 15–20.

8 And Whitney Smith, *The Bibliography of Flags of Foreign Nations*, G.K. Hall, Boston, 1965; and J. Kelly and V. Paul, *Flags of Convenience: The Emerging Regime and the Canadian Experience*, with the assistance of T.L. McDorman, Research Report no. 9, Canadian Marine Transport Centre, Dalhousie University, Halifax, Nova Scotia.

9 Hans Horstmann, *Vor – Und Frühgeschichte des europäischen Flaggensvessens*, Schunemann, Bremen, 1971; or his earlier book dtv – *Lexikon politischer Symbole*, Munich, dtc. 1970.

10 There were four conventions but only the second, i.e. on the High Seas is generally cited. For details of the original texts see UN Doc. A/Conf. 13/L.52–L.55; and Misc. No. 15 (1958), Cmnd 584.

11 Only the Convention on the High Seas is generally declaratory of established principles of international law (see preamble) but the other three provide evidence of the generally accepted rules bearing on their subject matter, the cogency of this depending in part on the number of ratifications.

12 Article 4 of the Geneva Convention on the High Seas; also generally on the modern law of the sea, see McDougal and Burke, *The Public Order of the Oceans*, 1962.

13 Ibid., Article 5 (first half); for interpretations see Colombos, *International Law of the Sea*, 6th edn, 1967; H.R. Northrup and R.L. Rowan, *The International Transport Workers' Federation and Flag of Convenience Shipping*, Industrial Research Unit, Wharton School, University of Pennsylvania, Philadelphia, 1983, about 251pp.

14 Article 5(2) ibid.; but see generally Whiteman, *Digest of International Law*, iv, 1965; cf. M. Whitfield, 'Kloster cruise to flag out eight ships: transfer will save at least US $25m a year', *Lloyd's List*, no. 53438, Tuesday 18 November 1986, p. 1.

15 Article 6(1) ibid.; and Brownlie, *Principles of Public International Law*, 1973, pp. 183–251; see also 'Cyprus flag crackdown', *Lloyd's List*, no. 53439, Wednesday 19 November 1986, p. 1.

16 B. Hogan, 'Boat people at the mercy of pirates', *Lloyd's List*, 10 May 1985, p. 4; see also 'Call for cargo crime fightback', *Lloyd's List*, no. 53440, Thursday 20 November 1986, p. 3.

17 Article 6(2) ibid.; Brownlie, op.cit., pp. 257–9; Bowett, *The Law of the Sea*, 1967; cf. B. Hogan, 'Pledge on Liberian register standards', *Lloyd's List*, no. 53436, Saturday 15 November 1986, p. 3.

18 For the text of the Convention with Index and Final Act see United Nations Publication Sales No. E. 83, V.5, UN. New York, 1983; when ratified, the 1982 Convention will repeal and replace the 1958 Convention.

19 The Convention establishes a comprehensive framework for the regulation of all ocean space. It is divided into 17 parts and 9 Annexes, and contains provisions governing, *inter alia*, on navigation, seabed mining and exploitation of living and non-living resources.

20 Lewis M. Alexander, 'The Law of the Sea Conference: issues in current

negotiations' in R.B. Lillich and J.N. Moore, *Readings in International Law*, Newport, 1980, pp. 188–98.

21 Barry Buzan, 'Negotiating by consensus: developments in technique at the United Nations Conference on the Law of the Sea', *American Journal of International Law*, vol. 75, 1981, pp. 324–48.

22 J.K. Gamble, Jr., 'Post World War II multilateral treaty making: the task of the Third United Nations Law of the Sea Conference in perspective', *San Diego Law Review*, vol. 17, 1980, pp. 527–56.

23 Article 5 of 1958 is reproduced in notes 13–14 above; Article 10 of 1958 requires states to take such measures to ensure safety, i.e. collisions, manning and general seaworthiness of ships. Article 94 of 1982 is reproduced in the Annex at the end.

24 Article 217 of 1982 is a lengthy provision providing for certain enforcements by the flag states while Article 235 of 1982 relates to the responsibility and liability of states generally in international obligations.

25 D.S. Gandhi, 'Shipowners, mariners and the New Law of the Sea: the effect of technical, legal and political constraints upon the traditional users of the world's oceans', *Fairplay International Shipping Weekly*, 1977, p. 38.

26 See generally Osieke, 'Flags of convenience vessels: recent developments', *American Journal of International Law*, vol. 73, 1979, p. 604; see also I.M. Sinan, 'UNCTAD and the flags of convenience', *Journal of World Trade Law*, vol. 18, 1984, pp. 95–109.

27 J.N. Moore (Director of Centre for Ocean Law and Policy, University of Virginia) speaking at a 'panel discussion on Flags of Convenience', cited in *New Trends in Maritime Navigation, Proceedings of the 4th International Ocean Symposium*, Ocean Association of Japan, 1979, pp. 69, 70, 71.

28 Kano, 'Flags of convenience' in *New Trends in Maritime Navigation*, ibid., pp. 63 and 64; M. Whitfield, 'Japan's seamen seek more free flag jobs', *Lloyd's List*, no. 53213, Thursday 6 March 1986, p. 1.

29 Article 5(1) (second half) of the Geneva Convention on the High Seas; see also McDougal, Burke and Vlasic, 'The maintenance of public order at sea and the nationality of ships', *American Journal of International Law*, vol. 54, 1960, pp. 25 and 104.

30 Hence the spokesman for the Group of 77 saying '. . . The path to economic liberation passes across the sea', *Proceedings of the United Nations Conference on Trade and Development*, Manila, 1979, 5th session, vol. 1., 78, para 195.

31 See the *Draft Report of the First Committee* of the 1986 Convention Conference, UNCTAD Doc. No. TD/RS/CONF/C.1/L.1; for detailed discussions at UNCTAD Conference generally and leading to the Convention in particular see pp. 48–54 (post).

32 Cf. the enumerations of the FOC characteristics by the *Rochdale Report*, notes 54–55 (post); but for the first and classical work see B.A. Boszeck, *Flags of Convenience — An International Legal Study*, Harvard University Press, Cambridge (Mass.), 1962.

33 See, for instance, V. Brajkovik and E. Pallua, 'Lien substantiel et la nationalité des navires', *Jugoslovenska revija za medunaroduo pravo*, 1960.

34 International Court of Justice (ICJ) Reports 1953 (preliminary objection

1953). By an exchange of Notes, 1919–1920, Switzerland was responsible for Liechtenstein's foreign representation.

35 See also the *Pinsone Case* (1928) 5 RIAA 327 and *R v. Secretary of State, Home Department, Exporte Thakrar* [1974] 2 WLR 593; B. Hogan, 'UNCTAD close to treaty on registration', *Lloyd's List*, no. 53193, Thursday 30 January 1986, p. 1.

36 Cf. *Mavrommatis Palestine Concession* (Jurisdiction) (1924), Series A. No. 2, p. 12 (1 WCR 297, 302); cf. J.M. Wells, 'Vessel registration in selected open registries', *Maritime Lawyer*, vol. 6, 1981, pp. 221–45.

37 International Court of Justice (ICJ) Rep. 1955, pp. 4 and 24 (Second Phase); but see C. Mayer, 'Sea Docs Registry may collapse', *Lloyd's List*, no. 53437, Monday 17 November 1986, p. 1.

38 But see *Brazilian and Serbian Loans Case* (1929), Series A, Nos 20–21, p. 17 (2 WCR 340, 353); C. Arosemera, 'The enrolment of vessels under the flag of the Republic of Panama and the registration of mortgages thereon', *Current Issues in International Ship Finance*, 1984, pp. 149–75.

39 The United Nations Conference on the Law of the Sea (UNCLOS III), which reproduced the Convention on the Law of the Sea 1982 A/Conf. 63/122 Article 218 and 220 reflect this, providing for port and coastal state enforcement of vessel pollution standards.

40 E. Gold, 'Flags of Convenience Conference' in *New Directions in Maritime Law*, 1978, pp. 100–2 identified at least three discrete groups of shipowners who make use of FOC, some of whom fit the stereotype rationale outlined herein.

41 International Maritime Associates, *Economic Impact of Open Registry Shipping*, Washington, 1979, supports the view that, once it was discovered the solution could not be obtained via a legal regime, the debate shifted to the economic (link) regime.

42 See also UNCTAD, Report by the Secretariat of, *Action on the Question of Open Registries*, UN Doc. No. TD/B/C.4/220, March 1981, p. 11; B. Hogan, 'EEC intervention delays flag treaty', *Lloyd's List*, no. 53197, Tuesday 4 February 1986, p. 3.

43 An earlier report by the OECD *Maritime Transport*, 1971, p. 99, supports the point made by the UNCTAD study; M. Whitfield, 'BP Shipping to end direct employment', *Lloyd's List*, no. 53205, 9 January 1986, p. 1.

44 The UK, France, Norway, the Netherlands and the USA, because of defence considerations, supported Panama and Liberia.

45 *United Nations Conference on the Law of the Sea* (UNCLOS I) Geneva, vol. IV, 2nd Committee A/Conf. 13/40; V. Bishop, 'Manila to act over rogue crew agencies', *Lloyd's List*, no. 53437, Monday 17 November 1986, p. 1.

46 The issue was submitted to the ICJ for an advisory opinion: *Constitution of the Maritime Safety Committee of the Inter-Governmental Maritime Consultative Organisation* (IMCO — now IMO) [1960] ICJ Rep. 150.

47 Prof. S.G. Sturmey providing that last description. See also UNCTAD, 'Flags of convenience', *Journal of World Trade Law*, vol. 15, no. 5, September–October 1981, pp. 466–8.

48 R.S. Doganis and B.N. Metaxas, *The Impact of Flags of Convenience*, Research Paper no. 3, Transport Studies Group, Polytechnic of Central

London, 1976; see also *Flags of Convenience in 1978*, Discussion paper 8, November 1978.

49 S.J., *Buy the Flag: Developments in the Open Registry Debate*, Discussion paper no. 13, Polytechnic of Central London, Transport Studies Group, August 1983, p. 2.

50 Rodney Carlisle, *Sovereignty for Sale: The Origins and Evolution of the Panamanian and Liberian Flags of Convenience*, Naval Institute Press, Annapolis, Maryland, 1981.

51 A.J. Church, Jr., *Flags of Convenience or Flags of Necessity*, US Naval Institute Proceedings, vol. 106, no. 6, 1980, pp. 58–62.

52 A representative sample of definitions and/or descriptions worked out by the author accommodating all interests and views.

53 L.R. Harolds, 'Some legal problems arising out of foreign flag operations', *Fordham Law Review*, vol. 28, 1959, p. 295; see also M.L. Hathron, 'The Vessel Documentation Act of 1980', *Maritime Lawyer*, vol. 7, 1982, pp. 303–17.

54 The Report was also quoted verbatim by the OEEC *Maritime Transport 1971*, Paris, p. 86; see also C. Arosemera, 'Remedies available for creditors of ships enrolled under the Panama flag', *Current Issues in International Ship Finance*, 1984, pp. 177–206.

55 The *Rochdale Report* (Committee of Inquiry into Shipping – Report of, Chairman Lord Rochdale), London, May 1970, p. 51; see also Conference Report UNCTAD Doc. no. TD/RS/CONF/15.

56 E. Agirotto, 'Flags of convenience and sub-standard vessels: a review of ILO's approach to the problem', *International Labour Review*, vol. 110, 1974.

57 Ibid.; cf. M. Casanova, 'Requisiti di naxionlita e dismission di bandieva (Conditions for granting of nationality and change of flag) Studi in onori di Berlingieri', *Diritoo Maritimo*, 1964, pp. 137–53.

58 Ibid.; see also generally A.L. Kolodkin, *The Nationality of Seagoing Ships and the Principle of Genuine Link*, CEM II, 1961, M. 1962, pp. 227–40.

59 For details see generally Marshall Dimock, *Free Enterprise and the Administrative State*, University of Alabama Press, 1951; B. Hogan, 'Numast unhappy about UN registration talks', *Lloyd's List*, no. 53198, 5 February 1986, p. 3.

60 R. Carlisle, 'The American century implemented: Stettinus and the Liberian flag of convenience', *Business History Review*, vol. 54, 1980, pp. 175–91.

61 But see D.P. Currie, 'Flags of convenience, American labour and the conflicts of law', *Supreme Court Review*, 1963, p. 34; and Conference Report UNCTAD Doc. no. Td.RS/CONF/15/Add.1.

62 See Carlisle, *Sovereignty for Sale*, op.cit., for probably the best historical outline, pp. 1–19; R. Farndon, 'UK flag out shipping set to top domestic tonnage', *Lloyd's List*, no. 53424, Saturday 1 November 1986, pp. 1 and 2.

63 Ibid., pp. 19–37; see also 'EEC countries urged to create new Euroflag', *Lloyd's List*, no. 53420, Tuesday 28 October 1986, p. 1; see also the last item on Note 61, *supra*.

64 Ibid.; see also R.S. Karmel, 'Labour law, international law and the Panlibho fleet', *New York University Law Review*, vol. 3, 1961, p. 1342; E. Pallua,

'The nationality of ships in Yugoslavia law with reference to the present international developments' in *Essays on International and Comparative Law in Honour of Judge Erades*, The Hague, 1983, pp. 123-33.

65 See again R. Carlisle, *Sovereignty for Sale*, op.cit., chapter 5, 'Neutrality 1939-41', pp. 71-98; cf. *Text transmitted to the Drafting Committee by the First Committee*, UNCTAD Doc. no. TD/RS/CONF/C.1/CRP.1 (Identification and Accountability), Agenda Item N.8.

66 Ibid., pp. 15-18, 21-7 and 61-8; see also the *Draft Report of the Second Committee of the 1986 Convention Conference*, UNCTAD Doc. no. TD/RS/CONF/C.2/L.2.

67 Ibid., pp. 21-7; see also an addition to the Draft Report UNCTAD Doc. no. TD/RS/CONF/C.2/L.2/Corr. 1. Agenda Item 8; and Conference Report UNCTAD Doc. no. TD/RS/CONF/15/Add. 1/Corr. 1.

68 Ibid., pp. 61-8; but see an earlier *Draft Texts for Consideration by the Second Committee*, UNCTAD Doc. no. TD/RS/CONF/C.2/L.1 Agenda Item 8.

69 Ibid., pp. 6-7; cf. the above two with *The Proposal by the Chairman of the Second Committee*, UNCTAD Doc. no. TD/RS/CONF/C.2/CRP.1.

70 American Committee of the Flags of Convenience, *The Roles of the Flags of Necessity*, New York; but see the *Text Transmitted to the Drafting Committee by the First Committee*, UNCTAD Doc. no. TD/RS/CONF/C.1/CRP.2 (Bareboat Charter), Agenda Item 8.

71 See, for example, B.W. Lewis, 'The nationalization of British industry', *Law and Contemporary Problems*, Duke University School of Law, Durham, NC, Autumn 1951.

72 The classical statement in favour of *laissez-faire* is Adam Smith, *The Wealth of Nations*, Random House Inc., New York, 1937; and B. Hogan, 'Progress on UN Ship Register Treaty', *Lloyd's List*, no. 53199, Thursday 6 February 1986, p. 1.

73 OEEC, *Study on the Expansion of the Flags of Convenience Fleets and Various Aspects Thereof*, Doc. C(57) 246, 28 January 1958.

74 US Department of Commerce, Maritime Administration, *Ships Registered under the Liberian, Panamanian and Honduran Flags Deemed by the Navy Department to be under United States Effective Control*, Washington DC, 1968.

75 Ibid.; see also 'Changing loyalties as owners ship out', *Seatrade Business Review*, September/October 1986, pp. 6-9; but see *Conference Report*, UNCTAD Doc. no. TD/RS/CONF/19.

76 A.J. Hotz, 'Legal dilemmas: the Arab-Israeli conflict', *South Dakota Law Review*, vol. 19, 1974, pp. 242-8; see again the last item on Note 75.

77 W. Gorter, *The United States Merchant Marine Policies: Some International Economic Implications*, Department of Economics and Sociology, Princeton University, Princeton, 1955, 16pp.

78 OECD, *Maritime Transport*, Paris, 1971, pp. 85-109; see discussions (post) on the Registration Convention, especially *Draft Texts for Consideration by the First Committee* (Note by the Secretariat of UNCTAD), UNCTAD Doc. No. TD/RS/C.1/L.1, Agenda Item 8.

79 Committee of Inquiry into Shipping 1970; see also *Draft Tests for Consideration by the First Committee*, op.cit.

80 Ibid. para. 1373; E. Ion, 'Five of OSA's vessels to switch flag', *Lloyd's List*, no. 53407, Monday 13 October 1986, p. 1; *Conference Report*, op.cit., Corr. 1.

81 OECD, *Maritime Transport*, 1971, p. 99; J. Apter, 'France bids to stem flow to foreign flags', *Lloyd's List*, no. 53274, Thursday 8 May 1986, p. 1.

82 Ibid.; see also generally discussions in text (post) relating to the 1986 Convention, especially the *Statement of Administrative and Financial Implications Submitted by the UNCTAD Secretariat*, UNCTAD Doc. no. TD/RS/CONF/L.3/Add. 1, Item 8.

83 Ibid.; see also *Report of the First Committee of the United Nations Conference on Conditions for Registration of Ships*, UNCTAD Doc. no. TD/RS/CONF/L.4.

84 Ibid.; and text transmitted by the *Drafting Committee to the Conference*, UNCTAD Doc. no. TD/RS/CONF/L.5, Agenda Item no. 8.

85 Ibid.; but see *Checklist of Documents* therein listed in UNCTAD Doc. no. TD/RS/CONF/Misc. 1; H. Williams, 'Reagan vetoes US–flag ship loan pledges', *Lloyd's List*, no. 53423, Friday 31 October 1986, p. 1.

86 Ibid.; supplemented by another *Checklist of Documents*, UNCTAD Doc. no. TD/RS/CONF/Misc. 1/Rev. 1 (in English only); UNCTAD, *Conference Report*, op.cit., Add. 1/Cow. 1.

87 Ibid., p. 100; see also *Provisional List of Participants*, UNCTAD Doc. no. TD/RS/CONF/Misc. 1; H. Williams, 'Senate Studies US register plan for foreign ships', *Lloyd's List*, no. 53299, Saturday 7 June 1986, p. 1.

88 Ibid.; and *The Second Provisional List of Participants*, UNCTAD Doc. no. TD/RS/CONF/Misc. 2/Add. 1–2; J. Apter, 'Action by unions on Dreyffus register bid', *Lloyd's List*, no. 53380, Thursday 11 September 1986, p. 1.

89 Ibid.; cf. *The Final List of Participants*, UNCTAD Doc. no. TD/RS/CONF/INF. 1; S. Wood, 'Wallem to transfer office to Isle of Man', *Lloyd's List*, no. 53381, Friday 12 September 1986, p. 1.

90 Ibid.; cf. *Communication Received from the International Chamber of Shipping*, UNCTAD Doc. no. TD/RS/CONF/NGO/1 (Note by the UNCTAD Secretariat), Agenda Item no. 8.

91 Ibid.; and *Second Communication Received from the International Chamber of Shipping*, UNCTAD Doc. no. TD/RS/CONF/NGO/2 (Note by the Secretariat of UNCTAD), Agenda Item no. 8.

92 Ibid.; but see *Communication Received from the International Association of Dry Cargo Shipowners* (INTERCARGO), UNCTAD Doc. no. TD/RS/CONF/NGO/3 (Note by the Secretariat of UNCTAD), Agenda Item no. 8.

93 Ibid.; see also *Communication Received from the International Association of Independent Tanker Owners* (INTERTANKO), UNCTAD Doc. no. TD/RS/CONF/NGO/4 (Note by the UNCTAD Secretariat), Agenda Item no. 8.

94 Ibid.; cf. *Communication Received from the International Shipping Federation* (ISF), UNCTAD Doc. no. TD/RS/CONF/NGO/5 (Note by the UNCTAD Secretariat), Agenda Item no. 8.

95 Ibid., p. 101; see also C. Brown-Humes, 'Widespread backing for ship identity number plan', *Lloyd's List*, no. 53382, Saturday 13 September 1986, p. 3.

96 See also the *Working Paper by the President of the Conference*, UNCTAD Doc. no. TD/RS/CONF/CRP. 1; 'German flag exodus continues', *Lloyd's List*, no. 53424, Saturday 1 November 1986, p. 3.

97 R.A. Powell, 'New developments in taxation of shipping under flags of convenience' in *International Regulation of Maritime Transportation*, New York, 1978, pp. 211–29.

98 E.A. Wittig, 'Tanker fleets and flags of convenience', *Texas International Law Journal*, vol. 14, 1979, pp. 115–38; and UNCTAD *Conference Report*, op.cit., Add. 1/Corr. 2 (in Spanish only).

99 S. Farrell, 'The use of flags of convenience by Latin American shipping', *Maritime Policy and Management*, vol. 11, no. 1, 1984, pp. 15–20.

100 S.G. Sturmey, *British Shipping and World Competition*, Athlon Press, London, 1962, p. 223; 'Flagging out condemned by European Parliament', *Lloyd's List*, no. 53382, Saturday 13 September 1986, p. 1.

101 See *Draft Resolution Submitted by the President* of the 1986 Convention Conference, UNCTAD Doc. no. TD/RS/CONF/L.3, Agenda Item no. 8; see also second half of Note 192 (post) on the relationship between commodity interests and FOC registries.

102 *Lloyd's List*, 9 June 1981; see also 'Norwegian Union fights to maintain flag rights (flagging out)', *Lloyd's List*, no. 53392, Thursday 25 September 1986, p. 1.

103 D.E. Price, 'Sanctions on South Africa – implications for shipping', *Asian Shipping*, September 1986, pp. 43–4; E. Ion, 'How South Africa has coped with the oil embargo', *Lloyd's List*, no. 53385, Wednesday 17 September 1986, p. 3.

104 E. Wittig, 'Tanker fleets and flags of convenience. Advantages, problems and dangers', *Texas International Law Journal*, Winter 1979.

105 M. Scerni, 'La nationalita delle navi come oggetto delle morme internazionali' (Nationality of ships as an object of International Rules), *Communitazioni e Studi*, 1963, pp. 87–111.

106 E. Spasiano, 'Le discrimminazioni di bandiera' (flag discrimination), *Rivista di Diritto della Navigazione*, 1967(1), pp. 85 ss.

107 A. Vidal, 'El abanderamiento de bugues extranjeros en Espana' (Registry of foreign ships in Spain), *Ponencias odel v Congresso International de Derecho Comparado*, Barcelona, 1958, pp. 335–41.

108 US Department of Commerce, Maritime Administration, *Foreign Flag Merchant Ships Owned by US Parent Companies, as of December 31 1976*, GPO, Washington DC, 1978.

109 T.J. Romans, 'The American merchant marine – flags of convenience and international law', *Virginia Journal of International Law*, vol. 3, 1963, p. 121.

110 US Department of Commerce, Maritime Administration, *Foreign Flag Merchant Ships Owned by US Parent Companies as of June 30 1974*, GPO, Washington DC, 1975.

111 W.P. Carrell, 'A study of American owned vessels under the flags of Panama, Honduras and Costa Rica', unpublished Master's thesis, University of Virginia, Charlottesville, 1962.

112 Harbride House, *The Balance of Payments and the US Merchant Marine*, Boston, 1968; but see 'Seamen's strike sparks new rush to flag out', (Coastal shipping, West Germany), *Fairplay International Shipping Weekly*, 11 September 1986, pp. 53–6.

113 M.D. Wellington, 'The better part of valour — applicability of the Jones Act to the flags of convenience fleet', *San Diego Law Review*, vol. 7, 1970, pp. 674–83.

114 H.J. Manning, 'Liberia exploits the flags of convenience practice', *Bulletin of the African Institute of South Africa*, vol. 15, nos 5–6, 1967, pp. 186–90.

115 John G. Kilgour, 'Effective United States control', *Journal of Maritime Law and Commerce*, vol. 8, 1977, p. 377; C. Mayer, 'Liberia makes cuts in ship register fees', *Lloyd's List*, no. 53372, Thursday 4 September 1986, p. 1.

116 L.C. Kendall, *The Business of Shipping*, Cornell Maritime Press, Cambridge Md., 1974; L. Buckingham, 'Shell to switch entire UK fleet to IOM register', *Lloyd's List*, no. 53338, Wednesday 23 July 1986, p. 1.

117 League of Nations, 'The comparative study of national laws governing the grant of the right to fly the merchant flag', *League of Nations Official Journal*, vol. 12, 1931, p. 1631.

118 Republic of Liberia, *Liberia — 25 Years as a Maritime Nation*, International Trust Company, Monrovia, 1972; R. North, 'Norway owners applaud move on flagging out', *Lloyd's List*, no. 53384, Tuesday 16 September 1986, p. 1.

119 R. Rienow, *The Test of the Nationality of a Merchant Vessel*, Columbia University Press, New York, 1937; M. Barber, 'Irish line set for transfer to new register', *Lloyd's List*, no. 53392, Thursday 25 September 1986, p. 1.

120 R.G. Vamberg, 'Nationalism in shipping', *Maritime Studies and Management*, vol. 1, 1974, p. 243; M. Whitfield, 'IOM register is expected to double in size', *Lloyd's List*, no. 53318, Monday 30 June 1986, p. 1.

121 E.D. Naess, *The Great Panlibho Controversy — The Fight Over Flags of Convenience*, Gower Press, Essex, 1972.

122 Republic of Liberia, *Liberian Code of Laws of 1956 Adopted by the Legislature of the Republic of Liberia*, 22 March 1956, Cornell Maritime Press, Ithaca, NY, 1957.

123 Y.S. Hernandez, *Pabellones de Conveniencia* (Flags of Convenience), Comite de Derecho Maritimo, Barcelona, 1960; but see UNCTAD *Conference Report*, op.cit., Add. 1/Corr. 3 (in French only).

124 D.H.N. Johnson, 'The nationality of ships', *Indian Yearbook of International Law*, vol. 8, 1959, p. 3; M. Whitfield, 'Marpol adoption sets the stage for major Manx register growth (IOM)', *Lloyd's List*, no. 53318, Monday 30 June 1986, p. 3.

125 H.P. Drewery, *World Shipping Under Flags of Convenience*, London, 1975, p. 70; L. Buckingham, 'Luxembourg in move to start vessel register', *Lloyd's List*, no. 53431, Monday 10 November 1986, p. 1.

126 C.R. Hallberg, 'Shipping under flags of convenience: maritime safety aspects' in *International Regulation of Maritime Transport*, New York, 1978, pp. 231–40.

127 K. Ewing, 'Union action against flags of convenience. The legal position in Great Britain', *Journal of Maritime Law and Commerce*, vol. 11, no. 4, 1980, pp. 503–8.

128 L.L. Herman, 'Flags of convenience — new dimensions to an old problem', *McGill Law Journal*, vol. 24, 1978, pp. 1–28; L. Hagberg (ed.), *Handbook on Maritime Law: Vol. 111-A: Registration of Vessels: Mortgages on Vessels: Argentina–Norway*, written by Members of the Committee on Maritime and Transport Law of the Section on Business Law of the International Bar Association, Kluwer, Deventer, 1983, about 400pp.

129 A.F. Ceres, *Merchant Marine: National Necessity*, US Naval Institute Proceedings, vol. 53, 1927, p. 570.

130 T. Coleman, *The Liners: A History of the North Atlantic Crossing*, Allen Lane, London, 1976; B. Wilson, 'How Stena made major reductions in fleet costs', *Lloyd's List*, no. 53308, Wednesday 18 June 1986, p. 4.

131 The Economist Intelligence Unit, *Open Registry Shipping*, London, 1979; B. Hogan, 'Shipping contribution to Danish exchequer falls', *Lloyd's List*, no. 53419, Monday 27 October 1986, p. 3.

132 J. Fabrega, *Consular Traffic of Panama*: Decree 41 of 1935, Panama, 1951; A. Spurrier, 'Fourteen French ships in Kerguelen flag switch', *Lloyd's List*, no. 53398, 2 October 1986, p. 1.

133 'Liberia: plugging some leaks', *The Economist*, 8 May 1971; E. Simon, 'Exodus from W. German flag gains momentum', *Lloyd's List*, no. 53414, Tuesday 21 October 1986, p. 3.

134 S.W. Emery, 'The effective United States control fleet', *US Naval Institute Proceedings*, vol. 96, 1970, p. 160.

135 R.D. Gatewood, 'Seapower and American policy', *US Naval Institute Proceedings*, vol. 53, October 1927, p. 1070; 'Norway may start free flag to halt decline', *Lloyd's List*, no. 53303, Thursday 12 June 1986, p. 1.

136 L.F.E. Goldie, 'Recognition and dual nationality: a problem of the flags of convenience', *British Yearbook of International Law*, 1963, p. 220.

137 Heine and Co., *An Analysis of the Participation of US and Foreign Flag Ships in the Oceanborne Foreign Trade of the US* 1937, 1928, 1951–60, Government Printing Press, Washington DC, 1962.

138 Y. Alexander and N.N. Kittrie (eds), *Crescent and Star: Arab–Israeli Perspectives on the Middle East Conflict*, AMS Press, Toronto, 1973, p. 310; B. Hogan, 'Ship registration treaty is uncertain of support', *Lloyd's List*, no. 53200, Friday 7 February 1986, p. 1.

139 Hein, *An Analysis of the Ships under Effective US Control, and Their Employment in the US Foreign Trade During 1960*, Maritime Administration, Washington DC, 1962.

140 R.W.R. Flourney, Jr., *A Collection of Nationality Laws of Various Countries as Contained in Constitutions, Statutes and Treaties*, Oxford University Press, Oxford, 1929.

141 E.A. Duff, *The United Fruit Company and the Political Affairs of*

Guatemala 1944–1954, Master's thesis, University of Virginia, Charlottesville, 1957.

142 R.E. Anderson, *The Merchant Marine and World Frontiers*, Cornell Maritime Press, Ithaca, NY, 1945; Reprint, Greenwood, Westpoint, Conn., 1978.

143 Hein, *Effective US Control of Merchant Ships: A Statistical Survey*, GPO, Washington DC, 1970; B. Hogan, 'Radical shipping industry plan to be put to UNCTAD', *Lloyd's List*, no. 53420, Tuesday 28 October 1986, p. 1.

144 R. Engler, *The Politics of Oil*, Macmillan, New York, 1961, p. 156; R. Engler, *Brotherhood of Oil*, University of Chicago Press, Chicago, 1970.

145 Chinua Achebe, *Things Fall Apart*, op.cit.; see also H.P. Drewery, *US Oil Imports, 1971–1985: Repercussions on the World Tanker and Oil Industries*, London, 1973.

146 David Stonebridge, 'Impact of the falling dollar on shipping: real costs and revenues highly sensitive to changes in parity', *Asian Shipping*, January 1986, pp. 9–10.

147 P. Ehlermann, 'Aspects of ship financing in the FRG', *Current Issues in Shipping Financing*, vol. 1, 1983, pp. 85–121; R. North, 'Norwegian flagging out approval likely', *Lloyd's List*, no. 53308, Wednesday 18 June 1986, p. 1.

148 'T-men eye overseas tax havens', *Business Week*, McGraw-Hill Inc., New York, 24 December 1960; see also *Revenue Act of 1962*, Report 1881, US Senate Committee on Finance.

149 N.K. Jones, *Flags of Convenience in the Pacific: Prospects for Proliferation, Impact and Regulation*, HAWAU-T-75-004; B. Hogan, 'How the UN reached a ship registration treaty', *Lloyd's List*, no. 53202, Monday 10 February 1986, p. 3.

150 R. Laishley and T. Bruley, 'What future for flags of convenience?', *African Business*, March 1980, pp. 13–14; 'Why Third World needs shipping aid', *Lloyd's List*, no. 53420, Tuesday 28 October 1986, p. 3.

151 B.N. Metaxas, 'OECD study of the flags of convenience', *Journal of Maritime Law and Commerce*, vol. 4, 1973, pp. 231–54.

152 B. Hogan, 'Christian Haaland announces re-flagging', *Lloyd's List*, no. 53398, Thursday 2 October 1986, p. 1.

153 Drewery Shipping Consultants, *The Involvement of Oil-Exporting Countries in International Shipping*, London, 1976; G. Whittaker, 'Vanuatu appoints a Piraeus agent', *Lloyd's List*, no. 53308, Wednesday 28 June 1986, p. 5.

154 G. Dalton, 'History, politics and economic development in Liberia', *Journal of Economic History,* vol. 25, 1965, p. 569.

155 L. Ealy, *The Republic of Panama in World Affairs 1903–1950*, Pennsylvania State University Press, 1951; Reprint: Greenwood, Westport, Conn., 1970.

156 UNCTAD Report by the Secretariat, *Economic Consequences of the Existence or Lack of a Genuine Link between Vessel and Flag of Registry*, UNCTAD Doc. no. TD/B/C.4/168/Add. 1, December 1977, p. 9.

157 O. Knudsen, *The Politics of International Shipping*, Lexington Books, New York, 1973, p. 46; G. Whittaker, 'Greek register's future hangs in the balance', *Lloyd's List*, no. 53419, Monday 27 October 1986, p. 1.

158 J.E. Oribe Stemmer, 'Flag preference in Latin America', *Journal of Maritime Law and Commerce*, vol. 10, October 1978, pp. 123–34; R. North, 'Exodus

of ships from Norwegian flag', *Lloyd's List*, no. 53419, Monday 27 October 1986, p. 3.

159 A.J. Garvey, *Garvey and Garveyism*, Macmillan, New York, 1970, pp. 61-2; 'Norway international register plans backed', *Lloyd's List*, no. 53420, Tuesday 28 October 1986, p. 3.

160 S. Hlophe, 'A Class Analysis of the Politics of Ethnicity of the Tubman and Tolbert Administration in Liberia', Paper read at *Liberian Studies Association*, Macomb III, 2 April 1977.

161 International Labour Office, *Conditions in Ships Flying the Panama Flag: Report of the Committee of Enquiry of the International Labour Organisation*, ILO, London, May–November 1949, 1951.

162 C.W. Jenks, 'Nationality, the flag and registration: criteria for demarcating the scope of maritime conventions', *Journal of Comparative Legislation and International Law*, vol. 19, 3rd series, 1937, p. 245.

163 R.S. Karmel, *Labour Law, International Law and the Panlibho Fleet*, op.cit., p. 1342; M. Whitfield, 'Norway to review its policy of flagging out', *Lloyd's List*, 28 December 1985, p. 1.

164 'Under two flags: foreign registry of American merchantmen', *Stanford Law Review*, vol. 5, 1953, pp. 797ff; 'Isle of Man puts out the flag for management companies', *Shipbroker International*, April 1986, p. 15.

165 See again E.A. Duff, *The United Fruit Company and the Political Affairs of Guatemala 1944-1954*, op.cit.; 'Flagging out gathers momentum, promotes new concerns over Norway's maritime environment', *Lloyd's Ship Manager*, vol. 6, no. 9, December 1985, pp. 75-7.

166 E.P. Hanson, *United States Invades Africa*, Harpers, February 1947; P.A. Giles, 'Registration of a British flag vessel in the port of Hong Kong and registration of mortgages', *Current Issues in International Ship Financing*, vol. 1, 1983, p. 191.

167 R. Lansing, *Notes on Sovereignty from the Standpoint of the State and the World*, Carnegie, Endowment for International Peace, Washington DC, 1921.

168 F. Pratt, 'Commerce destruction, past, present and future', *US Naval Institute Proceedings*, vol. 54, 1934, p. 1513; 'West European flag fall (World Fleet)', *Lloyd's Shipping Economist*, March 1986, p. 4.

169 See also the *Report of the United Nations Conference on Conditions for Registration of Ships on the First Part of its Session, Held at the Palais des Nations*, Geneva, from 16 July to 3 August 1984, UNCTAD Doc. no. TD/RS/CONF/10/Add. 2/Annex v, p. 3.

170 R.W. Bixler, *The Foreign Policy of the United States in Liberia 1819-1955*, Pageant Press, New York, 1957; A. Marshall, 'Owners welcome new Norwegian Register plan', *Lloyd's List*, no. 53304, Friday 13 June 1986, p. 3.

171 C. Berguido *et al., Manual for Masters and Seamen on Ships under the Panamanian Flag*, Philadelphia, 1957; R. North, 'Norway's shipowners in call for dual register', *Lloyd's List*, no. 53397, Wednesday 1 October 1986, p. 3.

172 For the text of the Convention, including IMCO recommendations see Singh, *International Maritime Law Conventions*, vol. 2, pp. 980-1052;

'EEC countries urged to create new Euroflag', *Lloyd's List*, no. 53420, Tuesday 28 October 1986, p. 1.

173 For the text of the Convention of 1962 which amended the 1954 Convention, see Singh, *International Maritime Law Conventions*, op.cit., vol. 3, pp. 2233-72.

174 P. Cummins, 'Oil tanker pollution control: design criteria v. effective liability assessment', *Journal of Maritime Law and Commerce*, vol. 7, 1978, p. 169.

175 J.C. Davies III, *The Politics of Pollution*, Pegasus, New York, 1970; B. Hogan, 'Owners urged to ignore captive open registries', *Lloyd's List*, no. 53393, Friday 26 September 1986, p. 3.

176 Ibid.; see also L.F.E. Goldie, 'International principles of responsibility for pollution', *Columbia Journal of Transnational Law*, Autumn 1970.

177 Republic of Liberia, 'Board of Investigation (into the Torrey Canyon)', *International Legal Materials*, vol. 6, 1967, p. 480; V. Bishop, 'Dual HK register set to start in 1991', *Lloyd's List*, no. 53409, Wednesday 15 October 1986, p. 1.

178 See again E. Agirotto, 'Flags of convenience and substandard vessels: a review of the ILO's approach to the problem', op.cit., p. 437.

179 E.D. Brown, 'The lessons of the Torrey Canyon: International Law Aspects', *Current Legal Problems*, 1968, p. 113; M. Whitfield, 'Free flag growth attacked by the ITF', *Lloyd's List*, no. 53317, Saturday 28 June 1986, p. 3.

180 But see E. Cowan, *Oil and Water: The Torrey Canyon Disaster*, Lippincott, New York, 1968; G. Durairaj, 'Evergreen to transfer ships to Malaysian flag', *Lloyd's List*, no. 53411, Friday 17 October 1982, p. 2.

181 *Rochdale Report*, op.cit., pp. 183-98; see also I.M. Sinan, 'UNCTAD and flags of convenience', *Journal of World Trade Law*, vol. 18, no. 2, March–April 1982, pp. 95-109.

182 L.F.E. Goldie, 'Liability for oil pollution disasters: international law and the delimitation of competencies in a federal policy', *Journal of Maritime Law and Commerce*, vol. 6, 1975, p. 303.

183 Chida, 'Characteristics of vessels operating under flags of convenience' in *New Trends in Maritime Navigation — The Future of the Law of the Sea and Economy*, op.cit., pp. 56 and 545.

184 UNCTAD, *Action on the Question of Open Registries*, UNCTAD Doc. no. TD/B/C.4/220, March 1981, p. 11; see UN Doc. no. Ref A/Conf.62/122, 7 October 1982.

185 R.A. Humphrey, 'The open registry phenomena: some economic and political aspects' in *New Trends in Maritime Navigation*, op.cit., pp. 57 and 58.

186 'No sign of agreement in UNCTAD talks', *Lloyd's List*, 8 November 1983; see again the *Provisional Agenda, Annotations to the Provisional Agenda and Suggestions for the Organization of the Week of the Conference*, UNCTAD Doc. no. TD/RS/CONF/1/Corr. 1, Agenda Item 4.

187 Ibid.; 'Free flag states plan break away', *Lloyd's List*, 21 November 1983; *Provisional Agenda, Annotations to the Provisional Agenda . . .*, op.cit., Agenda Item 5.

188 Ibid.; 'Economic link a stumbling block in flag controversy', *Lloyd's List*, 15 December 1983; 'UNCTAD flags of convenience convention finalised', *Bulletin of Legal Developments*, 1986, p. 55.

189 L. Juda, 'World shipping, UNCTAD, and the New International Economic Order', *International Organisation*, vol. 35, 1981, pp. 493 and 494.

190 Point noted by the Committee on Shipping of UNCTAD, in Resolution 43 (S-111) on open registry fleets; M. Whitfield, 'A land register proposed for Finnish fleet', *Lloyd's List*, no. 53433, Wednesday 12 November 1986, p. 1.

191 Ibid.; report produced in UNCTAD Doc. no. TD/B/C.4/L.152, June 1981; see also *Financial Times*, 7 February 1986, p. 7 for the Report on the UN Convention on Ship Registration.

192 UNCTAD, *Action on the Question of Open Registries*, UNCTAD Doc. no. TD/B/C.4/220, 3 March 1981, p. iii; E.G. Frankel, 'Global economics — commodity trade and shipping development', *Bulk Handling of Transport*, vol. 5 (Conf.), 1985, pp. 13–16.

193 *UN Conference on Conditions of Registration of Ships*, UNCTAD Doc. no. TD/RS/Conf/G/L.2, First Committee, pp. 4–5.

194 Ad Hoc Intergovernmental Group on the Economic Consequences of the Existence or Lack of Genuine Link between Vessels and Flag Registry.

195 Ibid.; *Report of the Preparatory Committee for the United Nations Conference on Conditions for Registration of Ships*, Palais des Nations, Geneva, 7–18 November 1983, UNCTAD Doc. no. TD/RS/CONF/3; (see also UNCTAD Doc. no. TD/B/C.4/AC).

196 See *Report of the Preparatory Committee for Registration of Ships*, Palais des Nations, Geneva, 7–18 November 1983, UNCTAD Doc. no. TD/RS/CONF/PC/4.

197 Ibid.; see also *Report of the First Session*, 6–10 February 1978; cf. *Draft Provisional Rules of Procedure*, UNCTAD Doc. no. TD/RS/CONF/2/Corr. 1 (Note by the UNCTAD Secretariat), Agenda Item 3.

198 Ibid.; and *Draft Final Provisions for an International Agreement on Conditions for Registration of Ships*, UNCTAD Doc. no. TD/RS/CONF/4/Corr. 1 (Report by the UNCTAD Secretariat), Agenda Item 8.

199 Ibid.; see also UNCTAD Doc. no. TD/B/C.4/177; cf. *Communication Received at the Secretariat from the United Kingdom Submitting a Proposal on Behalf of Group B*, UNCTAD Doc. no. TD/RS/CONF/5/Corr. 1, Agenda Item 8.

200 Ibid.; see also the *Report by the Chairman of the Committee in Pre-Conference Meeting of Senior Officials*, Palais des Nations, Geneva, 12-13 July 1984, UNCTAD Doc. no. TD/RS/CONF/6.

201 See also *Report of the Second Session*, 14–22 January 1980; and *Rules of Procedure of the United Nations Conference on Conditions for Registration of Ships*, UNCTAD Doc. no. TD/RS/CONF/8, Agenda Item 3.

202 Ibid.; cf. *Report of the United Nations Conference on Conditions for Registration of Ships on the First Part of its Session*, Palais des Nations, Geneva, 16 July-3 August 1984, UNCTAD Doc. no. JD/RS/CONF/10/Ass. 1-2, Item no. 11.

203 Ibid.; see also UNCTAD Doc. no. TD/B/C.4/AC.1/8; and the *Report of the Credentials Committee*, UNCTAD Doc. no. TD/RS/CONF/9, Agenda Item no. 7(a).

204 Ibid.; but see the *Draft Report of the United Nations Conference on Conditions for Registration of Ships*, Palais des Nations, Geneva, 16 July–3 August 1984, UNCTAD Doc. no. TD/RS/CONF/L.1/Add 1–4, Agenda Item 11.

205 Ibid.; and UNCTAD Doc. no. TD/B/C.4/191; see also the *Report of the Second Committee*, UNCTAD Doc. no. TD/RS/CONF/L.2.

206 Ibid.; and *Report of the Preparatory Committee for the United Nations Conference on Conditions for Registration of Ships*, UNCTAD Doc. no. TD/RS/CONF/3/Corr. 1.

207 Ibid.; and UNCTAD Doc. no. JD/B/784 as well as the *Draft Final Provisions for an International Agreement on Conditions for Registration of Ships*, op.cit.

208 Ibid.; cf. *Communication from the United Kingdom Submitting a Proposal on Behalf of Group B*, op.cit.

209 See *The Proceedings of the Intergovernmental Preparatory Group on Conditions for Registration of Ships*, op.cit.; R. Scott, 'Bermuda faces US tax set-back', *Lloyd's List*, no. 53432, Tuesday 11 November 1986, p. 2.

210 Ibid.; see also the *Pre-Conference Meeting of Senior Officials*, Palais des Nations, Geneva, 12–13 July 1984, UNCTAD Doc. no. TD/RS/CONF/6.

211 Ibid.; and UNCTAD Doc. no. TD/B/AC: 34/4; see also generally the *Agenda for the United Nations Conference on Conditions for Registration of Ships*, Geneva, 16 July–3 August 1984, UNCTAD Doc. no. TD/RS/CONF/7.

212 Ibid.; however, see *Rules of Procedure of the United Nations Conference on Conditions for Registration of Ships*, UNCTAD Doc. no. TD/RS/CONF/8.

213 Ibid.; *Report of the Group on its First Session*, for the *Report of the Proceedings of the Group on its Second Session*, Geneva, 8–26 November 1982; see *Documents List* in UNCTAD Doc. no. TD/RS/CONF/10/Add. 2, Annex IV, p. 3.

214 Ibid.; and *Report of the Preparatory Committee for the United Nations Conference on Conditions for Registration of Ships*, op.cit.

215 Ibid.; and UNCTAD Doc. no. TD/B/Ac. 34/8; *Report of the Preparatory Committee for the United Nations Conference on Conditions for Registration of Ships*, op.cit.

216 Ibid.; but see the *Preparation of a Draft International Agreement on the Conditions for Registration of Ships — A set of basic principles concerning the conditions upon which vessels should be accepted on national shipping registers*, UNCTAD Doc. no. TD/RS/CONF/PC/2.

217 Ibid.; and *Report of the Group on its Second Session*; see the *Draft Provisional Rules of Procedure on the United Nations Conference on Conditions for Registration of Ships*, Geneva, 16 July–3 August 1984, UNCTAD Doc. no. TD/RS/CONF/2.

218 Ibid.; and *A Set of Basic Principles Concerning the Conditions Upon Which Vessels should be Accepted on National Shipping Registers — Comments by Governments*, UNCTAD Doc. no. TD/RS/CONF/PC/3/Add. 1–3.

219 UNCTAD, *Beneficial Ownership of Open Registry Fleets*, UNCTAD Doc. no. TD/222/Supp. 1; but see *Communication Received from the Government of Liberia*, UNCTAD Doc. no. TD/B/AC.34/7.

220 Ibid.; cf. *Practices in Relation to Recording of Operators, the Use of Bearer Shares and Bareboat Charter*, UNCTAD Doc. no. TD/B/Ac. 34/6; see also Article 12 of the Convention on Bareboat Charter.

221 UNCTAD, Report by the Secretariat of, *Trade Routes of Open Registry Vessels*, UNCTAD Doc. no. TD/222/Supp. 5; M. Whitfield, 'Furness Withy to switch vessels to HK', *Lloyd's List*, no. 53432, Tuesday 11 November 1986, p. 1.

222 UK on behalf of Group B Countries, *A Set of Principles Concerning Conditions upon which Vessels should be Accepted in National Registries as Proposed by the Inter-governmental Preparatory Group* at 2nd Session, Geneva, November 1982, UN Doc. no. TD/RS/CONF/PC/3, 18 May 1983, p. 14.

223 Ibid.; and *Report of the Intergovernmental Preparatory Group on Conditions for Registration of Ships on its Second Session*, Geneva, 8–26 November 1982, UNCTAD Doc. no. TD/B/935.

224 Tache, 'The nationality of ships: the definition and controversy and enforcement of the genuine link', *International Lawyer*, vol. 16, 1982, p. 301.

225 Ibid.; and *Report of the Intergovernmental Preparatory Group on Conditions for Registration of Ships on its Second Session*, op.cit.

226 R.A. Humphrey, 'The open registry phenomena: some economic and political aspects', op.cit.

227 Proceedings of UNCTAD, Manila, 1979 5th Session, vol. 1, 78, para. 105, 'The spokesman for the Group of 77'; see also documents listed in UNCTAD Doc. no. TD/RS/CONF/10/Add. 2/Annex IV, p. 3.

228 'Economic Impact of Open Registry Shipping', *International Maritime Association*, 1979; see also UNCTAD, *Conditions for Registration of Ships*, op.cit.

229 *Report of the Intergovernmental Preparatory Group on Conditions for Registration of Ships on its First Session*, op.cit.

230 For details of these conditions see the *UN Conference on Conditions of Registration of Ships, First Committee*, UN Doc. no. TD/RS/CONF/C.1/ L.2, 1 August 1984.

231 UNCTAD, *Action on the Question of Open Registries*, UN Doc. no. TD/B/C.4/220, 3 March 1981, p. iii; and *Communication Received from the Government of the Union of Soviet Socialist Republics*, UNCTAD Doc. no. TD/B/AC.34/3.

232 *UN Conference on Conditions of Registration of Ships*, UN Doc. no. TD/RS/CONF/C.1/L.2. First Committee, pp. 4–5; V. Bishop, 'HK hints at rethink on taxes for new register', *Lloyd's List*, no. 53431, Monday 10 November 1986, p. 3.

233 Opening Statement of the US, Geneva, 16 July–3 August 1984, Conference on Conditions for Registration of Ships.

234 UN Doc. no. TD/RS/CONF/3; see also *The Third Special Session of the Committee on Shipping*, Geneva, 27 May–6 June 1981, UNCTAD Doc. no. TD/B/C.4/227.

235 UN Doc. no. TD/RS/CONF/4; see also *The Official Records of the Trade and Development Board — Twenty-third Session*, Suppl. no. 3, UNCTAD Doc. no. TD/BB/855.

236 UN Doc. no. DAFFE/MTC/84.7; *Report of the Intergovernmental Preparatory Group on Conditions for Registration of Ships on its First Session*, op.cit.

237 UN Doc. no. TD/RS/CONF/C.2/L.2 Annex; UNCTAD, Report by the Secretariat, UNCTAD Doc. no. TD/B/C.4/220, *Open Registry Fleets*.

238 Ibid.; *Working Paper* no. 2, p. 2; see also UNCTAD, Report by the Secretariat, *Beneficial Ownership of Open Registry Fleets, 1983*, UNCTAD Doc. no. TD/B/C.4/261.

239 'Liberian register: limited room for manoeuvre', *Lloyd's Shipping Economist*, November 1986, pp. 11–12; see also N.J. Lopez, 'The Hong Kong Register of Shipping — general principles examined', *Asian Shipping*, November 1986, pp. 21–5; and G. Clark, 'Positive government attitude bodes well for Cyprist fleet', *Fairplay International Shipping Weekly*, 13 November 1986, pp. 36–9.

240 Ibid., p. 7 and Annex, p. 2; UNCTAD, Report by the Secretariat, *Beneficial Ownership of Open Registry Fleets, 1979*, UNCTAD Doc. no. TD/B/C.4/AC.1/7/Corr. 1.

241 Ibid., p. 3; and UNCTAD, Report by the Secretariat, *Beneficial Ownership of Open Registry Fleets, 1980*, UNCTAD Doc. no. TD/B/C.4/218; B. Hogan, 'EEC protests blamed for delay', *Lloyd's List*, no. 53202, Monday 10 February 1986, p. 3.

242 Lawrence Juda, 'World shipping, UNCTAD and the New International Economic Order', op.cit.

243 P. Birnie, 'Contemporary maritime legal problems' in Barston and Birnie (eds), *The Maritime Dimension*, 1980, p. 169; 'New registry will benefit service industries', *Lloyd's List*, no. 53434, Thursday 13 November 1986 (Hong Kong Special Report), pp. 5–12.

244 Transport Canada, *Shipping Policy for Canada*, 1979, p. 16; UNCTAD, Report by the Secretariat, *Beneficial Ownership of Open Registry Fleets, 1981*, UNCTAD Doc. no. TD/B/C.4/231.

245 E. Naess, *The Great Panlibho Controversy* op.cit., p. 162; cf. UNCTAD, Report by the Secretariat, *Beneficial Ownership of Open Registry Fleets, 1982*, UNCTAD Doc. no. TD/B/C.4/255.

246 But see Panel Discussion in *New Trends in Maritime Navigation*, 4th International Ocean Symposium, Ocean Association of Japan, 1979, p. 49; 'ITF warns on erosion of vessel standards', *Lloyd's List*, no. 53434, Thursday 13 November 1986, p. 1.

247 Giles Clark, 'Owners consider a doubtful future now that the euphoria is over', *Fairplay International Shipping Weekly*, 9 October 1986, pp. 16–21.

248 'Changing loyalties as owners ship out (ship registry)', *Seatrade Business Review*, September–October 1986, pp. 6–9; M. Whitfield, 'Yugoslavia may open flag to foreign owners', *Lloyd's List*, no. 53435, Friday 14 November 1986, p. 1.

249 For full list of participants see UNCTAD, *UN Conference on Conditions for*

Registration of Ships, UNCTAD Doc. no. TD/RS/CONF/22, 7 February 1986, para. 3.

250   UNCTAD, *Final Act of the United Nations Conference on Conditions for Registration of Ships*, op.cit.; UNCTAD, Report by the Secretariat of, *Review of Trends 1977/78 (in open registry)*, UNCTAD Doc. no. TD/222/Supp. 6.

251   Ibid., Fourth Part, Geneva, 20 January 1986, Agenda Item no. 8; UNCTAD, Report by the Secretariat of, *Trade Routes of Open Registry Vessels*, UNCTAD Doc. no. TD/222/Supp. 5.

252   UNCTAD, *United Nations Convention on Conditions for Registration of Ships*, TD/IMD/1770, 7 February 1986; cf. UNCTAD, Report by the Secretariat of, *Comparative Labour Costs*, UNCTAD Doc. no. TD/222/Supp. 4.

253   Ibid., p. 1; and *The Proceedings of the Fifth Session of the United Nations Conference on Trade and Development*, Manila, 7 May–3 June 1979, UNCTAD Doc. no. TD/269 (vol. 1: Report and Annexes).

254   Ibid.; and *Report of the Preparatory Committee for the Conference*, UNCTAD Doc. no. TD/RS/CONF/3; see also generally UNCTAD, Report by the Secretariat of, *Merchant Fleet Development*, UNCTAD Doc. no. TD/222.

255   Ibid.; and UNCTAD, Report by the Secretariat of, *Beneficial Ownership of Open Registry Fleets*, UNCTAD Doc. no. TD/222/Supp. 1.

256   The Geneva Convention on the High Seas 1958 and UNCLOS III 1982; cf. UNCTAD, Report by the Secretariat of, *Merchant Fleet Development: Statistical Annexes on Cargo Flows*.

257   For the text of the Convention see *Final Act of the United Nations Conference on Conditions for Registration of Ships*, UNCTAD Doc. no. TD/RS/CONF/22, 7 February 1986.

258   UNCTAD Doc. no. TAD/INF/1770, 7 February 1986, p. 1; and UNCTAD, Report by the Secretariat of, *Maritime Transport of Hydrocarbons*, UNCTAD Doc. no. TD/222, Supp. 3.

259   Ibid.; see *Legal Mechanisms for Regulating the Operations of Open Registry Fleets during the Phasing Out Period*, UNCTAD Doc. no. TD/B/C.4/AC.1/6.

260   Thus, 'recognition' in 1958 and 1982 was replaced by 'option' in 1986: *Repercussions of Phasing Out Open Registries*, UNCTAD Doc. no. TD/B/C.4/AC.1/5.

261   That 'giving in' or 'compromise' marked a landmark in the conclusion of the Convention and was to prove costly to the anti-FOC league once more.

262   TAD/INF/1770, p. 2; *Report of the Intergovernmental Working Group on the Economic Consequences of the Existence or Lack of a Genuine Link between Vessel and Flag of Registry*, UNCTAD Doc. no. TD/B/C.4/AC.1/8.

263   Ibid., p. 3; for the inception of 'option' see *Report of the Ad Hoc Intergovernmental Working Group on the Economic Consequences of the Existence or Lack of a Genuine Link between Vessel and Flag of Registry*, UNCTAD Doc. no. TD/B/C.4/191.

264   See *Final Act of the Conference* as signed on 14 February 1986 for this Article in particular and the whole text in general.

265   Ibid., see also *Report of the Ad Hoc Intergovernmental Working Group on the Economic Consequences of the Existence or Lack of a Genuine*

Link between Vessel and Flag of Registry at its Second Session, op.cit.

266 That was also the explanation provided by Mr Lamina Fadika; and *Verbale Government replies to the Secretary of UNCTAD's of 20 June 1977,* UNCTAD Doc. no. TD/B/C.4/AC.1/2/Add. 1-3.

267 Article 7 introduces the 'option' while Article 13 deals with 'joint ventures'; cf. *Economic Consequences of the Existence or Lack of a Genuine Link between Vessel and Flag of Registry,* op.cit.

268 Article 9, *United Nations Convention on Conditions for Registration of Ships,* Geneva, 7 February 1986; V. Bishop, 'Taxation plans threaten proposed HK register', *Lloyd's List,* no. 53429, Friday 7 November 1986, p. 2.

269 *Economic Consequences of the Existence or Lack of a Genuine Link between Vessel and Flag of Registry,* op.cit.

270 See *The Economic Consequences of the Existence or Lack of a Genuine Link between Vessel and Flag of Registry,* op.cit.

271 Article 10 is entitled *Role of Flag States in Respect of the Management of Shipowning Companies;* see also L. Hagberg (ed.), *Handbook on Maritime Law: Vol. III-A: Registration of Vessels: Mortgages on Vessels: Pakistan-Yugoslavia,* written by Members of the Committee on Maritime and Transport Law of the Section on Business Law of the International Bar Association, Kluwer, Deventer, 1983, about 296pp.

272 On the whole there are quantitative but not qualitative changes between the 1982 Convention on the one hand and the 1982 and 1958 Conventions on the other.

273 Since the main criticism against the liner conferences, at least by the DMNs, has been their *remote control* operation from bases in the TMNs, far removed. 'USL brings over half its fleets home', *Lloyd's List,* no. 53449, Monday 1 December 1986, p. 1.

274 Article 5(1); but see the *Official Records of the Trade and Development Board at its Fourteenth Session — Supplement 2,* UNCTAD Doc. no. TD/B/C.4/123. L. Buckingham, 'Flag rights in wartime confirmed by Liberia', *Lloyd's List,* no. 53447, Friday 28 November 1986, p. 3.

275 TD/INF/1770, 7 February 1986, p. 2, and *Report of the Committee on Shipping on its Sixth Session,* UNCTAD Doc. no. TD/B/521; G. Wittaker, 'Crewing moves to halt Greek flag exodus', *Lloyd's List,* no. 53447, Friday 28 November 1986, p. 1.

276 One does not envisage the DMNs having elaborate institutions so as to emulate the USA but the principle is that they should have some nationally based authority at least.

277 Cf. especially Articles 90-94 of the 1982 Convention; see also UNCTAD Doc. no. TD/RS/CONF/10/Add. 2/Annex IV, p. 1; M. Whitfield, 'Unions will not IOM a free flag register', *Lloyd's List,* no. 53340, Friday 25 July 1986, p. 3.

278 There is nothing to prevent a country from establishing a mere domestic token office to satisfy the minimum requirement of the Convention. P. Green, 'Growing pressure against switch to Dutch Antilles (Holland flagging out)', *Lloyd's List,* no. 53446, Thursday 27 November 1986, p. 3.

279 See also Article 6 on *Identification and Accountability* for which detailed earlier debate is recorded in Annex I, issued separately in UNCTAD Doc. no. TD/RS/CONF/10/Add. 1.

280 Even members of the shipping industry itself do not find it satisfactory; see Note 281 below and text to UNCTAD Doc. no. TD/RS/CON/CRP1.

281 TAD/INF/1770, 7 February 1986, p. 5; itself supplementing UNCTAD, *Trade and Development Board Decision 294*, (XXVIII) 6 April 1984. D. Mott, 'Register plan may be advanced: warning of RCCL reflagging', *Lloyd's List*, no. 53446, Thursday 27 November 1986, p. 1.

282 Ibid.; and UNCTAD Doc. no. TD/RS/CONF/10/Add. 2, Annex II; as well as the *General Assembly Resolution 37/209* of 20 December 1982. 'Norway crew to strike over flag transfer', *Lloyd's List*, no. 53442, Saturday 22 December 1986, p. 1.

283 Article 6; see also generally UNCTAD Doc. no. TD/RS/CONF/10/Add. 2, 12 October 1984; see also Annex II of this document. D. Mott, 'UK owner warns over the rate of flagging out', *Lloyd's List*, no. 53422, Saturday 22 December 1986, p. 1.

284 Ibid.; for details see the main body of the Report issued in TD/RS/CONF/ 10 – originally circulated in TD/RS/CONF/L.3/Add. 1. A. Spurrier, 'Kerguelen transfer rise', *Lloyd's List*, no. 53455, Monday 8 December 1986, p. 3.

285 TAD/INF/1770, 7 February 1986, p. 1; Annex 1, containing the composite text, was issued in TD/RS/10/Add. 1; 'Plea for flag treaty ratification', *Lloyd's List*, no. 53203, Tuesday 11 February 1986, p. 3.

286 Ibid., p. 2; for different versions of the motions tabled see UNCTAD Doc. no. TD/RS/CONF/10/Add. 1/Corr. 1, 30 October 1984. E. Sinon, 'W. German flag loses 60 vessels', *Lloyd's List*, no. 53455, Monday 8 December 1986, p. 3.

287 Ibid., p. 3; for the basis of the French spokesman's claims see UNCTAD Doc. no. TD/RS/CONF/10/Add. 1 and Corr. 1 and Add. 2. M. Whitfield, 'Panamanian labour law ruling', *Lloyd's List*, no. 53455, Monday 8 December 1986.

288 Ibid., p. 4; see the proposals which the President of the Conference prepared for submission in UNCTAD Doc. no. TD/RS/CONF/12; but see D. Mott, 'Norwegian seamen plan attack on UN ship treaty', *Lloyd's List*, no. 53205, Thursday 13 February 1986, p. 1.

289 Ibid.; for details see under rule 3 of the rules of procedure of the Conference – UNCTAD Doc. no. TD/RS/CONF/8; the composite text of the agreement accepted by the Plenary Conference is the UNCTAD Doc. no. TD/RS/CONF/L.13.

290 Ibid., p. 3; this is because, at the first part of its session, the Conference approved the allocation of these items to be considered by the two main committees – see UNCTAD Doc. no. TD/RS/CONF/10, paras 403 and 404.

291 Ibid. This conforms to the rules of procedure the details of which are embodied in UNCTAD Doc. no. TD/RS/CONF/8. 'UN Conference on Conditions for Registration of Ships – Third Session, Geneva, July 8-9 1985' (North-South Monitor), *Third World Quarterly*, vol. 8, no. 1;

Third World Foundation for Social and Economic Studies, January 1986, pp. 280-1.

292 Ibid.; see also Resolution I adopted by the Conference, UNCTAD Doc. no. TD/RS/CONF/10/Add. 2, Annex II. See also 'UN Conference on Conditions for Registration of Ships, Fourth Session. Geneva, 20 January-7 February 1986' (North-South Monitor), *Third World Quarterly*, vol. 8, no. 3, Third World Foundation for Social and Economic Studies, July 1986, pp. 1032-3.

293 Ibid., but note *Group B Reaction to UNCTAD Trade and Development Board — Decision 303* (XXIX) of 21 September 1984 by which a provision was made for the resumed session to be held from 28 January to 15 February 1985.

294 Cf. Geneva Convention (High Seas) 1958 Articles 4-6; see also *Neue Züricher Zeitung*, 8 February 1986, p. 18, on the Report of the UN Convention on Ship Registration 1986.

295 Cf. *The Report of the Conference on the First Part of its Session* issued as UNCTAD Doc. no. TD/RS/CONF/10 and Add. 1 and Corr. 1 and Add. 2. See also 'Conference on Conditions for Registration of Ships, Geneva, 16 July-4 August 1984' (North-South Monitor), *Third World Quarterly*, vol. 7, no. 1, Third World Foundation for Social and Economic Studies, January 1984, pp. 147-8.

296 Article 1, *Objectives*, 1986 Convention; see also the *Report of the Conference on the Resumed Session*, Geneva, 28 January 1985, Agenda 5, UNCTAD Doc. no. TD/RS/CONF.11, 12 November 1984.

297 *Seatrade*, March 1986, p. 19; see also *The Rules of Procedure of the Conference*, UNCTAD Doc. no. TD/RS/CONF/10/Add. 2; G. Marston, 'The UN Convention on Registration of Ships', *Journal of World Trade Law*, vol. 20, no. 5, September-October 1986, pp. 573-8.

298 M. Whitfield, 'Free flag attacked by the International Transport Workers Federation', *Lloyd's List*, 28 March 1986, p. 3. See also *UNCTAD Press Release* TD/INF/1708, 22 July 1985.

299 'Ship Registration Agreement finally signed in Geneva', *Fairplay International Shipping Weekly*, vol. 296, no. 5342, 13 February 1986, p. 8; see also *The Guardian*, London, 20 July 1985.

300 S.R. Tolofari, K.J. Button and D.E. Pitfield, 'Shipping costs and the controversy over open registry', *Journal of Industrial Economics*, vol. 34, no. 4, 1986, pp. 409-22.

301 S. Wade, 'Anti-FOC lobby marshalls forces with the ILO (Port State Control)', *Fairplay International Shipping Weekly*, vol. 147, 1986, pp. 12-15; see also *Financial Times*, London, 22 July 1985; and UN Press Release, TAD/INF/1708, 22 July 1985.

302 V. Walker, 'Owners threaten to pull down the flag', *Shipbroker*, March 1986, pp. 7-9; for the text of the resolution, see Annex II of the *Conference Report*, UNCTAD Doc. no. TD/RS/CONF/8 (Article 29).

303 M. Whitfield, 'Norway to review its policy of flagging out', *Lloyd's List*, 28 December 1985, p. 1; cf. UNCTAD Doc. no. TD/RS/CONF/10, Add. 2. See also *Le Monde*, Paris, 22 and 24 July 1985 and *UN Press Release* TAD/INF/1707, 9 July 1985.

304 'Flags of convenience: a flatter', *The Economist*, 12 July 1986, pp. 68–70; also UNCTAD Doc. no. TD/RS/CONF/10, Add. 1/Corr. 1. See also *UNCTAD Press Release*, TAD/INF/1587, 16 July 1984 and *UNCTAD Bulletin*, no. 203, June 1984.

305 See again M. Whitfield, 'Free flag attacked by the international free trade unions', op.cit., and UNCTAD Doc. no. TD/RS/CONF/10, Add. 1. See also *International Herald Tribune*, Paris, 7 August 1984, p. 9 and *West Africa*, London, 30 July 1984, p. 1543.

306 TAD/INF/1770, 7 February 1986, p. 5; but see *The Report of the Conference on the First Part of its Session*, op.cit.; also *Financial Times*, 7 February 1986.

307 Ibid.; see also *UN Conference on Conditions for Registration of Ships. Resumed Session*, Geneva, 28 January 1985, UNCTAD Doc. no. TD/RS/CONF/12, 13 December 1984; also *The Guardian*, 8 February 1986 and *The Times*, 14 February 1986.

308 S. Bertram, 'The internationality of shipping', *The Institute of Transport Journal*, May 1969, pp. 140–7; 'US flag shipping faces upheaval as companies face judgment by the bottom line', *Fairplay International Shipping Weekly*, 5 June 1986, pp. 31–3.

309 Article 19; G.E.C. Maitland, 'Registration of ships' mortgages under the laws of Liberia, pending change', *Current Issues in Ship Financing*, vol. 1, Practising Law Institute, pp. 233–94.

310 TAD/INF/1770, 7 February 1986, p. 2; S. Dune, 'Registration of vessels and mortgages in developing open registries in the Caribbean', *Current Issues in Ship Financing*, vol. 2, Practising Law Institute, pp. 7–8.

311 H.R. Northrup and R.L. Rowan, *The International Transport Workers' Federation and Flags of Convenience Shipping*, 1983. See *The Far Eastern Economic Review* (Hong Kong), 6 March 1986 and UNCTAD Bulletin (Geneva), February 1986.

312 F.J.J. Cadwallader, 'Flag discrimination or something more?', *Current Legal Problems*, 1976, pp. 99–111; M. Whitfield, 'CP to transfer tankers to IOM [Isle of Man] register', *Lloyd's List*, no. 53320, Wednesday 2 July 1986, p. 1. See also *UN Press Release*, TAD/INF/1767, 21 January 1986.

313 'Is the Convention on Registration really necessary?' in UNCTAD Registration of Ships Conference 1984 sponsored by the Liberian Shipping Corporation. See also *UN Press Release*, TAD/INF/1776, 24 January 1986.

314 S.G. Sturmey, *The Open Registry Controversy and the Development Issue*, Book Series no. 8; 'Sea Docs Registry could be shelved', *Lloyd's List*, no. 53429, 7 November 1986, p. 1. See also *UN Press Release*, TAD/INF/1770, 7 February 1986.

315 Ibid.; see also S.G. Sturmey, 'CONVENIENCE: food for thought [flags of convenience]', *Motor Ship*, vol. 65, no. 776, March 1985, p. 90; 'Canaries register is pondered by Spain', *Lloyd's List*, no. 53427, Wednesday 5 November 1986, p. 1.

316 B. Hogan, 'Ship registration treaty expected', *Lloyd's List*, 20 January 1986, p. 1; see also *Neue Züricher Zeitung*, 11 February 1986, p. 12, for Report of the UN Conference on Ship Registration.

317 Lawrence Juda, 'World shipping, UNCTAD, and the New International Economic Order', op.cit., pp. 493 and 494; 'Register: time ticks away as embattled owners set deadline for international register', *Shipping News International*, November 1986, pp. 31–3.
318 M.L. McConnell, *JMLC*, vol. 16, no. 3, 1985, p. 1.

PART II
SHIPPING IN
INTERNATIONAL
TRADE RELATIONS

3 Shipping preferences in international trade

Introduction

The first of the mechanisms used to aid and protect merchant shipping is flag preference. However, this mechanism is similar to, and has the same characteristics as the others. No suitable definition of flag preference exists yet but the nearest is that of the OECD Maritime Transport Committee.[1]

> By various measures, discrimination is practised in favour of ships of the national flag and against ships of other countries' flags. Such measures are, for example:
> (a) Measures in the field of exchange control.[2]
> (b) Legislative provisions in favour of the national flag.
> (c) Arrangements made by governmental or semi-governmental organisations giving preferential treatment to national flags.[3]
> (d) Preferential shipping clauses in trade agreements.[4]
> (e) The operation of import and export licensing systems so as to influence the flag of the carrying ship.
> (f) Port regulations.[5]
> (g) Taxation measures.[6]

However, flag preference, like the other major forms of restrictive shipping practices, is a:

> State shipping policy that discriminates between different flags in giving

153

cargo by preferring or giving priority to the domestic flag in giving cargoes and/or granting privileges.[7]

There are a dozen or more categories of flag preference practised by some or all the TMNs, DMNs and the STNs. For our purposes these can be grouped into four major categories:

1   Type 1: Cargo reservation
    (i)   Cargo-sharing
    (ii) Cargo preference
    (iii) Cargo reservation
2   Type 2: Exclusions and trade arrangements
    (i)   Cabotage restrictions
    (ii) Bilateralism
    (iii) Multilateralism
3   Type 3: State-financed cargoes
    (i)   Foreign aid cargoes
    (ii) Agricultural relief cargoes
    (iii) State-financed cargoes
4   Type 4: Miscellaneous flag preferences
    (i)   Foreign-parity flag preference
    (ii) Inland-parity flag preference
    (iii) Miscellaneous flag preference

These are only broad categories and the list is by no means exhaustive.[8] No doubt more practices will develop with time.

Cargo Reservation

Cargo reservation is the most popularly known of the flag preference mechanisms. This too is only a generic term encompassing cargo-sharing and cargo preference.

Cargo-sharing

Cargo-sharing was the original idea at the inception of restrictive shipping practices and, although it has since crystallized into a distinct practice, it is still, by and large, often confused with flag dis-crimination, discussed in Chapter 4. Authors tend to juggle with these terms whenever it suits them, yet they convey different concepts. In the first place, cargo-sharing is not, or at least is not intended to be, discriminatory; it is possibly the oldest known and most acceptable of the restrictive shipping practices.[9] Secondly, it may only be

154

preferential in the sense that State A may prefer, for various reasons, to share her cargoes with the flags of State B rather than with those of State C. Thirdly, cargo-sharing may contain an element of cargo reservation but this is only in so far as it applies to that state's portion of a given cargo; in other words, a state could reserve, say, 50 per cent of the cargoes of her national flag and yet still participate in (cargo) sharing of the remaining 50 per cent unreserved portion.[10]

Normally, the verb 'to share' connotes the principle of partaking or parity. As will be evident in the succeeding chapters, cargo-sharing is the most fair of the restrictive shipping practices and the one akin to the liberal principles of reciprocity, most favoured nation treatment, foreign parity standards and, indeed, national treatment and flag equality.[11] Cargo-sharing means literally 'sharing' whereas cargo preference, cargo reservation and flag discrimination may import the element of 'winner takes all'. The principles behind cargo-sharing may involve a number of parties, for example two (on a 50–50 basis), and a variety of other different proportions, such as that proposed, as a guideline, by the UN Code of Conduct for Liner Conferences of 40–40–20.[12]

Cargo-sharing, like all the other mechanisms, is used for establishing and developing national merchant marines. The idea behind it is that it guarantees automatic supply of cargoes, which generates demand for national flag carriers and so on. As the OECD Maritime Transport Committee was, correctly, to point out:

> Since the war the principle of shipping freedom is being increasingly threatened by administrative and other measures taken by the governments of various countries to protect their national fleets or even to create such fleets.[13]

It would appear that it is the general rule, rather than the exception that the less restrictive countries prefer cargo-sharing to either cargo preference or cargo reservation and flag discriminations. This is particularly true when it comes to the TMNs. It may denote a position of superiority and confidence in competitiveness in the sense that the most restrictive countries are the STNs and DMNs whose merchant fleets are either still non-existent or, when they do exist, are disadvantaged in one way or another:[14]

> In most cases, these countries are newcomers to the maritime world and have built up their fleets for reasons of prestige or in the belief a lifeline in times of war is thereby assured . . . .[15]

Cargo preference, on the other hand, is a bit more restrictive than cargo-sharing as a flag preferential method of establishing and developing national fleets.

Cargo Preference

The similarities and distinctions between cargo preference and flag discrimination will be sufficiently outlined in Chapter 4. Suffice it to say at this stage, however, that the distinctions may appear cosmetic — if not theoretical. Be that as it may, the term 'cargo preference' is used interchangeably with cargo-sharing and cargo reservation.[16] Indeed, there does not appear to be an appropriate definition of cargo preference (as distinct from flag discrimination) since most authors tend to combine or use the two interchangeably. However, the underlying principles are different: in our view, both cargo-sharing and cargo preference constitute a governmental intervention in the structure of the existing maritime system, subdividing the freight market by adopting legislation or concluding treaties that set up an order for carrier preference.[17]

In other words, such cargo preference seeks to reserve a portion of the volume of cargo flowing between the trading partners, with the object of directly favouring certain ship owners, usually — but not always, adopting the flag as the operative criterion. The principle involved in cargo preference is that, when there is cargo available, instead of market forces governing its distribution, the state intervenes and allocates that cargo, giving first priority to the domestic flag, or where domestic tonnage is not available or incapable of meeting the demands required, then to foreign flag carriers. And even among foreign flags, friendly flags (by treaty or otherwise) will be preferred to ordinary third-party flags.[18]

Another method of effecting cargo preference is to award high (freight) quality cargoes to domestic flag carriers and the bulky, low-quality cargoes to the others. Both flag discrimination and flag preference, as controls over a portion of the demand for maritime transport, are formidable instruments that may be employed to foster the establishment and development of certain merchant marine industries for economic or political purposes.[19] Without singling out one country in particular, it would be fair to point out that cargo preference as a method of fostering national fleets is common to both the USA and the DMNs, especially those of Latin America:

> In some cases such practices are resorted to by countries with limited resources and little or no experience in ship management, who find that they cannot attract business except by the imposition of discriminatory measures.[20]

156

Otherwise, cargo preference is a subdivision of flag preference, which is in turn a type of, or a subdivision of, flag discrimination — but a discrimination which applies only to cargoes. Cargo preference may — and often does — take the form of giving preferences to the national flag, then to flags enjoying national treatment, flags of most favoured nations, flags of trading partners, and finally other flags; whereas flag discrimination may — but does not have to — take these degrees of priority into consideration.[21]

Cargo Reservation

Without further analysis, it can safely be summarized that cargo reservation is a form or a subdivision of flag preference, itself a form of flag discrimination. Its principles, characteristics, criteria and other features are nonetheless similar to those of cargo-sharing and cargo preference. Even at the level of semantics, the term 'preference' comes from the verb 'to prefer' or 'preferred', meaning possessing or accorded priority, advantage or privilege, and generally denoting a prior or superior claim or a right of payment as against another thing of the same kind.[22] 'Reservation', on the other hand, comes from the verb 'to reserve', meaning to keep back, set aside, to retain or to keep in store for a future time.[23] Thus, bearing in mind the aforementioned and relating it to maritime transport, cargo reservation would likewise denote state action aimed at reserving a certain portion of exports and/or imports for vessels flying the national flag. In other words, cargo reservation is an admission (or guarantee) by that state to her national lines: 'We shall put aside cargo for you no matter whether you are inefficient or late or what . . . '[24] Like all the other mechanisms, cargo reservation is resorted to for the same reasons — to enable the speedy establishment and development of national merchant marine fleets. However, although a practice predominating among the DMNs, it is not altogether unknown among some TMNs (such as the USA) and (as is to be expected) among the STNs, some of which are fairly sophisticated.[25]

> In other cases, however, the countries practising discrimination are larger and more highly developed. In many of them either the whole or part of the merchant fleet is owned by the state and in some much of the export and import trade is in the hands of the state as well.[26]

It also goes without saying that almost all the countries that practise some form of cargo-sharing, cargo preference and flag discrimination inevitably also practise cargo reservation, for the simple reason that one would have to reserve cargoes away from flag A, for example, before assigning the same cargo to the preferred flag B.[27] Both cargo preference and cargo reservation may take the form of percentages (e.g. 40 per cent), fractions (e.g. one-third), quality (e.g. all electronic goods), freights or tonnage of cargoes. In the final analysis it should be observed that it would be quite reasonable for a country to reserve a certain portion of cargo sufficient to maintain her flag as a commercial entity, particularly if her fleet cannot be assured of cargo in the open market or on the homeward journey.[28]

The legitimacy of the wishes of these countries is recognized by the OECD. The only objections are the methods used to advance and achieve this objective:

> At their meeting in Tokyo in February 1971 (——), ministers of the Consultative Shipping Group adopted a resolution on flag discrimination. This resolution expressed concern at the increasing application of such measures by governments. Ministers did, however, recognize the legitimate wishes of the developing countries to build up and expand their merchant fleets.[29] They agreed that these aspirations would be best realised if developing countries aimed at establishing and operating their shipping on a competitive, economically viable basis, and they agreed to consider requests for financial and technical assistance for this purpose sympathetically . . .[30]

Exclusions: Unilateralism, Bilateralism and Multilateralism

The second type of flag preference is exclusions and trade arrangements and consists of three main categories. The first is the unilateral total exclusion of foreign flags from a particular area, the best example being restrictions in coastal waters known alternatively as cabotage restrictions. The other two result from trade arrangements, either through the home country and another country (bilateral), or through or by a group of countries (multilateral).

Unilateralism: Cabotage Restrictions

The term 'cabotage' is a nautical term derived from Spanish, literally denoting navigating from cape to cape along the coast without going out into the open sea — i.e. in territorial waters. Thus, in international law generally, and maritime trade in particular, cabotage is identified with coastal trade so that it means navigating and trading along the coast between the ports thereof.[31] Since it is a relatively new concept, there are no suitable definitions of this kind of restrictive shipping practice. The nearest we can get to a definition are descriptions and/ or explanations. In that sense cabotage is discriminatory, being the practice of keeping foreign flags out of coastal waters. Since coastal waters are regarded as internal waters, cabotage trade is therefore regarded as internal trade.[32] By totally excluding foreign flags and therefore foreign competition, the idea behind cabotage restrictions is the same as outlined above — to promote the establishment and development of national merchant marines in a particular trade area through guaranteed supply and demand.[33]

In this case, state intervention negates competition and replaces the market forces of demand and supply. In that respect cabotage restrictions are a form of flag preference but with as far-reaching effects as flag discrimination; whereas cargo preference refers to preferential treatment, cabotage does not allow for that kind of comparison.[34] In that respect, cabotage can be likened to cargo reservation in as far as coastal trade is reserved for the national flag. But that is as far as the analogy goes; cabotage differs from reservation in that, in the former, reservation is normally 100 per cent and not just a portion of the cargo as would normally be the case with cargo reservation and cargo-sharing.[35]

The only limitations on cabotage are where the coastal waters form part of an international waterway (for example, the Suez and the Panama Canals) or the international strait; although in these areas the coastal state has jurisdictional sovereignty similar to that on international rivers and landmasses.[36] Apart from the coastal states' obligations under international trade law, most states adopt a protectionist approach for more than economic reasons, and cabotage restrictions are no different.[37] However, discussion here will be limited to the economic rationale — i.e., that cabotage restrictions are resorted to as a means of establishing and developing national merchant marines.[38]

Bilateralism

The second type of flag preference mechanism used for this purpose is trade agreement or arrangement, and is bilateral. Bilateralism is not a total exclusion of foreign or third party flags as is cabotage and, although bilateralism may have the development of national fleets as its principle aim, it is also part of the practice of international commerce.

As indicated above bilateralism in maritime commerce is borrowed from the international trade practice of bilateral negotiations and agreements — 'bi' implying transactions and negotiations between two parties. The term is generally used to refer to trade agreements between two countries. For instance, there are bilateral clearing agreements, bilateral payments' agreements and, of course, bilateral trade agreements. Bilateral trade and payments' agreements are substitutes for more efficient and economic multilateral trade.[39] However, except for limited advantages in periods of disturbances, bilateral agreements are usually harmful to world trade and to countries participating in them and, as such, shipping arrangements are no exceptions. This may be noted as one of the disadvantages of bilateralism in shipping. When trade between any two countries is conducted through bilateral agreements, it tends to be reduced to the level at which the value of goods moving in one direction exactly equals the value of goods moving in the other direction.[40]

It is this fact which appeals to the maritime nations that practise bilateralism. However, as a result, less effective use might be made of the world's resources, since there are fewer opportunities to take advantage of international specialization. Moreover, trade is directed from its normal channels into channels that are determined by the central system and not by market forces.[41] Many countries lacking foreign exchange seek bilateral agreements to overcome this shortage, and it is not difficult to see why this appeals to shipping where the balance of payments' argument ranks very high. It is also not difficult to realise why the DMNs, especially, resort to bilateralism in both ocean-borne and ordinary international trade.[42] A further disadvantage of this kind of approach is that, once it begins, it has a tendency to spread; when, for instance, nations placed at a disadvantage, because of exchange controls, adopt controls themselves as a means of striking back at other countries — thereby countervailing flag discriminations.

Applying this analogy to maritime commerce, a kind of picture emerges. Two countries conclude a trade agreement with a maritime clause, or alternatively a purely maritime agreement, that seeks to divide cargo involved in the trade between them between their two respective national flag fleets. This is fast becoming the most common and acceptable practice in international maritime commerce. Normally it is in the ratio of 50–50 and may be embodied in a treaty, an understanding or, indeed, a convention.[43] Originally, the 50–50 division restricts the shares between only the two parties to the treaty and/or understanding, excluding any other third parties. Although bilateralism is now almost universally recognized and accepted, the interests of third parties who might have customarily plied that trade are not entirely forgotten.[44] So this formula or guideline is now extended from 50–50 to 40–40–20, or some other similar arrangement worked out by the parties.

Our first example is therefore that of the UN Code of Conduct for Liner Conferences, which embodies the spirit of this guideline, and could not have better suited the aspirations of the DMNs in their endeavour to establish and develop their own national fleets. This Code is therefore the first application of the use of bilateralism as a mechanism to achieve this objective,[45] and was the underlying objective of the DMNs when they piloted it, as a tool of development, into an international convention. It will be remembered that the spirit of the Code is that:

> The group of national shipping lines, if any, of two countries, the foreign trade between which is carried by the conference, shall have equal rights to participate in the freight and volume of traffic generated by their mutual foreign trade carried by the Conference.[46]

Although this applies only to the liner conference portion of ocean-borne trade, and although the 40–40–20 split is not explicit or rigid in the proposed convention, nevertheless it is useful, and a recognition of the rights of states to partake in the cargoes generated by their trade.[47] The DMNs have further interpreted this as the international recognition of their legitimate right to use bilateralism as a mechanism to establish and develop their own national merchant marines. It is yet to be seen how this will become a practical reality.[48]

Our second example of bilateralism in international shipping is that involving the USSR and the USA which will be discussed extensively, not simply because it involves the leading TMN and STN and also the world's largest trading partners, but because of the light it sheds on bilateralism in ocean-borne commerce. No doubt the two countries have bilateral maritime arrangements with other countries but of immediate concern is the US/USSR Maritime Agreement of 1972,[49] as amended and updated from time to time, and which was entered into simultaneously with a general trade agreement. Although its objective appears to be to foster US–Soviet maritime commerce (by opening commercial ports and affording both the US flag vessels and Soviet flag vessels the opportunity to participate equally, and substantially, in the carriage of all cargoes moving by sea between the two nations), which objective is typical of maritime bilateral treaties anyway, the underlying objective must surely be to enable both countries to expand their merchant marines generally and on this route in particular.[50]

In the said treaty this equal and substantial share is defined as not less than one-third of the bilateral government-controlled trade. Secondly, any inequality in the division of the uncontrolled cargoes between the flag fleets of the two states is to be adjusted through the allocation of controlled cargoes. The definition of controlled cargoes applied to the USA conforms with that used in prior domestic US legislation.[51] The Soviet definition of controlled cargoes, however, is much more expansive and includes all bilateral cargoes imported into, or exported from, the territory of the USSR where a commercial body or other authority or entity of the USSR has, or would have, the power at any time to designate the carrier. It would appear that the effect of this inclusive language is to expand the coverage of the agreement's cargo preference provisions to a substantial portion of the US–Soviet bilateral trade.[52] However, in the case of the USA this agreement only covers government-controlled cargoes, whereas in the USSR (an STN) such division is superfluous.

This agreement marks a landmark in maritime jurisprudence. In the first place, it created a shipping trade where none existed before, which must have (one way or the other) aided the expansion of the merchant marine of the two parties — a hypothesis quite consistent with our contention.[53] Secondly, although there are no statistics relating to US growth there are, however, indications that the Soviet merchant marine has almost doubled over this decade. Though this cannot be attributed entirely to such bilateral arrangements as the one in question, since there is no statistical evidence, some part of the expansion must be attributed to it.[54] Thirdly, as the first known major treaty between an STN and a TMN, it could easily be interpreted as a free trade recognition of restrictive practices as a means of development and expansion of national fleets through trade expansion.[55] Fourthly, the importance of the participation of third flag vessels was recognized, emphasizing the absence of any conflict with any treaty obligations to other TMNs and other maritime states. This refutes the jurisprudence prevalent among the liberal TMNs that there is an irreconcilable conflict of laws in the trade between market and planned economies.[56] Finally, this maritime agreement has become a firmly established part of the trade policies of the USA and the USSR. Recently, the USA and USSR reaffirmed their commitment to foster bilateral trade through preferential regulation by renewing the maritime agreement,[57] all of which must surely lead, indirectly, to the further expansion of both parties' merchant marines.

Multilateralism

The third mechanism of the second type of flag preference is exclusion of other flags through a multilateral trade agreement, sometimes known simply as multilateralism. This is yet another of the principles derived from international trade, meaning trade between more than two nations. In the free trade sense, it is supposed to be the means of extracting the maximum gains from international trade and the division of labour.[58] It contrasts with bilateralism, in which one country makes an agreement to trade with another. Bilateralism places limits upon consumers' freedom to buy goods in the cheapest market and prevents the realization of full international specialization with each country producing, for export, the product in which it has the largest comparative advantage.[59]

A further disadvantage is that if, on the other hand, a country adopts bilateralism when the rest of the world is trading multilaterally, and there are no serious problems of unemployment at home, it cuts itself off from the advantages of free trade and lowers the standard of living of its inhabitants. It is also worth remembering, however, that multilateral trading may be difficult to maintain if a major currency becomes scarce, as occurred after the Second World War when the dollar became scarce because the rest of the world was anxious to buy from the USA and ran into deficits with her. This is thought to have resulted in protectionism in international trade generally, and maritime commerce in particular.[60] This situation was aggravated by the fact that some countries discriminated in their commerce not only against the hard currency area, but also against other countries that insisted on trade deficits being settled in gold or dollars. A case in point was when France tried to cut down her imports from Germany in order to keep her gold and dollars to pay for imports from the USA.[61]

Governments and international institutions, such as GATT (General Agreements on Tariffs and Trade) and the IMF (International Monetary Fund), have tried to restore free multilateral trade. They have been helped by the gradual disappearance of the dollar problem; the successful reconstruction of Europe after the War; the relative stability, until recently, of the US economy; and an increase in world liquidity through the media of the IMF, European Payments Union (EPU) and the policies of the US Export–Import Bank, discussed later (pp. 172–3). [62] Thus, international shipping has to learn and borrow from international trade by adopting these principles and practices through treaties, agreements and conventions or merely memoranda of understanding. The UN Code of Conduct for Liner Conferences is yet another example of international efforts at both bilateral and multilateral approaches; bilateral, when it seeks the 50–50 basis, and multilateral, when it adopts the 40–40–20 approach.[63] The other examples of multilateralism in international shipping are the maritime clauses of regional groupings, free trade areas and economic communities, such as COMECON (Commission for European Cooperation), the EEC, the Lome Convention, etc.

What must constantly be borne in mind is that the motive behind multilateralism in ocean-borne commerce is the desire to develop and expand the national merchant fleets of the parties involved, individually or severally. Apart from the above-listed examples, one of the earliest known attempts by the TMNs is the British Commonwealth Merchant Shipping Agreement.[64] At the other end of the spectrum, probably one of the finest examples of multilateralism among the DMNs in particular and international shipping in general is the solution chosen by the Latin American countries. It will be remembered that one of the first outcomes of the Latin American Free Trade Association (LAFTA) was the Convention on Water Transport of May 1966,[65] providing for a flag preferential system – although, by then, national preference legislation and cargo-sharing treaties were already common, covering both regional and international trade.[66] Of specific relevance is Article 4 of the Convention which reserves the carriage of the seaborne trade between the contracting parties to their national vessels, in equality of treatment and other conditions established in the Convention and its associated regulations.[67]

Needless to say, the preferential regime thus envisaged is multilateral, and its implementation gradual in time and volume, following the growth of the transport capacity of the contracting parties. However, vessels of non-contracting parties, operating regular and traditional services, will be allowed to participate in transportation between the contracting parties if they fulfil the following requirements:[68]

(a) Their participation does not constitute an obstacle to free trade between the contracting parties and the stable expansion of their merchant marines (the emphasis clearly conveying the development objective of the multilateral convention);[69]
(b) Their normal schedule is between ports of their own country and those of the contracting parties;[70]
(c) Their countries do not implement restrictive measures on traffic with, or against, vessels belonging to the contracting parties (a clause forestalling countervailing actions);[71]
(d) They abide by trade tariffs established by the Conference or similar bodies set up by the treaty.[72]

Although multilateralism in shipping may have its advantages it also has its disadvantages as a departure from freedom of shipping. Although departure from the traditional patterns has evident advantages from the point of view of the operation of vessels, its implementation is difficult. Basic sources of disagreement are the criteria adopted for the distribution of reserved shipments.[73] Countries controlling a large volume of trade will still aspire to reserve a substantial part for their own carriers. On the other hand, members whose foreign trade is insufficient to sustain the development of the viable merchant marine industry will favour an integrated multilateral approach, expecting to obtain a share in the carriage of trade between their bigger partners.[74] Herein lies the root cause and the problems of shipping preferences and discriminations; those who have nothing to contribute and therefore nothing to share will quickly advocate sharing, on the failure of which they resort to the restrictive lever; those who have something to contribute and therefore have everything to lose, advocate free trade. On a global scale, the DMNs represent the former while the TMNs represent the latter.[75]

In quite a different context, this analysis of the inherent conflict of interests may explain why ratification did not take place until 1975, no less than a whole decade after the signing of the treaty.[76] It is also significant that, as of then, the two major trading countries of the continent – Argentina and Brazil – had not ratified it.[77] The Convention eventually did not take off due to insufficient ratifications, and even if it had there would probably be no evidence to suggest it would have achieved its objective of expanding the contracting parties' national merchant marines. Nevertheless, it was a brave attempt at multilateralism in shipping.[78]

It is true that most of the DMNs' restrictive shipping practices are implemented by the Latin Americans. It is also true that the fleets of these countries have grown a great deal since the inception of these restrictive practices, demonstrating that the practices could have fulfilled their desired objective of aiding the establishment and development of national merchant marine fleets.[79] On the other hand, it could also have been a coincidence since these countries also generate sufficiently substantial trade to maintain viable national merchant marine fleets in any event.[80] Assuming that the metaphor 'trade follows the flag' is true, it is difficult to envisage a country with an insufficient ocean-borne trade of its own being able to establish, develop and sustain a national merchant marine fleet purely on the basis of restrictive practices.[81]

The principle behind multilateralism in shipping in general, and the lesson of the LAFTA Convention in particular, is that it can be possible for a group of countries to agree to pool their reciprocal ocean-borne commerce in order to create a wider freight market to be shared, at least in principle, by their national flag vessels with equality of conditions.[82] Their multilateral preferences may be introduced in isolation or in the context of a wider process of economic integration as was the case with the LAFTA Convention on Water Transport.[83] Whereas these are actions that several governments can take jointly, there are still many actions they take unilaterally, one of these being our third type of flag

165

Table 3.1 US government-sponsored cargoes – calendar year 1983[1]

Public Law 664 Cargoes:

Shipper	US Flag Revenue ($1,000)	Total Metric tons	US Flag Metric tons	Percentage US Flag tonnage
Agency for International Development (AID):				
Loans and grants	62,157	1,245,658	559,887	45[3]
PL 480 – Title II	102,417	1,869,604	902,961	48[3]
Section 416	3,815	44,645	20,986	47[3]
Board of International Broadcasting	19	137	122	89
Department of Agriculture:				
PL 480 – Title I	123,328	3,674,699	1,772,069	48[3]
Department of Commerce: Industry and Trade Administration Other Agencies	410	1,611	496	31[4]
Department of Defence:				
Military Assistance Program and the Foreign Military Sales Credit Program	34,001	115,581	89,575	78[5]
Corps of Engineers	2,698	8,226	8,218	100[5]
Naval Facilities Engineering Command (Diego Garcia)	8,172	23,486	23,486	100
Naval Facilities Engineering Command (Somalia)	1,896	4,281	4,281	100
Department of Energy:				
Bonneville Poser Administration	19	842	110	13[4]
Strategic Petroleum Reserve	74,200	11,687,165	9,539,292	82[6]
National Aeronautics and Space Administration	235	596	263	44[3]
Tennessee Valley Authority	12	115	88	77
Department of the Treasury:				
Chrysler Corporation	2,466	22,893	14,070	61[7]
General Services Administration stockpile	8,372	805,428	805,394	100
Department of Transportation:				
Urban Mass Transportation Administration	3,338	23,398	11,592	50[2]
Federal Railroad Administration	83	4,248	2,246	53
US Information Agency	374	1,203	1,175	89
Department of State: Foreign Building Office (not including AID)	559	3,620	3,522	97
Other Agencies	206	238	201	84[8]

Table 3.1 (cont.)

Public Resolution No. 17 Cargoes:

	Total Metric tons	US Flag Metric tons	Total Freight Revenue ($)	US Flag Freight Revenue ($)	Percentage US Flag
	100,273	86,152	39,739,883	32,474,602	82[10]

Agency for International Development (AID)/Israeli
Agreement–Cash Transfer Program

US Flag Revenue ($)	Total Metric tons	US Flag Metric tons	Percentage US Flag tonnage
36,871,000	1,667,848	814,353	49[9]

Notes:
1. Includes civilian agencies, Department of Defence Foreign Military Sales Program, Military Assistance Program, US Army Corps of Engineers – NEGEV – Oman and the Naval Facilities Engineering Command – NAVFAC (Diego Garcia and Somalia). Other Department of Defence cargoes not included.
2. Agencies' tonnages are reflected in metric tons for uniformity only. Cargo preference compliance for those programmes involving high cube/low density cargoes, is achieved on a gross revenue ton basis for such programmes do not necessarily represent the exact extent of the programme's compliance with the statute.
3. This programme did not meet the minimum 50 per cent US flag participation level. US flag service was available on a timely basis to have enabled the agency to meet the cargo preference requirement.
4. Agencies complied with the statute as the imbalance in favour of foreign-flag shipments was due to non-availability of US flag service.
5. Documents were only received from Honduras, Oman and Saudi Arabia projects.
6. MARAD monitors the SPR programme on the basis of long-ton miles (LTM). In CY 1983, this programme provided a total of 33,922,489,645 LTM of which US flag carriers derived 20,884,507,992 LTM or 61 per cent.
7. The three-year Chrysler Guarantee Loan programme was terminated on 15 August 1983.
8. Cargo of government and private agencies that generated less than 100 metric tons of cargo in 1983. The agencies which reported in 1983 are: Action, Agriculture Marketing Service, Agriculture Research Service, American Battle Monuments, Animal, Plant Health Inspection Service, Centre for Disease Control, Defence Accounting Office, Department of Defence, Drug Enforcement, Drug Enforcement Administration, Federal Aviation Administration, Foreign Agricultural Service, Federal Bureau of Investigation, Federal Highway Administration, General Accounting Office, Geological Survey, Health and Human Services, Immigration and Naturalization Service, International Exchange Service, Labour Department, Library of Congress, Narcotics Assistance Unit, National Oceanic and Atmospheric Administration, National Park Service, National Science Foundation, Peace Corps, Smithsonian Institute Soil Conservation Service, Treasury Department, US Custom Services, US Trade Representatives, and Veterans' Administration.
9. While statistics are shown for CY 1983 shipments, the Israeli cash transfer programme is maintained on a fiscal year basis. This reflects the terms of the side letter executed each year between the government of Israel (GOI) and AID. On a fiscal year (1983) basis, GOI shipped exactly 50 per cent on US flag vessels.
10. Compliance based on freight revenue only.

Source: Maritime Administration (USA), 1985, pp. 24–5.

preference — that pertaining to state-financed cargoes, discussed below.

State-financed Cargoes

State-financed cargoes are a type of flag preference practised mainly by the (aid-giving) wealthier nations.[84] Although it is probable that most TMNs include such maritime clauses in trade agreements with the recipient DMNs, notable among them is the USA. In June 1954, for instance, the then Organization for European Economic Co-operation (OEEC) Maritime Transport Committee noted with concern that preferential shipping regulations, applicable under Public Law No. 17 of 26 March 1934, to the carriage of all cargo financed by loans made by instrumentalities of the USA government were also being applied to cargo financed by US private banking institutions against guarantee by US government banking agencies. These regulations were being applied to a loan financed by 14 private banks which had been guaranteed by the Export–Import Bank of Washington.[85] The Maritime Transport Committee considered that the application of Public Law No. 17 in the circumstances represented an unjustified extension of the preferential measures at present in force which would affect all the maritime transport countries if the ruling was to pass unchallenged.[86] State-financed cargo–flag preference represents the sophistication that has been reached in using all the means available to a state to establish and/or expand her national fleet.[87] State-financed cargo is really a broad category which includes foreign aid cargo preference, surplus agricultural commodities and relief aid, and government-financed cargo preferences. The other rationale and motives for resort to this particular mechanism will be apparent in the ensuing discussion. For the US practice see Table 3.1.

'Foreign aid cargoes' preference

Foreign aid shipments, as a type of preference, is a brainchild of the USA, which is hardly surprising; the USA is the biggest aid-donor country in the world and although many other aid-donors occasionally resort to this restrictive practice, our leading example will inevitably be that of the USA. The main operative legislation in this respect is Public Law No. 664[88] — the Cargo Preference Act 1954,[89] which amended Section 901 of the Merchant Marine Act 1936.[90] It will be remembered that the former legislation codified various references in existing American foreign aid programmes — for example, the original Economic Cooperation Act 1948.[91] The principles and objectives behind cargo preference in foreign aid cargoes is that the act applies where American aid is furnished without provisions for reimbursement, which presumably means and includes aid cargoes which, although technically sold by the USA, are, in reality, given away for a purely nominal or token sales price.

It would appear that this reimbursement provision was intended to exclude from the coverage of the legislation instances where the US government acts simply as an agent, on a reimbursable basis for the foreign aid recipient nation.[92] The Cargo Preference Act 1954 came in to fill a lacuna as, before it, there had been many instances where, for example, fertilizers and other economic-aid commodities were purchased from a European country for delivery to the Far East on a laid-down cost basis under which American flag vessels were effectively frozen out because of the lower rates quoted by low-cost foreign competitors.[93] Here is another classic example of a restrictive practice being used first to negate or displace market forces and second to support a high cost, and probably an inefficient, merchant marine.

There are few agencies involved in the administration of the aid programme. The statute is applicable principally to shipments financed by loans or grants of the Agency for International Development (AID).[94] There is some indication that the use of this particular preference is beginning to pay off. The fact that AID will not finance delivery services aboard foreign flag vessels has resulted in the use of the US flag vessels considerably in excess of the minimum 50 per cent requirements. This is coupled with an orchestrated 'Ship American' campaign waged by the Federal Maritime Commission (FMC), Department of Commerce (DOC), Department of Trade (DOT), American shipowners and other American vested shipping interests.[95] This success would not have been possible without these flag preference requirements since — as indicated above — American vessels would be very uncompetitive; their freight rates quotations being higher due to higher running costs. Thus, therein lie the motives and/or rationale behind flag preference.[96]

This type of flag preference has, moreover, been given a boost. The US Foreign Operations Administration (FOA) was frequently thought to be the main agency shipping offshore procurement cargo in foreign bottoms. But the 1954 Cargo Preference Act applies whether cargoes are procured within or without the USA: this extraterritoriality, if we may call it such, guarantees the US flag vessels a wider market in addition to guaranteeing them the domestic market.[97] Otherwise the cargo preference requirement of offshore procurement applies to given supplies as well. Lastly, the responsibility for the enforcement of the applicable 50–50 provision is placed on the cooperating countries by the FOA's successor, the International Cooperation Administration (ICA), regulation: if the 50–50 requirement is not met by geographical areas[98] for any three-month period, the recipient country has to refund ICA reimbursements for commodities, insurance and freight as the ICA Director, in his discretion, shall consider necessary to effect a compliance by the cooperating country with the foreign requirement for the period of time.[99]

In conclusion, therefore, the Merchant Marine Act 1936, the Cargo Preference Act 1954 and the Economic Cooperation Act 1948, *ejusdem generis*, place an obligation on AID, ICA, etc.[100] These statutes require that whenever the USA purchases, donates or finances any equipment, materials, or commodities, or merely guarantees the convertibility of foreign currencies in any of these transactions, the appropriate federal agency must ensure that, if ocean transportation is required, at least 50 per cent of the gross tonnage of such cargo moves aboard privately-owned US commercial flag vessels to the extent that such vessels are available at fair and reasonable rates.[101] If the US flag vessels can be guaranteed 50 per cent, where under normal circumstances they would probably have competed for 10 per cent or so, then this is consistent with the presumption that the merchant marine fleet would expand to meet this guaranteed demand. These statutes are applicable principally to shipments financed by loans or grants from AID but also apply to surplus agricultural commodities.

'Surplus Agricultural Commodities
and Relief Aid' Preferences

Although this is really part of foreign aid cargo flag preference, its importance merits a separate discussion and lengthy emphasis. It, too, is a creation of the USA, from where, naturally, the highlights come. However, this time the operative legislation is Public Law No. 17,[102] as amended. Briefly, this legislation states that exports of agricultural or other products fostered by government loans are to be carried exclusively in vessels of US registry unless it is determined by the Maritime Administration (MARAD) that such vessels are not available in sufficient numbers, or in sufficient tonnage capacity, or on necessary sailing schedules, or at reasonable rates. It would be worth noting a short history of this piece of legislation in order to appreciate its role in the development and expansion of the US merchant marine. What initiated this particular flag preference programme was that agricultural exports, which hit new heights during the Korean War, fell off rapidly from late 1952, causing the surplus to build up to alarming proportions.[103] In Congress emphasis centred on measures to overcome the farm surplus situation and stimulate the export of agricultural commodities, which measures involved the sale of price support stocks to commercial firms, donations for relief use, and the inclusion of sales for foreign currencies in Mutual Security Programmes.[104]

Since the merchant marine is the twin-arm of international trade, this stimulation of exports of agricultural commodities had to go hand-in-hand with the promotion of the use of US flag vessels through this cargo preference clause. This, *inter alia*, was the string attached to this aid programme. In 1954, therefore, the 83rd Congress confirmed substantial authorization for this purpose and established an additional programme of sales for foreign currency under Title 1 of the Agricultural Trade Development and Assistance Act (ATDAA). Housed under Public Law No. 480,[105] this programme seems to have paid off. This particular flag preference example underlines the fact that maritime trade and practice not only serves but follows international trade policies. For instance, in the first five years of the programme it is estimated that agreements totalling some US$5,000 million were signed with foreign countries, including over US$40 million for ocean freight to be paid by the Department of Agriculture,[106] which boasted, then, that the 50–50 cargo preference provision had added at least US$12 million to reducing the cost of the farm subsidies.

However, it is the Department of State which negotiates surplus agricultural agreements with foreign countries. Thus, as far as the USA was concerned, the idea was 'we give you the food, but on our plates', which gave the recipients no choice. In any case, it would be very generous for the USA to allow the benefits of their enormous surplus agricultural aid and foreign trade to foreign (though cheaper and much more efficient) vessels which had done nothing to earn it.[107] Apart from certain limited exemptions the tendency is to apply the Act whenever cargo is 'touched anywhere along the line by the hand of the government'.[108] The stress on government benefit in disposing of products at the highest price obtainable would tend to ignore legislative history that the reimbursement exception to the Act's coverage was intended to take care of situations where the government only acted as agent rather than selling the products itself.[109] Be that as it may, this particular flag preference legislative scheme has been one of the most effective in keeping the US merchant marine afloat.[110] However, the greatest objection to this pedigree of flag preference has been that relating to government-financed cargoes.

This category is in many ways similar to the cargo preferences attached to foreign aid and surplus agricultural and relief supplies. However, in some cases it also differs from the two as herein outlined. In principle these are cargoes arising from purchases or transactions using government loans, or other assistance to the buyer, in a foreign country or to that foreign country itself.[111] In many countries restrictions are imposed on the shipment of this type of cargo; preference, in part or in whole, being given to national flag carriers. One would normally expect this sort of relationship in a trade agreement between a developed and developing country — hence the label 'aid with strings'. Once again, the USA is a TMN that practises this kind of flag preference.[112] The operative legislation is Public Law No. 17, which stipulates that shipments financed by the Export–Import Bank (EXIMBANK) of Washington will include in their credit agreements a requirement that cargo shipment be made in US flag vessels, unless the requirements are waived by MARAD (later FMC).[113] In certain circumstances, notwithstanding the availability of US flag vessels, vessels of the recipient nation may be allowed to share up to 50 per cent of the EXIMBANK-financed cargoes under general waivers of Public Law No. 17 which are usually good for the life of a particular credit.

Otherwise, general waivers are granted only when the FMC is satisfied that parity of treatment is extended to US flag-vessels in the trade of foreign nations as in the National Treatment Preference (pp. 173–6).[114] And even if a general waiver is granted, it applies only to vessels of the recipient nation registry to the extent of their capacity to carry the cargo under the credit. Suppose that the aid recipient is, for example, Uganda, a land-locked country with no merchant marine of her own; what it means is that such cargoes would have to be carried 100 per cent in US flag vessels.[115] As expected, third flag vessels (i.e. of countries other than the USA or the recipient) are barred from competing for EXIMBANK cargoes unless the US flag vessels are not available, and if so, at reasonable rates.[116]

In the operation of this scheme, in addition to its own banking operations, the EXIMBANK conducts special leading operations for other agencies involved in the game. For example, it funds loans for the Office of Defence Mobilization under the 1950 Defence Production Act[117] and it performs several functions for the ICA: credits under the Mutual Security Act 1954;[118] emergency wheat loans; or, for example, the US$100 million credit to the former European Steel and Coal Community under the 1951 Mutual Security Act;[119] and ICA investment guarantees (currency transfer and loss by war or confiscation.[120] As noted above, the last category is not covered by the Cargo Preference Scheme, nor is the Bank's insuring, for example, of a consignment of cotton bales against war risk and expropriation.[121] However, ICA regulations apparently subject the remaining cargoes to cargo preferences. It is this kind of use of flag preference by the USA and other countries, to establish and expand their national merchant marine fleets irrespective of the sound economic criteria, which has infuriated the other OECD members, among others.[122] At the inception of this programme, and on the proposal of the then-OEEC Maritime Transport Committee, the Council of the OEEC adopted a resolution requesting the US government to reconsider the practice of applying the provisions of this Public Law No. 17 to transactions which, but for the existence of guarantee from the EXIMBANK, would be of an ordinary commercial character.[123]

Miscellaneous Flag Preferences

There are many other forms of flag preference, all of them designed to improve the position of the national fleet. We shall combine them under three broad categories: foreign parity, inland parity and miscellaneous flag preferences.

Foreign Parity Flag Preference

In purely international trade terminology, foreign parity is alternatively known as the conditional Most Favoured Nation Clause (MFNC); the supposedly non-discriminatory aspect of the principle of national treatment. In a way it is related to bilateralism and multilateralism.[124] The MFNC is employed in international commercial agreements, which are treaties in which tariff privileges accorded by a country to any other countries are also automatically extended to all other countries with which it has treaties – awarding them MFN or national treatment. For example, an MFNC in a treaty between Country A and B might state that B's goods entering A's ports would not be subject to duty higher than that levied on similar goods from any other country, and vice-versa.[125] The two countries thus receive in principle an assurance of treatment in tariffs at least as good as that enjoyed by any other country and a safeguard against tariff discrimination and consequently flag preference.[126]

This, however, is only true of the unconditional MFNC which automatically extends the benefits of tariff and maritime concessions to all countries enjoying foreign parity status with the tariff-reducing country, whether the concessions are given freely or reciprocally (i.e. in return for counter-concessions).[127] Of late, however, many countries, especially the DMNs, have made departures from the classical theory of unconditional MFNC in favour of the conditional MFNC; the latter makes extensions of the privilege dependent upon the grant of similar concessions by the country benefiting from them.[128]

It will be remembered that before 1914 the unconditional MFNC in bilateral trade agreements was thought to be influential in promoting free trade (although in practice the automatic extension of the benefits was often nullified by administrative devices such as tariff descriptions designed to confine concessions to one country). Between the Wars the effectiveness of the concession was subsequently weakened by the use of the conditional form and, more importantly, by the growth of quotas.[129] It would therefore appear that maritime flag preferences and flag discriminations have their roots in the conditional MFNC, which now forms the basis of negotiations based on the MFNC principle. The unconditional clause could deter tariff concessions whenever a bilateral agreement to reduce tariffs threatened to result in both parties giving other countries more benefits than they received themselves.[130]

After the Second World War, the search for a way out of this difficulty, while preserving the benefits of the MFNC, led to the GATT. This provided for simultaneous bilateral tariff agreements between pairs of countries, the concessions being generated by the use of the MFNC and incorporated into a single multilateral agreement. Thus originated the bilateral and multilateral maritime preferences as we know them today.[131] Probably the best examples of these in maritime treaties are those of the USA — the details of which are given in the annexes at the end of the book.

All the examples of the bilateral and multilateral approaches already discussed can also be attributed to the foreign parity flag preference.[132] The other aim of the principle of national treatment, which relates it more to maritime practices, is the inland parity flag preference.

Inland Parity Flag Preference

The standard of national treatment or inland parity means that the parties accord to each other's nationals the same treatment as they accord their own nationals. This is sometimes known as equality of treatment or the standard of reciprocity which means that one party accords the other exactly the same rights and advantages that the other accords in return.[133] National treatment has been the standard

174

predominantly applied to shipping since the beginning of the free trade era.[134] It will be remembered that the authoritative pattern had been set by the Cobden Treaty of 1860 which was concluded between France and Great Britain and which in general provided for MFN treatment but, with respect to merchant marines, granted national treatment of reciprocity or equality or inland parity preferences.[135]

The example of the Cobden Treaty was followed by a great number of commercial treaties of this period. The view that national treatment was the most equitable standard for shipping has indeed been accepted not only on a bilateral but also on a multilateral basis, as evidenced above.[136] The outstanding treaty in this respect is the IMCO Convention and Statute on the International Regime of Maritime Ports of 9 December 1923. This provides, *inter alia*, that as regards the access to, and the use of, ports, every contracting state undertakes to grant the vessels of every other contracting states equality of treatment with its own vessels.[137] However, although this Convention, which has been ratified by twenty-three states, has done much to facilitate the commercial operations of ships in ports, it is not easily applied to the participation of ships in maritime transport as such.

As a result, the application of national treatment to this field also has been frequently advocated. It is accepted that national treatment represents the highest standard that could be granted because it can be assumed no state treats its own nationals on a less favourable basis than foreigners.[138] If, however, this standard is to be made the basis of a reciprocal agreement, the state expected to grant this standard must ask itself what benefit it will get in return for its own nationals − i.e., what is the status enjoyed by the nationals of the other contracting party? Obviously certain differences in the material status of the nationals of both states will always be found, but if these differences exceed a certain measure it is plain that the agreement on national treatment would create unwarranted restrictions for the nationals of the one and unjustified benefits for the nationals of the other state.[139]

This, then, is the natural limit for the application of this standard. One can then understand the reluctance and the predicament of the STNs. It is precisely for this reason that there has been a marked departure from this principle in international trade generally, and maritime trade in particular; hence all the discriminatory and preferential maritime policies.[140] It may not be safe to assume that because of the above factors, this principle of national treatment in public international law and trade has therefore been abandoned; but it may be true to say this constitutes an exception to the practice even though not a total abandonment.

In order to extend the applicability of inland parity, an attempt has been made to add to an agreement on national treatment a clause providing that neither party could claim inland parity in order to receive rights which extend further than those it is granting its own nationals.[141] This means, however, that a combination is sought of two standards which are quite different and which therefore amount to a contradiction in terms. If a combination of such types could be held valid at all, it would impart a mere exception rather than a general rule.[142]

Miscellaneous Flag Preferences

The flag preference headings discussed above are merely broad generalizations. It has not been, and indeed, it would not be, possible to deal with all the various types of preferences that may be open to states.[143] The above list is further supplemented, and complemented, by the discussion of such similar topics in Chapter 4 and Chapter 8 generally.[144] Nevertheless, the discussion would not be complete without considering some, but not all, of the miscellaneous categories which pertain particularly to the USA.[145] For instance, even though there seems to be no regulation or policy statement on the subject, it would appear that in returns under the Mutual Defence Assistance Act of 1949, certain equipment, for example from the UK,[146] would still be subject to cargo preference,[147] since the UK makes delivery alongside the ship at the point of origin. Similarly, transportation to Italy, for instance, of surplus Defence Department property for sale there,[148] would be subject to the same requirement as that relating to surplus agricultural commodities and relief aid. However, when transportation follows purchase, the opposite result should obtain about stipulations in the contract of sale.[149]

Equally applicable are student exchange programmes for which the government provides funds, including transportation of effects,[150] but these would seem not to be subject to cargo preference.[151] Furthermore, the Cargo Preference Act 1974 expressly exempts from its requirements cargoes carried in the three ships of the Panama Canal Company, a government-owned corporation which primarily serves the needs of the Panama Canal and its workers.[152] The list could be endless. The contributions of flag preferences towards the establishment and/or expansion of national fleets may be indirect rather than direct, largely political rather than purely commercial, but they are nevertheless there. They may be gradual and not easily compatible.

Notes

1 OECD, *Maritime Transport*, 1960, p. 10.
2 See Chapter 5 at pp. 240-2 and also Chapters 9-10 generally.
3 (a) and (b).
4 E.g. bilateralism.
5 E.g. berth and port discriminations.
6 For fiscal and financial relief see Chapter 8.
7 W.R. Malinowski, 'Towards a change in the international distribution of shipping', *International Conciliation*, no. 582, March 1972.
8 UNCTAD Secretariat, *Report*, Doc. no. TD/B/C.4/63, 4 November 1970, 1 of 3.
9 Metaxas, *Economics of Tramp Shipping*, 1971, pp. 24-6.
10 The *Rochdale Report* (Committee of Inquiry into Shipping – Report of Chairman Lord Rochdale), London, May 1970, paras 136-40, p. 51.
11 Black, *Law Dictionary*, rev. edn., 1968, p. 1542; and Chambers, *Twentieth Century Dictionary*, p. 1244.
12 UNCTAD, *Code of Conduct*, Article 4(2); UNCTAD *Conference of Plenipotentiaries on the Code*, vol. II, TD/Code/13/Add. 1.
13 OECD, *Maritime Transport*, 1961, p. 53.
14 US Dept. of Commerce, MARAD, *Maritime Subsidies*, 1978, p. 52.
15 OECD, *Maritime Subsidies*, 1961, Chapter 1.
16 C. O'Loughlin, *Economics of Sea Transport*, 1st edn, Pergamon Press, Oxford, 1967, pp. 149, 156-9, 163.
17 G.H. Hearns, 'Cargo preference and control', *Journal of Maritime Law and Commerce*, vol. 2, no. 3, pp. 481-2.
18 C.F.E. Cufley, *Ocean Freights and Chartering*, 1974 (reprint), Chapter 10.
19 Ibid., pp. 316, 317-18.
20 OECD, *Maritime Transport*, 1962, p. 18.
21 Cufley, 'The Movements and the Development of World Merchant Shipping', in op.cit., pp. 309-36 at pp. 319-20.
22 A.M. Macdonald, OBE, Chambers, *Twentieth Century Dictionary*, 1977 Rev., p. 1057.
23 Ibid., p. 1148.
24 H. Olof, *Flag Discriminations: Purposes, Motives and Economic Consequences*, Publication of the Swedish School of Economics, no. 3, 1956, p. 39.
25 W. Gorter, *United States Shipping Policy*, for Council of Foreign Relations, Hemper & Brothers, New York, 1956.
26 OECD, *Maritime Transport*, 1953, p. 42.
27 Cufley, 'Flag discriminations and trade reservations', op.cit., pp. 318-19.
28 UNCTAD, Doc. no. TD/B/C.4/38/Rev. 1, paras 337-40, p. 91.
29 Ibid.
30 OECD, *Maritime Transport*, 1964, p. 39.
31 R.O. Goss, '(Preferences, peoples' expressions of) advances in maritime economics', *CUP*, 1st edn., 1979; in Introduction especially at p. 14.
32 *Rochdale Report*, op.cit., paras 141, p. 41.
33 Ibid., Chapter 5, Coastal and Short Sea Trades, paras 296-320, pp. 60-2.

34 Ibid., paras 220(1) and 222(1).
35 Ibid., para. 220(1), p. 60.
36 E.g. treaty between the Argentine Republic and Chile defining the boundaries between the two countries (Tierra del Fuego, neutrality of Straits of Magellan, etc.) signed at Buenos Aires, 23 July 1881, British and Foreign State Papers, pp. 1104-5.
37 UNCTAD Doc. no. TD/B/B.C/4/63-3 of 3.
38 Ibid.
39 R.F. Mikesell, 'Foreign Exchange in the Postwar World', *Twentieth Century Fund*, New York, 1954.
40 See also text under 'Multilateralism', p. 162.
41 As to its advantages/disadvantages see end of Part I and also Part III of this book.
42 H. Chalmers, *World Trade Policies*, University of California Press, Berkeley, California, 1953.
43 W. Friedman, *The Changing Structure of International Law*, Feffer and Simons, New York, 1964, chapter 5, pp. 51-9.
44 Ibid., pp. 196-201 — i.e. 'Less developed countries and the universality of international law'.
45 Ibid., 'Conflicts of ideology and universality of international law', pp. 202 to the end.
46 Article 4(2)(a) of Code of Conduct for Liner Conferences.
47 Ibid., Article 4(2)(b).
48 Ibid.
49 US Department of State *Bulletin*: Agreement Regarding Trade Act, 18 October 1972, no. 595, 1972.
50 P.B. Fitzpatrick, 'Soviet-American Trade 1972-74; a summary', *Virginian Journal of International Law*, 15, 1974, p. 39.
51 US-USSR Maritime Agreement, 1972, Annex 111(a).
52 Ibid., 'White House Fact Sheet'.
53 US Department of State *Bulletin*, no. 661, 1972, Annex 111(1)(c)(iii).
54 Though this agreement was interrupted by the US embargo following the Afghan crisis.
55 This treaty is in line with Soviet (and STNs) concepts of international trade relations and law being concluded only through treaties.
56 US Department of State *Bulletin*, no. 96, 1976; Agreement Regarding Certain Maritime Matters, 29 December 1975.
57 The six-year agreement, which went into effect 1 January 1976, was signed on 19 December 1975 and expired on 29 December 1981.
58 See again generally R.F. Mikesell, 'Foreign exchange in the postwar world', *The Twentieth Century Fund*, New York, 1954; H. Chalmers, *World Trade Policies*, University of California Press, Berkeley, California, 1953.
59 G.C. Hufbanner, *et al.*, 'The GATT codes and unconditional MFN principle', 3rd Article in the *Symposium on the Multilateral Trade Agreements II*, vol. 12, ILJ Geon, Washington University, no. 1, 1980, pp. 59-95.
60 A.P. Rubin, 'The international legal aspects of unilateral declarations', *AJIL*, vol. 71, 1977, pp. 1-30.
61 M. Hardy, 'The UN and General Multilateral Treaties concluded under the

auspices of the League of Nations', *British Yearbook of International Law*, vol. 39, 1963, pp. 425–40.

62 D.R. Anderson, 'Reservations to multilateral conventions: a re-examination', *International Contemporary Law Quarterly*, vol. 13, 1964, pp. 450–81.

63 S.G. Sturmey, 'The development of the Code of Conduct for Liner Conferences', *Maritime Law and Management*, vol. 3, no. 2, April 1979, pp. 133–48.

64 Commonwealth Shipping Agreement of 1931.

65 W.D. Buss, 'The basic international structure of LAFTA and the proposals for its modifications: intergovernmentalism v. regionalism', Case WRJ, *International Law*, vol. 2, 1969, pp. 34–57.

66 J.E. Oribe-Stemmer, 'Flag discrimination in Latin America', *Journal of Maritime Law and Commerce*, vol. 10, no. 1, p. 129.

67 R.B. Brown, *Transport and the Economic Integration of Latin America*, Brookings Institution, Washington DC, 1966, pp. 153–4.

68 Ibid., chapter 6, i.e. 'Latin American shipping policies and the LAFTA Maritime Convention', pp. 88–94.

69 Ibid., i.e. 'Shipping rates and service and draft LAFTA Treaty', pp. 153–4.

70 K.R. Simmonds, 'The Central American Common Market: an experiment in regional integration', *Int. & Comp. LQ*, vol. 16, 1967, pp. 911–45.

71 A.F.V. Garcia *et al.*, 'Institutional and economic perspectives on Latin American integration', *Proceedings of American Society of International Law*, vol. 61, 1967, pp. 167–86.

72 Brown, op.cit., 'Latin American shipping policies', pp. 107–13.

73 Article 4 of LAFTA Water Convention.

74 J.E. Oribe-Stemmer, op.cit.

75 Brown, op.cit.,. 'Present maritime service within LAFTA Water Convention area', pp. 124–31.

76 W.R. Pawson, 'Resource allocation and integration in the Central American Common Market', *NUJ International Law and Politics*, vol. 3, 1970, pp. 107–35.

77 Brown, op.cit., 'Effect of imbalances of trade flows, other views of the rate problem, and the reservation of cargo for LAFTA ships', pp. 154–6.

78 Ibid., pp. 138, 145–9.

79 Brazil, Argentina, Venezuela and Mexico account for about half of the LAFTA economic trade by country.

80 The LAFTA Water Convention was terminated and replaced by a new and hopefully more viable Maritime Economic Treaty.

81 Brown, op.cit., chapter 9, pp. 216–17.

82 Ibid., 'Transport policy', pp. 218–20.

83 Ibid., 'Conclusion relating to LAFTA', pp. 221–4.

84 S.J. Rubin, *The Conscience of the Rich Nations, The Development Assistance Committee and the Common Aids Efforts*, Harper & Row, New York, 1966.

85 Note that Japan too has an EXIMBANK.

86 OECD, *Maritime Transport*, 1954, para. 68.

87 Hence state intervention, ibid., p. 54.

88 68 Stat., p. 832, 1954.

89 46 ISC 1241(b), 1964.

90 49 Stat., p. 2015.

91 1954 *House Hearings*, p. 92.

92 S. Rep. no. 1584, p. 2.

93 'Contribution of federal aid to trade', Appendix 2, at 15 of *Public Law*, p. 480.

94 Agricultural Trade Development and Assistance Act, 68 St. stat.; 445, 1954, as amended, 7 USC, paras 17-19, 1964, Titles I, II, pp. 1721-4.

95 See also 73 Stat. 610, 1959, as amended, 7 USC, 1964, Title IX, paras 1731-6.

96 I. Foighel, 'Aid to developing countries – a legal analysis', *Novdisk Tid. Int. Ref.*, vol. 40, 1970, pp. 87-175.

97 M.W. Perry *et al.*, 'US foreign policy and emerging legal policy issues of technology transfer', *Proc. Am. Soc. International Law*, vol. 70, 1976, pp. 1-10.

98 S. Rep. no. 2286, 87th Congress, 2nd Session, 44, 1962.

99 68 Stat. 832, 1954, as amended, 46 USC, 1964, para. 1241(b).

100 Ibid.

101 See also *Rochdale Report*, op.cit., para. 150, p. 43.

102 US Maritime Research Committee, 'An analysis of the application of Public Law 664 (50-50) to the disposal of agricultural surplus under Title I Public Law 480', reprinted in *Senate Hearings*, p. 108.

103 J.N. Hyde, 'Economic development agreements', *Hague Recueil*, vol. 105, 1962, pp. 267-74; R. Triffin, *The World Money Maze: National Currencies in International Payments*, Yale University Press, New Haven, 1966.

104 48 Stat. 500, 1934, 15 USC, para. 616(a), 1964.

105 H.C. on Merchant Marine and Fisheries, 'Cargo preference and its relation to the Farm Surplus Disposal Program', H.R. Rep., no. 1818, 84th Congress, 2nd Session, 6, 1956.

106 Ibid., 5 June 1956, 7 UST DIA 7071 *TIAS*, no. 3588 (effective 5 June 1956).

107 See also *TIAS*, no. 3989 (effective 3 February 1958).

108 US Department of Agriculture, *Export Credit Programs for Financing Dollar Sales of US Agricultural Commodities*, 1959.

109 1954, *Senate Hearings*, H.R. Rep. 2329, p. 2.

110 Ibid., p. 97; see generally International Cooperation Administration, *Investment Guarantee Handbook*, GPO, Washington DC, 1957.

111 Construction Reserve Fund, 12 CRF, para. 402 3(a), 1963.

112 R. Greiger, 'The unilateral change of economic development agreements', *Int. & Comp. LQ*, vol. 23, GPO, Washington DC, 1974, pp. 73-104.

113 US Department of Commerce, MARAD, *Statement on Public Resolution No. 17*, 24 July 1959, reprinted in *Alcoa SS Co. v. Cia Anomima Venezuela de Navegacion*, 7 FMC 345, 737, 1962; affirmed sub-nom. *Alcoa SS Co. v FMC*, 321 F. 2d 756 (DC Cir. 1963).

114 See Annex on MFN and National Treatment.

115 The US was a major donor to the Eastern African Disaster Relief, 1979-81.

116 Cf. G. Schwarzenberger *et al.*, 'Equality and discrimination in international economic law', *Yearbook World Affairs*, vol. 25, 1971, pp. 163-81.

117 1956 *Senate Hearings* 125.
118 Contra, the 151 Act.
119 1954 *Senate Hearings*: 'Defence Department Directive on Mutual Defence Shipments'.
120 68 Stat. 832, 1954.
121 46 USC, para. 1241 (Suppl. V 1958).
122 *Rochdale Report*, op.cit., para. 151, p. 43.
123 Ibid.
124 J. Viner, *International Economics*, The Free Press, Glencoe, New York, 1951.
125 L.G. Jahnkel, 'The EEC and the MFNC', *Canadian Yearbook of International Law*, vol. 1, pp. 252-71.
126 S.G. Sturmey, op.cit., 'Flag discrimination and import tariff', pp. 102, 114.
127 S. Murase, 'The MFN in Japan's treaty practice during the period 1854–1905', *American Journal of International Law*, vol. 70, 1976, pp. 273-97.
128 G.P. Verbit, *Trade Agreements for Developing Countries*, New York, 1969.
129 Timberg *et al.*, 'Control of international restrictive business practices', *Proceedings of American Society of International Law*, vol. 69, 1975, pp. 170-92.
130 Anon., 'Tariff surcharges and Article II of GATT', *University Journal of International Law and Politics*, vol. 5, New York, 1972, pp. 341-56 at pp. 349 and 351.
131 S.G. Sturmey, op.cit., pp. 194-8, 206-7, 405, 409-10, i.e. 'Flag discrimination in bilateral trade agreements and the 50-50 Rule'.
132 R.E. Hudec, *The GATT Legal System and World Diplomacy*, Praeger, New York, 1975.
133 US Department of Trade, Memo submitted to the President's Advisory Committee, August 1965.
134 H.G. Rohreke, *The Formula and Material Concept of Flag Equality*, Institute of Shipping Economics, Bergen, 1961, p. 1.
135 Treaty of Friendship, 'Commerce and Navigation between the US and West Germany', Article IV(1), *TIAS*, no. 3593.
136 For this Convention, see *Great Britain Treaty Series*, no. 24, 1925.
137 N. Singh, 'International Conventions on Merchant Shipping', *British Shipping Laws*, vol. 8, 1963, pp. 1558-68.
138 Note 135 above, Article IV(2).
139 G.H. Hackworth, *International Law*, vol. 5, 1943, p. 272.
140 'John T. Bill Co. v. US', 104 F. 2d 67 (CCPA 1939) in W.W. Bishop, *International Law Cases and Materials*, 3rd edn, Little & Brown, Boston, 1971, pp. 160-4.
141 Article 1(1), US–West German Treaty; *Bill Co. v. US*, p. 161.
142 Ibid., proclaimed 14 October 1925, 44 Stat. 2132, Article VII.
143 UNCTAD Doc. no. TD/B/C.4/63 1, 2, 3. Corrigenda and Addenda 1-2.
144 Article XII, US–Belgium Treaty, 1875, (19 Stat. 628, 1 Mallay Treaties 90).
145 Indeed most examples are from the USA: e.g. *House Hearings*, no. 2329, p. 2.
146 US–UK Agreement, 13 May 1957, para. 3, 1957, 8 UST & OIA 835, *TIAS*, no. 3843.

147 Presumably to the 100 per cent American Flag Shipping requirements of 32 CFR, para. 1.309(b) (2) (Suppl. 1958).

148 US–Italy Agreement, 22 June 1957, 8 UST & DIA 881, *TIAS*, no. 3850.

149 1954 *House Hearings*, p. 63.

150 See text under '"Surplus agricultural commodities and relief aid" preferences', pp. 170–71.

151 See Commission for Education Exchange Agreement between US and Paraguay, April 1957, 1957 SUST & DIA 946, *TIAS*, no. 3856.

152 Cargo Preference Act 1954 as amended by Cargo Preference Act 1974.

4 Shipping discriminations in international trade

Introduction

Flag discrimination is a development from flag preference; it is a less liberal mechanism designed to strengthen development and protective measures. In many respects it has all the characteristics of flag preference, being its continuation and having the experience of flag preference behind it. 'Discrimination' derives from the verb 'to discriminate' meaning: to note the difference of or between; to select from others; treat differently because of prejudice.[1]

Flag discrimination has its roots in the USA where, with reference to common carriers, especially railroads, it involves a breach of the carrier's duty to treat all shippers alike, and afford them equal opportunity to market their products. Although originating as an interstate and non-discriminatory concept of a carrier's failure to treat all alike under similar conditions, flag discrimination was developed in the USA and used as a protective and expansionist device directed against foreign flags in export and import trade.[2]

Thus, in merchant marine terms, discrimination and the criteria of flag discrimination were outlined in the preceding chapter and will be developed more fully in the succeeding chapters. As noted earlier, no suitable definition as yet exists for this term, except that it is a generic term for a series of activities directed mainly at a foreign flag with regard to access to cargoes, ports or services with the objective of making it less competitive.[3] Therefore, for the purposes of this discussion, the actions in question may be described and explained thus:

> Flag discrimination is a measure employed by a state which interferes with international maritime transport and provides less favourable treatment for other flags than for the national flag.[4]

Though sometimes mistaken for, and used interchangeably with, flag preference, flag discrimination can frequently be distinguished in that it covers a wider area than flag preference which, in most cases, is a restrictive discrimination regarding cargoes. It will become apparent from the examples in both cases that flag preference is more common and probably more tolerated than flag discrimination.[5] The varied categories of flag discrimination practices can be grouped under the following four major headings:

1 Port surcharges
   (a) Berth and port discrimination
   (b) Fees and surcharges
2 Scheduled cargoes
   (a) Itemized cargoes
   (b) Energy transportation
   (c) Defence transportation
   (d) Government supplies
3 Essential trade routes and others
4 CIF/FOB and miscellaneous discriminations

However, these are only broad categories and the list is by no means complete.[6] In addition, some of these categories might overlap with examples listed under flag preference and state intervention respectively. For example, scheduled cargoes have many characteristics in common with state-financed cargoes. Although there are also many basic differences, the two concepts share the same principles and objectives, namely: first, to protect national fleets from external competition; and, second, to aid their development or expansion. This is probably true despite the occasional denial by the practising countries that this is not the case.[7] Indeed, in an elaborate questionnaire sent by the UNCTAD secretariat to all maritime nations, requesting them to list the types of flag discrimination, flag preference, maritime subsidies and state intervention practised by them, very few bothered to reply. And even the few who did reply largely denied imposing any restrictions in favour of their national flags against foreign flags.[8]

Port Surcharges and Discriminatory Fees

The point of contact between a nation and the outside world regarding international commercial exchanges is at international airports and seaports[9] and at road and rail border posts. Discrimination is therefore bound to occur at any of the last three points, since only an insignificant amount of trade is airlifted. Here we shall concern ourselves with seaports, since the concept of flag is more associated with ships and aircraft than railroads or road transport.

Port Discriminations

From a purely commercial point of view this is perhaps the least subtle flag discrimination; not to mention probably one of the most unfair and least tolerated. In many ways this discrimination is related to the subsequent example of discriminatory fees. However, as in all other restrictive shipping practices, the idea behind port and berth discrimination is principally twofold: to give preference to national carriers and, at the same time, to discriminate against foreign flag vessels.[10]

The first instance is the treatment of ships in port. This practice can take the form of hindering the activities of selected countries' ships by placing them in a worse position than the national ships. Thus, for example, unloading and loading of the said ships in the port is sometimes deliberately delayed.[11] The demurrage and other surcharges incurred prevent the affected ships from obtaining freight incomes. Also, it is not unknown for a country to have higher tariffs for foreign ships and lower (or no) tariffs for their own flag vessels.[12]

The same discriminatory principles are repeated as regards access to berths, so that permission to berth is not granted on a first-come-first-served basis as would normally be the case. A domestic liner that comes in later would receive berth clearance before an earlier-arriving foreign flag vessel.[13] Alternatively, a certain sector of modern, well-equipped and efficient berths may be reserved for domestic vessels only, with foreign flag vessels being directed to wait or to proceed to outmoded, less sheltered and probably inefficient ports or berths at some distance away.[14] We have already seen that, where the ports are not seaports but inland river ports, cabotage restrictions may be used as another argument for discriminating against foreign flags. Consequently, in terms of giving the home flags an unfair lead or economic advantage, port and/or berth flag discrimination may be totally unjustified,[15] especially where it ranges from allocating cargo 'to national flags first' to all sorts of absurd practices.

However, besides the justification of having to ensure some trade for the national flag, other perceptible advantages, accruing to the interests of ocean-borne commerce and which may often be labelled flag discrimination, can be gained from port regulations and planning. In the case of port congestion, there is good reason to want to re-route other vessels to other berths or even other ports. This is more so as regards lucrative ports and/or central-popular berths.[16] Unfortunately, the vessels re-routed may happen to be mainly foreign flags. Another reason could be that the particular port is government-controlled, for example, where government supplies (see pp. 193–5) and, at times, urgently required emergency relief cargo is loaded and unloaded.

Such discrimination might be unpopular but should be understandable. Moreover, it is not entirely without precedent in other forms of transportation — for example, in air transport.[17] Just as the national airlines might enjoy priority at national airports where the national headquarters are located, it may be only fair that similar treatment is accorded or extended to national merchant marine vessels in national seaports, a place they should, after all, regard as home.[18]

Not all port discrimination is practised for commercial reasons or with the aim of protecting and expanding national merchant fleets. There are those which function solely in support of a principle. For example, most, if not all, socialist countries do not allow FOCs into their ports as a policy which constitutes their contribution to the UNCTAD efforts to discourage and eventually phase out open registry.[19] That would doubtless form a valid rationale, in some circles, for port discrimination. Yet other forms of flag discrimination may result from a country's commitment to fulfil an international obligation. As in the case of sanctions' discrimination in support of UN embargoes, discussed later (pp. 206–7), certain countries discriminate against South African or Israeli flag vessels by total exclusion from their seaports, airports and air space in case of hostile aircraft.[20] Beyond isolating this as a form of flag discrimination, its merits and demerits are beyond our scope to question.

I have also consistently maintained the defence and security aspects of flag discrimination, the full impact and examples of which will be dealt with later.[21] Suffice it to say, at this stage, that some ports with, or near naval, military or other similar installations vital to a country's national interest may be exclusively out of bounds to foreign flags and what would normally be regarded as hostile or not-too-friendly states. The reasons behind this policy may be economic as well as protective of security — i.e. fear of espionage and sabotage.[22] This is particularly so if the same principles are applied to berths or ports within proximity of economic and research installations — for example, space research stations, oil terminals or rigs, and other offshore activities. This is particularly common in the TMNs. This discussion confirms our argument that flag discrimination arises partly from states' mistrust of each other as well as in the belief that restrictions can be used for advancing economic, political and security objectives.[23]

Another example of this kind of discrimination is expenditure that particularly affects foreign vessels and cargo carried by foreign vessels — commonly known as discriminatory fees and surcharges.

Discriminatory Fees and Surcharges

The object of this kind of flag discrimination is to institute some kind of resource transfer from foreign vessels to the home governments; these resources would then hopefully be redeployed in the establishment, development and expansion of national fleets, with some part being applied to improve the domestic port systems and other maritime-related infrastructures. But it is an abhorrent type of resource transfer, being mandatorily applied.[24] The other objection to this taxation-type transfer is that it is penal. The first category, therefore, involves tonnage measurement, whereby the fleets of different countries are classified in different ways, by means of which discrimination is exercised. Fees based on such classifications are also varied — to the benefit of the home fleet.[25] The second category is discrimination relating to consular fees which affect the ships of different nations to different degrees. Such measures can be significant when the consular fees are very high. For instance, the charges for small quantities of cargo can be almost as high as the freight itself.[26] Thirdly, there are discriminations in charging pilot fees which points to the hardships and extra costs to foreign flag vessels.[27]

Then there are taxes on the freight incomes of foreign shipping companies. On the one hand, expenditure that affects cargo carried by foreign vessels is more of an island or internal measure. On the other hand, there is discrimination with respect to railway tariff rates, whereby goods that have been brought into the country by the country's own ships are allowed lower railway freight rates.[28] Paradoxically, the freights of the home-flag vessels can, as a consequence, be charged at a higher rate than those of the foreign flag vessels — higher (not lower), in order to make it lucrative for the internal railway system to pick it up first.[29] Then there is discrimination concerning duties, whereby cargoes which arrive by foreign flag ships are taxed with a higher duty, which is discriminatory against foreign shipping companies.[30]

The list is endless. Among the few advantages of this type of flag discrimination is that it enhances the competitiveness of the home flag and raises revenue which in some cases may be badly needed. As to whether a significant amount can be raised to be ploughed back into port investments is another matter.[31] Apart from being penal there is the danger that foreign flags could be driven away by prohibitive charges thereby defeating the whole purpose of the scheme. O'Loughlin noted correctly that: 'In practice there have been cases of these taxes being so penal as to constitute virtual prohibition of the foreign flag vessel.'[32] The other point worth noting is that such taxes are always passed on to the customers, thereby making the goods passing through a discriminating port very expensive. There is also the question whether ports ought to be making excessive profits, or any at all, as opposed to providing a service and only charging enough to cover their operational costs.[33] One would tend to agree with the *Rochdale Report* that:

> In principle, we consider that the charge payable should be related to the length of time for which a ship uses the port facilities and the nature of the facilities required. In this way the charges paid by a ship using them would be related to the costs incurred by the port authority in providing them . . . .[34]

and that these proposals are consistent with the long-term policy, set out in paragraph 18 of the White Paper, *Nationalised Industries, A Review of Economic and Financial Objectives*, which states that:

> . . . pricing policies should be devised with reference to the costs of the particular goods and services provided . . . . The aim of pricing policy should be that the consumer should pay the true costs of providing the goods and services he consumes, in every case where these can be sensibly identified.[35]

Scheduled Cargoes

Where surcharges are not the criteria, scheduled cargoes may be the yardstick for flag discriminations. Flag discrimination implies that a country's national flag has to carry most, if not all, of the export and import cargoes generated by that country's international trade.[36] Nowhere is this better illustrated than in relation to that cargo which the country is best able to produce, by virtue of the law of comparative advantage, or that which that country considers to be of vital priority and in the national interest.[37] It is presumed that in most cases such cargoes, if artificially directed to the home flag, would alone manage to sustain a viable national fleet. These fall under four major headings:

1 Itemized or designated cargoes
2 Energy transportation
3 Defence and security transportation
4 Government supplies.

Itemized or Designated Cargoes

Known alternatively as essential commodities, this discriminatory scheme, referring to both exports and imports,[38] is used to exclude foreign merchant marines altogether from certain selected cargoes. Briefly, there are certain cargoes that are of crucial or strategic importance to particular nations for various reasons, and such cargoes are consequently recommended to be carried only, or as much as possible, in national flag vessels. They could comprise a particular country's major exports and, therefore, its largest foreign exchange earner; this would be the case especially with a single-crop country,[39] which would wish freight from its transportation to go to the national flag. As in the case of Japan, the scheme could be directed specifically at less bulky, but high-value freight especially compact computers, hi-fis and other valuable electronic or communications equipment.[40]

But a classic example of the use of scheduled cargo discrimination as a means of developing a country's national fleet is when a country wishes to diversify its fleet by developing a particular type of vessel regarded as crucial but not already forming part of its fleet.[41] The argument normally advanced by the country concerned is that necessity is the mother of invention. Demand generates supply: make the cargo scheduled and you will obtain the type of vessel that carries it.[42] It is conceivable that this is how modern prestigious ships such as ROROs, LASH (Lighters Aboard Ship), LNGs (Liquefied natural gas carriers), OBOs (oil-bulk-oil combine carriers), supertankers, etc., were originally acquired by the flags who own them.[43] Spain, presumably for this reason, restricts many scheduled imports, such as petroleum, tobacco, cotton, etc., to national vessels through state monopolies.[44] But the absurd way in which such a development objective can be stubbornly pursued, regardless of any notions of sound economic principle, is well illustrated by the American case.

The experience of the Pacific Coast apple industry illustrated this callous disregard of commercial considerations, and the administrative rigidity that has characterized the USA's requirement to diversify her fleet by the use of scheduled cargo processes.[45] The case in point arose when the required refrigerator tonnage off the West Coast for sales to Europe was virtually non-existent in 1952-53 even though there was a 'reefer' tonnage available on the East Coast.[46] The Federal Maritime Board (FMB) insisted on a protracted delay until a refrigerator was built, and refused application for waiver under the 50-50 cargo preference provision which, *inter alia*, could have meant using the already available reefer tonnage lying idle on the East Coast.[47] Thus, despite these difficulties, the importance of the time involved and the fact that the government would have suffered no loss (these being surplus agricultural commodities and relief shipments), the Department of Agriculture persisted in applying the 1954 Cargo Preference Act[48] to the letter on a commodity-by-commodity basis.

So the apple sellers could not rely on the possibility of commodity waivers as these would be offset in shipments of some other commodity. The Christmas 1952-3 trade with Britain, for example, was lost as a result, even though there was never any question that the waiver would have been in order. The same situation held for the sales of surplus fresh fruit products as well as animal products.[49] The FMB might have ended with a diversified merchant marine, with the addition of the refrigerated vessels, but with no cargo to carry that year since the crop was lost. About thirty years later, the development argument was still fanatically being pursued by the Americans, this time in the form of energy transportation.

Energy Transportation

This time the use of flag discrimination for development purposes manifested itself in the controversial Energy Transportation Security Act of 1975[50] which requires a minimum of 20 per cent cargo reservation for American flag vessels.[51] But, at its initial stages, the bill surmounted stiff opposition in both Houses to get its development provisions accepted. President Ford at first vetoed it, stating that the development requirements would have an adverse impact on foreign relations, and would create serious inflationary pressures by increasing oil costs.[52] However, because of the consequences of the Arab-Israeli war (which the bill was out to remedy in the first place) and intense lobbying,[53] it was eventually passed by Congress on the basis of:

1   national security;
2   recent administrative action supportive of flag discrimination;
3   increased domination of foreign trade by flag fleets of foreign states.[54]

To emphasize further the security reasons for the use of flag

190

discrimination it was asserted that the USA must be able to supply its armed forces and domestic consumers with fuel and supplies in times of crisis. It was pointed out by the pro-development lobby group that, at that time, there was a reliance upon large numbers of tankers and ships which sailed under foreign flags,[55] but which were owned by USA citizens or corporations. Such vessels were subject to requisitioning by the Secretary of Commerce: 'Whenever the President shall proclaim that the security of the national defence makes it advisable, or during any national emergency declared by proclamation of the President.'[56] The use of flag discrimination for development purposes seems to grow from strength to strength whenever the merchant marine industry finds itself playing a leading role in national defence. For instance, in the American case, an incident that added urgency and necessity to energy transportation flag discrimination concerned the Arab–Israeli war.[57] Despite the fact that the Panlibho fleets are entitled to US war-risk insurance in return for being US 'effective control fleets', the Liberian restrictions on the use of these vessels, by the US for military purposes, questioned the legal basis of the US requisition claim in the event of the flag state opposition. And reports, at the time, that oil shipments to US armed forces were withheld by oil companies during the 1973 Arab–Israeli war,[58] alarmed the Americans and encouraged the initiation of this legislation.

For this reason, Representative Frank Clark, reflecting the position of many of the bill's supporters argued that: 'Today we are engaged in a worldwide conflict for oil. For the good of our country, we must never forget that in this conflict foreign flag tankers are manned by mercenaries . . . .'[59] Thus, in this context energy transportation flag discrimination had economic as well as defence and security elements. No doubt, after the crucial role that the merchant navy played in the Falklands crisis, the Development School, on both sides of the Atlantic, will be in greater ascendency regarding both energy transportation and the defence transportation itself.

Defence and Security Transportation

Defence and national security, in addition to politics and economics, are fast emerging as the major motives for flag discrimination and flag preference.[60] Supposedly for fear of espionage and sabotage, various countries are keen to prevent what they schedule as security shipments falling into enemy hands through the use of foreign and often unfriendly flag vessels. For this purpose, defence and security means and includes shipments for a country's own or allied defence (as, for example, in the NATO and Warsaw Pact), and shipments of defence aid to other friendly countries.[61] Although this type of cargo could

191

be airlifted (where urgently required) or shipped in existing normal vessels, including those belonging to allies and other friendly nations, countries have often ignored these alternatives and insisted on establishing and/or developing their national merchant fleets for the purpose[62] — the argument being that it would be very unwise to entrust supplies for immediate combat use to foreigners. And this argument includes not only the cargoes in question but encompasses a wider jurisprudential meaning: military intelligence, political, diplomatic, economic and almost all confidential and top security shipments.[63]

To get an idea of what this means, a few examples can be given, especially from the TMNs. In Portugal, for instance, without prejudice to bilateral agreements, all Portuguese cargoes shipped to the military or scientific research bases existing or to be established in Portuguese territory must be carried exclusively in the national bottoms.[64] However, the most noteworthy example of this flag discrimination comes from the USA. The first cargo preference statute of that country provided that ocean transportation for the army and navy coal, fodder supplies and provisions must be carried on US flag vessels.[65] This statute is still operative, though in an amended form.[66] Secondly, exclusive use of US flag vessels is required for shipments owned by the government and in possession of the Military Department, and which are intended for the use of the military department — whatever all that elaboration means.[67]

The discrimination extends beyond the usual exclusion coverage, for instance with respect to: 'Supplies for the use of the United States which are contracted for and require subsequent delivery to a military department but are not owned by the government at the time of shipment . . . .'[68] Private vessels (if available at fair and reasonable rates) must be employed to transport at least 50 per cent of the aggregate gross tonnage and tankers' capacity.[69] There are no statistics available to show that this type of flag discrimination has aided the expansion of the US flag fleets despite the fact that, since 1904, these items have included enormous shipments of coal, provisions, fodder or supplies,[70] and despite the fact that the list has been lengthened to include federal officers and employee travel,[71] as well as transportation of effects and automobiles.[72]

At the other end of the spectrum, in the DMNs, a random example is provided by the Philippine practice. Inevitably, however, this is all tied in with the American example. The Philippines,[73] like most of the other members of the Association of South East Asian Nations (ASEAN) with a mutual defence pact with the USA through the South East Asian Treaty Organization (SEATO), is another of these security-conscious nations. For example, all imports of US agricultural commodities under s.402 of the US government's Mutual Defence Security Act (Public Law No. 480)[74] which are in excess of the 50 per cent required to be carried on US flag vessels, must be shipped in Philippine flag vessels when available. One can understand the advantage of a nation having a merchant marine capable of coping with wars, hostilities and emergencies; but its economic opportunity cost must be enormous.[75]

One must be aware that wars are not fought all the time and that there is the danger of establishing and expanding a large war-footing merchant navy which would be expensive to maintain but idle most of the time.[76] This is so because such a merchant navy would have to be larger than was necessary for the trade requirements of a nation at any given time. Even if that were not the case, as the Falklands crisis has shown, its application to defence seriously interrupts the normal economic activities of a merchant navy.[77] On the other hand, rather than having an economically useless standing naval reserve, disruption of economic life is the price the community would have to pay whenever the merchant marine is diverted to fight wars. One problem that remains, however, is the difficulty of distinguishing defence and security shipments from purely government shipments.[78]

Government Supplies

We should note that government supplies are not necessarily the same as the state-financed cargoes discussed above.[79] Although there is a great deal of similarity between the two, government supplies should be understood to mean supplies intended for use by the central government and its departments, including the public sector.[80] Alternatively known as government-controlled cargoes, they are mainly imports intended for government use or exports intended for diplomatic and consular use.[81] In this latter aspect, they include vehicles, stationery, diplomatic bags, provisions and even food rations. Government supplies would not normally include military hardware and provisions — these would belong to the categories of defence and security — but modern requirements imply that the bulk of government supplies is based on military considerations.[82]

Another factor that adds importance to this scheme of flag discrimination is that currently there are so many foreign troops from the powerful nations stationed abroad, normally in the less developed and deprived world, that enormous shipments are continuously being made for home ports to support them and their dependants.[83] Among the TMNs, only one other example, apart from the USA, is worth mentioning. I mentioned earlier that, in Portugal, all cargoes shipped by the public sector entities must be carried in Portuguese flag vessels or foreign flag ships chartered by Portuguese shipowners, except in the case of reciprocal or international agreements providing for other arrangements.[84] Up to 50 per cent of such cargoes can be carried on ships of the importing or exporting country, if the laws of that country concede equal treatment for Portuguese flag vessels.

However, as indicated above, by far the most outstanding illustration remains that of the USA. In addition to examples given above, supplies for research purposes (e.g., space programmes or for outposts in the Arctic and the Antarctic) and to those countries heavily dependent on US foreign aid fall under this category.[85] Undoubtedly, the Department of Defense is the largest shipper of government supplies and, further, categorizes its supplies into two main types for purposes of flag discrimination: government-owned supplies in its possession or that of a contractor; and government supplies, including those for foreign aid, contracted for but not owned by the government at the time of shipment.[86] For instance, supplies of the first category, when for the use of military departments, are subject to the 100 per cent US flag preference, unless US flag vessels are not available at fair and reasonable rates.[87] Both the motives for, and the sophistication of, the application of modern flag discrimination is ensured by requiring insertion of one of three clauses in any contract under which title to property may pass to the government prior to shipment[88] − a clause is inserted in the contract requiring the shipment only as directed by the contracting officer who is guided by the regulations and applicable departmental procedures.[89] The shipment must be made only by US flag vessels in the circumstances discussed above. Secondly, when the supplies are contracted for, but not government-owned at the time of shipment, a clause is inserted in the contract allowing the contractor to choose his own method of transportation, but requiring him to furnish to the contracting officer one copy of the applicable ocean shipping documents indicating, for each shipment under the contract, the name and nationality of the vessel and the measurement tonnage shipped on such a vessel.[90] Thirdly, the defence regulations also provide that additional provisions concerning vessels to be used may be inserted in accordance with departmental procedures.[91] Accordingly, Navy procurements directives permit additional provisions allowing the contracting officer to determine, where possible, in large shipments, when and how compliance with the 50 per cent requirement is to be achieved.[92] However, none of these Department of Defense regulations applies to shipments of classified supplies where the classification prohibits the use of non-governmental vessels.[93] Furthermore, the use of government vessels is encouraged to meet essential military requirements involving special transportation services which cannot be

194

performed by the privately owned and operated merchant fleet; such a category may include peacetime troop transport taken over by private American shipowners.[94]

As regards flag discrimination of government supplies in the DMNs, one example that immediately comes to mind is that of Ecuador.[95] In this latter case all imports and exports which are the property of the government or its enterprises, or of public entities or private institutions which are intended for social or public purposes, as well as cargo belonging to mixed companies in which the government owns more than 50 per cent of the capital, are obliged to be transported in vessels owned by national shipping companies or by those which cargo reservation laws consider as such. However, 59 per cent of the cargo may be transported on vessels belonging to the importing or exporting country provided this is done on the basis of reciprocity.[96] There is not much emphasis on defence-related cargoes in the DMNs as regards government supplies. However, in modern times the distinction between government supplies and defence shipments may be very thin indeed or even non-existent.[97]

The merits of state supplies as a motive for flag discrimination cannot be overemphasized. Security compels states to restrict defence shipments to their own national flags or those of military allies.[98] However, this kind of flag discrimination is practised more for policy than development reasons. Even if it were for the latter reasons these cargoes normally constitute a very small proportion of any country's shipments. Not only are they insignificant, therefore, but they are also normally referred to as non-commercial cargoes,[99] and are only available for ordinary private merchant vessels where military or government-owned vessels are unavailable. Figures are not available to indicate the extent to which this type of flag discrimination might have contributed towards the expansion of the merchant marines of those countries that practise it.[100] A mechanism most likely to influence such expansion is essential routes flag discriminations.

Essential Trade Routes Discriminations

As in most of the other forms of discrimination, the essential trade routes doctrine has its origins in American jurisprudence. Resorted to for both policy and development motives, there appear to be two categories of essential trade routes: those that are not commercially viable and therefore need subsidies and the protective measures of flag discrimination; and those that are both commercially viable and geopolitically strategic.[101] The strategic importance of the latter indicates their being set aside exclusively for the domestic flags. To the former category belong sea routes leading to remote and normally underdeveloped regions within the country itself, the neglect of which may lead to the stagnation or lagging behind of the affected districts.[102] These routes are normally commercially unprofitable but politics dictate their maintenance nevertheless.

In the first place, these routes are declared designated or simply essential routes.[103] Secondly, services to these areas are maintained or only made possible through maritime transportation subsidies. The next step is that the said routes become sheltered from competition through flag discrimination and other preferential means. In the case of the United Kingdom such essential trade routes may be those serving the outlying islands, like the Shetlands and the Hebrides in the North of Scotland.[104] In the case of the DMNs, such as the archipelagic countries of South East Asia, the routes may be to one of the deprived islands.[105] The second category normally consists of militarily strategic and/or economically lucrative routes, such as the North Atlantic which serves North America and Western Europe, and carries the largest volume of trade linking the world's most industrialized regions. And from the security point of view it is the mainstay of NATO.

Since the doctrine is essentially an American creation, and although many other countries have since adopted the practice in designating their own essential trade routes, it is nonetheless to the USA that we shall turn for the definition, descriptions, principles and motives involved.[106] It will be remembered that there are links with the condition attached to the recipients of foreign aid. For example, to qualify for a maritime subsidy (discussed below), shipping companies must, *inter alia*, operate vessels on what are designated as essential trade routes. But what exactly are essential trade routes? MARAD has defined an essential trade route as:

> A route between ports of the United States coast area or areas to foreign markets which has been determined by the Maritime Administration to be *essential for the promotion, development, expansion, and maintenance of the foreign commerce of the United States.*[107] [Emphasis added]

By 1952, thirty-one essential trade routes had been designated on the basis of considerations involving economic, geopolitic, national defence and steamship economics. Emphasizing its economic role, the *Murray Report*, for instance, declared that:

> The essential trade route concept is sound and has contributed to the economic stability of the liner segment of our merchant fleet in the foreign

trades. However, constant scrutiny of all trades should be given in order to ensure that the granting of subsidy aid is in keeping with the traffic needs of essential trade routes.[108]

The link between maritime subsidies and flag discriminations and the policy issues involved in both perhaps comes out most clearly in the operation of essential trade routes.

Operating differential subsidies, for instance, were granted only to companies that scheduled sailings on one or more of the USA's then thirty-one essential trade routes. It may be interesting to note that those routes were designated essential by the FMC on 20 May 1946, and were found to be, in the words of the Merchant Marine Act 1936, also 'essential for the promotion, development, expansion and maintenance of the foreign commerce of the United States'.[109] Further, under Section 211 of the Act, the FMC was instructed to:

> . . . give due weight to the cost of maintaining each of such steam ship lines on essential trade routes, the probability that any such line cannot be maintained except at heavy losses disproportionate to the benefit accruing to foreign trade, the number of sailings and types of vessels that should be employed in such lines and any other facts and conditions that a prudent businessman would consider when dealing with his own business, with the added consideration, however, of the intangible benefits the maintenance of any such line may afford to the foreign commerce of the United States and to the national defence.[110]

The proponents of maritime subsidies and flag discriminations have always justified them on the grounds that they have been recognized by this piece of legislation. For instance, in reviewing the essential trade routes, as early as 1953, the FMC noted that:

> . . . present day influences in the world are different from those influences which exerted force in 1936 when the initial concepts regarding trade routes existed . . . . As a result of recent world events other factors . . . must be considered, for the reason that their influence is, of increased importance to the national welfare of the United States.[111]

Therein lie the origins, purposes, characteristics, and importance of flag discriminations and maritime subsidies, in general, and the essential trade route doctrine in particular, seen, at least, from the US point of view.

As mentioned above, MARAD also listed four basic areas of consideration as paramount in the determination of essential trade routes. Under the first category of economics, the factors considered in designating and operating a subsidized essential trade route generally underline the said objectives. These are:

1 Comparison of the trade area with total trade as to exports, imports, dollar balance exchange, and post-war and pre-war trends in these items;
2 The significance of the trade to the economy of the USA as measured by such factors as the importance of exports and imports to the US economy, the competition between American and foreign goods, and raw materials and resource potentials;
3 Domestic industrial relocation and development as they are related to trade;
4 Trade inhibitions — tariffs, currency restrictions, quantitative restrictions and licencing systems.[112]

These criteria are quite in line with the general purposes of the establishment and development of national merchant marines, and this is a conclusive and self-explanatory list of these objectives. Neither is there anything unusual about the geopolitical factors, which include:

1 Climate, geographical position and strategic position;
2 Aid programme;
3 United States and its defence;
4 Political effects of US flag shipping on the routes;
5 Influence of the trade route on so-called fringe nations;
6 Development of trade and of trade possibilities because of political factors;
7 The competitive position of the products of the changed political status of foreign areas.[113]

And, as expected, military considerations include such factors as:

1 Direction of movement of military cargoes;
2 Stock-piling activities;
3 The advantages of increased exports to areas near trade routes essential to the national defence.[114]

These objectives would seem to cover almost every other aspect of the national economy — especially those pertaining to trade. And, finally, steam ship economics encompasses judgements about many matters, among them:

1 Delimiting the trade areas to conform to economic ship-operating practices;

2 The service requirements of the areas, and the characteristics of
   the vessels to be employed;
3 The type of foreign competition to be encountered.[115]

As in all the other aspects of the use of flag discrimination as a
tool for development, it is not possible to determine with acceptable
accuracy the effects of the policy of fixing essential trade routes
upon the USA or, indeed, any national merchant marine and its
foreign competitors. MARAD will not release data that would reveal
the percentage of cargoes carried by subsidized operators on each
trade route for fear of competition and, probably, the figures would
not be particularly encouraging. However, in 1952, liners of all flags
lifted about 35 million long tons of dry cargo on the US essential
trade routes alone, with the US flag vessels managing only 35 per
cent of that. These do not appear to be encouraging statistics but
then essential trade route flag discriminations had just come into
operation. Although subsequent figures have not been available
from which to appraise the scheme, at least for that year, subsidized
liners were overwhelmingly important in carrying the US flag vessels'
share of dry-cargo tonnage on essential trade routes and was far
higher than on other unprotected routes though, again, the data do
not permit the inference that the establishment of certain routes as
essential has attracted US liners to them.

There may be indications that the designation of a trade route as
essential, plus the presence of subsidized operators, does not necessarily lead to US shipping companies and, indeed, shipping companies
of any other nations, gaining a sufficiently large share of available
dry cargoes to enable their expansion. It also appears that the mere
designation of a route as essential by MARAD does not necessarily
adversely affect foreign shipping lines.[117] Essential trade route
designation only indirectly affects foreigners or the discriminated
flag. Non-subsidized American as well as foreign flags are also
affected. Finally, the granting of operating differential subsidies
only to the liner operators on essential trade routes gives a substantial assistance.[118] This seems to be the case whether the
discriminating country is a TMN or DMN.

At the other end of the spectrum, an example of essential trade
route flag discrimination from a DMN is that of the Republic of
South Korea, which in many respects is almost identical with the
US policy. In South Korea, too, the government may order any
maritime transportation businessman receiving subsidy or loan, to
operate his ship on a specific domestic or international essential
trade route for a fixed period.[119] Any loss from this service will be
compensated in a manner prescribed by a Presidential Decree. When

the ship concerned in the subsidized essential trade route is considered too old for its purpose, the government may order the substitution or improvement of the ship and may itself bear the loss caused by such substitution or improvement. However, there is an element of internal flag discrimination as well.[120] Government substitution and improvement is not confined to operators in essential trade taking precedence over others in the domestic construction of ships. Likewise, when a maritime transportation businessman operates his ship on a regular international and/or essential trade route for the promotion of foreign trade and to earn foreign currency the government may subsidize any loss he sustains, as prescribed by the said Presidential Decree.[121]

South Korea is one of the emerging NICs with a good economic performance. She is also one of the many DMNs relying heavily on maritime subsidies and flag discrimination. She has achieved a marked expansion in her foreign trade with a corresponding expansion of her merchant marine and shipbuilding to match that trade boom. It is not clear how much of that establishment and expansion is attributable to maritime subsidies and flag discrimination, generally, and essential trade routes designation in particular.[122] Despite this, most other DMNs, who are not also NICs, have not achieved similar expansions in their merchant marines, despite heavy dependence on maritime subsidies and flag discrimination. Although South Korea's expansion in the maritime sector can be linked directly to her better overall economic performance, yet there might be some correlation between the flag discrimination, trade performance and expansion of the merchant marine sector.[123] It could be the case of the flag following trade rather than vice versa.

CIF Discriminations

There are many other flag discriminatory mechanisms operated by various countries in an effort to develop and expand their national merchant fleets. I am unable to discuss all of them for reasons of time and space. Even if that were not the case I do not think the said mechanisms would markedly aid the merchant marines to any significant level. One or two are, however, worth mentioning. The first of these are CIF shipments. The letters CIF when used in a mercantile agreement for the sale of goods involving shipment, denote that the sum named in the agreement includes the cost of the goods, insurance during the transit to the purchaser and freight: CIF (cost insurance freight) for short.[124]

A. The seller must:

1 Supply the goods in conformity with the contract of sale together with such evidence of conformity as may be required by the contract.

2 Contract on usual terms at his own expense for the carriage of the goods to the agreed port of destination by the usual route, in a sea-going vessel (not being a sailing vessel) of the type normally used for the transport of goods of the contract description, and pay freight charges and any charges for unloading at the port of discharge which may be levied by regular shipping lines at the time and port of shipment.[125]

3 At his own risk and expense obtain any export licence or other governmental authorization necessary for the export of the goods.

4 Load the goods at his own expense on board the vessel at the port of shipment and at the date or within the period fixed or, if neither date nor time has been stipulated, within a reasonable time, and notify the buyer, without a delay, that the goods have been loaded on board the vessel.

5 Procure, at his own cost and in a transferable form, a policy or marine insurance against the risks of carriage involved in the contract. The insurance shall be contracted with underwriters or insurance companies of good repute on FPA terms, and shall cover the CIF price plus ten per cent. The insurance shall be provided in the currency of the contract, if procurable.[126]

Unless otherwise agreed, the risks of carriage shall not include special risks that are covered in specific trades or against which the buyer may wish individual protection. Among the special risks that should be considered and agreed upon between seller and buyer are theft, pilferage, leakage, breakage, chipping, sweat, contact with other cargoes and others peculiar to any particular trade.

When required by the buyer, the seller shall provide, at the buyer's expense, war risk insurance in the currency of the contract, if procurable.

6 Subject to the provisions of article B.4 below, bear all risks of the goods until such time as they shall have effectively passed the ship's rail at the port of shipment.[127]

7 At his own expense furnish to the buyer without delay a clean negotiable bill of lading for the agreed port of destination, as well as the invoice of the goods shipped and the insurance policy or, should the insurance policy not be available at the time the documents are tendered, a certificate of insurance issued under the authority of the underwriters and conveying to the bearer the same rights as if he were in possession of the policy and reproducing the essential provisions thereof. The bill of lading must cover the contract goods, be dated within the period agreed for shipment, and provide by endorsement or otherwise for delivery to the order of the buyer or buyer's agreed representative. Such bill of lading must be a full set of 'on board' or 'shipped' bills of lading, or a 'received for shipment' bill of lading duly endorsed by the shipping company to the effect that the goods are on board, such

endorsement to be dated within the period agreed for shipment. If the bill of lading contains a reference to the charter-party, the seller must also provide a copy of this latter document.

8   Provide at his own expense the customary packing of the goods, unless it is the custom of the trade to ship the goods unpacked.[128]

9   Pay the costs of any checking operations (such as checking quality, measuring, weighing, counting) which shall be necessary for the purpose of loading the goods.

10   Pay any dues and taxes incurred in respect of the goods up to the time of their loading, including any taxes, fees or charges levied because of exportation, as well as the costs of any formalities which he shall have to fulfil in order to load the goods on board.

11   Provide the buyer, at the latter's request, risk and expense, (see B.5) with the certificate of origin and the consular invoice.

12   Render the buyer, at the latter's request risk and expense, every assistance in obtaining any documents, other than those mentioned in the previous article, issued in the country of shipment and/or of origin and which the buyer may require for the importation of the goods into the country of destination (and, where necessary, for their passage in transit through another country).[129]

B. The buyer must:

1   Accept the documents when tendered by the seller, if they are in conformity with the contract of sale, and pay the price as provided in the contract.

2   Receive the goods at the agreed port of destination and bear, with the exception of the freight and marine insurance, all costs and charges incurred in respect of the goods in the course of their transit by sea until their arrival at the port of destination, as well as unloading costs, including lighterage and wharfage charges, unless such costs and charges shall have been included in the freight or collected by the steamship company at the time freight was paid.
     If war insurance is provided, it shall be at the expense of the buyer (see A.5).[130]

3   Bear all risks of the goods from the time when they shall have effectively passed the ship's rail at the port of shipment.

4   In case he may have reserved to himself a period within which to have the goods shipped and/or the right to choose the port of destination, and he fails to give instructions in time, bear the additional costs thereby incurred and all risks of the goods from the date of the expiration of the period fixed for shipment, provided always that the goods shall have been duly appropriated to the contract, that is to say, clearly set aside or otherwise identified as the contract goods.

5   Pay the costs and charges incurred in obtaining the certificate of origin and consular documents.

6   Pay all costs and charges incurred in obtaining the documents mentioned in article A.12 above.

7　Pay all customs duties as well as any other duties and taxes payable at the time of or by reason of the importation.

8　Procure and provide at his own risk and expense any import licence or permit or the like which he may require for the importation of the goods at destination.

It is the duty of the buyer to take up the documents and pay for them, and this is so whether or not the goods arrive, for if they are lost he will have the benefit of insurance.[131] The FOB contract, on the other hand, means 'Free on Board'. Under an ordinary FOB contract the seller puts the goods safely on board,[132] pays the charges of doing so, and for the buyer's protection — but is not under a mandate to do so except only upon terms of a reasonable and ordinary bill of lading or other contract of carriage[133] — and gives up possession of the documents to the ship. There is no further contractual liability on the seller as soon as he delivers the goods to the carrier; his obligations cease at that point. The buyer under an FOB contract cannot claim delivery of the goods before shipment.[134] So much for the purely legal position of the parties. The relevance of CIF and FOB shipments, regarding trade policies, lies especially in the way they affect the preferential and discriminatory status of various flag vessels in relation to access to cargoes and other related treatments.[135]

There are certain loopholes in the mechanism of the CIF and FOB contracts that have been exploited by national entities for discriminatory purposes. The disadvantage of the CIF, for instance, is that the consignor or seller has the right to choose the carrier and that could mean any carrier other than the flag carrier of the consignee's nationality or choice: thus, where flag discrimination exists in the consignor's country he would be duty-bound to use his national carrier for such exports. Where discrimination exists it is probable that the consignee's country would have preferred otherwise; this in effect involves loss to the consignee's national flag vessels not only of the freights but also of insurance premiums and the consequential loss of the foreign currency that would be involved.[136] On the FOB contracts, however, the situation is reversed; it is the consignee or buyer who chooses the carrier, and the assumptions are that he would prefer to be compelled to choose his national carrier. That being the case, freight and premiums will be earned by the consignee's national flag carrier and local insurance firms, respectively.[137]

In previous cases we saw how policy decisions interfere with or replace market forces. In this respect we see how policy decisions utilize the loopholes in the operation of market forces. In both cases, the sum total of the effects is that the choice and competition element is negated. There is, however, an element of consideration in return for the consignor/consignee's undertaking to ship with the national flag.[138] It will be apparent in the second part of this inquiry that, in return for subsidies, incentives, inducements and benefits, the consignors and consignees enter contracted undertakings with their governments to use domestic flags to make earnings and savings of foreign currency that would have been spent on foreign flags. It is assumed that national sentiment can also provide sufficient inducements to opt for the national flag.[139] We have had to discuss this at length, not because it makes a large contribution to the expansion of national fleets, but because of the light it sheds upon the complex mechanism that now constitutes modern flag discrimination.

FOB Discriminations

Another example of this type of flag discrimination is where it is stipulated that imported goods are to be quoted FOB after which currency is allotted with preference for cargoes shipped on the country's own keels, where a bilateral maritime agreement exists between the consignee and the consignor's countries.[140]

A. The seller must:

1 Supply goods in conformity with the contract of sale, together with such evidence of conformity as may be required by the contract.

2 Deliver the goods on board the vessel named by the buyer, at the named port of shipment, in the manner customary at the port, at the date or within the period stipulated, and notify the buyer, without delay, that the goods have been delivered on board.

3 At his own risk and expense obtain any export licence or other governmental authorization necessary for the export of the goods.

4 Subject to the provisions of articles B.3 and B.4 below, bear all costs and risks of the goods until such time as they shall have effectively passed the ship's rail at the named port of shipment, including any taxes, fees or charges levied because of exportation, as well as the costs of any formalities which he shall have to fulfil in order to load the goods on board.

5 Provide at his own expense the customary packing of the goods, unless it is the custom of the trade to ship the goods unpacked.

6 Pay the costs of any checking operations (such as checking quality, measuring, weighing, counting) which shall be necessary for the purposes of delivering the goods.

7 Provide at his own expense the customary clean document in proof of delivery of the goods on board the named vessels.

8   Provide the buyer, at the latter's request and expense (see B.6) with the certificate of origin.

9   Render the buyer, at the latter's request, risk and expense, every assistance in obtaining a bill of lading and any documents, other than that mentioned in the previous article, issued in the country of shipment and/or of origin and which the buyer may require for the importation of the goods into the country of destination (and, where necessary, for their passage in transit through another country).

B.   The buyer must:

1   At his own expense, charter a vessel or reserve the necessary space on board a vessel and give the seller due notice of the name, loading berth of and delivery dates to the vessel.

2   Bear all costs and risks of the goods from the time when they shall have effectively passed the ship's rail at the named port of shipment and pay the price as provided in the contract.

3   Bear any additional costs incurred because the vessel named by him shall have failed to arrive on the stipulated date or by the end of the period specified or shall be unable to take the goods or shall close for cargo earlier than the stipulated date or the end of the period specified and all the risks of the goods from the date of expiration of the period stipulated, provided, however, that the goods shall have been duly appropriated to the contract, that is to say, clearly set aside or otherwise identified as the contract goods.

4   Should he fail to name the vessel in time or, if he shall have reserved to himself a period within which to take delivery of the goods and/or the right to choose the port of shipment, should he fail to give detailed instructions in time, bear any additional costs incurred because of such failure, and all the risks of the goods from the date of expiration of the period stipulated for delivery, provided, however, that the goods shall have been duly appropriated to the contract, that is to say, clearly set aside or otherwise identified as the contract goods.

5   Pay any costs and charges for obtaining a bill of lading if incurred under article A.9 above.

6   Pay all costs and charges incurred in obtaining the documents mentioned in articles A.8 and A.9 above, including the costs of certificates of origin and consular documents.

Examples of this exist in the DMNs. In the Republic of Korea, for instance, the government encourages the use of Korean flag vessels by awarding some government procurement contracts on an FOB, rather than a CIF basis, thereby enabling these ships to compete on a more equal basis with the established fleets of the TMNs.[141] The extent to which this policy is successful is indicated by the relatively large ratio of cargoes carried by its ocean-going merchant fleet. During 1975, for instance, South Korean vessels carried about 33 per cent of Korean ocean-borne foreign trade. Furthermore, it was expected that South

Korean flag vessels would be handling approximately 44 per cent of the country's trade by 1978; that is an excellent ratio by any international standard, let alone by a DMN one.

Of course, the result could not entirely be attributable to the CIF/FOB policy, or indeed flag discrimination in general.[142] As noted above, the difficulty in making any inference is compounded by the fact that, South Korea being an NIC, its economy was expanding rapidly at the time. Nevertheless, it would be fairly safe to assume that the expansion of the South Korean merchant fleet is due, to a certain extent, to the operation of flag discrimination in general, and to CIF/FOB mechanisms in particular.

Our final illustration is also from a DMN, another Far Eastern NIC, the Philippines.[143] The Philippine Presidential Order No. 37, provides that all purchase of Filipino imports be made on an FOB basis; that all freight payments be made in pesos in the Philippines; and that preference on the carriage of imports be given to Philippine flag vessels. As in the case of South Korea, the Philippine CIF/FOB policy also seems to have aided the expansion of the national merchant fleet.[144] Though the Philippine record on this is not as impressive as that of her South Korean neighbour, it is nevertheless quite good. For example, largely due to the CIF/FOB policy, Philippine flag vessels carried an average close to 22 per cent of Philippine foreign trade in 1970 (24.3 per cent of imports and 19.4 per cent of exports). Figures for 1978 onwards are not yet available, but on this basis they would be good, if not better than the South Korean ones.[145] That being the case, just as in the South Korean example, the Philippines CIF/FOB policy would seem to have paid off.

Sanctions Discriminations

Finally, there are the types of discrimination which may not have direct bearing on the developments of national fleets. One of these comprises sanctions discriminations[146] which, though effected by a state, nonetheless support political and international obligations.

In international trade relations economic sanctions are a coercive but unenforceable measure that calls for the complete or partial interruption of economic relations with an unruly and perverse nation in an attempt to make it conform to international law.[147] Such a sanction is usually adopted by an international organization in dealing with the affairs of an uncooperative nation. In 1935, for example, the League of Nations imposed sanctions against Italy in an attempt to prevent its aggression against Ethiopia. These sanctions included an arms embargo, a financial embargo and a shipping embargo by way of trade restrictions against materials that were essential to Italy's war machine.[148] The Charter of the UN provides the groundwork for such action by that organization. Other regional organizations also impose sanctions; an example of the latter being the imposition of sanctions on the Dominican Republic by the members of the Organization of American States (OAS).[149]

Thus, sometimes a country is faced with a dilemma of having to discriminate against other and/or foreign flags for economic or any other reasons but in the furtherance of that country's obligations imposed on her by the international community under international law.[150] A more recent example concerned the United Kingdom. In 1965, Southern Rhodesia (now Zimbabwe), then a British colony, made a Unilateral Declaration of Independence (UDI) under settler leader Ian Smith. This was not only treason against Her Majesty's Government but also a contravention of the UN (Committee) De-colonization Policy.[151] Thus, there was a moral duty on the United Kingdom, as the Decolonizing Power and Permanent Member of the Security Council. Consequently the UN General Assembly passed a Resolution imposing sanctions on Rhodesia which the United Kingdom could not veto.[152]

These consisted of economic trade sanctions in general and an oil embargo in particular. The burden fell on the United Kingdom to ensure that neither exports nor imports entered or left Rhodesia. In fulfilment of this obligation the United Kingdom was duty-bound to maintain a naval fleet[153] at the Mozambican ports of Beira and Lourenço Marques (now Maputo) to ensure that merchant ships with cargo destined for Rhodesia did not enter and those with cargo from Rhodesia did not leave. For Britain this meant discriminations against the affected ships, including some of her own, that had attempted sanction-breaking.[154] Similar actions have been called against South Africa for her refusal to end racial discrimination (apartheid) by the minority whites against the majority black population. This demonstrates further how in international trade relations, shipping has played a crucial part in national life, international affairs, and economic and political functions.[155] The other type of sanctions involves discrimination by private individuals or private institutions (like conference discriminations) which might aid national shipping but are not actively encouraged by the state.

Notes

1 Black, *Law Dictionary*, rev. edn., 1968.
2 OECD, *Maritime Transport*, 1969, p. 59.

3 Ibid.
4 H.G. Rohreke, *The Formula and the Material Concept of Flag Equality*, Institute of Shipping Research, Bergen, 1961.
5 Ibid.
6 The *Rochdale Report* (Committee of Inquiry into Shipping — Report of Chairman Lord Rochdale), London, May 1970, para. 147, pp. 42-3.
7 UNCTAD Doc. no. TD/B/C.4/63.
8 OECD, *Maritime Transport*, 1967, p. 41.
9 For coastal states.
10 UNCTAD Doc. no. TD/B/C.4/38 Rev., para. 333, p. 91.
11 Ibid., para. 333.
12 UNCTAD, Doc. no. TD/B/C.4/63, op.cit.
13 House Report No. 1419, 87th Congress, 2nd Session, *The Ocean Freight Industry*, GPO, Washington DC, 1962, pp. 110-25.
14 UNCTAD Doc. no. TD/B/C.4/38 Rev., op.cit., paras 335, p. 91.
15 US Federal Maritime Commission, Docket No. 65-34.
16 UNCTAD Doc. no. TD/B/C.4/38 Rev. 1, op.cit., para. 335, p. 91.
17 Ibid.
18 S.G. Sturmey, 'The development of the Code of Conduct for Liner Conferences', *Maritime Law and Management*, vol. 3, no. 2, April 1979, pp. 133-48.
19 US Federal Maritime Commission, Docket No. 65-45 'Investigation of ocean freight rate structures in the trade between the US North Atlantic Ports and ports in the UK and Eire — Agreement Nos. 7100 and 5850'.
20 US Congress: Joint Economic Committee, *Hearings before the Sub-Committee on Federal Procurement and Regulation, Discriminatory Ocean Freight Rates and the Balance of Payments*, Part 1, GPO, Washington DC, April 1965, p. 1.
21 S.G. Sturmey, 'Flag discrimination against panlibho', *British Shipping and World Competition*, Athlon Press, London, 1962, pp. 220-1.
22 See also 'Sanctions Discriminations', pp. 206-7.
23 UNCTAD Doc. no. TD/B/C.4/38 Rev., chapter 10, section 3, paras 336, p. 91.
24 H. Olof, *Flag Discriminations: Purposes, Motives and Economic Consequences*, Publication of the Swedish School of Economics, no. 3, 1956, pp. 44-5, i.e. 'Expenditures that affect foreign vessels'.
25 US Federal Maritime Commission, Docket No. 66-49, November 1967: 'North Atlantic Mediterranean Freight Conferences — Rates on Household Goods', GPO, Washington DC, p. 10.
26 UNCTAD Doc. no. TD/B/C.4/63.
27 C. O'Loughlin, *Economics of Sea Transport*, 1st edn, Pergamon Press, Oxford, 1967, pp. 94, 115 and 178.
28 S.G. Sturmey, op.cit., pp. 18, 30, 33.
29 House Report No. 1419, Congress, 1st Session, *The Ocean Freight Industry*, op.cit., pp. 123 and 124.
30 UNCTAD Doc. no. TD/B/C.4/38 Rev., para. 323, p. 89.
31 Ibid., para. 324, p. 59.
32 C. O'Loughlin, op.cit.

33 OECD, *Maritime Transport*, 1965, p. 50.
34 *Rochdale Report*, op.cit.
35 *Nationalized Industries: A review of Economic and Financial Objectives 1967*, Cmnd. 3437, HMSO, para. 18.
36 Hence the spirit of Article 4(2)(a) of the UNCTAD Code of Conduct for Liner Conferences.
37 National interest is a lucid term; but see also the 'Energy Transportation', pp. 190–1.
38 'Report on United States Department of Transportation Research Study', *Lloyd's List and Shipping Gazette*, London, 20 August 1968.
39 UNCTAD Doc. no. TD/B/C.4/38 Rev., op.cit., para. 341.
40 Ibid.
41 Diversification and self-reliance are strong motivations for the establishment/development of national fleets.
42 US Department of Commerce, MARAD, *Maritime Subsidies*, 1978, pp. 149–252.
43 That is certainly true of Algeria and the USA.
44 UNCTAD Doc. no. TD/B/C.4/38 Rev., op.cit., chapter 10, i.e. 'Discriminations between products and shippers'.
45 Ibid., para. 34, i.e. 'Limits to overall discrimination versus individual product discrimination'.
46 Apart from the said American efforts to develop the refrigerated carriers in 1954, the other is the Algerian one to develop the LNG.
47 Hearings on Operation and Administration of Cargo Preference Act before the House on Merchant Marine and Fisheries, HR Rep. No. 1818, p. 12.
48 Ibid. See also 84th Congress, 2nd Session, 2, 1956.
49 Senate Committee on Agriculture and Forestry, *Amendments to Public Law 480*, 83rd Congress, S. Rep., No. 2290.
50 Kilgour, 'The energy transportation security act 1974', *Journal of Maritime Law and Commerce*, vol. 7, 1976, p. 557.
51 Senate Hearings on S.2089 and HR8193, supra, note 21, p. 7.
52 *Washington Post*, 17 December 1974, para. A, p. 2; and 1974 *Published Papers* 786.
53 *Washington Post*, 1 January 1975, para. A, col. 1, p. 12.
54 HR Rep. No. 1003, 93rd Congress, 2nd Session 2, 1974.
55 C.C. Joyner, 'Latin America's communal response to the energy crisis. The Latin American Energy Organization (OLADE)', *Lawyer of Americas*, vol. 6, 1974, pp. 637–61.
56 Note: 'The American merchant marine, flags of convenience and international law', *Virginian Journal of International Law*, vol. 3, 1963, p. 121.
57 Exec. Order No. IV, 2 November 1973, reprinted in Senate Hearings on S.2089 and HR.8193, supra, note 21, p. 210.
58 E.D. Naess, *The Great Panlibho Controversy — The Fight over Flags of Convenience*, Gower Press, Essex, 1972.
59 HR8193, 93rd Congress, 2nd Session, 1974; reprinted in Senate Hearings S.2189 and HR8193, supra, note 21, p. 7; 93rd Congress, 2nd Session, 1974, reprinted in id., p. 5.

60 See also *Rochdale Report* – last sentence of para. 147 and opening sentence of para. 150, both at p. 43.

61 L. Henkin *et al.*, 'The social scientist looks at international law of conflict management', *Proc. Am. Soc. Int. Law*, vol. 65, 1971, pp. 96–106.

62 *Rochdale Report*, chapter 21, 'National security', paras 1400–15, pp. 371–4.

63 US Department of Commerce, MARAD, *Maritime Subsidies*, op.cit., pp. 137–9 with 'Flag discrimination', p. 138.

64 33 Stat. 518, 1904.

65 70A Stat. 146, 1956; 10 USC, para. 2631, 1964.

66 Armed Services Procurement Regulations 1–1402(1)(A)(II), 1960.

67 Ibid., (1)(B) 1963.

68 Stat. 2051, 1936; 46 USC, para. 1241, 1952.

69 33 Stat. 518, 1964; 10 USC, para. 2631 (Supp. V, 1958).

70 70 Stat. 187, 1956; 36 USC, para. 1241 (C).

71 10 USC, para. 5748, 6157, 19748 (Supp. V. 1958) (Army, Navy and Airforce, respectively).

72 17 Stat. 405, 1932; 5 USC, para. 173(c), 1952.

73 US Department of Commerce, MARAD, *Maritime Studies*, 1978 – see under Philippines.

74 D. Rather, 'The best congress money can buy', *CBS News Reports*, 31 January 1975.

75 Ibid.; *Washington Post*, 10 August 1976, para. A3, col. 1.

76 46 USC, paras 1742 and 1283, 1970.

77 Trade Act 1974 (Public Law No. 93–618), see Preamble.

78 See also 88 Stat. 1978 (codified in large at USC, paras 2101–2487, Supp. 78 V. 1975).

79 In Chapter 3, pp. 168–73.

80 *Rochdale Report*, op.cit., paras 150–1.

81 See further for definitions of government supplies.

82 S.G. Sturmey, *British Shipping and World Competition*, op.cit., pp. 33, 124–5, 202–4, 206–8, 226, 375, 385.

83 E.g. Nato troops in Europe, Cuban/Soviets in Angola, French troops in Francophone Africa, etc.

84 *Maritime Subsidies*, op.cit., pp. 137–9.

85 Such outposts are in Greenland, Iceland, etc.

86 32 CFR, para. 1.309 (Supp. 1958).

87 Ibid., para. 1.309(b)(2).

88 See US–Spanish Agrt., 30 July 1954, para. 2(9)(ii), 1954, UST & DIA 2328 TIAS, no. 3094.

89 32 CFR, para. 1.309(d)(1)(Supp. 1958).

90 Ibid., para. 1.309(d)(2).

91 'Military sea transportation service' by 32 CFR, para. 1.309(e)(1)(ii) (Supp. 1958).

92 Navy Procurement Directive 1–307(e)(1).

93 32 CFR, para. 1.309(c)(2)(v) (Supp. 1954).

94 HR Dep., No. 2329, p. 3.

95 *Maritime Subsidies*, op.cit., pp. 38–9.

96 Ibid., p. 39.
97 American Legion, *Merchant Marine Bulletin*, March 1958, p. 4.
98 US–West German Agrt., 4 April 1954, para. 2(a)(III).
99 Ibid., 1957, 8 UST & DIA 497, TIAS, No. 3804 (effective 7 February 1957).
100 See also final paragraphs of last chapter.
101 UNCTAD Doc. no. TD/B/C.4/38 Rev. 1, para. 337.
102 W. Gorter, *United States Shipping Policy for Council of Foreign Relations*, Hemper & Bros, 1956, pp. 162–8.
103 UNCTAD Doc. no. TD/B/C.4/38 Rev. 1, paras 337–40, Table 49, p. 92.
104 HMSO, *Report of the Committee of Inquiry into the Major Ports of Great Britain*, London, Cmnd. 1824, September 1962.
105 Ibid., chapter 40, pp. 196–8; some of these islands (300 miles apart) are urgently in need of such schemes.
106 Section 714, Merchant Marine Act 1936.
107 W. Gorter, op.cit., chapter 4, p. 131.
108 Ibid., p. 121.
109 US Department of Commerce, *Review of Essential US Foreign Trade Routes*, GPO, Washington DC, 1953, p. 4.
110 Ibid., p. 6.
111 W. Gorter, op.cit., chapter 8, p. 163.
112 Ibid., p. 163.
113 Ibid., p. 164.
114 Ibid., p. 164.
115 Ibid., p. 164.
116 US Department of Commerce, *Review of Essential Trade Routes*, op.cit., pp. 6–7.
117 US Department of Commerce, MARAD, *US Oceanborne Foreign Trade Route Traffic Carried by Dry Cargo Ships, Calendar Year 1948, 1950 and 1953*, GPO, Washington DC, 1953, part 2, p. 5.
118 US Department of Commerce Bureau of the Census, *US Waterborne Trade*, GPO, Washington DC, 24 June 1955, p. 10.
119 Drewery Shipping Consultants, *The Emergence of Third World Shipping*, no. 6, 1978, para. 2.1, p. 12.
120 Ibid., para. 2.1.1, p. 13.
121 *Maritime Subsidies*, op.cit., pp. 95–8, p. 98, para. H.
122 Probably a large portion.
123 As are indeed for most of the other NICs in South East Asia.
124 D.M. Sassoon, *British Shipping Laws*, 2nd edn, vol. 5, 1975.
125 *Renter v. Sala*, 4 CPD, 1979, p. 239.
126 *Biddel Bros. v. E. Clements Horst Co.*, 1KB 214, 1911, p. 220.
127 *Wilson Holgate & Co. v. Belgian Grain Produce Co.*, 2 KB, 1920, p. 1.
128 *Diamond Alkali Export Corporation v. F.L. Burgeors*, 3 KB, 1921, p. 443.
129 *Re Keighley Maxted & Co. v. Bryan, Durant & Co.*, 70 LT, 1894, p. 155.
130 Ibid.
131 *Weis v. Produce Brokers Co.*, 7 LLLR211, 1921.
132 Per Lord Porter in *Comptoir d'Achat et de Neute due Boerenbond Belge*

S.A. v. Louis de Ridder Linitada (The Julia), AC 293, 1949, p. 309; 1949 1 All ER 269, p. 274.

133 *Olearia Tirvena S.P.A. v. N.V. Algenieene Oliehandele*, 1 LLR, 1972, p. 341.

134 In *Wimble v. Rosenberg*, 3 KB, 1913, p. 743.

135 Section 32(3) Sale of Goods Act 1893.

136 'Preferential treatment: a new standard for international economic relations', *Harvard International Law Journal*, vol. 18, Winter 1977, pp. 109–35.

137 A.G. Guest, *Benjamin's Sale of Goods*, 1st edn, 1974, pp. 687–910.

138 Learning Resources Centre, Plymouth Polytechnic, Maritime Studies, *Current Awareness Bulletin*, no. 369, 19 June 1981.

139 J. Lebuhn, 'Practising CIF and FOB today', *Eur. Trans. Law*, vol. 16, no. 1, 1981, pp. 24–36.

140 *United Baltic Corporation v. Burgett and Newsman*, 8 LLLR, 1921, p. 190.

141 Drewery Shipping Consultants, *Emergence of Third World Shipbuilding*, op.cit., p. 13.

142 *Maritime Subsidies*, op.cit., p. 96.

143 *Rochdale Report*, op.cit., p. 437.

144 Ibid., p. 439.

145 *Maritime Subsidies*, op.cit., p. 97.

146 H.C. Taubenfeld *et al.*, 'Economic sanctions as a means of influencing governments', *Proceedings of the American Society of International Law*, no. 58, 1964, pp. 183–218.

147 Ibid.; see also R. St. J. Macdonald, 'The resort to economic coercion by international political organisations', *University of Toronto Law Journal*, vol. 17, 1967, pp. 86–169.

148 See the Covenant of the League of Nations, article 16; also R. St. J. Macdonald, 'Economic sanctions in the international system', *Canadian Yearbook of International Law*, vol. 7, 1969, pp. 61–91 where the Italian invasion is discussed in detail.

149 See the Charter of the United Nations; also P.W. Bonsal, 'OAS recommends further action regarding Dominican Republic', *Department of State Bulletin*, February 1961, pp. 273–6.

150 C. Oliver *et al.*, 'International law and the quarantine of Cuba', *American Journal of International Law*, vol. 57, 1963, pp. 373–7 and 588–604 examining arguments for and against US action regarding its legality and her obligation under the UN Charter and international law.

151 R.M. Cummings, 'The Rhodesian Unilateral Declaration of Independence and the Britain of the international community', *New York University Journal of International Law and Politics*, vol. 6, 1973, pp. 47–84, discusses these issues, especially Britain's obligations.

152 See Security Council Resolution SC. Res. 216 (1965) of 12 November 1965, condemning the Rhodesian Unilateral Declaration of Independence.

153 Ibid.; see also SC. Res. 217 (1965) of 20 November 1965 calling upon all states to break off economic relations with Southern Rhodesia and imposing an oil embargo: see especially the Preamble.

154 Ibid.; see also SC. Res. 221 (1966) of 9 April 1966, reaffirming an oil embargo of Southern Rhodesia and calling upon the UK to prevent, by force if necessary, oil for Rhodesia reaching Beira.

155 See SC. Res. 181 (1963) of 7 August 1963, calling for a voluntary arms embargo against South Africa; also SC. Res. 282 (1970) of 23 July 1970 calling upon states to observe strictly the arms embargo against South Africa; also SC. Res. 418 (1977) of 4 November 1977, strengthening the existing arms embargo against South Africa.

PART III
SHIPPING IN
INTERNATIONAL POLITICS

5 Political intervention in shipping

Introduction

Although state intervention is the latest development in restrictive practices in international shipping, it is really both a form and a continuation of flag discrimination. This is because, although like the others it does not have a precise definition, it nevertheless has a description similar' to that of flag discrimination. It will be remembered that:

> Flag discrimination is more easily recognised than given a comprehensive description. It comprises above all any action by which governments restrict the freedom of traders to choose the ships in which cargo may be carried and thus places impediments in the path of the free flow of international trade. Examples are:
>
> (a) cargo preference laws;
> (b) measures in the field of exchange control;
> (c) preferential shipping clauses in trade agreements;
> (d) the operation of import and export licencing systems so as to influence the flag of the carrying ship;
> (e) port regulations; and
> (f) taxation measures.[1]

In some respects items (a), (c), (e) and (f) have already been covered. Whereas flag discrimination and maritime subsidies were mainly internally oriented, state intervention is geared much more to external trade and an integration of the merchant marine fully into the national economy, international trade and tariff operations generally. It has, therefore, both a wider and a deeper application.

'Interference' or Intervention

By this we mean the nature of the main responsibilities which governments or states have assumed towards the merchant marine industry.[2] Government shipping policies are welcomed in certain sectors and resented in other circumstances.[3] Where these policies are welcome, especially when they provide relief or constitute positive reactions from one's own government, they are referred to as intervention.[4] However, when similar policies are adopted by foreign governments or consist of supposedly negative reactions from domestic governments, they are interpreted simply as interference.[5] This ability to switch sides has characterized the mixed feelings with which the industry, especially among the TMNs, has responded to bold moves by states towards the industry. Besides the industry being predominantly in private hands in these countries, there is a general belief that the least active governments are the best governments.[6]

Government involvement, however, dates back to the emergence of maritime subsidies. In my view, therefore, both flag discrimination and maritime subsidies are a form of state intervention; negative and positive reactions, respectively, at least from the industry's viewpoint.[7] Whereas the object of subsidies was to save the industry from collapse, flag discrimination and state intervention are designed to avoid the benefits of subsidies extending to foreign flags. In other words, the former two were the beginning of and the natural progression to the latter. The general direction of all, however, is to establish, protect and develop national merchant fleets for political, security and economic reasons.[8]

Nevertheless, state intervention takes as many forms as has been broadly indicated.

> The Government's responsibilities towards the industry fall into two categories. The first, . . . is a general responsibility concerning the industry's commercial interest both at home and overseas, and promoting its contribution to the national well-being; the second . . . is a more detailed regulatory function, established by statute, for the safety of ships and the welfare of seafarers.[9]

Under the first category fall the kinds of actions described above; the actions of the second category are either not relevant, or only remotely so, to the establishment and expansion of national fleets.

Some of these regulations are, no doubt, common to the general industrial and commercial sector,[10] but quite a few are peculiar to the merchant marine industry. What has provoked an outcry from some is the fact that, in the past, industry in general and shipping in particular were left to the private sector to manage and control. This was no longer the case following the two World Wars.[11] But the main reason for exceptions, especially among the shipowners in the TMNs, was the disadvantage to which they were put by the massive state support and protection by the DMNs, not to mention the fact that the emerging fleets of the DMNs cut into the previous monopoly-like position of the TMNs' fleets.[12] Of late, however, state intervention has assumed international proportions, with the international community adopting a common policy towards shipping as envisaged by the UNCTAD Code of Conduct for Liner Conferences.

Nature and Development of Intervention

Comparing modern shipping with what it was before the Second World War, and for some time after 1945, there can be no doubt that the industry has taken a battering and has undergone a major change,[13] the implications of which affected its very existence and in particular the position of the private and commercially operating shipowners. I refer to the steady increase of state intervention.[14] Serious government intervention in the shipping industry commenced after the Second World War when the DMNs, in an effort to promote their national shipping industries, used unilateral legislation to preserve a good part of their exports and imports for their national flags.[15] The real breakthrough came in the 1960s when Brazil, for instance, introduced a law protecting as much as 50 per cent of its trade for its national flag and virtually compelled foreign shipping companies to accept the position.[16] Within a relatively short period of time, almost all Latin American and a number of other DMNs followed this pattern and the traditional carriers in those trades had to cut back their participation considerably, to the benefit of, and in the face of fierce competition from, the newly emerging national lines.[17]

Parallel with this development, many of the said countries tried to use the membership of their lines in the respective liner conferences to influence the level of rates in the tariffs, paying particular attention to their basic export commodities.[18] Since it is normal practice in many conferences that general increases have to be agreed almost unanimously by all members, this indirect government intervention proved to be quite successful, and in fact still is today.

Another type of government intervention is the regulation of conferences through national legislation. As will be apparent later, a typical example is provided by the US Shipping Act 1916, particularly as revised in 1961.[19] One aspect of the regulation which was resented by the shipping conferences in that country was the requirement that the people running these services spend more than half of their time on bureaucratic red-tape. The other objection was that everyday conferences in the US trades must comply with countless rules and orders of the FMC in order to prove that they are not violating the anti-trust regulations.[20] A further disadvantage of this kind of state intervention, as claimed by the private sector, is that, even with the best of intentions, this is a difficult task and the shipping industry has to emply an army of lawyers to help them interpret legal language in order to avoid possible treble damage suits and other penalties.[21] Hence, the criticism that state intervention and flag discrimination cause inefficiency leading to high costs and higher freight rates. In fact, on the North Atlantic route, the shipping companies came to the conclusion that, in one particular year, their lawyers' fees had been considerably higher than the lines' collective profits. State intervention through national legislation does take place in a number of the TMNs (other than the USA), such as Canada and Australia, as well as in many DMNs.[22] The USA example, however, has by far the most far-reaching effect since compliance with its laws can be time-consuming and costly; for even small and accidental violations can be dangerous due to anti-trust implications. The most annoying aspect, to the private operators, is that many commercial plans and objectives are virtually paralysed by this over-regulation.[23]

Another example of government intervention involves the STNs' ocean-borne commerce.[24] Perhaps the word intervention is inappropriate here — it is rather complete government control.[25] As in flag discrimination, through FOB purchases, CIF sales and the exclusive involvement of state agencies in the export and import trade, the mechanism does not leave the slightest freedom for private operators in these countries. Consequently, national ships are used almost exclusively.[26] Closely related to the practices of STNs, is of course bilateralism — i.e. the strict bilateral shipping arrangements between two countries, mostly on a 50–50 basis.

Bilateralism is the common procedure adopted between and amongst STNs and DMNs.[27] As noted earlier, it can safely be assumed that any country whose shipowners want to participate in its shipments to and from the USSR, for instance, can only achieve this aim if a bilateral shipping agreement is reached on an equal access basis, and tariffs with a viable rate level are accepted. Where this is not the case, USSR ships will carry almost the entire trade in both directions, leaving third flag carriers no chance at all.[28] The shipping agreement signed between the USA and USSR in 1972, and renewed in 1976, also follows this plan. This kind of state intervention seems to have become internationally acceptable with the advent of the UNCTAD Code of Conduct for Liner Conferences.[29]

However, it is no exaggeration to assert that far more than 50 per cent of all the world's ocean-borne trade was already, to a greater or lesser degree, affected by government intervention before the discussion about the UNCTAD Code even started.[30] To many people this Code appeared to be the culmination of state involvement; to others (and I am one of them) there are a number of positive aspects involved, not only with the UNCTAD Code, but with state intervention generally.[31]

State intervention takes many forms. We have been able to isolate state control, state participation, state aid and others, and will proceed to discuss them below, starting with state control.

State Control

The reconstruction of the TMNs' fleets after the war involved a large outlay of capital, the replacement of obsolete uneconomic tonnage demands, and further large investments.[32] A reasonable and relatively stable freight level and a fiscal system which permits owners to accumulate sufficient funds for replacement or expansion are the two factors requisite for the maintenance, on a commercial basis, of efficient and cheap overseas shipping services.[33] In their turn, these basic factors are essential to the proper functioning and development of international maritime trade generally. However, conditions are no longer ideal for the operation of these market forces. Rather, violently fluctuating freight markets, resulting in periods of unhealthy boom and acute depressions, are the order of the day.[34] They are as unwelcome to shipowners and governments as they are to everyone else, since they increase the difficulties of planning ahead and lead at times to laid-up tonnage and periods of unemployment.

This, plus the desire of states to establish, develop and expand national fleets of their own, has led various governments to intervene and control the industry[35] through supervisory planning, directives and approvals, regulatory agencies, domestic registry and control of foreign participation, all of which are discussed below.

Supervisory Planning

State planning of the economy is no longer the monopoly of STNs and DMNs; it is now widely accepted as a fact of life. Neither is the shipping industry to be viewed outside this government in industry and commerce.[36] What differs, however, is the degree of planning; ranging from total (in the case of STNs), through mixed economies (in the case of DMNs), and semi-control (in the case of TMNs).[37] What is generally agreed is that the planned economy is a system in which some or all of the decisions on allocation, production, investment and distribution are made by a central government agency. The collective economic planning used in a typically planned economy is based on the assumption that social welfare can be recognized and pursued more effectively under centralized planning.[38]

The predominantly private shipping concerns among the TMNs are, however, quick to point out that this assumption denies the advantages to which it is said to lead and results in chaotic disharmony between production and consumption.[39] They further point out that, in planned shipping, the initiative for economic activities and decisions concerning them do not originate with the shipping entrepreneurs.[40] And, of course, they resent the idea that the government should start with an overall plan of major objectives and then attempt to achieve the fullest possible utilization of available resources in line with the state objectives. Nevertheless, for the reasons stated above, the shipping industry accepts some form of state intervention on the basis that, in modern times, there is, after all, no single government that does not act as the overall overseer of the economy.[41] But that is about all they are prepared to accept.

The shipowners and shipping companies fear the elimination of the market mechanism in price formation and the government undertaking to replace the market functions that exist in completely planned economies. They further fear that the planned shipping agencies (pp. 225-7)[42] created in various countries, to set up production goals, resource allocations and decision-making regarding production and investment, are steps towards totalitarianism. Such systems exist even in such pro-Western DMNs as Taiwan, where shipments are planned under the supervision of the Ministry of Commerce, with first priority being given to vessels built under the Measure for the Joint Development of Trading, Shipping and Shipbuilding, for instance.[43] In the Taiwanese example, second priority is given to ordinary vessels of Taiwanese nationality and third choice to other vessels. One can detect the discrimination practised in this for development objectives.[44]

The nature, extent and policy underlying merchant marine planning in Taiwan is such that when shipping companies plan to build new vessels, they must first seek domestic shipbuilding companies.[45] If the latter are unable to undertake the construction, only then can private shipowners place orders with foreign shipyards, and even then only after gaining Ministry of Commerce approval.[46] And, as expected, in line with the development objectives of state planning, high priority is given to the building of such vessels as container ships, multipurpose cargo ships and special ships for carrying imported bulk grains and minerals.[47] With the exception of constructions for foreign shipowners, it can only be assumed that the types of vessels listed above are those in shortest supply with the national flag or in response to the national flag demands to service international trade, or both.[48]

However, these vessels must carry the Taiwanese flag, sail in lanes pertinent to the international trade of Taiwan, and not be leased out but run by the Taiwanese owners.[49] Finally, the domestic ship-building price under the Measure cannot exceed 5 per cent of the international price for similar vessels of the same type and function. The down payment must be 20 per cent of the total price before the ship is handed over to the shipowner; the period of payment of instalments is not less than seven years.[50] There is a subsidy to enable local owners to purchase on credit over longer periods. Thus, the previously predominantly privately-owned merchant marine industry now finds itself having to comply with state supervisory planning requirements. These range from external commerce to shipping and shipbuilding, of which the Taiwanese case is but one example.[51]

Government Directives and Approvals

Sometimes government directives and requirements for government approval are used instead of supervisory planning to control the merchant marine. This state direction of the merchant marine industry is conducted for precisely the same objectives outlined in state planning above, and the principles applied in employing both mechanisms are about the same.[52] It will, no doubt, be clear by now that in the government direction of the economy there are two types of modern approach. One is the partial directive that has evolved under the private enterprise system and with which the TMNs' shipping industries are acquainted:[53] it is this approach on which we shall therefore focus attention. It will also be remembered that, under this system, government direction may be applied through the general economic policy that is designed to smooth economic fluctuations experienced in the free enterprise system.[54] This may take the shape of actions to offset a recession, the initiation of general shipbuilding projects to provide employment, the reduction of taxes to increase the purchasing power of shipowners and shippers, and the lowering of interest rates to encourage investments.[55] Government policies to prevent inflation and to encourage economic growth are also examples of limited instances where government directives and requirements for government prior approvals may be necessary.[56]

As in the case of flag discriminations and maritime subsidies, government directives and approvals take many forms, such as proclamations, byelaws, pronouncements, decrees, etc.[57] It is unnecessary to emphasize that these directives and approvals are more common among the STNs and DMNs. A typical example is the case of Israel, where government approval is necessary before foreign ships can be chartered by an Israeli party. Such approval is obtainable only if domestic ships are unavailable on competitive terms, or when special-lift ships are required.[58] Secondly, under Israeli law on this point, a ship must have at least 50 per cent Israeli ownership to be registered under the Israeli flag. Perhaps all these stringent requirements are necessary given Israel's volatile position in the Middle East. Besides, as in most DMNs, shipping is of extreme importance to Israel since almost all her foreign trade is seaborne.[59] In fact, shipping has become Israel's second most important foreign exchange earner, behind tourism, and is expanding at an accelerated rate. In 1969, for instance, Israeli flag ships carried approximately 50 per cent of her foreign trade — by far the highest proportion outside the STNs. Not all of this can be attributed to the approval policy, but a large percentage must have been due to it.[60] So, in a way, the government feels vindicated for initiating and continuing the intervention policy and, through it, the control of the merchant marine industry directives and requirements for approvals.[61] Of course, these approvals and directives are most common in flag discriminations and subsidies. It should also be noted that these government directives are often initiated and justified as a *quid pro quo* for state subsidies to the merchant marine industry; it is the price the industry has had to pay in return for state aid.[62]

In this respect, we should remember the case of South Korea. The South Korean government may direct any maritime transportation owner receiving subsidy or loan under the applicable law to operate his ship on a specific domestic or international route for a fixed period.[63] Any loss from this service is compensated in a manner prescribed by a Presidential Decree.[64] Thus, the government is prepared to offer a double subsidy, as in this case, in return for compliance with its directives. We also noted furthermore that, when the ship concerned in the above item is considered too old for the promotion of public or national interest, the government may direct that the ship be substituted or improved, itself bearing any resultant loss to the owner.[65] Moreover, this process takes precedence over others in the domestic construction of ships. Finally, in 1976 the South Korean government directed that, where possible, all new ships for the Korean merchant fleet would be built at the country's own yards, again with the government undertaking to subsidize owners and yards.[66] Non-compliance with such directives can have very serious consequences, including treating the vessels concerned as foreign for the purposes of flag discrimination and subsidies, and/or outright acquisition. The approval requirement enables the government to plan maritime services not according to market requirements but rather according to national needs.[67] We do not single out South Korea other than for using this as a typical example of this kind of state intervention. This intervention is normally effected through a licensing system.

Regulatory Agencies

Nowhere is state intervention illustrated better than through regulatory agencies[68] and, as noted in the section on the nature and development of state intervention, regulatory control through state agencies marked the beginning of unilateral actions by various governments aimed at controlling the liner conference sector in particular.[69] Many statutes, commissions and reports were introduced in various countries with varying degrees of success. In the final analysis, regulatory shipping agencies were set up, including associations and councils, aimed at self-regulation.[70] Although they may play only a small or non-existent role in aiding the establishment, development and expansion of national fleets, they are nevertheless worth discussing, being the finest example of state intervention in the merchant marine industry through control mechanisms. The best known of these are the General Council of British Shipping (GCBS) and the FMC.[71]

But it is the US version (FMC) that has raised protests from the world shipping community. The US government as a large shipper, shipowner and operator, and as the agency responsible for the national welfare, is in an anomalous position as regards the adoption of an appropriate policy towards shipping generally and shipping conferences in particular.[72] It wants competition to be free enough to ensure rates at a level approximate to those that would be established in a free competitive market, and also wants stable rates which can best be obtained by permitting ship operators to form monopolistic combinations,[73] the formation of which is not ordinarily favoured by the government. The US government and public have a deep traditional anti-trust feeling which can be detected not just in the FMC, but also in the other agencies, such as the DOJ (Department of Justice), DOC, DOT, DOA (Department of Agriculture) etc. On this matter, the government, as represented by these institutions, and the shipping industry do not see eye-to-eye[74] and are as far apart as they can possibly be. The private operators, on the one hand, claim that the overtonnaging of some trades — often a concomitant of the monopolistic combinations reminiscent of what they (private operators) would wish — may, after all, be in the interest of their national defence.[75] The government's argument, on the other hand, is that the conflicting interests and desires cannot be reconciled in the US government's policy towards liner conferences in particular and the merchant marine industry generally.[76]

It is because of this that Section 14 of the Shipping Act 1916 prohibits the formations of combinations, the use of fighting ships, retaliation against any shipper for non-compliance with combination agreements, and use of unfair or unjust discriminatory contracts.[77] Section 14(a) provides the means of disciplining foreign lines participating in liner conferences affecting the USA for such breaches.[78] Section 15 requires all liner conferences affecting the US flag lines in US foreign trade to be filed with the FMC; and Section 16 forbids unreasonable discrimination for or against persons, localities and classes of traffic.[79] Further regulations are provided in the Merchant Marine Act 1920 and the Merchant Marine Act 1936, as amended from time to time.

It is interesting to note that the USA, which prohibits flag discrimination, is also the major practitioner of it.[80] However, in reading these laws one must remember that the government cannot directly regulate the rates of services established by international liner shipping conferences. Though the law may appear to give the government the right to regulate rates, this applies only to domestic operations.[81] The American attempt to extend this regulation, in some respects, beyond her borders has met with a stiff response from other countries. So for the moment at least, the US government can exact indirect control over international liner conference agreements only by refusing to approve the participation of US flag vessels, by penalizing them if they do so, and by refusing certain port privileges to the foreign flag vessels involved.[82]

The limited power of any national government prevents it from effectively controlling international shipping, and this is true even of the USA. For the USA, this fact has been particularly vexing because of the said anti-monopoly and anti-control bias of government policy.[83] For the most part, most other TMNs do not share this bias and accept cartels with little official animosity. The USA, on the other hand, accepts liner conferences but puts restrictions on their US members. In short, the US flag vessel operators are not forbidden to join conferences but they must not engage in certain practices adopted by some conferences.[84] This intervention has had no bearing

226

on the expansion of the US fleet: it has probably retarded it. One area, however, where the USA has been successful, and which is relevant to the expansion of its national fleet, is the control of foreign participation in domestic shipping. This will be discussed in a wider context in the section on state participation with respect to the financing and managing of a national fleet (pp. 231–2).[85]

Control of Foreign Participation

Permitting foreign investment to participate in one's national economy can lead to expansion, but again it may retard expansion of certain sectors which rely heavily on foreign capital and foreign skills. Foreign investment, in this case, would be the acquisition by a government or its citizens,[86] of assets abroad, or by the government or citizens of other states in a given country. Such investments may take the form of bank deposits, foreign government bills, government or industrial securities, or titles to land, buildings, capital equipment related to the merchant marine industry, or the vessels themselves.[87] Private investment abroad will normally be made in the hope of a higher interest, dividend, or other income than can be obtained at home,[88] or in the expectation of alterations in exchange rates, or out of fear of political or taxation changes at home, as was the case with foreign registry.[89]

Government investments, on the other hand, are undertaken for political, diplomatic, military or other reasons that may pay little attention to the yield of the investment. An example is provided by the TMNs' loans to the DMNs.[90] The problem is to weigh the political and other advantages, which are difficult to judge, against the additional yield the investments would have earned elsewhere. The benefits to a country as a whole from investment abroad, as compared with investment at home, are not confined to the monetary interest or yield received by the investor, because they may affect employment, the productivity of labour, or the terms of trade and state revenue.[91] It does not, however, necessarily follow that foreign investment yields a lower social return than investment at home. It may be higher, for example, where it reduces the price of imports. It also does not follow that foreign investment should be made exclusively by governments, which are able to take indirect social effects into account, because government investment tends to become political investment whereas the errors of individual investors tend to cancel out.[92] From a recipient country's point of view, foreign investment can lead to control of certain sectors of national economic life by foreigners. This can be unwise. There is no country in the world which does not have foreign investment on her soil, including the USA.[93] However, noting the defence importance of shipping, an attempt has been made by various countries to either control or eliminate foreign participation in this sector.

Yet again, the best example is probably that of the USA.[94] Section 27 of the Jones Act 1952,[95] for instance, sets out four conditions for foreigners engaging in US domestic cargo trade. The first is the documentation requirement which prohibits all but US flag vessels from participating in this trade. The idea is that such vessels could then be subject to other policies reflected in US domestic laws; requiring documentation under US laws would probably facilitate conforming to these laws.[96] Examples of these laws are those relating to the regulation, expansion and defence roles of national fleets. The second requirement is the construction requirement which specifies that vessels engaged in the domestic trade must be built in the USA.[97] This requirement, however, neither permits alien investment in the ship construction industry nor operations by aliens of vessels as domestic carriers. It may negatively affect the possibility of a foreign carrier competing in the domestic trade because of the likelihood that most of its fleet would have been built outside the USA.[98]

The third requirement is that of ownership or management. Section 27 requires the individual owner to be a citizen and, by reference to Section 2 of the Shipping Act 1970, the corporate owner to be domestically organized and owned, to the extent of 75 per cent of the ownership interest, by US citizens.[99] The same ownership interest requirement applies to partnerships.[100] In addition to the Chief Executive Officer, the Chairman of the Board of a corporate owner must be a US citizen and the number of alien directors, if any, must be less than the quorum of the board.[101] In addition, aliens who invest in domestic enterprises unrelated to the maritime industries generally[102] must arrange their business so that all water cargo transportation is handled by carriers rather than by the business itself.[103] Even though the business itself could handle the carriage most efficiently, the cost of transport is increased and the potential profitability lowered.[104] Thus, this restraint might prove to be an indirect impediment to foreign investment in other industries as well.[105]

The fourth and final requirement relates to environmental protection, safety and other regulatory concerns, all of which are served by easing the flow of funds into the merchant marine, especially by aliens. The investment restraint prohibits the entry of new foreign competitors into the field.[106] This control of foreign investments in the US merchant marine serves to prevent foreigners from gaining a foothold in the industry and aids expansion and

228

employment efforts. It may retard rapid expansion, by denying vital foreign investments, but at the same time it ensures that whatever expansion takes place is truly American, which is good for security, political and economic reasons.[107] If this policy results in the development of a truly national fleet then it is that kind of fleet that this inquiry is all about.

State Participation

Closely related to state control is actual state participation. All the previous forms of protection and intervention by the state have been from a distance — detached. However, with the benefit of hindsight, many countries discovered that the most effective means of control, and the fastest way to expand, is through direct state participation in the financing, management and direction of the merchant marine industry.[108] In that way, governments are kept in touch with the problems and needs of the industry, etc., and also take part in the daily routine and decision-making process; being able to influence these important decisions and being party to them.[109] State participation gives the industry more protection — the necessary stability for expansion. This is true, at least of the STNs and DMNs. State participation in the merchant marine industry is effected through joint ventures and partnerships, state ownership, nationalized industries and through arrangements to award a monopoly to state contracts and state purchases.

Joint Ventures and Partnerships

Joint ventures initially meant an association of individuals on firms formed to carry out a specific business project.[110] Now, of course, parties may include state and state institutions. Although a joint venture is very similar to a partnership, it differs in that it is limited to the success or failure of the specific project for which it was formed. As in the case of a partnership a joint venture is formed by a contractual agreement in which each partner assumes unlimited liability for the organization's debts.

The other mechanism of state intervention is through partnership.[111] Ordinarily, a partnership is a type of business in which two or more persons (or states in this case) agree on the amount of their contribution (capital and effort), and on the distribution of profits, if any. Partnerships are more common in the retail trade, accounting and law than in expensive and heavy industries like merchant shipping.[112]

Since the partners pool their capital, partnerships are generally larger than, say, proprietorships, which also exist in shipping; but they are still relatively small when compared with shipping corporations (pp. 78–9). In many respects, however, shipping partnerships are similar to shipping proprietorships.[113] But the distinct feature is that these are different from ordinary partnerships. They are subject to government regulations and are not characterized by unlimited liability, which means that not all the partnership assets are available as security for their creditors. Thus, one of the most effective ways of state control of the merchant marine industry is through part-participation.[114] This is particularly true of the DMNs. These ventures and partnerships are normally in association with local or foreign business investments. The important point to note, in this respect, is that state participation involves majority shares for the purposes of maintaining control. Control is the objective of the exercise or the operative word from the state's point of view.[115]

Shipping ventures and partnerships are sometimes regional exercises, as in the case of Colombia. It is understandable why Colombia would, for instance, seek to control her shipping; it is special to Colombia with its two coastlines and its large coffee exports which supply some 50–55 per cent of foreign exchange earnings.[116] The Colombian flag line, Flota Mercante Grancolombiana, is such an exercise in regional ownership. Colombia's National Federation of Coffee Growers controls approximately 80 per cent of the ownership, with the remaining 20 per cent controlled by the Development Bank of Ecuador.[117] At one time the Venezuelan government also participated in Flota's ownership. As might have been expected, there were strings attached to this state participation; although there were no legal requirements, in effect, imports for governments or quasi-government agencies were generally carried by Flota.[118] There were also benefits: close ties with the Colombian government and publicity for the advantages of shipping via Flota account for the shipping line's strong position.

In Egypt, too, joint ventures in the maritime transport industry are encouraged by awarding such ventures tax-free operations for the first five years and other fringe benefits.[119] And in South Korea companies wishing to receive government assistance must have a minimum tonnage of 20,000 grt, and minimum capital of 500 million won; joint ventures with overseas interests are permitted, provided that national interests are 51 per cent or more and the Board of Directors is at least 60 per cent South Korean.[120] Liberia, on the other hand, became a partner through the Liberian Shipping Corporation (LSC) in two shipping companies incorporated in Liberia, the Total

Investment Shipping Company (TISC) and the Provident Shipping Company (PSC).[121] The LSC owns 50 per cent of TISC, the remainder being shared equally by Dutch and Israeli interests. The PSC is owned jointly by the Liberian government and the Graengesburgh Company of Sweden, a large stockholder in Liberian Mining Company (LAMCO) mines.[122] Finally, the Malaysian government signed an agreement to establish a major shipyard at Johore Bharn on a joint venture basis with Japanese and other investors. When completed, it will be one of the largest in SEA.[123]

In some cases these efforts have assisted in the establishment and expansion of national fleets; in others, they have served to hinder that progress. What is not denied is that they have enabled governments to control and direct shipping.[124] Not all governments have been satisfied with part-participation as a method of state intervention: quite a few have opted for total control — nationalizations of at least certain sectors of shipping and shipbuilding — hoping this would speed up the establishment and development of national fleets.

Nationalized Shipping and Shipyards

Nationalization is, of course, an act by which a government takes over the ownership and operation of a shipping company or shipyard which was previously in the hands of foreign or private citizens.[125] These governments argue that such nationalizations increase productive efficiency by permitting the direct investment of public funds, by enlarging the scale of operations, and by coordinating operations more effectively.[126] On the other hand, private shipping concerns and other opponents of nationalizations, especially among the TMNs, state that the record of private shipping enterprises is such that government takeovers are unnecessary,[127] and that government ownership is usually characterized by excessive costs because of elaborate over-centralized organization.[128] However, as will be evident in the succeeding chapters, nationalization and other forms of state inter-vention have been used by some countries purely as a means of eliminating foreign ownership of their merchant marine industries or as part of a policy of the wholesale nationalizing of all major industries, as in the UK.[129]

In the latter case, for instance, on 1 July 1977, 19 shipbuilding companies, 5 diesel marine engine manufacturers and 3 training companies were nationalized to form the British Shipbuilders' Corporation (BSC).[130] Labour, industry and government were represented in a management which planned to use economies of scale to obtain more orders for the industry.[131] The docks too, were nationalized and operated under the BTDB. The BTDB were returned to private concerns in 1983 under the new name of Associated British Ports (ABP). The shipyards, however, remain decentralized so that individual shipyard performance can be measured. The pooling of orders takes place only when required to facilitate the securing of orders.[132]

The other example from the TMNs is provided by Portugal, where, by Decree Laws 205-C/77 and 205-D/75 of 16 July 1975, the Companhia Nationale de Navegaco and the Companhia Portuguese de Transporto Maritimas respectively were nationalized.[133] The same decree nationalized the shares of Sociedade Portuguesa de Navios Tanques, Lda Soponate. In addition, Resolution No. 153/77 of 5 May 1977 called for the creation of Navis-Navega Cus de Portugal to function as a coordinator and supervisor of the public business management of these firms, already established in the field of sea navigation, without prejudice to the anatomy and legal individuality of the latter.[134] The Law Decree of 16 November 1977 established NAVIS. These nationalized shipping organizations, therefore, became state-owned. State-owned shipping does not normally exist on its own. Many countries have had to start new national fleets where none existed before.[135]

State-owned Shipping

State-owned shipping, which has mushroomed, especially among the DMNs, is not only another alternative method of state intervention in the industry, but is, perhaps, the only true case of states establishing their own national fleets.[136] Often this development exists either side-by-side with joint ventures, partnerships and nationalized shipping, or is the only form permitted to operate. Whereas such ownerships would have been unthinkable about a century ago, today public ownership of merchant shipping is the general rule rather than the exception.[137] In such cases, then, the industry becomes part of the government ownership and operation generally. The principle involved is that the government replaces private shipowners as the supplier of capital. Thus, the government supplies the capital and determines the maritime facilities to be provided.[138]

In addition, the government chooses the management, assumes the responsibility of paying labour, purchasing supplies, setting the prices for ocean-borne trade and maritime services, determining the freight rates, and reaping profits or meeting deficits if they are incurred.[139] This governmental act of removing private ship ownership and assuming the operation of the shipping enterprise is what is called government or public ownership. It may come about through the creation of parastatal shipping bodies or, assuming what was already in existence, through nationalization. However, as in the case of STNs and DMNs, perhaps the term 'state intervention' then loses its meaning.[140] Intervention ends with nationalization and other previously mentioned methods of state control. But when there is a concern created by the government from public funds it would be an anomaly to refer to government direction of it as intervention or even participation. This is true of state shipping and all government holdings.[141]

Sometimes state shipping companies deliberately put pressure on the private sector to conform to state control. The action of the Irish government is an example of the former; the Irish Shipping Company (ISC) and the British and Irish Steam Packet Company Limited (BISPCO) seem to have been created because the government was dissatisfied with the way private shipping behaved.[142] By 31 May 1978, shortly after coming into being, the ISC, which operates mainly in the deep sea trade on charter and tramping and had only eight bulk carriers of 142,943 grt, soon became effectively the owner of the St Patrick and St Killian car ferries. These ferry companies had previously resisted compliance to and control by the government. But when the government undercut their operations they had no choice but to allow themselves to be taken over.[143]

Otherwise government ownership does not exclude, and often invites, partnership, as in the above-discussed incidents or the cases of FINMARE (Financia Maritima) of Italy.[144] FINMARE is a holding company in which the IRI, an agency of the Ministry of State Holdings, owns 75 per cent of the shares and the public owns 25 per cent. Shareholdings in FINMARE and IRI in shipping companies entitled to government subsidies are shown in Table 5.1.[145]

Table 5.1 State ownership of shares (Italy)

Company	FINMARE (%)	IRI (%)	Tirrenia (%)
Italia	90	10	
Lloyd Triestino	80	20	
Adriatica	60	40	
Tirrenia	80	20	
Torremar	48.51		51.49
Caremar	48.51		51.49
Siremar	48.51		51.49

In addition, approximately 80 per cent of the shipbuilding in Italy is owned and operated by FINCANTIERI, a holding company in which IRI owns 100 per cent of the stock.[146] In accordance with the Comitato Interministeriale per la Programmazione Economica (CIPE) recommendations of 7 October 1967, the shipyards under FINCANTIERI control were reorganized under a new entity called ITALCANTIERI which now includes the Sestri, Monfalcone and Castellamere shipyards.[147]

The immediate motive behind these forms of state intervention, i.e. participation and control, is to enable the state to integrate shipping into the general industrial, economic and commercial planning programmes. The immediate objective is to enable the swift establishment and expansion of national fleets.[148] The intention may be good, but as to whether these measures deliver the goods is a different matter. We have been able to outline several options open to governments but we have no feedback and therefore no way of knowing whether the overall objectives have been or will be achieved through these mechanisms.[149]

The other alternative similar to, but different from, state ownership is state purchase.

State Purchase

State purchase of ships is not a type of ownership but rather a state subsidy with active state participation.[150] The programme involves state provision of credit facilities, to the national lines, for the purchase of ships and favouring the said lines for any purchases the state makes. The purchase could be of foreign flag vessels or domestic vessels registered abroad.[151] The country where such practice is prominent is Greece, where more often than not the aim of the scheme is: 'In order to attract foreign economic interests, including shipping companies which may or may not be controlled by Greek interests, for the purposes of establishing regional or home offices in Greece . . . .[152] This is perhaps a much clearer and more direct method of attempting to establish and develop a national fleet than most of the others we have touched on. First, in order to purchase foreign flag ships, to promote the modernization of Greece's merchant fleet, the Greek government (as we noted) has authorized local banks to issue letters of guarantee covering up to 50 per cent of the total value of vessels flying foreign flags, which are bought in order to be subsequently registered under the Greek flag.[153] The balance of the cost of these vessels must be provided by the purchaser himself in foreign exchange. Credits to be extended to purchasers, on the bases of the bank letters of guarantee mentioned above, should be repayable in no less than a year in equal annual or semi-annual instalments.[154] This is a type of state subsidy but one with a difference;

first because it involves active state action and, second, because it involves state participation. Vessels to be purchased under the foregoing scheme must be less than twelve years old. In cases where the purchase involves coastline cargo vessels and coastline passenger vessels (including passenger ferry boats/ships) flying foreign flags, a scheme similar to the one outlined above is applicable.[155] Under the scheme, bank letters of guarantee may cover up to 80 per cent of the total value of the ships purchased provided, however, that the total value of each vessel does not exceed US $1,000,000 and its age is not less than eight years.[156]

Insurance of bank letters of guarantee for the purchase of ships whose value is in excess of US $1 million shall be contingent upon special approval by the Greek Currency Committee. However, to qualify for the benefits extended under the above schemes, prospective purchasers of foreign flag vessels should undertake a commitment to register such vessels under the Greek flag.[157] The second category is that of purchases of national flags registered abroad. Again in the Greek example, local banks are authorized to extend loans for the purchase of ships flying the Greek flag provided that:

(a) The vessel to be purchased is less than fifteen years old;[158]
(b) The amount of the loan does not exceed 50 per cent of the value of the vessel or the maximum of US $10,000,000 for each vessel.[159]

Otherwise the loans are repayable in three years (five equal semi-annual instalments) with a period of grace of one year. And, finally, loans intended to finance purchases of ships in general (Greek flag or foreign flag) bear a minimum interest rate of 14 per cent p.a.[160]

This Greek scheme seems to be achieving its objectives. In fact, there have been indications that the Greek flag has grown ever since. But this is not a point that should be overstressed. This programme lays emphasis on modernization rather than general expansion.[161] Even if that were not the case, Greece is one of those countries with many flags registered abroad and it is these which are returning. That puts Greece in a unique position that cannot be compared with many other countries. At any rate attracting back one's own flags can hardly be called expansion.[162] The fact that the scheme seems to be successful in this case does not warrant a generalization that state purchase is a viable mechanism for every nation to establish and expand its national fleet.[163] Thus, as it relates to Greece, state purchase as a form of state intervention must be seen in that limited extent. What might, however, justify general application are state contracts.

Originally known as admiralty contracts, state contracts are, strictly speaking, a kind of discrimination or preference that favours domestic construction companies with access to government contracts.[164] In a wider sense, however, these contracts involve payment for keeping units of the merchant navy in reserve for the navy's account. Such contracts also have a more cost-motivated form inasmuch as they include a special compensation for armaments.[165] Here we shall restrict ourselves to the non-military aspects of admiralty contracts. Inevitably this type of contract is linked to the construction subsidy.[166] In Argentina, for instance, the benefits of state contracts are applicable only to companies owned or controlled by resident Argentine citizens.[167]

Australia, on the other hand, provides a bounty for the construction of ships built in registered Australian shipyards for use in Australian waters or as an Australian vessel for use in overseas trade.[168] A better example still is the Canadian Government Purchasing Scheme under which government contracts have generally been restricted to Canadian shipyards and, since 1965, have been awarded to the lowest qualified bidder — an exception being a submarine built abroad.[169] More and more maritime nations now adopt this form of intervention. A fairly recent example arose in 1976, when the South Korean merchant fleet was to be built at the country's own yards with the government undertaking, as usual, to subsidize owners and yards.[170]

However, by far the most elaborate scheme is that operated by the Peruvian government. The Law of 9 January 1962, authorized the establishment of a naval construction industry providing for 5 per cent state participation. The cost is provided by the revenue from export and import trades.[171] After the government has fulfilled its obligations to this industry, the remainder of the money goes to the Compania Panana de Vapores (Chile) (CPV) for the purchase of ships or for their construction in Peru.[172] Secondly, by the Ministerial Resolution of 12 June 1972, no more purchases are allowed in Peru of foreign vessels similar to those built in Peru until the National Industry Commission (NIC), formed earlier in the same month for this purpose, has presented its recommendations to the government on the effect of such requests upon the development of the naval industry.[173] Finally, all Peruvian flag vessels must be repaired only by Peruvian shipyards or dry-docks, unless the owners can show that the national shipyards do not have the capacity for a specific job. Repairs abroad may be made only in case of emergency.[174] In addition to such legislation, another statutory requirement,[175] restricting the construction of national flag ships to domestic shipyards for operation in a nation's foreign and domestic trade, specifies that materials and component parts for the construction of ships and their maintenance and repair, as well as food, stores and supplies, be purchased domestically.[176] These aid requirements are no different from any of the interventionist schemes discussed above. The objectives remain the establishment and/or expansion of the national fleet.

The third major form of state intervention, for the same purpose, is state aid to ocean-borne trade.[177]

State Aid to Ocean-borne Commerce

The establishment and/or development of a national fleet would be meaningless unless matched by a demand for transportation of the nation's ocean-borne trade. Where such trade is non-existent, or in its infancy, governments have sought to create and sustain it through the same mechanisms.[178] This has been done through export promotion, import restrictions, and manipulation of exchange control regulations.

Export Inducements and Incentives

No other mode of transportation has had an equivalent effect upon all types of exchange of goods and services between different countries as has merchant shipping.[179] Business firms from the TMNs sell machinery and equipment to DMNs, which in turn sell raw materials to firms in the former.[180] The growth of ocean-borne trade has been greatly helped by modern techniques of merchant shipping transportation and communications.[181] These relatively new merchant marine developments have brought countries closer together than they had ever been in the past and have made the conduct of ocean-borne trade easier.[182]

More up-to-date and complete international economic information, too, has made the consignor and consignee more knowledgeable regarding available products and markets.[183] It is the realization of these potentials, and the desire to tap these resources, that has led various states to actively assist the foreign-trade-promoting aspects of their national merchant marines.[184] One of the most effective ways of achieving this objective has been through incentives and/or inducements — made possible due to the close proximity between merchant marine transportation, ocean-borne trade and international trade[185] — and now a common practice among states, TMNs and DMNs.

Take, for example, the case of the Philippines. Presidential Decree 806 of 3 October 1975,[186] states that the government will take all steps necessary, including the provision of direct incentives to Filipino flag vessels and national shipping lines, to enable them to carry a substantial and increasing share of the cargo generated by Philippine foreign trade.[187] The same legislation also states that Philippine flag vessels and those which are owned, controlled, or chartered by Philippine nationals, shall carry at least an equal share of cargo as that carried by vessels of the other country involved in that particular trade.[188] Furthermore, exporters will be able to deduct from their taxable incomes an amount equivalent to 150 per cent of overseas freight expenses and charges in Philippine ports incurred in shipping export products, provided they are Philippine flag carriers.[189]

So, often, aid to ocean-borne trade is operated together, and simultaneously, with that to international trade. In the Philippine example, enterprises registered with the Board of Investments will also be allowed to deduct from their taxable income 200 per cent of shipment costs incurred in the transport of their raw materials and products to and from foreign ports, provided the shipments are on Filipino flag vessels.[190] Similar inducements, of a subsidy nature, are provided for in the general export promotion exercises.[191]

Export Promotions

This scheme relates to the export of actual goods, commodities or services shipped from one country or area to another in the conduct of foreign trade, and operates on the same principles and criteria as the inducements and incentives above.[192] Again, in South Korea such a scheme is operated under five main categories according to the Law of 28 February 1967:[193]

1 The government may give encouragement subsidies to maritime transportation businessmen operating or utilizing Korean flag ships in international trade, which contribute towards earning or conserving foreign currencies.[194]

2 The government shall assist and foster a maritime transportation organization whose objective is to enhance the status of and to encourage international activities of maritime transportation businessmen.[195]

3 When a maritime transportation businessman operates his ship on regular international routes for the promotion of foreign trade and to earn foreign currency, the government may subsidize any loss he sustains, as prescribed by the said Presidential Decree.[196]

4 The government may order any maritime transportation business-

man receiving subsidy or loan under applicable law to operate his ship on a specific domestic or international route for a fixed period. Any loss from this service will be compensated in a manner prescribed by Presidential Decree.[197]

5 The government or any individual shall, for transport of cargo by ship, use a Korean flag ship or ship chartered by a Korean national where available or not in violation of international agreements.[198]

That the requirement be in accordance with international agreements probably refers to the rule against discrimination and equality in the GATT and other international conventions to which South Korea is a signatory or which it has ratified.[199] This provision marks a departure from the practices of other countries. Nevertheless, these and other measures are aimed at export promotion in the national flag vessels.

However, besides these measures, there are also measures aimed specifically at the export of the vessels themselves, equipment and parts thereon, as well as of technical know-how.[200] These too operate by way of subsidies. One of these schemes involves ship export credits.

Ship Export Credits

So often we forget that ships and aircraft, besides being carriers of physical goods and services, are at the same time themselves subjects of international trade, and perhaps more lucrative ones at that. Ship export, like shipbuilding, is still largely a monopoly of the TMNs. Take, for example, three leading TMNs.[201] First, West Germany: since 1961, in order to reduce the cost of export credits for ships, the government has made available ERP (European Recovery Programme) loans and interest subsidies to bring credit terms in relation to ship exports approximately to the internationally prevailing level.[202] The reduction of the interest rate applies solely to that portion of the purchasing price for which payment is deferred.

The amount of the reduction of interest rate is dependent on the current interest rates of the capital market; it must not exceed 12 per cent.[203] Needless to say, assistance will be given in accordance with the Understanding on Export Credit for Ships in its most recent valid version. The Ninth Shipbuilding Assistance Programme for ship exports in the period 1979–82 has been finalized in its implementation.[204] The Tenth Programme is running late. Transactions not financed by a shipyard or its bank are granted to the shipyards in the form of loans by the Combined EXIMBANK of Japan.[205]

The Japanese EXIMBANK is the equivalent of the US EXIMBANK and is supported by the government. However, the bank's loans are supplemented by those of the private banks which cover at most

60 per cent of the total ships' price.[206] Present conditions for the said loans are normally as follows:

1 EXIMBANK loans cover 55 per cent of the combined loans (i.e. 33 per cent of the total price). The term of an EXIMBANK loan is seven years after completion of the ship;[207]
2 Private banks will finance the shipyard with the remainder of the combined loans (i.e. 27 per cent of the total price).[208]

The financing terms of the EXIMBANK are so decided in order that the combined loans meet the OECD Understanding on Export Credits for Ships.[209] However, the shipyard which enjoys these credits will grant a deferred payment to the shipowners abroad on the same conditions as the combined loans. These include payment spread over seven years, at approximately 5 per cent interest rate, and a down payment of at least 30 per cent of the price by delivery time.[210] These credits are mainly directed at expansion of shipbuilding and, through it, ship exports. They may have no direct relation to the expansion of the national fleet itself. The latter objective may be achieved through the manipulation of foreign exchange regulations.[211]

Foreign Exchange Considerations

Foreign Exchange Exemptions

In an economic context, foreign exchange is the system whereby one currency is exchanged for (or converted into) another, though sometimes the term is used as if it were synonymous with the exchange itself.[212] The three main types of foreign exchange systems are:

1 The gold standard in its various forms;
2 Freely fluctuating exchange rates;
3 Several varieties of exchange control.

The fact that each country has its own monetary system is one of the principal complications of international trade. The use of foreign exchange is a country's principal means of selling its transactions and controlling its foreign trade with other countries.[213] Thus, a country's demand for foreign exchange depends on the amount of goods that it wants to import, while the supply of foreign exchange available to it depends on the amount of goods and services it can export. When a nation imports a greater amount of goods and services than it exports,[214] so that foreign exchange expenditure exceeds foreign exchange receipts, the nation is said to have a balance of payments deficit which it must finance either from borrowing or reserves of foreign exchange accumulated in the past. Alternatively, that country will impose exchange restrictions.[215]

Occasionally, however, governments do the opposite (exempt certain sectors) to achieve various objectives in international trade generally, and in the merchant marine industry in particular.[216] This is because the merchant marine industry, both in its physical exports as well as in export of services in the form of carriage of goods, is regarded as one of the major earners of foreign exchange. This correlation between foreign exchange and merchant shipping has been utilized by many nations. One country which manipulates foreign exchange is Greece.[217] Under the programme Greek seamen and workers are permitted to open deposits in convertible foreign currencies with the Greek Commercial Banks, the Agricultural Bank, the National Mortgage Bank, and the Posts and Savings Bank. The interest rates on such deposits are as follows: savings deposits 6.25 per cent, time deposits 6.75–8 per cent depending on the duration of deposits, and sight deposits 3 per cent.[218]

The curious thing to note is that these interest rates are higher than normal. Secondly, these deposits, including accrued interest, are regarded as convertible currencies and not as deposits in local currency. The convertibility of such deposits is valid for the entire time of the depositor's stay abroad.[219] As regards seamen, this privilege is extended for a further three-year period from the date of the retirement, while for other workers for three years after final repatriation.[220] It will be apparent by now that this measure, and the one noted earlier on subsidies, which also offers a higher yield than corresponding deposits in local currency, was adopted in order to attract part of the large overseas deposits by Greek workers, especially seamen, abroad.[221] It is, of course, part of the Greek government's general drive to attract foreign flags and also her own vessels currently operating in open registry or under flags of convenience back to the Greek flag.[222] It is hoped that such moves may rejuvenate the dwindling and ageing Greek fleet as well as improve the country's balance of payments and, consequently, its international trade position. Foreign exchange manipulation has both exemptive and restrictive aims.[223]

Foreign Exchange Restrictions

However, the Greek case is a peculiar example and there is no evidence that the overall experiment is working. On the contrary, most countries prefer to restrict foreign exchange dealings[224] to try and improve their international trade positions.[225] In this latter policy the lead is given by Chile where, for instance, on the basis of Decree No. 179 of 19 February 1968, the Chilean lines receive a 20 per cent advantage upon liquidation of foreign currency received from incomes in the transport of cargo and passengers to and from Chile and between foreign ports.[226] In Pakistan, on the other hand, shipping companies receive a 30 per cent bonus on foreign exchange turned into the government for rupees.[227]

However, one fine example from the TMNs, albeit rather an old one, is that of Spain. Prior to 1958 the Spanish government had imposed foreign exchange restrictions on the convertibility of Spanish pesetas to dollars.[228] These restrictions made it difficult for US flag operators, among others, to solicit for cargo. An additional regulation published by the Spanish government in 1957 made it mandatory for Spanish importers to certify that no Spanish ship was available to carry the material before they would be allowed to utilize the US flag or any foreign flags to lift cargo.[229] These two sets of regulations were no doubt part of the state intervention to aid the merchant marine in particular and international trade generally.

The combination of the two sets of regulations, however, proved a great handicap for attracting foreign operators, especially American, into Spanish foreign trade.[230] In 1958, therefore, the US government refused to grant waivers of Public Resolution No. 17 to Spain on the grounds that Spanish actions were discriminatory against US shipping.[231] This was the origin of and justification for countervailing or retaliatory flag discrimination that will be referred to shortly. The Spanish government subsequently revoked the discriminatory regulations. US and other foreign operators were now considered to have an adequate opportunity for soliciting cargoes in Spanish foreign trade and waivers were granted accordingly[232] allowing Spanish flag vessels to participate in EXIMBANK-financed cargoes.

This serves to illustrate the kind of international effects and therefore reactions that can follow from a country's unilateral intervention to try to improve her foreign shipping trade.[233] The point to be made is that this was a genuine attempt to use restrictive regulations on foreign currency for the promotion of the national fleet and foreign trade.

Import Restrictions

Sometimes a ban is imposed on physical goods instead, and import restrictions provide another example of such measures.[234] In ordinary circumstances imports are goods or services received, in the course of foreign trade, by the country from a foreign country or area imported either in response to direct orders or on consignment.[235] In this case, however, the term 'import' means and includes goods and services and also the importation of vessels, maritime equipment, spare parts, shipping services and insurance.[236] In an effort to establish and develop merchant marines of their own, as well as to improve their foreign trade position, many countries impose restrictions on both sets of imports.[237] These imports from abroad are therefore restricted by:

1 Tariffs;
2 Import quotas;
3 Restrictions of foreign exchange to importers, who do not use the national flag (as in the previous paragraph);
4 Direct prohibitions.[238]

The aim of such an exercise is either to protect domestic shipping or manufactures, or to try to correct an adverse balance of payments, or indeed to prohibit goods harmful to health or morals.[239] However, as indicated by the Spanish–US example above, large-scale restrictions on foreign currency and/or imports generally lead to a fall in exports, since it reduces other countries' earnings of foreign currency. This, in contrast to the original objective, reduces foreign trade leading to reduced national fleets.[240] As intimated earlier, the import licence is yet another weapon in the arsenal of state intervention. Despite the 1958 incident in Spain, imports of ships from all countries are subjected to the prior procurement of an import licence; one would expect Spain to have learnt her lesson.[241]

Under some systems of foreign exchange control (and again in Spain), shipping merchants are only permitted foreign exchange to pay for ship imports sanctioned by the maritime authorities. In such cases licences have to be obtained before the vessels can be imported.[242] Similarly, where imports of vessels are subjected to quotas as demanded, for instance, by the Canadian Maritime Transport Ministry, ocean-going vessels can be imported only by shipowners who have obtained the necessary licence.[243] Quotas are, of course, the other alternative to tariffs and licences, as a means of restricting imports. The number of vessels to be imported during a period is first determined, and then licences are issued to the shipbuilding (supplying) countries, assigning a quota to each.[244]

These mechanisms are not restricted solely to state intervention in the merchant marine; rather they are universally recognized, though not acceptable, as a means of state regulation of its foreign trade or protection of domestic industry.[245] Most other maritime nations, especially the DMNs, use import duties (i.e. taxes) imposed on the equipment and services of vessels entering the country, the purpose being either to increase a state's revenue or to protect home shipowners and shipbuilders by making the imported vessels more expensive.[246] This is imposed in addition to the customs, taxes and excise exemptions which should have been imposed on home operators, but from which they are exempted. For example, all imports to Argentina consigned to the federal, provincial or municipal governments, which have entered the country on a foreign flag vessel, will only be cleared after the presentation at the Custom House Offices and/or reception offices of the Certificate of Cargo Loaded on Foreign Flag Vessel — Law No. 18250.[247]

In order to obtain this certificate, the importer must submit an application in triplicate to the National Administration of Maritime Interests thirty days before the cargo-loading date. This application must contain a description of the type of cargo, its weight and/or volume, the type of cargo packing, the measure unit and quantity, the country of foreign loading port,[248] the loading date, and the name and nationality of the shipping line and the unloading port. Thus, the idea is to discourage use of foreign flags in favour of national fleets by setting up almost insurmountable obstacles for the shippers who would otherwise have chosen foreign flags.[249]

The list of mechanisms for state intervention could be endless. We shall, however, simply summarize the others.

Other Mechanisms of State Intervention

Below there follows a series of other measures, some of which may not have a direct bearing on the establishment and/or expansion of national fleets, but which may nevertheless assist the state concerned in assessing the overall view of its national fleet.[250]

Domestic Ship Registry

State regulation of shipping through registration, though operating like state intervention through a licensing system, is not a unilateral act but a right granted by an international convention because: 'Each state whether coastal or not has a right to sail ships under its own flags on the high seas.'[251] This privilege includes the right to stipulate the conditions for such registration and the rights of national jurisdiction over such vessels:

> Each state shall fix the conditions for the grant of its nationality to ships for the registration of ships in its territory . . . , in particular the state must

effectively exercise its jurisdiction and control in administration, financial and social matters on ships flying its flag . . . .[252]

However, various countries have exercised these rights to enable them to intervene in, and control, the merchant marine industry in their territory in different ways and in circumstances that could not have been intended by the Convention. One of these adverse uses is discriminating against foreign flags with the ultimate aim of aiding the establishment and/or expansion of the domestic fleet.[253] As we have discussed, the stringency of these registration requirements varies from country to country. The common, immediate objective of all countries is to have a rough idea of the strength of the merchant marine force and to ensure that shipping falls within the planning requirements of the national economy.[254] Of course, there is some revenue to be raised from the registration fees but this is a very minor benefit. There do not seem to be major problems caused by stringent national requirements for registration. Even where these are discriminatory, they may be protected by principle sovereignty.[255]

A trend which is causing grave concern is the registration of vessels under so-called 'flags of convenience'. This is, of course, quite a different problem from that of flag discrimination or state intervention. The latter practices stand condemned[256] because interference by governments with the free competition of shipping services, in international trade, is inimical to the interests of all trading nations whether maritime or not. On the other hand, resort to flags of convenience may not be directly instigated by governments though their actions, particularly in the field of taxation, may indirectly create conditions in which the practice presents attractions to shipowners.[257] How far these attractions are real and permanent may be open to question, but there is no doubt that they can easily bring about conditions which sooner or later provoke countermeasures. Of significance however, is that, of late, countries have resorted to actively encouraging foreign registry as a way of aiding their merchant shipping.[258]

Foreign Ship Registry

Whether there are already grounds for action by governments and, if so, what lines such action should take or whether the remedy lies in the shipowners' hands are matters requiring the most careful study.[259] Alternatively known as open registry or flags of convenience, foreign registry is the national flag flown by a merchant ship that has been registered in a country other than that of its owners in order to escape higher domestic wages and taxes. There is no exhaustive definition of flags of convenience which would effectively encompass their significance and characteristics.[260] In 1958, however, the Maritime Transport Committee of the OEEC (now OECD) defined them as:

> The flags of such countries as Panama, Liberia, Honduras and Costa Rica whose laws allow and, indeed, make it easy for ships owned by foreign nationals or companies to fly these flags. This is in contrast to the practice in the maritime countries (and in many others) where the right to fly the national flag is subject to stringent conditions and involves far-reaching obligations.[261]

The origins of foreign registry are as old as those of flag discrimination and maritime subsidies.

The reasons for the spread of the concept, however, are to be found in the reconstruction efforts following the Second World War with its ensuing recession and soaring costs.[262] The principal sources of open registry are the USA, Greece, Italy, UK, Scandinavia, Japan and Western Europe; while the principal destinations are Liberia, Panama, Singapore, Cyprus, Lebanon, Somalia, Honduras, Costa Rica, etc.[263] The disadvantages of open registry (e.g. poor safety records and pollution) far outweigh its advantages, such as the said easing of competition, reductions in running costs, law taxation (in the tax havens) and relaxed regulations, etc. A detailed study of open registry, including the current international efforts to gradually phase it out, has been discussed extensively in Chapter 2.[264]

The relevance, and the point to be made here, is that the named TMNs use open registry as a means of solving their maritime problems and promoting their foreign trade.[265] Let us look at a few examples. About 40 per cent of Dutch-owned shipping tonnage is registered under foreign flags. The Royal Netherlands Shipowners Association attributes this fact to the absence of adequate fiscal measures in the Netherlands.[266] Secondly, since late 1975 the Norwegian government has granted permission for Norwegian shipowners and operators to register some of their tonnage in foreign countries under certain circumstances, e.g., where running costs are too high on a particular type of vessel, or as a way of accommodating the cargo preference rules of other countries.[267]

Finally, since early 1977, Swedish shipowners have received permission to register older, less sophisticated vessels under third flags provided a special allowance is granted and a new Swedish vessel is taken into service.[268] This is the nearest Swedish equivalent to the American trade-in trade-out scheme through which so many US vessels have found their way to foreign registry.[269]

Notes

1 OECD, *Maritime Transport*, 1956, para. 82, p. 63.
2 See case of *Trust Co. of New Jersey v. Greenwood Cemetery*, 21 NJ Misc. 169, 32 A. 2d, 519, p. 523.
3 Also the case of *State v. First State Bank of Ind.*, 52 ND 231, 202 NW 391, p. 402.
4 Meaning to save the situation from getting out of hand; towards or back to the normal course.
5 Simply called encroachment among the TMNs.
6 For details see L.E. Piffer, *The Closing of the Public Domain*, Stamford University Press, California, 1951.
7 See also the origin of maritime subsidies in the previous chapter.
8 And the section on the justification for maritime subsidies, ibid.
9 *Rochdale Report*, (Committee of Inquiry into Shipping – Report of Chairman Lord Rochdale), London, May 1970, chapter 22, 'Role of government shipping policy', para. 1417, p. 375.
10 See also M. Clawson and B. Held, *The Federal Lands: Their Use and Management*, The Hopkins Press, Baltimore, 1957.
11 For comparison see L.C. Sorrell, *Government Ownership and Operations of Railways for the United States*, Prentice-Hall Inc., Englewood Cliffs, NJ, 1939.
12 See also 'The nationalisation of British industries', *Law and Contemporary Problems*, vol. 16, no. 4.
13 Even shipping, which had always been conservative, could not ignore technological change, for instance.
14 Attributed to the fact that now three times as many nations own merchant marines than was the case before the War.
15 See Chapter 3 on flag preference; the *Rochdale Report*, op.cit., Appendix 4, pp. 437–40.
16 Brazilian National Shipping Policy, see Preamble to Decree Law No. 60679 of 3 May 1967.
17 R.B. Brown, *Transportation and the Economic Integration of Latin America*, Brookings Institution, Washington DC, 1966, p. 105.
18 See also T. Lawrence, *Liner Conferences and the Developing Countries*, Tanker Bulker International, vol. 4, no. 5, May 1978, pp. 181-9.
19 K.E. Bakke, 'US regulation of international internodal ocean cargo movements', *International Container Industry Conference Proceedings*, November 1977, pp. 23-7.
20 Bors, 'Regulatory and political restraints and their effects on liner shipping', ibid., pp. 17–22.
21 R.T. Young, Chairman, American Bureau of Shipping, in his Address to the Conference on 'The United States and international shipping: the economic future', *Lloyd's Shipping Economist*, 1980, pp. 1-5.
22 M. Ratcliffe, 'The economics of international shipping – the world trade cycle and its long-term effect on shipping markets, politics and their short-term disruptions to markets', ibid., pp. 1-9.

23 H. Levy, 'United States liner shipping policy: a call to reason', *International Container Conference Proceedings*, op.cit., pp. 80-1.

24 L. von Misco, *Socialism, and Economic and Social Analysis*, The Macmillan Co. New York, 1936.

25 A.C. Pigou, *Socialism and Capitalism*, The Macmillan Co., London, 1937; J.A. Schumpeter, *Capitalism, Socialism and Democracy*, Harper & Row, New York, 1942.

26 But see P.M. Sweeny, *Socialism*, McGraw-Hill Book Co., New York, 1949.

27 See also, 'State trading shipping lines', OECD, *Maritime Transport*, 1985, p. 18.

28 G. Bayley, 'Problems ahead with Soviet tanker surplus', *Fairplay International Shipping Weekly*, vol. 265, no. 4927, 9 February 1978, pp. 7-8.

29 K.H. Sager, 'Russia has signed the UNCTAD (Liner) Code, but will she ratify?', *Norwegian News*, no. 17, 1 September 1978, pp. 8-11.

30 C. Landauer, *The Theory of National Economic Planning*, 2nd edn, University of California Press, Berkeley, California, 1947.

31 For some of these positive aspects see Chapter 3.

32 Both world wars marked the starting-point for many changes in national and international shipping.

33 However, the overriding concern for all these changes is that of maintaining shipping on a commercial and profitable basis.

34 The breaking-point came when it was no longer possible to achieve these objectives under the said prevailing conditions.

35 This, then, is when governments came up with what is popularly known as state intervention.

36 S.E. Harris, *Economic Planning*, Alfred Knopf Inc., New York, 1949.

37 J.E. Meade, *Planning and the Price Mechanism: The Liberal-Socialist Solution*, The Macmillan Co., New York, 1948.

38 V. Packard, *The Waste Makers*, David McKay Co. Inc., New York, 1960.

39 S.H. Britt, *The Spenders*, McGraw-Hill Book Co., New York, 1960.

40 See the case *State v. Manning*, 220 Iowa 525, NW 213.

41 They are prepared to accept the FMC.

42 'Far-Eastern report' (shipping, shipbuilding, shipbreaking, liner trade, Hong Kong), *Fairplay International Shipping Weekly*, vol. 270, pp. 42-52.

43 A.M. Smith, 'Taiwan's restraint is unleashed' (container shipping), *Containerisation*, vol. 13, no. 5, May 1979, pp. 17-20.

44 See the case of *Kemp v. Stanley*, 204 La., 110 15 SO., 2nd. 1, p. 11.

45 'China: trade explosion boosted by boom in bulkers', *Lloyd's Shipping Economist*, vol. 1, no. 1, February 1979, pp. 8-11.

46 'Japan dazzled by prospects of China's surge forward' (shipping), *Zosen*, vol. 23, no. 9, December 1978, pp. 22-4.

47 No other DMNs' practice is comparable to that of Taiwan.

48 For approval see case of *Rooney v. South Sioux City*, 111, 1 February 1955, NW 474, p. 475.

49 See also *State v. Duckett*, 133 SC 85, 130 SE 340, p. 342.

50 And *McCarten v. Sanderson*, 111 Mont. 407, 109P, 2nd. 1108, p. 1112, AIR 1229.

51 It is therefore fair to assume state intervention has become common and acceptable.
52 See again case of *Rooney v. South Sioux City*, op.cit., p. 478.
53 And *State v. Duckett*, op.cit., p. 345.
54 Provision of employment is predominantly an economic consideration for state intervention.
55 U. Wasserman in 'Key issues in developments: interview with UNCTAD secretary general', *Journal of World Trade Law*, vol. 10, no. 1, January–February 1976, p. 17.
56 For détente see *State v. Oregon-Washington R. & Nav. Co.*, 128 Wash. 365, 223P. 600, p. 608.
57 'Israeli shipping', *Sapanut*, vol. 7, no. 3, December 1977, pp. 1–2.
58 Ibid., p. 11.
59 Ibid., p. 12.
60 I. Gal-Edd, 'Israeli foreign trade', *Journal of World Trade Law*, vol. 3, no. 1, January–February 1969, p. 1.
61 Intervention aims to stop, limit or minimize foreign flags from utilizing/ benefiting from subsidies to national flags.
62 J.L. Hazard, *Transportation; Management Economies; Policy*, Cornell Maritime Press, Cambridge, Md., 1977.
63 'Growth and future plans for Korean shipbuilding industry', *Asian Shipping*, May 1978, pp. 30–2.
64 Law of 28 February 1967.
65 H. Gomer, 'Tanker scrapping — a small contribution to a big problem', *Seatrade*, vol. 17, no. 12, December 1977, pp. 41 and 43.
66 'Korea shipbuilding complete second of parcel tanker series', *Asian Shipping*, no. 5, September 1978, pp. 17–18.
67 Article 4, Geneva Convention of the Law of the Sea (High Seas).
68 Ibid., Article 5(1).
69 See *Graves v. People of State of New York*, ex. rel. O'Keefe, NY, 306, US. 466, 59, S. Ct. 595, p. 597, 83L. Ed. 927, 120 ALR 1466.
70 R.J. Sampson in the *Proceedings of the Colloquium Series on Transportation 1967–68 Winnipeg*, Centre for Transportation Studies, University of Manitoba, 1968.
71 But the nerve centre of British shipping is regulated by the Board of Trade under the Department of Industry.
72 See again K.E. Bakke, op.cit., pp. 23–7.
73 A. Phillips (ed.), *Promoting Competition in Regulated Markets*, Brookings Institution, Washington DC, 1975.
74 K.J. Kryvoruka, 'American ocean shipping and the anti-trust laws revised', *Journal of Maritime Law and Commerce*, pp. 67–107.
75 Ibid., p. 107.
76 C.J. MacGuire and R.E. McDaniel, 'Conquering the maze: a proposed re-organisation of the US shipping laws', *Proceedings of the Maritime Safety Council*, vol. 38, no. 4, June 1981, pp. 93–9.
77 G.W. Mason, 'Regulation, public policy and efficient provision of freight transportation', *Transport Journal*, Autumn 1975.
78 Ibid.

79 J. Lansing, *Transportation and Economic Policy*, Free Press, New York, 1966.

80 See also D. Munby, *Transport: Selected Readings*, Penguin Books, Baltimore, 1968.

81 I. Middleton and A. Renouf, 'Washington doors close' (US Maritime Policy), *Seatrade*, vol. 10, no. 10, November 1979, pp. 691-701.

82 W.L. Bush, 'Steamship conference contract rate agreement and the dual rate system', *ICC Practitioner's Journal*, November-December 1972.

83 M. Gray, 'United States: the building of a maritime policy', *Fairplay Shipping International*, vol. 272, no. 4015, 11 October 1979, pp. 6-11.

84 J. Chiarbas, 'Murphy's second law' (US maritime proposals), *Seatrade*, vol. 9, no. 7, July 1979, pp. 3-5.

85 Anon., 'US edges slowly towards stricter liner control', *Seatrade*, vol. 8, no. 3, March 1978, pp. 19 and 21.

86 See *Securities and Exchange Commission v. Wickham*, D.C. Minn. 1gF. Suppl. 245, p. 247.

87 See also *Drake v. Crane*, 127 no. 85, 29SW 990, 27. LRA653.

88 M.J. Kust, *Foreign Enterprise in India: Law and Policies*, University of Carolina Press, Chapel Hill, 1964.

89 M.S. McDougal *et al.*, 'Maintenance of public order at sea and the nationality of ships', *American Journal of International Law*, vol. 54, 1960, pp. 25-116.

90 J. Tinbergen, *Shaping the World Economy*, Twentieth Century FWd, New York, 1962.

91 C. Oliver, 'The American foreign investment code', *American Journal of International Law*, vol. 60, pp. 763-84.

92 J.N. Hyde, 'Economic development agreements', *Hague Recueil*, vol. 105, 1962, pp. 267-374.

93 See also *Stramann v. Scheefen*, 7 Colo., App. 42, p. 191; *Una v. Dodd*, 39 NJ Eq. 186.

94 D.M. Phillips, 'Restraints on foreign investments in the merchant marine — an asset or liability to the US interest?', *Cornell International Law Journal*, vol. 11, no. 1, Winter 1978, pp. 1-49.

95 46 USC, para. 883 (Suppl. V. 1975).

96 D.P. Hanson, 'Regulation of the shipping industry: an economic analysis of the need for reform', *Law of Politics and International Business*, vol. 12, no. 4, 1980, pp. 973-1001.

97 46 USC, para. 883, 1970.

98 7 US Department of Commerce, Foreign Direct Investment in the US, App. K, 1976, at K. 65.

99 G. Jantscher, 'Bread upon the waters: federal aid to the maritime industries 80', 1975, note 28, p. 51.

100 46 USC, para. 802(a) (1970). But seen Anon., 'The rising tide of reverse flow', *Michigan Law Review*, vol. 72, 1974, pp. 551-91.

101 Ibid., also L.B. Barnes, 'State regulation of foreign investment', *Cornell International Law Journal*, vol. 9, no. 1, Winter 1975, pp. 82-100.

102 46 USC, para. 802(c), 1970.

103 46 USC, para. 883-1, 1970.

104 46 USC, para. 835, 1970.
105 See generally S. Rep., No. 2145, 85 Cong. 2d Sess., 1958; reprinted in *US Code Cong. and Ad. News*, 5190, 1958.
106 See also Act of 14 July 1956, Pub. Law No. 8474, para. 1,70 Stat. 544.
107 D.F. Vagts, 'The corporate alien: definitional quations in federal restraint on foreign enterprise', *Harvard Law Review*, vol. 74, 1960–61, pp. 1489–551.
108 Ibid.
109 R.J. Blackwell, 'Implementation of the Merchant Marine Act of 1970', *Journal of Maritime Law and Commerce*, January 1974.
110 A. Berglund, *Ocean Transportation*, Longmans, Green & Co., New York, 1931.
111 A.E. Waugh, *Principles of Economics*, McGraw-Hill Books, New York, 1947, chapters 4 and 8; see also the case of *Lobsitz v. E. Lissberger Co.*, 168 App. Div. 840, 154, NYS 556, p. 557.
112 A. Marshall, *Principles of Economics*, Macmillan, London, 1920, p. 51; see also the case of *Preston v. State Industrial Accident Commission*, 174, Ov. 553, 149 P. 2d. 957, pp. 961 and 962.
113 J.H. Bonneville *et al.*, *Organising and Financing Business*, Prentice-Hall Inc., Englewood Cliffs, NJ, 1959.
114 W.G. Friedman and G. Kalmanoff, *Joint Internation Ventures*, Columbia University Press, New York, 1961.
115 L. Gorton, 'Joint ventures in shipping law', *Journal of Business Law*, July 1978, pp. 238–44.
116 L.A. Keith and C.E. Gubellin, *Introduction to Business Enterprise*, McGraw-Hill Book Co., New York, 1962.
117 B.S. Whebie, 'Cooperation through trade facilitation', *ICC International Shipping Conference*, May 1977, pp. 89–96.
118 G.H. Upolla, 'IMCO: an effort in Latin America', *Latin American Shipping*, 1979, pp. 61–3.
119 A.G. Clement, 'A promising future for owners and builders', *Latin American Shipping*, 1979, p. 13.
120 'Egypt' (investments, post Suez Canal), *Shipbroker*, vol. 6, no. 2, February 1980, pp. 21–7.
121 'South Korea, shipping and shipbuilding' (special report), *Lloyd's List*, 11 January 1979, pp. 4–6.
122 E.D. Naess, 'Liberian flag shipping, the industry's perspective', *Seatrade Publications*, pp. 117–26.
123 The LSC was created by the Act of 18 April 1961.
124 'Malaysia shipyard and engineering pulling out of the recession', *Norwegian Shipping News*, vol. 37, no. 6, May 1981, pp. 23–6.
125 State control is not an end in itself but a means to an end — the establishment and development of national fleets.
126 Nationalization originates from Spanish or Mexican Law Nationalization: Hall, *Mexican Law*, para. 749.
127 M. Domke, 'Foreign nationalisations', *American Journal of International Law*, vol. 55, 1961, pp. 585–616.

128 R.S. Miller and R.J. Strangler in *Essays on Expropriations*, Ohio State University Press, Columbus, p. 165.

129 O. Knudsen, *The Politics of International Shipping: Conflict and Interaction in a Transitional Issue-Area, 1946-1948*, Lexington Books, Mass., chapter 3 in 2.

130 B.W. Lewis, *British Planning and Nationalisation*, The Twentieth Century Fund, New York, 1952.

131 'The nationalisation of British industries', *Law and Contemporary Problems*, Autumn 1951.

132 *Rochdale Report*, op.cit., para. 637, p. 776.

133 Ibid., paras 274-80, pp. 77-9.

134 'Portugal: special report' (shipping ports, shipbuilding, etc.), *Lloyd's List*, 18 March 1980, pp. 5-15.

135 'Portugal' (survey – shipping and ports), *Shipbroker*, vol. 6, no. 3, March 1980, pp. 23-8.

136 The other TMNs with nationalized sectors are Australia, Canada, Finland, France, Ireland, Italy, Netherlands, New Zealand, Norway, Spain, Sweden, etc.

137 See B.W. Lewis, *British Planning and Nationalisation*, The Twentieth Century Fund, New York, 1952, p. 85.

138 And 'The nationalisation of British industries', *Law and Contemporary Problems*, Duke University Law School, Durham NC, Autumn 1951.

139 US Department of Commerce, *Survey of Current Business: National Income Supplements*, July issues.

140 H.C. Prichett, *The American Constitution*, McGraw-Hill Book Co., New York, 1959, chapter 36, for comparison of state ownership, nationalization and eminent domain.

141 See again L.E. Piffer, *The Closing of the Public Domain*, op.cit.

142 *Beekman v. Saratoga and S.R. Co.*, 3 paige, NY 45, 73 Am. Cas. 1914C, p. 1266.

143 'Ireland' (survey of shipping ports, etc.), *Lloyd's List*, 14 March 1978, pp. 9-10.

144 See also 'Irishman' (tug), *Fairplay International Shipping Weekly*, vol. 265, no. 4940, 4 May 1978, pp. 26-7.

145 FINMARE is a public holding; cf. *Harrison v. Big Four Bus Lines*, 217.

146 'Italian marine industries' (survey), *Fairplay International Shipping Weekly*, vol. 265, no. 4938, 20 April 1978, pp. 41-57.

147 Ibid.; almost all the leading DMNs operate from state ownership with the exception, perhaps, of Cyprus, Saudi Arabia and the UAE.

148 See again *Fairplay International Shipping Weekly*, vol. 255, no. 4938, op.cit., pp. 41-57.

149 B.J. Abrahamson and M.A. Singer, 'A shipping research program with particular reference to smaller nations', *Journal of Israeli Shipping*, April 1972.

150 C.E. Fayle, *A Short History of the World's Shipping Industry*, Allen & Unwin, London, 1933.

151 *Oklahoma City v. Board of Education of Oklahoma City*, 181 Okl, 539, 75P 2d 201, involving state contracts.

152 Irving, *The Purchasing Power of Money*, The Macmillan Co., New York, 1912.
153 US Department of Commerce, MARAD, *Maritime Subsidies*, 1978, p. 67.
154 Emergency Law No. 465 Amending and Supplementing Certain Provisions of Law No. 1880/1951 Concerning Government Purchases of Ships.
155 Ibid., published 9 July 1968; became effective 1 January 1968.
156 On 17 April 1970 Legislative Decree No. 509 was enacted to extend the purchasing powers of Law No. 465.
157 Provided by legislation governing taxation of ships of all types and/as codified under Royal Decree No. 800 of 1 December 1970.
158 Ibid., applicable only to flags owned by Greeks.
159 The law provides for two categories of vessels herein designated as (a) and (b).
160 This condition applies to both categories with each category further subdivided into 4 sub-categories, a–d.
161 See Laws Nos 465/68 and 509/70 as codified by Law No. 800.
162 See also G. Alexanderson and G. Norstrom, *World Shipping*, John Wiley and Sons, New York, 1963.
163 E. Frankel and H.S. Marens, *Ocean Transportation*, MIT Press, Cambridge, Mass., 1972.
164 L.C. Kendall, *The Business of Shipping*, Cornell Maritime Press, Cambridge, Md., 1973.
165 S.G. Sturmey, *British Shipping and World Competition*, Athlon Press, 1962, p. 104.
166 Ibid., p. 105, note 1; US Maritime Commission, *Economic Survey of the American Merchant Marine* (Kennedy report), 1937, p. 58.
167 D. Wettery, *High Speed Surface Craft*, vol. 19, nos 9 and 10, June–July 1980, p. 24.
168 'New building finance: no abatement in the subsidy scramble', *Fairplay International Shipping Weekly*, vol. 273, no. 5034, 21 February 1980, pp. 25–7.
169 F. Phillips, 'The innovative line' (Australian national line), *Containerisation*, vol. 14, no. 3, March 1980, pp. 26–30.
170 R.A. Black, 'The Australian shipper — his shipping needs', *Australian Symposium on Shipping and Management* (conference proceedings), November 1977: vol. I, pp. 17–22; vol. II, pp. 1–2.
171 'South Korea: growth and future plans for Korean shipbuilding industry', *Asian Shipping*, no. 3, May 1978, pp. 30–2.
172 Done under Decree Law of 9 January 1962.
173 Authorized under Decree Law No. 20759 of 15 October 1974.
174 See also Supreme Decree, effective 26 March 1976.
175 Decree Law No. 22067 of 11 January 1978.
176 Decree dated 30 December 1969.
177 The Law of 8 February 1957.
178 The other TMNs that practise this are Canada, Iceland, the Scandinavian countries, Spain and the USA; the majority of the other DMNs do.
179 S.A. Lawrence, *US Merchant Shipping Policies and Politics*, Brookings Institution, Washington DC, 1966.

180 See *Tennessee Oil Co. v. McCanless*, 178 Tenn. 683, 157 SW 2d, p. 272.

181 See also *An Introduction to Doing Import and Export Business*, Chamber of Shipping of the US, Washington DC, 1962.

182 E.E. Pratt, *Modern International Commerce*, Allynand and Bacon Inc., Boston, 1956.

183 For inducement see *State v. Stratford*, 55 Idaho 65. 37P. 2d 681, p. 682.

184 See also J.M. Clark, 'Business accelerations and the laws of demand: the technical factor in economic cycles', reprinted in *Readings in Business Cycle Theory*, McGraw-Hill Book Co., New York, 1964.

185 And D. Hamburg and C.L. Schultze, 'Autonomous investment v. induced investment', *Economic Journal*, Royal Economic Society, London, March 1961.

186 G. Ackley, *Macro-economic Theory*, The Macmillan Co., New York, 1961, pp. 485–93 and 518–29.

187 'Marcos manoeuvres Philippine flag' (shipping), *Containerisation*, vol. 13, no. 3, March 1979, pp. 49–51.

188 G.F. Tanesco, 'The ambitious achievements and developments of the Philippine shipping industry', *Seatrade*, Hong Kong Conference, November 1978, pp. 31–41.

189 See also the Philippines Overseas Shipping Act of 1975.

190 The Development Bank of the Philippines authorized to do so by Presidential Decree Order No. 37 and Presidential Decree 806 of 3 October 1975.

191 The other TMNs doing this are Canada, Denmark, Finland, France, Germany (FRG), Greece, Japan, Spain and Sweden; most DMNs do.

192 See *US v. Hill*, CCA, NY 34F 2d. 133, p. 135.

193 Commonly known as The Shipping Promotion Law enacted by the Republic of Korea on 28 February 1967.

194 Ibid., para. D; also A.M. Smith, 'Korea mixes its Pacific presence' (profile of 3 container shipping companies), *Containerisation*, vol. 15, no. 6, June 1981, pp. 32–6.

195 Ibid., para. E; see also 'South Korea's high-riding yards strive to achieve a balance', *Seatrade*, vol. 11, no. 6, June 1981, pp. 21–3.

196 Ibid., para. F; ASEAN (Malaysia, Singapore, Thailand, Philippines, Indonesia), *Lloyd's List, Special Report*, 7 August 1980, pp. 5–12.

197 Ibid., para. G; J.M. Featherstone, 'Through transport and the total export concept', *Conference on Maritime Commercial Practices*, November 1978, pp. 1–8.

198 Ibid., para. F; also 'The shipbuilding industry in South Korea and its development', *Schiff und Haven Komm*, no. 4, April 1979, pp. 271–3.

199 See Shipping Protection Law of 28 February 1967.

200 Thus the above law covers (1) importation, (2) improvements, (3) repairs and (4) chartering of a ship on condition the ship will take the Republic of Korea nationality.

201 Y.O. Maruno, *Practice and Law of International Ship Finance*, PhD thesis, Southampton University, 1978.

202 R.A. Ramsay, 'World trade versus the supply of shipping and ships', *Marine Policy*, vol. 4, no. 1, January 1980, pp. 63–7.

203 J.A. Cassing, 'Trade pattern production and resource allocation in a model with jointly supplied international transport services', *Transportation Economics*, vol. 6, no. 3, December 1979, pp. 293-309.

204 See 'German shipping industries determinedly optimistic despite difficulties', *Asian Shipping*, no. 22, October 1980, pp. 19-23.

205 'Finance' (shipping investment, second-hand market), *Marine Week*, vol. 6, no. 5, 21 December 1979, pp. 27-30.

206 'Policy amendments to boost shipping industry' (Japan), *Zosen*, vol. 24, no. 5, August 1979, pp. 14-16.

207 See also 'Japanese shipping activities last year', *Norwegian News*, no. 2, 26 January 1979, pp. 23-8.

208 W. Uchi, 'Close relationships between shipbuilding industry in Japan and shipowners in Greece', *Zosen*, vol. 25, no. 3, June 1980, pp. 36-9.

209 'IBJ surveys Japanese shipping and shipbuilding industry', *Zosen*, vol. 24, no. 3, June 1979, pp. 14-16.

210 J.J.R. Luthwaite, 'The Japanese problem — bankers opt for prudence as small and medium sized [ship] builders crumble', *Fairplay International Shipping Weekly*, vol. 265, no. 4938, 20 April 1979, pp. 21 and 23.

211 OECD European Conference of Ministers of Transport, *Report of the International Symposium on Theory and Practice in Transportation Economics*, 1964-65, Paris.

212 R. Mikesell, *Foreign Exchange in the Post World War*, Twentieth Century Fund, New York, 1954.

213 See also F. Southard Jr, *Foreign Exchange Practice and Policy*, McGraw-Hill Book Co., New York, 1940.

214 F. Machlup, 'The theory of foreign exchanges' in H. Ellis and L.A. Metzler, *Readings in the Theory of International Trade*, McGraw-Hill Book Co., New York, 1949.

215 See 'Strong DM threat to German shipping', *Norwegian News*, no. 17, 1 September 1978, pp. 5-7.

216 R. Adams, 'Pricing in foreign currencies: financing international trade' (conference proceedings), November 1977, p. 4.

217 H. Williams, 'Impact of exchange rates, charges on shipping costs and revenues', *Norwegian News*, vol. 37, no. 7, May 1981, pp. 23-6; also reported in *Asian Shipping*, April 1981, pp. 58-9.

218 *Continental Grain Export Corporation (US) v. STM Grain Ltd* (Charles E. Ford Ltd), 1979, 2 Lloyds LR, p. 64.

219 Law No. 465, published September 1968.

220 See also 'Greece adjusts to new realities', *Seatrade*, vol. 8, no. 6, June 1978, pp. 3-4.

221 And Legislative Decree No. 509, 17 April 1970; M. Ratcliffe, 'Greek shipping — going bust waiting for methavrio [the day after tomorrow]', *Tanker Bulker International*, vol. 4, no. 5, May 1978, pp. 5 and 7.

222 Under the Royal Decree No. 800; also 'Greek marine' (safety, casualties, shipping), *Nautical Review*, vol. 3, no. 8, August 1979, pp. 32-40.

223 Laws 465/68 and 509/70, codified by Law 800.

224 Article 23, Greek Constitution 1968; cf. Law 465/1968.

225 Governed by Laws 1880/60 and 3415/55 as amended by Legislative Decree 4094/60 and 4419/64.
226 See *An Introduction to Doing Import and Export Business*, op.cit.; and D.D. Humfrey, *American Imports*.
227 See *Cunard Steamship Co. v. Melton*, 43 S.Ct. 504, 26 US, 100, 67 L.Ed. 894, 2 ALR 1306.
228 The Conqueror 49, Fed. 99.
229 H.B. Kellough and L.M. Kellough, *Economics of International Trade*, McGraw-Hill Book Co., New York, 1948.
230 P.T. Ellsworth, *The International Economy*, The Macmillan Co., New York, 1958.
231 C.P. Kindleberger, *International Economics*, Richard D. Irwin Inc., Homewood, Ill., 1958.
232 C. Brock, *The Control of Restrictive Practices from 1956*, McGraw-Hill Book Co., New York, 1966.
233 Heydon, *The Restraint of Trade Doctrine*, Butterworths, London, 1971.
234 V. Korah, *Competition Law of Britain and the Common Market*, Penguin Books, London, 1968.
235 OECD, *Guide to Legislations on Restrictive Business in Europe and North America*, Paris, 1964.
236 For GATT see A.H. Peck, *International Economics*, Thomas Y. Crowell Co., New York, 1957, chapter 11.
237 See again *Cunard Steamship v. Melton* (note 227 above).
238 See also H.B. Kellough and L.M. Kellough, *Economics of International Trade*, op.cit.
239 C.P. Kindleberger, *International Economics*, op.cit.
240 P.T. Ellsworth, *The International Economy*, op.cit.
241 C. Brock, *The Control of Restrictive Practices from 1956*, op.cit.
242 Heydon, *The Restraint of Trade Doctrine*, op.cit.
243 V. Korah, *Competition Law of Britain and the Common Market*, op.cit.
244 A.H. Peck, *International Economics*, op.cit.
245 OECD, *Guide to Legislations*, op.cit.
246 Income Tax Act; see also 'Canada' (shipowners, shipbuilding, arctic ports), *Marine Week*, no. 44, 9 November 1979, pp. 18–23.
247 C. Hayman, 'Canadian shipowners make their feelings known', *Seatrade*, vol. 8, no. 7, July 1978, p. 15.
248 J.L. Shaw, 'Europressor Lineas Maritinas Argentinas SA. Co. profile', *Asian Shipping*, May 1981, pp. 7–9.
249 Ibid.; see also 'Argentina: cargo reservation threat grows', *Lloyds Shipping Econ.*, vol. 1, no. 5, June 1979, pp. 11–14.
250 See also 'Back from the brink' (UNCTAD Code), *Seatrade*, vol. 8, no. 11, November 1978, pp. 3–4.
251 See, for instance, 'Canada, shipping and shipbuilding', *Marine Week*, vol. 5, no. 8, August 1979, pp. 65–7.
252 Act 4, Geneva Convention – Law of the Sea – High Seas.
253 Ibid., Act 5(1).
254 *Rochdale Report*, op.cit., paras 824–5, 1530, 84, 89–90, 101.
255 US Department of Commerce, MARAD, *Maritime Subsidies*, 1978, p. 104.

256 See also Article 5(2), Geneva Convention on the High Seas.
257 OECD, *Maritime Transport*.
258 C. Rodney, *Sovereignty for Sale*, Naval Institute Press, Annapolis, Maryland, 1981.
259 H.J. Darling, 'The elements of an international shipping policy for Canada', *Transport Canada Marine*, 1974.
260 American Committee for Flags of Necessity, *The Role of Flags of Necessity*, New York, 1962.
261 K. Grundey, *Flags of Convenience in 1978*, Polytechnic of Central London, November 1978, pp. 1-3.
262 *Rochdale Report*, op.cit., para. 183, p. 51.
263 P. Yang, 'The ITFW disputes over flags of convenience', *Asian Shipping*, November 1980, pp. 46-8.
264 'Open for compromise' (likely outcome of UNCTAD's Committee on Shipping Meeting on Open Registry), *Seatrade*, vol. 11, no. 4, April 1980, pp. 13-15.
265 'Exposed: how flags of convenience shipping threatens to hand down the red duster', *The Seaman*, July 1981, Suppl. 11pp.
266 US Department of Commerce, MARAD, *Maritime Subsidies*, 1978, pp. 113-15, p. 113.
267 Ibid., pp. 119-23; also 'Basic industries also in the future' (Norwegian shipping), *Norwegian News*, no. 1, 25 January 1980, pp. 68-70.
268 Ibid., pp. 153-6; also D. Parton, 'Swedish yards on the brink — but where there is life . . .', *Seatrade*, vol. 10, no. 2, February 1980, pp. 65-7.
269 Ibid., pp. 168-76; K. Grundey, 'Research into flags of convenience at the PLC', *Pynda Leader*, Winter 1979, pp. 21-4.

6 State ownership and participation in shipping

Introduction

A national merchant fleet is believed to be of vital economic and security interest by many of the world's governments, and in order to ensure that these interests are upheld, many governments have developed myriad aids and subsidies in support of their merchant fleet.[1] It has also been the case that governments of most nations possessing merchant fleets, whether state- or privately-owned, offer some form of special assistance to their maritime industries to further their commercial and political interests.[2] The forms in which these assistances occur have been dealt with in Chapters 3 and 4 — i.e. preferences and discriminations respectively. Special aid to the industry by various governments has been the subject of Chapter 5 — i.e. state intervention.[3] Many governments are, however, unhappy with merely controlling and aiding what are still largely privately-owned industries. Thus, quite a few governments, not content with regulating the industry, have sought state participation and/or ownerships.[4] This chapter attempts to outline the form and content of state ownerships of the merchant marines and their related maritime industries. It also seeks to provide some rationales for such state actions.

The great trading nations have developed huge merchant fleets that have an impact all over the world, and many others are seeking, in various degrees, to follow suit.[5] The costs of developing and

258

operating a merchant fleet vary tremendously from country to country. A nation possessing an advantage on one particular cost factor will probably be suffering from a disadvantage in another cost area. Be that as it may, international maritime law not only recognizes but also makes provisions for such eventualities.[6] Articles 27 and 28 of UNCLOS I are applicable to government ships when operated for commercial purposes. Thus:

SUBSECTION B. RULES APPLICABLE TO MERCHANT SHIPS AND GOVERNMENT SHIPS OPERATED FOR COMMERCIAL PURPOSES

Article 27
Criminal jurisdiction on board a foreign ship

1. The criminal jurisdiction of the coastal State should not be exercised on board a foreign ship passing through the territorial sea to arrest any person or to conduct any investigation in connection with any crime committed on board the ship during its passage, save only in the following cases:

a) if the consequences of the crime extend to the coastal State;
b) if the crime is of a kind to disturb the peace of the country or the good order of the territorial sea;
c) if the assistance of the local authorities has been requested by the master of the ship or by a diplomatic agent or consular officer of the flag State; or
d) if such measures are necessary for the suppression of illicit traffic in narcotic drugs or psychotropic substances.

2. The above provisions do not affect the right of the coastal State to take any steps authorized by its laws for the purpose of an arrest or investigation on board a foreign ship passing through the territorial sea after leaving internal waters.

3. In the cases provided for in paragraphs 1 and 2, the coastal State shall, if the master so requests, notify a diplomatic agent or consular officer of the flag State before taking any steps, and shall facilitate contact between such agent or officer and the ship's crew. In cases of emergency, this notification may be communicated while the measures are being taken.

4. In considering whether or in what manner an arrest should be made, the local authorities shall have due regard to the interests of navigation.

5. Except as provided in Part XII or with respect to violations of laws and regulations adopted in accordance with Part V, the coastal State may not take any steps on board a foreign ship passing through the territorial sea to arrest any person or to conduct any investigation in connection with any crime committed before the ship entered the territorial sea, if the ship, proceeding from a foreign port, is only passing through the territorial sea without entering internal waters.

Article 28
Civil jurisdiction in relation to foreign ships

1. The coastal State should not stop or divert a foreign ship passing through the territorial sea for the purposes of exercising civil jurisdiction in relation to a person on board the ship.

2. The coastal State may not levy execution against or arrest the ship for the purpose of any civil proceedings, save only in respect of obligations or liabilities assumed or incurred by the ship itself in the course or for the purpose of its voyage through the waters of the coastal State.

3. Paragraph 2 is without prejudice to the right of the coastal State, in accordance with its laws, to levy execution against or to arrest, for the purpose of any civil proceedings, a foreign ship lying in the territorial sea, or passing through the territorial sea after leaving internal waters.[7] While Articles 29–32 are the rules applicable when ships are operated by governments for non-commercial purposes.

SUBSECTION C. RULES APPLICABLE TO WARSHIPS AND OTHER GOVERNMENT SHIPS OPERATED FOR NON-COMMERCIAL PURPOSES

Article 29
Definition of warships

For the purposes of this Convention, 'warship' means a ship belonging to the armed forces of a State bearing the external marks distinguishing such ships of its nationality, under the command of an officer duly commissioned by the government of the State and whose name appears in the appropriate service list or its equivalent, and manned by a crew which is under regular armed forces discipline.

Article 30
Non-compliance by warships with the laws and regulations of the coastal State

If any warship does not comply with the laws and regulations of the coastal State concerning passage through the territorial sea and disregards any request for compliance therewith which is made to it, the coastal State may require it to leave the territorial sea immediately.

Article 31
Responsibility of the flag State for damage caused by a warship or other government ship operated for non-commercial purposes

The flag state shall bear international responsibility for any loss or damage to the coastal State resulting from the non-compliance by a warship or other government ship operated for non-commercial purposes with the laws and regulations of the coastal State concerning passage through the territorial sea or with the provisions of this Convention or other rules of international law.

Article 32
Immunities of warships and other government ships
operated for non-commercial purposes

With such exceptions as are contained in subsection A and in articles 30 and 31, nothing in this Convention affects the immunities of warships and other government ships operated for non-commercial purposes.[8]

Rationale for Government Ownership Operations

In fact the Convention makes allowance for the UN and its constituents to operate ships. Thus there is provision for ships flying the flag of the United Nations, its specialized agencies and the International Atomic Energy Agency:

> The preceding article does not prejudice the question of ships employed on the official service of the United Nations, its specialised agencies or the International Atomic Energy Agency, flying the flag of the organisation.[9]

Although warships are not commercial vessels and are therefore not the subject of this discussion, nevertheless they are government-owned ships and are, accordingly, provided for under Immunity of Warships on the High Seas:

> Warships on the high seas have a complete immunity from the jurisdiction of any state other than the flag State.[10]

Even ships that are used on non-commercial services have immunity so long as they are operated and/or owned by states and/or governments, under Immunity of Ships used only on Government Non-commercial Service:[11]

> Ships owned or operated by a state and used only on government non-commercial service shall, on the high seas, have complete immunity from the jurisdiction of any state other than the flag State.[12]

Further provisions relating to government-owned and/or operated ships, as warships or for commercial and non-commercial purposes are to be found in Articles 110(1)(a), 110(1)(e) and 110(2) of the Convention.[13]

The rationale for state participation should not be too difficult to find. National security and defence has already been mentioned, as has the crucial role of shipping in international economic, political, trade and financial relations. Another reason is that certain governments, both DMNs and market economy TMNs, believe in a certain amount of public ownership: that is, the government ownership and operation of a business enterprise.[14] Under public ownership, the government replaces the private owner as the capitalist. Thus, the government supplies the capital and determines the facilities to be provided.[15] It also chooses the management, and assumes the responsibility of paying labour, purchasing supplies, setting the price for its goods and services, and reaping profits or meeting deficits if they are incurred. Many governments (e.g. UK) have embarked on this course through nationalization: a government act of removing private ownership and assuming the operation of the enterprise.[16] These governments argue that nationalization increases productive efficiency by permitting the direct investment of public funds, by enlarging the scale of operations, and by coordinating operations more effectively.[17] They cite, in support of their arguments, the fact that many of the TMNs are enjoying their current strong positions because their governments resorted to nationalization and public ownership of the industries following the Second World War.[18]

The most outstanding example of public ownership has been in the USA: namely, the Tennessee Valley Authority, which is concerned with conservation and power production in the Tennessee Valley area.[19] Nationalization has been used by some countries purely as a means of eliminating foreign ownership of their basic industries, which is perfectly legitimate. The other rationale for government ownership or participation is on ideological grounds, such as the STNs who operate planned economics or state trading.[20] The STNs, mainly of Eastern Europe, operate an economic and political system in which some or all of the decisions on allocation, production, investment and distribution are made by a central government agency.[21] The collective economic planning used in a planned economy is based on the assumption that social welfare can be recognized and pursued more ably under centralized control. This is the antithesis of private enterprise, which is said to lead to chaotic disharmony between production and consumption.[22] In a planned economy, the initiative for economic activities and decisions concerning them do not originate with the shipping entrepreneur. Rather, the government starts with an overall plan of major objectives and then attempts to achieve the fullest possible utilization of available resources in line with state objectives.[23] In a completely planned economy, the market mechanism in price formation is eliminated, and the government undertakes to replace the market functions. The planning agency gets all the goals for production, allocates scarce resources among competing users, makes decisions on production and investment, and distributes the output to consumers.[24] In this way, the planned economy claims to achieve maximum social welfare. Shipping has to fall in line with these plans, and it is against this background that the nature and extent of state ownership and/or participation in the industry can best be appreciated.[25]

State Ownership of Shipping in Africa

North Africa

Algeria   Algeria's state-owned shipping line, Compagnie Nationale Algérienne de Navigation (CNAN) has as its major goal the carriage of 50 per cent of the country's foreign trade. In early 1979 it was reported that the line was conveying about 25 per cent of all dry cargo traffic[26] — 13-15 per cent in its own ships and 10 per cent in chartered vessels. Article 1 on Algerian Law No. 78-02 of February 1978 states that:

> In accordance with the provisions of the national charter, and applying Article 14 of the Constitution, import and export of goods, supplies and services of all kinds are under the exclusive control of the state.[27]

It also states that:

> Contracts of a commercial agency or of representation whose purpose is the realisation of the import or export of merchandise or the use of services, can only be concluded with foreign companies, wherever they may be, in Algeria or abroad, by an organization of the State.[28]

Otherwise the CNAN and the Société Nationale pour la Recherche, la Production, le Transport, la Transformation et la Commercialisation des Hydrocarbures (SONATRACH) are state-owned concerns. Algeria owns a 13.7 per cent share in the Arab Maritime Petroleum Transport Company (AMPTC).[29] Two vessels of the Compagnie Algéria–Libyenne de Transport Maritime (CALTRAM), a joint Algerian–Libyan venture, fly the Algerian flag. Algeria also holds a 49 per cent interest in the Algerian–Beninese shipping line (the Republic of Benin owns the remaining 51 per cent).[30] The US EXIMBANK financed traffic between the USA and Algeria, which was equally divided between vessels of each country.

Egypt   In Egypt, on the other hand, the government owns the Egyptian Navigation Company and the Petroleum Organization of Egypt. The Alexandria shipping and Navigation Company is a Pan-Arab Company with Egyptian, Jordanian, Kuwaiti and Saudi-Arabian participation.[31] Until recently, Egypt was also involved with Syria and Libya in a joint venture called the Federal Arab Maritime Company (FAMCO).

Libya   The Libyan government owns the General Maritime Transport Company (GMTC), which in turn owns virtually the entire Libyan fleet[32] and also controls all shipping activities in Libya. The entirely state-owned, Universal Shipping Company (USC), Benghazi, is the sole agent of tanker shipping in all of Libya.

The government of the Turkish Republic and the Socialist Peoples' Libyan Arab Jamahiriya have established a joint maritime transport stock company.[33]

Morocco   In Morocco, the government owns the Compagnie Marocain de Navigation (COMANAV). Both COMANAV and the state-owned Office Chirifione de Phosphate (OCP) are involved in a joint maritime transport venture, MARPHOCEAN, with the French firm GAZOCEAN.[34] COMANAV has formed a pool with the French firm FABRE to share cargo between the French Mediterranean and Casablanca on a 40–40–20 basis. A similar pool has been formed with French firms (including GEM and UIM) for the northern French ports of Rouen and Le Havre. A West German shipping firm, OPDR, also has a successful similar pool with COMANAV for cargoes between Hamburg, Bremen, Rotterdam, Antwerp and Morocco.[35]

West Africa

Gabon   In Gabon, Société Nationale des Transports Maritimes is the state-owned shipping line. Gabon has developed two major port systems: Owendo and Port Gentil. The port of Libreville has been relegated to handling the tourist trade. A government decree signed on 7 September 1978 confirms the division of cargo, using UNCTAD's 40–40–20 formula with the qualification that government and quasi-government cargo be expressly reserved for Gabonese flag vessels.[36]

Ghana   Ghana achieved independence in 1957, and its only shipping company, the Black Star Line became fully Ghanian owned in 1967 when the government of Ghana acquired all the ZIM shares.[37] Most cargoes ordered by the Ghana Supply Commission, the government's purchasing organization, are handled by the Black Star Line as shipping agents,[38] although cargo is moved by the first available conference vessel.

Liberia   Liberia presents a curious picture. The world's largest merchant fleet (about 10-15 per cent of the total world fleet) operates under the Liberian flag, and these vessels play a vital role in the country's economy through their registration fees and tonnage.[39] It is estimated that Greek interests own some 30-35 per cent, and Hong Kong interests own about 10-15 per cent; the remainder is owned by almost everybody in the world. Uniterwyk Liberia Lines, owned by Uniterwyk Corporation and Libyan citizens was declared a national line in 1978.[40] As a Liberian corporation partially owned by Liberian citizens, the newly designated national line uses Liberian seamen. The government supports a maritime institute, being established at Marshall City, to provide training for Liberian seamen.

Nigeria   Nigeria is the only other country of any significant holding in West Africa. The Nigerian National Shipping Lines Ltd was incorporated on 5 February 1959 by the federal government as part of its policy of participation in private industries of importance to the national economy. Plans were for the company to enlarge its fleet to thirty-one vessels by the beginning of the 1980s. Nigeria plans to transport 50 per cent of its oil production in its own vessels.[41] As of the late 1970s, it had just one tanker of some 270,000 dwt capable of carrying about 2 million barrels of crude oil. About 90 per cent of Nigeria's reserve is derived from oil imports which represents 58 per cent of Nigeria's total oil exports.[42]

Nigeria's national policy on liner shipping follows the cargo-sharing principles of the UNCTAD Code. However, it also requires all importers and exporters whose business is registered in Nigeria to grant priority of their sea freight to the Nigerian National Shipping Line (NNSL), in order to give the national line effective cargo control.[43] The NNSL will then be responsible for carving up the cargo on the 40-40-20 basis retaining 75 per cent of the total Nigerian allocation for itself, and apportioning the remaining 25 per cent amongst the other Nigerian lines.

South-East Africa

The only other countries with significant national fleets, outside North and West Africa, are South Africa and probably Zaïre.[44]

South Africa   Foreign trade is of vital importance to South Africa, whose imports equal nearly 19 per cent of the Gross Domestic

Product (GDP) and whose exports provide nearly 14 per cent of the Gross National Product (GNP). Consequently, shipping is of great interest to South Africa. The merchant fleet is growing, as is the ship-repair industry which benefited from the increased traffic around the Cape of Good Hope, resulting from the Suez Canal's temporary closure.[45] Cape Town and Durban are the centres of the country's ship-repair and shipbuilding activities. South African flag vessels carried approximately 32 per cent of South Africa's ocean-borne foreign trade in 1977 (38 per cent of imports and 26 per cent of exports) — themselves impressive figures.[46] Apart from that there is no data available to indicate state ownership and/or participation, but it is very substantial indeed, given the secretive and sensitive nature of the regime. What is known is that the government has promulgated measures for the promotion of the South African shipping, shipbuilding and ship-repair industries.[47]

Zaïre   In Zaïre, Law 74-014 (7-10-74) gives Compagnie Maritime Zaïroise (CMZ) the monopoly of the sea transport of exports from the Republic of Zaïre and the monopoly of all the products imported with the assistance of the Bank of Zaïre. Since 25 July 1977, Zaïre belongs to the Code of Conduct of Maritime Conferences.[48] This Code emphasizes the distribution of the freight on the 40–40–20 basis for reasons of efficiency of this monopoly. The CMZ sought the creation of a Zaïrian Council of Freighters responsible for the control of imports and exports. Imports and exports between Zaïre and ports in Belgium, the Federal Republic of Germany, The Netherlands, and the Scandinavian countries must be shipped in vessels participating in the Conferences of the Associated Central West African Lines (CEWAL).[49] Imports and exports financed by the Executive Council (the government) will have to be shipped by Zaïrian vessels; but for reasons of emergency or lack of CMZ ships available, other ships might assume the shipment of all SOZACDM products to the countries listed above.[50] In the case where these products would be carried by foreign ships, CMZ will receive a retrocession or reservation commission. In cases of emergency aids, the food products, raw materials, auto parts for cars sold to Zaïre, and vehicle equipment granted to Zaïre by the above-mentioned countries, the priority of shipment will be 50–50 for Zaïrian and CEWAL vessels. Other imports and exports will be carried by CEWAL vessels.[51]

State Ownership of Shipping in the Americas

North America

Canada   Until recently, Canada was one of the very few TMNs that observed free trade. The majority of the vessels under the Canadian flag were not involved in ocean-going foreign trade, but were utilized in domestic traffic and trade with American ports on the Pacific, Gulf and Atlantic coasts, the St Lawrence seaway and on the Great Lakes.[52] In 1978, for example, Canadian flag vessels carried some 87.8 per cent of the tonnage in Canadian international waterborne trade, including the Great Lakes; this participation amounted to 46.7 per cent of inbound tonnage and 17.9 per cent of outbound tonnage. Excluding trade with the USA, there was minimal Canadian flag participation in transporting international cargo tonnage.[53] So it appears that Canada divested itself of its deep-sea fleet shortly after the Second World War, relying on competition amongst foreign carriers to keep freight rates at a reasonable level. Studies on the need for a Canadian-flag deep-sea fleet have been conducted[54] and, while the government is developing its policy towards this, the Canadian Seafarers' Unions have signed an agreement with some Canadian ship companies to place Canadian crews on some of their vessels operating under foreign registry. Against this background, it further appears that there is no government ownership of the merchant fleet, with the exception of ferry vessels which are almost exclusively directly or indirectly government-owned.[55]

The British Columbia Ferry Corporation, a Crown Corporation of the British Columbia Provincial Government, owns a large number of ferries and operates an extensive ferry system on the West Coast. CN Marine, a wholly owned subsidiary of the Crown Corporation, owns and operates extensive ferry and coastal shipping services on the Atlantic Coast.[56] In addition, all provinces own and operate various small ferries and the federal government owns a number of ferries which are chartered to private operators who, in all cases, receive some form of subsidy. Cannactic Shipping Limited, a government industry consortium with 51 per cent federal government participation, operates the MV *Arctic*, an experimental ship that combines features of both contemporary cargo ships and ice-breakers.[57] Government contracts have generally been restricted to Canadian shipyards and, since 1965, have been awarded to the lowest qualified bidder (an exception was a submarine built abroad). At one time, a foreign-built vessel could, with the consent of the Minister of Transport, be registered in Canada without the payment of duty and taxes but, when so registered, could engage only in international trade.[58] All industries are entitled to receive aid under various general programmes covering 50 per cent of the approved research grant.

USA   There is no direct state ownership in the USA, except for the liberty ships, survey ships and vessels engaged in naval duties, and patrol boats.[59]

Central America

Brazil   The Brazilian government is by far the largest stockholder of Liner Brasileiro, and of the Vale de Rio Doce Navegaco SS (DOCENAVE) (for coal and iron ore), as well as of the national tanker fleet, Flota Nacionale de Petroleiros (FRONAPE).[60] Incentives in the form of fiscal accounting measures extended to exporters utilizing bilateral agreements (including Brazil) were ended at the end of 1979.

Colombia   With a coastline of about 5,000 miles and with the current importance of foreign trade to the country's economy, shipping is of major importance to Colombia with its two coastlines and its large exports of coffee,[61] which supply some 50–55 per cent of the country's foreign exchange earnings. The Colombian merchant fleet, Flota Mercante Grancolombia, is an exercise in state and regional ownership. Colombia's National Federation of Coffee Growers controls approximately 80 per cent of the ownership, with the remaining 20 per cent controlled by the Development Bank of Ecuador.[62] At one time, the Venezuelan government also participated in Flota's ownership. Although there are no legal requirements in effect, imports for government or quasi-government agencies are generally carried by Flota. These informal ties with the Colombian government and publicity for the advantages of shipping via Flota account for the shipping line's strong position.[63]

Finally, two US shipping lines operate in association with Gran Colombia service routes to and from Colombia; Delta Lines covering US East Coast traffic, and Lykes Brothers covering US Gulf Coast traffic.

Ecuador   In Ecuador, TRANSNAVE is a state commercial shipping enterprise belonging to the national fleet with its own heritage, legal character and an autonomous administration. All hydrocarbons, 50 per cent of general, 50 per cent of refrigerated and 50 per cent of bulk cargoes are reserved exclusively for state companies or mixed companies in which the state has 51 per cent (control) of the participation in social capital. The National Council of Marine and

Ports is responsible for fixing the respective percentages when applying the Cargo Reservation Law to traffic which is not covered by the Law. Fifty per cent of the cargo can be carried in ships of the importing or exporting countries if it is done in a reciprocal manner. Cabotage traffic is exclusively reserved for Ecuadorian flag vessels or vessels chartered by national shipping enterprises, either private or state.[64] All state, municipal and government-sponsored cargoes must be conveyed in Ecuadorian bottoms.

Mexico During 1970 Mexican flag vessels carried 15 per cent of the country's ocean-borne foreign trade. The government subsidizes the cost of vessel's fuel to the extent of 50 per cent of the total fuel expenses. Coastal trade and Petroleos Mexicanos (PEMEX) traffic are restricted to national flag ships when available. The government agency PEMEX owns and operates the country's longest fleet of merchant ships consisting primarily of tankers which move all of its crude and refined products. A wholly government-owned bulk carrier operation, Compania Naviere Minera de Golfo, SA de CV, was constituted in 1979 under the Secretaria de Portrimonis y Formentoi Industrial as part of Mexico's national development programme.[65] Transportacion Maritima Mexicana (TMM) is operated as a private concern although in 1962 the government − i.e. the Bank of Mexico, the National Bank of Foreign Commerce and the government's investment corporation, Nacional Financiera − purchased 30 per cent of TMM's stock. TMM receives neither an operating nor construction subsidy.[66] The government has guaranteed loans made by TMM for new construction and, in some cases, ships have reportedly been purchased with partial payment in commodities or fishing vessels. The Government of Mexico participates in the Caribbean basin regional multilateral shipping line NAMNCAR.[67] Mexico's major shipyards have been nationalized, although there are a number of small private shipyards producing small vessels for the domestic fleets. The government is investing some US $22 million to start up the first parastate shipyard, Astilleros Unidos de Veracruz which is expected to turn out tankers of up to 80,000 dwt for PEMEX.[68]

Peru Ocean transportation is of particular importance to Peru because of the country's 1,250-mile coastline and poor land access to neighbouring markets. Approximately 98 per cent of Peru's foreign trade moves by sea. Peru's most important shipping firms are Consorcio Naviera Peruoma SA (CNAP) and the state-owned Corporacion Peruana de Vapores (CPV), which control most of Peru's ocean-going tonnage.[69] CPV is wholly government-owned and the naval shipyards (SIMA) have been converted into a state-owned company.

Venezuela   Finally, in Venezuela, the economy depends to a large extent on the petroleum industry. In 1978, for example, petroleum averaged 2,362,736 barrels a day. Ninety per cent of Venezuela's foreign trade is carried by sea and it is therefore in its interest to maintain a sufficient and adequate merchant fleet to handle this trade.[70] The Venezuelan flag transports nearly 30 per cent of its general cargo trade — i.e. approximately 10 million tons in 1980. Its participation in the carriage of petroleum is minimal though. The CA Venezuelana de Navigacion (CAVN) is a state enterprise operating as a totally distinct government agency, but paying all its taxes, including income tax, the same way as any private enterprise: it does not enjoy any type of operating subsidy or favours as one would have expected.[71] Diques y Astilleros Nacionales, CA (DIANCA), located in Puerto Corbelos is a government-owned dry-dock. There is a shipyard construction project in Los Toques, Isla de Paraguana, being built as a joint venture with the Spanish government: Venezuela retains 55 per cent of the investment.[72]

South America

Argentina   The state-owned Empressa Lineas Maritimas Argentinas (ELMA) is expanding and updating its fleet with a ten-year plan (1979–88), a US $632 million programme which will include the purchase of 120 ships totalling 470,000 dwt. One-third of the cost of the programme was to be borne by ELMA without recourse to national treasury funds,[73] but the plan was probably adversely affected by the Falklands conflict of 1982. With over 95 per cent of Argentina's foreign trade being ocean-borne, this updating and expansion would enable Argentine flag lines to carry a larger percentage. The government owns ELMA, the principal company operating in international trade, as well as the major oil company, Yacimientos Petroliteros Fiscales (YPF), and one river fleet, all of which total about 48 per cent of the merchant fleet.[74] There are at least six privately-owned shipping companies with more than 100,000 tons, and about six others with more than 50,000 tons.

Chile   Most of Chile's foreign trade moves by sea. Its 2,630-mile-long coastline is one of the longest in the world and has many seaports. Approximately 38 per cent of Chile's imports move through Valipariso, Chile's major port. Chile's exports, mainly copper and other minerals, move through the ports of Huasco, Topocilla, Charmal and Coquimbo.[75] Chilean flag vessels carry approximately 22 per cent of Chile's imports and 40 per cent of its exports. The government owns the Empressa Maritima de Estardes. The company is authorized to operate in foreign trade should circumstances make it advisable, but so far it has limited its activities to domestic routes and to a few trips abroad conveying livestock.[76] The government also owns about 25–30 per cent of Compania Sudamericana de Vapores (CSAV).

There are one or two other measures that assist state participation. First, by Decree No. 179 of 19 February 1968, the Chilean line receives a 20 per cent advantage upon liquidation of foreign currency received from incomes in the transport of cargo and passengers to and from Chile and between foreign ports.[77] Second, changes have been insufficient to cover costs and a subsidy from the fiscal budget is necessary to maintain port operations. Port rates are the same for all shipping and there appears to be no discrimination in berthing, as is usually the case in other protective countries.[78] Third, and finally, Chilean shipping companies must insure the hulls, machinery and equipment of their vessels with Chilean insurance companies. Expenditure, protection and indemnity or any other contingency insurance must be purchased by Chilean shipping companies from Chilean insurance companies.

Panama   Finally, although Panama is technically a Central American country, it will nonetheless be mentioned here (rather than there) due to the peculiar nature of its registrations and holdings. Panama's merchant fleet is almost entirely foreign-owned. It is estimated that US interests comprise about 51 per cent of the tonnage and that most of the remainder is owned by Hong Kong, and Italian and Japanese interests.[79] While there is no restriction to the operation of foreign ships in Panama's territorial waters, coastal shipping is restricted to the almost insignificant number of Panamanian flag ships. And finally, a fishing licence is required for all vessels fishing for commercial purposes in the navigable waters of the Republic of Panama.[80] Failure to obtain the licence results in a fine from US $10,000 to US $100,000.

Uruguay   Uruguayan flag vessels carry about 15 per cent of imports and 6 per cent of exports. Montevideo is Uruguay's principal port. Government policy is to facilitate merchant marine operations, but it appears to grant no direct subsidy, and operates tax benefits, cargo preferences and loans.[81] Through the National Ports Administration, the government owns and operates two small river boats; two ocean-going and one coastal vessel through the National Fuels, Alcohol and Portland Cement Administration (ANCAP); and, through the Ministry of Defence, two large tankers are chartered to ANCAP for the transportation of crude to the refinery in Montevideo.[82]

State Ownership of Shipping in Asia

North-East Asia

Japan   Although it is second to Liberia in the world league, in reality Japan is the largest shipping, and second largest trading nation in the world (behind the USA). Since it is an island with poor natural resources, it has to import a large proportion of foodstuffs as well as a major part of raw materials for industrial production.[83] Shipping and shipbuilding are therefore extremely important to the country's economy, and both the government and private firms have made an effort to encourage these industries. In 1978 Japanese flag vessels carried 39.2 per cent of Japan's ocean-borne foreign trade (41.6 per cent of Japan's imports and 20.8 per cent of exports).

The state seems to have gone in for massive subsidies rather than direct ownership or participation.[84] For example, a subsidy for Island/Mainland services in the amount of approximately 2,346 million yen was allocated for the fiscal year 1979. The Ministry of International Trade and Industry underwrites export insurance policies to cover a wide range of commercial and political risks in addition to ship export credits, loans, tax benefits, and grants. Otherwise the government owns relatively small tonnage as compared with Japan's private sectors.[85] The total value of the orders placed by the Defence Agency and the Maritime Safety Agency was 104,115 million yen in 1977 and 137,375 million yen in 1978.

South Korea   The Republic of South Korea's exports have been expanding at about 42 per cent every year since 1960, when exports totalled US $33 million. Foreign trade, both exports and imports, has been increasing by about 36 per cent each year since 1967.[86] The Korean government implemented a five-year shipbuilding programme with the aim of expanding the country's ocean-going fleet to 12 million grt by 1986 and increasing the earnings of its people from the shipping industry to US $1.8 billion by 1981. During 1975, Korean vessels carried 35 per cent of Korea's ocean-borne foreign trade.[87] Korean flag vessels handled approximately 47 per cent of the country's trade in 1979. Otherwise, apart from tax benefits, subsidies (operational and constructional) loans and cargo preferences, the government is content to take a back-seat except for retaliatory measures when necessary: for instance, when a foreign operator of a vessel is deemed to have committed acts hindering the development of Korea's maritime transportation, or to have confused the order of trade routes, the Korean government may take the necessary countermeasures.[88] Finally, in 1976, the Korean government proclaimed that, where possible, all new ships for the Korean merchant fleet would be built at the country's own yards with the government undertaking to subsidize owners and yards.

Philippines   Shipping is of major interest in the Philippines, with its 74 national ports, 528 municipal ports and about 220 private ports under 18 different port management units, spread throughout the 7,100 islands. There is extensive inter-island shipping and a growing participation in international shipping.[89] In 1978, Philippine flag vessels carried 19.4 per cent of Philippine foreign trade (21.34 per cent of imports and 16.67 per cent of exports) in terms of volume. In 1974, the Maritime Industry Authority (MARINA) was established to coordinate activity in the field of maritime development. It gives special attention to the expansion of the merchant fleet, focusing on the early replacement of obsolete and uneconomic vessels, and the raising of domestic capability for shipbuilding and repair.[90] The government embarked on a ten-year plan to invest US $1 billion in shipbuilding for the years 1981–90. In addition the government operates tax incentives, loans and interest on loans, government incentives and cargo preferences in favour of the national fleet. The government-owned Philippine National Lines was established by Presidential Decree No. 900 in March 1976.[91] Its objective is to assist in the private sector's acquisition programme and to supplement shipping services provided by private shipping companies. It undertakes all manner of business activities for the establishment of a reliable shipping service that includes but is not limited to the ownership, lease, charter, management and operations of merchant vessels[92] whether for cargo or for passenger on a scheduled, non-scheduled or charter basis, on domestic- and/or international-scale ship brokerage and other related or supportive activities; and the ownership, establishment, management and operation of shipbuilding and ship repair facilities in order to provide adequate services to the shipping industry.[93]

South-East Asia

Indonesia   As in the Philippines, inter-island shipping is of major importance to Indonesia and occupies the bulk of the Indonesian flag merchant fleet. As of the end of 1970, some 404 ships of 390,175 dwt were in the inter-island services and in 1970 these ships carried 1,790,000 metric tons of cargo. The Indonesian government has separated ports into those admitting foreign trade, and those restricted to insular traffic.[94] Many of the forty-seven ports open to foreign trade move only special cargoes such as lumber, ore, and equipment related to the oil industry. There are port expansion plans for the Port of Tandjung Priok, near Djakarta, which handled 8.7 million tons of cargo in 1975.[95] In 1976, Indonesian flag vessels carried 22 per cent of its dry cargo and palm oil trade, and 8 per cent of its crude oil traffic. The government grants no subsidies to its maritime industries, but it does operate import tax exemptions, cargo preferences and bilateralism. In addition, the government owns the Indonesian National Shipping Company (PERNI), the national inter-island fleet, which runs and operates more than half of Indonesian flag tonnage;[96] Djakarta Lloyd which is the nation's international shipping line; and PN Pertania, the oil enterprise. It also owns the following docks/shipyards:

PT Dock Tandjung Priok at Tandjung Priok, Djakarta;
PT Dock Tandjung Perak at Tandjung Perak, Surabaja;
PT Kodja at Djakarta and Palembang;
PT Ippa Gaya Baru at Djakarta, Tjirebon, and Semarang;
PT Waiame at Ambon;
PT Industrial Korpal Indonesia at Gresik, Padang, Manado and Ujung Pandang.[97]

Taiwan On the other hand, Taiwan intends to raise the capacity of its fleet of merchant ships to a level of carrying 70 per cent of bulk and 40 per cent of miscellaneous imports and exports. The government operates cargo preferences, loans, customs and tax benefits and subsidies (construction and depreciation) to the industry. There is only one publicly-owned shipyard, China Shipbuilding Corporation in Taiwan, which is capable of building large ships exceeding 100,000 dwt[98] with shipways in production to build vessels under 30,000 dwt. China Merchants Steam Navigation Company and the Taiwan Navigation Company are also publicly owned. Young Ming Marine Transport Corporation is a subsidiary of China Merchants Steam Navigation Company and is its operating arm.[99]

South-West Asia

India India is one of the leading shipping nations generally and in the DMNs in particular, and her flag vessels cover about 32 per cent of general cargo exports and 52 per cent of general cargo imports. Indian flag vessels have about a 40 per cent share of total trade. In order to qualify for Indian registry, ship-owning companies have to register in India under national laws and regulations and must be at least 60 per cent owned by Indian nationals.[100] Government aids include subsidies (operating, construction, loans, interests and depreciation), cargo preference coverage and bilateralism. For every ton of her ships ordered from overseas yards, an Indian shipowner must place orders for comparable tonnage in India. The government has instituted a ban on the registry of ships that could otherwise be built in India. The General Insurance Corporation (including marine) which, with its subsidiaries, has the exclusive privilege of carrying out general insurance in India, was nationalized in 1971.[101] The two government-owned shipping lines in India, the Shipping Corporation of India (SCINDIA) with 137 ships and the Mogul Line Ltd with 17 vessels account for 54 per cent of Indian tonnage ownerships.[102]

The Hindustan Shipyard at Visakhapatham is owned by the government, as is a second yard at Cochin. The Garden Reach Workshops at Calcutta were acquired by the Ministry of Defence in 1960. This shipyard is now building cargo liners of about 26,000 dwt. Mazagon Dock Ltd, Combay, another shipyard under the Ministry of Defence, is capable of building merchant ships up to 16,000 dwt, and Cochin Shipyard has commenced construction of its first Panarmax vessel of 75,000 dwt with completion originally scheduled for late 1986, but running about a year late.

Malaysia   Shipping is vital to Malaysia due to its heavy dependence on foreign trade and the separation by water of West from East Malaysia.[103] Malaysia's fleet is one of the fastest growing in the world. In just seven years (1971–78) the Malaysian International Shipping Corporation (MISC) built up a diverse modern fleet of vessels, and planned to double the tonnage in the years 1978–85. However, MISC has only managed to lift a 20 per cent share of Malaysia's foreign trade.[104] In 1973 the Malaysian government signed an agreement to establish a major shipyard at Jahore Bharu on a joint venture basis with Japanese and other investors. When completed it will be one of the largest in South-West Asia. The government has more than a 51 per cent interest in MISC and a 50 per cent interest in the shipyard at Jahore Bharu.[105]

Pakistan   Pakistan's fleet was nationalized in 1974. The major shipping company is the National Shipping Corporation which specializes in liner services, while nine smaller companies, which have been merged to form the Pakistan Shipping Corporation, concentrate on the pilgrim-passenger services and dry cargo tramp operations. Under the 1975–80 plan period, the government expected to arrange funds to acquire 19 vessels of various types. Approximately 15 per cent of Pakistan's trade is carried on Pakistan flag vessels. Pakistan operates a subsidy, tax benefits, loans, cargo preferences, cabotage and bilateralism. The National Shipping Corporation was established by the government in September 1963 with a 25 per cent share of capital in the public sector and the balance of 75 per cent in the private sector, but was nationalized in 1974, as was the Pakistan Shipping Corporation (a merger of nine smaller companies). The Karachi Shipyard and Engineering Works Ltd,[106] the only national shipbuilding yard, is run on commercial lines and is controlled by a semi-autonomous body, the West Pakistan Industrial Development Corporation.

Singapore   The Singapore government has equity participation in the Neptune Orient Lines Ltd, the Keppel Shipyard and the Sembawang Shipyard Ltd.[107] It also has partial ownership of the Jurong Shipyard, Mitsubishi Singapore Heavy Industries and a number of smaller shipyards.[108]

State Ownership and Participation in Europe

North-East Europe

Denmark   Almost entirely surrounded by water and possessing a coastline of some 4,600 miles, Denmark has a major interest in both shipping and shipbuilding. More than 90 per cent of the earnings of the Danish merchant fleet is derived from cross-trade, i.e. trade exclusively between non-Danish ports. In 1979 Danish vessels engaged in external trade (non-coastline) contributed about 9.2 per cent of the total foreign exchange earnings.[109] In 1978, Danish flag vessels carried 11.1 per cent of Denmark's seaborne foreign trade (7.7 per cent of imports and 25.3 per cent of exports). The government operates tax exemptions, stamp credits (insurance and exports), depreciation subsidy, cargo preference and cabotage. The government also owns and operates coasters which are confined essentially to services serving internal routes and routes between Denmark and Sweden or Germany, and to vessels operated by the Greenland Trade Department.[110] Financial support amounting to about US $0.5 million per annum is given by the government to institutions engaged in shipbuilding research. In terms of value, the Danish government's share in the total Danish building of ships has varied considerably. On average for the years 1976–81 it amounted to about 5 per cent.

Finland   Shipbuilding is one of Finland's major industries and about 90 per cent of deliveries are exported. Finnish yards specialize in all types of high-technology vessels such as ice-breakers, ro-ros, LNG carriers and luxury passenger vessels.[111] The government operates subsidies (operating, construction, interest loans), credits (home and export), tax (benefits and duty) and cargo preference. In addition, it has a small interest in Finnlines Ltd, and owns several non-merchant type ships such as ice-breakers and survey ships. The government also has the controlling interest in Valmet Oy, which is one of the country's most important producers of ships and machinery.[112] On average, shipbuilding accounts for 15–20 per cent of the country's total turnover. Government grants, based on research contracts, concluded between the government and a firm or laboratory and relating to a particular research project, can amount to 50 per cent of the direct costs of a project. Ship-related research and development projects received approximately 2 per cent of the contributions between 1970–72.

West Germany   The West German merchant fleet is eleventh in the world in terms of size. It is an overwhelmingly modern fleet with 86 per cent of its registered tonnage less than ten years old.[113] The government operates subsidies (loans, construction, depreciation), credits (guarantees, export, insurance), tax benefits (including customs), countervailing policies, cargo preference and contribution to research. Ownership of the shares of one big shipyard is distributed as follows: 75 per cent held by a state-owned steel mill having the form of a joint stock company; 25 per cent by State Schleswig Holstein. State Bremen owns 39 per cent of the shares of a medium-sized shipyard.[114] Both yards are managed as private enterprises though they account for slightly less than 20 per cent of German yards' total capacity in merchant shipbuilding. Finally, government contributions to shipyards' and institutes' research projects amounted to DM 5.1 million in 1977 and DM 8 million in 1978.

Norway   Shipping is one of Norway's most important industries, providing in 1979 about 22 per cent of Norwegian foreign exchange earnings. About 92 per cent of Norwegian tonnage is employed in third-flag or foreign-to-foreign trade (cross-trade) and 95 per cent of the shipping receipts originate from non-Norwegian sources.[115] Norway possesses the fifth largest fleet in the world, and Norwegian flag vessels carried 37 per cent of Norway's ocean-borne foreign trade during 1979. The fleet is relatively young and has a high number of specialized vessels. In 1979 16 per cent of total production hours at Norwegian shipyards were connected with oil activities, 57 per cent with new buildings and the remainder with repair, conversions, and varying types of industrial production. The government operates subsidies (operation, depreciation, interest, loans, construction), tax (benefits, customs) and research grants.[116] Norway is one of the few governments that positively encourages flagging-out as an international shipping policy.

Sweden   Formerly, the bulk of the production of Sweden's shipbuilding industry was for export but nowadays the largest part is for domestic owners.[117] The government has nationalized most of the major shipyards, placing them under a holding company called the Swedish Shipyards Corporation. Under certain restrictions tonnage transfers, mainly to other TMNs, are permitted.

North-West Europe

Belgium   Apart from subsidies (loans, interest, depreciation), credits (export, insurance) and tax benefits, there is no evidence of direct public ownership in Belgium.

France   On the other hand, the French also operate subsidies (operating, construction, modernization, depreciation), tax (benefits, rebates and customs), cargo preference, bilateralism and reimbursement of part-cost due to accidents and/or sickness and also has one of the most extensive public ownership networks.[118] The government owns the principal shares in the largest shipping company, the Compagnie Generale Maritime (French Line Services), which was formed by the consolidation of the Compagnie Generale Transatlantique and the Compagnie des Messageries Maritimes. In 1969 the French Line and the Compagnie de Navigation pooled their activities in the Mediterranean and formed a new shipping line, the Compagnie Generale Transmediterrannée.[119] A decree of 26 February 1974 approved the creation of a partly (17 per cent) state-owned company, Société Française d'Endes et de Realisations Maritimes, Partnaires et Navales, in order to promote and disseminate French methods and techniques in the fields of sea transport, shipbuilding, ship-repair and port industries.

   The government's interest in owning so large a part of the shipping industry is consistent with the French policy of maintaining a certain amount of state control in those industries which are in national interest — e.g. shipping, railways, electricity, gas and coal.[120] There is also a practice, dating from 1610, of the use of a Courtier Maritime or a maritime broker: a unique phenomenon peculiar to France. The Courtier Maritime is an officer of the government, appointed by due process of law and as such he is entrusted the duty of performing the necessary (maritime) formalities required by French customs. His fee is set by the government and is based on a pre-calculated scale. But over and above his official duties he may, upon request, be authorized to act as an independent agent in the commercial maritime brokerage business for which he may charge a fee or percentage based on tonnage loaded or unloaded as would any other broker or forwarder professionally engaged in this field.[121]

The intervention of the Courtier Maritime is not obligatory. The owner and/or captain of the foreign vessel, if either speaks and reads French, or the consignee/forwarder may and can attend to all customs formalities. It is only when they do not themselves attend to such matters that (mainly for their own protection) they must utilize the services of French accredited brokers. This service is officially recognized by the French government and must meet and conform to government standards and requirements.

Republic of Ireland   The Irish Republic is another country with a substantial public sector of the merchant maritime industry. Tonnage on the Irish register has been increasing steadily over the last few years and a wide variety of scheduled services from Ireland are provided for passengers and freight worldwide. The large Gulf Oil petroleum terminal on Whiday Island in Bantry Bay has been gaining importance as a petroleum transshipment port in Western Europe: it can handle tankers of up to 350,000 dwt and above.[122] The government operates a construction subsidy and tax benefits. But, above all, Irish Shipping Ltd and B&I Company (The British and Irish Steam Packet Company Ltd) were until recently both state-owned. On 31 March 1978 Irish Shipping Ltd, which operates mainly in the deep-sea trade on charter and tramping, had eight bulk carriers of 142,943 grt. It also effectively owns the *St Patrick* and *St William* car ferries which are operated by Irish Continental Line (a subsidiary company of Irish Shipping Ltd) and provide a direct passenger and ro-ro freight service on the Rosslare/Le Havre and Rosslare/Cherbourg routes. On the same date, the B&I owned three car ferry vessels[123] and a freight vessel. A new car ferry, at present under construction at Veroline Cork Dockyard, was scheduled for the end of 1986. The B&I Company provides passenger/car services to the UK, and unit-load ro-ro and lo-lo (lift on, lift off) freight services to the UK, Europe and throughout the world.[124]

The Netherlands   Rotterdam, in the Netherlands, is the world's foremost port. However, mainly for fiscal motives, about 40 per cent of Dutch-owned shipping tonnage has not been registered in the country. The government operates subsidies (direct, interest, depreciation), exemptions (tax, customs, duty) credit guarantees, reorganization and conversion assistance, contribution to research and other forms of state aids. In addition, the government holds a majority of the shares in the NV Swomvaart Maatscharppij Zeeland, a company operating a ferry service jointly with the British Ranbourgs across the North Sea.[125] This company operates on a commercial basis but, in connection with the restructuring of the shipping (in which the Dutch are currently involved), it has been necessary for the government to take part in the enlarged share capital to strengthen the financial position of some yards. In November 1978, for instance, the Amsterdam Drydock Company took over the NDSM repair yards from the Rhine-Schelde-Verolme (RSV) group.[126] However, the government and ADM each have a 35 per cent share in this the new company, Netherlands Shipbuilding (NSM); RSV owns the remaining 30 per cent. The government is handling the cost of integration and through the National Investment Bank, is participating in the share capital.[127]

UK   The UK has been a maritime nation throughout its history and, as an island nation, has had a very heavy dependence on foreign trade. The British fleet is one of the most modern and diversified in the world, and is a substantial and consistent contributor to the balance of payments. There are 300 ports (90 per cent of them handling foreign trade) handling about 350,000 tons of cargo annually. Until recently, the British government operated subsidies (operating, construction, loans), tax benefits and customs rebates, and credit facilities for export orders,[128] and also had one of the largest public ownerships and substantial shareholding as follows:

On 1 July 1977, 19 shipbuilding companies, 5 diesel marine engine manufacturers and 3 training companies were nationalized to form the British Shipbuilders Corporation (BSC).[129] One further ship-building company and six ship-repairers were subsequently acquired by BSC. The latter's corporate strategy aimed to reduce capacity to about 400,000 compensated grt per annum and to concentrate activity on core yards which BSC considered could be competitive internationally.

The government had the following shipping interests:

1   An interest in British Petroleum, the parent company of BP tankers;
2   An interest in the nationalized British Rail Board, which owned ferry boats and the Central Electricity Generating Board, which owned ships employed in coastal trade.

The publicly-owned sector including the Harland and Wolff shipyard in Belfast, accounts for about 97 per cent of merchant shipbuilding,[130] 99 per cent of warship building, 100 per cent of slow-speed diesel manufacture, and some 50 per cent of ship-repair activity. The Harland and Wolff shipyard is separate from BSC and its shares are entirely owned by the Northern Ireland Department of Commerce. With EEC approval, that Department created an intervention fund of approximately $57 million to assist in winning new orders during the period 1980–81.

Southern Europe

Italy   The Italian government operates subsidies (operating, construction group and building, depreciation, loans, interest, reorganization and yard conversion), tax benefits and customs duties rebates, cargo preference, cabotage, contribution to research, and miscellaneous assistance.[131] Italy also has the largest section of the maritime industry in Southern Europe set out as follows.

FINMARE is a holding company in which the Instituto per la Ricostruzione Industriale (IRI), an agency of the Ministry of State Holdings, owns 75 per cent of the shares. Shareholdings of FINMARE and IRI in shipping companies entitled to government subsidies are as follows:

	FINMARE	IRI
Italia	90%	10%
Lloyd Treiestino	80%	20%
Adriatica	60%	20%
Tirrenia	80%	20%

	FINMARE	TIRRENIA
Torremar	48.51%	51.49%
Caremar	48.51%	51.49%
Siremar·	48.51%	51.49%

Approximately 90 per cent of the Italian shipbuilding industry is owned and operated by Finanziaria Cantieri Navali (FINCANTIERI), a holding company in which IRI owns 100 per cent of the stock. In accordance with the CIPE (Comitato Interministeriale per la Programmazione Economica) recommendations of 7 October 1967, the shipyards under FINCANTIERI control were reorganized under a new entity called ITALCANTIERI which now includes the Sestri, Monfalcone, and Castellamare shipyards.[132]

Portugal   There do not seem to be any more public holdings in Portugal after 1980, the reason being that Decree Law No. 77/80 of 16 April 1980 ended the public status of Navegacas de Portugal (NAVIS), Companhina Nacional de Navegacos (CNN), and Companhina Portuguesa de Transportes Maritimas (CTM). Likewise, until 1973, the fund for the renovation of the merchant marine (FRMM) has stopped loan grants, except guarantees, to the maritime industry.[133]

Spain   In complete contrast to Portugal, neighbouring Spain has a particular interest in international shipping because most of the country's foreign trade is seaborne. In 1976 Spanish flag vessels lifted 46.2 per cent of the country's foreign trade (53.6 per cent of imports and 27.5 per cent of exports). Spain operates subsidies (operating, construction, loans, interest), tax benefits, customs duty exemption, cargo preference and import restrictions.[134] In addition, Spanish government participation in shipping companies represents about 11 per cent of the total number of ships of 100 grt and over. These ships are operated primarily through the INI-owned Empressa National 'Elcano' and the state-owned Compania Arendataria Monopolio de Petroleos SA (CAMPSA). The government also purchased the transmediterranean shipping line. The government controls 100 per cent of Empressa National Bazan de CNMSA (Bazan) which manages the naval dockyards and also builds merchant vessels, and Astilleros y Talletes del Noroesle SA (ASTANO) and most of the shares of Astilleros Espanoles SA (AESA).[135] The three companies function as private firms, receive no preferential treatment, and represent 92 per cent of Spain's shipbuilding capacity. Imports of ships from all countries are subject to the prior procurement of an import licence. These are granted with some reluctance, but some ships are nevertheless imported.

Switzerland   Finally, although the Swiss government permits up to 50 per cent of the financing of Swiss flag seagoing vessels to be foreign financed there are nevertheless very tight conditions — for instance, at least 75 per cent of all shares and the entire origin and capital must be held by stockholders residing in Switzerland. Indeed, Switzerland is one of the very few landlocked countries operating deep-sea merchant shipping. The government maintains tight control over the registration of ocean-going vessels under the Swiss Flag: corporations owning ships under Swiss registry must be listed in the Swiss Commercial Register; must have their operating headquarters and centre of activity in Switzerland; and all of their managers, associates and partners must be Swiss citizens — in the case of partners, they must also be resident in Switzerland. There are no statistics available as to the percentage

282

of Switzerland's foreign trade carried by Swiss Flag vessels. In peacetime ships are trading in free competition and most of the goods carried are for foreign account.

Cyprus   Apart from a 10-year waiver of taxation on Cypriot owners' income, there is no state or public authority in Cyprus.

Greece   The Greek-owned fleet, as opposed to the Greek flag fleet, is possibly the largest merchant fleet in the world. The government has been making efforts to attract Greek-owned vessels to Greek registry, and there were indications that these efforts were meeting with some qualified success until the current worldwide wave of flagging-out. Otherwise the Greek government, too, provides the traditional subsidies, tax benefits, loans and interest on loans, credit facilities for the purchase of both foreign and Greek flag ships, loans for working capital, preferences, cabotage, bilateralism, training and welfare benefits.[136] In addition to which, the National Bank of Greece and the Hellenic Industrial Bank both of which are state-owned, own 85 per cent of Nearian Shipyard on the Aegean island of Syros.[137]

State Ownership and Participation in the Middle East

Iran   Petroleum has accounted for about 76 per cent of Iran's export earnings and revolutionized the country's economy. The country now possesses the world's largest crude petroleum loading terminal at Kharg Island which can handle up to 14,786 tons per hour, although its operations have been severely contained by the Gulf War. There are cargo preferences but no government subsidies in Iran. In terms of state ownership, Arya Shipping Lines of Iran was nationalized on 7 August 1979 in line with the government policy of taking control of all major industries in the country.[138] In 1980 its name was changed to Islamic Republic of Iran Shipping Line.

Iraq   As to Iran's arch-enemy — Iraq — the oil tanker enterprise is a division within the state-owned Iraq National Oil Company. Dry cargo operations are the responsibility of the Iraq Maritime Transport Company which is under the direction of the Ministry of Transportation. An Iraqi–Soviet agreement provides for the transport of Soviet goods exported to Iraq on Iraqi vessels and the assignment of Soviet crews to some Iraqi vessels.[139]

Israel   Shipping is of extreme importance to Israel since almost all of Israel's foreign trade is seaborne. Shipping has become Israel's second most important foreign exchange earner, behind tourism, and is expanding at an accelerated rate. ZIM Israel Navigation Company is spearheading the expansion drive with a ten-year construction programme of thirty-three new vessels costing about $300 million.

Haifa and Ashdod have been Israel's primary ports. Eilat and Ashkelon have lost their importance because of the situation in Iran and the discontinuance of fuel imports from Iran.

In 1969, Israeli flag shipping carried approximately 50 per cent of Israel's foreign trade.[140] The government operates customs duties, tax concessions and cargo preferences in favour of the fleet and, in addition, public ownership is as follows:

1 ZIM Israel Navigation Company, the national shipping line, is owned by four partners: the Israel Corporation, owned by Jews abroad (50 per cent), the government (30 per cent), the Histadrut (National Labour Union) (10 per cent), and the Jewish Agency (10 per cent).
2 ZIM Israel Navigation Company owns Petroleum Tankers Ltd.
3 The government owns Israel Shipyards Ltd the only yard capable of building ships of over 1,000 gross tons and which has already built vessels of about 9,000 tons.[141]

Other:

1 Shipping companies and the government share 50–50 in all costs of training officers.
2 Government approval is necessary to charter foreign ships by an Israeli party. Approval is given only if domestic ships are unavailable on competitive terms or when special lift ships are required.
3 Under the Israeli Merchant Shipping (vessels) Act 1960, a ship must have at least 50 per cent Israeli ownership to be registered under the Israeli flag.[142]

Kuwait Kuwait possesses one of the world's largest known reserves of oil. About 70 billion barrels of oil and petroleum make up 98 per cent of Kuwait's exports and provides about 93 per cent of the government's revenue. Kuwait can refine up to 530,000 barrels of petroleum per day which is to be expanded by 1989 to 750,000 barrels daily.

Some of Kuwait's ports are geared to the petroleum industry with the port at Mina Al-Ahmadi and the offshore Sea Island Terminal capable of handling the largest existing tankers. The most important non-petroleum port is Shuwaikh which currently can handle about

5 million tons of cargo and receive about 2,100 ships a year.[143] The first stage of North-East Extension Plan will add to the existing port facilities nine additional berths, three of which will be container berths, one for ro-ro ships and the remaining five for general cargo vessels, thus providing a total number of 27 berths.

The Kuwaiti government crude oil sales contracts include terms which require that cargo preference be given to Kuwaiti flag tankers.

Kuwait Shipping Company is in the process of liquidation and the Kuwait Oil Tankers Company has been totally state-owned since 29 June 1976.[144]

Saudi Arabia On the other hand, in the kingdom of Saudi Arabia, the state flag vessels receive markedly lower bunkering rates. A Royal Decree requires that Saudi flag vessels be used provided they are equal in ability, quality and performance.

Turkey Only three Turkish shipyards, all state-owned, can currently build large ocean-going vessels. These are the Comiatti,[145] Taskizak shipyards and Crolenk naval yard. Meantime there are also privately-owned shipyards that are capable of building cargo vessels of up to 15,000 dwt. In addition to loans, cargo preferences and cabotage there are also state ownerships. Turkish Cargo Lines is a state-owned company in possession of a fleet consisting of 58 vessels totalling 1,072,789 dwt, broken down as follows:[146]

1	Dry cargo vessels	247,770 dwt
2	Bulkers	406,170 dwt
3	Tankers	413,352 dwt
4	Ro-ro ships	5,497 dwt
Total		1,072,789 dwt

Furthermore, eight container ships each 5,500 dwt, five bulkers each 18,000 dwt and four coasters each 2,700 dwt of capacity are under construction in Turkish shipyards and are expected to join the company's fleet in the very near future whereas, according to un-official sources, Turkish flag ships on order are reported to total 270,000 dwt, out of which 144,800 dwt are orders placed by the Turkish Cargo Lines for the construction of the vessels mentioned above.[147]

Turkish Cargo Lines has the most potential and is the largest shipping company of Turkey acting as liner and tramp operator with a modern fleet servicing almost all ports of the world with thoroughly experienced and competent maritime personnel.

UAE   In the United Arab Emirates, the Abu Dhabi National Tanker Company is a wholly-owned subsidiary of the state-controlled Abu Dhabi National Oil Company. The government of Dhubai owns 30 per cent of the equity in the Dhubai Maritime Transport Company.[148]

State Ownership and Participation in Oceania

Australia   With more than 12,000 miles of coastline, virtually every major Australian city is a seaport. Considerable port expansion has taken, and is still taking, place throughout the country. This includes two new container terminals at Port Botany (Port of Sydney) and one at Fisherman Islands (Brisbane). In addition, new bulk loading facilities particularly to handle increased exports of coal, are being developed at various ports around the coast.[149]

In 1978–79 Australian flag vessels carried 2.65 per cent of Australia's ocean-borne foreign trade (3.9 per cent of imports and 2.44 per cent of exports). Over the same period, Australian flag vessels lifted 9.8 per cent of cargoes carried in all Australia's overseas liner trades, 12.0 per cent of imports and 7.3 per cent of exports.[150]

Depreciation is allowable in respect of plan on articles owned by a taxpayer and (a) used by him during the year of income for the purpose of producing assessable income; or (b) installed ready for use for that purpose and held in reserve by him. The date from which depreciation of a new ship should commence, for income tax purposes, may vary according to the facts of each individual case. The date on which ownership is acquired would be appropriate if, at that time, the ship required no further fitting out in order to begin service and if, at that time, the ship was at a port from which it would normally take on passengers or cargo. For example, a ship intended for an Australian coastal run would not be regarded as 'installed ready for use' for the purpose of providing assessable income merely upon delivery at a foreign shipyard. It is considered that depreciation of such a ship would commence, for income tax purposes, when it reached the first port of its Australian run.[151]

Australia's coastal trade is reserved for vessels licensed under the Australian Navigation Act; i.e. those which comply with conditions and wages made in accordance with Australian industrial awards.

Australia's public sector is divided as follows:

(a) *Commonwealth*   The Australian Shipping Commission, which was established in 1956, operates the Australian National Line, a

Commonwealth-owned merchant shipping authority. Until 1969 the Australian National Line operated vessels principally in the Australian coastal trade. However, since 1969, the Line has developed services in international liner and bulk cargo trades. As of 30 June 1979 the Line had thirty-five ships (1,362,060 dwt), twelve of which were operating in overseas trades. About 80 per cent of the coastal cargoes carried by the Australian National Line are bulk items, principally iron ore and bauxite.[152]

The Cockatoo Island Dockyard at Sydney is owned by the Commonwealth and is leased to Vickers Cockatoo Dockyard Pty Ltd. Work at this yard is confined mainly to naval vessels.

(b) *States*   The Western Australian Coastal Shipping Commission operates a cargo service with three vessels principally on the west coast of Australia.

The Tasmanian Transport Commission operates one small vessel engaged in intrastate trading in Tasmania and between Tasmania and Victoria.

Amongst others, the State Dockyard at Newcastle, New South Wales, is involved in shipbuilding and ship-repair activities. The dockyard has a floating dry-dock which can accommodate vessels of up to 22,000 dwt for repairs.[153]

New Zealand   There is no evidence of state ownership or participation in New Zealand. Tonnage elsewhere in Oceania and Australasia is too insignificant to merit mention.

Notes

1 For maritime subsidies as a method of developing national fleets see Ademuni-Odeke, *Protectionism and the Future of International Shipping*, Martinus Nijhoff, 1984, chapter 5.
2 Ibid.
3 Ibid., chapter 6.
4 Either through outright nationalization or equity participation.
5 The DMNs seem to have learnt a lot from the TMNs in giving aid to and protecting national fleets.
6 For instance, agreements with state traders is currently recognized as a legitimate form of business dealings.
7 UN *Official Text* of the United Nations Convention on the Law of the Sea with Annexes, New York, 1983, pp. 9–10.
8 Ibid., p. 10.
9 Ibid., Article 94, p. 31.
10 Ibid., Article 95, p. 32.

11 Ibid., Articles 27–32.

12 Ibid., Article 96, p. 33.

13 Ibid., pp. 35–86.

14 For an examination of public ownership of railroads in the USA, see L.C. Sorrell, *Government Ownership and Operations of Railways for the United States*, Prentice-Hall Inc., Englewood Cliffs, NJ, 1939.

15 Ibid.; for a modern statement of the doctrine see H.C. Simons, 'A positive program for *laissez-faire*', *Economic Policy for a Free Society*, The University of Chicago Press, Chicago, 1948.

16 For an examination of public ownership in Great Britain see 'The Nationalisation of British Industries', *Law and Contemporary Problems*, vol. 16, no. 4, Duke University School of Law, Durham, North Carolina, 1957.

17 Ibid.; see also J.M. Keynes, *The End of Laissez-Faire*, L. & V. Wolf, London, 1926; and F.A. van Hayek, *The Road to Serfdom*, The University of Chicago Press, Chicago, 1944.

18 For additional details, see L. Piffer, *The Closing of the Public Domain*, Stanford University Press, Stanford, California, 1951.

19 Ibid.; see also the classic statement in favour of *laissez-faire* in Adam Smith, *The Wealth of Nations*, Random House Inc., New York, 1937.

20 See also M. Clawson and B. Held, *The Federal Lands: Their Use and Management*, The John Hopkins Press, Baltimore, 1957.

21 Ibid.; cf. M. Dimock, *Free Enterprise and the Administrative State*, University of Alabama Press, Alabama, 1951.

22 For further information see C. Landauer, *The Theory of National Economic Planning*, 2nd edn, University of California Press, Berkeley, California, 1947.

23 See also S.E. Harris, *Economic Planning*, Alfred A. Knopf Inc., New York, 1949.

24 Ibid.; see also J.E. Meade, *Planning and the Price Mechanism: The Liberal-Socialist Solution*, The Macmillan Company, New York, 1948.

25 But see L. Kelso and M.J. Adler, *The Capitalist Manifesto*, Random House Inc., New York, 1958; and National Association of Manufacturers, Economic Principles Commission, *The American Individual Enterprise System*, McGraw-Hill Book Company, New York, 1946.

26 Agreements to divide cargo on either a 50–50 basis or on the UNCTAD 40–40–20 basis have been signed with France, USSR, Bulgaria, Guinea, Brazil, the German Democratic Republic, the People's Republic of China and the Republic of Cape Verde.

27 Article 1, Algerian Law No. 78–02 of 11 February 1978.

28 Ibid., except for crude oil, traffic between the ports of metropolitan France and Algerian ports is reserved for Algerian and French flag vessels.

29 Ibid., and Article 1 of the Algerian Constitution.

30 The next five-year plan calls for several new ships to be built, which should increase CNAN's participation in the carriage of Algeria's foreign trade.

31 Joint ventures in the marine transport industry are encouraged under Law No. 43 by according such ventures tax-free operation for the first 5–8 years and other fringe benefits. See also Article 1 of Ministerial Decree 221 of 1974.

32 Department of Transportation, MARAD, *Maritime Subsidies*, Government Printing Office, Washington DC, p. 104.

33 See also A. Clincop, *The Libyan/Malta Continental Shelf Case International Insights*, vol. 2, 1980, pp. 43–9.

34 Morocco is the only African community with access to both the Mediterranean Sea and the Atlantic Ocean, which is one reason why 99 per cent of its foreign trade is seaborne.

35 The government of Morocco requires that 40 per cent of imports and 30 per cent of exports must move on Moróccan vessels. On 5 November 1979, Morocco and France reached an agreement to split maritime cargo 50–50 on a case-by-case basis.

36 See also generally, B.A. Grodana, *Africa's Share of Water Resources: Legal and Institutional Aspects*, Frances Pinter, London and Boulder, 1985.

37 For details see ZIM Lines under Israel, pp. 283–4; see generally, UNDP, 'Environmental Management Problems in Resource Utilisation and Survey of Resources in the West and Central African Region', *UNEP Regional Studies*, no. 37.

38 For the origin of the Black Star Line, see Garvey and Garveyism, pp. 61–2.

39 Approximately 5–8 per cent of Liberia's annual budget comes from registration fees which are equal to about 1.7 per cent of Liberia's GNP.

40 Although ownership by a Liberian entity is a requirement of registration, it is estimated that a small portion of the Liberian fleet is beneficially owned by Liberians.

41 Ibid.; however, it also requires all importers and exporters whose business is registered in Nigeria grant priority of their sea freight to the Nigerian National Shipping Line (NNSL) in order to give the national line effective cargo control.

42 Ibid.; the NNSL will then be responsible for carrying up the cargo on the 40–40–20 basis, retaining 75 per cent of the total Nigerian allocation for itself and apportioning the remaining 25 per cent amongst the other Nigerian lines.

43 Ibid.; see also Note 37 supra; and J.S. Meyer, 'In another country: the effect of mandatory port law upon mandatory duties of discharge and delivery: Torpco Nigeria v. m/v Westwind', *Maritime Lawyer*, vol. 9, pp. 123–37.

44 Zaïre is treated here as falling in the South-East African region although geographically it is a South-West or Central African country.

45 Two container berths are operative at Cape Town providing, among other things, stacking space for 13,900 containers for international trade and 4,240 containers used in the constant or domestic trade.

46 At Durban, South Africa's biggest port, a container terminal has been established on a 125.7 hectare site, with five deep-sea container berths.

47 At Port Elizabeth, container facilities capable of handling 5,000 containers per month, have been provided.

48 Law 74-014 of 7 October 1974.

49 Ibid.; see *The Implementation of the New Law of the Sea in West Africa: Prospects for the Development and Management of Marine Resources*, Dalhousie Ocean Studies Programme, Dalhousie University, Halifax, 1985.

50 Ibid.; and M.A. Robinson and R. Lawson, 'Some reflections on aid to fisheries in West Africa', *Marine Policy*, vol. 10, 1986, pp. 101-10.

51 In fact the statistics relating to these are usually omitted in the two countries' ocean-borne commerce.

52 The government operates an operating subsidy or aid, Canada Task Force on Deep-Sea Shipping. *Task Force on Deep-Sea Shipping: Report to the Minister of Transport*, Transport Canada, Ottawa, 1985.

53 Ibid.; and a construction subsidy or aid; D. Napier *et al.*; Canadian Transport Commission, Research Branch, *Multinational Transport in Canadian International Trade*, Transport Industries Analysis, Ottawa, 1982, p. 102.

54 Ibid. Export credits are also available to Canadian shipyards through the Export Development Corporation.

55 Demolition and/or modernization subsidies are also provided under the Income Tax Act.

56 Ibid.; including non-payment of customs on ships imported into Canada to engage exclusively in international trade.

57 Cabotage restrictions are in operation with effect from 1 January 1966. Withdrawal from the central clauses of the British Commonwealth Merchant Shipping Agreement in 1975 freed Canada from the obligation to give preference to Commonwealth built and registered vessels in the coasting trade.

58 Ibid. This Agreement was totally abandoned in 1977 by the unilateral decision of the remaining members. The coasting laws of Canada are presently under review for purposes of revision.

59 Office of Technology Assessment, *Alternative Approaches to Cargo Policy: A Supplement to an Assessment of Maritime Trade and Technology*, Washington DC, 1985, p. 45.

60 See also Decree Law No. 60679 May 1967 which created the Merchant Marine Refinancing Fund, Law No. 4622 of 3 May 1975, as amended, Decree Law 666 of 2 July 1969.

61 See Decree Law No. 1208 of July 1969, Articles 1 and 2.

62 Ibid. See also Decree No. 994 of 1966, Articles 1 and 2.

63 Ibid.; and Decree Law No. 616 of 1972 and Article 29 of Decree 2349 of 1971.

64 Nevertheless, transport can be limited to 50 per cent of the cargo in cases where it is specified in the granting of a credit.

65 See the Mexican International Multimodal Container Transport Decree.

66 Ibid.; see also Decree of 28 April 1966.

67 And Decree of 30 January 1967.

68 Ibid.; and a Decree effective 1 January 1966; as well as the Certificate of Rebates of Indirect Taxes System (CEDIS) which was rehabilitated in 1977.

69 See the Law of 9 January 1962; The Ministerial Resolution of 12 June 1972; Peruvian Government Decree of 25 January 1966; Decree of 2 June 1970, Decree 22067 of 11 January 1978 and The Law of 8 February 1957.

70 See the Law for the Protection and Development of the National Merchant Marine.

71 See also Article 24 of the General Resolutions of the Pilotage Law.

72 Note also that in 1966 the USA and Venezuela made an arrangement by which bilateral cargoes protected by official laws and regulations of either country are equally distributed.

73 See Article 13 of Law No. 20,447 of 22 May 1974.

74 Ibid. See also Law No. 22,016 which made state-owned firms subject to taxation.

75 See Decree No. 179 of 19 February 1968.

76 Ibid.

77 Ibid.

78 Ibid.

79 See Article 708 of the Fiscal Code of Panama.

80 Ibid.; see also Cabinet Decree No. 15 of 27 January 1972.

81 Law No. 14,650. The government-owned shipping lines are exempt from some taxes, and the import of ships of more than 1,000 dwt intended for the national merchant navy are exempt from consular fees and any other taxes.

82 Ibid.; Uruguay has agreements with Brazil and Argentina which provide for an equal sharing of the cargo carried between them.

83 Export of credits for ships are granted to the shipyards in the form of the Combined Export Import Bank of Japan (supported by the government) and private bank loans which cover almost 70 per cent of the total ship's price.

84 Loans for ship exports accounted for approximately 18 to 22 per cent of total EXIMBANK loans during the fiscal years 1977 and 1978.

85 Financing terms of the EXIMBANK are decided in order that the combined loans meet the OECD 'Understanding an Export Credit for Ships'.

86 M. Chang, *The UNCTAD Model Marine Hull and Cargo Insurance Clauses: Recent Developments in Marine Insurance Law from Korean Perspective*, LM thesis, Dalhousie University, 1985.

87 Ibid.; and B.K. Min and J.M. West, 'Limitation of shipowners' liability under the Commercial Code of Korea', *Journal of Maritime Law and Commerce*, vol. 16, 1985, pp. 21–37.

88 Ibid. S.H. Lee, 'Distant water nations' response to extended fisheries jurisdiction: the case of South Korea', *Maritime Policy Reports*, vol. 6, no. 5, 1984, p. 6.

89 See Presidential Decree No. 764 signed on 7 August 1975; also Presidential Decree No. 1221.

90 Ibid.; and Presidential Decree No. 215 of 16 June 1973; also Presidential Decree No. 806.

91 Ibid.; and A Memorandum of the President to the Central Bank and to MARINA dated 5 March 1975; cf. Presidential Decree No. 894 of 26 February 1976.

92 Ibid.; and Presidential Decree No. 760 of 31 July 1975; also Presidential Decree No. 744 Part cf. Presidential Decree No. 1466.

93 Ibid. Cf. Presidential Decree; and Presidential Decree No. 664 of 5 March 1975; as well as Presidential Decree No. 666.

94 Indonesia allocates 45 per cent of European cargoes for own vessels.

95 The 50 per cent of cf fertilizer imports (100 per cent of FOB fertilizer imports) must be carried on Indonesian flag vessels.

96 Priority for bunkers is given to vessels carrying food imports and those carrying essential export commodities, such as oil, cement and timber.

97 Note that materials for the Japanese-financed Asahana hydro-electric aluminium project in Sumarna must be carried 50–50 by Japanese and Indonesian vessels.

98 There is no duty on items imported for building and fitting out ships and income taxes do not apply to newly built ships registered in Taiwan for a period of five years.

99 Shipments are planned under the supervision of the Ministry of Commerce with first priority being given to vessels built under the measure for the Joint Development of Trading, Shipping and Shipbuilding.

100 See also N. Chandrahasan, 'Indian Ocean peace zone proposal: is it valid today?', *Journal of the Indian Ocean Law Institute*, vol. 26, 1984, pp. 543–55.

101 P. Kurani (ed.), *Bombay: Shipping Handbook*, Bombay Shipping and Allied Services, 1983.

102 S.P. Jagota, 'India and the Law of the Sea', *Archiv des Valkerrechts*, vol. 22, 1984, pp. 49–68; see also R. Puri, *India and National Jurisdiction in the Sea*, New Delhi ABC Publications House, 1985.

103 On 1 January 1980 the Malaysian government instituted a policy whereby all coastal traffic is restricted to ships that are registered in Malaysia and priority is given to ships owned by Malaysians.

104 In 1979 only about 40 per cent of the vessels participating in coastal shipping were Malaysian registered.

105 All official and semi-official agencies (except those importing goods under the United States Agency for International Development Programs) purchase maritime insurance from such Pakistani companies as have joined the national co-insurance scheme administered by the Pakistan Insurance Corps.

106 Coastal shipping is restricted to Pakistani flag ships when available. Half of US and World Bank aid is reserved for national flag ships.

107 Singapore–Soviet Shipping Company (SINSOV) is a 50/50 venture between Soviet and Singapore interests.

108 The Singapore Shipping Association and the Indonesian Shipowners' Association signed an agreement in 1975 which provided for 50–50 cargo-sharing by association members in the trade between the two countries.

109 See Statutory Notice 564 of 8 November 1978.

110 Effective from 31 July 1973 any sea transport of goods from Denmark to Greenland requires a permit from the minister of Greenland. Exempt from this requirement are Danish government institution ships, and transport by sea of goods required for the operation of the Danish–American defence areas.

111 See the Act of Tax Allowances for the Promotion of Production and Exports of Shipbuilding and Other Metal Industries of 1956.

112 Ibid.; as amended in 1970.

113 See under the 'Principles for the Promotion of the German Merchant Marine', German Federal Register No. 94 of 20 May 1965.

114 Ibid. See also the OECD Understanding on Export Credits for Ships in the

292

most recent versions (from 1 December 1979 onwards); and measures against detrimental shipping policies of foreign countries.

115 Hence, according to the decision of Parliament of 29 April 1975, the Ministry of Commerce and Shipping may issue guarantees for loans from foreign credit institutions.

116 See also the scope of Norwegian Guarantee Institute for Ships and Drilling Vessels established in December 1975.

117 The System, in effect since 1973, was continued under the Shipping Act of 6 June 1980. Note also that the Swedish Export Credit Board was authorized to finance Swedish ship exports on OECD forms to the end of June 1981.

118 For Belgium see the Act of 23 August 1948 modelled on the French lines.

119 See the Decree of 26 February 1974.

120 See also the reimbursement of part-cost pursuant to Article 79, title 'Accidents and Illness Occurring on Board or in Course of Embarking'.

121 The equivalent in English jurisprudence would probably be general maritime agent.

122 See also E.J. Donelan, 'Offshore exploration and exploitation: the legal regimes of the United Kingdom and the Republic of Ireland', *New Law Journal*, vol. 133, 1983, pp. 461–4.

123 C.R. Symmens and P.R.R. Gardiner, 'Marine scientific research in offshore areas: Ireland and the Law of the Sea Convention', *Marine Policy*, vol. 7, 1983, pp. 291–301.

124 F. Forde, *The Long Watch: The History of the Irish Mercantile Marine in World War II*, Grill and Macmillan, Dublin and New York, 1981, p. 147.

125 H. Hoorn, G. Peet and K. Wieriks, 'Harmonising North Sea policy in the Netherlands', *Marine Policy*, no. 9, 1985, pp. 53–61.

126 Environmental Resources Ltd, *The Law and Practice Relating to Pollution Control in the Netherlands*, 2nd edn, Graham and Trotman, London, 1982, p. 133.

127 V.M. Brown, 'Legislacion y jurisprodencia holandesa en 1981', *Anuario de Deredo Maritimo*, 1984, pp. 329–40.

128 Export credit finance for merchant vessels arranged through banks in the UK is normally available with the official support of the Export Credit Guarantee Department (ECGD).

129 See also the Industry Act 1972.

130 Ibid., as amended by the Industry Act 1975 and the Shipbuilding Act 1979.

131 See Law No. 684 of 20 December 1974 and Law No. 231 of 25 May 1978.

132 Ibid. See also Law No. 720 of 23 December 1975 and Law No. 26 of 2 February 1974.

133 Ibid.; see Law No. 234 of 25 May 1978 and Law No. 259 of 5 May 1976.

134 See Resolution No. 283/77 of 5 November 1977 and Resolution 78/78 of 24 May 1978 of Portugal; see also Resolution No. 102/78 of 26 June 1978.

135 See Resolutions 265/79 of 18 August 1979; Resolution 359/79 of 21 December 1979; Resolution 144/80 of 24 April 1980; Resolution 145/80 of 24 April 1980; and Decree-Law No. 77/80 of 16 April 1980.

136 See Law No. 378-68 and Law No. 89/1967 and compare them to Law Nos 465 (9/7/68), Decree 509, Decree 800 (1/12/70), Law 27/75 (22/4/75).

137 See also Article 23 of Greek Constitution of 1968 and Article 107 of 1975 Constitution which became effective on 11 June 1975, and Law No. 81411 Supplementing and Amending Tax and Certain Other Relating Provisions which became effective on 13 September 1978.

138 Iranian Decree No. 35510 of 23 August 1976 created the bureau at the Ministry of Commerce for the purpose of planning and programming the importation and shipment of government goods.

139 The Gulf (or Iran–Iraq) War has adversely affected the shipping of not only the two combatants but of the neighbouring countries as well as international oil shipping.

140 Equipment, machinery and materials required to build Israel Shipyards Ltd are exempt from customs and duties and indirect taxes.

141 Tax advantages are given to shipyards at all stages of the implementation of the project and of its subsequent operation. These tax concessions are also available to any approved industrial commercial enterprises.

142 Requirements for the use of Israeli bottoms for carrying meat to Israel are negotiated with the exporting country. Financial regulations of October 1972 require the purchase of import licences on an FOB basis, thereby giving the government of Israel control over the choice of vessel and the placement of cargo insurance. In November 1977 this regulation was changed and many items no longer need an import licence.

143 US Department of Commerce, MARAD, *Maritime Subsidies*, 1981, p. 100.

144 Ibid., p. 101.

145 Coastal trade is reserved to Turkish flag ships; A. Wilson, *The Aegean Dispute*, London International Institute for Strategic Studies, (Adelphi Papers; 155), 1979.

146 The Turkish government encourages the building of ships in Turkey and fleet renewal with modern tonnage by offering loans to both the private and public sector.

147 G. Blake, 'Marine policy issues for Turkey', *Maritime Policy Reports*, vol. 7, no. 4, 1985, p. 6.

148 J.O.S. Kennedy, 'Australian fisheries management: industrial transferable quotas for southern blue fin tuna', *Marine Policy Reports*, vol. 8, no. 4, 1986, p. 6.

149 J.R.V. Prescott, *Australia's Maritime Boundaries*, Australia National University, Department of International Relations, Canberra, 1985.

150 Ibid.

151 A. Bergin, 'Australian ocean policy: the need for review', *Marine Policy*, vol. 10, 1986, pp. 155–8.

152 I.A. Shearer, 'Australia and the International Law of the Sea', *Archiv des Volkerrechts*, 1986, pp. 22–40.

153 Australian Bureau of Transport Economics, *Marine Oil Spill Risk in Australia*, Report no. 53, The Bureau, Canberra, 1983.

PART IV
SHIPPING IN
INTERNATIONAL
ECONOMICS

7 Shipping and the provision of employment

Introduction: Towards a Definition of Employment

Of the economic rationale for state aid to the merchant marine, the most often quoted is the provision of employment. This argument is more relevant in the UK with unemployment currently over 10 per cent and rising fast. The recession has hit the UK merchant fleet hardest.[1] Like any other industry the benefits of merchant shipping should be the creation and/or the preservation of employment. But what is employment? It is submitted that employment is the state of being employed. According to the UK Department of Employment for instance,[2] persons who work for pay or profit are employed. This includes all persons who work for 15 hours or more without pay in a family business or farm. It would therefore appear that the definition would include even those who are unpaid but who nevertheless add to the GNP.[3]

In the UK total unemployment is normally measured each month by the number registered by the job centres and the DHSS for the Department of Employment. The criteria have now been limited to only those actually claiming unemployment benefit[4] which would exclude those employable but unemployed, such as housewives. It also includes those who may not wish to claim for various personal reasons or those simply ineligible to claim under the new means test. Proprietors, self-employed persons[5] and domestic servants, and others, all qualify as employed. With the current worldwide recession and inflation and with over 3 million people out of work in Britain alone, unemployment is one of the key issues facing the western economies in particular and the world economies as a whole.[6]

With its strong correlation with international trade merchant shipping has not escaped the devastating effects of this worldwide recession. On the contrary, as the principal conveyor of world trade, it has been hit hardest.[7] These after-effects have doubtless been most felt in the TMNs such as the UK. The undesirable opposite of employment is unemployment. In Britain, anyone sixteen years of age or over who is not in full-time education, able-bodied, not working and is looking for a job qualifies as an unemployed person.[8] This would include the thousands of school-leavers who are unemployed but are nevertheless kept occupied by the government under the new Youth Training Schemes (YTS) or the Youth Opportunity Programmes (YOPS) as well as other displaced workers in various retraining schemes.[9]

For the statistical summary of the maritime working population in Britain as of March 1984 see Table 7.1. Also counted among the employed are:

(a)   those persons who are waiting to be called back to a job from which they have been laid off;[10]
(b)   those waiting to report to a new job scheduled to begin within thirty days;[11] and
(c)   those who are out of work but are not looking for a job because of temporary illness or because of a belief that no work is available in their line or in their community.[12]

The list does not include the voluntary and compulsory redundancies, early retirements and natural wastages; schemes developed to deal with unemployment in the UK.[13]

Most nations have employment legislations which place the official responsibility for promoting stability in the labour sector in the hands of the governments.[14] An essential objective of such legislations is the maximum utilization of available resources which means a low unemployment level and a high rate of utilization of industrial facilities. The legislations further create a government body, like the Department of Employment in the UK,[15] for the management of the national economic programmes and establish additional machinery, such as the National Development Council (NEDCO), to achieve better understanding and focusing of attention on the important problems of the economy.[16] For a statistical summary of the employees in employment in the UK, see Table 7.2.

It will be remembered that crucial to the understanding of

Table 7.1 Registered dockworkers, average daily disposition of workers' register by local board (UK): 1984

Number

	Employed	Surplus	Sick/injured	Holiday	Authorized absence	In dispute	Other absence	Dormant release register	All RDWs	of which Permanent	Supplementary	Temporary unattached
London	2,020	287	138	305	13	218	3	23	3,007	2,983	–	24
Medway and Swale	402	33	11	65	–	16	6	–	533	533	–	–
South Coast	833	132	21	143	1	102	1	1	1,234	1,233	–	1
Plymouth	27	9	1	5	–	1	–	–	43	43	–	–
Cornwall	73	12	5	13	1	3	–	–	107	107	–	–
Bristol and Severn	427	110	14	83	1	47	1	–	683	683	–	–
South Wales	522	120	29	87	–	70	2	–	830	830	–	–
Liverpool[1]	1,531	193	58	230	3	224	11	–	2,250	2,249	–	1
Manchester[2]	117	45	4	22	–	14	–	1	203	202	–	1
Fleetwood	72	9	1	10	–	8	–	–	100	100	–	–
Cumbria	34	16	–	6	–	3	–	–	59	50	9	–
Ayrshire	8	5	1	2	–	1	–	–	17	17	–	–
Clyde	130	56	13	26	1	19	1	–	246	245	–	–
Aberdeen	198	4	9	30	1	16	3	1	262	255	6	1
Other East Scotland	284	93	24	51	4	37	3	–	466	458	8	–
Tyne and Wear	134	117	6	31	–	9	–	–	297	297	–	–
Middlesbrough and Hartlepool	404	95	22	66	1	40	3	4	635	631	–	4
Hull and Goole	662	232	64	122	7	100	1	–	1,158	1,157	–	1
Grimsby and Immingham	592	87	19	91	3	41	4	–	837	828	9	–
Wash ports	120	32	8	20	–	5	–	–	185	185	9	–
East Anglia	164	32	11	26	–	7	1	–	251	246	5	–
All	8,754	1,669	459	1,434	36	981	40	30	13,403	13,333	37	33

[1] includes Birkenhead, Bromborough and Garston
[2] includes Salford, Ellesmere Port, Runcorn and Weston Point

Source: Department of Transport, British Ports Association, 1984, table 4.13.

Table 7.2 Registered dockworkers, average daily disposition of workers' register (UK): 1965–1984

	1965	1970	1975	1980	1981	1982	1983	1984
Employed	—	34,373	22,471	16,048	13,577	11,825	10,311	8,754
Surplus	—	2,336	4,951	4,103	3,828	2,018	1,744	1,669
Sick/injured	—	3,345	1,483	1,163	838	578	444	459
Holiday	—	3,441	3,190	2,489	2,246	1,802	1,684	1,434
Authorized absence	—	193	126	86	65	57	42	36
In dispute	—	2,465	1,102	447	357	409	339	981
Other absence	—	706	278	116	84	61	42	40
On dormant and release register	—	53	37	40	27	38	25	30
All RDWs	65,128	46,912	33,638	24,492	21,022	16,788	14,631	13,403
Permanent	—	45,639	32,102	24,420	20,984	16,721	14,582	13,333
Supplementary	—	782	1,483	21	4	25	20	37
Temporarily unattached	—	491	53	51	34	42	29	33

Source: Department of Transport, British Ports Association, 1984, table 4.12.

Table 7.3 Employment in the port transport industry (UK): 1965–1984

Thousands

JUNE	1965	1970	1975	1976	1977	1978	1979	1980	1981	1982	1983	1984
Males	122.9	96.6	63.1	60.9	60.4	58.5	56.6	53.9	49.4	42.6	38.2	34.9
Females	6.1	5.7	4.2	3.9	4.3	4.1	4.1	4.3	4.2	4.0	3.8	4.0
All persons	128.9	102.4	67.3	64.9	64.7	62.6	60.7	58.2	53.6	46.7	42.0	38.9

Source: Department of Transport, British Ports Association, Port Statistics 1984, table 4.10.

employment situation in the merchant marine sector is the relationship between the employers (government and shipowners) and employees (trade unions).[17] The employees in merchant shipping are represented principally by The National Union of Seamen (NUS) whose main function is to protect the jobs and the living standards of the shore, seagoing and all other labour forces employed in the industry.[18] The industry may not be the one largest single employer but it is nevertheless a major one and an integral part of any economy. It includes those employed directly in shipping, transport equipment, transport, insurance and other related services.[19] For a statistical summary of this in relation to UK employees in employment, for the port transport industrial sector, see Table 7.3.

Shipping and Employment

The Theory of Employment and Merchant Shipping

It is true to say that any industry can only be a source of secure employment if it is profitable or aided. The aim of any government is full employment at all levels and that includes the merchant shipping industry.[20] Thus it is not only the shipping industry that is established and aided for this purpose. The situation in which the demand for labour equals the supply forthcoming at the given level of real wages is ideal. In these circumstances there can be some unemployment if it is balanced by unfilled vacancies. A situation with no unemployment at all is both unattainable[21] (except in Utopian and static societies) and undesirable because it would leave no room for adaptation to changing circumstances and because it would be chronically inflationary. Most western governments have realistically resigned themselves to a situation of some permanent unemployment at least.[22]

Several kinds of unemployment may exist under full employment:

1 *Seasonal* In some industries, as in agriculture and shipbuilding, work is dependent on the weather. In others the demand for products (clothing, food, etc.) varies with the weather. Firms in these industries may therefore require fewer workers in slack periods. This explains why subsidies are necessary in the merchant marine and agricultural sectors − to help eliminate the cause of seasonal unemployment.[23]

2 *Frictional* The merchant marine industry also happens to be one of these where frictional unemployment is rampant even during

periods of full employment. The structure of the industry is constantly changing and labour must move from declining firms and industries to others which are prospering and expanding. However, where no other sectors are prospering and expanding then the solution would be to grant more subsidies to the merchant marine industry to contain this frictional unemployment.[24] Otherwise such workers may be unemployed for quite a period because the transition may require time and cost in moving home or training for new jobs, there may be opposition from trade unions to entry of new workers, reluctance to move into new areas, hope of inducing the government to establish new industries, etc.[25]

3 *Structural* This is the name given to unemployment if the transition (mentioned in frictional unemployment) is very long. It results from the inability of the economy to re-employ the displaced labour especially seamen, shipbuilding workers and those in the related maritime sector.[26]

4 *Voluntary* More rarely, some employees are content to be unemployed either because they do not see much hope or are uninterested in retraining. This may not be the case with seagoing personnel, due to the occupational hazards.[27]

Today in the 1980s the world is witnessing mass unemployment similar to that of the 1930s. The merchant marine industry has no doubt had her share of that unemployment, and it will be a long time before the situation improves. Indeed, the situation could get worse if further state aid is not extended to industry generally[28] and the maritime industry in particular. It will be remembered that, in 1944, a British government *White Paper* advising on post-war government policies recommended that, to avoid a repetition of the 1930s when a large proportion of the working population were unemployed,[29] economic policy should aim at securing a high and stable level of employment. Lord Beveridge's Report on the Social Services had defined full employment as a situation in which the number of vacancies exceeded the number of men unemployed so that the demand for labour was larger than the supply.[30]

Were that position to be attained it would be ideal for the merchant marine or, indeed, any industry. Full employment in Lord Beveridge's sense had existed in Britain since the war except for short periods. Lord Beveridge's target for unemployment was 3 per cent;[31] in post-war Britain it seldom rose above 2 per cent. However, unemployment is currently running at a national average of 10 per cent with the merchant shipping and shipbuilding areas registering about 12 per cent in the North-East and Upper Clyde. This is a far cry from thirty years ago when, at its peak,[32] British merchant shipping alone employed some 200,228. That was about 40 per cent of the total workforce then employed in the OEEC; the latter total then stood at some 504,587 in 1955, excluding Japan which joined the expanded OECD in 1961.[33] For details see Table 7.4.

Table 7.4   Crews employed in the merchant fleets of the participating and associated countries 1955 (ships 100 grt and over)

Country	Deck Officers	Engineers	Deck and Engine Room Hands	Catering Staff	Total
Belgium	444	658	1,201	999	3,302
Denmark[1]	1,850	2,400	5,500	2,850	12,600
France	4,150	3,300	18,450	9,050	34,950
Germany[2]	4,322	3,124	17,398	6,942	31,786
Greece[3]	3,837	3,537	13,117	4,866	25,357
Italy	6,055	6,358	13,663	11,770	37,846
Netherlands	5,194	5,579	17,223	10,939	38,935
Norway[4]	6,501	4,382	25,844	10,350	47,077
Portugal	587	531	2,325	1,838	5,281
Sweden[5]	5,070	3,000	13,000	5,800	26,870
Turkey[6]	5,762	4,632	17,044	3,295	30,733
United Kingdom[7]	24,334	25,945	51,958	48,991	151,228
Total P.C.	68,106	63,446	196,723	117,690	445,965
Canada	157	164	586	215	1,122
United States					57,500
Total					504,587

[1] Including 155 foreigners.
[2] Including crews of all seagoing vessels regardless of tonnage. Including 17 foreigners.
[3] Including Greek sailors employed under foreign flags.
[4] Including 7,214 foreigners.
[5] Including 7,403 foreigners.
[6] Including crews of small coastal schooners.
[7] Excluding some 49,000 Indians, Pakistanis, Chinese, etc. serving on UK registered ships on articles opened and closed outside the UK.

Source: OEEC, *Maritime Transport*, 1955–56, p. 30.

The true figure of British employment in the maritime sector as a whole at the time was probably about 500,000. The above figure of 200,228 was only for ships of over 100 grt. To obtain a figure resembling reality[34] one would have to consider and include the labour force in all vessels regardless of size and function. That would include fishing vessels, merchant ships, passenger liners, as well as supply vessels for the oil industry. Also included would be the labour force in the maritime-related or supporting services[35] such as shipbuilding, repairs and salvage operations, insurance, brokerage, catering, etc. The UK figures for 1955 were 2 per cent up on the previous year when the UK total was about 197,618 out of the OEEC total of 442,769 (49 per cent)[36] excluding Canada, Japan and the USA. See Table 7.5 for the previous year (1954).

Table 7.5 Crews employed in the merchant fleets of the OEEC participating countries 1954

Country	Deck Officers	Engineers	Deck and Engine Room Hands	Catering Staff	Total
Belgium	490	767	1,222	828	3,307
Denmark	1,900	2,500	6,500	3,200	14,100
France	3,963	2,981	17,572	9,460	33,976
Germany	3,893	2,756	14,668	5,949	27,266
Greece**	6,086	2,460	16,209	2,850	27,605
Italy	5,170	5,034	26,553	15,279	52,036
Netherlands	5,622	6,205	11,254	8,177	31,258
Norway	6,033	4,015	19,611	7,936	37,595*
Portugal	619	549	2,499	1,887	5,554
Sweden	5,005	2,914	12,829	5,602	26,350
Turkey**	5,530	4,470	22,571	2,533	35,104
United Kingdom	24,485	25,455	51,891	46,787	148,618
Total participating countries	68,796	60,106	203,379	110,488	442,769

*Excluding 5,494 foreigners.
**Including crews of small coastal ships.

Source: OEEC, *Maritime Transport*, 1954, table 20, p. 18.

Merchant Shipping, Inflation and Employment

Full employment, or as near there as possible, is the desire of most economies, and industries; the merchant marine being no exception. But this desire too has its own problems. Some maritime transport economists distinguish between *full employment* as defined above and *over-full employment*,[37] when the demand for labour exceeds the supply and the number of vacancies is larger than the number unemployed. The problem for the economic policy is generally held to be the maintenance of full employment while yet avoiding inflation; it is made more difficult by the uncertainty on when the point of full employment is reached.[38] The British experience of full or over-full employment has been almost inevitably accompanied by inflation. Inflation leading to recession or vice-versa can be the worst moment for the merchant marine. With a small amount of cargoes available to many ships it leads to overtonnaging[39] and, sometimes, to the collapse of smaller or less competitive shipping companies.

In a pure economic context, inflation is a condition in which the total demand for goods and services in the economy is larger than their supply, and it is characterized (if unchecked) by a constantly rising level of prices.[40] In merchant shipping terms it is a situation of overtonnaging leading to the laying up of ships and/or the breaking up of tonnage. It is this factor, among others, that drove certain flags away from national registrations to flags of convenience,[41] i.e. cheap labour, substandard registration requirements and low taxation. Recession leading to overtonnaging and laying up of tonnage tends to sharpen the contradictions between labour and shipowners. This normally results in some owners selling off, transferring registration and capital investments abroad in order to maintain or increase profits.[42] For the average monthly employment of the US maritime workforce, see Table 7.6.

Table 7.6   US maritime workforce average monthly employment

	Average monthly employment in fiscal year:	
	1983	1984
Seafaring shipboard jobs	20,695	19,193
Shipyards*	106,446	105,072
Production workers	84,713	82,976
Management and clerical	21,733	22,096
Longshore	34,727	32,116

*Commercial yards in the active shipbuilding base, constructing new ships and/or seeking new construction orders.

Source: MARAD, Maritime Subsidies, 1985, p. 36.

Once inflation is under way, rising industrial costs tend to be followed by rising prices. Wages (and other pay) increases are sought to compensate for the decline in real wages and they are granted because they can be passed on in higher prices to the consumer,[43] for example, in this case, in higher freight rates. This further increases costs, and (in the absence of action by the monetary authorities) the cycle becomes self-perpetuating. A policy of full employment that leads to over-full employment can start off an inflation.[44] In the merchant marine industry this is the state referred to as overtonnaging or *over-capacity*. Since labour is fully employed, the shipowners must pay higher wages to attract sufficient onshore and ocean-going employees.[45]

If, however, prices and wages are rising together, as is usually the case, *real* wages may not rise, and the Seamens' Unions try to keep ahead of inflation by demanding increases in money wages. An inflationary spiral can also be initiated by increases in other costs[46] or by autonomous price rises due to changes in the conditions of demand arising from increasing incomes or changing social habits. Various methods of mastering or controlling the inflation accompanying full employment have been suggested.[47] Some maritime transport economists argue that a degree of inflation be accepted as a stimulus for growth. The weaknesses of this policy are that continued inflation tends to distort the structure of production, and to bear heavily on the fixed-income classes (whose real income is constantly reduced by rising prices).[48]

Sooner or later the policy may bring pressure on the balance of payments (as exports increase in price and become less competitive abroad) and that inflation may not remain moderate for long. Other economists believe that a wage policy[49] might prevent wage increases from initiating or feeding an inflation, and that this can be achieved by publishing an incomes policy figure calculated by the government as the highest *average* increase in earnings and salaries compatible with a stable level of prices[50] and persuading the Seamens' Unions not to exceed it. One difficulty is that, in a changing economy, some industries and firms (notably the merchant marine and related services) will have to pay more than this figure, others less.[51]

In that case either more aid will have to be poured into the merchant marine industry or unemployment will rise to above average in the sector. The government may be able to apply the policy to its employees in the public sector, at least for a period[52] until recruitment becomes difficult and employees are lost to private industry (e.g. the merchant marine) where employees and unions make their own settlements, and if a free market in labour is thought desirable, the government can only advise and persuade, and not direct.[53] Thus, this kind of policy will work only if collective bargaining is abandoned or limited.

There is a third category of economists who have argued that there is no other way of avoiding inflation except by the revision of the post-war British full employment policy stated above.[54] This view has been further reinforced by statistical studies showing a close relationship between the level of unemployment and the corresponding rate of wage increases. Herein lies the root causes of subsidies in the maritime sector and protectionism[55] in industry generally; the aim being the creation and/or the maintenance of full employment. The alternative to this policy is the current cut-backs in shipbuilding, the steep decline of the merchant marine and the successive rise in the balance of payments deficit[56] that has been evident in the UK lately.

The Full Employment Argument

In the TMNs (with which we have mainly concerned ourselves so far), an unemployment rate nearer 2 per cent than 10 per cent would ease the pressure on resources — especially on labour. Government measures would ensure that most unemployment was only transitional.[57] The difficulty is to know precisely when full employment is reached or when the demand for labour equals the supply. I urge that it is better to put a brake on economic expansion *before* demand is equal to supply than to risk over-full employment.[58] Whatever the answer to the problems created by full employment, it would seem that every government will adopt economic policies that ensure *a high and stable level of employment*, if not full employment, and assist the unemployed to find new work more quickly and help them more generously until it is found.[59]

A method advocated by this study is state assistance to the industry concerned. In this case it happens to be the merchant marine and its related industries. The two limbs of this method are maritime subsidies and protectionism, the latter consisting of cargo preferences,[60] flag discriminations and direct state intervention. In this respect protective policies are often invoked as a means to cure unemployment. When large numbers are unemployed the imposition of extra mechanisms[61] such as tariffs or some other systems of protection is extremely tempting. Indeed, in the 1930s the existence of large-scale unemployment was in many countries the most frequently used argument for protection. There is little doubt that in the short run, a tariff can provide a higher level of domestic employment.[62]

Protection brings about some switch in demand from imports towards home-trade products. It is difficult to envisage such a switch taking place without some of the slack being taken up in the domestic economy, particularly if there is a strong multiplier effect.[63] But this is a short-term view. In the first place it assumes that the foreign repercussions are negligible. In fact a reduction in supplying countries' exports resulting from the tariff will cause a fall in these countries' domestic incomes which in turn brings about some reductions in their imports.[64]

On the other hand if the tariff-imposing country exports to these countries there will be a drop in its exports, and hence a fall in employment in its export industries. Thus the imposition of a tariff in a given country might well rebound to the disadvantage of its

307

export industries[65] even in the absence of deliberate retaliation. In the real world, however, deliberate retaliatory policies are likely — particularly if protection is introduced in times of general recession as is the case now. There is then a danger of beggar-my-neighbour tariff-building which tends to follow, as indeed occurred in the 1930s.[66] Even apart from foreign repercussions, it is important to know whether the unemployment which it is hoped to alleviate is the kind which can be appropriately reduced by domestic protection. There are certain types of unemployment that might not be easily cured by protection[67] — at least not in the short run.

Some, or most, of these occur in the merchant shipping industries. We noted that unemployment might be *structural*, that is due to internal technological changes such as the low manning requirements introduced by computerization, use of straddles for loading/ unloading, containerization, etc.[68] The appropriate remedy in this case may not be a tariff, which although temporarily creating more jobs, does so only at the cost of slowing down economic growth. The correct policy in such a situation is an overall economic development policy providing alternative employment[69] and training facilities for seamen displaced by technological changes. However, the seagoing traditions may take long to adapt to onshore employment let alone

Table 7.7   Crews employed in the merchant fleets
of the OEEC participating countries 1953

Country	Deck Officers	Engineers	Deck and Engine Room Hands	Catering Staff	Total
Belgium	600	825	1,550	925	3,900
Denmark	1,900	2,200	5,900	2,700	12,700
France	3,963	2,981	17,572	9,460	33,976
Germany	3,619	2,384	12,517	5,415	23,935
Greece	1,179	1,033	4,045	1,363	7,620
Iceland	n.a.	n.a.	n.a.	n.a.	n.a.
Ireland	n.a.	n.a.	n.a.	n.a.	n.a.
Italy	4,700	4,577	24,139	13,890	47,286
Netherlands	3,602	4,649	16,818	9,325	34,394
Norway	5,815	3,933	19,211	8,336	37,295
Portugal	n.a.	n.a.	n.a.	n.a.	n.a.
Sweden	4,556	2,862	12,881	6,051	26,350
Turkey	4,765	3,926	20,779	2,227	31,697
UK	20,848	24,128	51,914	47,654	144,544
Total participating countries	55,547	53,498	187,326	107,346	403,697

Source: OEEC, *Maritime Transport*, 1954.

to the idleness characteristic of unemployment.[70] In terms of full employment in the OECD maritime industry, the best times were 1953–85 (Tables 7.4 and 7.5). See Table 7.7 for the 1953 figures.

The Under-Employment Argument

An aspect of the industrialization argument which has received considerable attention in recent years is under-employment especially in the merchant marine sector. While Manoilesco maintained that the marginal productivity of labour in shipping was low, modern authors and scholars[71] have gone further, suggesting that, in the case of some countries, it might even be zero. In other words the degree of under-employment in the merchant marine in certain countries is such that part of the labour force could be removed from the industry without a fall in total output.[72] Indeed, owing to present overmanning, output might actually rise (in which marginal productivity is negative). This is the concept of under-employment or *disguised* unemployment, developed by Professor Arthur Lewis. The solution to this problem is what is termed in modern economic slang as *thinning down*, or *pruning*, or *streamlining*, or simply *rationalization*.[73]

This is what has recently happened to the British shipbuilding, mining and steel industries, to mention but a few examples. Unemployment in the merchant shipping industries is often said to be associated with fixed technical coefficients of production.[74] Thus, it is claimed that a certain number of workers are required to man a vessel or work in a building or repair yard. Beyond a certain point, the addition of managerial limits of labour to given quantities of land and other factors results in no increase in aggregate output — perhaps even a decrease.[75] This would be more like the case of sub-site family agriculture in a developing country than that of a merchant marine industry in an industrialized world. The examples may be two extremes — i.e. from two opposite ends of economic development and/or industrialization — but the analogy is nevertheless useful.[76]

In the former case the peasant is not only likely to be ignorant of cost considerations, he might also be expected to provide employment for the extended family, for whom few opportunities for outside employment exist. In the latter case the overmanning of ships can lead to the destruction of profitability.[77] The problem is especially serious where the growth of population leads to yet more unemployment in the shipping terminals and shipbuilding regions. It should be noted that such *under-employed* shipworkers and seamen may not necessarily be idling.[78] They could in fact be using

Table 7.8 Employment in transport and communications (UK)

(a) Employees in employment at June: 1974–1984

Thousand

	SIC 1980	1974	1975	1976	1977	1978	1979	1980	1981	1982	1983	1984
Railways	71	195.4	201.8	193.7	182.2	183.9	182.3	181.4	175.8	168.1	160.5	153.2
Other inland transport	72	467.2	465.2	453.7	451.2	449.2	454.0	447.7	409.8	397.3	392.3	387.3
Road passenger transport*	721	—	—	—	—	—	—	—	—	190	189	188
Road haulage	723	—	—	—	—	—	—	—	—	191	186	184
Other	722 726	—	—	—	—	—	—	—	—	16	17	15
Sea transport	74	84.3	85.0	76.8	79.8	77.0	74.2	70.3	65.8	58.1	48.7	41.1
Air transport	75	47.0	46.5	47.3	48.9	51.5	54.6	56.4	55.1	46.6	42.3	44.6
Supporting services to transport	76	116.6	113.6	112.2	113.7	114.9	115.9	115.4	110.1	101.7	96.2	92.5
Inland	761	—	—	—	—	—	—	—	—	17	17	17
Sea	763	—	—	—	—	—	—	—	—	50	45	42
Air	764	—	—	—	—	—	—	—	—	35	35	34
Miscellaneous transport and storage	77	120.8	125.7	128.6	141.7	158.9	160.7	163.0	157.4	152.8	144.8	148.2
Postal services and telecommunications	79	434.2	438.6	421.6	410.7	406.5	413.4	427.8	428.7	426.6	421.1	417.7
All transport and communication	7	1,465.4	1,476.3	1,433.9	1,428.2	1,442.2	1,455.0	1,462.1	1,402.6	1,351.1	1,305.9	1,284.5
All industries and services		22,297	22,213	22,048	22,126	22,274	22,638	22,458	21,386	20,927	20,587	20,694

*Scheduled

(b) Employees in employment: by sex and employment status

SIC 1980	June 1981 Male	June 1981 Female Part-time	June 1981 Female All	June 1983 Male	June 1983 Female Part-time	June 1983 Female All	June 1984 Male	June 1984 Female Part-time	June 1984 Female All
Transport and communication 7	1,128.9	55.2	273.6	1,048.2	53.3	257.7	1,022.4	55.0	262.0
Railways 71	163.5	0.8	12.3	150.0	0.7	10.5	143.3	0.7	9.9
Other inland transport 72	857.9	16.2	51.8	342.0	15.9	50.3	337.3	16.1	49.9
Sea transport 74	58.7	0.6	7.1	43.6	0.5	5.2	36.7	0.4	4.3
Air transport 75	37.3	0.6	17.8	29.5	0.5	12.8	29.9	0.6	14.7
Supporting services to transport 76	94.1	3.0	15.9	81.5	2.7	14.7	78.1	2.5	14.4
Miscellaneous transport and storage 77	95.2	11.8	62.2	85.4	10.9	59.4	85.8	12.2	62.4
Postal services and telecommunications 79	322.2	22.3	106.5	316.2	22.2	104.9	311.3	22.5	106.3

(c) Employees in employment: by standard region: June 1984

SIC 1980	North	Yorkshire & Humber	East Midlands	East Anglia	South East	South West	West Midlands	North West	Scotland	Wales	Great Britain
Transport and communication 7	55.2	93.5	73.0	39.0	563.1	79.1	84.4	139.7	114.2	43.3	1,286.6

Source: HMSO Department of Transport, *Transport Statistics Great Britain 1975–1985*, table 1.27.

up a great deal of physical energy. They are, however, under-employed in the sense that they are relatively unproductive. Neither is it necessarily true to say that they require fewer calories of food intake than if they were employed in other factories.[79]

Accordingly, Lewis and others argue that the transfer of such labour to the towns would neither diminish the output of the merchant marine industry nor increase aggregate demand for maritime services. Hence a tariff might improve the allocation of resources.[80] The under-employment argument using tariffs has been criticized, notably by Haberber, Viner and Meiner. First, they argue that technical production coefficients are less rigid than proponents of the transfer of the workers as previously assumed. Viner, for example, finds it 'impossible to conceive'[81] of a shipping company on which some addition to the output might not be secured by using additional labour in more careful selection and planning of the industry or in more intensive use of the yards. By the same token there would be some decrease in absolute shipping output if some workers were to leave the industry.[82]

Secondly, where a labour market exists, it is difficult to see why any shipowner should engage labour, the marginal rate of which he knows to be less than its marginal cost (i.e. wage rate). Of course, through sheer ignorance, he might continue to employ workers who do not justify their wages.[83] In the merchant marine industry the likelihood of workers not earning their keep is of course much greater, although given some mobility of labour it seems likely that, even in this case, in the long run there would be a movement out of the shipping sector.[84] From this brief outline of some of the issues involved in economic development of the DMNs especially, we can hopefully appreciate some of the complexities of the questions raised by protectionism in such countries.[85]

Today, few economists would argue that developing nations should never foster the development of their own national merchant marines by protective means. However, protective policies should be undertaken only after careful consideration of their implications.[86] A general blanket protection granted to each and every industry might well involve such a country in high and quite unnecessary costs. Before we go on to examine the balance of payments' argument, we should take a glance at Table 7.8 showing employees in transport and communications employment in Britain as of June 1984.[87] Of particular interest are the figures in the box (c), i.e. transport and communication and supporting services to transport in which sea transport features prominently.

Employment and the Balance of Payments

The Earnings and Savings of the Balance of Payments Arguments

In the 1930s arguments for protection based upon the desire for fuller employment were closely linked with those concerned with the balance of payments. If there had been no balance of payments' constraint, Keynes's employment argument for the tariff would not have been advanced.[88] There are other and better ways of securing a higher level of domestic demand than recourse to protection. But given the balance of payments' difficulties, governments are tempted to reduce external deficits by means of domestic protection. This is especially true of the developing nations[89] whose development programmes often entail substantial strain on limited foreign exchange resources. In fact the GATT agreement expressly permits a member country to impose trade controls (as a temporary measure) in case of balance of payments disequilibrium, and in the post-war world a very high proportion of trade and payments' restrictions exist precisely in order to safeguard countries' balance of payments.[90]

For example, the UK import surcharge of 1964 was imposed for this reason and the UK Exchange Controls (removed in 1979) had the same objective. But, on the whole, similar criticisms can be levied against protective policies imposed for the balance of payments' reasons as against those invoked to maintain full employment.[91] For example, if country A's exports and country B's imports policies which deliberately restrict A's exports have an adverse effect upon incomes in B and hence upon B's imports as applied by country A, the reduction on country B's imports could well have an adverse effect upon country A.[92] Suppose, further, that country C is introduced into the equation. Even if B imports nothing from country A, it will almost certainly import from third countries, such as country C, which may happen to be country A's markets. In this example protection in any one of these three countries is bound to affect all.[93]

Of course, even if protection succeeds in correcting the balance of payments disequilibrium (or unemployment), it does not follow that protection is the best policy to attain this end. It is simply one method of switching demand from imports to home-produced substitutes and in this respect may be regarded as an alternative (and in many respects a second-best alternative) to devaluation.[94] Finally, as with all arguments for protection (except perhaps those relating to infant industries and developing countries), it should be remembered that protection by insulating, in part or in whole, the

313

industries of a country from foreign competition removes one of the strongest possible incentives for efficiency.[95]

A tariff might strengthen a country's balance of payments or trade but the gain is temporary if the industries fostered became inefficient so that, when protection is removed, their ability to compete on world markets is diminished.[96] The main argument concerning the role of the merchant marine in the savings and earnings of the balance of payments is to be found in Chapter 8. The main argument to be made here is the strong link between foreign exchange reserves and domestic levels of employment.[97] Nowhere would this be more relevant than in a foreign exchange-earning industry like merchant shipping. Be that as it may, the other argument for protection of the merchant marine industry is allegedly to provide employment for national seafarers or to protect the merchant marine fleet in the face of severe competition.[98]

Protection of the Merchant Marine Industry

These two aims — the provision of employment for national seafarers and/or the protection of the merchant fleet in times of severe crisis — can be considered together as the main concern for protectionism.[99] Both deal with periods of depression. Protection concerns tramp ships and tankers when rates are between the normal level and that lower level at which national ships would move into lay-ups. Protection concerns liners when capacity utilization falls as a result of falling trade volumes or increased capacity.[100] The employment aim is mainly concerned with non-liner tonnage when rates reach the lay-up level. It is characteristic of non-liner shipping that very slight variations in demand lead to very high changes in freight rates.[101]

The structure of costs, with overheads accounting for over one-half of total costs, gives rise to a situation in which the fall in demand at the end of the boom leads to rapidly falling freight rates but the emergence of very little over excess capacity.[102] Once rates fall to the level of the voyages' costs minus lay-up costs of the highest cost ship, the rate of fall in freight rates is damped by a movement of ships with lay-up. But when rates have reached this level all but the most economic tramps are unprofitable. As demand continues to fall, rates fall, the volume of laid-up tonnage rises[103] and the proportion of the vessels remaining in service, which are covering the total costs, decline for tramp shipping and, although it is receipts which are deficient, paradoxically most attempts to increase receipts will fail to achieve the aim. The only viable policy, in this respect, would be an operating subsidy.[104]

If, in the early stages of a depression, the problem is that the high costs of national ships make them among the first to move into lay-up then cost-reducing subsidies would be appropriate. As the depression deepens, however, the level of national costs in relation to international costs[105] becomes less relevant and so a subsidy to make up the difference between the actual and the viable level of freight rates becomes appropriate. If the only concern is with employment, then a cost-reducing subsidy, which reduces the voyage costs of national shipowners to those of the lowest in the world market, remains appropriate.[106] Such a subsidy would leave shipowners and shipping companies making unchanged losses, but would keep ships out of lay-ups until they were due for survey. As each ship's survey date arrived additional action would be needed.[107]

Provision of Employment Argument

In the depression situation envisaged, liner operators will be operating below capacity. Here preference legislation would help to increase cargoes. These help the national merchant marine by removing cargo from foreign ships and so are likely to lead to retaliation by countervailing actions.[108] Only the use of operating subsidies will avoid this. The natural outcome of the lay-ups is the unemployment of seamen. To strengthen the national argument for providing employment, there has been action at international level. There are a couple or so conventions on this point.[109] The first one is concerned with the establishment and maintenance of an efficient and adequate system for financing employment for seamen. It notes that the business of finding employment for seamen is not to be carried out for pecuniary gains; presumably the duty is of right and on principle.[110]

The convention provides further that any company or agency which has been engaged in such work as a commercial enterprise for pecuniary gain, however, may be permitted to continue temporarily if the work is conducted under government supervision and inspection.[111] All member nations ratifying the convention agree, first, to take all necessary steps to abolish the practice of finding employment for seamen as an enterprise for pecuniary gain, as soon as possible. Secondly, the contracting states, when ratifying,[112] undertake to organize and maintain an efficient and adequate system of public employment offices for finding employment for seamen without charge. This is the first international convention to expressly provide for, and charge, national governments with the duty of providing employment for their seamen.[113]

Thus, the provision of employment becomes a public, national and international obligation. It has also become such a duty to maintain continuity of employment in the merchant marine industry. The purpose of the second convention is therefore to have each member state[114] 'encourage all concerned to provide continuous or regular employment for qualified seafarers in so far as this is practicable, and in so doing, to provide shipowners with a stable and competent work force'.[115] The ways and means of achieving this objective may include: contracts or agreements providing for the continuance of regular employment with a shipping undertaking or an association; or the establishment and maintenance of a register or list of categories of qualified seafarers.[116]

The registers are to be reviewed so as to achieve the levels needed for the maritime industry. When reduction in the lists become necessary, all measures should be taken to minimize the harmful effect to seafarers.[117] Third, and finally, is the convention's recommendations along similar lines to those discussed above. This recommendation provides for the continuous or regular employment of all qualified seafarers. When continuous or regular employment is not practicable, guarantees of employment and/or income should be provided. When registers or lists of qualified seafarers[118] are used to obtain regular employment for seafarers, criteria should be established for determining who will be included on such a list. The convention, in fact, goes further than the maintenance of a mere list, to the provision of alternative employment where possible, particularly where reduction of the list may be inevitable.[119]

For example, if reduction of the list is unavoidable, help should be given to aid seafarers in finding alternative employment through retraining facilities and the assistance of the public employment services.[120] Finally, the termination of employment is to be based on agreed criteria as far as possible, and be subject to adequate notice and accompanied by such payments as unemployment insurance, severance benefits or any combination of benefits provided for by national legislations, regulations or collective agreements.[121]

Supporters of protectionism for employment provision tend to point to the large number employed in the merchant navies of the OECD countries. Table 7.7 (p. 308) shows figures for the first time the OEEC Maritime Transport Committee published its annual report in 1953.[122] Then the total employed in the then OEEC was about 457,487 (i.e. the given total of 403,697 plus the 4,790 and 49,000 foreigners in Portugal and the UK. Even then that was only true of the fourteen member countries who replied to the Committee's questionnaire.[123] It should also be pointed out that then Canada, Japan and the USA were not members of the OEEC. The new expanded OEEC (the OECD) has twenty-three members (nine more). At that time, the UK was the largest single employer with about 193,544 seamen (the given total of 144,544 plus 49,000 foreigners).

316

Compare this to Table 7.4 (p. 303) when the OEEC maritime employment was at the peak with a total of 553,587[124] seamen (the given total of 504,587 plus 49,000 foreigners in the UK fleets). It will also be noted that the UK figure was 200,228 (the given 151,228 total plus the 49,000 foreigners). However, the 553,587 total was of only fourteen of the current twenty-three member states of the OECD;[125] and only of ships of 100 grt and above.

Maritime Employment in the OEEC/OECD Countries

The importance of the merchant marine industry as a source of maritime employment is therefore further emphasized by the example obtainable from the OECD countries. In addition to the statistics detailed above, Table 7.9 shows the principal results of an inquiry into the composition of the crews by nationality.[126] Of the fourteen countries for which sufficient information was available in 1968, five employed only nationals and two (Finland and France) employed foreigners only as an insignificant part of the total personnel.[127] All in all foreigners accounted for 13 per cent of the total personnel of the merchant marines of Denmark and the Federal Republic of Germany, for about 25 per cent in the fleets of Belgium and Norway and for little over one-third in the Dutch and Swedish fleets.[128]

Table 7.9   Foreign personnel employed in the merchant marines of OECD member countries, 1968

							Persons employed
	EEC	Other Europe	Africa	Asia	Latin America	Others or not specified	Total foreigners
Belgium	186	356	176	8	8	15	749
Denmark	248	1,101	150	524	191	114	2,328
Finland	38	183	·8	1	19	26	275
France	1	1	322	85	19	–	428
Germany	172	3,914	193	1,277	39	364	5,959
Iceland[1]	–	–	–	–	–	–	–
Ireland[1]	–	–	–	–	–	–	–
Italy[1]	–	–	–	–	–	–	–
Netherlands	60	3,189	31	5,382	37	200	8,899
Norway	947	6,724	153	5,025	1,058[2]	184	14,091
Portugal	–	–	–	–	–	–	–
Spain	–	–	–	–	–	–	–
Sweden[1]	–	2,169	–	–	–	4,001	6,170
Switzerland	277	90	7	–	20	–	394

[1] 1967 data.
[2] Including North America.

Source: OECD, *Maritime Transport*, 1968, p. 56.

In the early 1970s and early 1980s the total employment was down on the above figures;[129] it was 50,000 in 1981 and 49,000 in 1982. By the early 1980s contraction in the industry, due to the beginning of the worldwide economic depression, had already begun.[130] At the boom periods the number employed in these countries was about one-and-a-half times more. Supporters of protectionism for the provision of employment in the merchant marine contend that unless massive state aid is available[131] to the industry this figure could slump even further with the resulting massive unemployment. Even then the 222,810 of the personnel employed in the merchant marines of all the twenty-three OECD member states by occupation was only 40 per cent of the same number from only twelve member states at the peak in 1955 (Table 7.4, p. 303).[132]

In just one year the figure fell by about 50 per cent from 384,257 in 1981 to 222,810 at the end of 1982. The same figures broken down in terms of nationality (excluding fishing vessels) was 167,682 in 1982 falling from some 308,945 the previous year.[133] Some countries, notably Canada, Greece, Iceland and the UK either do not keep the latter records at all or did not respond. Others like Australia, Ireland, Japan and Sweden provided only part of the statistical records. The most alarming records are revealed by the British statistics.[134] She remains by far the largest employer or the most overmanned merchant navy with 53,772 out of the whole OECD total of 222,810 by occupation in 1982 — i.e. about 25 per cent with the remaining twenty-two participating countries providing 75 per cent.[135]

It will be further evident that the figures for Britain represent a decline of 75 per cent (53,772 in 1982) from 200,228 at the peak thirty years ago in 1955. In fact Britain was then employing the equivalent of the current OECD total strength.[136] However, these statistics in themselves can be misleading if taken literally. There should be some caution in interpreting the figures. First, they do not represent the true number of personnel employed in the merchant navy but rather on only ships of 100 grt and over.[137] The 1982 figures also exclude fishing vessels which are included in our definition of the merchant marines. Secondly, as evident therein, the figures are not complete as not all the participating countries responded fully to the committee's surveys.[138]

Lastly, they probably do not include offshore oil supply vessels which tend to be less than 100 grt but quite numerous in the OECD. Offshore operations are in most cases a very recent phenomena.[139] The true strength of personnel employed in the merchant marines would have to include both ocean-going and coastal operations, as well as the other related services such as shipbuilding, insurance, catering, passenger liners, ferries, hovercrafts, dry docks, repairs, salvage, labour and port operators.[140] The only conclusion to be drawn from the figures is that of an industry in fast decline and therefore in dire need of state assistance, if this steep decline is to be arrested. The alternative to these nations would then be a contraction in their commitments to the Employment Guarantee Convention;[141] hence the protection of employment argument.

The Protection of Employment

Shipping and Keynes' Theory of Employment

In spite of the limited nature of the argument for protection as a means of countering domestic unemployment, it was the one most frequently advanced in favour of the British tariff, for example in the 1930s. Indeed before Britain left the Gold Standard, Keynes[142] himself used a somewhat sophisticated version of the unemployment argument for protectionism. In common with most of his contemporaries (economists of the Cambridge School), Keynes had been brought up as a free-trader. It was he, however, who in 1923 evoked somewhat rhetorically: 'Is there anything tariff can do, which an earthquake cannot do better?'[143] This would not have been to the benefit of those who have sought Keynes' theory to protect industry and therefore jobs — especially those who have sought its extension and/or application to merchant shipping.[144]

But in 1930, in his *A Treatise on Money*, Keynes appeared to perform a U-turn. He, instead, was considering a tariff as a means of attaining a higher level of employment than would have been possible under free trade.[145] This is when Keynes made his suggestion of a 15 per cent duty on all manufactured and semi-manufactured goods with a 5 per cent duty on foodstuffs and certain raw materials. This was carried in the popular article in the *New Statesman* and *Nation* in the Spring of 1931.[146] His conversion to protection as the proper policy for Britain had also become clear in his contribution to the work of the Macmillan Committee, of which he was an influential member. It would appear that, at that time, Keynes was aware of the difficulty for Britain of implementing a full employment policy without taking steps to safeguard the gold reserves.[147]

We shall soon note, in Chapters 9 and 10, the strong link between foreign exchange reserves and the level of employment, and how this affects the merchant navy. In the context of a fixed exchange rate, a domestic financial policy sufficiently expansionist[148] to make a substantial inroad into unemployment policy would have weakened Britain's external position. Keynes argued that in this situation the

319

correct policy was domestic expansion accompanied by devaluation. Before the pound sterling began to lose ground against the dollar[149] this had been the policy put forward by the British National Union of Seamen. But since then (unlike now) the government appeared determined at all costs to maintain the exchange rate, the necessary degree of domestic expansion would only be feasible if it took place behind a tariff wall.[150]

Hence Keynes advocated a tariff, not as the best possible policy but as the one which would be preferable to allowing the economy to stagnate. It was a second-best remedy. Behind the moderate tariff wall, policies for full employment could be formulated without fear of serious external repercussions.[151] Such a tariff would not harm Britain's trading partners but merely offset the external consequences of internal expansion, by making sure that expansion would not result in a substantial increase in imports. Although a tariff is still a useful tool for protectionism[152] in international trade relations, its modern shipping equivalents are cargo preference, flag discriminations and direct state intervention. Among the latter mechanisms are measures such as state directives backed up by countervailing actions.[153]

There was no question of deliberately reducing imports as the result of the measures Keynes advocated. Accordingly, Keynes denied that the tariff involved a beggar-my-neighbour policy. Indeed, if Britain's trading partners agreed to adopt expansionist policies,[154] the need for a tariff would probably disappear. But since this seemed unlikely, the tariff was the only way in which the correct internal policy could be followed without damage to the balance of payments. Transport and shipping economists have sought to relate Keynes' theory[155] of protection of employment in the economy, generally, to the merchant marine industry in particular. Policy-makers in the DMNs have seized and capitalized on this. 'What is good for Britain is good for the rest of the world', they say.[156] Hence the employment protection argument.

Shipping and the Protection of Employment Argument

Thus, the employment argument, as developed by Keynes, was in a sense one resting upon a particular set of circumstances and was probably not intended to be a general justification for protection. Nevertheless, the argument seems to be revived and extended to the merchant navy[157] whether or not currently the general economic and/ or shipping conditions is anything to be compared with Keynes' times. Keynes, though, believed that the best way to secure full employment was by appropriate domestic economic policies. If external factors[158] made the implementation of such policies impossible, some degree of insulation from the world economy might be desirable. In such circumstances the loss of advantages of international division of labour might be preferable to that resulting from under-utilization of resources.[159]

The gist of the argument, as applied to shipping, is that if the merchant marine industry is not aided but allowed to shrink or die those deriving their livelihood, directly or indirectly, from it would be unemployed.[160] And that, in a chain reaction, this would affect the whole economy and consequently the country's international trade, balance of payments position and international relations. In the British example one needs to know how many people are employed in the merchant marine and related industries[161] to realize what a disaster this would be. It would affect a cross-section of the shore-based labour force, seagoing personnel, shipbuilding and the steel industry who supply them, ship repairs contractors and heavy engineering industries that supply them, insurance companies, docks, banks, freight and transport services etc.[162]

This is not to mention the dependants thereon such as the catering and invisibles. For the figures of the UK registered seamen employed and unemployed for the decade 1974–84 (end of year), see Table 7.10. It is a far cry from the good days of the early 1950s,[163] and shows a decline in line with that in the merchant marine and related industries. It is precisely to protect these and their own jobs that the British transport and seamen's unions constantly strike.[164] The consequences of lack of aid to the merchant marine industry would drive the national fleets out of international competition, or to the

Table 7.10   United Kingdom shipping industry:
             seamen on UK register (end of year)

Thousands

	1974	1975	1976	1977	1978	1979	1980	1981	1982	1983	1984
Registered seamen[1]											
Employed	75.4[2]	76.2	73.4	70.4	68.8	66.3	62.6	57.8	51.3	43.2	37.1
Unemployed	1.3[2]	1.3[2]	1.3[2]	1.3	1.2	1.4	2.0	3.5	3.5	2.9	1.7
Total[3]	76.7	77.5	74.7	71.7	70.0	67.7	64.6	61.3	54.8	46.1	38.8

[1] Includes officers and cadets as well as ratings.
[2] Estimated figure.
[3] Excludes seamen remaining temporarily on the register although no longer seeking work.

Source: HMSO, Department of Transport, *Transport Statistics Great Britain 1974–1984*, table 4.22.

foreign registry with further loss of jobs to the nationals arising from the transfer of the said jobs to foreign nationals and fleets.[165]

Protection of employment in the merchant marine industry became a strong reason in many traditional maritime nations in the early 1930s when considerable unemployment arose. This trend seemed to have improved until the late 1970s and early 1980s[166] with another worldwide recession which the merchant marine industry has not escaped. For this reason, opponents of protectionism to the industry argue that, since it has not yet been necessary, it will probably not be so again, as in the future it can be reckoned that state institutions[167] in the advanced maritime nations will generally intervene to create employment which should also be more *productive* than formerly. We can reason: should seamen's wages be protected or should they be retrained and given other forms of employment at corresponding wages?[168]

This will be a question of where the use of labour is supposedly more productive. The problem is difficult principally because its solution will depend on the target at which the measures should be aimed — and this is very difficult to determine.[169] What is more difficult to determine, though, is the direct relationship between employment generally and the seamen's wages in particular, and the standard of living.[170] We shall, therefore, turn our attention to this problem in the remaining paragraphs of this chapter.

Shipping, Employment and the Standards of Living

The state of national employment determines the cost of living and, therefore, the population's standards of living. Protection of the latter is often cited as the rationale for the maintenance of the former. Standards of living, with reference to a person,[171] a family, or a body of people, means the extent to which they can satisfy their wants. Thus, if they can afford only the minimum amount of food, clothing and shelter their standard of living would be described as very low. It is in relation to this that developing countries differ from the richer nations.[172] A low standard of living is usual for most seamen from the poorer countries of the world. If, on the other hand, they are able to enjoy a great variety of food, a good supply of good clothing and live in well-furnished houses and in addition are able to satisfy a wide variety of other wants, then clearly people are enjoying a high standard of living.[173]

So far the latter has been the case with people (including those employed in the merchant marine industry) in the advanced countries of the north. But this privileged position has recently come under severe threat following recession and, therefore, massive unemployment of the labour force[174] generally and those in the merchant marine industry in particular. But there are other external reasons for this, A people's standard of living first depends on the size of the national income and, second, on the manner of distribution of that national income.[175] People in the less developed regions of the world are described as 'poor' because the national income as an average per head is low. Wide differences in the standard of living in the same country are normally the result of a very unequal distribution of the national income, among other factors.[176]

The higher standard of living of the advanced maritime nations is due to those countries having large stocks of up-to-date capital, well-trained labour and, probably, the willingness of the people themselves to work for that higher standard of living.[177] Currently there is also less inequality of income in the advanced economies of the industrialized world than in the less industrialized parts of the emerging maritime nations. A great deal is being done to raise the standard of living in the less economically developed economies,[178] since the accumulation of capital proceeds more rapidly the more a country has and this, therefore, otherwise tends to widen the gap between the developed and the developing maritime nations.[179]

The need to protect the standard of living in the merchant marine industries of the western nations is generally firmly maintained. The reason for this is demonstrated first and foremost by the labour unions.[180] As the white collar unions are increasingly adopting the same way of thinking as the labour unions, it is probable that they will try to make themselves heard in the discussion on the same lines. On the whole seamen's and shipping executives' wages tend to reach the same level as wages in general in the country in question.[181] This is partly a result of economic realities but partly of the principle of wage equality. If a maritime nation wants a higher wage level than another it would have to use other means other than protectionism. Hence the protection of wages argument.[182]

Protection of Seamen's Wages and Employment

Flag discriminatory measures towards achieving competition mean that they cannot overcome the obstacles of subsidies or extra charges that the state raises; or at least they cannot do so easily. In this way there is room for higher wages. In the USA[183] for example, higher wages have come about through an official decrease. The US Merchant Marine Act 1936 includes regulations dealing with the minimum wages of officers and crew on board the shipping vessels. It can be argued that the mercantile maritime is hereby assured a higher general quality of men serving on board[184] than if wage rates were set without

323

Table 7.11   Employment of US flag ocean-going fleets — 30 September 1984[1]

	Total		Vessel type									
			Passenger Pass./cargo		General cargo		Intermodal		Bulk carriers		Tankers	
Status and area of employment	No.	Deadweight tons (000)	No.	Deadweight tons (000)	No.	Deadweight tons (000)	No.	Deadweight tons (000)	No.	Deadweight tons (000)	No.	Deadweight tons (000)
Grand total	**749**	**23,965**	**34**	**268**	**268**	**3,188**	**150**	**3,299**	**25**	**1,121**	**272**	**16,089**
Active vessels	**408**	**16,459**	**9**	**75**	**54**	**763**	**116**	**2,671**	**22**	**999**	**207**	**11,951**
Foreign trade	140	4,320	3	29	33	503	74	1,924	6	435	24	1,429
Nearby foreign[2]	3	55	—	—	—	—	2	18	—	—	1	37
Great Lakes–Seaway foreign	—	—	—	—	—	—	—	—	—	—	—	—
Overseas foreign	137	4,265	3	29	33	503	72	1,906	6	435	23	1,392
Foreign to foreign	20	1,112	—	—	—	—	5	90	1	127	14	895
Domestic trade	183	9,606	2	14	1	18	25	393	13	388	142	8,793
Coastwise	30	1,318	—	—	—	—	—	—	5	148	25	1,170
Intercoastal	76	3,024	—	—	—	—	—	—	6	184	70	2,840
Noncontiguous	77	5,264	2	14	1	18	25	393	2	56	47	4,783
Other US agency operations	65	1,421	4	32	20	242	12	264	2	49	27	834
MSC charter	54	1,336	—	—	15	210	12	264	2	49	25	813
BB charter & other custody	11	85	4	32	5	32	—	—	—	—	2	21
Inactive vessels	**341**	**7,506**	**25**	**193**	**214**	**2,425**	**34**	**628**	**3**	**122**	**65**	**4,138**
Temporarily inactive	9	371	—	—	—	—	4	87	1	82	4	202
Laid-up (privately owned)	91	4,266	1	6	18	227	23	372	2	40	47	3,621
Laid-up (privately owned/ NDRF)	4	110	—	—	2	24	2	86	—	—	—	—
Laid-up (MARAD-owned) pending disposition[3]	9	99	2	19	7	80	—	—	—	—	—	—
National Defense Reserve Fleet	228	2,660	22	168	187	2,094	5	83	—	—	14	315

[1] Excludes vessels operating exclusively on the inland waterways and Great Lakes, those owned by the US Army and Navy, and special types such as tugs, cable ships, etc.

[2] Nearby foreign trade includes Canada, Mexico, Central America, West Indies, and North Coast of South America.

[3] Other than vessels in the National Defense Reserve Fleet.

Source: MARAD, *Maritime Subsidies*, 1985, p. 11.

interference. The question that arises is whether the quality is so much better that it balances the larger costs borne by the state. It is very difficult to get a valid answer to the question without more thorough investigations of the entire situation.[185] However, see Table 7.11 for the employment of US flag ocean-going fleets as of 30 September 1984 and compare with the UK figures in Table 7.10 (p. 321).

It may be surmised, however, that it is very doubtful whether the shipowners obtain greater efficiency by these regulations. On the contrary, it seems most reasonable to presume that the regulations regarding minimum wages might have the effect of increasing freight rates.[186] An increase in the income of one wage-earning group which is not based on an increase in production must essentially mean that the national income must be redistributable. The wage earners concerned obtain a rise that is taken from another group of wage earners, and possibly also from the owners of capital or land.[187] A basic line of economic thought to which no objection can be made is that, in the long run, an increase in wage levels can only go hand-in-hand with increased productivity and/or an increased supply of capital and land.[188]

In the long run, a nation as a whole cannot therefore be said to have an economic advantage by excluding the merchant marine fleets of other nations alone and simply by protectionism.[189] This is the argument used by the critics of protection for the protection of seamen's wages[190] and living standards.[191] We can here establish a connection with the current literature in the subject by quoting Onlin:

> Considering the obvious advantages that the international exchange of goods and the distribution of labour between different countries brings to all parties, it may seem strange that there can be no such widespread conceptions as that the obstruction of this exchange of goods can itself improve the possibilities of production and increase the national income. Probably the explanation of this misconception lies in the fact that protection of certain goods or increase in the customs duties can undoubtedly involve considerable profits for the manufacturers and sellers of goods.[192]

However, the protectionist argument is that protection would boost the manufacture and export of goods and services. This would in turn lead to a better balance of payments and national income position.[193] High national income would, of course, mean full employment and higher standards of living for the seamen and the country's population as a whole. This argument is disputed by the anti-protectionist economists along the lines outlined by Onlin's statement above.[194] Onlin further states that:

The advantages of protection are concentrated on a smaller number of people, while the burden of the rise in prices is more or less distributed among the whole of the country's buying public. It is a well-known fact that those who gain by a certain procedure are very easily convinced that their own interests and the interests of the community run parallel. Furthermore, it can easily be seen that the protected production thrives, while it is not so apparent that other production is held back and delayed in its development through protection.[195]

The reasons for protecting one's own (and the country's) wages and social conditions are obviously of less importance to the same degree if the merchant marine fleet of a country does not have its own officers and crew. Without any nationals at all from the country to run the vessels, the rationale would, no doubt, cease to hold.[196] If, however, one wishes to have other nationals employed on board for reasons of efficiency, or anything less, one has to protect the domestic merchant marine fleets to such an extent that it can be treated in exactly the same way as emoluments.[197] In reality they comprise indirect wage allowances and benefits in kind that are directly concerned with special working conditions on board and service in certain foreign countries.[198]

Notes

1 'British and French shipbuilding: the industrial relations of decline', *Industrial Relations Journal*, vol. 16, part 4, 1985, pp. 7–16; 'Minister blames lack of world orders for inability of BS to maintain its present capacity', *The Times*, 15 May 1986, p. 1d.
2 A.P. Learner, *Economics of Employment*, McGraw-Hill Books, New York, 1951, p. 10.
3 This would include those who are not gainfully employed such as volunteers; special section on the countries of the Pacific Ocean area, see *Fairplay International Shipping Weekly*, no. 297, 22 May 1986, Supplement, p. 1.
4 This seems to have reduced the official employment statistics by probably as much as 25–50 per cent; see also 'Shipbuilding in Belgium', *Shipping World and Shipbuilder*, vol. 182, May 1986, p. 203.
5 See also *Employment of Older Men and Women*, Report of Walkinson Committee, 1953; but see 'Shipbuilding in France', *Shipping World and Shipbuilder*, vol. 182, May 1986, p. 197.
6 Ibid., Report of 1955; and 'Shipbuilding in the Netherlands', *Shipping World and Shipbuilder*, vol. 182, May 1986, p. 185; 'Minister accused by Labour MPs of being indifferent to imminent collapse of industry', *The Times*, 15 May 1986, p. 1d.
7 See 'Recession also hits towing, salvage and heavy lift', *Motor Ship*, vol. 67, no. 789, April 1986, pp. 52–4; 'PM urged to adopt scrap and building policy

to help industry through its crisis', *The Times*, 16 May 1986, p. 16.

8 Unemployables are people who on account of mental or physical disability, are unable to follow normal employment. They are no longer included in the numbers of the unemployed; 'Shipping correspondence', *The Times*, 24 May 1986, p. 7e.

9 These number around 500,000 by 1986 figures; R. Scott, 'South Korean shipping', *Fairplay International Shipping Weekly*, vol. 298, June 1986, pp. 27-30; 'Demise of British industry discussed', *The Times*, 15 May 1986, p. 2d.

10 See the Preamble to the Unemployed Workman Act 1905; cf. 'Swedyards — down but by no means out', *Fairplay International Shipping Weekly*, vol. 298, 12 June 1986, pp. 17-18; 'Shipping diary note', *The Times*, 16 May 1986, p. 10a.

11 Unemployed Workman Act 1905; cf. Bernard Brown, *Human Factors in Australian Shipping*, National Institute of Labour Studies, Flinders University, Bedford Park, South Australia, 1966; 'The taxing question of priorities', *The Times*, 18 May 1986, p. 29a.

12 Unemployed Workman Act 1905; see also Malathi Bolan, *The Shipping Industry in India, Strategic Factors in Industrial Relations Systems*, International Institute for Labour Studies; 'Shipping correspondence', *The Times*, 19 May 1986, p. 13d.

13 Unemployed Workman Act 1905; and M. Muller, 'Strikes: strike of crew members supported by the ITF held unlawful by Dutch court applying Philippine law: *The Sandi Independence*', *Journal of Maritime Law and Commerce*, vol. 16, 1985, pp. 423-6.

14 See, for instance, Unemployment Assistance Act 1934; see also generally David R. Norman, 'Has something been lost? An analysis of a seldom utilised concept in maritime law', *Loyola Law Review*, vol. 30, 1984, pp. 875-900.

15 Created by the government in 1962 to examine the economic performance of the nation with special reference to the future plans in the private and public sectors of industry consider the obstacles to faster growth, methods of improvements and competitiveness.

16 Those problems were reviewed in the report: *Growth of the United Kingdom Economy to 1966*, published in 1963. A further report discussed 'Conditions Favourable to Faster Growth'.

17 Martin Whitfield, 'Crewing terms in British Petroleum switch shock unions', *Lloyd's List*, 14th Journal, 1986, p. 1; Martin Morris, *The Law of Seamen*, 4th edn, Lawyers Co-operative Publication, Bancroft-Whitney, Rochester, San Francisco, 1986.

18 Ibid.; see also 'Merchant Navy settles for 5.9%', *Industrial Relations Review and Report* (Pay and Benefits Bulletin), no. 359, 1986, p. 708; Joanne Lawistoski, 'Limitation of liability for stevedores and terminal operators under the carriers bill of lading and COGSA', *Journal of Maritime Law and Commerce*, vol. 16, 1985, pp. 337-8.

19 Ibid.; but see also 'The General Council of British Shipping makes first pilotage change protest', *Lloyd's List*, 16 January 1986, p. 1; International Labour Organization, *Conventions des recommendations sur le travail maritime*, Geneva, 1983.

20 See 'Full employment and full utilisation of our ships', pp. 196–201 of Robert Earle Anderson's *The Mechanical Marine and World Frontiers*, CIO Maritime Postwar Programme Series, Cornell Maritime Press, New York, 1945.

21 Arthur Seldon and F.G. Pennance, *Everyman's Dictionary of Economics*, Dent and Sons, London, 1965, p. 431; National Dock Labour Board, *Annual Report and Accounts*, 1975; Clark Kincaid, 'Wallsend site to be closed by end of year', *The Times*, 15 May 1986, p. 1d.

22 According to the OECD Reports and Forecasts; see also National Dock Labour Board, *The Dock Worker Employment Scheme 1967*; and 'Putting the buoyancy into shipping', *The Times*, 18 May 1986, p. 29a.

23 Seldon and Pennance, op.cit., p. 431; National Dock Labour Board, *The Place of the Shipping Industry in the National Economy*, Derek Bibby, 1964.

24 Ibid.; see also Northwestern University Transportation Centre, *Collective Bargaining and Technological Change in the Transportation Industry*, 1971.

25 In Britain labour exchanges were established in 1912, largely because of the economic investigations and advocacy of W.W. (later Lord) Beveridge in the effort to adjust supply and demand.

26 Also known as general unemployment which results from a general falling off in the demand for labour caused, for example, by a reduction in the total amount of spending in the economic system.

27 This was the most evident symptom of the down-turn in the trade cycle before World War II. It was Klyne's argument that, at such times, the government should maintain the demand for labour by keeping up the supply of money and spending by low interest rates, tax reliefs, and undertaking public works.

28 See Katsuhiko Hattori, 'Analytical review of overtonnaging of large tankers', *Tamri Report*, no. 10, July 1985; but see K.H. Kwik, 'Collision rate as a danger criterion for marine traffic', *Journal of Navigation*, vol. 39, May 1986, pp. 203–12.

29 *Employment Policy*, White Paper, 1944; see also Reese (ed.), *Merchant Marine Policy*, 1963; 'Shipping miracle is slipping into the past', *Fairplay International Shipping Weekly*, vol. 297, 22 May 1986, p. 28.

30 Lord W. Beveridge, *Full Employment in a Free Society*, Longmans, London, 1931, a Postscript to which he described the White Paper as epoch-making.

31 Ibid.; like Lord Beveridge himself, the White Paper regarded controlled location of industry as an essential prerequisite to the success of any full employment policy.

32 Then Britain held about 50 per cent of world tonnage; see also Craig Forsyth, 'Sea Daddy: an excursion into an endangered social species (the stereotype American merchant seaman)', *Maritime Policy and Management*, vol. 13, no. 1, pp. 53–60.

33 For Japanese entry into the OECD, see OECD, *Maritime Transport*, Paris, 1962; see also National Maritime Board, *Yearbook, 1976–7* (summary of agreement), 1978.

34 These figures include only vessels of 100 grt and above thereby excluding probably another 50 per cent of vessels and seamen.

35 What is commonly known as 'shipping and the invisibles', the mathematics of

which is that for every directly related job in shipping, there are probably five others in the indirectly related areas.

36 Table 7.5. The methods in use in the various countries for compilation of crew statistics differ as explained in the notes below the table.
37 See also Employment Protection Legislations since the Employment Protection Act 1975; C.E. McDowell and H.B. Gibbs, *Ocean Transportation*, McGraw-Hill, New York, 1954, p. 105.
38 J.L. Hanson, *A Dictionary of Economics and Commerce*, 5th edn, Macdonald and Evans, 1977, p. 217; R. Hope, 'The political economy of marine transportation', *Marine Policy and the Coastal Community*, Croom Helm, London, 1976, p. 103.
39 Ibid.; see also p. 158; A.Y. Benham, 'A study of the value of national fleets and shipping policies in developing countries', unpublished Masters Thesis, UWIST, Wales, 1974.
40 Ibid.; and UNCTAD, *Establishment and Expansion of Merchant Marines in Developing Countries*, 1969; see also Betham, 'Political factors and the evolution of national fleets in developing countries', *Maritime Studies and Management*, vol. 3, 1976, p. 131.
41 Paul A. Giles, 'Registration of a British flag vessel in the port of Hong Kong, and registration of mortgages', *Current Issues in Ship Financing*, Practising Law Institute, vol. 1, 1983, p. 191.
42 Ibid.; see also G.E.C. Maitland, 'Registration of ship mortgages under the laws of Liberia, pending change', *Current Issues*, op.cit., pp. 233–94.
43 See again 'British and French shipbuilding; the industrial relations of decline', *Industrial Relations Journal*, op.cit., pp. 7–16.
44 Ibid.; see also Michael Maitland, 'Shipping cycles II', *Seatrade*, February 1986, pp. 19–23; see also E. Chrzanowski, 'Current aspects of international shipping policy', *Maritime Policy and Management*, vol. 5, 1978, p. 289.
45 R. North and D. Watt, 'Ten man crew is proposed by Norway owner', *Lloyd's List*, 17 February 1986, p. 1; A.S. Banks (ed.), *Political Handbook of the World 1977*, McGraw-Hill, New York, 1978, p. 535.
46 Hanson, op.cit., p. 262; Currie, 'Flags of convenience, American labour and the conflict of laws', *Supreme Court Review*, 1963, p. 34.
47 Ibid., p. 263; David W. Robertson, 'Current problems in seamen's remedies: seamen status, relationship between Jones Act and LHWCA, and unseamanworthiness actions by workers not covered by LHWCA', *Louisiana Law Review*, vol. 45, 1985, pp. 875–906.
48 Seldon and Pennance, op.cit., p. 223; Graydon Starring, 'Meting out misfortune: how the courts are allotting the costs of maritime injury in the eighties', *Louisiana Law Review*, vol. 45, 1985, pp. 907–26.
49 Martin Whitfield, 'B.P. shipping to end direct employment', *Lloyd's List*, 9 January 1986, p. 1; A.H. Hansen, *Economic Policy and Full Employment*, McGraw-Hill Books, New York, 1947, pp. 57–77, pp. 65–6; D. Watts, 'Protection of merchant ships', *British Yearbook of International Law*, vol. 33, 1977, pp. 52 and 84.
50 Martin Whitfield, 'Sealink men want guarantees: five week "sit in" at Harwich over job security', *Lloyd's List*, 16 January 1986, p. 3.
51 Ibid.; see also 'MP to question BP crewing in Commons', *Lloyd's List*,

20 January 1986, p. 3; G.J. Mangove, *Marine Policy for America*, Lexington Books, 1977, pp. 175-6.

52 Hanson, op.cit., p. 224; Hurn, 'Nationalism and internationalism in shipping', *Journal of Transport Economics and Policy*, vol. 3, no. 6, 1969.

53 Ibid., p. 225; Mankabady, 'Rights and immunities of the carrier's servants or agents', *Journal of Maritime Law and Commerce*, vol. 5, 1973, p. 111.

54 Ibid., p. 440; Sher, 'Federal Maritime Commission and labour related matters', *Journal of Maritime Law and Commerce*, vol. 3, p. 677.

55 David Serko, 'Protectionism: sentiment is extremely high', *Worldwide Shipping*, vol. 48, no. 7, December–January 1986, pp. 17-20; J. Myles *et al.*, *The Political Order of the Oceans*, Yale University Press, 1962, chapter 6.

56 For the balance of payments generally and in relation to Great Britain in particular, see Chapter 10 of this book where the subject is adequately covered.

57 Shutz, 'Industrial unrest in the nation's maritime industry', *Labour Law Journal*, vol. 15, 1964, p. 337; A.D. Couper, *The Geography of Sea Transport*, Hutchison, London, 1972, p. 121.

58 Note: 'Effect of United States labour legislation on the flags of convenience fleet: regulation of shipboard labour regulations and remedies against shoreside picketing', *Yale Law Journal*, vol. 69, 1960, p. 498.

59 Note: 'Flags of convenience and NLRB jurisdiction', *Newark University Law Review*, vol. 60, 1965, p. 195; 'SDP Conference condemns shipyard closures and demands government action to reverse them', *The Times*, 19 May 1986, p. 49.

60 Igor Averin, 'Protectionism may deepen East/West split' (EEC shipping policy effects on Soviet shipping), *Motor Shipping*, vol. 66, no. 788, March 1986, p. 78.

61 See, again, David Serko, 'Protectionism: sentiment is extremely high', *Worldwide Shipping*, op.cit., pp. 17-20.

62 Jose Paul, 'The impact of port charges on shipping freight rates', *Dock and Harbour Authority*, vol. 66, no. 777, March 1986, pp. 256-60.

63 But see Bridget Hogan, 'Protectionism hits bulk trade in Third World', *Lloyd's List*, 20 December 1985, p. 4; Edgar Gold, *Ocean Shipping and Commercial Viability*, p. 257.

64 Cf. Peter Polonska, *Ocean Politics in South-East Asia*, Singapore Institute of South East Asian Studies, 1978; UN, *The Sea: A Selected Bibliography on the Legal, Political and Technological Aspects*, E/F 76.1.6, New York, 1976.

65 Ibid.; and Michael A. Morris, *International Politics and the Sea*, Westview Press, Boulder, Colorado, 1979; E. Gold, 'The rise of the coastal state in the Law of the Sea', *Marine Policy and the Coastal Community*, London, 1960, pp. 13ff.

66 Note: 'Foreign shipowners equitable relief against shoreside picketings', *Stanford Law Review*, vol. 13, 1961, p. 321.

67 J. Shootwell (ed.), *The Origins of the International Labour Organisation*, 1934; J.K. Gamble Jr. (ed.), *Law of the Sea, Neglected Issues*, University of Hawaii, Honolulu, 1979.

68 But see 'Container efficiency and shipping problems confronted', *Cargo Systems International*, February 1986, pp. 14-17.

69 Cf. 'The container market to 1990s (global box requirements)', *Cargo Systems International*, February 1986, pp. 19–21.

70 'IMO and the training of maritime personnel', *IMO News*, no. 4, 1985, pp. 12–14; and 'High stakes in Manila', *Seatrade*, vol. 9, 1979, p. 3,4 (editorial).

71 Dr Morse, *The Origin and Evolution of the ILO and its Role in the World Community*, 1969; E. Fayle, *A Short History of the World's Shipping Industry*, Allen and Unwin, London, 1983, pp. 294 *et seq.*

72 But see Kenneth A. Witherspoon, 'Watch out watchmen! Congress has excluded security employees from maritime employment coverage under the Longshore and Harbourworkers' Compensation Act Amendments of 1984', *San Diego Law Review*, vol. 22, 1985, pp. 941–62.

73 Constitution of the International Labour Organization 1948, Art. 4, 62 Stat. 3485, 15 UNTS.35 as amended 25 June 1953.

74 But see Norman J. Lopez, 'Mariner's view (crewing, manning, certification . . .)', *Asian Shipping*, January 1986, pp. 19–20; Grammonos Bank, *Finance for Ship Purchasing*, University of Wales, Bangor, 1979.

75 David Mott, 'New Navy transfer scheme to be launched for Merchant Navy officers', *Lloyd's List*, 17 December 1985, p. 2.

76 Norman J. Lopez, 'A training treaty to tame the laws (Convention on standards of training, certification and watch keeping for seafarers)', *Asian Shipping*, December 1985, pp. 19–22.

77 Bridget Hogan, 'Seafarers seek support for Co-ops: lawyer close to first deal in plan for networks of co-operative shipping lines', *Lloyd's List*, 10 January 1986, p. 4.

78 Ibid.; cf. E.W.S. Gill, 'Containerisation, a seaman's view point (job satisfaction in a changing industry)', *Asian Shipping*, December 1985, pp. 29–32.

79 G.R. Hughes, 'Nautical institutes' response to economic and social pressures arising from shipping: the President's Address to the 1986 AGM', *Seaways*, July 1986, pp. 3–5.

80 W.A. Lewis, *The Theory of Economic Growth*, Allen and Unwin, London, 1955, p. 320; Jenks, 'The significance of the International Law of Tripartite Character of the International Labour Organisation', *Transactions of the Grotius Society*, vol. 22, 1937, p. 45.

81 See J. Viner and G. Meir, *Leading Issues in Development Economics*, OUP, Oxford, 1964, p. 81; Hours of Work (Industry) ILO Convention 1919, *Conventions and Recommendations*, 1966, p. 1; Nautical Institute, *Conference on International Shipping*, London, 1979.

82 See W.A. Lewis, op.cit., p. 327; also mandatory Medical Examination (Seafarers) 1946 ILO Convention, p. 214, *UNTS*, p. 233; Gosoric, *UNCTAD: Conflict and Compromise*, Sithhoff, Leiden, 1972, pp. 80–3.

83 S. Haberler, *Theory of International Trade with its Application on Communal Policy*, New York, 1950, p. 56; Basil Mogridge, 'Labour relations and labour costs' in Prof. F.G. Sturmey, *British Shipping and World Competition*, The Athlon Press, University of London, 1962, chapter 12, pp. 283–321.

84 'Watchkeepers' in R.H. Thornton, *British Shipping*, Cambridge University

Press, 1939, chapter XIV, pp. 229–46; ILO Convention No. 22 Seamen's Articles of Agreement 1926, *UNTS*, vol. 38, p. 295.

85 Ibid., *The Men*, chapter XIII, pp. 211–18; for Statutory Form of Articles of Agreement see 46 USC 563–575 (1974 Suppl.).

86 See 'The political environment in shipping' in Thorsten Rinman and Rigmor Linden (eds), *Shipping, How It Works*, Elanders Boktryckeri AB, Kingsbackar, 1978, pp. 141–8.

87 For recommendations concerning hours of work on board ship 1936 see *British Shipping Laws*, vol. 8, 1973, p. 1183 and Recommendation No. 109 Concerning Wages, Hours of Work on Board Ship and Manning 1958, *British Shipping Laws*, vol. 8, 1973, p. 1213.

88 John Maynard Keynes, *General Theory of Employment, Interest and Money*, 1936. In fact the Coalition Government's *White Paper on Employment Policy*, 1944, marked the acceptance of the Keynesian revolution.

89 See also Resolution XII concerning the Basic Minimum Wage for Able Seamen adopted by the 55th Maritime Session of ILO 1970, *British Shipping Laws*, vol. 8, 1973, pp. 1320–1.

90 Note: 'Flag of convenience shipping: NLRB interest authority over labour disputes when virtually none of the responses of a foreign shipowner to the picketing of his vessel would be limited to a wage-cost decision', *Vanderbelt Journal of Transnational Law*, vol. 8, 1974, p. 239.

91 For earlier studies see J.S. Smith, *Foreign Commerce Weekly*, Washington DC, 22 September 1945; ILO Convention and Recommendation concerning Minimum Standard in Merchant Ships, *International Legal Materials*, vol. 15, 1976, p. 1288.

92 Ibid.; see also H.F. Karreman, 'Methods of improving world transport accounts applied to 1950–53', Technical Paper 15, *National Bureau of Economic Research*, USA, 1961.

93 Ibid.; and *Review of Economics and Statistics*, February 1958 (Supplement); and articles by I.S. Lloyd in *The Times*, 5 and 6 July 1961; *British Shipping Laws*, vol. 8, 1973, p. 1218.

94 See, for example, A.R. Ferguson *et al.*, *The Economic Value of the US Merchant Marine*, Transport Centre, Northwest University, Illinois, 1961.

95 Dr D.L. McLachlan, 'The price policy of liner conferences', *Scottish Journal of Political Economy*, vol. 10, November 1963.

96 R.M. Thwaites, 'The economics of shiptime', *Transnational North East Coast Institution of Engineers and Shipbuilders*, vol. 75, part 1, 3 January 1959.

97 National Maritime Board, *Yearbook*, 1964, p. 108; R. Morris, 'The Melabourne dock war', *Maritime Policy and Management*, vol. 10, no. 1, pp. 53–6.

98 Ministry of Labour *Gazette*, May 1964; B. Metaxas, 'Maritime economics: problems and challenges for the future', *Maritime Policy and Management*, vol. 10, no. 3, pp. 145–64.

99 *Report of the Committee of Inquiry into the Major Ports of Great Britain* (*Rochdale Report*), Cmnd. 1824, HMSO, p. 112; Editorial, 'The role of the entrepreneur and the shipping industry', *Maritime Policy and Management*, vol. 8, no. 3, pp. 137–40.

100 See also (UK) Shipping Companies Exemption Order 1948; but see B.J. Thomas, 'The changing structure of the UK port industry and its impact on stevedoring costs', *Maritime Policy and Management*, vol. 8, no. 3, pp. 141–62.

101 Capt. J.P. Williams, 'The problems facing Australian shipping in the next decade', unpublished paper delivered to the Economic Society of Australia and New Zealand, Melbourne, April 1960, table 6.

102 Canadian Maritime Transport Commission, *Cargo Reservation and Liner Conference Shipping Serving Canada. An Analysis Related to the UNCTAD Code of Conduct*, Ottawa, 1979.

103 E.G. Frankel, J. Arnold and P. Read, 'Impact of cargo sharing on US liner traders', *Marine Policy*, vol. 5, 1981, pp. 23–39.

104 Gerald Jantscher, *Bread upon the Waters: Federal Aid to Maritime Industries*, The Brookings Institution, Washington DC, 1975, p. 164.

105 Bremen Institute of Shipping Economics, *Monthly Figures of Shipping, Freight Markets Sea Trade, Ports and Sea Canals* 1985 — see the monthly crew costs according to selected flags and crew sizes compared by ship type and according to selected flags.

106 Lloyds Ship Manager, Lloyds of London Press, *Survey of 1986*, especially the operating costs (bankers and labour).

107 Japanese Shipowners Association, *Review of Japanese Shipping, 1970*, issue — see especially the number of officers and ratings.

108 OECD, *Maritime Transport*, Paris, 1954 — on effects of protectionism.

109 See Multilateral Convention No. 9 of 1920 for 'Establishing Facilities for Finding Employment for Seamen', *International Legislation*, no. 25, 12 December 1920, p. 515; Bremen Institute of Shipping Economics, *Shipping Statistics Yearbook*: facts and figures about shipping, shipbuilding, seaports and seaborne traffic, 1956; cf. FRG and OECD figures in view of the ITF worldwide scale and Far East scale effective as of 1 September.

110 See also Article 1 of the Convention; also UK Department of Trade (Marine Division) London, *1986 Annual Report*. Examinations for Certificates of Competency in the Merchant Navy Statistics, see the relevant text under the 'foreign-going vessels'.

111 But Article 3 of the Convention; cf. UK Department of Employment, *British Labour Statistics Yearbook*, 1976, HMSO, London. See especially the earnings and hours/employees in employment/numbers of employed persons in the sea transport section.

112 And Article 3 of the Convention; also UK Central Statistical Office, *Annual Abstracts of Statistics* (whose section on employment replaced the *British Labour Statistics Yearbook*, op.cit., last published in 1976), HMSO, London, see employees in employment (sea transport) and numbers unemployed (sea transport).

113 But see Article 4 of the Convention; see also GCBS, *British Shipping Statistics*, London, 1986 — see the text under employment and the table under the number of seafarers.

114 ILO Maritime Conventions: Convention Concerning Continuity of Employment for Seafarers (no. 145 of 1976); British Shipping Federations (which gave way to the General Council of British Shipping GCBS), London, 1968.

333

See especially manning level in June, and the expected manning changes in the UK-registered home- and foreign-going vessels.

115 Article 2 of Convention 145 of 1976; Brian Yolland, 'Crew costs and international shipping' (contained in 'IS IT RIGHT?'), *Lloyd's World of Shipping Conferences in Hong Kong, 12–16 October 1981*, Lloyd's of London Press Ltd, London, 1982. Compare the Singapore, Indonesia, Burmese, Panama, UK, S. Korea and Finnish figures.

116 Article 3 of Convention 145 of 1976; see Westinform, *Manning the Merchant Fleets of the World*, Westinform Shipping Reports, no. 299, Westinform Services, 1973; cf. especially the number of ratings on board ships engaged in international trading to personnel per ship/personnel per 1000 grt 1965–70.

117 Article 4 of Convention 145 of 1976; US Department of Transportation, MARAD, Maritime Manpower Report, *Seafaring, Longshore, and Shipyard employment as of April 1977*, Report no. MAR 4055, Washington DC. These include privately owned ships as well as MSC/MA/BBC/GAA and Navy ships.

118 Recommendations Concerning Continuity of Employment for Seafarers (Recommendation 154 of 1976); cf. Sealife Programme, *Report on an Examination of the Validity of the Flanesburg Project Data with Respect to its Applicability to the UK Merchant Marine (Coastal Vessels)*, Sealife Project, Report no. 2, 1976.

119 Articles 2–4 of ILO Recommendation 154 of 1976; Sealife Programme, *Report on an Examination of the Validity of the Flanesburg Project Data with Respect to its Applicability to the UK Merchant Marine*, Sealife Project 1, Report no. 1), London Sealife Project Office, 1975.

120 Article 5 of ILO Recommendation 154 of 1976; Sealife Programme, *Central Manpower Supply to the Merchant Navy: Second Report and Recommendations*, London Sealife Project Office, 1978; cf. The seasonal employment of ratings from a sample of ferry ports and the total number of fixings via local establishment offices. May 1977–April 1978.

121 Article 6 of ILO Recommendation 154 of 1976; Sealife Programme, *Central Manpower Supply to the Merchant Navy: Intermediate Report*, London Sealife Project Office, 1978. Pay particular attention to the Net change in jobs on foreign-going vessels 1972–77, Trends in merchant navy employment, and Changes in foreign-going jobs at sea by sector.

122 OEEC, *Maritime Transport*, Paris, November 1953, table 22; see also H. Sasaki, *The Shipping Industry in Japan*, Strategic Factors in Industrial Relations Systems — Research Series no. 3, International Institute for Labour Studies, Geneva, 1976.

123 See Table 7.10 for the list; in the same series, see S. Rubenowitz and A. Gleerup, *The Shipping Industry in Sweden*, Strategic factors in Industrial Relations Systems — Research Series no. 25, International Institute for Labour Studies, Geneva, 1977.

124 See also National Union of Seamen, *Flags of Convenience: the Unacceptable Force of Shipping*, London, 1981. See especially the statistical table of the number of seamen employed, for comparative figures for the late 1970s and early 1980s.

125 But see National Board for Prices and Incomes, *Pay and Conditions of Merchant Navy Officers*, presented to (HE) Parliament by the First Secretary of State and Secretary of State for Economic Affairs and the Minister of Labour, June 1967 (Report no. 35), HMSO, London, 1967 which shows the annual return on 30 June 1966 of Merchant Navy officers.

126 OECD, *Maritime Transport*, Paris, 1969, para. 131, p. 76, 'Personnel employed in the merchant fleets of the OECD member countries'.

127 Ibid.; see also table XXXiii(a) 'Personnel employed in the merchant marines of OECD member countries', p. 146. D. Chappell (commentary), 'A note on the optimal handling capacity at Aberth', *Maritime Policy and Management*, vol. 6, no. 1, pp. 69–72.

128 Ibid.; see also table XXXiii(b), p. 147; J. Kind, 'The adequacy of ships and the competence of seamen', *Maritime Policy and Management*, vol. 6, no. 1, pp. 1–5.

129 Ibid. at end year 1968; B.J. Thomas, 'Port management development – a strategy for the provision of a training capability in developing countries', *Maritime Policy and Management*, vol. 8, no. 3, pp. 179–90.

130 Ibid. at end year 1969; Jim McConnille, 'Changing patterns of manpower and management in the UK shipping industry', *Maritime Policy and Management*, vol. 6, no. 1, pp. 39–48.

131 OEEC, *Maritime Transport*, Paris, 1956 (for 1955 figures), p. 27; B. Nolan, 'Triple doses: a view of seamen's health', *Maritime Policy and Management*, vol. 6, no. 2, pp. 119–28.

132 Ibid., table XII, p. 30; M.H. Smith and J. Roggema, 'Emerging organisational values in shipping: Part I: Crew stability', *Maritime Policy and Management*, vol. 6, no. 2, pp. 129–44.

133 OECD, *Maritime Transport*, Paris, 1983 (for 1982 figures), p. 68; E. Rosenstein *et al.*, 'Nautical framing systems and the occupational behaviour of seamen: the Israel experience', *Maritime Policy and Management*, vol. 5, no. 1, pp. 5–18.

134 Ibid., p. 69; M.H. Smith and J. Roggema, 'Emerging organisational values in shipping: Part 2, Javando a redistribution of responsibility on board ship', *Maritime Policy and Management*, vol. 6, no. 2, pp. 145–56.

135 Ibid., table XXI(a), p. 138; editorial, 'Discipline in British merchant ships', *Maritime Policy and Management*, vol. 5, no. 2, pp. 73–4.

136 Ibid., table XXI(b), p. 139; R. Morris, 'Labour relations in the Hong Kong merchant navy', *Maritime Policy and Management*, vol. 5, no. 2, pp. 107–16.

137 OECD, *Maritime Transport*, Paris, 1984 (for 1983 figures), p. 77; J. Kinahan, 'Maritime industrial relations', *Maritime Policy and Management*, vol. 4, no. 1, pp. 97–106.

138 For 1982 figures, see OECD, *Maritime Transport*, 1983, p. 78; also M. Evez, 'Retraining of ratings for officer rank: biographical characteristics and motivational determinants of willingness to be retrained', *Maritime Policy and Management*, vol. 5, no. 4, pp. 307–14.

139 Ibid., table XXI(a), p. 182; see also J. Jackson and R. Wilkie, 'General purpose manning: a case study of organisation innovation. Part 3', *Maritime Studies and Management*, vol. 3, no. 1, pp. 21–6 for offshore figures.

140 Ibid., table XXI(b), p. 183; W. Burger and A.G. Corbet, 'Training in maritime technology', *Maritime Studies and Management*, vol. 3, no. 2, pp. 81–6.

141 See notes 114–125; also K.A. Moore, 'Development of USSR and CMEA shipping' contained in *GREENWICH FORUM VI World Shipping in the 1990s*: Records of a conference at the Royal Naval College, Greenwich 23–25 April 1980, Westbury House, Guildford, 1981.

142 B.N. Metaxas, *The Economics of Tramp Shipping*, Athlon Press, London, 1971; J. Jackson and R. Wilkie, 'General purpose manning: a case study of organisational innovation, Part I', *Maritime Studies and Managements*, vol. 2, no. 3, pp. 132–7.

143 J.M. Keynes, 'Free trade and unemployment', *Nation and Athenaeum*, November 1923, p. 1; Jim McConville, *The Shipping Industry in the United Kingdom*, Strategic Factors in Industrial Relations Systems – Research Series no. 26, International Institute for Labour Studies, 1977.

144 International Maritime Associates Inc., *Economic Impact of Open Registry Shipping*, commissioned by the Bureau of Maritime Studies, Ministry of Finance, Republic of Liberia (s.1): (s.p.), 1979.

145 J.M. Keynes, *A Treatise on Money*, vol. 1, pp. 131–2; UK, *Working Group on the Employment of Non-domiciled Seafarers*, HMSO, London, 1978; see also D.H. Moreby, 'On the management of nautical colleges', *Maritime Studies and Management*, vol. 2, no. 3, pp. 129–31.

146 'Proposals for a revenue tariff', *New Statesman and Nation*, 7 March 1931; J.J.M. Hill, *The Seafaring Career*, The Tavistock Institute of Human Relations, London, 1972; W.R. Rosengren and M.S. Bassis, 'Ship contingencies and nautical education: a problem of level and scope of certification', *Maritime Policy and Management*, vol. 2, no. 3, pp. 154–64.

147 J.M. Keynes, *A Treatise on Money*, op.cit., pp. 326–63; International Labour Conference: *Report of the Director General*, first item on the agenda, Report no. 1, 62nd (maritime) session, Geneva, 1976.

148 J.M. Keynes, *A Treatise on Money*, op.cit., vol. 2, pp. 184–9; UK, *Steering Committee on the Safety of Merchant Seamen at Work*, HMSO, London, 1978; W.W. Pilcher, 'Some commitments of maritime employment: the longshore case', *Maritime Studies and Management*, vol. 2, no. 4, pp. 195–201.

149 *Addendum to the Report of the Committee on Finance and Industry (Macmillan Report)*, HMSO, London, 1931; E.G. Frankel, *Regulation and Policies of American Shipping*, Auburn House Publishing Company, Boston, Mass., 1982 – distribution of US ocean going shipboard jobs.

150 UK Department of Transport, *Transport Statistics Great Britain 1971-81*, HMSO, London, 1982 – especially section on Employment in Sea Transport; editorial 'High stakes at Manila', *Seatrade*, vol. 9, June 1979, p. 3.

151 J.M. Keynes, letter to *The Times*, 29 September 1931; Economist Intelligence Unit, *Open Registry Shipping*, London 1979 – fleet manning by nationalities and crew costs; UNCTAD, *Report and Annexes*, Third Session, Santiago de Chile, vol. 1.

152 Sir Roy Harrods, *Life of John Maynard Keynes*, Macmillan, London, 1952, p. 424; UK Department of Trade and Industry, *Census of Seamen April 26,*

1971, Vessels Registered in the UK, HMSO, London, 1972; UNCTAD, Fourth Session, Nairobi.

153 Sir Roy Harrods, op.cit., especially p. 424, notes ff; ESCAPE, 'Regional Economic Co-operation in Asia and the Far East', *Report of the ESCAPE Working Party on Shipping and Ocean Freight Rates and Related Papers*, Regional Economic Co-operation Series, no. 5, UN, New York, 1968.

154 UK, *Committee of Inquiry into Shipping Report* (Chairman The Right Hon. The Viscount Rochdale, OBE, TD, DL), Cmnd. 4337, HMSO, 1967.

155 Sir Roy Harrods, op.cit., p. 425; M. Barry, *Occupational Health and Safety of Seafarers: Survey of Statistics: preliminary report*, Sealife Programme 1979 (see also the earlier Sealife Programme reports, op.cit.).

156 H. Randall, *Keynesian Commercial Policy*, Dobson, London, 1927, p. 100; see also Economic and Social Committee of the European Communities: *EEC Shipping Policy: Flags of Convenience Opinion*, Brussels, 1979 — employment and unemployment in the shipping industry 1.1.1978 and employment figures of the seagoing staffs (CAACEE).

157 R.S. Doganis and B.N. Metaxas, *The Impact of Flags of Convenience*, Polytechnic of Central London, London, 1976 — crew cost and comparison of basic wages.

158 H. Randall, op.cit., p. 101; see also Drewery Shipping Consultants Ltd, *The Impact of Inflationary Costs Tendencies on Dry Cargo Shipping Operations*, Survey no. 25, London, 1982.

159 H. Randall, op.cit.; J. Jackson and R. Wilkie, 'General purpose manning: a case study of organisational innovation, Part II', *Maritime Studies and Management*, vol. 2, no. 4, pp. 215-20.

160 Jim McConville, 'Collective bargaining in the shipping industry', *Maritime Studies and Management*, vol. 1, no. 1, pp. 74-97.

161 The exact figure is not known but the estimate, according to the OECD Maritime Transport, was about 50,000 in direct maritime employment.

162 A realistic estimate should be to table the 50,000 to about 150,000 as the total workforce; R.A. Ramsay, 'Organisation of shipping', *Ocean Yearbook I*, Chicago, 1978, p. 211ff.

163 W.R. Rosengren editorial, 'A sociological approach to maritime studies: a statement and example', *Maritime Studies and Management*, vol. 1, no. 2, pp. 71-3.

164 William L. Standard, *Merchant Seamen: A Short History of their Struggles*, Coleman, Stanferdville, 1979; C. French, 'Poor nations may rock the boat at Manila Conference', *Globe and Mail*, Toronto, 22 March 1979, p. 1310.

165 See also Edward E. Swanstrom, *The Waterfront Problems of Labour*, Fordham University Press, New York, 1938; UNCTAD, *Guidelines for the Study of the Transfer of Technology to Developing Countries*, Doc. no. E.72.11.D.19.

166 R.O. Goss, 'Some economic aspects of flag discrimination', *Maritime Policy and Management*, vol. 13, no. 3, 1986, pp. 245-50; *Lloyd's Nautical Yearbook*, 1979, pp. 325-33.

167 See also A.H. Vanagas, 'Flag discrimination: an economic analysis' in R.O. Goss, *Advances in Maritime Economics*, CUP, London, 1977, chapter 1, pp. 37-64.

168 See also Paul S. Taylor, *Sailors Union of the Pacific*, Ronald Press, New York, 1923; S.A. Lawrence, *International Sea Transport: The Years Ahead*, Lexington Books, 1972, p. 253.

169 And the Proceedings of the Convention of the International Seamens Union of America held in Washington, February 1937; 'Conflict within Govt. over whether MOD frigate orders should be placed to ease crisis rather than to obtain best value for money for defence budget', *The Times*, 17 May 1986, p. 20.

170 Richard E. Madigan, *Taxation of the Shipping Industry*, Cornel Maritime Press, 1982; Alisa Ferguson, 'Troon Yard to close by end of year', *The Times*, 15 May 1986, p. 1d.

171 F.S. Wolfgang and P.A. Samuelsen, 'Protection and real wages', *Review of Economic Studies*, 1941, p. 100; see also Grant Uder, *British Ships and Seamen* (Book II. The Seamen), Macmillan, London, 1969; see also 'BS expected to demand big job cuts when it meets unions for pay talks', *The Times*, 14 May 1986, p. 1d.

172 Wolfgang and Samuelsen, op.cit., p. 101; J.M. McConville, *The Shipping Industry in the UK*, Strategic Factors in Industrial Relations Systems, Research Series no. 26, International Institute of Labour Studies, 1977.

173 P.M. Alderton, *Sea Transport: Operation and Economics*, Thomas Reed, London, 1973, especially chapter 5 on The Crew, pp. 64–72; 'Govt. confirms BS plans for 3,500 redundancies', *The Times*, 15 May 1986, p. 1d.

174 See 'The merchant seamen' in Ralph Davis, *The Rise of the English Shipping Industry in the Seventh and Eighteenth Centuries*, Macmillan & Co., London, 1962, chapter 6, pp. 110–32.

175 Ibid., chapter VII, 'The pay and conditions of merchant seamen', pp. 133–58; 'Shipbuilding and Allied Management Association: Annual Conference backs emergency motion for calling ballot on industrial action over British Shipbuilders redundancy plans', *The Times*, 18 May 1986, p. 2h.

176 Clement Jones, *British Merchant Shipping*, Edward Arnold & Co., 1922, chapter VII, pp. 116–39 on The Crew; but see 'BS managers may join workers in strike over redundancies', *The Times*, 18 May 1986, p. 2h.

177 But see chapter VII of Peter Duff and Colin Anderson's *British Ships and Shipping*, George G. Harrap & Co. Ltd, London, 1949, pp. 137–8, on Merchant Seamen; 'BS seeks deal on new-style apprenticeships system', *Times Educational Supplement*, 23 May 1986, p. 13a.

178 See also 'Wages and conditions of work for the common seamen' in Dorothy Burwash, *English Merchant Shipping 1460–1540*, University of Toronto Press, 1947, chapter 2, pp. 35–81; see the leading article (on shipping) in *The Times*, 15 May 1986, p. 19a.

179 N. Perry and R. Mike, 'Social theory and shipboard structure. Some reservations on an emerging orthodoxy', *Maritime Studies and Management*, vol. 1, no. 1, pp. 31–9; 'Shipping discussed in Parliament', *The Times*, 15 May 1986, p. 4a.

180 'The face of seamen' in Michael R. Banquet, *No Gallant Ship: Studies in Maritime Local History*, Halis and Conter, London, 1959, chapter 13, pp. 163–76; 'Shipping discussed in Parliament', *The Times*, 16 May 1986, p. 4f.

181 See again, 'Full employment and full utilisation of our ships' in E. Anderson, *The Merchant Marine and World Frontiers*, Cornell Maritime Press, New York, 1945, pp. 196–201.

182 Cf. Bridget Hogan, 'Protectionism hits bulk trade in Third World', *Lloyd's List*, 20 December 1985, p. 4; 'Shipping discussed in Parliament', *The Times*, 22 May 1986, p. 4e.

183 W.F. Stolper, *Readings in the Theory of International Trade*, Allen and Unwin, 1980, p. 205; Paul David, 'The politically unsafe ports', *Lloyds Maritime and Commercial Law Quarterly*, February 1986, pp. 112–28; 'Shipping discussed in Parliament', *The Times*, 23 May 1986, p. 4f.

184 W.F. Stolper, op.cit.; I. Middleton and J. McCallum, 'Never mind the politics — what about the economy?', *Seatrade*, February 1986, pp. 4–7; for further details see *The Times*, 15 May 1986, p. 2d.

185 Olav Knudsen, *The Politics of International Shipping Conflict and Inter-action in a Transnational Issue — Area 1946–1968*, Lexington Ky; D.C. Heath, Farnborough, 1973.

186 C.P. Scrivasstava, 'International shipping law and the developing countries', *Maxims*, no. 21, Nordik Institute for Research, Oslo, 1977.

187 Stephen A. Shefton, 'Federal Maritime Policy', *International Regulation of Maritime Transportation*, Annual Proceedings of the Fordham Corporate Law Institute, pp. 351–6.

188 Ralph Michael Gilberman, 'Cargo preferences: The United States and the future regulation of international shipping', *Virginia Journal of International Law*, vol. 16, 1976, pp. 865–901.

189 Juan E. Oribe-Stemmer, 'Flag preference in Latin America', *Journal of Maritime Law and Commerce*, vol. 10, 1978, pp. 123–34; 'Tory MP urges government to support the merchant navy', *The Times*, 15 May 1986, p. 1e.

190 A.H. Vanagas, 'Flag discrimination: an economic analysis' in R.O. Goss (ed.), *Advances in Maritime Economics*, CUP, 1977, pp. 37–64.

191 Magims Wijkman, 'Effects of cargo reservation: a review of UNCTAD's Code of Conduct for Liner Conferences', *Marine Policy*, vol. 4, 1980, pp. 271–89.

192 N. Perry and R. Wilkie, 'Social theory and shipboard structure II: Models, metaphors and ships', *Maritime Studies and Management*, vol. 1, no. 3, pp. 136–46.

193 W. Gorter, *United States Merchant Marine Policies: Some International Economic Implications*, Princeton University Press Essays in International Finance, Princeton, New Jersey, 1955.

194 I. Haji, 'UNCTAD and shipping', *Journal of World Trade Law*, vol. 6, 1972, p. 58; 'Scott-Lithgow-Britoil confirms compensation claims against Trafalgar House over late delivery of drilling rig could total £12m', *The Times*, 15 May 1986, p. 25e.

195 International Chamber of Shipping, *Third UN Conference on the Law of the Sea — Canacas 1974: The Shipping Issues*, ICS, London, 1974.

196 S.A. Lawrence, *United States Merchant Shipping Policies and Politics*, Brookings Institution, Washington DC, 1966: 'Smith's Docks to be closed by end of year', *The Times*, 15 May 1986, p. 1d.

197 L.M.S. Rajwar *et al.*, *Shipping and Developing Countries*, International
Conciliation no. 582, Carnegie Endowment for International Peace, 1971.
198 Ibid.

8 Employment of economic resources in shipping

The acceptable face of state intervention has taken the form of maritime subsidies which, as the title to this chapter implies, consist mainly of financial aid and fiscal relief to shipping and shipbuilding.

Financial Aid and Relief to Shipping and Shipbuilding

The majority of countries provide significant assistance to shipping, some as an overall assistance to industry generally and others specifically to the merchant marine industry. Some countries on the other hand give little or no assistance to shipping, and originally only a small fraction of the TMNs' fleets received operating subsidies.[1] In some cases, a considerable share of all assistance is reserved for coastal shipping, where it is sometimes given in exchange for contractual services within the national transportation system. We shall not attempt here to measure specific amounts but only seek to review the development effects on the international level of financial aid[2] and fiscal relief to shipping and discuss the reasons for such assistance and the forms in which it is extended. By their nature, the international effects of such assistance are entirely different from those which may be caused by flag discrimination.[3]

The main reasons for financial aid and fiscal relief to shipping have been the need to establish and develop merchant fleets (by reconstruction or renovation), to remedy financing problems and exceptionally high operating costs, or the need to compensate for special services.[4] The main forms of financial aid are operating subsidies and various financing aid schemes. Fiscal relief is mainly extended in the form of various depreciation privileges. This chapter therefore contains an historical account of the reasons which have led a number of countries to grant financial aid or fiscal relief to their shipping industry, and of the types of aid which have recently been in force.[5] There are distinctions between financial aid and fiscal relief, aid to shipping and to shipbuilding, assistance to coastal shipping and to vessels operating in international ferries to which we shall return later. The similarities are that they are all forms of subsidy.[6]

What is a Subsidy?

In an economic context a subsidy is a payment to individuals or businesses by government for which it receives no products or services in return. The purpose of such payments is to maintain a particular service — in this case a maritime transport service — at a price that the public can readily afford but that cannot otherwise be profitably supplied at this price. The particular service or product should be essential to the public welfare and/or national interest. The government would therefore find it necessary to subsidize the enterprise in order to keep it operating and producing the service or product.[7] In the USA, for instance, federal subsidies are given to airlines to carry mail; to railroads and other means of public transportation of commuters; to farmers under the various agricultural programmes; and last, but not least, to the merchant marine industry to build and operate ships. In the USA the term 'subsidy' has also been used to include governmental payments to other governments, now referred to as grants-in-aid.[8] On the other hand, in a legal context, a subsidy is: 'Something, usually money, donated or given or appropriated by the government through its proper agencies, in this country by the Congress'.[9] In US law, therefore, a subsidy is a grant of money made by the government in aid of the promoters of any enterprise, work or improvement in which the government desires to participate, or which is considered a proper subject for state aid because it is likely to be of benefit to the public and/or the national interest.[10] The fact that the merchant marine is subsidized means that it is regarded as essential.

What is worth noting is that, firstly, subsidies are payments by the state to producers or distributors in order to reduce prices, and secondly, that subsidies are inevitably linked to transportation and international trade. In this respect it will be further remembered that the earliest known subsidies are those on exports in order to encourage their sale abroad. Thirdly, subsidies can be provided indirectly or directly by deliberately running the merchant marine, and other means of transportation, at a loss between manufacturing centres and ports.[11] Fourthly, and finally, however, subsidies, like tariffs, do interfere with the operation of the principle of comparative costs and so do not benefit the whole world. It is in this context that we focus attention on maritime subsidies; subsidies made to the merchant industries for various reasons and purposes noted earlier and below. Maritime subsidies take different forms and are not limited to the discussion in this chapter. As we noted, there were elements of subsidy in flag preference and discrimination and further examples in Chapter 5 which dealt with state intervention.[12]

Maritime Subsidies

Maritime subsidies, *inter alia*, are at the forefront of current controversy in international maritime trade and transportation. Consequently, some knowledge of transport economics and international trade is a prerequisite for a fuller appreciation of maritime subsidies in particular, and state aid to the merchant marine industry generally. The two are interrelated and one affects the other. It would appear also that one would require some understanding of the structural set-up of the political economy of both the TMNs and DMNs.[13] This might dispel the popular opinion in shipping circles that it is the STNs and DMNs which normally resort to the malpractice of maritime subsidies. The argument continues that these two, with their autocratic political system and planned economies, are encroachments on, and a hindrance to, established liberal international trade principles and the embedded market-economy doctrine of free trade.[14]

As this inquiry will hopefully show, this belief may be popular but is not necessarily true. I may not feel competent to speak for the STNs but I may feel duty-bound to do so on behalf of my origins — the DMNs — in their attempt to establish, develop and/or expand their merchant marine fleets through subsidies. Besides, whatever the prejudices, since the Second World War there has been a marked shift in the capitalist economies towards mixed enterprises.[15] together with some limited economic planning and outright nationalization in certain essential sectors. The result is that it is now the general rule rather than the exception that almost all countries are involved, in one way or the other, in planning and participation in both national and international economics.[16]

The *laissez-faire* doctrine — at least the classical kind — seems to have been eroded. In the final analysis, therefore, government participation in, and government control of, the economy is no longer the exclusive monopoly of the STNs, with their so-called clients, the DMNs. This is true of subsidies to industry in general and maritime subsidies particularly. This inquiry may prove the accuracy or inaccuracy of this proposition.[17] The DMNs have laid themselves open to such accusations by making demands on the established TMNs, but there is ample evidence to show that both camps share responsibility for resorting to maritime subsidies and state intervention in favour of the merchant marine industry, with development objectives in mind. This can be traced from the origins of maritime subsidies. For centuries before the DMNs emerged as national entities, the TMNs already practised maritime subsidies.[18]

Origins of Maritime Subsidies

Subsidies, maritime or otherwise, are neither new concepts nor new practices.[19] In early English law, a subsidy was already known as:

> An aid, tax or tribute granted by parliament to the King for the urgent occasions of the Kingdom to be levied on every subject of ability according to the value of his lands.[20]

At about the same time international law also recognized subsidies, albeit for motives far removed from what we know today, as:

> The assistance given by one nation to another to enable the latter to carry on a war, when such a nation does not join directly in the war.[21]

So much for the general outline of the origins of subsidies by parliament and in international law.

Maritime subsidies also probably date from the same period. As early as the seventeenth and eighteenth centuries maritime subsidies were already a common feature in British industry and took a variety of forms.[22] Japan, too, gave certain types of subsidies to her merchant marine industry as early as the eighteenth century for the purposes of its establishment and expansion.[23] Noting the current strength of the Japanese merchant marine industry it must be admitted that the effort succeeded. The Japanese example has been imitated by others, notably by the DMNs. The belief is, 'if they can do it so can we'. Be that as it may, the USA was not left out either; she too entered the race immediately before the nineteenth century and continued through into the twentieth.[24] Thus, maritime subsidies are not a new phenomenon, nor were they started by the DMNs, as we would be led to believe.

Table 8.1 Maritime subsidies before 1914[a]

Country	Type of maritime subsidy				
	Postal subvention	Operational subsidy	Construction subsidies	Indirect subsidies	Cargo preference
Austria Hungary[b]	X	X	X	X	
Brazil[c]	X	X		X	
Denmark	X				X
Egypt[c]	X				
France	X	X	X	X	
Germany[d]	X				X
Greece	X				X
Italy	X	X	X		
Japan	X	X	X		
Mexico[c]	X	X			
Netherlands	X				
Portugal	X				
Russia[e]	X	X	X	X	X
Spain	X		X		
Sweden	X				X
United Kingdom	X				
United States	X				X

[a]Excluding cabotage restrictions.
[b]Now Austria and Hungary.
[c]Only developing maritime nations then (DMNs).
[d]Now East and West Germany.
[e]Before the 1917 Revolution; now USSR.

Source: Sturmey, Sig. *British Shipping and World Competition*, p. 28.

It will be apparent from Table 8.1 that, of the seventeen examples considered, only three (Brazil, Egypt and Mexico) are DMNs. The above examples, however, take the form of indirect subsidies. Although nowadays operational and constructional subsidies would be categorized as direct, and cargo preference as a form of flag discrimination, at that time they were all classified together as subsidies. However, before the First World War, shipbuilding subsidies were granted in Austria, Greece, Japan, Italy and Russia and were continued between the wars almost to halt the contraction in the industry during the slump, or to enable it to contract on a rational basis.[25] Therein lie the other motives for granting maritime subsidies. O'Loughlin, however, notes that direct subsidies have been common since the Second World War, although there have been a number of minor subsidies, some in the smaller DMNs.[26]

This is probably the earliest known form of direct maritime subsidy. At present it has been phased out by most, if not all, maritime nations, and is only discussed here for historical purposes. Sturmey notes that, as early as the nineteenth century, aid to shipping predominantly took this form and that Britain took the lead.[27] Thornton, however, points out that there was little to be proud of at the time (1837) in the British merchant marine, no doubt due to the role of this form of subsidy.[28] As to its value, he confirms that the decision to put the carriage of mails out to contract was one of the commercial importance of which it 'cannot be too strongly emphasized. The . . . mail policy of the British government . . . gave the British ocean shipping a start it never lost'.[29] Unfortunately, and inevitably, the British have lost that lead ever since. Sturmey concurs with Thornton's contention and, although the policy was a naval one, intended to expedite the mails and reduce the cost of carrying them by replacing the alarmingly inefficient naval services, the 'mail subventions were of profound consequence in bridging the gap between the known high costs of steamship operation and commercial revenue obtainable'.[30] It would appear that the majority of the TMNs followed the British lead. Sturmey further notes that these early postal subventions may be considered as examples of infant industry subsidies which succeeded in their aim precisely because they were working with, and not against the economic tide.[31] And that in their other aim, that of providing ships as reserves for the navies of the countries concerned, the policy was less successful. For example, the large express ships of the North Atlantic in particular were extremely useful in the First World War in the unsuspected roles of troopships and hospital ships, but early in the war the navies of both Britain and Germany became convinced that they had made a mistake in subsidizing mail ships for use as auxiliary cruisers.[32] This realization seems to have virtually ended the use of mail subventions as subsidies for this purpose. Following the Second World War, and with further technological advancement, particularly the advent of diesel engines, mail subventions were replaced by more modern and more direct subsidies.[33]

Direct Subsidies

Direct subsidies are granted to both coastal vessels engaged in domestic trade and to ocean shipping, i.e. vessels operating on international services. In line with the general development objective, assistance to coastal shipping may be necessary to redress the coastal fleet's structural problems in cases where owners of small coastal vessels have insufficient access to the capital market,[34] or in exchange for certain contractual services which are in the public interest but are not attractive to private shipowners. The common characteristics of aid schemes for the reserved sector of coastal shipping are the intimate relations with other fields of national economic policy and the absence of immediate and noticeable effects on international shipping.[35]

Direct aid to vessels operating in international services, on the other hand, is designed to improve the international competitive position of the vessels receiving such aid, or to make possible the construction and operation of vessels which otherwise might not have been able to face international competition.[36] This may of course be detrimental to the competitive position of other vessels not in receipt of such aid and may introduce distortions into the general international shipping scene. On the other hand, it can also be argued that assistance to ocean shipping may be necessary because of special internal circumstances for which the national shipping industry cannot be held responsible.[37]

Financing problems have been mentioned most frequently as reasons for government assistance. The high proportion of capital costs in the total cost of shipping makes the industry particularly sensitive to conditions in the capital market.[38] New vessels are usually built with a considerable amount of credit and even small differences in credit conditions, and especially in rates of interest, can considerably affect the economics of new building. In countries with an insufficient capital market, shipping investments may thus encounter particular difficulties.[39] High domestic interest rates and tight credit conditions are not only typical for some of the developing OECD member countries, but have been specifically mentioned by the more industrialized TMNs, such as Germany and Japan, as consequences of the war and, therefore, as reasons for post-war government assistance to shipping.[40]

Reasons for Direct Subsidies

Other countries refer to lack of interest in shipping investments. It appears that the high risks of the industry have led even the more advanced TMNs with more developed capital markets to grant assistance in order to encourage private investments in shipping.[41] Germany, for example, mentions the precarious structure of owners' finances due to war and it appears probable that similar problems existed in the other TMNs. Finland and Sweden at the time did call

347

attention to the special problems of small shipowners who may have insufficient access to the capital market.[42] A number of different reasons have led the governments of both TMNs and DMNs in recent years to grant aid to their shipping industries. Leaving aside for the moment the question of compensation for special services (which we have touched on briefly and to which we shall return shortly) deemed necessary in the public national interest,[43] governmental assistance to shipping is motivated either by problems of the national shipping sector, or even more frequently, by particular conditions of the national economy outside the shipping sector. The need for reconstruction or renovation of the fleets has also been mentioned by a number of countries as a reason for government assistance.[44]

Certain TMNs, in the course of their industrial development, have granted aid with a view to the modernization of their ocean fleets and their adaptation to present-day competitive conditions. Exceptionally high operating costs can be due to numerous reasons which are more or less beyond the control of the shipowner.[45] A high national wage level, for instance, puts the operation of US vessels at a particular disadvantage; while France has problems with its special maritime system of social security, as an important factor contributing to a higher than average level of operating costs, and has called attention to the considerable impact of the different methods of financing maritime social security in various countries.[46]

The position of the vessel or a shipping company in international competition can be influenced by any of the major cost items. Besides capital costs and operating costs, the fiscal conditions of the country of registration may be a reason for competitive disadvantage.[47] Public assistance is often granted for special services. The public utility aspects of certain remunerative coastal services, especially of passenger services, or services between the mainland and the outlying islands has been mentioned. In some of these cases rates or fares are controlled by or subject to governmental approval.[48]

Special service obligations are, however, not confined to such domestic services. All countries giving direct subsidies to international deep-sea operations make this aid conditional upon the operation of certain services deemed essential in the national interest.[49] Thus, financial or fiscal aid has been described, in practically all cases, as due to particular conditions within the individual country or its shipping industry. Some TMNs, however, have mentioned that they were occasionally obliged to extend special aid to a number of shipping companies when continuing depressed conditions on the world shipping market made the servicing of certain loans impossible.[50] In the domain of direct financial aid, direct operation and constructional subsidies, allowances or grants constitute the most easily discernible form of assistance. [51]

Operational Subsidies

The operational subsidy in the USA probably best exemplifies all the principles and characteristics of this particular category. An operating [52] differential subsidy is granted to US ship operators to place the operating costs of US flag vessels on a parity with those of foreign competitors. [53] The subsidy is based on the difference between the fair and reasonable cost of insurance (protection and indemnity and hull and machinery premiums), maintenance, repairs not compensated by insurance, wages (officers and crew), and subsistence of officers and crews on the passenger vessels, and the estimated costs of the same items if the vessels were operated under foreign registry. [54]

Subsidy is paid pursuant to operating subsidy contracts between the government and the operators. [55] Authority for the payment of the subsidy under these contracts is contained in Title VI of the Merchant Marine Act 1936, as amended. [56] In accordance with government or industry efforts to reduce government expenditures on privately-owned merchant shipping, recently executed operating subsidy contracts have not included subsidy for hull and machinery insurance premiums, and maintenance and repair costs, pursuant to the provisions of Section 603 of the Act. This section permits the parties to the operating subsidy contracts to agree to a lesser amount of subsidy than that which is necessary to achieve parity. [57] Under Title VI, the operators holding subsidy contracts must be US citizens and must possess certain other qualifications. The Secretary of Commerce must determine that the subsidized vessels are of US construction and that the operation of such vessels in an essential service is required to meet the foreign flag competition and to promote the foreign commerce of the USA. [58] See Table 8.2 for the US Operational Differential Subsidy (ODS) accruals and outlays between 1 January 1937 and 30 September 1984.

Under certain circumstances, for example, to passenger vessels, in addition to the liner trades, an operating subsidy is also authorized for the cruiser trades. With respect to cargo vessels, prior to the enactment of the Merchant Marine Act 1970, which extensively amended the 1936 Act, the operating subsidy was payable only to liner-type vessels with scheduled sailings on established trade routes. [59] The 1970 amendments broadened the scope of the term 'essential service' to authorize the payment of an operating subsidy to aid in the operation of bulk carrier type vessels, whether or not operating on particular services, routes or amended Title VI of the 1926 Act,

Table 8.2 US ODS accruals and outlays – 1 January 1937 to 30 September 1984

Calendar year of operation	Accruals			Paid in FY 1984	Outlays	
	Subsidies	Recapture	Subsidy accrual		Total amount of net accrual	Net accrual liability
1937–1955	$682,457,954	$157,632,946	$524,825,008	$ –0–	$524,825,008	$ –0–
1956–1960	751,430,098	63,755,409	687,674,689	–0–	687,674,689	–0–
1961	170,884,261	2,042,748	168,841,513	–0–	168,841,513	–0–
1962	179,396,797	4,929,404	174,467,393	–0–	174,467,393	–0–
1963	189,119,876	(1,415,917)	190,535,793	–0–	190,535,793	–0–
1964	220,334,818	674,506	219,660,312	–0–	219,660,312	–0–
1965	183,913,236	1,014,005	182,899,231	–0–	182,899,231	–0–
1966	202,734,069	3,229,471	199,504,598	–0–	199,504,598	–0–
1967	220,579,702	5,162,831	215,416,871	–0–	215,416,871	–0–
1968	222,862,970	3,673,790	219,189,180	–0–	219,198,180	–0–
1969	230,256,091	2,217,144	228,038,947	–0–	228,038,947	–0–
1970	232,541,169	(1,908,643)	234,449,812	–0–	234,449,812	–0–
1971	202,440,101	(2,821,259)	205,261,360	–0–	205,261,360	–0–
1972	190,732,158	–0–	190,732,158	–0–	190,732,158	–0–
1973	219,475,963	–0–	219,475,963	–0–	219,475,963	–0–
1974	219,297,428	–0–	219,297,428	40,515	219,297,428	–0–
1975	260,676,152	–0–	260,676,152	153,748	260,676,152	–0–
1976	275,267,465	–0–	275,267,465	–0–	275,267,465	–0–
1977	294,779,691	–0–	294,779,691	–0–	294,779,691	–0–
1978	285,075,424	–0–	285,075,424	643,692	285,075,424	–0–
1979	279,347,879	–0–	279,347,897	1,035,299	279,347,897	–0–
1980	385,399,792	–0–	385,399,792	4,628,490	385,399,792	–0–
1981	350,299,767	–0–	350,299,767	6,678,675	350,299,767	–0–
1982	364,833,552	–0–	364,833,552	18,195,591	364,833,552	–0–
1983	275,821,894	–0–	275,821,894	30,200,977	266,253,931	9,567,963
1984	338,789,000	–0–	338,789,000	322,682,687	322,682,681	16,106,313
Total Regular ODS	$7,428,747,325	$238,186,435	$7,190,560,890	$384,259,674	$7,164,886,614	$25,674,276
Soviet Grain Programmes	$ 147,132,626	–0–	$ 147,132,626	–0–	$ 147,132,626	–0–
Total ODS	$7,575,879,951	$238,186,435	$7,337,693,516	$384,259,674	$7,312,019,240	$25,674,276

Source: MARAD, 1984, p. 14.

permits the payment of operating subsidy on leased as well as owned vessels.[60] The subsidized operators under the operating–differential subsidy contracts must assume the obligations of a replacement programme. Under this scheme they are contractually required to construct new vessels to replace the existing vessels in their subsidized fleets as the existing fleets become obsolete.[61]

The number of vessels to be built under the replacement programme and the vessels' designs are agreed upon after negotiations between the subsidized operators and the US government Department of Shipping.[62] Since the enactment of Public Law 93-603, permitting the payment of an operating subsidy on leased vessels, many of the ship operators, in order to raise the large amounts of capital necessary for the construction of modern vessels, have taken advantage of the leverage lease financing methods to lower the shipbuilding costs.[63] Under this arrangement, the ownership of the newly constructed vessels is vested in the financial institutions and the vessels leased to the subsidized operators under bareboat charters. This method of financing, however, is not used solely in connection with the construction of vessels by operators who are receiving an operating subsidy.[64] The total amount of subsidy paid under the operating-differential subsidy contracts during the fiscal year 1977–78 was US $344 million. Subsidy paid during the fiscal year 1977 under the special operating–differential subsidy executed in connection with the shipment of grain to the USSR was US $34.3 million.[65] See Table 8.3 for the US operational differential subsidy accruals and outlays between 1 January 1937 and 30 September 1984.

Constructional Subsidies

Besides direct operating subsidies, several countries do give construction subsidies. Among the TMNs these are tied to construction in domestic yards and are designed to decrease domestic building costs in order to approximate them to those of foreign builders.[66] It can be assumed that these subsidies do not include any element of assistance to the shipowners concerned. Figures of expenditure under this heading are not available but, as in the case of operating subsidies, all these schemes are subject to certain conditions being fulfilled on the part of the beneficiary.[67] It should also be noted that in some countries these schemes are not limited to shipping but that a large range of industries are also eligible for these grants. Construction subsidies, to the extent that they benefit the shipowner, can obviously stimulate the construction of modern vessels and can help to improve productivity and foster the technical progress of a country's fleet − a prerequisite for fleet expansion.[68]

Table 8.3 US ODS accruals and outlays by lines – 1 January 1937 to 30 September 1984

Lines	Accruals			ODS paid	Net accrued liability
	ODS	Recapture	Net accrual		
Aeron Marine Shipping[9]	$ 24,587,408	$ —0—	$ 24,587,408	$ 23,736,756	$ 850,652
American Banner Lines[1]	2,626,512	—0—	2,626,512	2,626,512	—0—
American Diamond Lines[1]	185,802	28,492	157,310	157,310	—0—
American Export Lines[2]	693,821,868	10,700,587	683,121,281	683,121,281	—0—
American Mail Lines[3]	158,340,739	7,424,902	150,815,837	150,815,837	—0—
American President Lines[3]	972,633,361	17,676,493	954,956,868	952,161,414	2,795,454
American Shipping[9]	14,645,061	—0—	14,645,061	13,847,387	797,674
American Steamship	76,462	—0—	76,462	76,462	—0—
Aquarius Marine Co.[9]	18,645,750	—0—	18,645,750	18,024,224	621,525
Aries Marine Shipping	24,923,374	—0—	24,923,374	24,923,374	—0—
Atlantic & Caribbean S/N[1]	63,209	45,496	17,713	17,713	—0—
Atlas Marine Co.	18,567,577	—0—	17,093,785	17,093,785	1,473,792
Baltimore Steamship[1]	416,269	—0—	416,269	416,269	—0—
Bloomfield Steamship[1]	15,588,085	2,613,688	12,974,397	12,974,397	—0—
Chestnut Shipping Co.	33,099,918	—0—	33,099,918	31,817,510	1,282,408
Delta Steamship Lines	567,705,491	8,185,313	557,520,178	555,030,592	2,499,586
Ecological Shipping Co.	4,860,743	—0—	4,860,743	4,860,743	—0—
Farrell Lines	540,926,955	1,855,375	539,071,580	538,473,091	598,489
Prudential Lines[4]	618,494,723	24,223,564	594,271,159	593,104,378	1,166,781
Gulf & South American Steamship[5]	34,471,780	5,226,214	29,245,566	29,245,566	—0—
Lykes Bros. Steamship	1,233,915,527	52,050,598	1,181,864,929	1,181,364,929	500,000
Margate Shipping	55,814,697	—0—	55,814,697	53,731,600	2,083,097
Moore McCormack Bulk Transport[10]	42,960,530	—0—	42,960,530	41,280,084	1,680,446
Moore McCormack Lines[1]	669,642,384	17,762,445	651,879,939	650,121,627	1,758,312
N.Y. & Cuba Mail Steamship	8,090,108	1,207,331	6,882,777	6,882,777	—0—
Oceanic Steamship[6]	113,947,681	1,171,756	112,775,925	112,775,925	—0—
Ocean Carriers[9]	27,381,462	—0—	27,381,462	26,881,462	500,000
Pacific Argentina Brazil Line[1]	7,963,936	270,701	7,693,235	7,693,235	—0—

Pacific Far East Line[7]	283,693,959	23,479,204	260,214,755	260,214,755	–0–
Pacific Shipping Inc.	17,894,201	–0–	17,894,201	15,839,371	2,054,830
Prudential Steamship[1]	26,352,954	1,680,796	24,672,158	24,672,158	–0–
Sea Shipping[1]	25,819,800	2,429,102	23,390,698	23,390,698	–0–
States Steamship	231,997,100	5,110,997	226,886,103	226,869,100	17,003
United States Lines[8]	682,932,432	54,958,689	627,963,743	627,105,726	868,017
Waterman Steamship	227,170,916	–0–	227,170,916	225,689,786	1,481,130
Worth Oil Transport	17,168,742	–0–	17,168,742	15,023,661	2,145,081
South Atlantic Steamship[1]	96,374	84,692	11,682	11,682	–0–
Seabulk Transmarine I & II, Inc.	12,693,932	–0–	12,693,932	12,193,932	500,000
Equity	629,504	–0–	629,504	629,504	–0–
Total Regular ODS	$7,428,747,325	$238,186,435	$7,190,560,890	$7,164,886,614	$25,674,276
Soviet Grain Programmes	$ 147,132,626		$ 147,132,626	$ 147,132,626	–0–
Total ODS	$7,575,879,951	$238,186,435	$7,337,693,516	$7,312,019,240	$25,674,276

[1] No longer subsidized or combined with other subsidized lines.
[2] AEL was acquired by Farrell Lines, 29 March 1978.
[3] APL merged its operations with AML's, 10 October 1973.
[4] Changed from Prudential-Grace Lines Inc., 1 August 1974.
[5] Purchased by Lykes Bros. Steamship Co. Inc.
[6] Went into receivership 2 August 1978.
[7] Ceased to be subsidized line in November 1970.
[8] Included 33 subsidized ships in November 1979.
[9] Accruals to be adjusted in Fiscal Year 1984.
[10] Purchased by United States Lines October 1983.

Source: MARAD 1984, p. 15.

For the disbursement of the US Construction Reserve Funds see Table 8.4.

Table 8.4 US Construction Reserve Funds – 30 September 1981

Company	Balance (dollars)
Cargo Carriers Inc.	1,675,000
Central Gulf Steamship Corp.	1,000
Gulf Mississippi Marine Corp.	100
Ingram Industries Inc.	85,000
Joan Turecamo Inc.	3,876
Lee-Van Ltd	650,000
Mobil Oil Corp.	3,283,438
National Marine Service Inc.	1,145,300
Total, 30 September 1981	6,843,714
Net decrease fiscal year 1981	8,663,628

Source: MARAD, 1981, p. 13.

Among the TMNs, the system operated by the Irish Republic is probably a much more elaborate example, where state subsidies, for this purpose, are payable for ships built in Irish yards.[69] The Shipping Financing Corporation, a subsidiary of the Industrial Credit Company, a government investment bank, provides loans at low interest rates towards the cost of ships built domestically so that credit facilities can be extended to shipowners comparable to those available in other countries. The only substantial shipbuilding yard in Ireland, however, is the Verolme Cork Dockyard (VCD) in which there is a substantial state investment by way of loans, grant contributions and share subscriptions. In addition to its shipbuilding facilities, the yard has extensive ship repair and general engineering units.[70]

There have been two forms of state aid available for shipbuilding at VCD:

1 Credit facilities and subsidized interests for shipowners (i.e. shipping finance);
2 Maximum loss subsidy of 7 per cent of the contract price of a vessel.[71]

Under the Shipping Finance Scheme, which is administered by the Shipping Finance Corporation (a subsidiary of the Industrial Credit

Co.), credit is provided for shipowners ordering vessels from VCD. The credit terms which comply with OECD and EEC regulations, are limited to 70 per cent credit over seven years at no less than 8 per cent interest.[72] VCD also had the benefit of a subsidy scheme to offset losses incurred in shipbuilding. The operation, however, expired at the end of 1977. The limit to the subsidy was 7 per cent of the contract price of the vessel[73] or the loss incurred in building a vessel after depreciation, whichever was the lesser.[74]

India, on the other hand, provides the example from the DMNs: the government owns the Hindustan shipyard at Visakhapatnan, and the Cochin shipyard.[75] Subsidy is paid directly to the yard and varies according to the cost of construction of a ship. Until 31 March 1976 it was 5 per cent of the international price of the ship which was fixed at the average of the valuation received from reliable foreign ship valuers in three or four leading shipbuilding countries.[76] This government assistance to the shipyard is to be reduced at the rate of 1 per cent every two years. Shipbuilding is also assisted to the extent of an actual price differential between the indigenous price and the lowest international price of six vital items of machinery subject to a ceiling of 10 per cent of the international price. This pricing policy is currently under government review.[77] Construction subsidy is sometimes known, loosely, as modernization.

Modernization Subsidies (Scrap and Build and Demolition)

We noted earlier that the need for reconstruction or renovation of fleets has been given by a number of countries as a reason for government assistance.[78] It will also be recalled that Germany and Japan, for instance, granted considerable assistance during the post-war years in order to help the reconstruction of the ocean-going fleet which had been almost entirely lost during the war. Certain countries, in the course of their industrial development, have granted aid with a view to the modernization of their ocean-going fleets and their adaptation to present-day competitive conditions.[79] Among the TMNs, some — for example, France and Sweden — have aided the modernization of their coastal fleets, and certain others — including the USA — have granted assistance to ocean shipping with the specific purpose of promoting the construction of modern vessels.[80]

The first type of modernization is what is known in the trade as scrap and build.[81] For instance, the Italian Law No. 622 of 24 July 1959, as amended, provides shipowners (who scrap vessels and contract to build new units of a gross tonnage amounting to at least 50 per cent of the scrapped vessels) with a subsidy of 30,000 Italian lira per ton weight of the new vessel.[82] When the gross tonnage of the new vessel exceeds 75 per cent of the scrapped vessel's tonnage, the grant is also limited to 75 per cent of the scrapped vessel's gross tonnage.[83] Vessels scrapped must be at least fifteen years old and have been registered in Italy for at least five years. However, Law No. 720 of 23 December 1975 extended this subsidy, with some modifications, until 31 December 1980.[84] However, since then, the programme seems to have ended.

Japan, on the other hand, introduced the scrap and build system in 1961.[85] In the Japanese case when a shipowner intends to scrap a superannuated home-trade cargo ship, and build a new one of the same type, he may be granted permission to utilize the measures by which part of the construction is financed by the Maritime Credit Corporation on condition that he shares the ownership of such a ship with the Corporation.[86] The terms of such financing vary. The total amount of finance in the fiscal year 1976, for instance, was 12,400 million yen.[87]

The other TMN is the USA.[88] It will be remembered that Section 510 of the Merchant Marine Act 1936 authorizes MARAD to acquire privately owned obsolete vessels[89] in exchange for an allowance of credit payable to the shipowner or shipbuilder on the construction of new vessels. It also provides for the acquisition of marine class vessels constructed under Title VII of the Merchant Marine Act 1926[90] and Public Law 911, and other suitable vessels constructed in the USA, which have never been under foreign documentation, in exchange for obsolete vessels in the National Defence Reserve Fleets.[91]

A second category of state aid is known properly as modernization subsidy. By modernization we mean the installation of technologically advanced machinery in place of old machinery.[92] The merchant marine industry has not escaped the effects of technological advances. In some cases there has been merely substitution. Modernization by the substitution of new machinery for similar but older machinery because of the modern equipment's superiority is attributable to technical improvements rather than to mere newness.[93] However, a substantial amount of outmoded plant and equipment is still being used by the merchant marine industry. Moreover, the development of new technological improvements is making recently-introduced production techniques obsolete, hence the necessity of state subsidies to keep abreast. A number of the TMNs have definite schemes in this respect. In the USA, modernization subsidy is directed mainly towards the renovation of the vessels for the National Defence Reserve although, according to Table 8.5, that number is fast dwindling.

In Canada, for instance, modernization is known alternatively as demolition subsidy.[94] The Income Tax Act, as amended from time

Table 8.5   US National Defence Reserve Fleet 1945-84

Fiscal year	Ships	Fiscal year	Ships
1945	5	1965	1,594
1946	1,421	1966	1,327
1947	1,204	1967	1,152
1948	1,675	1968	1,062
1949	1,934	1969	1,017
1950	2,277	1970	1,027
1951	1,767	1971	860
1952	1,853	1972	673
1953	1,932	1973	541
1954	2,067	1974	487
1955	2,068	1975	419
1956	2,061	1976	348
1957	1,889	1977	333
1958	2,074	1978	306
1959	2,060	1979	317
1960	2,000	1980	320
1961	1,923	1981	317
1962	1,862	1982	303
1963	1,819	1983	304
1964	1,739	1984	386

Source: MARAD, 1984, p. 38.

to time, provides a tax deferral on insurance proceeds arising from the involuntary disposition of a vessel, provided that these funds are re-invested in a replacement vessel. Under the programme instituted in 1976, money spent by shipbuilders on the modernization of equipment will be matched by the government to a limit of 3 per cent of the value of the new construction.[95] In France, on the other hand, investment subsidies are available to owners on certain conditions for the modernization of cargo liners wherever built.[96] Also equipment grants were payable during the period of the Seventh Plan (1976-80) at rates varying from 2-15 per cent of the contract price, depending on the type of ship, and totalling not more than US $222 million.[97] However, passenger ships and long-range tankers do not qualify for these grants. The programme has been continued and is now into the Ninth Plan (1986-90).

In Belgium, modernization subsidies fall under the depreciation accounting category. Under this scheme, expenditure for modernization of existing ships or loss of major repairs and alterations on the acquisitions of second-hand ships are subject to the same schedule of depreciation.[98] However, the objective behind modernization subsidies, as in the other cases, is to increase efficiency and competitiveness.[99] The third and final heading of modernization subsidy is a combination of yard conversion and part expansion subsidies. In quite a few countries these are treated as modernization or construction subsidies.[100]

This is not entirely accurate, however, for, whereas the former relate to the ocean-going vessels themselves, the latter are much more applicable to the shipyards and ports — the fixed structures,[101] the only common denominator being that all are building subsidies. A couple or so of the TMNs have definite programmes regarding yard conversions. In France, for example, the government supports a programme for the conversion of the shipyards and the retraining of shipyard employees for other industrial activities.[102] Investment grants of up to 20 per cent of the cost of equipment have been available for the conversion of small and medium-sized shipyards since the decree of 27 December 1960.[103]

On the other hand, in Norway, government loans can be granted for the restructuring of shipyards over twelve years with no interest or down payment during the first three years.[104] The loans may cover up to 40 per cent of the cost involved. For the fiscal year 1978, US $7 million were granted for this purpose. This is a follow-up of a parliamentary decision taken in 1977 granting loans, limited to US $91 million, for restructuring and employment purposes. And in Spain, government approval must be obtained for expansion or conversion of shipyards.[105] As to port expansion subsidies, one distinct example is West Germany, where credits are granted to port operators to enlarge facilities. Interest is 5.5 per cent with repayment periods of twelve years.[106]

Among the DMNs, because the Chilean charges have been known to be insufficient to cover costs, a subsidy from the fiscal budget was found necessary to maintain port operations.[107] Even then, port rates in Chile remain identical for all shipping and there is no evidence of port or berth flag discrimination of the kind we saw earlier operating in some ports. In contrast, being an archipelagic country, Indonesia has so many ports dotted on numerous islands that they could hardly be developed without some form of assistance.[108] Port expansion is therefore needed and planned for several Indonesian ports, the most important expansion plans being for the port of Jandjung near Djakarta.[109] Having said that, however, it is difficult to differentiate between modernization and depreciation subsidies (described below) particularly when it comes to accounting systems.

Actual Depreciation Subsidies

Actual depreciation is a reduction in the value of fixed assets.[110] The most important causes of depreciation are wear and tear (loss of value

358

caused by the use of an asset), the effects of the elements (i.e. decay or corrosion), and gradual obsolescence, which makes it unprofitable to continue using the same assets until they have been fully exhausted.[111] The annual amount of depreciation of an asset depends on its original purchase price, its estimated useful life, and its estimated salvage value. A number of different methods of assessing the amount of depreciation have been developed and a number of such various references are made in this chapter.[112] Using the simple straight line method (post), which considers depreciation to be a function of time, the annual depreciation cost is calculated by dividing the cost of the asset (original minus salvage cost) equally over its entire life.

When the life of a fixed asset, like a ship, is a function of use rather than of time, industry employs the production method, in which depreciation is calculated in proportion to the use (generally expressed in terms of hours of operation or units produced) which has been made of the asset.[113] There are also a number of decreasing-charge methods, such as the diminishing-value method and the sum-of-the-digits method which allocate higher depreciation costs to the initial years of an asset's operation and lower depreciation costs to the latter years. These methods assign the greatest decrease in the resale value which normally occurs. Such accelerated depreciation methods (post) can be used in conjunction with the tax laws to reduce the overall cost of new capital investments.[114]

These economic bases are used to evaluate maritime direct depreciation subsidies. Take the case of West Germany. In that country the depreciation of ships is based on a regular useful life of fourteen years for dry cargo ships, and twelve years for tankers, reefers, special container ships and LASH ships. The twelve-year period is also applied to dry cargo ships delivered after 31 December 1972.[115] The ships may be written off in unchanging amounts (straight line method) or in annually decreasing amounts (regressive method). In the latter case, the percentage of the ships' value used to calculate the depreciation must not amount to more than the double percentage applicable in using the straight line method (for ships chartered after 31 August 1977, 250 per cent). Depreciation must neither exceed the acquisition value nor go below the scrap value of the vessel (US $20 per grt).[116]

A special depreciation allowance may be requested by German owners for new vessels, either built on demand or purchased from stock. This allowance may also be used in the first years of the vessel's life including the year of its construction or purchase. The cumulative amount of special depreciation was originally up to 30 per cent of the acquisition costs.[117] This special depreciation is accorded in

359

addition to the ordinary depreciation and may only be used if the ship is being depreciated according to the straight line method. The special depreciation percentage was raised from 30 per cent of the vessel's constructed or purchased cost from 1975 to 1978, and the scheme was extended for four additional years. After five years of the vessel's life, the remaining value is depreciated in a straight line over the rest of the vessel's useful life. Vessels covered by this special depreciation may not be sold within eight years of construction or purchase.[118]

Still in the German case, special depreciation on ships ordered in or after 1971, may only generate an accounting loss for the owner if no less than 30 per cent of the ship's construction costs have been financed from the owner's capital funds. If this requirement is met, special depreciations are admissible, but any accounting losses resulting therefrom must not exceed 15 per cent of the vessel's value. This regulation does not apply to ships of less than 1,600 gross tons (except tankers, seagoing tugs and special prospecting vessels).[119] But not all depreciations are special and actual, nor are subsidies limited to them only; there is also accelerated or anticipated depreciation. In the economic context this is a faster-than-historical rate of depreciation of fixed assets for income tax purposes. It is a method of depreciation that makes the depreciation allowance, and hence the tax allowance, available earlier in the life of the asset. Since fiscal relief is discussed later under indirect subsidies (pages 364–5) it suffices here to refer to one example, i.e. special allowances for depreciation of more than 100 per cent of a new vessel's purchase price. A large number of countries grant a certain latitude in respect of depreciation provisions or the formation of tax-free reserves, thus giving various possibilities to defer tax payment.[120] In this respect, numerous different provisions exist in the various countries, some permitting the constitution of tax-free reserves, others allowing depreciation periods of less than the physical life of a ship, or permitting various forms of acceleration — i.e. higher rates of depreciation during the early life of a vessel.[121] Accelerated depreciation either takes the form of constant depreciation percentages (reducing balance method) instead of linear depreciation or of special depreciation allowances during the first years of the vessel's life — of the kind discussed above.[122]

Accelerated Depreciation Subsidies

Provisions for accelerated depreciation must be considered in view of today's rapid technical progress and the correspondingly early economic obsolescence of assets typical of the shipping sector. Once free depreciation is permitted, a new vessel could be written off entirely during the first year.[123] Although this takes account of the fluctuating character of shipping profits, few companies make enough profits to postpone a significant amount of tax. It seems worth noting, however, that attitudes of the fiscal authorities in different countries with regard to the accounting life of a ship vary considerably, and that normal depreciation periods are between five and twenty-five years.[124] By using the liberalized provisions for computing depreciation, in the USA, for instance, a business can recapture almost 50 per cent more of its investments in a fixed asset during the first half of the asset's useful life than it could when it was limited to a straight line depreciation.[125]

Again in the USA, rapid tax amortization certificates issued during the Second World War and the Korean conflict in order to stimulate defence-supporting investment, permitted the US shipping companies to write off within five years assets that would normally have been depreciated over a longer period.[126] Accelerated depreciation in any form does not increase the total tax-free allowances for capital consumption. This applies to the merchant marine as to any other industry. In Australia, for instance, this kind of depreciation is allowable in respect of a plant or articles owned by the taxpayer[127] and:

(a) used by him during the year of income for the purpose of producing assessable income; or
(b) installed ready for use for that purpose and held in reserve by him.[128]

Thus in Australia, as in the USA, the date from which depreciation of a new ship should commence for income tax purposes may vary according to the facts of each individual case. The handover date would be appropriate if, at that time, the ship required no further fitting out in order to begin service and if the handover point was at a port from which the ship would normally take on passengers or cargoes.[129] For instance, a ship intended for an Australian coastal run would not be regarded as installed-ready-for-use for the purposes of proving assessable income merely upon delivery at a foreign shipyard. It is not considered that the depreciation of such a ship would commence for income tax purposes, when it reached the first port of its Australian run.[130]

Loans Subsidies

Loans by governments or public financing institutions for new vessel building, purchase or repairs are given by many countries, making this the category of aid most frequently granted. The conditions under which such loans are given vary between countries and often between individual loans.[131] In the various examples we encountered, interest rates varied between 2.5 per cent and 6.5 per cent, repayment periods between five and twenty-five years, and loans granted varied between 30 per cent and 80 per cent of the ship's value. All loan subsidies offer some advantage over commercial loans but these advantages are of significant importance.[132] In limited cases it appears that the loan conditions and terms closely approach those of the open capital market. In these cases, as in the others, lack of access to the normal capital market for certain owners (small or medium-sized firms) seems to be the primary motive for government intervention. As will be apparent, most countries limit loans to building, purchase or conversion of coastal vessels. In a few others, loans are conditional upon building in national yards and the shipbuilding sector is in fact the beneficiary.[133]

The impact of shipbuilding loans on the public purse and the significance of such loans for the individual recipient are difficult to assess. While it may be possible to estimate, in individual cases, the subsidy element of a loan received at less than the market rate of interest, other factors such as prolonged repayment periods, higher borrowing rates with respect to the ship's value and easier access to loan capital, can hardly be quantified.[134] It may be somewhat easier to assess actual or hypothetical cost to governments of special credit schemes, but we have not (and indeed could not) have attempted it here. It seems probable, however, that loans on advantageous terms have in some countries played a considerable role in stimulating investment in certain types of shipping and have possibly been effective in this respect at relatively low cost to the government by combining aid with a large element of self-help.[135]

From this point of view, the Swedish Ship's Mortgage Bank presents an interesting example. While the government contributes the original stock, the institution raises capital on the open market and gives mortgages on commercial terms for vessels under 3,000 grt. This makes it one of the most common types of direct subsidies outside the building subsidies.[136] In addition, the Swedish government provides subsidies, within certain limits, for loans obtained by Swedish shipyards from domestic or foreign credit institutions.[137] Detailed discussion of this Swedish illustration provides illuminating examples of this type of subsidy.[138] In Swedish terms, the aim of these subsidies is to help shipyards refinance part of their outstanding construction credits to Swedish and foreign shipowners. In this respect, it resembles a construction subsidy, but that is as

362

far as the similarity goes, since the latter subsidies are used primarily as collateral security for loans secured by mortgage.[139]

The Swedish system, in effect since 1936, was continued under the Shipbuilding Act of 2 November 1978. According to the legislation, the actual volume of the guarantees was to be allowed to increase by US $1.1 billion to the extent of US $3.8 billion before the end of 1981.[140] Swedish owners, ordering from Swedish yards, receive a five-year, interest-free 'unit-off-loan' of a maximum of 25 per cent of the new-building price. After five years the ship is assessed and if the ship's value has increased the gain will be divided equally between the state and the owner.[141] In addition, credit guarantees of a maximum of 70 per cent of the building price can also be obtained. The loans covered by the guarantees may have a maturity period of twelve years maximum. To receive a 'write-off-loan' and/or credit guarantees the order had to be placed with a Swedish yard before the end of 1979 — the ship to be delivered before the end of 1980.[142]

The Swedish Ship's Mortgage Bank grants credits to Swedish shipowners against a mortgage within 50–70 per cent of the estimated value of a new ship. The credit period is fifteen years for loans with 50 per cent of the value and ten years for those between 50–70 per cent of the value. The loans are redeemable by annual instalments of one-fifteenth and one-tenth per cent per annum, respectively.[143] The rate of interest is dependent on the current rate of interest ruling on the bond market at the time of the grant, but remains unchanged during the credit period. Outstanding loans amounted to about US $250 million on 31 December 1977. To meet temporary economic difficulties the Bank has been given facilities to postpone the annual instalment payment provided that the risk is acceptable.[144]

Since 31 July 1977, the government could issue guarantees for loans to Swedish shipowners. The aim of this guarantee system is to prevent modern Swedish ships being sold at extremely low prices. The ships must belong to shipping companies with a clear ability to overcome their economic problems and remain profitable in the future.[145] The total volume of these guarantees for Swedish owners amounted to US $115 billion. In the Act, resulting from the Bill to Parliament of 2 November 1978, the two major Swedish shipping companies, the Salen Shipping Group and the Bostrom Shipping Group were expected to receive specially designed support by government guarantees and loans for the period 1979–82 for the Salen Shipping Group, and 1979–83 for the Bostrom Shipping Group, respectively. The Bostrom Shipping Group was also expected to receive a direct financial contribution of US $18 million.[146] The programme has, however, been scaled down now that Sweden has opted to purchase from foreign yards rather than build in expensive domestic yards.

Interest Subsidies

The last, but not least, significant direct subsidy is the interest subsidy. Closely related to public loans with advantageous conditions are interest subsidies, usually for commercial loans, reportedly in operation by four TMNs, one of which has since discontinued its scheme.[147] Japan, for instance, had been granting a 3 per cent subsidy on private loans and a 2.5 per cent one on Development Bank Loans, while Italy provided up to 3.5 per cent on certain loans. In France, the interest subsidies were designed to bring interest rates for commercial loans down to a minimum of 3 per cent under certain conditions.

Interest is of course the price paid for the use of loan monies over a period of time. Individuals, businessmen and governments buy the use of loan monies to purchase ships[148] and other capital goods, because they can increase production and productivity through the introduction of new plants and new machines. Likewise, consignors and consignees pay interest for the use of loan monies, because they wish to make purchase of goods and services in excess of their current income.[149] Even governments pay interest for the use of loan monies because their expenditure usually exceeds their receipts.

According to the loanable funds theory of interest — the details of which are now relevant here — the price of monies equals the price paid for the use of loanable funds.[150] The intersection of the supply and demand curves of loanable funds designates the rate of interest. In most economies, therefore, businessmen look to governments not only for loans and loan subsidies, but for interest subsidies as well. Shipowners and shippers are no exceptions; on the contrary they are at the forefront.[151] Most maritime nations resort to some type of interest subsidies. In the Netherlands for instance, the government grants interest subsidies to Dutch shipbuilders enabling them to furnish credits at reduced rates to both domestic and foreign customers.[152] However, in conformity with the Understanding of the OECD, the Dutch government grants such subsidies for credits of up to 70 per cent of the cost of ships for export, for a maximum duration of seven years.[153] The interest subsidy consists of the difference between the current market rate of interest, based on the yield of State Bonds, and the minimum net interest rate of 8 per cent mentioned in the Understanding. Besides, only those shipyards that are prepared to rationalize their programmes in mutual co-operation and collaborate in research and cost-saving are eligible for this interest subsidy.[154] Since most TMNs are members of the OECD, their conditions and terms for granting interest subsidies would be similar, if not identical, to that of the Netherlands. The fact that direct maritime subsidies have become the general rule rather than the exception underlines their importance in the protection and development of industries generally and merchant marine industries in particular.[155]

Indirect Subsidies

Where direct subsidies are denied or unavailable, they are often substituted by indirect subsidies,[156] although at times, the difference between the two can be very thin or indeed non-existent. Direct subsidies normally fall into the domain of financial aid, whereas indirect subsidies are sometimes referred to as fiscal relief. In examples such as the granting of special depreciation allowances exceeding the original cost of the vessel, the two are interrelated.[157] Otherwise indirect subsidies, or fiscal relief, are normally granted in the form of permission to carry forwards or backwards losses and various possibilities of deferring tax-payments and credit guarantees — for example, through free or accelerated depreciation to assets or through the formation of tax-free reserves.[158] However, the most commonly recognized example is the investment allowance.

Investment Allowances and Grants

Within this category are investment promotion allowances, investment grants, etc. One type of fiscal relief is closely related to direct financial assistance to shipping. Investment allowances — that is, special allowances for depreciation of more than 100 per cent of the purchase price of a new vessel or asset — are granted by many countries, some of which have recently discontinued the scheme and replaced it with investment grants (page 370) which are assumed to have a similar effect, but are demanding on the public purse.[159] One notable example is that of Australia, where, for instance, a plant ordered or contracted for between 1 January 1976 and 30 June 1978 attracted an investment allowance of 40 per cent of the plant's cost provided that the plant was first used or installed ready for use by 30 June 1979. The allowance, combined with depreciation allowances, results in total deductions equivalent to 140 per cent of cost.[160] However, for plant ordered or contracted for before or between 1 July 1978 and 30 June 1985, the investment allowances were at the rate of 20 per cent, but the plant needed to be first used or installed ready for use by 1 July 1986. The income tax deduction for the investment

Table 8.6 US Federal ship financing guarantee (Title XI Programme Summary — statutory limit $9.5 billion) principal liability on 30 September 1984

Vessel types	Contracts in force		Active applications	
	Vessels covered	Principal amount $	Vessels covered	Principal amount $
Deepdraft vessels				
Tankers	81	1,903,314,358	1	3,200,000
Cargo	126	1,042,007,884	4	12,800,000
LNGs	16	1,181,552,000	1	11,300,000
Bulk/OBOs	22	377,521,286	0	0
Cruise ship			1	99,000,000
Total	245	4,504,395,528	7	126,300,000
Other types:				
Drill rigs/ships	78	868,504,269		
Tugs/barges/drill service	3,713	1,661,084,297	62	18,000,000
Miscellaneous	24	224,553,703	6	63,800,000
Total	3,815	2,754,142,269	68	81,800,000
Total vessels	4,060	7,258,537,797	75	208,100,000
Shipboard lighters	1,975	44,666,684	0	0
Total	6,035	7,303,204,481	75	208,100,000

*Rounded to the nearest dollar.

allowance becomes available in the financial year in which the plant is first used or installed ready for use.[161] However, capital expenditure on the purchase of a new ship would attract the investment allowance, provided that the ship was to be used wholly or exclusively in Australia for the production of assessable income. A ship that sails between Australia and overseas ports would not meet this requirement.[162] This is rather unusual since most assistance is geared to aiding international trade.

Investment allowances are known by different names and are operated as different schemes in different countries depending on the accounting system in existence. In West Germany, the same category of subsidy is known as an Industrial Investment Promotion grant. Under this scheme, in the first half of 1975, for instance, the German government introduced a 7.5 per cent investment promotion grant for all German investors who realized certain investments within a given period of time.[163] Many German shipowners seem to have made use of that opportunity by placing new orders, a great deal of them with foreign yards. However, the programme seems to have ended in mid-1976 and has been replaced by grants and guarantees.[164] The final two types of financial assistance most frequently granted by the TMNs are investment grants and credit guarantees, usually for commercial loans. These were prevalent in Belgium, the USA and Denmark; the latter country reserving the guarantee for the building or converting of freighters of 500 grt and less.[165] Such guarantees can lower the rate of interest by the difference between the government and commercial long-term borrowing rates without actually incurring any outlay for the government. The government is thus taking some of the commercial risks involved and may, of course, incur expenditure in case of default of the firms concerned.[166] Thus, unlike the promotional allowances, the guarantees are a kind of government insurance against the risks of inconvertibility or expropriation of foreign shipping investments. Table 8.6 gives an example of the operation of the scheme in the USA. See also the next subsection for a further discussion of the scheme.

Investment Guarantees and Deferred Credits

The investment guarantee programme was first undertaken by the US merchant marine to encourage the flow of AID programmes to the DMNs.[167] Shipowners making approved direct foreign investments, particularly in the developing countries, had to purchase protection against the risk of being unable to convert foreign shipping earnings into dollars, and the risk of expropriation or confiscation by the government of the country in which the investment was made.[168] This example further illustrates how much international shipping is interrelated with international trade and with foreign aid and foreign investments. Foreign investment guarantees were offered by the UN Food and Agricultural Programme (FAO), as provided for under the Mutual Security Act 1951. However, the guarantees do not protect the investment against ordinary business risks, but only against adverse actions by foreign governments.[169] Besides, the foreign elements have not been used very extensively and have not achieved their aim of significantly expanding the merchant marine fleet or increasing the flow of private merchant marine capital into the developing countries.

The latter objective was only achieved by the encouragement and promotion of FOCs, while the former could only be achieved by the alternative method of extending the guarantees to domestic merchant marine investment.[170] The states of Hamburg, Bremen, Biedersachsen (Lower Saxony) and Schleswig-Holstein also accord, to a limited extent, guarantees for credits for the purchase of new commercial ships built in local yards, when such credits cannot be covered by usual ship mortgages.[171] These credit guarantees are available to German nationals and, according to the arrangements between the coastal states, they are also available to other EEC and OECD nationals.[172] The other example is from the Netherlands where, in exceptional cases, government-guaranteed commercial loans may be given to shipping companies for investment purposes.[173] However, unlike West Germany, no provision is made for any facility with regard to the interest to be paid or to the period of redemption — a characteristic which would tend to assimilate this scheme to deferred credits or outright loans.[174]

On the other hand, the deferred credit, as a form of investment allowance subsidy, is sometimes known as loss carrying. In a business subject to strongly fluctuating trade conditions, such as shipping, the permission to carry forward losses in order to deduct these from future profits or to carry back losses to diminish the taxable profit of a previous year may be of considerable significance.[175] Permission to carry forward losses is given in most countries. It should be noted however that in most cases, the schemes apply not only to shipping but to all industries. In quite a few countries losses may be carried forward for an unlimited number of years; a number of countries allow five years and some permit ten years.[176] In Singapore, a DMN where this type of subsidy is predominant, the programme is executed under the scheme: 'Deferred Credit for Financing Vessels Built in Singapore'. This recently-announced ship-financing scheme is available for the construction of vessels under 5,000 dwt under the following terms:[177]

- Loan quantum — Up to a maximum of 50 per cent of contract value.
- Interest rate — Fixed rate of 9.5 per cent or thereabouts during the tenure of the loan.
- Repayment — Up to a maximum of seven years after delivery.
- Disbursements — In accordance with making progress.
- Currency — In Singapore dollars.
- Types of vessels — Generally for vessels over 100 grt and tug-boats over 500 bhp. Each case is decided on its own merits. Military craft and all types of drilling equipment are excluded.

The scheme is designed partially to finance deferred credits granted by local shipyards to the owners of the vessels under construction,[178] and the vessels to be financed must be completely built in Singapore. In the event that the deferred credit granted by a shipyard exceeds 50 per cent of the contract value, additional financing may be made available to the shipyard on commercial terms — i.e. without subsidy elements. The interest rate would most likely be on a floating basis.[179] Within the scheme of deferred credit subsidies is the financing of yard construction expansion and yard equipment under the following terms:

- Amount   50 per cent of cost facilities.
- Interest rate   9.5 per cent or thereabouts.
- Duration   Up to eight years.

But perhaps the most elaborate indirect subsidy consists of a series of tax exemptions, allowances, deductions, etc. normally considered under the umbrella term 'tax benefits'.

Tax Benefits

The fiscal system relating to the taxation of shipping may, under certain conditions, have similar beneficial effects for the shipowners as financial assistance. However, fiscal provisions most often apply to income tax liability and consequently will usually be relevant provided that profits are made.[180] For many shipping companies in the TMNs, profitability has in recent years been very poor, rendering them unable to exploit fully the available fiscal relief opportunities of direct tax benefits and customs duty exemptions.[181] The US programme is not only the most elaborate and most comprehensive, but is also the one that brings out clearly all the important principles, features, characteristics and motives for and of maritime tax benefits. For this reason it will be dealt with at some length.[182]

In general shipping is treated similarly to other industries, except where US citizens owning or leasing eligible vessels may obtain certain tax benefits through the maintenance of the Capital Construction Fund (CCF) and the Construction Reserve Fund (CRF). The CCF programme is a method of aiding US vessel operators in accumulating capital necessary for the construction, reconstruction and acquisition of vessels of US registry built in the USA.[183] Its purpose is to remove certain competitive disadvantages that US operators encounter relative to foreign flag operators. The CCF extends tax deferral privileges to vessel operators in US foreign commerce and in the non-contiguous and Great Lakes domestic trades.[184] It is authorized by Section 607 of the Merchant Marine Act 1936, as amended, and arose from the 1970 amendments to the Act. Prior to 1970 only subsidized operators had tax deferred funds, under Section 607.[185]

Table 8.7 US Capital Construction Fund holders — 30 September 1984

A & A Boats, Inc.
Aeron Marine Shipping Co.
Alaska Riverways, Inc.
Amak Towing Co. Inc.
AMC Boats, Inc.
American Atlantic Shipping, Inc.
American President Lines, Inc.
American Shipping, Inc.
Andover Co., L.P.
Aquarius Marine Co.
Ashland Oil, Inc.
Atlantic Richfield Co.
Atlas Marine Co.
Bankers Trust of New York Corp.
Bethlehem Steel Corp.
Binkley Co., The
Blue Line, Inc.
Brice Inc.
C & G International, Inc.
C & G Marine Service, Inc.
Cambridge Tankers, Inc.
Campbell Towing Co.
Canonie Offshore, Inc.
Canonie Transportation, Inc.
Cement Transit Co./Medusa Corp.
Central Gulf Lines, Inc.
Citimarlease (Burmah I), Inc.
Citimarlease (Burmah Liquegas) Inc.
Citimarlease (Fulton), Inc.
Citimarlease (Whitney), Inc.
Cleveland-Cliffs Iron Co., The
Crowley Maritime Corp.
CSI Hydrostatic Testers, Inc.
Delta Steamship Lines, Inc.
Dillingham Tug & Barge Corp.
Edison Chouest Boat Rentals, Inc.
Edward E. Gillen Co.
El Paso Arzew Tanker Co.
El Paso Howard Boyd Tanker Co.
El Paso Southern Tanker Co.

Eserman Offshore Service, Inc.
Exxon Shipping Co.
Falcon Alpha Shipping, Inc.
Falcon Capital, Inc.
Falcon Funding, Inc.
Falcon World Shipping, Inc.
Farrell Lines, Inc.
Ford Motor Co.
Foss Alaska Lines, Inc.
Foss Launch and Tug Co.
Fred Devine Diving & Salvage, Inc.
Garber Bros Inc.
GATX Corp.
G & B Marine Transportation, Inc.
General Electric Credit and Leas. Corp.
General Electric Credit Corp, of Delaware
General Electric Credit Corp. of Georgia
Gilco Supply Boats, Inc.
Graham Boats, Inc.
Great Lakes Towing Co.
Hannah Brothers
Hannah Marine Corp.
Houston Natural Gas Corp.
Hvide Shipping, Inc.
Inter-Cities Navigation Corp.
Intercontinental Bulktank Corp.
Interstate Marine Transport Co.
Interstate Towing Co.
ITC Towing Co.
John E. Graham & Sons
Kinsman Lines, Inc.
Lepaluoto Offshore Marine, Inc.
L & L Marine Services, Inc.
Luedtke Engineering Co.
Lykes Bros. Steamship Co.
Madeline Island Ferry Lines, Inc.
Matson Navigation Co. Ltd.
Middle Rock, Inc.

Miller Boat, Inc.
Monticello Tanker Co.
Montpelier Tanker Co.
Moody Offshore, Inc.
Moore McCormack Resources, Inc.
Mount Vernon Tanker Co.
Mount Washington Tanker Co.
National Marine Service, Inc.
Neuman Boat Line, Inc.
Nicor, Inc.
O.L. Schmidt Barge Lines, Inc.
Ocean Carriers, Inc.
Offshore Marine, Inc.
Ogden Corp.
Oglebay Norton Co.
Overseas Bulktank Corp.
Pacific Hawaiian Lines, Inc.
Pacific Shipping, Inc.
Petro-Boats, Inc.
Petrolane Inc.
Prudential Lines, Inc.
Reynolds Leasing Corp.
Ritchie Transportation Co.
Seabulk Tankers, Ltd.
Sea Savage, Inc.
Smith Lighterage Co. Inc.
State Boat Corp.
Steel Style Marine
Sun Co., Inc.
Tidewater Inc.
Toterm Resources Corp.
Transway International Corp.
Tug Alaska Mariner, Inc.
Tug Western Mariner, Inc.
Union Oil Co. of California
United States Cruises, Inc.
Waterman Steamship Corp.
Western Pioneer, Inc.
Windjammer Cruiser, Inc.
Young Brothers Ltd
Zidell, Inc.

Source: MARAD, 1984, p. 7.

The revised CCF programme under Section 607 is now available to both subsidized and non-subsidized operators, and the old CRFs have been phased out of existence. Briefly, Section 607 allows for deferment of income tax payments on certain deposits of money or other property, if the funds are used to construct vessels in US shipyards.[186] An operator's earnings or gains are realized from the operation of an agreement vessel, from the net proceeds arising from the sale or other disposition of the vessel or from insurance or indemnification for the loss of such a vessel. Also included are earnings from the investment or re-investment of amounts on deposit in the CCF. In general the operator's taxable income is reduced to the extent that deposits of money are made into the fund under these categories.[187] Table 8.7 shows a list of the US CCF holders in 1984.

Construction Deposits

An operator may also deposit in a CCF amounts allowable as a depreciation deduction with respect to agreement vessels. Such deposits do not directly reduce taxable income, but the earnings from such funds may be accumulated on a tax-deferred basis.[188] By the investment of assets in the CCF, a fundholder may compound the fund benefits and develop an expanded pool of tax-deferred funds. However, the investment of the funds in securities and stocks is subject to certain restrictions which are intended to preserve the fund's integrity. A fund established pursuant to Section 607,[189] is maintained in three accounts: an ordinary income account, a capital gains account, and a capital account. The manner in which the funds would be taxed if not deposited is the primary determinant of the account to which a deposit is credited.[190]

When qualified withdrawals are made from the fund for the construction, reconstruction or acquisition of vessels, barges, or containers, certain basic adjustments are made to the assets being acquired depending upon the account from which the monies are withdrawn.[191] Withdrawals from the ordinary income account reduce the tax basis of the acquired vessel by an amount equivalent to the amount withdrawn; withdrawals from the capital gains account result in a partial reduction basis; and withdrawals from the capital account do not reduce the tax basis of the acquired vessel.[192] If a withdrawal is made from the fund for other than a qualified purpose, any amounts withdrawn from the ordinary income and capital gains accounts are taxable as earned in the year of withdrawal. Additionally, the tax attributable to the non-qualified withdrawal is subject to an interest charge for the period between the year the account was deposited and the year the withdrawal was made.[193] Since the tax

Table 8.8   US maritime subsidy outlays — 1936–85

Fiscal year	New construction CDS $	Re-construction CDS $	Total CDS $	ODS $	Total ODS & CDS $
1936–55	248,320,942[1]	3,286,888	251,607,830	341,109,987	592,717,817
1956–60	129,806,005	34,881,409	164,687,414	644,115,146	808,802,560
1961	100,145,654	1,215,432	101,361,086	150,142,575	251,503,661
1962	134,552,647	4,160,591	138,713,238	181,918,756	320,631,994
1963	89,235,895	4,181,314	93,417,209	220,676,685	314,093,894
1964	76,608,323	1,665,087	78,273,310	203,036,844	281,310,254
1965	86,096,872	38,138	86,135,010	213,334,409	299,469,419
1966	69,446,510	2,571,566	72,018,076	186,628,357	258,646,433
1967	80,155,452	932,114	81,087,566	175,631,860	256,719,426
1968	95,989,586	96,707	96,086,293	200,129,670	296,215,963
1969	93,952,849	57,329	94,010,178	194,702,569	288,712,747
1970	73,528,904	21,723,343	95,252,247	205,731,711	300,983,958
1971	107,637,353	27,450,968	135,088,321	268,021,097	403,109,418
1972	111,950,403	29,748,076	141,698,479	235,666,830	377,365,310
1973	168,183,937	17,384,604	185,568,541	226,710,926	412,279,467
1974	185,060,501	13,844,951	198,905,452	257,919,080	456,824,532
1975	237,895,092	1,900,571	239,795,663	243,152,340	492,948,003
1976[2]	233,836,424	9,886,024	243,712,448	386,433,994	630,146,442
1977	203,479,571	15,052,072	218,531,643	343,875,521	562,407,164
1978	148,690,842	7,318,705	516,009,547	303,193,575	459,203,122
1979	198,518,437	2,258,492	200,776,929	300,521,683	501,298,612
1980	262,727,122	2,352,744	265,079,866	341,368,236	606,448,102
1981	196,446,214	11,666,978	208,113,192	334,853,670	542,966,862
1982	140,774,519	43,710,698	184,485,217	400,689,713	585,174,930
1983	76,941,138	7,519,881	84,511,019	368,194,331	452,705,350
1984	13,694,523		13,694,523	384,259,674	397,954,197
Total	3,563,715,715	264,904,682	3,828,620,397	11,140,639,637	11,140,639,637

[1] Includes $131.5 million CDS adjustments covering the Second World War period, $105.8 million equivalent to CDS allowances which were made in connection with the Mariner Ship Construction Programme, and $10.8 million for CDS in fiscal years 1954 to 1955.
[2] Includes totals for FY 1976 and the Transition Quarter ending 30 September 1976.

Source: MARAD, 1981, p. 52.

paid is on non-qualified withdrawals, no adjustments to the basis arise as a result of a non-qualified withdrawal.

The CRF authorized by Section 511 of the Merchant Marine Act 1936, as amended, is also a financial assistance programme which provides tax deferral benefits to US shipowners.[194] Through the CRF, shipowners operating vessels in US foreign or domestic commerce can defer the gains attributable to the sale or loss of a vessel.[195] The proceeds deposited must be used to construct, reconstruct or acquire vessels of US state registry built in the USA. Although any gains on such transactions are not recognized for income tax purposes, nevertheless, if the deposits are properly expended for a vessel, the basis for determining appreciation of such a vessel is reduced by the amount of any such gains.[196]

The ability to defer gains on certain transactions through deposits to the CRF applies only to vessel owners. Citizens operating a vessel owned by another party cannot benefit from the provisions. Section 511 also permits a vessel owner or operator to deposit in the CRF earnings from the operation of US registry vessels and earnings from the investment of such funds.[197] Such deposits do not exempt the taxpayer from tax liability for the earnings, nor do they postpone the time such earnings are includable in the gross income. However, earnings so deposited are considered to have been accumulated for the reasonable needs of business and are not subject to accumulated earnings tax.[198] This ability to accumulate funds for the construction, reconstruction, or acquisition of a vessel is the only benefit available through the CRF to a non-owner operator of a vessel. Other forms of tax subsidies are customs duties exemption for domestic flag vessels. In that respect they resemble flag discrimination.[199] For these and other related subsidies operated in the USA, see Table 8.8.

Customs Exemptions

Exemptions from customs duties operate on the same principles and, sometimes, in lieu of general tax benefits. Again this is but an umbrella term for numerous, but related, subsidies, which are referred to under different titles in different countries.[200] In Australia, for instance, they are known simply as fees and are operated on the principle that machinery and equipment used in the construction of new ships in Australian yards may, in some circumstances, be imported duty-free when equivalent goods are not reasonably available from Australian manufacturers.[201]

In Canada, on the other hand, this kind of fiscal relief for the merchant marine industry is known by its traditional name of customs duties and is not payable on ships imported into Canada to engage exclusively in international trade.[202] Secondly, vessels constructed and registered in Commonwealth countries are free to engage in the Canadian coastal trade, with the exception of that within the Great Lakes and St Lawrence River Basin, which is restricted to vessels registered in Canada. Also, upon payment of a duty of 25 per cent[203] vessels of Commonwealth registry entitled to the MFN tariff treatment may engage in the Canadian coastal trade which is excluded to vessels of other registry. This is a good example of aid to shipping which is combined with the MFN principle as well as with flag discrimination. However, when a suitable Canadian vessel is not available,[204] there is provision for the temporary use of non-Commonwealth registered ships in the coastal trade. In such circumstances, the vessel is subject to the same duty prorated for each month in service in Canada. Otherwise materials imported for the building of ships for export are duty-free; for ships for the domestic market, duty is payable at the normal rate.[205] This illustrates the fact that more emphasis is placed on aiding ocean-going vessels and, therefore, ocean-borne commerce.

However, the more common practice among the TMNs is that of Spain, where it is known as customs duty exemption. In this case imported material for incorporation in ships for export is considered as a temporary import and is therefore exempted from customs duty.[206] To take account of customs duties paid on imported material and equipment for ships for the domestic market a rebate of 7 per cent is granted which partly offsets these duties; the rebate is reduced to 4.5 per cent in the case of imported propulsion gear and equipment for fishing vessels. In the case of ships for export, the rebate is calculated after deducting, from the value of the ship, the value of materials imported under the system governing temporary imports.[207] The DMNs follow similar principles. In Argentina, for instance, the Empressa Lineas Maritimas Argentinas (ELMA) is exempt from all taxes and the Income Tax Act, as amended from time to time, establishes promotional regulations for private ship enterprise.

Compensatory Subsidies

Some countries prefer actual direct payment to mere tax exemptions.[208] This is akin to direct assistance and is known as compensatory subsidy. Compensatory subsidy to the merchant marine industry is, of course, only part of a wider governmental compensatory fiscal policy[209] towards industry generally. Normally, a government resorts to this kind of indirect aid in the management of government finance to compensate for fluctuations in national income and employment — compensatory fiscal policy, which combines deficit and surplus financing and attempts to achieve a high level of employment by maintaining a high level of national income.[210] It uses taxation and spending to produce the desired balance. To maintain the desired level of income during a business decline any decrease in private spending or investment must be balanced by a government policy of either increasing government spending (raising total government purchases from private business) or reducing taxes (increasing the income of consumers, business or both).[211] To maintain the desired level of income during a period of expansion and inflation, government policy should comprise reduction in expenditure borrowing, a possible increase in taxes, or both. If such government action is timely, and the amounts involved are large enough, substantial fluctuations in national income and employment may be avoided.[212] Thus, in many countries, aid to the merchant marine industry has to be viewed in the general context of the national income and employment policy. National merchant marines are gradually becoming integrated into general national budgetary and economic planning; it was originally largely a private sector in private hands. Generally, private consumption is relatively stable in the short run, while private investment is relatively volatile.[213]

The foregoing analysis is more applicable to the private sector, and more so to the merchant marine industry which is an industry still largely in private hands,[214] in the TMNs at least. It was in recognition of this fact that this kind of fiscal relief or indirect maritime subsidy was devised.[215] There is both the direct compensatory and the inflation/cost escalation subsidy. Both examples are illustrated by the French practice. Describing its action as 'Reimbursement of Part-Cost Pursuant to Article 79',[216] the government decided in 1966 to reimburse shipowners for part of the cost incurred pursuant to Article 79, entitled 'Accidents and Illness Occurring on Board in Course of Embarking' — a rather clumsy heading[217] obscuring the real purpose of the subsidy scheme. Nevertheless, these kinds of costs are peculiar to French shipowners, and constitute one of the elements of their handicap with regard to foreign shipowners,[218] rather than aid in the protection and/or expansion of the national fleet. I, for one, prefer to refer to this subsidy by its customary name: insurance and/or insurance subsidy.

Inflation and Insurance Subsidies

However, the decision to reimburse part of these costs has the same motivation as the decision concerning the allowance for compensatory subsidies and/or inflation subsidies. Thus, in France, together with compensatory subsidies, the Ministry of Transport administers a programme that guarantees compensation for increases in shipbuilding costs, that exceed a set threshold (currently 7.3 per cent).[219] Note, however, that inflation subsidies are quite different from export credit insurance.[220] To illustrate this difference, take the case of Denmark which administers the latter. Danish export credit insurance is based on purely commercial insurance principles rather than subsidy principles.[221] The scheme is voluntary and no lower limit is set for such insurance; premiums vary between 0.125 per cent and 0.25 per cent p.a. of the outstanding debt and 0.3 per cent p.a. of outstanding debts for political risks. These principles are, however, not applicable to inflation subsidy.[222] In contrast, inflation subsidies are more akin to the credit guarantee subsidies discussed earlier.[223] Perhaps inflation subsidies are more appropriately practised in the UK where they are referred to as cost escalation insurance or simply deflation allowance.[224] The British government operates a temporary scheme of cost escalation insurance on sales by British shipbuilders to both the domestic and export markets.[225] Within the development objective the scheme is designed to give shipbuilders a measure of protection against exceptional and unpredictable increases in UK costs.[226] To qualify for cover, however, a prospective contract for the supply of items must reach an individual unit value of about £500,000, have a manufacturing period of at least two years, and have a basic contract price of at least £2 million.[227]

We have so far concentrated on subsidies that involve machinery and services; we have hardly mentioned those relating to labour. Indeed subsidies for machines, without corresponding subsidies for the men who operate the machines, would be an incomplete scheme.[228]

Seamen's Welfare Benefits

The list of indirect subsidies operated by different countries is endless. There are many varieties all aimed at protecting and expanding the national merchant marines in one way or another.[229] We shall, however, limit ourselves here to two main types: seamen's welfare benefits, and subsidies to research and maritime academies. With regard to the first of the two examples we have already mentioned the French maritime social insurance. The other illustration from a TMN is that of Greece. It is interesting to note that this is part of the new Greek drive and initiative to attract back to the Greek flag Greek seamen and vessels currently operating under FOCs.[230] Interesting, because whereas other countries' expansion policies are directed at new building and protectionism, the Greek initiative is moving in exactly the opposite direction – to attract back her already existing fleet presently registered under different flags. Indeed, the scheme seems to have paid off with the return of many Greek flags from mainly FOC registries.

Thus, on the basis of legislation recently introduced,[231] persons of Greek descent who have an established permanent residence abroad, Greeks employed abroad and seamen serving on board ocean-going vessels are exempt from payment of transfer tax (which in other

376

cases ranges from 11-13 per cent) on the purchase of real property made through the importation of foreign exchange.[232] More specifically, persons of Greek descent who have resided abroad for at least five years are entitled to the above exemption provided they purchase real property in Greece within a period of five years at the latest from their return from abroad.[233] In addition, Greeks employed abroad as workers or employees should have completed at least three years' work abroad and receive their wages or salaries in foreign exchange to qualify for the above exemption subsidy.[234] Lastly, Greek seamen employed on board Greek or foreign flag vessels for at least three years and receiving their pay in foreign exchange are also eligible for this tax exemption. This inducement subsidy acts as an attraction for foreign exchange, in addition to its expansionist motive — hence the strong link between merchant shipping and balance of payments considerations.[235]

Conversely, the Italian approach seems to be designed more for the protection of the seamen themselves. For instance, an Italian law, which became effective in March 1977, makes maritime agents responsible for the social welfare, payment of salaries, and insurance coverage of all new crew employed.[236] However, the maritime agents must produce guarantees from FOC shipowners covering insurance and salaries before taking on new Italian crews.[237] Where their wages do not cover social benefits or are inadequate, the Italian government will subsidize the cost of sickness benefits, medical expenses, pensions etc.[238]

In the UK, as in France and West Germany, social benefits are part of the National Health Insurance scheme administered by the DHSS.[239] In addition, maritime welfare is part of the general subsidies to the merchant marine industry in general and shipbuilding in particular.[240]

Last, but not least, of the indirect maritime subsidies are the grants for research and the nautical maritime academies.[241] The rationale behind this is that unless the government intervenes, these expenses would otherwise be borne by the industry, thereby diverting valuable investments from direct ploughback.[242] It is hoped that money used for research in designs and maritime academies to train both the shore and seagoing officers and crew will improve efficiency, safety and productivity in the industry.[243] It will, of course, also create and/or protect jobs in addition to aiding the general purpose of expanding the national fleet and maintaining a pool of trained and skilled labour.

Ship Research Grants

Although the merchant marine industry is still largely in private hands, especially in the TMNs, governments nevertheless retain an overall interest and derive the greatest benefits. Rather than leave the private sector to go it alone, it is only reasonable that governments intervene whenever necessary. Thus in Canada, for instance, research grants are not restricted to the merchant marine industry. All industries are entitled to aid under various general programmes covering as much as 50 per cent of the cost of approved research.[244] State contribution to maritime research and maritime academies in Denmark, on the other hand, is in the form of financial support amounting to about US $0.15 million p.a. given by the government to institutions engaged in shipbuilding research.

Other governments are more heavily involved in such aid schemes.[245] Japan, for instance, has a fully established Ship Research Institute as well as a University of Mercantile Marine attached to the Ministry of Transport Science, Education and Industry, both of which had annual running costs of approximately 2,300,000 million yen in the 1976 fiscal year.[246] In addition, the Nuclear Ship Development Agency was established with government funds in 1963. The Netherlands maritime industry finances part of its maritime research programme with government funds,[247] while in Norway and Sweden various institutes work on a task basis and are becoming less dependent on government subsidy.[248]

In the UK, research related to shipbuilding is carried out by the state-run National Physical Laboratory.[249] The government also supports selected research and design (R & D) work done by firms or research associations, and gives specific aid to certain projects of the British Ship Research Association.[250] State aid for R & D work averages about £2 million p.a.[251] Benefits from such indirect subsidies are also indirect; they accrue over a long period of time and are therefore difficult to evaluate in the way they seem to achieve the objectives of aiding the expansion of national merchant marine fleets. It is no coincidence that the more advanced maritime nations, like Japan, UK, USA, West Germany and the Scandinavian countries, are also the largest investors in maritime subsidies generally and research and maritime academies in particular.[252]

Finally, mention should be made of the international efforts which culminated in the establishment of a UN/IMO World Maritime University (WMU) in Malmo, Sweden, in 1983.

Notes

1 OECD, *Maritime Transport*, 1971, p. 10.
2 US Department of Commerce, MARAD, *Maritime Subsidies*, 1978, p. 20.

3 See Chapter 10 on economic consequences.

4 Such as military services.

5 But this is not exhaustive.

6 See further on for details.

7 *US Joint Economic, Subsidy and Subsidy-like Programs of the US Governments*, GPO, Washington DC, 1960.

8 These programmes cost US $57.3 billion, 19 July 1950–30 June 1961 according to the above report.

9 Black, *Law Dictionary*, pp. 1596–1957.

10 *Kennecott Copper Corporation v. State Tax Commission, DC Utah*, 60.F. Suppl. p. 181, p. 182.

11 Utility to the public is an essential prerequisite for governments to grant subsidies.

12 Farm subsidies, i.e. 'Agricultural support subsidies' (UK) under The Agricultural Act 1947.

13 J.G. Kilgour, 'Double subsidy issue in shipping', *Journal of Maritime Law and Commerce*, vol. 4, no. 6, 1975, pp. 395–407.

14 *Readings in the Theory of International Trade* (Committee of the American Economic Association).

15 *The Rochdale Report* (Committee of Enquiry into Shipping — Report of Chairman Lord Rochdale), London, May 1970, paras. 170–82, pp. 48–57.

16 Note 14 (above) especially the Introduction.

17 *The Rochdale Report*, op.cit., also notes USA, UK, Japan, Italy, France and Spain for subsidies.

18 S.A. Lawrence, *International Shipping: The Years Ahead*, Lexington Books, Lexington, Mass., 1972.

19 C. O'Loughlin, *The Economics of Sea Transport*, 1st edn, Pergamon Press, Oxford, pp. 82–5.

20 Black, *Law Dictionary*, op.cit., p. 1597.

21 Ibid., p. 1597.

22 S.G. Sturmey, *British Shipping and World Competition*, Athlone Press, London, 1961, pp. 28–9.

23 Ibid., pp. 19–21 and 31–2.

24 Ibid., pp. 122–4, 128–36 and 188–91.

25 *State Aid to the Merchant Marine in Major Maritime Nations before the War*, US Department of Commerce, Maritime Administration, Washington DC, 1961.

26 O'Loughlin, op.cit., pp. 89–95.

27 S.G. Sturmey, op.cit., pp. 30–1.

28 R.H. Thornton, *British Shipping*, Cambridge, 1959, pp. 21–2.

29 S.G. Sturmey, op.cit.; see also F. Evershem, *Effects of Shipping Subsidization*, Bremen, 1958, p. 15.

30 S.G. Sturmey, op.cit.; R. Smith, *Influence of the Great War upon Shipping*, New York, 1919, p. 135.

31 *Report of the German Control Stations and the Atlantic Emigration Traffic*, Cmnd. 9092, November 1916, 1918.

32 J.E. Stanstad, *Shipping and Shipbuilding Subsidies*, US Department of Commerce, 1932, p. 326.

33 F. Evershem, op.cit., p. 15.

34 R. Smith, op.cit., p. 135.

35 E. Bennethan and A.A. Walters, *Port Pricing and Investment Policy for Developing Countries*, OUP, 1979.

36 See also J.W. Devanney, *Marine Decisions under Uncertainty*, Cornell Maritime Press, Cambridge, Md., 1971.

37 W.L. Grossman, *Ocean Freight Rates*, Cornell Maritime Press, Cambridge, Md., 1956.

38 See also P. Hanson, 'Soviet Union and world shipping', *Journal of Soviet Studies*, July 1970.

39 Lloyd's of London, *Lloyd's Calendar and National Yearbook*, (Annual), Lloyd's of London Press, London.

40 C.M. Moyer, 'A critique of the rationales for present US maritime programmes', *Transportation Journal*, Winter 1974.

41 C.S. Pearson, *International Marine Environment Policy: The Economic Dimension*, John Hopkins University Press, Baltimore, 1975.

42 J.R. Smith, 'Ocean freight rates', *Political Science Quarterly*, no. 2, 1906.

43 UN, *The Application of Modern Transport Technology to Mineral Development in Developing Countries*, New York, 1976.

44 US Department of Justice, Antitrust Division, *The Regulated Ocean Shipping Industry*, Report, 1977 (Stock No. 027-000-00474-1).

45 Z. Zannetos, 'Persistent economic misconceptions in the transportation of oil by sea', *Maritime Studies and Management*, no. 1, 1973.

46 US Congress, Senate Committee on Commerce, Science and Transportation, *Illegal Rebating in the US Ocean Commerce*, Hearings before the Subcommittee on Merchant Marine and Tourism, 95th Congress, 1st Session, serial no. 95-13, 1977.

47 See also US Congress, Joint Economic Committee, *Discriminatory Ocean Freight Rates and the Balance of Payments*, 89th Congress, 1st Session, 6 January 1965.

48 T. Thorburn, *The Supply and Demand of Water Transport*, Stockholm School of Economics, 1960.

49 B.N. Metaxas, 'Notes on the internationalization process in the maritime sectors', *Maritime Policy and Management*, January 1978.

50 FMC Fact Finding Investigation No. 6: *The Effect of Steamship Conference Organisation, Rules, Regulations, and Practices upon the Foreign Commerce of the US*, 1965.

51 US Senate, *Merchant Marine Study and Investigation* (Government Aid to Shipping), GPO, Washington, 1980.

52 US Maritime Commission, *Economic Survey of the American Merchant Marine*, GPO, Washington, 1937.

53 *Report to the President on Foreign Economic Policies*, GPO, Washington, 1980, p. 89.

54 Post-war Planning Committee, *Post-war Economic Outlook for American Shipping*, GPO, Washington, 1946, p. 4.

55 Treasury Department (Communication from the President), *Scope and Effects of Tax Benefits Provided to the Maritime Industry*, GPO, Washington, 1953.

56 US Department of Commerce, MARAD, *Review of Essential Foreign Trade Routes*, GPO, Washington, 1953, p. 14.

57 Ibid., p. 6; also Section 211 of the 1936 Act.

58 Ibid.; 'Employment of US Flag Merchant Fleet Seagoing Vessels, 1000 grt and over as of 31/12/55', *Report* 300.

59 US Congress, *Study of the Operations of MARAD and FMB*, Hearings before the Committee on Merchant Marines and Fisheries, 84th Congress, 1st Session, GPO, Washington, 1955, p. 20.

60 US Department of Commerce, MARAD, *US Oceanborne Foreign Trade Route Traffic (1948, 1950, 1951 and 1952)*, GPO, Washington, part 2.

61 US Department of Commerce, MARAD, *The Annual Report of MARAD on Fiscal Year 1972*, GPO, Washington, para. VII, pp. 84 and 85.

62 Ibid., *Fiscal Year 1973*, para. IV, p. 69.

63 *The Rochdale Report*, op.cit., para. 209, pp. 56–7.

64 US Department of Commerce, MARAD, *Maritime Subsidies*, GPO, Washington, 1978, pp. 169–70.

65 M.L. Fair and E.W. Williams, *Economics of Transportation and Logistics*, Business Publications, Dallas, 1973.

66 D.F. Pegrum, *Transportation: Economics and Public Policy*, 3rd edn, R.D. Irwin, Homewood, Illinois, 1973.

67 H.S. Norton, *Modern Transportation Economics*, 2nd edn, Charles E. Merrill Publishing Co., Columbus, Ohio, 1971.

68 'Irish container industry — tanked up for action' [tanker container manufacture], *Cargo Systems International*, vol. 7, no. 9, September 1980, p. 43.

69 US Department of Commerce, MARAD, *Maritime Subsidies*, GPO, Washington, November 1978, p. 80.

70 'Ireland' [features on Irish Offshore development], *Oilman*, 28 June 1980, pp. 14–17.

71 R. Legion, 'Shipping and the EEC', [EEC Regulations and decisions on shipping], *Seaways*, October 1980, pp. 13–16.

72 'Republic of Ireland' [Shipping, Shipbuilding, Ports, Finance, Oil], *Lloyd's List*, 5 April 1979, pp. 5–11.

73 The other TMNs are Canada, Denmark, Finland, France, Italy, Japan, Netherlands, Norway, Spain, Sweden, UK and USA.

74 'Indian container manufacturing plans hot up', *Cargo Systems International*, vol. 6, no. 7, July 1979, pp. 91–3.

75 'Nagpas v. India 2: Merchant marine — an evaluation', *Navy International*, vol. 83, no. 7, July 1978, pp. 26–8.

76 The other DMNs doing this are Argentina, Brazil, South Korea, Pakistan, Peru, Venezuela, etc.

77 Department of State *Bulletin*, 'Diplomatic adjustments by the maritime nations', 17 January 1966, pp. 78–85.

78 D. Marx, Jr., *International Shipping Cartels*, Princeton University Press, Princeton, NJ, 1953, chapter 2.

79 For the DMNs, see D. Tresselt, 'Shipping and shipping policy in Latin America', *Smaskrifter*, no. 21, Bergen, 1967, generally.

80 J. Puty, 'To scrap or not to scrap', *Nautical Review*, vol. 3, no. 3, March 1979, pp. 5–7.

81   'Italian marine industries' [shipping, RORO, liners, shipbuilding, ports, etc.], *Fairplay Shipping International*, vol. 270, no. 4990, 19 April, p. 33.

82   'Shipbuilding and allied activities in Italy' [shipbuilding, engine building], *Shipbuilding and Marine Engineering International*, vol. 102, no. 1229, June 1979, pp. 233–48.

83   'Italy' [shipowners, shipbuilding, ship repair, ports], *Norwegian News*, vol. 6, no. 48, 7 December 1979, pp. 19–23.

84   S.G. Sturmey, op.cit., p. 121.

85   T. Kadoi, 'Shipbuilding under reduced facilities' [outlook for shipbuilding in Japan], *Zosen*, vol. 24, no. 11, February 1980, pp. 17–19.

86   G. Nakamura, 'Diversification in Japanese shipbuilding industries', ibid., pp. 24–7.

87   'US Report' [shipping, trade, shipbuilding, energy, safety, technology], *Seatrade*, vol. 8, no. 6, June 1978, pp. 113–25.

88   Waitehouse, 'Maritime spring clean' [US shipping policy], *Seatrade*, vol. 8, no. 5, May 1978, pp. 3–4.

89   'US shipbuilding', *Marine Engineers Review*, July 1978, pp. 1–10.

90   'Review of the shipbuilding and ship repairing industries in the US east coast', *Shipping World and Shipbuilding*, no. 3927, January 1978, pp. 55–7.

91   D.M. Keezer *et al.*, *New Forces in American Business*, McGraw-Hill Book Co., New York, 1969, 1959, section on transport.

92   McGraw-Hill Survey 1958 revealed that the USA needed $95 billion to modernize.

93   Modernization in a maritime sense.

94   'Canada Report' [Arctic development, shipping, commodities, shipbuilding, ports], *Seatrade*, vol. 9, no. 8, August 1979, pp. 97–107.

95   'Canadian marine industries', *Lloyd's List*, Special Report, 30 April 1981, pp. 5–7.

96   D. Tinsley, 'Seeking greater freedom in La France Libre' [French shipping], *Fairplay Shipping International*, vol. 269, no. 4985, 18 March 1979, pp. 7–10.

97   M.D. Revel, 'Financial needs and trends of international shipping', *Maritime Management*, vol. 2, no. 2, March 1979, pp. 7–10.

98   'Belgian marine industries' [shipping, shipbuilding, ports], *Fairplay Shipping International*, vol. 269, no. 4984, 8 March 1979, pp. 37–45.

99   Ibid.

100   The other TMNs are Spain and the USA; there is evidence among the DMNs.

101   Normally yard conversion, port development and/or expansion go together.

102   J.P. Dobler, 'Restructuring French shipbuilding industry offers high technology', *Norwegian News*, vol. 37, no. 6, May 1981, pp. 87–90.

103   'French shipbuilding and allied industries' (survey), *Mot. Ship* (Suppl.), May 1981, pp. 5–15.

104   'Norway: land of the entrepreneurs' [shipping and shipbuilding], *Shipping World and Shipbuilding*, April 1980, pp. 231–4.

105   'Shipping in the Spanish national budget', *Norwegian News*, vol. 10, 17 November 1978, pp. 12–13.

106   'West German marine industries – a special report' [shipping, shipbuilding,

ports], *Fairplay Shipping International*, vol. 267, no. 4959, 14 September 1978, pp. 41-62.

107 A.G.A. Clement, 'A promising future for owners and builders', *Latin American Shipping*, 1979, p. 13.

108 R.N. Hornick, *Indonesian Maritime Law*, vol. 8, no. 1, October 1976, pp. 73-85.

109 'Still the world's ship repair bargain basement' [Singapore, Malaysia, Philippines, Indonesia, Hong Kong], *Shipcare Maritime Management*, vol. 12, no. 9, October 1980, p. 35.

110 *N.Y. Life Insurance Co. v. Anderson*, CCA, NY 263F 527, p. 529 for definition of another dispute following claims on depreciation.

111 *Boston & A.R. Co. v. New York Cent. R. Co.*, 256 Mass. 600, 166 Wis. 163 NW 652, p. 655.

112 That is, this para. and the next; and in this case *People ex rel. Adwondack Power & Light Co. v. Public Service Co.*, 193, NYS, 186, 191, 200 AD 268.

113 It represents only what observation and experience suggest as likely to happen, with a margin over.

114 *Southern Bell Tele & Bell Tele Co. v. Rail Commission of South Carolina*, DCSC 5F 2d, 77, p. 96, interpreting whether covered by the US tax system.

115 'Has shipbuilding a future in Western Europe?', *Norwegian News*, no. 17, 14 September 1979, pp. 29-31, discussing alternative interest subsidies.

116 'West German marine industries', *Fairplay Shipping International*, vol. 272, no. 5014, 4 October 1979, pp. 21-36.

117 Ibid.; H.L. Beth, 'Restructuring of European industries and shipbuilding', *European Shipping and Shipbuilding* (Conference Proceedings), 1978, pp. 99-116.

118 'West German marine industries', *Fairplay Shipping International*, vol. 267, no. 4959, pp. 41-62 at p. 50.

119 UNCTAD Secretariat, Report by, *International Transoceanic Transport and Economic Development*, Geneva and New York, 1969, para. 4.

120 The other TMNs are Australia, Belgium, Canada, France, Italy, Japan, the Netherlands, Norway, Sweden and the USA; the only other DMNs are Taiwan and India.

121 Ibid. in connection with ELOSOC Resolution 1372 (SLV).

122 Ibid., 'Concerning activities of the UN system of organisation in the transport field' (TD/B/C.4/46), 6 January 1969.

123 See also UNCTAD, Secretariat *Report* by, Document No. (TD/B/C.4/36), 13 December 1968.

124 H. Terborgh, *Realistic Depreciation Policy*, Machinery and Allied Products Institute, Washington DC, 1954, chapter 2.

125 E. Grant and P. Horton, Jr., *Depreciation*, The Ronald Press Co., New York, 1949, especially table 10.

126 H.A. Finney and H.E. Miller, *Principles of Accounting*, 5th edn, Prentice-Hall Inc., Englewood Cliffs, NJ, 1957, generally.

127 H. Bierman, *Managerial Accounting Introduction*, The Macmillan Co., New York, 1959, especially chapter 5.

128 US Treasury Department Publications 456 (7-62), *Depreciation Guidelines and Rules*, Rule 10.

129 R. Silto *et al.*, 'Depreciation: a special report', *Journal of Taxation*, May 1963, whole supplement.

130 'Australia' [shipping, trade unions, container services, shipbuilding], *Marine Week*, vol. 5, no. 23, 23 June 1978, pp. 9–14.

131 F.E. Phillips, 'The INNOVATIVE national line' [Australia national line], *Containerisation*, vol. 14, no. 3, March 1980, pp. 26–30.

132 R.M. Black, 'The Austra shipper — his shipping needs', *Australian Symposium on Shipping Management* (Conference Proceedings), vol. 1, November 1977, pp. 17–20 discussing the advantages.

133 Ibid., vol. II, pp. 1–2.

134 In re-Lallar's Estate, 362, III. 621 1 N.E. 2nd 50, 53 (American case on subsidies).

135 H.W. Carter and Y.W.P. Snaveley, *Intermediate Economic Analysis*, McGraw-Hill Book Co., New York, pp. 343–7.

136 J. Conrad, *An Introduction to the Theory of Interest*, University of California Press, Berkeley, Calif., 1959, pp. 100–3.

137 *McLondon v. Johnson*, 71 GA. App. 424, 31 S.E. 2nd, 89, p. 92 (Swedish vessel).

138 'Combating the loan shark', *Law and Contemporary Problems*, Winter 1941, pp. 25–6.

139 'The Swedish shipbuilding bill', *Norwegian News*, 23 November–8 December 1978, pp. 18 and 21.

140 B. Wallin, 'Sweden, one of the world's great carrying nations' [Survey], *Shipbroker*, vol. 4, no. 2, March 1978, pp. 21–9.

141 'Swedish marine industries: first signs of Spring?', *Fairplay Shipping International*, vol. 278, no. 5101, 4 June 1981, pp. 26–32.

142 'Scandinavia: marine industries survey', *Zosen*, vol. 25, no. 13, March 1981, 50pp.

143 J.S. Banks, 'Scandinavian liner companies — maintaining a bold front with a massive investment in ro-ro', *Cargo Systems International*, vol. 6, no. 2, February 1979, pp. 28–31.

144 'Report on Scandinavia' [shipping, shipbuilding], *Fairplay Shipping International*, vol. 270, no. 4992, 3 April 1979, pp. 8–14.

145 'Sweden' [special reports on shipping, shipbuilding, ports], *Lloyd's List*, 31 May 1979, pp. 5–13.

146 'Emerging maritime loans', C.1, S.2, *The Draco*, 7 February, Cas.1, 042.

147 W.W. Smith, 'Monetary theories of the rate of interest: a dynamic analysis', *Review of Economics and Statistics*, vol. XL, pp. 15–21.

148 'The loan shark problems today', *Law and Contemporary Problems*, Winter 1954; cf. Note 187.

149 J.M. Keynes, *The General Theory of Employment, Interest and Money*, Harcourt, Brace and World, Inc., New York, 1936, especially Introduction.

150 See again Fisher, I., *The Theory of Interest*, op.cit., New York, 1954.

151 'The case for maritime subsidies', *Tanker Bulker International*, vol. 4, no. 5, May 1978, pp. 18–19.

152 J. de Tony, 'Netherlands marine industries . . .', *Fairplay Shipping International*, vol. 276, no. 5076, 11 November 1980, pp. 27–33.

153 'The Netherlands . . .', *Lloyd's List*, 16 April 1981, p. 5015.

384

154 Ibid., p. 16.
155 See again 'The case for maritime subsidies', op.cit., p. 20.
156 The other TMNs besides the Netherlands are Denmark and the USA; there is no evidence of this practice among the DMNs.
157 Note that between 1 July 1950 and 30 June 1961 the USA spent $57.3 billion on this.
158 US Joint Economic Committee, *Subsidy and Subsidy-like Programs of the US Government*, GPO, Washington DC, 1960.
159 *Securities & Exchange Commission v. Wickham*, D.C. Minm. 12F, Suppl. 245, p. 247 on whether subsidized vessel should compete with an unsubsidized vessel.
160 'Australia — special report', *Lloyd's List*, 10 August 1978, pp. 4-15.
161 'East Asia and Australia' [Survey], *Nov. Oil*, vol. 5, no. 2, February 1978, pp. 63-5.
162 P.M. Heaton, 'In Eastern waters', *Sea Breezes*, vol. 53, no. 408, December 1979, pp. 761-5.
163 'West Germany' [Survey], *Marine Weekly*, vol. 5, no. 32, 1 September 1978, pp. 16-22.
164 The only other TMN is Japan; there is no evidence of any DMNs.
165 N. Buchanan and H.S. Ellis, *Approaches to Economic Development*, The Twentieth Century Fund, New York, 1955, chapter 16 on the OECD.
166 Commission of Foreign Economic Policy, *Staff Papers*, GPO, Washington DC, 1954, pp. 126-34.
167 C.W. Venhausser, 'The US merchant marine at the crossroads', *Port Baltimore Bulletin*, November 1980, p. 22.
168 L.C. Kendall, 'The modern American merchant marine', *US Naval Institute Proceedings*, October 1979, pp. 70-6.
169 See 'Germany' [Survey], *Asian Shipping*, no. 22, October 1980, pp. 19-23.
170 J. Pearson, 'Shipping and the EEC', *Seaways*, July 1981, pp. 11-15.
171 See 'The FRG', *Lloyd's List*, 16 April 1981, pp. 5-15.
172 The other TMNs are the UK and Greece; and the DMNs are China (Taiwan) and Singapore.
173 *Moore v. Sampson Country*, 220 N.C. 232, 17 S.E.2d, 22, at p. 23 (FRG company).
174 *US v. Marine Co.*, CCA Ill., 90F. 2d 549, p. 551 (FRG vessel).
175 See also 'Singapore' [Government subsidies], *Asian Shipping*, April 1981, pp. 57-8.
176 See also 'Singapore Report', *Shipcare and Maritime Management*, vol. 13, nos 18-26.
177 'Singapore Report', *Zosen*, vol. 25, no. 2, May 1980, pp. 16-18.
178 US Treasury Department, *Your Federal Income Tax Annually*.
179 L.H. Seltzer, *The Place of the Personal Exemptions in the Present Day Income Tax — Taxation Revision Compendium*, vol. 1, Tax Foundation, New York, 1959, pp. 449-514.
180 US Internal Revenue Code, US Treasury Department, *Our Federal Tax Annually*.
181 Ibid.
182 H. Kahn, *Personal Deductions in the Federal Income Tax*, National

Bureau of Economic Research Inc., Princeton University Press, NJ, 1960.
183 Customs exemptions (post) are also a form of tax relief.
184 J.R.C. Boyes, 'No quick fix for US marine industry', *Containerisation*, vol. 15, no. 15, 6 June 1981, pp. 32–6.
185 S. Wade, 'US shipping policy in the melting pot', *Fairplay Shipping International*, vol. 279, no. 6105, 2 July 1981, p. 47.
186 H. Levy, 'US liner shipping policy', *International Container Industry Conference Proceedings*, November 1977, pp. 17–22.
187 R.J. Blackwell, *Implementation of the Merchant Marine Act, 1970*, vol. 5, no. 2, January 1974, pp. 167–81.
188 R.S. Agman, 'Competition, rationalization and US shipping policy', *Maritime Law and Commerce*, vol. 7, no. 1, October 1976, pp. 1–50.
189 C.J. MacGuire and R.E. McDaniel in *Proceedings of the Maritime Safety Conference*, vol. 38, no. 4, June 1981, pp. 43–99.
190 'Midyear review', *Fairplay Shipping International*, vol. 267, no. 4950, 13 July 1981, pp. 48–89.
191 R.E. Madigan, *Taxation of the Shipping Industry*, Cornell Maritime Press, Cambridge, Maryland, 54pp.
192 *The Rochdale Report*, op.cit., para. 172, p. 49.
193 'US Report', *Seatrade*, vol. 81, no. 6, June 1978, pp. 113–25.
194 P. Goldman, 'Alternative proposal for US maritime policy', *Seatrade*, vol. 10, no. 1, January 1980, pp. 25–7.
195 46 USC Title 27 (1976 edn), p. 711.
196 46 USC Title 27 Section 1161.
197 Ibid., Section 1151.
198 Ibid., Section 1171 (g).
199 Ibid., Section 1161'1) on 'Taxation of deposits upon failure of conditions'.
200 Ibid., Section 1161 (n).
201 'Australia' [report], *Marine Week*, vol. 5, no. 23, 23 June 1978, pp. 9–14.
202 P.T. Ellsworth, *The International Economy*, The Macmillan Co., New York, 1958.
203 C.P. Kindleberger, *International Economics*, op.cit.
204 Ibid.
205 See 'Canadian Restrictive Trade Practices Commission', para. 437, p. 126 of *The Rochdale Report*, op.cit.
206 Cf. D.P. O'Connell, 'The federal problem concerning the maritime domain in Commonwealth countries', *Journal of Maritime Law and Commerce*, vol. 1, no. 1, October 1969–70, pp. 441–2.
207 C. Hayman, 'Canadian shipowners make their feelings known', *Seatrade*, vol. 8, no. 7, July 1978, p. 15.
208 J. Shaw, 'Empressor Maxitimas Lineas, Argentinas SA', *Asian Shipping*, May 1981, p. 709.
209 R.A. Musgrave, *A Theory of Public Finance*, McGraw-Hill Book Co., New York, 1959, part 1.
210 A.H. Hansen, *Fiscal Policy and Business Cycles*, W.W. Norton and Co. Inc., New York, 1941, pp. 58–9.
211 W.P. Engle, *Economic Stabilization*, Princeton University Press, NJ, 1952, pp. 75–6.

212 *Strustman v. Des Meines City Ry. Co.*, 180 Iowa, 524, 163, N.W. 580, p. 585 (the plaintiffs in this case relied on that argument).

213 P.A. Samuelson, *Economics*, 5th edn, McGraw-Hill Book Co., 1961, pp. 275-7.

214 G. Ackley, *Macroeconomic Theory*, The Macmillan Co., New York, 1961, pp. 424-39.

215 S.H. Slichter, *Reconciling Expansion with a Stable Price Level: Problems of the US Economic Development*, Committee for Economic Development, vol. 1, New York, 1958.

216 D. Tinsley, 'Knowing where one's strength lies' [French report], *Fairplay Shipping International*, 1979, pp. 13-15.

217 'France' [Survey], *Marine Week*, vol. 6, no. 30, 27 July 1979, pp. 21-5.

218 The other TMNs are the Netherlands and the USA; the DMNs are Brazil and South Korea.

219 W.L. Thorpe and R.E. Quandt, *The New Inflation*, McGraw-Hill Book Co., New York, 1959; see also Note 217.

220 'France's maritime strategy', *Navy International*, vol. 85, no. 10, October 1980, pp. 588-92.

221 US Chamber of Commerce, *An Introduction to Doing Business*, op.cit.

222 'Denmark' [Survey], *Shipbroker*, vol. 5, no. 6, November 1979, pp. 21-5.

223 W. Schmidt, 'No reduction in Danish fleet', *Norwegian News*, no. 5, 9 March 1979, pp. 5-7.

224 'British shipbuilders' [Survey report], *Mot. Ship.*, vol. 59, no. 704, March 1979, Suppl. 18pp.

225 'UK shipping' [Survey], *Shipping World and Shipbuilding*, vol. 175, no. 3978, July–August 1981, p. 8.

226 'British shipping: another year of crisis', *Norwegian News*, vol. 37, no. 1, January 1981, pp. 76-7.

227 See also *Seatrade*, vol. II, no. 1, January 1981.

228 US Joint Economic Committee, *Staff Report on Employment Growth and the Price Levels*, GPO, Washington DC, December 1959.

229 H.J. Richardson, *The Economics and Financial Aspects of Social Security*, University of Toronto Press, 1960.

230 'Greece' [Survey], *Norwegian News*, vol. 37, no. 1, January 1981, pp. 79-81.

231 'Greece' [Report], *Marine Weekly*, vol. 6, no. 11, November 1979, pp. 19-24.

232 'Greece' [Report], *Lloyd's Shipping Economist*, vol. 2, no. 9, September 1980, pp. 8-14.

233 'Greek shipbuilding', *Fairplay Shipping International*, vol. 274, no. 5046, 15 May 1980, pp. 51-69.

234 'Greek example', *Lloyd's Shipping Manager*, vol. 1, no. 2, May 1980, pp. 9-11.

235 E.M. Burns, *Social Security and Public Policy*, McGraw-Hill Book Co., New York, 1956.

236 'Italian' [Report], *Mot. Ship.*, Special Survey, 1980, 32pp.

237 'Italy' [Survey], *Marine Week*, vol. 6, no. 4, 26 January 1979, pp. 23-9.

238 'Italy' [Review], *Shipping World and Shipbuilding*, vol. 174, no. 3969, October 1980, pp. 8-14.

239 J. Press, 'The collapse of the contributory pension scheme', *Transportation History*, vol. 5, no. 2, September 1979, pp. 91-115.

240 Cf. 'Greek example', op.cit., pp. 9-11.

241 D. Bess, 'The maritime academics are all wet', US Naval Institute Proceedings, October 1979, pp. 70-6.

242 G. Rich, 'The Plymouth experience', *European Shipping and Shipbuilding* (Conference Proceedings), 1978, pp. 51-74.

243 V. Carlson, *Economic Security in the US*, McGraw-Hill Book Co., New York, 1962.

244 See 'Canadian shipping', *Lloyd's List*, 20 April 1978, p. 6.

245 Cf. A. Wallace, 'Denmark' [Report], *Fairplay Shipping International*, vol. 266, no. 4941, 11 May 1978, pp. 8-10.

246 Training, 'Governments, universities and industry involved', *Offshore Engineer*, February 1978, pp. 23-8.

247 'The Netherlands' [Special report], *Lloyd's List*, 17 April 1980, pp. 5-17.

248 'Dutch government sails in with rescue package', *Seatrade*, vol. 8, no. 4, April 1978, pp. 16-19.

249 *The Rochdale Report*, op.cit., paras 683-87, pp. 183-7.

250 Ibid., chapter 12, paras 649-779, pp. 180-221.

251 D.C. Watt, 'Integrated policy for the oceans — teaching in the university', *World Marine Policy*, vol. 4, no. 1, January 1980, pp. 67-9.

252 'Nautical colleges', *Seaways*, August 1980, pp. 18-22.

PART V
SHIPPING IN
INTERNATIONAL FINANCE

9 Shipping and foreign exchange

Introduction: Foreign Exchange Problems

Detailed analysis of the relationship between shipping and the balance of payments in a country's national and international economy is adequately covered in the *Rochdale Report*.[1] Further coverage is also provided in the next chapter including some mention of foreign exchange. This chapter is therefore a forerunner to the subsequent one. The main considerations for, especially, the DMNs establishing and/or developing their own national fleets are:[2]

1 The role of merchant marines as a factor in national or regional economic development and, in particular, the diversification of their economic structure;
2 The relative priority of investment in shipping as compared with investment in other sectors;
3 The net effect of shipping operations on the balance of payments generally, and theirs in particular;
4 National merchant marines as a factor in securing employment within a country; and
5 National merchant marines as an instrument for the promotion of exports from these countries.[3]

Thus, foreign exchange has already been established as a major factor in the shipping aspirations of the DMNs. There is in fact a correlation

Table 9.1 Shipping's contribution to the current accounts of leading maritime nations

(a) GREECE

(million SDRs/%)		1975	1976	1977	1978	1979
Current account						
Credits	(1)	3,621	4,346	4,932	5,488	6,844
Debits	(2)	4,343	5,150	5,859	6,264	8,308
Balance	(3)	-722	-804	-927	-776	-1,464
thereof shipment						
Credits	(4)	45	41	56	59	60
Debits	(5)	169	202	231	246	327
freight	(6)	145	173	199	212	282
insurance	(7)	24	29	32	34	45
Balance	(8)	-124	-161	-175	-187	-267
Percentages						
(4) : (1)		1.2	0.9	1.1	1.1	0.9
(6) : (2)		3.3	3.4	3.4	3.4	3.4
(8) : (3)		17.2	20.0	18.9	24.1	18.2

(b) JAPAN

(billion SDRs/%)		1975	1976	1977	1978	1979
Current account						
Credits	(1)	56.43	69.94	82.08	91.36	97.99
Debits	(2)	56.94	66.73	72.75	77.36	104.72
Balance	(3)	-0.51	3.21	9.33	14.00	-6.73
thereof shipment						
Credits (freight)	(4)	2.58	3.30	3.43	3.47	3.94
Debits (freight)	(5)	2.24	2.29	2.09	2.29	2.91
Balance	(6)	0.34	1.01	1.34	1.18	1.03
Percentages						
(4) : (1)		4.6	4.7	4.2	3.8	4.0
(5) : (2)		3.9	3.4	2.9	3.0	2.8

(c) NORWAY

(million SDRs/%)		1975	1976	1977	1978	1979
Current account						
Credits	(1)	10,085	11,443	12,553	13,722	16,669
Debits	(2)	12,135	14,721	16,893	15,397	17,564
Balance	(3)	-2,050	-3,278	-4,340	-1,675	-895

thereof shipment

		1975	1976	1977	1978	1979
Credits	(4)	2,439	2,530	2,548	2,504	3,161
Debits	(5)	164	166	181	157	184
Balance	(6)	2,275	2,364	2,367	2,347	2,977
Percentages						
(4) : (1)		24.2	22.1	20.3	18.2	19.0
(5) : (2)		1.4	1.1	1.1	1.0	1.0
(6) : (1)		22.6	20.7	18.9	17.1	17.9

(d) UNITED STATES
(billion SDRs/%)

		1975	1976	1977	1978	1979
Current account						
Credits	(1)	129.04	149.32	159.02	177.21	222.76
Debits	(2)	113.92	145.55	171.01	188.83	223.29
Balance	(3)	15.12	3.77	-11.99	-11.62	-0.53
thereof shipment						
Credits						
freight on export	(4)	0.97	1.20	1.06	1.14	1.34
ocean freight on other shipments	(5)	0.28	0.30	0.34	0.33	0.37
Debits						
freight on imports	(6)	2.51	3.44	3.96	4.26	4.65
passenger services						
Debits (ocean fares)	(7)	0.23	0.23	0.22	0.21	0.20
other transportation						
Credits						
charters	(8)	0.07	—	0.03	0.03	0.05
port disbursements	(9)	3.00	3.76	4.17	4.47	5.09
Debits						
charters	(10)	0.31	0.29	0.30	0.30	0.32
port disbursements	(11)	1.56	1.81	2.03	2.10	2.58
credits (4) + (5) + (8) + (9)	(12)	4.32	5.26	5.60	5.97	6.85
debits (6) + (7) + (10) + (11)	(13)	4.61	5.77	6.51	6.87	7.75
balance (12) – (13)	(14)	-0.29	-0.51	-0.91	-0.90	-0.90
Percentages						
(12) : (1)		3.3	3.5	3.5	3.4	3.1
(13) : (2)		4.0	4.0	3.8	3.6	3.5

Source: Blumenhagen, *Shipping and the Balance of Payments*, table 111/5, pp. 19–20.

393

between the indebtedness of the DMNs and the fact that they still largely depend on shipping and related services provided by foreigners — mainly by the TMNs.[4] On the basis of the reasons advanced by those DMNs that have established merchant marines, the main sources of indirect effects on the flow of income resulting from the establishment of a shipping fleet appear to have been expected through:[5]

1 Prevention of disruptions of shipping services during hostilities in which the country concerned is not directly involved;
2 Reduction of economic dependence;
3 Influencing conference decisions;
4 Economic integration;
5 Diversification of employment; and once more
6 Improvement of foreign exchange positions.[6]

All the other issues have been dealt with in the foregone chapters of this study with topics 5 and 6 being the subject-matter of this and the next chapter. The link between shipping and foreign exchange is due to the former's crucial role in development, fostering foreign trade and its dual role as both an item of foreign trade as well as its most important servant:[7] its conveyor. For shipping's contribution to the current accounts of the leading maritime nations, see Table 9.1.

Key Role of Shipping

Transport and Development

There is a strong link between transport and development, although shipping as an essential element of the transportation network is more related to international development. The objective of an international economic development policy[8] is to increase the real income of the world community, paying particular attention to means of increasing the rate of growth of real income per head especially in the DMNs. International transport has a role to play in this process. In order to achieve maximum rate of growth of real income,[9] countries must trade with each other in such a way that each makes optimum use of its specialized forms of production. Before this international trade can be effective in curing conditions of poverty, a number of conditions have to be fulfilled.[10] One is that all countries should have free access to the world markets, since, limitations affecting access to markets hampers the economic development of the DMNs especially. Another condition is that there must be adequate transport services[11] between countries, operated efficiently and charging the lowest prices consistent with the long-term maintenance of those services.

In the absence of international trade all countries are supposed to be self-sufficient in the sense that they can consume and invest only that which they have produced. On the other hand, international trade permits specializations in production, with each country producing those goods in which it has comparative advantage[12] and importing those which it cannot produce or can produce only at prohibitive costs. Hence the Law of Comparative Advantage or the principle of International Division of Labour. The process of development also includes the establishment or expansion of domestic industries.[13] Domestic industries are necessary because many economic activities which cannot form the basis of international trade are still an essential part of domestic development. But, like many elements in the infrastructure,[14] they are also needed to facilitate trade in the production of those goods which can be economically produced beyond the needs of the home market. Although domestic industries supplying the domestic market are important, economic development is always associated with the expansion of international trade.[15] The existing transport needs of the DMNs are the results of the past development in their economies which have led to particular trading patterns, with less emphasis on export trade.

Future development is likely to produce an increase in, and a changing pattern of, trading leading to both an increase in transport requirements and a change in the pattern of routes and types of facilities used.[16] The major mode of transport currently used in international trade is sea transport especially in cases where the trading partners are non-contiguous. However, in considering transport requirements, the needs for land transport between contiguous territories and for intermodal transport links in the case of landlocked countries must not be forgotten.[17] Besides, goods rarely travel from the point of supply to the point of demand entirely by sea and, as already mentioned, sea transport must essentially be regarded as one link in a transport chain which normally involves the use of two or more modes.[18] In addition the role of air freighting must be taken into account, although this is currently more important in trade between the TMNs than in the trade of the DMNs.

The aspect of air transport of greatest importance to the DMNs is its speed which makes it possible to reduce stockholding,[19] with consequent economies in the use of scarce capital for this purpose. If sea transport is used for goods with a fluctuating demand, the level of stocks in relation to the annual volume of trade has to be high if buyers are not to be kept waiting indefinitely for supplies.[20] Hence

Table 9.2 UK owned ships: receipts from international services and payments abroad

	1976 Dry cargo £mn	Tanker £mn	1976 Total £mn	1977 Dry cargo £mn	Tanker £mn	1977 Total £mn	1978 Dry cargo £mn	Tanker £mn	1978 Total £mn	1979 Dry cargo £mn	Tanker £mn	1979 Total £mn
RECEIPTS FROM INTERNATIONAL SERVICES												
Freights												
on UK imports	303	76	379	311	69	380	264	57	321	321	79	400
*on UK exports	403	23	426	474	23	497	392	26	418	406	37	443
**on cross-voyages	454	375	829	507	378	885	441	403	844	443	505	948
Total freights	1,160	474	1,634	1,292	470	1,762	1,097	486	1,583	1,170	621	1,791
Passenger revenue												
collected in UK	83	—	83	95	—	95	103	—	103	109	—	109
*collected abroad	141	—	141	162	—	162	170	—	170	202	—	202
Total passenger revenue	224	—	224	257	—	257	273	—	273	311	—	311
Time charter receipts												
*from abroad	367	239	606	377	195	572	280	183	463	294	306	600
from UK non-shipowners	18	1	19	16	1	17	3	2	5	13	3	16
Total time charter receipts	385	240	625	393	196	589	283	185	468	307	309	616
A Total receipts from international services	1,769	714	2,483	1,942	666	2,608	1,653	671	2,324	1,788	930	2,718
PAYMENTS ABROAD												
Disbursements abroad												
bunkers and lubricants	169	159	328	190	166	356	138	136	274	183	167	350
port and other expenditure	499	161	660	578	158	736	513	136	649	499	205	704
B Total payments abroad	668	320	988	768	324	1,092	651	272	923	682	372	1,054
A–B Total receipts from international services *less* total payments abroad	1,101	394	1,495	1,174	342	1,516	1,002	399	1,401	1,106	558	1,664
CONTRIBUTION TO BALANCE OF PAYMENTS												
a credits—receipts from abroad (total of items marked*)	1,365	637	2,002	1,520	596	2,116	1,283	612	1,895	1,345	848	2,193
b debits—total payments abroad	668	320	988	768	324	1,092	651	272	923	682	372	1,054
a–b Net contribution to balance of payments	+697	+317	+1,014	+752	+272	+1,024	+632	+340	+972	+663	+476	+1,139

Source: General Council of British Shipping, *British Shipping Statistics, 1979/1980*, table 5.1, pp. 88–9.

the important link between transport and development. Table 9.2 shows the receipts from international services and payments abroad for UK-owned shipping.

Shipping and Development

Already in these few pages the crucial role of transport generally and shipping in particular for development has been demonstrated. Some imports — for example, spare parts for capital equipment — are essential for development.[21] Arrangements with overseas suppliers under which goods ordered by cable are air-freighted can ensure quick delivery to customers without the need to hold stocks. Also, in comparison with sea transport, air transport can frequently lead to a reduction in the number of links[22] used in a transport chain, since airports, unlike seaports, are not restricted to locations on the coast or in estuaries. Although the DMNs' trade generates demand for transport facilities, the influence of the supply of transport facilities on the demand for such facilities must always be considered.[23] Where transport facilities of a particular type are provided, only trade which can use those transport facilities can take place. The trade of any country, whether developed or developing, can be hindered if transport facilities of the right type are not available.[24] Investment in the expansion of transport facilities may be induced, that is, arise from a change in the pattern or size of demand which comes clear to the transport operators. However, in the context of economic development, the most important type of investment in transport is likely to be that which is autonomous[25] — i.e. that which occurs before the need becomes manifest and in the expectation that the provision of appropriate transport facilities will generate the necessary trade to make the investment economic.

In the case of induced investments it might be expected that in a freely competitive system, the profit motive of transport operators would lead them to supply the transport facilities required. In certain important respects, however, international transport is not freely competitive.[26] Although, in the long run, it may be that potential needs are normally fulfilled by the supply of appropriate transport facilities, in the short run this is not however necessarily the case. Indeed, the short run may be quite long, since some years may elapse before the transport system leads to potential demands, the realization of which has been hindered by a lack of appropriate facilities.[27] Historically private enterprise has been an important source of autonomous investments in transport generally and maritime transport in particular. In the modern world, however, such investments in the DMNs depend largely on government action and on the provision of capital through international agencies.[28] However, the statement that there is a close relationship between the existence of a transport and economic development is not entirely true. Transport is of course, not the only determinant of economic development but it is a decisive factor.[29] Secondly, the causal relationship between the existence of a transport system and economic development is not one-way — in other words transport influences economic development but at the same time is influenced by it.[30]

Nevertheless, it can generally be said that the structure and the speed of development of a national economy largely depend on the extent, and even more on the quality, of a transport system. Whenever people consume more products or products other than those they produce themselves[31] a transport system is needed to bridge the gap between production and consumption centres. This can be the case within a national economy or it can involve foreign trade based on the international division of labour. Before embarking on the role of shipping in foreign trade it is perhaps worth a reminder that all this is supposed to assist economic development:[32] the process of growth in total and per capita incomes especially in the case of the DMNs, accompanied by fundamental changes in the structure of their economies. These changes generally consist of increasing the importance of industrial activities, lessening the dependence on imports for the more advanced products and consumer goods and on agricultural or mineral products as main exports, and finally diminishing reliance on aid[33] from other countries to provide funds for investments and thus building a capacity to generate growth themselves. Associated with this economic process would be important social and political reform, the main objective of economic development being to raise the living standard and general wellbeing of the people in the economy.[34] For the international seaborne trade of the UK by flag carrier, see Table 9.3.

Shipping and International Trade

International trade is a prerequisite for economic growth and welfare and is one of the decisive factors for stimulating industrialization and the growth of the local markets for goods and services. Furthermore trade fosters the development of an advanced agricultural sector and techniques and increases the speed of development.[35] In order to engage in international trade any country needs a functional transport system or ready access to a means of transport, such as shipping. While, in general, all means of transport can serve to foster international trade activities, shipping is of the utmost importance, especially in the foreign trade of the DMNs.[36] While its importance to

Table 9.3 International seaborne trade of the United Kingdom: by flag of carrier

Percentage

	Dry cargo				Tanker cargo				All cargo			
	1983		1984		1983		1984		1983		1984	
	Weight	Value	Weight	Value	Weight	Value	Weight	Value	Weight	Value	Weight	Value
Exports[1]												
United Kingdom	29.5	37.2	29.0	39.3	20.2	20.8	21.5	22.3	23.5	32.8	24.0	34.6
FR of Germany[2]	14.7	12.4	14.5	11.9	7.4	7.5	6.0	6.2	10.0	11.1	8.8	10.3
Norway	3.3	2.7	2.9	2.1	8.9	9.0	8.8	8.2	6.9	4.4	6.9	3.8
Netherlands	8.7	5.7	9.5	5.5	4.7	4.6	2.6	2.7	6.1	5.4	4.9	4.7
Liberia	1.1	0.9	1.4	1.0	12.1	11.9	12.1	12.1	8.2	3.8	8.6	4.1
Denmark	2.1	2.8	2.2	2.6	0.8	0.9	0.8	0.9	1.2	2.3	1.2	2.1
Other EC[3]	12.6	15.3	13.2	14.6	13.3	13.0	10.6	9.8	13.0	14.6	11.5	13.3
All other flags	28.0	23.0	27.3	23.0	32.6	32.3	37.6	37.8	31.1	25.6	34.1	27.1
All	100.0	100.0	100.0	100.0	100.0	100.0	100.0	100.0	100.0	100.0	100.0	100.0
Imports												
United Kingdom	28.8	38.3	26.6	38.8	18.3	19.5	14.3	15.2	25.4	36.3	22.2	35.8
Liberia	3.4	1.2	4.1	1.4	16.2	15.1	15.6	14.1	7.6	2.7	8.2	3.0
Norway	5.7	2.2	5.9	1.9	12.8	13.0	17.3	17.6	8.2	3.5	9.9	3.9
Greece	3.4	0.8	4.1	0.9	7.1	6.0	8.5	7.8	4.6	1.4	5.6	1.7
FR of Germany[2]	13.4	13.6	15.6	13.8	3.3	4.4	2.6	4.0	10.1	12.6	10.9	12.6
Netherlands	6.2	5.2	6.3	4.7	2.1	2.5	2.6	3.0	4.8	4.9	5.0	4.4
Other EC[3]	10.7	17.5	10.2	17.7	9.5	9.6	9.2	9.4	10.3	16.7	9.8	16.6
All other flags	28.4	21.2	27.2	20.8	30.7	29.9	29.9	28.9	29.0	21.9	28.4	22.0
All	100.0	100.0	100.0	100.0	100.0	100.0	100.0	100.0	100.0	100.0	100.0	100.0

[1] Including re-exports.
[2] Federal Republic of Germany.
[3] European Community.

Source: HMSO Department of Transport, *Transport Statistics Great Britain 1974–1984*, table 4.21.

the TMNs cannot be denied — especially in those countries where virtually all exports and imports are necessarily carried by sea because of geographic location — it can still be claimed that shipping is of relatively greater importance especially to the DMNs.[37] The main reason for this is that the DMNs' foreign trade structure often leaves little or no room for intraregional trade that could possibly be carried by land transport. Economies of neighbouring DMNs show a high degree of similarity in types of cargoes exported or imported.[38] Thus, raw materials and semi-finished products — the DMNs' major export cargoes — are shipped mainly to the industrialized TMNs, while imports originating from these countries consist principally of manufactured goods.

By contrast, the TMNs' foreign trade — particularly that of Western Europe — is directed mainly towards neighbouring countries within the region.[39] Thus, in terms of value, EEC exports in 1980 were directed mainly towards other partner countries (53 per cent) while 51 per cent of total imports originated in these countries. In contrast, in the same year only 4 per cent of imports and 3 per cent of exports of the African DMNs consisted of international trade.[40] Another reason for the heavy dependence of the DMNs' foreign trade on the TMNs originates in the historical ties that link many of them with the industrialized TMNs. This foreign trade dependence on the industrialized TMNs is also reflected in shipping arrangements, which have traditionally been geared to the needs and trading requirements of the TMNs.[41]

Two basic forms of shipping services and related market organizations have evolved over the past century — namely, liner shipping, characterized by the Liner Conferences System, and tramp shipping. Liner shipping as an organizational form has remained basically unchanged, with conferences still functioning in the same way as they did some 110 years ago when the India–Pakistan conferences were founded.[42] Tramp shipping, however, has lost most of its importance in its traditional form, with new shipping arrangements reflecting changing requirements and technological progress in shipping.

While it is not possible to arrive at exact trading shares reflecting the importance of either form of shipping organization, it can be estimated that, in terms of tonnage carried, about 10–20 per cent of world trade moves under liner arrangements.[43] However, the actual importance of liner shipping is only partially reflected in these figures because, owing to the types of cargo carried, its percentage share in value of world trade is considerably higher. These observations on the role of shipping in trade generally and in trade and development in particular apply equally to the provision of port services.[44] The role of seaports will not be covered in detail here save to say that seaports'

400

essential functions are the loading and discharge of ships at their interface with inland transport. Related functions also carried out are storage and import–export formalities. With the exception of land-locked countries, the DMNs almost exclusively use their own ports as gateways for their foreign trade.[45] The primary reason for this is the paucity of overland routes, but there are supporting reasons in the complexity of formalities for transit trade and the safeguarding of foreign exchange. Some foreign trade is virtually tied to national ports — and often to single ports — any inadequacies in port service have an automatic detrimental effect on foreign trade and hence foreign exchange.[46] In particular, if capacity is insufficient, then foreign trade is held up at enormous costs to economic development. Ports have also responded to developments in export practice by developing free ports and free trade zones, such as Southampton and Liverpool in the UK.

The Unique Character of Shipping

The Dual Character of Shipping

In addition to its function in fostering development and foreign trade, shipping has a further unique role.[47] It has a dual character being both a servant to international trade and an industry in its own right: a commodity in foreign trade and, therefore, a factor in the foreign exchange equation. Demand for shipping, as for any other transport service, is always a derived demand, the level of which depends on the type and quantity of goods traded as well as on the geographic trade structure.[48] The fact that there is no *original* demand for cargo ship-ping services underlines the close linkage between trade and shipping. Yet, more important is the fact that shipping services are at the dis-posal of the trading community.[49] Consequently, the shipping industry has not only reacted to trading requirements but has, in many cases, created the preconditions for the expansion of world trade based on an intensified international division of labour. An example of such development can be seen in the rapid growth of trade in bulk commodities over the last two decades, combined with similarly important changes in trading patterns.[50] Reduction in bulk shipping costs based on the exploitation of the economies of scale in transport have resulted in a reduction of economic distance.

The decreasing costs of transport have helped to open up geographically distant markets and thus to reduce if not eliminate the locational linkages between production and processing of raw materials. However it is not the existence of a shipping industry as such that preconditions the expansion of world trade, but rather the provision of services adequate to the different needs of various trading interests.[51] Such adequacy is relevant to all facets of qualitative characteristics of shipping services, that is, the availability of ships physically suitable for the particular transport needs; the frequency of services offered to avoid undue interruptions in commodity flows; and, the pricing of such services in line with the ability of the goods traded to bear the costs of transport.[52] Unless these criteria are met, shipping cannot fulfil its role as a catalyst in world trade. Experience has shown that countries which, for one reason or another, have not been provided with such adequate shipping services, or have been deprived of them, have faced considerable setbacks in their foreign trade and therefore foreign exchange, coupled with corresponding interruptions of their development process.[53] The most effective way of avoiding such disruptions and ensuring the availability of adequate shipping services has been found by most countries to be the maintenance of a certain minimum engagement in shipping.

National carriers can reasonably be expected to maintain a closer link with the particular trading interests of their countries than can foreign carriers.[54] Furthermore, by controlling substantial tonnage in the national foreign trades a country can exercise a countervailing power against practices of foreign carriers that are possibly detrimental to its interests in the trade concerned. This policy is vigorously pursued by the USA. However, these considerations do not justify limiting the role of shipping to that of a servant to trade,[55] for such a perspective would incur the danger of concealing inefficiencies and consequently misallocating resources. Yet they make it sufficiently clear that decisions to invest in shipping cannot be based solely on criteria of commercial profitability at firm level but have to take into account those of viability for the country's economy as a whole.[56] From this it also follows that to compare investment in shipping with that in other sectors of the economy on the basis of direct returns on investments is neither feasible nor meaningful. More attention is devoted to this factor in the next chapter.[57] Suffice it to add, however, that benefits from allocating resources to other sectors depend on the existence of a functional transport system, such as shipping and, conversely, the expansion of shipping activities in complete unison with the development of other sectors of the economy.[58] For the comparative contribution of shipping (sea transport) in both debts and credits in the UK's service summary, see Table 9.4.

Table 9.4 UK services summary

£ million

	1972	1973	1974	1975	1976	1977	1978	1979	1980	1981	1982
					Current prices						
Credits											
General government	72	104	110	139	215	241	318	330	381	439	435
Private sector and public corporations											
Sea transport	1,607	2,055	2,665	2,651	3,233	3,433	3,149	3,804	3,816	3,784	3,565
Civil aviation	410	480	625	780	1,049	1,203	1,455	1,755	2,210	2,359	2,471
Travel	576	726	898	1,218	1,768	2,352	2,507	2,797	2,961	2,970	3,184
Financial services[1]	529	601	785	1,025	1,303	1,391	1,539	1,588	1,601	1,971	2,145
Other services	1,094	1,330	1,645	2,044	2,710	3,283	3,754	4,202	4,818	5,348	5,782
Total credits	4,288	5,296	6,728	7,857	10,278	11,903	12,722	14,476	15,787	16,871	17,582
Debits											
General government	423	513	629	709	867	940	986	1,072	1,014	965	1,239
Private sector and public corporations											
Sea transport	1,688	2,160	2,776	2,562	3,155	3,345	3,162	3,677	3,675	3,944	3,908
Civil aviation	340	415	540	675	840	984	1,176	1,467	1,815	1,922	2,080
Travel	535	695	703	917	1,068	1,186	1,549	2,109	2,738	3,271	3,650
Other services	601	727	1,005	1,479	1,845	2,110	2,033	2,080	2,278	2,520	2,861
Total debits	3,587	4,510	5,653	6,342	7,775	8,565	8,906	10,405	11,520	12,622	13,738
Balance	+701	+786	+1,075	+1,515	+2,503	+3,338	+3,816	+4,071	+4,267	+4,249	+3,844
					Constant prices (1980 = 100)						
Total credits	80	86	93	94	100	103	103	103	100	94	92
Total debits	84	89	91	90	89	88	88	96	100	98	98

[1] Financial services are shown as credit entries only. Similar earnings in the United Kingdom by overseas financial institutions, which are considered negligible, are included in 'other services' debits.

Source: Central Statistics Office 1983, table 3.1.

403

The overall linkage between shipping, trade, development and foreign exchange can best be appreciated further in the light of the current distribution of maritime transport in international trade relations.[59] For, apart from providing a service to trade, shipping as an independent industry has a direct bearing on a country's development process. It helps to improve the foreign exchange situation, creates employment, fosters technology transfer and economic integration and helps to safeguard the national sovereignty, particularly in times of political crises.[60] Apart from these direct effects, shipping investment also contributes substantially to the diversification of the investing country's economy, as it requires a whole range of support industries and services. These include shipbuilding and repairs, supplies, equipment, insurance and banking services, catering, telecommunications, etc.

The problem, however, is the distribution of the industry.[61] The present-day merchant fleet is owned predominantly by the world's TMNs — a small group of countries which are now advanced in shipping and which have between them owned the bulk of world tonnage throughout the present century. They reached this position partly through the advantage of early industrialization and partly as a result of the trading needs of their colonial and associated territories (as in the case of the UK).[62] Furthermore, they reached this dominant position partly because the expansion of world trade provided opportunities for economic advancement in shipping, which the national resources of the countries did not otherwise provide (e.g. Norway);[63] and partly through deliberate assistance to their fleets for reasons of national policy (e.g. the USA).

Over the last half century four major factors appear to have led to the emergence of shipping fleets in many previously non-maritime countries.[64]

1 The disruption of shipping services caused by the withdrawal of tonnage from commercial services during the Second World War;
2 The balance of payments problems in the years following the Second World War which placed a premium on the savings of foreign exchange and gave rise to a great number of bilateral trading arrangements — many of which contained shipping clauses;
3 The attainment of independence by colonial territories and the subsequent emergence of national consciousness; and, most importantly,
4 The conscious efforts being made by countries with lower per capita income to develop and diversify their economies.[65]

Table 9.5 Services transactions of general government (UK)

£ million

	1972	1973	1974	1975	1976	1977	1978	1979	1980	1981	1982
Credits											
European Community Institutions	—	13	21	34	46	78	94	115	112	122	150
US forces expenditure	19	19	18	21	25	40	50	43	74	90	75
Other military receipts by UK government	22	45	38	42	84	63	116	94	108	127	119
Other receipts	31	27	33	42	60	60	58	78	87	100	91
Total credits	72	104	110	139	215	241	318	330	381	439	435
Debits											
Military											
General Federal Republic	184	248	304	350	439	541	540	607	629	636	728
Other	166	176	228	245	292	259	293	296	209	126	310
Administrative, diplomatic, etc.	73	89	97	114	136	140	153	169	176	203	201
Total debits	423	513	629	709	867	940	986	1,072	1,014	965	1,239
Balance	-351	-409	-519	-570	-652	-699	-668	-742	-633	-526	-804

Source: Central Statistics Office 1983, table 3.2, p. 21.

Mention should also be made of the development of fleets by the STNs, which has, in many cases, been related to the developments of shipbuilding industries to service these fleets. In some STNs, for example Poland and Yugoslavia, the shipbuilding part of the development has reached the point where it has become an important export industry in itself, selling ships to both the TMNs and DMNs.[66] The role played by shipping in the economic development of these countries is something which the DMNs might usefully consider in connection with the establishment and development of their own national merchant marines. Despite these changes, however, a considerable gap remains between the shipping capacity and international trade of the TMNs and DMNs respectively.[67] This point has been laboured before and will also be covered later. Suffice it to point out, however, that the DMNs owned 6.8 per cent of the world merchant fleet twenty years ago, whereas, during the same period, their share of world trade by weight was some 58.3 per cent of goods loaded and 14.2 per cent of goods unloaded.[68] A high proportion of the goods loaded consisted of oil which then (two decades ago) accounted for 55 per cent of world trade by weight. Of the total world trade in oil movements, then, which amounted to 747 million long tons, 663 million long tons (or 88.8 per cent) originated from the DMNs in the Caribbean, Middle East, North Africa, West Africa and South-East Asia.[69] However, there are other factors that enter into the balance of payments accounting system besides, or in addition to, shipping. One of them is the services transactions of general government. For the UK comparative table of this in relation to that of the FRG and the EEC, see Table 9.5.

The Experience of the TMNs

Despite all these enormous contributions to world trade, the DMNs' foreign exchange records have remained a nightmare to say the least. This is in marked contrast to the healthy position of the TMNs' shipping which continues to enjoy a favourable foreign exchange position.[70] The reconstruction of the TMNs' fleets after the War involved a large capital outlay and the replacement of obsolete uneconomic tonnage and demanded further large investments. A reasonable and relatively stable freight rates level and a fiscal system permitting owners to accumulate sufficient funds for replacement or expansion were the two indispensable factors in the TMNs' maintenance of efficient and cheap overseas shipping services on a commercial basis.[71] In turn these basic factors were essential for the proper functioning and development of international maritime trade generally and the acquisition of a dominant position by the

Table 9.6   Shipping contributions to the total balance of payments on current account in 1953 (OEEC)

$ million

Country	Current account			Maritime transport		
	Total receipt	Total expenditure	Net balance	Receipts	Expenditure	Net balance
Austria	673.1	600.0	+ 73.1	6.1[3]	50.2	− 44.1
B.L.E.U.	2,848.0	2,817.9	+ 30.1	156.5[3]	206.7	− 50.2
Denmark	1,163.0	1,152.0	+ 11.0	173.0	151.0	+ 22.0
France	3,274.0	3,335.0	− 61.0	109.0[3]	210.0	−101.0
Germany	5,340.0	4,372.2	+967.9	199.0	278.0	− 79.0
Greece	251.9	330.7	− 78.8	22.8	28.9	− 6.1
Iceland	71.6	76.9	− 5.3	7.8	8.4	− 0.6
Ireland[1]	540.0	577.3	− 37.3	4.5	−	+ 4.5
Italy	2,361.3	2,658.9	−297.6	219.9	196.8	+ 23.1
Netherlands	2,836.0	2,431.0	+405.0	230.0[3]	116.0	+114.0
Norway	1,106.5	1,256.5	−150.0	454.5	278.3	+176.2
Portugal	232.8	300.1	− 67.3	16.2	17.0	− 0.8
Sweden[1] [4]	2,010.0	1,948.0	+ 62.0	312.0	145.0	+167.0
Switzerland	n.a.	n.a.	n.a.	n.a.	n.a.	n.a.
Turkey	n.a.	n.a.	n.a.	n.a.	n.a.	n.a.
United Kingdom	10,704.0	10,249.0	+455.0	1,036.0	693.0	+343.0
United States	16,984.0	17,035.0	− 51.0	1,232.0	1,058.0	+174.0
Canada[2]	5,512.0	5,927.0	−415.0	159.0	382.0	−223.0

[1] Imports c.i.f.
[2] Million Canadian $.
[3] Including all transport.
[4] Receipt and expenditure in foreign trade only.

Source: OEEC, *Maritime Transport*, Paris, 1953.

TMNs in particular. That TMN dominance in international finance, trade, politics, and economy was to a large extent derived from the corresponding dominance in maritime transport.[72] Hence the strong linkage between international maritime transport and foreign exchange. Thus, as long ago as 1954 when the OEEC started publishing its annual reports of the Maritime Transport Committee, the TMNs had realized the value of foreign exchange from international shipping.[73]

Table 9.6 indicates for those OEEC-TMNs (now OECD-TMNs) member countries who were able to show their shipping account separately, the importance of their shipping earnings (then) to their foreign exchange.[74] To take a few examples, in both Denmark and Sweden the income from shipping amounted to about 15 per cent of the total income from foreign trade and the credit foreign exchange payments on shipping accounts contributed largely to those countries' total favourable credit balance.[75] In Norway, shipping receipts amounted to almost 45 per cent of the total receipts from foreign trade and the net balance of shipping account was US $176 million, thus providing a very large contribution to the net foreign exchange account. These figure ratios have decreased in some respects but, by and large, the contributions are still significant.[76] The UK's figures for shipping did not include tanker freights and disbursements but did include disbursements by foreign ships in the UK ports, even though the figures still represented almost 10 per cent of her total income from foreign trade. If it were possible to include earnings from tankers, the UK shipping foreign exchange earnings would be considerably increased.[77] In Italy receipts from shipping almost amounted to 10 per cent of total receipts in 1953 and, for the first time since the War, Italy had had a credit balance on shipping account. In the case of the Netherlands, transport represented approximately 30 per cent of the net balance on current account; of this a very substantial proportion was contributed by shipping.[78] Three decades later, today, the position has not changed much.

The Development of National Shipping

The Experience of the DMNs

The depressed experiences of the DMNs in this field is in marked contrast to the buoyant ones of the TMNs. It is not surprising, therefore, that the establishment of national fleets is widely regarded by the DMNs as a means of earning or saving foreign exchange.[79] This may arise from actual foreign exchange difficulties, in which case the establishment of a national merchant marine is seen as possibly contributing to the solution to these problems. Consideration of foreign exchange is not limited to countries which are actually experiencing difficulties since the maintenance of equilibrium in foreign exchange is desirable for all countries engaged in international trade.[80] The DMNs as a group have an unfavourable balance on maritime transport account of foreign exchange, this being implicit in their relatively small share of world tonnage as already indicated.[81] They also have an unfavourable balance on other trade accounts not connected with shipping, but that is a different matter altogether. Of course, as specialization is now the basis of trade, there is no reason why a particular country (or group of countries) should necessarily expect its international receipts and payments for any one type of economic activity to balance.[82] But it is natural that each country, in attempting to create or maintain good housekeeping in its international payments, should consider how deficits may be reduced as well as how credit terms may be increased. Unfortunately there is no statistical table available to demonstrate the experiences of the DMNs in this area, but for an example of a TMN (namely West Germany) see Table 9.7.

Table 9.7　Federal Republic of Germany: shipping's contribution to the balance of payments (in million DM/%)

		1975	1976	1977	1978	1979	1980
Sea transport account							
Credits	(1)	7,437	7,269	7,501	7,452	8,242	9,480
Debits	(2)	8,182	8,409	8,277	8,530	9,887	10,501
Balance	(3)	-744	-1,140	-777	-1,078	-1,644	-1,021
Total receipts from international services	(4)	6,870	6,590	6,992	6,430	7,243	8,276
Invisible account[1]							
Credits	(5)	53,881	61,323	64,134	71,567	78,256	89,516
Debits	(6)	69,401	75,491	82,371	86,917	99,160	114,181
Balance	(7)	-15,520	-14,167	-18,236	-15,349	-20,905	-24,666
Current account[2]							
Credits	(8)	274,366	315,476	336,361	357,260	391,360	436,274
Debits	(9)	267,499	308,098	328,701	342,261	403,588	470,337
Balance	(10)	6,867	7,378	7,660	14,999	-12,228	-34,063
Percentages	(3) : (7)	4.8	8.0	4.3	7.0	7.9	4.1
	(1) : (8)	2.7	2.3	2.2	2.1	2.1	2.2
	(4) : (5)	12.8	10.7	10.9	9.0	9.3	9.2
	(4) : (8)	2.5	2.1	2.1	1.8	1.9	1.9

[1] Excluding unrequited transfers.
[2] Excluding transit trade.

Source: Blumenhagen, *Shipping and the Balance of Payments*, table III/2, p. 14.

Each country will naturally be seeking the most economic use of its resources.[83] But as special difficulties may arise from existing forms of protection in world trade — such as tariffs, import quotas and other non-tariff measures — the combinations of resources which would be most economically desirable in a free trade situation may yield a product which, because of trade restrictions and barriers cannot, in practice, be sold in world markets at a price which is economic to the producer.[84] In such a situation, which is likely to be particularly relevant for the DMNs, it is not surprising that they should resort to measures which, under a regime of completely free and undisputed international trade, would constitute a considerably uneconomic use of resources.[85] Recourse to such measures by individual countries in the real world of trade restrictions may be a rational method of attempting to increase national income, in the sense that they lead to the attainment of a solution which is optimal within the existing constraints, although it would be sub-optional if the conditions could be changed by removing trade barriers for instance.[86] Whether the desire is to create industries with favourable foreign exchange effects in order to maintain equilibrium in the balance of payments, or to improve an adverse foreign exchange situation, investment in shipping is a possible avenue of approach.[87]

It was with a view to the continuing severe economic imbalance in the relations between the TMNs and DMNs, and in the context of the constant and continuing aggravation of this imbalance of the DMNs' economics and the consequent need for the mitigation of their economic difficulties, that urgent and effective measures needed to be taken by the international community to assist those countries.[88] This was done by the 'Declaration on the Establishment of a New International Economic Order' by the UN General Assembly Resolution at the Sixth Special Session 1974.[89] In order to ensure its application it was found necessary to adopt and implement, within a specified period, a programme of action of unprecedented scope and to bring about maximum economic cooperation and understanding among all states — particularly between the TMNs and the DMNs — based on the principle of dignity and sovereign equality. That was in fact the 'Programme of Action for the Establishment of a New International Economic Order'[90] also passed by a Resolution at the Sixth Special Session of the UN. These two were preceded by the 'Declaration on Permanent Sovereignty over Natural Resources and Declaration of the Charter of Economic Rights and Duties of the States'. With regards to transport[91] and insurance the Programme action provided that:

All efforts should be made:

(1) To promote an increasing and equitable participation of developing

410

countries in the world shipping tonnage;

(2) To arrest and reduce the ever-increasing freight rates in order to reduce the cost of imports to, and exports from, the developing countries;

(3) To minimise cost of insurance and reinsurance for developing countries and to assist the growth of domestic insurance and reinsurance markets in developing countries and the establishment to this end, where appropriate, of institutions in these countries or at the regional level;

(4) To ensure the early implementation of the code of conduct for liner conferences;

(5) To take urgent measures to increase the import and export capacity of the least developed countries and to offset the disadvantages of the adverse geographic situation of landlocked countries, particularly with regard to their transportation and transit costs, as well as developing island countries in order to increase their trading ability; and

(6) By the developed countries to refrain from imposing measures or implementing policies designed to prevent the importation, at equitable prices, of commodities from the developing countries or from frustrating the implementation of legitimate measures and policies adopted by the developing countries in order to improve prices and encourage the export of such commodities.[92]

The two Declarations and Programme of Action came in the mid-1970s during the UN's Second Development Decade.

The United Nations Development Decades

With regard to foreign trade (both visible and invisible), and therefore foreign exchange, the NIEO was preceded by the UN Development Decades. The First UN Development Decade was in the 1960s just when the DMNs were both attaining political independence and becoming involved in shipping.[93] Since the start of the Second UN Development Decade in 1971, economic and political relations have changed dramatically: the worsening of the world situation in 1972, 1973 and the 1980s; the deterioration of the international monetary system; and increased inflation and unemployment in the TMNs.[94] In particular, the debt, energy and (recently) the famine crisis led to the emergence of a new group or subset of DMNs — the most seriously affected countries — and it was in this context that the Sixth Special Session of the General Assembly was held from 9 April to 2 May 1974.[95] Initiated on 30 January 1974 by Algeria on behalf of the group of 77 countries, its purpose was to study the problems of raw materials and development. At this Special Session, the General Assembly adopted the Declaration on and Programme of Action for the Establishment of New International Economic Order outlined above.[96] Detailed analysis thereof is beyond the scope of this study save for issues that affect shipping, insurance and other invisible transactions: those areas that have a direct bearing on shipping and foreign exchange have also been outlined immediately above.[97]

These were supplemented by the International Development Strategy for the Second UN Development Decade which lays down the general objective to be achieved during the Decade and details of which will be discussed later. Suffice it to mention at this stage, however, that in the field of invisibles including shipping, the strategy provides that:[98]

> The Objective is to promote, by national and international action, the earnings of the developing countries from invisible trade and to minimise the net outflow of foreign exchange from these countries arising from invisible transactions including shipping.[99]

Thus, so far as shipping is concerned, the achievement of this general objective called for action covering a number of fields and by all groups of countries. While the cooperation of other countries was required in order to achieve the goals, in the case of shipping much of the initiative for action lay with the DMNs themselves.[100] The role of other countries was only to facilitate and not to inhibit the realization of their initiative. The statement of the objective laid considerable stress on the question of foreign exchange. Clearly many different policy measures could contribute to the achievement of the objective, but the most important matter in this specific context was the corresponding share of ocean-borne trade carried by DMNs' ships.[101] However, it is important to note at this stage that there are two quite distinct aspects performed by shipping: foreign exchange earning and foreign exchange saving.

In the past the DMNs have often shown a major interest in saving foreign exchange in their maritime transport operations and have therefore concentrated on entry into liner trades serving their own ports. In cases where such countries have owned tankers and tramp ships they have likewise tended to use these vessels in the national trade.[102] There are other reasons why such actions might be desirable, but from the point of view of foreign exchange it is only one side of the picture. The earnings of foreign exchange through shipping had been very much neglected by the DMNs and it is not surprising that this was the aspect which had to undergo the greatest change during the Second UN Development Decade.[103] It is still important that the distinction between foreign exchange earning and foreign exchange savings be kept clear, for a fundamental objective of the Strategy was stated in terms of the share of the cargoes carried by DMNs' ships.[104] If the effort was concentrated on the savings of foreign exchange, then

412

the objective regarding the share of the cargoes carried would relate to the trade of each DMN, and it would be possible to evaluate, country by country, the extent to which each country had succeeded in increasing the share of its own trade carried by its own ships.[105] Many of these are implicit in the Development Strategy to which we now turn our attention.

The International Development Strategy

According to the International Development Strategy for the Second UN Development Decade when the criterion is the earning of foreign exchange through shipping, the picture broadens and is not restricted to the trade generated by each DMN but covers the share of total world trade carried by DMNs' ships.[106] Ships can operate as foreign exchange earners by entry as third flag carriers or cross-traders in conference trades or by entering the general world oil and dry bulk cargo trades. It is for this reason that the International Development Strategy for the Second Development Decade provided in the relevant section that:[107]

Invisibles including shipping

(53) The objective is to promote, by national and international action, the earnings of developing countries from invisible trade and to minimize the net outflow of foreign exchange from these countries arising from invisible transactions, including shipping. In pursuance of the objective, action held shall be taken, inter alia, in the following areas, by Governments and International Organisation and, where necessary, appropriately, involving Liner Conferences, Shippers' Councils and other relevant bodies:

(a) The principle that the national shipping lines of developing countries should be admitted as full members of liner conferences operating in their national maritime trade and have an increasing and substantial participation in the carriage of cargoes generated by their foreign trade should be implemented in the Decade;

(b) Further, Governments should invite liner conferences to consider favourably, fairly and on equal terms application of the national shipping lines, in particular of developing countries, for admission as full members to way-port trades related to these countries' foreign trades, subject to the rights and obligations of conference membership, as provided in paragraph 4, Section II of resolution 12(IV) of 4 May 1970 adopted by the Committee on Shipping;

(c) In order that the developing countries have an increasing and substantial participation in the carriage of maritime cargoes, and recognizing the need to reverse the existing trade whereby the shares of the developing countries in the world merchant fleet has been declining instead of increasing developing countries should be enabled to expand their national and multinational merchant marines through the adoption of such measures as may be appropriate to permit their shipowners to compete in the international freight market and thus contribute to a sound development of shipping;

(d) It is also necessary that further improvements be made in the liner conference system, and all unfair practices and discrimination where such exist in liner conference practices should be eliminated;

(e) In the determination and adjustment of liner freight rates, due consideration should be given, as is commercially possible and/or appropriate to

(1) The needs of the developing countries, in particular their efforts to promote non-traditional exports;

(2) The special problems of the least developed among the developing countries, in order to encourage and promote the import and export interests in these countries;

(3) Port improvements leading to a reduction of the cost of shipping operations in ports;

(4) Technological developments in maritime transport; and

(5) Improvements in the organization of trade.

(f) Governments of developed countries members of the United Nations Conference on Trade and Development should, upon request made by developing countries within the framework of their overall development priorities, duly consider extending, directly or through international institutions, financial and technical assistance, including training, to developing countries to establish and expand their national and multinational merchant marines, including tanker and bulk carrier fleets, and to develop and improve their port facilities. Within assistance programmes, special attention should be paid to projects, including training projects, for developing the shipping and ports of the least developed among the developing countries and for reducing their maritime transport costs;

(g) The terms and conditions on which bilateral aid and commercial credit are available for purchase of ships by developing countries should be kept under review in the light of relevant resolutions of the United Nations Conference on Trade and Development, namely, Conference Resolution 12(II) of 24 March 1968, and Resolution 9(IV) of 4 May 1970 adopted by the Committee on Shipping.

(h) Freight rates, conference practices, adequacy of shipping services and other matters of common interest to shippers and shipowners should be the subject of consultation between liner conferences and shippers and, where appropriate, shippers' councils or equivalent bodies and interested public authorities. Every effort should be made to encourage the institution and operation of shippers' council, where appropriate, or equivalent bodies and the establishment of effective consultation machinery. Such machinery should provide for consultation by Liner Conferences well before publicly announcing changes in freight rates;

(i) In view of the common interest of member countries in the United Nations Conference on Trade and Development, Shippers and Shipowners in improving imports, thus covering the cost of maritime transport and permitting reductions in freight rates, a concerted national and international effort should be evolved in the course of the Decade to promote the development and improvement of port facilities of developing countries;

(j) Maritime transport costs, the level and structure of freight rates, conference practices, adequacy of shipping services and related matters should continue to be kept under review within the United Nations Conference on Trade and Development, and additional measures to attain the objectives set out in this field should be considered within the whole programme of the permanent machinery of the Conference.[108]

In the first case entry is controlled by their liner conferences, but the free market trades are not subject to the control of bodies of this type. The ships employed for carrying oil, ore and other bulk cargoes, and tramp ships, are owned partly by industrial companies and partly by shipowners without other industrial interests.[109] It is with expansion of shares carried by own ships and, therefore, foreign exchange considerations that the DMNs got so worked up about cargo-sharing in the liners and bulk trades as well as the reforms of FOCs.[110]

For the DMNs wishing to expand their national fleet for the purposes of entering the foreign exchange-earning trades, the purchase of second-hand tonnage is always a worthwhile proposition. Owing to a sharp rise in labour costs in most TMNs, the operation of smaller oil and dry bulk carriers is becoming increasingly unprofitable, except during boom periods.[111] For the DMNs, however, with their generally lower wage rates, it would appear that the operation of these smaller ships can remain economic, particularly if ships already in operation are bought. DMNs entry into third-flag trades would contribute to the achievement of the foreign exchange objectives of the International Development Strategy for the Second UN Development Decade.[112] So far as the carriage of cargo by sea is concerned, the objectives stated in paragraph 53(e) of the Strategy (above) have two aspects, only one of which is covered by entry into cross-trades. The first concerns the cargo generated by the DMNs' foreign trade, in the carriage of which the ships of these countries' share have an 'increasing and substantial proportion' as is required by the Liner Code.[113] The second concerns maritime cargoes in general and is referred to in the passage which states that the shipowners in the DMNs should be enabled 'to compete effectively in the international foreign markets'. Entry into third-flag trades is directly relevant to the second aspect, but not the first.[114] Either way, the primary objective remains the earning and saving of foreign exchange — a theme which runs through the UN's Third Development Decade.

The North–South Perspective

The International Development Strategy for the Third UN Development Decade, was adopted by the General Assembly in December 1980. It sets out the major objectives and policies for the economic and social development of the DMNs during the 1980s.[115] With regard to invisibles, including shipping, it is not a marked departure from the International Development Strategy for the Second UN Development Decade of 1970; it merely reinforces and supplements it. Thus, it will not be necessary to go into its details for fear of repetition.[116] However, a high-level Intergovernmental Group of Officials convened to consider the Review and Appraisal of the Strategy. As part of UNCTAD's role in monitoring the Strategy, and adapting it to changing conditions, representatives from 100 countries examined developments in some of the crucial and most contentious areas, including international trade, maritime transport, commodities and financial and monetary questions.[117] The debt (and therefore foreign exchange) problems of the DMNs surfaced very often. Because they could not resolve long-standing North–South divisions on these issues, a composite text had to be drafted indicating the main areas of disagreement. These included the state of protectionism and structural adjustment, including structural reform of the international monetary system.[118]

They also considered the IMF's less severe conditionality practices and the need for compensatory financing of export earnings shortfalls; in brief, a coded phrase for the acute foreign exchange problems of the DMNs.[119] As was expected, disappointment resulted from the refusal of the TMNs to take up the call for new or revised policies in the TMNs.[120] Although the UN Strategy foresaw an average annual growth rate of 7 per cent during the decade – that is, an annual increase of about 4.5 per cent in per capita GDP – growth in GDP declined to 1.3 per cent in the 1980–84 period compared to 5.8 per cent in the First Development Decade, i.e. the 1960s.[121] By the end of 1984, for instance, the per capita income in the DMNs as a whole was 5 per cent lower than at the beginning of the Third Development Decade, i.e. 1980. The net transfer of financial resources dropped by US $4 billion, compared to US $55 billion in 1981. Meanwhile, the terms of trade of the DMNs deteriorated by about 1.6 per cent per annum in the same period.[122] The intransigence of the TMNs over the international economic environment is likely to reinforce these trends, since few DMNs have domestic markets of sufficient size to avoid the domination of overall economic conditions by their foreign exchange.

The fight against inflation in the TMNs is set to prolong the escalation of inflation rates in the DMNs, thereby worsening the latters' foreign exchange problems, largely as a result of the adverse external positions and the policies of currency devaluation often insisted upon as part of the IMF conditionality.[123] But what have these got to do with shipping and/or foreign exchange, one may ask? The answer to this is partly provided already: linking transport to foreign exchange. The other half of the answer is simple. The supplier of a transport service requires to be paid in his own currency, in a fully convertible currency or in goods, as, for example, a shipping clause included in a bilateral trade contract would stipulate.[124] Consequently, where transport is provided internationally, the costs involved normally enter into the foreign exchange account together with other costs. In considering the foreign exchange questions, only the part of the costs involved which have to be paid for in foreign currency is important. In the case of imports these costs are also defrayed in foreign currency.[125] Freight charges and insurance are also normally payable in foreign currency if the goods are not transported in nationally owned ships, although these charges may be partly offset by expenditures incurred by the foreign ships in the ports of the importing country — for example, expenditure by crews, purchase of stores, etc.[126] For an example of the comparative advantages enjoyed by the North — i.e. the TMNs — in the foreign exchange sphere, see the UK summary balance of payments in Table 9.8.

Transport and Foreign Exchange

Thus, transport, *per se*, has enormous bearing on a country's foreign exchange equation. Those countries which are suppliers of transport services therefore receive freight payments in foreign currencies but have also to make payments in foreign currencies for the overseas expenditures incurred by their ships,[127] any imported components of the operational inputs of the ships and the imported components of the capital invested in the ships themselves. These two issues (earnings and savings of foreign exchange) are discussed in detail in the next subsection.[128] They are also treated comprehensively in the next chapter. For the UK sea transport account for the decade 1972–82, see Table 9.9.

It only remains to add here, however, that those countries which are demanders/users of transport facilities have to make payments for transport in foreign currency and receive payments for expenses

Table 9.8 Summary balance of payments[1] (UK)

£ million

	1961	1962	1963	1964	1965	1966	1967	1968	1969	1970	1971
Current account											
Visible balance	−140	−100	−119	−543	−260	−108	−599	−712	−209	−34	+190
Invisibles											
Services balance	+21	+18	−31	−50	−36	+31	+168	+357	+422	+481	+625
Interest, profits and dividends balance	+254	+334	+398	+394	+435	+388	+378	+334	+498	+554	+502
Transfers balance	−88	−97	−123	−159	−169	−181	−216	−223	−206	−178	−193
Invisibles balance	+187	+255	+244	+185	+230	+238	+330	+468	+714	+857	+934
Current balance	+47	+155	+125	−358	−30	+130	−269	−244	+505	+823	+1,124
Financial account											
Investment and other capital transactions	−316	−3	−99	−311	−316	−579	−504	−755	−169	+549	+1,792
EEA loss on forward commitments	–	–	–	–	–	–	−105	−251	–	–	–
Allocation of SDRs	–	–	–	–	–	–	–	–	–	+171	+125
Gold subscription to IMF (−)	–	–	–	–	–	−44	–	–	–	−38	–
Official financing											
Net transactions with overseas monetary authorities[2]	+370	−375	+5	+573	+599	+625	+556	+1,296	−699	−1,295	−1,817
Foreign currency borrowing (net)	–	–	–	–	–	–	–	–	+56	+	+82
Official reserves (drawing on +/ additions to −)	−31	+183	+53	+122	−246	−34	+115	+114	−44	−125	−1,536
Balancing item	−70	+40	−84	−26	−7	−98	+207	−160	+351	−85	+230

Table 9.8 (cont.)

£ million

	1972	1973	1974	1975	1976	1977	1978	1979	1980	1981	1982
Current account											
Visible balance	−748	−2,586	−5,351	−3,333	−3,929	−2,284	−1,542	−3,449	+1,233	+3,008	+2,119
Invisibles											
Services balance	+701	+786	+1,075	+1,515	+2,503	+3,338	+3,816	+4,071	+4,267	+4,249	+3,844
Interest, profits and dividends balance	+538	+1,257	+1,415	+773	+1,365	+116	+661	+990	−186	+1,257	+1,577
Transfers balance	−268	−436	−417	−468	−775	−1,116	−1,777	−2,265	−2,079	−1,967	−2,112
Invisibles balance	+971	+1,607	+2,073	+1,820	+3,093	+2,338	+2,700	+2,796	+2,002	+3,539	+3,309
Current balance	+223	−979	−3,278	−1,513	−836	+54	+1,158	−653	+3,235	+6,547	+5,428
Capital transfers	–	−59	−75	–	–	–	–	–	–	–	–
Financial account											
Investment and other capital transactions	−673	+178	+1,602	+154	−2,975	+4,166	−4,263	+2,157	−1,887	−7,594	−2,851
Allocation of SDRs (+)	+124	–	–	–	–	–	–	+195	+180	+158	–
Official financing											
Net transactions with overseas monetary authorities	+449	–	–	–	+984	+1,113	−1,016	−596	−140	−145	−163
Foreign currency borrowing (net)	–	+999	+1,751	+810	+1,791	+1,114	−187	−250	−941	−1,587	+26
Official reserves (drawings on +/ addition to −)	+692	−228	−105	+655	+853	−9,588	+2,329	−1,059	−291	+2,419	+1,421
Balancing item	−815	+89	+105	−106	+183	+3,141	+1,979	+206	−156	+202	−3,861

[1] Figures for earlier years are published in earlier editions of this publication and are given back to 1946 in United Kingdom Balance of Payments 1971, and also in Economic Trends Annual Supplement (1979 and later editions).
[2] Including transfers from dollar portfolio to reserves in 1966 and 1967.

Source: Central Statistics Office 1983, table 1.1.

£ million

Table 9.9 Sea transport: total (UK)

	1972	1973	1974	1975	1976	1977	1978	1979	1980	1981	1982
Credits											
Ships owned by UK operators											
Freight on exports	191	224	326	374	426	497	418	443	445	363	327
Freight on cross-trades	401	531	712	646	829	885	844	948	1,020	1,164	1,059
Charter receipts	184	264	448	505	606	572	463	600	537	560	566
Passenger revenue	88	81	92	122	141	162	170	202	237	242	251
Total	864	1,100	1,578	1,647	2,002	2,116	1,895	2,193	2,239	2,329	2,203
Ships on charter to UK operators											
Freight on exports	18	23	30	26	51	68	89	81	101	82	71
Freight on cross-trades	527	684	701	559	698	709	583	864	756	590	482
Charter receipts	7	18	63	55	45	40	50	49	48	62	67
Total	552	725	794	640	794	817	722	994	905	734	620
Overseas operators											
Disbursements in the United Kingdom	191	230	293	364	437	500	532	617	672	721	742
Total credits	1,607	2,055	2,665	2,651	3,233	3,433	3,149	3,804	3,816	3,784	3,565
Debits											
Ships owned by UK operators											
Disbursements abroad	429	494	746	790	988	1,092	920	1,049	1,089	1,206	1,159
Ships on charter to UK operators											
Charter payments	628	778	799	659	802	837	716	727	634	623	604
Disbursements abroad	129	167	317	299	350	340	319	397	393	356	314
Total	757	945	1,116	958	1,152	1,177	1,035	1,124	1,027	979	918
Overseas operators											
Freight on imports	475	690	877	766	965	1,030	1,160	1,436	1,477	1,673	1,738
Passenger revenue	27	31	37	48	50	46	47	68	82	86	93
Total	502	721	914	814	1,015	1,076	1,207	1,504	1,559	1,759	1,831
Total debits	1,688	2,160	2,776	2,562	3,155	3,345	3,162	3,677	3,675	3,944	3,908
Balances											
Ships owned by UK operators	+435	+606	+832	+857	+1,014	+1,024	+975	+1,144	+1,150	+1,123	+1,044
Ships on charter to UK operators	-205	-220	-322	-318	-358	-360	-313	-130	-122	-245	-298
Overseas operators	-311	-491	-621	-450	-578	-576	-675	-887	-887	-1,038	-1,089
Sea transport	-81	-105	-111	+89	+78	+88	-13	+127	+141	-160	-343

Source: Central Statistics Office 1983, table 3.5.

incurred in their ports by foreign-owned ships and for any inputs in the current operational or capital costs of these ships they supply,[129] while the crews of ships customarily spend part of their wages ashore. The DMNs' foreign exchange problems are further aggravated by the fact that any meagre foreign currency they may earn is always spent in the TMNs since the DMNs do not generally have sufficient commodities to satisfy consumer demands of their populations — especially those with foreign tastes who may also have easy access to foreign markets.[130]

This last-mentioned item is important in the case of liners which spend long periods in port, but is unimportant for tankers and bulk carriers which do not. As the interplay of this factor in the balance of payments equation is discussed in both the next subsection and the next chapter, there is no need to repeat the discussions here.[131] However, it must be noted that, in the supply of any goods or services in international trade, foreign exchange costs and receipts are involved. Transport generally and maritime transport in particular are not in any way exceptional. Nevertheless, it has particular aspects from the foreign exchange perspective[132] in that entry into international transport does not require specific resource endowments such as are required for entry into international trade in commodities or manufactured goods. For this reason it may be attractive, for foreign exchange reasons, for a country to seek to become a supplier of transport facilities, whether as an import substitution or as an export-earning industry.[133] The consideration of the foreign exchange aspects of transport facilities reverts to the issue discussed above. To the extent that a country's trading can be organized on a scale which makes it economic for specialized shipping offices to be established, payments in foreign currency are reduced, since the services of foreign freighting agents are also reduced.[134]

At the same time, even if national flag vessels are not utilized, favourable foreign exchange effects arise from reductions made in transport charges. This question is also considered in the UNCTAD *Secretariat Report on Terms of Shipment*[135] but it is of sufficient importance to deserve high priority when resources can be released from other research projects in progress. Being the mode of transport more related to foreign trade, shipping therefore exerts more influence on foreign exchange earnings and savings than any other form of transport.[136] An example of the contribution of transport generally and sea transport in particular is that provided by the UK as indicated in Table 9.10.

It has been said repeatedly that, together with employment, economic diversification, economic self-sufficiency and other political and security factors, the foreign exchange issue has been foremost in the list of rationales for states' involvement in maritime transport.[137] Like many other politically laden claims it has been rather difficult to obtain direct evidence for it, although of course indirect or circumstantial evidence is abundant. In 1982, for instance, total freight payments of IMF member countries amounted to SDR 75.5 billion and freight receipts to SDR 47.0 billion.[138] This large discrepancy between receipts and disbursements shows the major difficulty of determining the global contribution of shipping to foreign exchange payments. About one-third of world tonnage is registered under FOCs and services to international trade of this tonnage are duly recorded as debits in the foreign exchange statistics of those countries using these services.[139] The corresponding credits, however, are not recorded, as the flag state regards the companies that own and operate these fleets as extraterritorial entities. Thus, the major countries providing FOC facilities such as Liberia and Panama, do not show any credit entries in their freight accounts,[140] making it much more difficult to ascertain the accurate contributions of shipping to foreign exchange. All that can be said from available statistics is that they are substantial.

When comparing foreign exchange contributions of shipping in the TMNs and the DMNs, the TMNs' earnings should therefore be adjusted by these shortfalls in credit entries as their nationals are the major beneficial owners of open registry tonnage (discussed in Chapter 2). Consequently, the freight entries of the TMNs and the DMNs membership of the IMF compare as follows:[141]

	Credits			Debits		
	1980	1981	1982	1980	1981	1982
Developed market-economy countries						
Original	35,452	37,886	36,342	33,852	36,151	35,058
Adjusted*	50,276	56,287	53,388	33,852	36,151	35,058
Developing countries	6,346	7,683	10,745	32,670	40,088	40,439

*Adjusted by 60 per cent of the asymmetry.

Source: UNCTAD Document no. TD/B/1013, p. 13.

Thus the DMNs' deficit in the sea transport balance amounted to some SDR 26.3 billion (US $34.2 billion) in 1980, SDR 32.4 billion

	1972	1973	1974	1975	1976	1977	1978	1979	1980	1981	1982
Credits											
Ships owned by UK operators											
Freight on exports	185	215	312	363	403	474	392	406	400	318	293
Freight on cross-trades	207	277	385	341	454	507	441	443	524	537	579
Charter receipts	100	139	255	298	367	377	280	294	261	227	188
Passenger revenue	88	81	92	122	141	162	170	202	237	242	251
Total	580	712	1,044	1,124	1,365	1,520	1,283	1,345	1,422	1,324	1,311
Ships on charter to UK operators											
Freight on exports	13	18	26	22	42	54	67	55	62	54	50
Freight on cross-trades	22	28	55	30	53	51	79	73	92	100	107
Charter receipts	3	3	10	14	17	18	14	6	7	13	11
Total	38	49	91	66	112	123	160	134	161	167	168
Overseas operators											
Disbursements in the United Kingdom	181	216	273	330	393	451	491	559	617	664	679
Total credits	799	977	1,408	1,520	1,870	2,094	1,934	2,038	2,200	2,155	2,158
Debits											
Ships owned by UK operators											
Disbursements abroad	316	359	486	553	668	768	648	677	752	723	748
Ships on charter to UK operators											
Charter payments	31	46	83	69	85	110	101	77	88	105	115
Disbursements abroad	23	29	52	40	70	81	111	105	126	129	135
Total	54	75	135	109	155	191	212	182	214	234	250
Overseas operators											
Freight on imports	347	502	681	586	765	860	1,020	1,268	1,380	1,550	1,684
Passenger revenue	27	31	37	48	50	46	47	68	82	86	93
Total	374	533	718	634	815	906	1,067	1,336	1,462	1,636	1,777
Total debits	744	967	1,339	1,296	1,638	1,865	1,927	2,195	2,428	2,593	2,775
Balances											
Ships owned by UK operators	+264	+353	+558	+571	+697	+752	+635	+668	+670	+601	+563
Ships on charter to UK operators	-16	-26	-44	-43	-43	-68	-52	-48	-53	-67	-82
Overseas operators	-193	-317	-445	-304	-422	-455	-576	-777	-845	-972	-1,098
All dry cargo	+55	+10	+69	+224	+232	+229	+7	-157	-228	-438	-617

Source: Central Statistical Office, 1983, table 3.3.

(US $32.7 billion) in 1982.[142] The current order of magnitude of freight payments of some US $40 billion contributes considerably to the existing imbalance of trade and the invisibles, and thus to the DMNs' debt problems. The only way to remedy this situation is to pursue a consistent policy of import substitution and export promotion of shipping services.[143]

However, when evaluating the actual and potential contribution of a national fleet to foreign exchange acquisition and/or savings it has to be borne in mind that, although the total freight paid to the national line in the country's foreign trade represents a gross foreign exchange saving and/or earning, the net effect on foreign exchange account will be considerably less,[144] depending on the degree to which national resources can be used in providing such services. The most important outflows in foreign exchange stemming from an engagement in shipping are financing costs for ships purchased abroad and bunker costs incurred in ports.[145] Consequently, the net foreign exchange effect of an investment in shipping differs considerably from country to country, with available figures ranging from 10 to 70 per cent of gross revenues depending on a variety of factors. Thus, even on the basis of a conservative estimate of only 30 per cent of gross foreign exchange savings representing actual net savings,[146] the DMNs could reduce their foreign exchange outflows by some US $6 billion if half the present outflows to foreign carriers could be channelled to national carriers. These are more than ample economic considerations for the establishment and/or development of national fleets:[147] itself a rebuff to critics who argue that there are no justifiable rationales for the DMNs' entry into international shipping, or that the motives for the DMNs' interests in shipping can only be political if not sinister. For the breakdown of the sea transport (dry cargo) contribution to the UK balance of payments, see again Table 9.10.

Concluding Remarks

The problem with this field of international trade relations is to identify the possible sources for improvement to foreign exchange from the establishment of national maritime fleets. The subject is complex, although an attempt has been made to present it here in a simplified form. It is even more complex since the potential net gain is the sum of many flows of payments and receipts recorded in the foreign exchange accounts of the country concerned, as well as many other flows which may not necessarily appear in the foreign exchange accounts of any nation as now compiled by the national authorities concerned and as published by the IMF. Shipping is only one of those flows although it is the thesis of this study that it is one of the essential elements. Otherwise the actual and potential gains to the foreign exchange account of a country which establishes a merchant marine is composed of (a) freight payments saved on carrying imports, *plus* (b) freight payments earned on carrying exports, *minus the sum of* (c) disbursements formerly made by foreign shipping owners now foregone, *and* (d) disbursements now made overseas.

Another point which needs to be considered is the opportunity cost to foreign exchange accounts of establishing a national merchant marine. It has been argued above that the net contribution to foreign exchange earnings or savings of a merchant marine is substantially lower than the gross freight earnings of the merchant fleet.

Without pre-empting discussions on this in the next chapter, it should perhaps be pointed out at this stage that the actual net gain of investment in shipping depends on

(a) the extent of national manning which can be achieved, particularly of deck and engine-room officers;
(b) whether ships can be built in domestic yards and, if so, the size of the import content of such ships;
(c) whether repairs and surveys can be carried out in domestic yards;
(d) the extent to which fuel and stores can be provided from domestic production;
(e) the nature of the trades in which ships engage, i.e. whether national trades, cross-trades or a mixture of both; and
(f) the terms of payment for ships purchased abroad.

In conclusion three points seem to come to mind. The first point is that shipping is a form of transport and, in all transport undertakings, the indirect and external benefits are important. It was noted that these include contributions to national economic development and the promotion of international trade — both as a servant to and, itself, an item of international trade. An aspect of this point that was taken for granted is that entry to tramping services on the world market may yield very few indirect benefits compared with entry to liner services catering for the trade of the nation. But it does yield the benefit of experience, which could be utilized later by entering national trades using liners.

The second point is that other benefits which may flow from a national merchant marine are external to the enterprise itself, although direct and measurable rather than indirect. The third point is a consideration of the ways in which investment in shipping might exert a specific, but indirect, effect on income flows: for example, by improving the foreign exchange positions; gaining a direct voice in conference decisions on rates and services and so securing decisions more favourable to the country than might otherwise have been obtained; increasing the trade of the country; assisting the pursuits of national and regional integration; and diversifying the employment base of the country. Of these the effects on foreign exchange are considered to be the most important although these factors are all interrelated.

Finally the contribution of transport generally and shipping in particular was considered. The method by which such contribution can be assessed is shown and the experiences of the TMNs and DMNs are considered in the light of available tables and other statistical evidence. It is therefore concluded that, in most cases, countries can actually improve their foreign exchange positions by entering shipping, the improvements being anything up to 80 per cent of the gross foreign earnings — especially when ships are purchased from overseas.

Notes

1 *Committee of Inquiry into Shipping*, Report by the Chairman, Lord Rochdale, Cmnd 4337, 1970, chapter 19, paras 1284-1399, pp. 342-70; US Congress, Senate Committee, *Rates and the Balance of Payments* 1965; S.G. Sturmey, *British Shipping and World Competition*, Athlone Press, London, 1961, p. 417.

2 UNCTAD, Report by the Secretariat of, *Establishment or Expansion of Merchant Marines in Developing Countries*, UNCTAD Doc. no. TD/26/Rev. 1, p. 31; A.J. Merchant and Sykes, *The Finance and Analysis of Capital Projects*, Longmans, London, 1963, pp. 118-19.

3 Ibid., p. 1; see also the Proceedings of UNCTAD, *Final Act and Report*, vol. 1, UN Publications Sales N.64.11.B.11, annex A.IV.22, p. 54; M.M. Dryden, 'Capital budgeting: treatment of uncertainty and investment criteria', *Scottish Journal of Political Economy*, Edinburgh, November 1964.

4 Ibid.; see also *Official Records of the Trade and Development Board*, Fifth Session, Suppl. no. 2, p. 26; M. Rakowski (ed.), *Efficiency of Investment in a Socialist Economy*, Pergamon Press, Warsaw, London, 1966; American Bureau of Shipping, *Surveyor*, August 1967, pp. 15-20.

5 See, again, UNCTAD Doc. no. TD/26/Rev. 1, op.cit., p. 1; as to the application of the theory of comparative advantage on shipping affairs compare H. Bohme, 'Die deutsche Seeschiffahrt im Strukturwandel der Weltwirtschaft. Wettbewerbsgrundlagen — Anpassungserfordernisse — Entwicklungsmoglichkeiten' in *Weltwirtschaft*, no. 1, 1979, pp. 159-95.

6 Ibid.; cf. UNCTAD Report, *Establishment or Expansion of Merchant Marines in Developing Countries*, op.cit.

7 UNCTAD, Report by the Secretariat of, *Review of Developments in Shipping*,

UNCTAD Doc. no. TD/B/C.4/25 and Corr. 1 and 2, paras 8–11; see also UK Chamber of Shipping, *Annual Report 1966–67*, Witherby and Co. Ltd, London.

8 For details on this see UNCTAD, Report by the Secretariat of, *International Transoceanic Transport and Economic Development*, UNCTAD Doc. no. TD/B/C.4/46, 6 January 1969, paras 3–11, pp. 3–5; *Ship Sale and Purchase Market Report*, Million and Co. (Shipping) Ltd, London, July–September.

9 Ibid.; see also the report of the UNCTAD *Trade and Development Board, Committee on Shipping*, Third Session, Geneva, 9 April 1969, Item II of the provisional agenda; *Fearnley's Review 1980*, Oslo, 1981; Lloyd's Register of Shipping, *Annual Report 1985*, London, p. 91.

10 Ibid.; and the Report by the UNCTAD Secretariat in connection with Economic and Social Council Resolution 1372 (XLV) concerning activities of the UN system of organizations in the transport field (submitted to the committee for information).

11 By resolution 1372 (XLV) adopted at its forty-fifth session the Economic and Social Council invited the Secretary-General of the United Nations to prepare, in consultation with UNCTAD and other interested bodies, the above report; S.N. Sanklecha, 'Development of Indian shipping and foreign exchange earnings', *Foreign Trade Review*, Indian Institute of Foreign Trade, New Delhi, July–September 1967.

12 Ibid.; known as 'a report on the major transport problems of developing countries in the context of their economic and social development, with special reference to the latest technological developments and their impact on the programmes and activities of the organisation of the United Nations system designed to assist the developing countries in the improvement of their transport facilities' − HMSO, *Report of the Shipbuilding Inquiry Committee 1965–66* (Geddes Report), Cmnd Paper 2937, London, March 1966, para. 47.

13 Ibid.; in pursuance of this resolution the UNCTAD Secretariat prepared the above report concerning the contribution of international transoceanic transport to the development of developing countries.

14 Ibid.; however, because the seaborne carriage of goods is normally one part only of the total transport chain linking the buyer and seller of a product, the report at times ventures beyond the transoceanic aspect.

15 Ibid.; that it does so is further evidence of the need for cooperation among all parts of the UN system concerned with the transport problems of, especially, developing countries.

16 These approaches are fully discussed in many books on economic development. See, for example, P N. Rosenstein-Rodan, Problems of industrialisation of Eastern and South-Eastern Europe', *The Economic Journal*, June 1943 (Quarterly Journal of the Royal Economic Society); *ECGD Services*, London Export Credits Guarantee Department and Central Office of Information, 1966, p. 16.

17 Ibid.; see also G. Ranis and J.C.H. Fei, *Development of the Labour Surplus: Theory and Policy*, R.D. Irwin, Homewood, Illinois, 1964; the effects of flagging out which also bears on foreign exchange was discussed in Chapter 2; *Financial Times*, London, 4 May 1967, p. 7.

18 For a full discussion see, for example, A.O. Hirschman, *The Strategy of Economic Development*, Yale University Press, New Haven, 1958; R.O. Goss, 'Investment in shipping and the balance of payments. A case study of import substitution policy', *Journal of Industrial Economics*, March 1965.

19 But see S. Scitovsky, 'Growth — balanced and unbalanced' in M. Abramoritz *et al.*, *The Allocation of Economic Resources*, Stanford University Press, Palo Alto, 1959; Comité des Armateurs de France, *Effects de l'invêtissement maritime sur la balance des paiements*, Paris, 1967.

20 Ibid.; cf. P. Streeten, 'Unbalanced growth', *Oxford Economic Papers*, Oxford, June 1959; J. Casas, *Shipping Costs and Revenues*, Institute of Shipping Economics, Lectures and Contributions no. 31, Bremen, 1981; *Lloyd's List*, 9 August 1967, p. 3.

21 See also H.B. Chenery, 'Comparative advantage and development policy', *American Economic Review*, March 1961; *Journal de la Marine Merchande*, Paris, 17 August 1967, p. 1855.

22 Bank of Israel Research Department, *The Israel Merchant Marine, an Economic Appraisal*, Jerusalem, 1962, p. 31; General Council of British Shipping, *British Shipping Statistics 1979/1980*, September 1980; see also IBRD/IDA *Annual Report 1966–67*, pp. 66 and 67.

23 IBRD *Annual Report*, ibid., p. 34; problems arising in the treatment of ships (and aircraft) manufactured in one country for another or sold by one country to another without moving from the one to the other tend to cause a lot of problems (see Note 24 below); IBRD, *The World Bank, IFC and IDA, Policies and Operations*, April 1985.

24 IBRD *Annual Report*, ibid., p. 40; the problems of sale of ships and aircrafts are discussed in United Nations, Department of Economic and Social Affairs, *International Trade Statistics — Concepts and Definitions*, Series M, no. 52, New York, 1970, pp. 11–14; also IBRD/IDA, *Annual Report 1966–67*, pp. 66 and 67.

25 IBRD *Annual Report*, ibid., p. 99; as to consequences of cafs on export industries cf. I.F. Reitze, *Wahrungszuschlage in der Schiffahrt und ihre Auswirkungen auf die Exportwirtschaft*, Forschungsinstitut für Wirtschafts-politik an der Universität Mainz, 1980.

26 Industrial Bank of Japan, 'The Economics of Shipping' in *Survey of Japanese Finance and Industry*, 1964, p. 13. More details of cafs are discussed in H.L. Beth, *Fluctuations of Exchange Rates — their Impact on Shipping*, Institute of Shipping Economics, Lectures and Contributions, no. 26, Bremen, 1979.

27 Ibid., p. 14; in this case, a counter-cyclical influence means an inflow of foreign exchange partly or totally compensating for the initial decrease of the foreign exchange reserves (in a system of fixed parities) respectively a move of the foreign exchange rate towards the original level initiated by the reactions in the shipping sector (in a system of flexible exchange rates).

28 See 'National income', *Polish Perspectives*, Warsaw, February 1967, p. 50; in this model any variations of exchange rates and their impact on the financial position of the domestic industry are excluded by the assumption that the trade balance does not change.

29 Ibid.; see also E. Krzeezkowaski, 'Sraveniia natsional nogo dokhoda PNR i

nekotorykh evropeiskikh stran' (Comparisons of national incomes of PPR and certain European countries), *Vestnik Statistik*, no. 2, Moscow, 1966, p. 37; IDB, *Seventh Annual Report, 1966*, Washington DC, 1967, p. 2.

30   R.T. Brown, *Transport and the Economic Integration of South America*, Brookings Institution, Washington DC, 1966, p. 95; HMSO Central Statistics Office, *Monthly Digest of Statistics*, no. 429, September 1981.

31   Industrial Bank of Japan, op.cit., table 4; H. Williams, *The Impact of Exchange Rate Changes in Shipping Costs and Revenues*; M.H.P. Drewery (Shipping Consultants) Ltd, *Shipping Statistics and Economics*, no. 125, London, March 1981, pp. 2–3.

32   Instituto de Estudios de la Marina Mercante, *Law Marina Mercante Argentina, 1961*, Buenos Aires, 1961, p. 31; IMF, *Annual Report on Exchange Arrangements and Exchange Restrictions*, Washington DC, 1981.

33   Ibid.; quoted in free translation by R.T. Brown, op.cit., p. 104; see also *Consultation in Shipping*, UN publication, Sales no. 68: II.D.I; IMF, *World Economic Outlook*, Washington DC, May 1980.

34   J.B. Condliffe, *The Commerce of Nations*, W.W. Norton & Co. Inc., New York, 1950; cf. E.A. Georgandopolous, *Shipping in Developing Countries — Problems and Prospects*, Institute of Shipping Economics, Lectures and Contributions, no. 20, Bremen, 1978, p. 5.

35   Ibid.; see also, generally, H. Deck, *Foreign Commerce*, McGraw-Hill Book Co., New York, 1953; cf. C. O'Loughlin, *Economics of Sea Transport*, Oxford, 1967, p. 40; *British Shipping Business*, 11 September 1981, pp. 67–70.

36   See, generally, F. Machlup, 'The theory of foreign exchanges' in H.S. Ellis and L.A. Metzler, *Readings in the Theory of International Trade*, McGraw-Hill Book Co., New York, 1949, chapter 5.

37   But see also R.F. Mikesell, *Foreign Exchange in the Postwar World*, The Twentieth Century Fund, New York, 1954.

38   Ibid.; and also F. Southard, Jr., *Foreign Exchange Practice and Policy*, McGraw-Hill Book Co., New York, 1940; J.N. Wood, 'Shipping and the UK economy' in *Maritime Studies and Management*, vol. 3, no. 2, 1975, p. 78.

39   For further information on foreign trade generally, see US Chamber of Commerce, *An Introduction to Doing Import and Export Business*, Washington DC, 1962.

40   UNCTAD, Report by the Secretariat of, *Shipping in the Context of Services and the Development Process*, UNCTAD Doc. no. TD/B/1013, 9 November 1984, p. 5; cf. F.M. Fisher, *Tramp Shipping*, Bremen, 1957, p. 83.

41   See also E.E. Pratt, *Modern International Commerce*, Allyn and Bacon Inc., Boston, 1956; cf. UNCTAD, *Establishment or Expansion of Merchant Marines in Developing Countries*, op.cit., p. 83.

42   T.K. Sarangan, *Liner Shipping in India's Foreign Trade*, UN Publications, Sales no. 67.11.D.25, chapter 1, para. 43; cf. T. Totland, 'Protectionism in international shipping and some economic effects' in *Maritime Policy and Management*, vol. 7, no. 2, 1980, pp. 103–14.

43   T.K. Sarangan, op.cit., chapter IX, para. 62 and chapter 1, para. 9. The relevant tonnage is deemed to be that reported in Lloyd's Register of

Shipping *Shipping Statistical Tables* 1973, table 2 'World fleets — analysis by principal type' in respect of general cargo (including passenger/cargo) ships and container (fully cellular) ships, exclusive of the US reserve fleet and the US and Canadian Great Lakes.

44 A. Hunter, 'Some notes on national shipping lines: the Australian case', leaflet, extract from the *Economic Record*, Australia, March 1967 (Journal of the Economic Society of Australia and New Zealand, Australia National University), p. 43.

45 US Department of Commerce, *Assistance to Maritime Industries in Western Hemisphere Nations*, Washington DC, December 1965, p. 13; see also Edgar-Forrester, *Sale and Purchase Report*, October 1981.

46 But see 'Convenio de Transporte por agua de la associacion Latinamericana de Libre Comercio' (LAFTA: Convention on Transport by Water) drawn up at Montevideo, 30 September 1966; cf. A. Pedohl, *Verkehrspolitik*, Gottingen, 1958, p. 83.

47 For details see UNCTAD, Report by the Secretariat of, *Shipping in the Context of Services and the Development Process*, op.cit., paras 42–7, pp. 11–12; cf. B. Sonderstein, *International Economics*, 2nd edn, 1980, chapter 1.

48 *Indian Shipping*, vol. III, no. 4, Bombay, April 1951, p. 18; cf. Deutsche Bundesbank, *Die Zahlungsbilanz der Bundesrepublik Deutschland 1977 bis 1980 nach Regionen*; Bellagezu, 'Statistische Belhefte zu den Monatsberichten der Deutschen Bundesbank' Reihe 3, *Zalhungsbilanzstatistik*, no. 7, July 1981, p. 41, footnote 8.

49 See also W.A. Radius, *United States Shipping in Trans-Pacific Trade, 1922–1938*, Stanford University Press, Palo Alto; changes in the share of seaborne foreign trade in the total foreign trade are excluded in the following.

50 Cf. A.R. Ferguson *et al.*, *The Economic Value of the United States Merchant Marine*, Transportation Centre, Northwestern University, Evanston, Illinois, 1961, p. 256. Of course, the ability of a shipowner to introduce his vessels on another route depends on the character of the ship among others.

51 C.F.H. Cufley, 'The bulk carrier revolution', text of the lecture given at Thurrock Technical College, Grays, Essex, England, 15 February 1967, p. 9.

52 Z.S. Zannetos, *The Theory of Oil Tank Ship Routes*, Cambridge, Mass. Institute of Technology Press, 1967, footnotes, p. 99.

53 US Department of Commerce, *Assistance to Merchant Marines in Western Hemisphere Nations*, op.cit., p. 13; cf. F.M. Fisher, *Tramp Shipping*, op.cit., p. 81; P. Garoche, 'The effects of handling charges on ships' operations costs', UN *Transport and Communications Review*, vol. 3, April–June, 1981.

54 See, again, A. Ferguson *et al.*, op.cit., p. 308; cf. H. Kreussler, 'Auswirkungen, der Dollarkursverluste auf die deutsche Seeschiffahrt' in *Hansa*, no. 19, 1978, pp. 1588–91.

55 Ibid., p. 3091. This is based on the arbitrary, but generally acceptable, assumption that the importer pays the freight. As to the limits of this approach cf. A. Stromme Svendsen, *Sea Transport and Shipping Economics*, Bremen, 1958, pp. 421–3.

56 But see D.L. McLachlan, 'The price policy of liner conferences', *Scottish Journal of Political Economy*, vol. 10, Edinburgh, November 1963, p. 331;

cf. A. Renouf, 'Under-rated dollar — over-rated problem?' in *Seatrade*, September 1978, pp. 3–4.

57 But for now see 'Five ships fight a sacred cow', *The Sunday Times*, 10 September 1967; cf. R.G. Mendoza, 'Currency fluctuations in the shipping industry — a banker's view' in *Money and Ships, 1979*, Transcript, London, 1979, p. 18.

58 Ibid. The entry of the Atlas line into the Australia–Far East trade was partly a reaction by the liner owners who formed the line in the possibility that the use of containers on their major trading routes might make their conventional liner tonnage obsolete.

59 For details of the organization of maritime transport see UNCTAD, *International Transoceanic Transport and Economic Development*, op.cit., paras 12–22, pp. 5–10.

60 See also UNCTAD, Report by the Secretariat of, *Freight Markets and the Level and Structure of Freight Rates*, Doc. no. TD/B/C.4/38, chapter VII for a discussion of the incidence of these costs.

61 Cf. OECD Maritime Transport Committee, *Ocean Freight Rates as Part of Total Transport Costs*, OECD Doc. no. MT(68)7, May 1968, para. 38; cf. R.G. Mendoza, 'Currency fluctuations in the shipping industry — a banker's view', op.cit., pp. 13–21.

62 This is because where goods are carried on foreign-owned liners, cargo handling changes are usually included in the freight payment made in foreign exchange. However, that part of the handling charges which is incurred in national ports will be recouped by the country, thus reducing the net foreign exchange outflow.

63 See UNCTAD Doc. no. TD/B/C.4/38, op.cit., chapters I to IV for a description of these countries commonly known in the business as cross-traders; see *United Nations Conference of Plenipotentiaries on a Code of Conduct for Liner Conferences*, vol. II — Final Act (including convention and resolutions), Part One, Annex I (article 49(1) of the Convention, and Part Two).

64 These four major factors are quantifiable, i.e. are economic. There is a further (or fifth) factor, namely national defence and security, generally known as the geopolitical or strategic factors.

65 For a detailed discussion of these and other related issues see, again, UNCTAD Doc. no. TD/26/Rev. 1, op.cit., paras 2 and 26–53, pp. 5–12; see Institute of Shipping Economics, *Shipping Statistics*, no. 9, September 1981, pp. 16–19.

66 See again UNCTAD Doc. no. TD/B/C.4/38, op.cit., paras 32–5; this is true also for shipowners and operators in those countries where the currency is pegged to the dollar, as far as they get revenues in other currencies and/or make payments in ports of countries the currency of which fluctuates against the dollar.

67 For a discussion of the effects of the use of different terms of shipment see generally, UNCTAD Doc. no. TD/B/C.4/36, op.cit.; cf. for example, B. Sonderstein, op.cit., part IV.

68 United Nations, *Monthly Bulletin of Statistics*, January 1967, based on figures given in metric tons; cf. W. Gosele, 'Grundzug des europäischen

Warhrungssystems' in *Kredit und Capital*, no. 12, 1979, pp. 377–404 (Summary in English).

69 Ibid.; see also British Petroleum Company Ltd, *Statistical Review of the World Oil Industry*, 1965, p. 11; with regard to imports these questions are discussed in United Nations, *International Trade Statistics*, op.cit., pp. 46–7.

70 See Board of Trade and Central Statistics Office, *Input–Output Tables for the United Kingdom, 1954*, HMSO, London, 1961; see also H.F. Karreman, *Methods of Improving World Transport Accounts*, New York, 1961.

71 'Freight indices, from facts and figures about shipping, shipbuilding, seaports and seaborne trade', *Norwegian Shipping News*, Weltschiffahrts Archiv, Bremen, 1959, p. 27; IMF, *Balance of Payments Yearbook*, vol. 31, December 1980.

72 See also German 'Freight indices from facts and figures about shipping, shipbuilding, seaports and seaborne trade', op.cit., p. 294; cf. H.F. Karreman, op.cit., p. 8.

73 OEEC, Maritime Transport Committee, Paris, December 1954, OEEC Doc. no. MT(54) 17; according to UNCTAD, the 'beneficial owner' is the person, company, or organization which gains the pecuniary benefits from the shipping operations. Cf. UNCTAD, *Review of Maritime Transport, 1980*, op.cit., p. 12.

74 Ibid., chapter 1 'Importance of shipping to the participating countries' especially part B 'Shipping as an item in the balance of payments', pp. 11–12.

75 See also OECD, Maritime Transport Committee, Paris, December 1973, OECD Doc. no. MT(73) especially Part V 'The role of shipping in the national economy of the OECD member countries'; cf. OECD, *Maritime Transport 1973*, op.cit., pp. 108–9.

76 Ibid., 'The shipping industry in national accounts', pp. 91–8; methodical problems as to considering ships classified according to different countries of registry as 'residents' in the balance of payments are discussed in second half of Note 77.

77 Ibid., 'Analysis of the consolidated accounts of national shipping industries', pp. 98–104; see C. O'Loughlin, *The Economics of Sea Transport*, op.cit., pp. 31–3; cf. O'Loughlin, op.cit., pp. 36–7.

78 Ibid., but see especially 'The shipping sector in the balance of payments' and the tables given therein, pp. 104–12; it is generally accepted that international transactions of movable capital goods do not enter into the capital accounts, but into the merchandise accounts.

79 Based on the information made available to UNCTAD by Policarpo Gutierrez, Director of the Flota Mercante Grancolombiana; see also Institute of Shipping Economics, *Shipping Statistics*, no. 9, September 1981.

80 But see again UNCTAD Doc. no. TD/26/Rev.1, op.cit., chapter V in particular; cf. OECD, Maritime Transport, 1973, *A Study by the Maritime Transport Committee*, Paris, 1974, p. 89.

81 In this connection see also UNCTAD, Report by the Secretariat of, *Development of Ports*, UNCTAD Doc. no. TD/B/C.4/42; sometimes the current account and the long-term capital account are taken together: the so-formed balance is called basic balance.

82 In this connection see also UNCTAD, Report by the Secretariat of, *The Economic Position of Landlocked Developing Countries*, UNCTAD Doc. no. TD/B/206, which outlines the proposals of the UNCTAD Secretariat for research in this field.

83 Proposals were laid before the committee on Shipping at its third session for the inclusion of a specific item in the work programme of the committee covering technological progress; in this study the international transactions in the field of cabotage are excluded.

84 UNCTAD, *Development of Ports*, op.cit.; see also C.N. Brower and J.B. Tepe, 'The Charter of Economic Rights and Duties of States', *International Lawyer*, vol. 9, 1975, pp. 295–318.

85 A progressive report on conferences' practices and adequacy of shipping services was also submitted to the third session of the Committee on Shipping.

86 UNCTAD, Report by the Secretariat of, UNCTAD Doc. no. TD/B/C.4/39; J.C. Vanzant, 'The Charter of Economic Rights and Duties of States: a solution to the development-aid problem?', *Georgia Journal of International and Comparative Law*, vol. 4, 1974, pp. 441–62.

87 In this connection, the Trade and Development Board had before it, at its twenty-ninth session, a report by the UNCTAD Secretariat *Services and Development Process*, UNCTAD Doc. no. TD/B/1008 and Corr.1.

88 See the 'Preamble' to the *Programme of Action for the Establishment of a New International Economic Order*, G.A. Res 3202 (S-VI) of 1 May 1974; S.A. Tiewul, 'The United Nations Charter of Economic Rights and Duties of States', *Journal of International Law and Economics*, vol. 10, 1975, pp. 645–88.

89 For the Declaration on the Establishment of a New International Economic Order itself see the General Assembly Resolution of the Sixth Special Session, G.A. Res 3201 (S-VI) of 1 May 1974.

90 See Note 88 above; but see M.E. Kreimin and J.M. Finger, 'A critical survey of the New International Economic Order', *Journal of World Trade Law*, vol. 10, 1976, pp. 493–572; cf. OECD, *Maritime Transport, 1973*, op.cit., p. 107.

91 For the Declaration on Permanent Sovereignty over Natural Resources see General Assembly Resolution GA 1808 (SVII) of 14 December 1986; see also the International Covenant on Economic, Social and Cultural Rights of 16 December 1966, Art. 1, para. 2; infra, International Covenant on Civil and Political Rights of 16 December 1966; Art. 1, para. 2.

92 Part I, Article 3(b)(i-vi) of the Programme of Action, op.cit.; and T.M. Frank and E.R. Chesler, 'At arm's length: the coming law of collective bargaining in international relations between equilibriated states', *Virginia Journal of International Law*, vol. 15, 1974–75, pp. 579–609.

93 For the Declaration of the First United Nations Development Decade see UN General Assembly Resolution GA Res 1710 (XVI) of 19 December 1961; see also GA Res 1715 (XX) of 19 December 1961 and GA Res 2084 (XX) of 20 December 1965.

94 The Second UN Development Decade was proclaimed by the GA Res 2626 (XXV) of 24 October 1970. Its programme began on 1 January 1971; see also ECOSOC Res 1556 (XLIX) of 31 July 1970.

95 The International Development Strategy for the Second UN Development Decade can be found in GA Res 2626 (XXV) of 24 October 1970, op.cit.; but see G.A. Zahiriou, 'The UN Economic Charter and US investment policy', *Mercer Law Review*, vol. 27, 1976, pp. 749–80.

96 For the Declaration of the New Order see GA Res 3201 (S-VI) of 1 May 1974, op.cit.; see also F.G. Dawson *et al.*, 'Towards a New International Economic Order', *Virginia Journal of International Law*, vol. 76, 1975, pp. 297–353; General Council of British Shipping, *Survey of British Shipping*, 1960.

97 See Note 92 above; see also E. McWhinney, 'The international law making process and the New International Economic Order', *Canadian Yearbook of International Law*, vol. 14, 1976, pp. 57–72; S.G. Sturmey, *British Shipping and World Competition*, Athlone Press, London, 1962, pp. 193–6.

98 The International Development Strategy for the Second UN Development Decade can be found in GA Res 2626 (XXV) of 24 October 1970, op.cit.; but see J.F. Dorsey, 'Preferential treatment: a new standard for international economic relations', *Harvard International Law Journal*, vol. 18, 1977, pp. 109–35.

99 The opening of paragraph 53 of the International Development Strategy adopted by the UN General Assembly Resolution 2626 (XXV) of 24 October 1970, op.cit.; see also S.J. Rubin *et al.*, 'The Charter of Economic Rights and Duties of States', *Proceedings of the American Society of International Law*, vol. 69, 1975, pp. 225–46.

100 General Assembly Resolution 3577 (XXX) of 15 December 1975 contains a mid-term review and appraisal of progress in the implementation of the International Development Strategy for the Second UN Development Decade.

101 The First Biennal Over-all Review and Appraisal of Progress in the Implementation of the International Development Strategy for the Second UN Development Decade can be found in GA Res 3176 (XXVIII) of 17 December 1973; cf. IMF, *Balance of Payments Yearbook*, vol. 3, December 1980, p. xii.

102 For the implementation of the international development strategy in shipping and ports see, generally, UNCTAD, Report by the Secretariat of, *Shipping in the Seventies*, UNCTAD Doc. no. TD/177.

103 For shipping policies for the implementation of the strategy see the United Publication Sales no. E.72.11.D.15, chapter 1; see also the figures taken from the United Nations, *Monthly Bulletin of Statistics*, vol. XXXCV, no. 6, June 1981, pp. XXIV–XXV.

104 Ibid.; pp. 27–38; see also C.D. Mervis, 'The United Nations Seventh Special Session: proposals for a New World Economic Order', *The Vanderbilt Journal of Transnational Law*, vol. 9, 1976, pp. 601–39.

105 For instance all tonnage figures relating to the DMNs which are normally cited in reports either exclude or include Liberia and Panama, since the fleets registered in these two countries, *inter alia*, are believed to be effectively controlled by interests foreign to those countries.

106 For specific measures in the implementation of the Second UN Development Decade, see chapter 11 of UNCTAD, *Shipping in the Seventies*,

op.cit.; as to the composition of each country group compare World Bank, *Annual Report*, Washington DC, 1981, p. 21.

107 Part 4 'Invisibles including shipping', Article 53 of the Development Strategy for the Second UN Development Decade; for a full copy of the text see also Ademuni-Odeke, *Protectionism and the Future of International Shipping*, Martinus Nijhoff, Dordrecht, 1984, pp. 488–509.

108 Ibid., especially paras (c), (f) and (g) for expansion of national and multinational fleets of the developing countries; see also United Nations, Sales no. E.75.11.D.12; and World Bank, *Annual Report*, op.cit., 1981, p. 21.

109 Ibid., paras (a), (b), (d) and (j) for Entry to conference lines of the developing countries; see also UNCTAD, Report by the Secretariat of, *Final Report of the Group of Experts on Model Rules for Multimodal Container Tariffs*, UNCTAD Doc. no. TD/B/C.4/267.

110 Ibid., paras (a), (c), (d) and (j) for increasing and substantial participation in the carriage of maritime cargo; see again UNCTAD, *Final Report of the Group of Experts on Model Rules for Multimodal Container Tariffs*, op.cit.

111 Ibid., paras (d), (h) and (j) for freight rates; see also UNCTAD, Report by the Secretariat of, *Guidelines on the Introduction of Containerisation and Multimodal Transport and the Modernization and Improvement of the Infrastructure of Developing Countries*, UNCTAD Doc. no. TD/B/C.4/238 and suppl. 1–4.

112 Ibid., paras (e) and (h) for consultation; for a more detailed discussion of this and the problems of containerization and modal transport, see, *inter alia*, the report by the UNCTAD Secretariat, *Following Report on Aspects of Economic and Social Implications of International Multimodal Transport in Developing Countries*, UNCTAD Doc. no. TD/B/C.4/181.

113 Ibid., paras (e) and (i) for improvement of ports; see also UNCTAD, Report by the Secretariat of, *Report of the Group of Experts on Problems Faced by Developing Countries in the Carriage of Bulk Cargoes on its Second Session*, UNCTAD Doc. no. TD/B/C.4/234.

114 See UNCTAD, Report by the Secretariat of, *Review of Maritime Transport 1970*, tables 13 and 15. The increase in the tonnage of other dry cargo ships, (i.e. not bulk carriers), was a modest 40 per cent over the decade.

115 Preparations for the International Development Strategy for the Third UN Development Decade stated at the end of the 1970s; F. Eversheim, *Effects of Shipping Subsidization*, Institute for Shipping Economics, Bremen, 1958, p. 15.

116 For the text of the Declaration of the Third UN Development Decade, see UN General Assembly Resolution no. GA Res 33/197 of 1979; *Investment Incentives*, Cmnd Paper 2874, HMSO, London, January 1966, p. 18.

117 For the text of the International Development Strategy for the Third UN Development Decade see UN Doc. no. A/35/464 of 23 October 1980; *Afro-Asian Co-operation on Shipping Report of the Fleet Committee*, Cairo, 8–11 May 1967.

118 For the international reform aspect of the International Development Strategy for the Third UN Development Decade, see UN Doc. no. A/35/465 of 14 October 1980; OECD, *Maritime Transport*, Paris, 1966, p. 149.

119 For the international monetary reform (shipping and the invisibles) aspects

of the International Development Strategy for the Third UN Development Decade see UN Doc. no. A/35/465/Add.1 of 27 October 1980.

120 For the consolidation and progressive development of the principles and means of international economic law relating in particular to the legal aspects of the new international economic order see UN Doc. no. A/35/466 of 10 October 1980.

121 See also 'High-level intergovernmental group of officials to consider the review and appraisal of the International Development Strategy for the Third UN Development Decade' (North–South Monitor), *Third World Quarterly*, vol. 6, no. 3, July 1984, p. 733.

122 See also UNCTAD, *Bulletin*, no. 199 of February 1984; see also UN Doc. no. A/AC.1906/L/Add.1; cf. Draft Report UN Doc. no. A/AC/196/L.3 of 12 April 1979; S.A. Lawrence, *United States Merchant Marine, Policies and Politics*, Washington DC, 1966, p. 142.

123 Ibid.; see also UNCTAD Press Release TAD/INF/1534 of 1 February 1984; see also UN Doc. no. A/AC/196 of 29 September 1979; see also UNCTAD, Report by the Secretariat of, *UNCTAD Activities in the Field of Shipping*, UNCTAD Doc. no. TD/278 and Corr.1, op.cit.

124 Ibid.; and UNCTAD Press Release TAD/INF/1538 of 8 February 1984; see also UN Doc. no. A/AC/1961-3; for the period 1979-82, the prices of coconut oil and sisal hemp, for example, were taken from UNCTAD, *Monthly Commodity Bulletin*, in the December issue of the respective following year.

125 Ibid.; and UNCTAD Press Release TAD/INF/1542 of 13 February 1984; but see UN Doc. no. A/AC/196/L.1. The list given at the end of Note 127 below would include tanker cleaning surcharge (for coconut oil only), port delay and additional surcharges and a low productivity surcharge (for Colombia only).

126 The consensus text of International Development Strategy for the Third UN Development Decade was adopted on 15 September 1980 during the General Assembly, Eleventh Special Session on International Economic Cooperation – see again, UN Doc. no. A/35/64.

127 UNCTAD, Report by the Secretariat of, UNCTAD Doc. no. TD/B/C.4/46 of 6 January 1969, op.cit.; for foreign exchange purposes, freight rates include, where applicable, Suez Canal surcharges, bunker and currency adjustment factors, etc.

128 Ibid., especially 'Transport and balance of payments', Part D, paras 27–9, pp. 11–12. For example, the conversion of rates to other currencies was based on parities given in *International Financial Statistics* published by the International Monetary Fund.

129 Ibid.; see also UNCTAD, Report by the Secretariat of, *Shipping in the Context of Services and the Development Process*, op.cit. Annual freight rates were calculated by taking a weighted average of various freight rates quoted during the year, weighted by their period of duration.

130 Ibid., especially 'Balance of payments' considerations', paras 48–51, pp. 12–13; see also United Nations Publications, Sales no. E.70.11.D.7; UNCTAD, Report by the Secretariat of, *Review of Maritime Transport 1983*, UNCTAD Doc. no. TD/B/C.4/266, table 22.

131 See 'Shipping and foreign exchange', next subsection and notes to the text therein; and Chapter 10 'Shipping and the balance of payments'.

132 Ibid., United Nations Publication, Sales no. 69.11.D.1, chapter V, op.cit.; but see United Nations Publications, Sales no. E.70.11.D.9; see also UNCTAD Doc. no. TD/B/1013, op.cit., table 1, p. 19.

133 See UNCTAD, Doc. no. TD/B/C.4/36, op.cit., chapter XI; but see UNCTAD, Report by the Secretariat of, *The Liner Conference System*, Doc. no. TD/B/C.4/62/Rev.1; and UNCTAD, Report by the Secretariat of, *Protection of Shippers' Interests*, Doc. no. TD/B/C.4/176.

134 See, again, UNCTAD Doc. no. TD/26/Rev.1, op.cit., 'Balance of payments', paras 51–3, p. 11; for detailed discussions of this see UNCTAD, Report by the Secretariat of, *Adequacy of Services and Level and Structure of Freight Rates*, UNCTAD Doc. no. TD/B/C.4/62/Rev.1.

135 Ibid., chapter V, generally and 'Shipping and the balance of payments'; and UNCTAD, Report by the Secretariat of, *Report of the Group of Experts on Problems Faced by the Developing Countries in the Carriage of Bulk Cargoes* on its Second Session, Doc. no. TD/B/C.4/234, Geneva, 1981.

136 Ibid., chapter 5, subsection 1, 'The balance of payments problems', paras 149–51, p. 31; see also the *Report of the Group of Experts on International Sea Transport of Liquid Hydrocarbons in Bulk* on its Second Session, UNCTAD, Report by the Secretariat of, Doc. no. TD/B/C.4/263, Geneva, 1984.

137 Ibid., chapter 5, subsection 2, 'Shipping in the balance of payments', paras 152–67, p. 31; This is also according to H.P. Drewery, *Shipping Statistics and Economics*, no. 154, August 1983.

138 On the basis of the STNs' share in world trade, worldwide freight payments can thus be estimated to be the equivalent of approximately SDR 82.0 billion; see United Nations Publication, Sales no. E/f 83.11.D.2, pp. 122–5.

139 The major countries providing FOC facilities, Liberia and Panama, do not show any credit entries in the freight account; see also United Nations Publication, Sales no. E/F 83.11.D.2, pp. 142–5.

140 See IMF, *Balance of Payments Statistics*, vol. 34, Yearbook, Part 2, Washington DC, 1983; but see UNCTAD, Report by the Secretariat of, *Handbook of International Trade and Development Statistics*, 1983.

141 Conversion into US dollars on the basis of the following exchange rates (dollars per SDR): 1980 -1.30; 1981 -1.18; 1982 -1.10; see also the terms of reference of the Committee on Shipping regarding multimodal transport, *inter alia*, UNCTAD, Doc. no. TD/B/740.

142 For a more detailed coverage of general aspects of this problem, see D. Blumenhagen, *Shipping and the Balance of Payments*, Lectures and Contributions of the Institute of Shipping Economics, Bremen, 1981.

143 See also generally UNCTAD, *Services and the Development Process*, op.cit.; see also UNCTAD Doc. no. TD/B/301 annex II.

144 In 1982, the deficit of the DMNs in the sea transport balance amounted to nearly US $33 billion, which has contributed considerably to the existing imbalance in the balance of trade and invisibles.

145 Ibid. This has contributed to the debt problems of the DMNs. One way to remedy this situation is the pursuance of a consequent policy of import

substitution and of export promotion in regard to shipping services.

146 See also *Proceedings of the United Nations Conference on Trade and Development*, Geneva, 23 March–16 June 1964; *Report of the Committee on Shipping on its Fourth Session, Official Records of the Trade and Development Board, Tenth Session*, suppl. no. 5.

147 Ibid., vol. 1, Final Act and Report, United Nations Publication, Sales no. 64.II.B.I, Final Act, Recommendation A.IV.22; and Rules of Procedure of the Main Committees of the Trade and Development Board, UNCTAD Doc. no. TD/B/740 annex II, United Nations Sales no. E.79.II.D.3.

10 Merchant shipping and the balance of payments

Introduction: What is the Balance of Payments?

Apart from the provision and maintenance of employment, the earning and/or saving of foreign exchange is the other economic argument often cited to justify the establishment and/or development of national fleets.[1] The close link between the balance of payments and the level of employment in an economy has been demonstrated. There is even a closer association between merchant shipping and foreign exchange and therefore the balance of payments.[2] As the principal conveyor of international trade, on which foreign exchange is earned or spent, shipping is largely responsible for the gain or loss of foreign exchange and, consequently, the balance of payments.[3] But what is the balance of payments? It is that part of the nation's accounts that shows payments by residents as compared with receipts from foreigners resulting from international transactions.

Most payments and receipts are for goods or services provided by the citizens of one country to those of others. Some payments are *unrequited* transfers such as gifts and loans. The items are therefore divided into several categories.[4] This is essential for deciding economic policy, because the respective remedies for a balance of payments deficit or surplus differ according to the causes, which emerge only from study of the items.[5] The main components of the balance of payments are as shown in Table 10.1.

Table 10.1 Balance of payments

Balance of Payments
(imaginary quantities)

current account

Receipts		£ million	Payments	£ million
(1)	Visible exports (a)	1,000	Visible imports	1,200
(2)	Invisible exports (b)	300	Invisible imports	250

Capital Account (c)

(3)	Borrowed	500	Lent	550
		1,800		2,000
(4)	Accommodating monetary movements (d) (Change in gold and dollar reserves)	200		–
		2,000		2,000

Key and explanation to the table:

(a) *Visible exports* are the receipts from sales to people in other countries of commodities produced or re-exported from a given country.[6]

   Visible imports are the payments to foreign nations for the goods they export to a given country.[7]

(b) *Invisible exports* are the receipts from and payments for shipping, insurance, banking, tourism, interests, profits and dividends, migrant funds, gifts and legacies.[8]

   Invisible imports are the payments to foreign nationals for the services (in (b)) they export to a given country.[9]

(c) *Capital account* shows the balance of lending between a given country and the rest of the world. It includes loans between that country and other governments as well as long-term and short-term private investments by citizens, of that country, in other countries and vice versa.[10]

(d) *Accommodating monetary movements* are the transfers of gold and convertible currency, so called because they result from and reconcile the decisions to import, export, borrow and lend taken by people in their own country of preference and other countries. Surplus or deficits on the total balance of payments cannot continue indefinitely because no country has indefinitely large reserves, and a surplus for one country implies a deficit for one or more other countries. Sooner or later a country which is in deficit has to take action to stop the outflow of its reserves. This means either reducing its payments to people in other countries, increasing its receipts from them, or both. Many ways of achieving this objective are available to governments, at least in theory. First, devaluation of exchange rates may stimulate exports and reduce imports. If the domestic economy can produce sufficient exports and substitute for imports without causing inflation, devaluation may solve the problem. Secondly, internal deflation may cure the trouble by restricting demand for imports and exportable goods and stimulating exports.[11]

Thus, the term balance of payments' surplus or deficit are often applied to the *current* section of the balance of payments. In this case both the surplus and deficit can continue for a long time — e.g. if a country is earning a large current surplus and is willing to lend it abroad[12] it can carry on earning surplus without placing its trading partners in difficulty. The UK followed this policy in the nineteenth century and West Germany for several years after the Second World War. Shipping and marine insurance are crucial to the balance of payments, as the income from them forms the largest proportion of the UK invisible earnings.[13] To most advanced shipping nations balance of payments deficits are normally offset only by such invisible imports. Were it not for shipping, insurance and other services, the UK balance of payments would be perpetually in the red.[14]

Thus, both the advanced and emerging maritime nations realize the key importance of the merchant marines' contributions to their respective balance of payments accounts. In the case of the UK, from Table 9.10 (p. 423) it will be apparent that the earnings from the carriage of dry cargo[15] (in sea transport) were composed of earnings by ships owned by UK operators (freight-on operators, cross-traders, charter receipts and passenger revenue); ships on charter to UK operators (freight-on exports, cross-traders and charter receipts); and overseas operators' disbursements in the UK.[16] Total credits on dry cargo operations amounted to £799 million in 1972 rising to £2,158 billion in 1982. Total debits amounted to £744 million in 1972 rising to £2,775 billion in 1982. The balance of payments on dry cargo operations was therefore +£55 million in 1972 rising to -£617 million in 1982.[17]

It is interesting to note that this branch of shipping operations was in balance of payments deficit for the first time ever in 1979 to the tune of -£157 million rising to -£617 million in 1982.[18] The actual balance of payments calculation is obtained by subtracting the disbursements to overseas operators from earnings from ships owned by UK operators and ships on charter to UK operators. The near deficit of 1973 can probably be attributed to the Arab–Israeli war[19] while the first deficits from 1977 onwards were probably due to: the oil crisis; the fall of the Shah of Iran; the devaluation of the pound following strikes and the 'winter of discontent'; the Russian intervention in Afghanistan; the beginning of the Iran-Iraq war; and the Lebanese crisis.[20]

Together with balance of payments, there are two other concepts — foreign exchange and exchange control — which directly affect international shipping and trade. These have been partly dealt with in Chapters 6 and 9 and will also be treated briefly below.

The Balance of Payments

Foreign Exchange and Merchant Shipping

Foreign exchange is the system whereby one currency is exchanged for (or converted into) another; though sometimes the term is used as if it were synonymous with *foreign currency* itself.[21] There are now four (formerly three) main types of foreign exchange systems:

1 The Gold Standard in its various forms;[22]
2 Freely fluctuating exchange rates;
3 The several varieties of exchange controls, and now;
4 Special Drawing Rights (SDR).[23]

The fact that each country has its own monetary system is one of the principal complications of international shipping in particular and international trade and the balance of payments generally. The barter system had many drawbacks but, under that system, exchange between shipping merchants of different nationalities was as simple as between people of the same nationality.[24]

When commodity money, such as cattle, came into use it was a type of money generally acceptable to people of many nationalities. In the days of Columbus, Magellan, Marco-Polo etc., the precious metals were even more generally acceptable[25] and even after they had been turned into coins the metals could be weighed and payments between different peoples were still relatively easy. In fact gold and silver coins of many different issuing authorities often circulated in trade.[26] It was when money reached its final stage of being merely paper that complications of exchange between shipping merchants of different nationalities really became complicated. So long as the paper was convertible into gold on demand the difficulties were less serious, but with the introduction and use of convertible paper money the real difficulties of foreign exchange began,[27] leading to the eventual introduction of foreign exchange controls.

But first a look at the contributions of tanker operations to the UK balance of payments shown in Table 10.2. The total credits were £808 million in 1972 rising by about 75 per cent in ten years to £1,407 billion in 1982.[28] The debts were £944 million in 1972 but rising by only 30 per cent in the ten years to £1,133 billion in 1982. Unlike the dry cargo sector, the tankers' operations had a balance of payments deficit of £136 million in 1972 falling to £20 million in 1978.[29] It will be remembered that 1973 was the year of the Arab–Israeli War and 1976 was the year when Britain was forced to borrow from the IMF due to the balance of payments' problems.

442

Table 10.2 Sea transport: tankers (UK)

£ million

	1972	1973	1974	1975	1976	1977	1978	1979	1980	1981	1982
Credits											
Ships owned by UK operators											
Freight on exports	6	9	14	11	23	23	26	37	45	45	34
Freight on cross-trades	194	254	327	305	375	378	403	505	496	627	480
Charter receipts	84	125	193	207	239	195	183	306	276	333	378
Total	284	388	534	523	637	596	612	848	817	1,005	892
Ships on charter to UK operators											
Freight on exports	5	5	4	4	9	14	22	26	39	28	21
Freight on cross-trades	505	656	646	529	645	658	504	791	664	490	375
Charter receipts	4	15	53	41	28	22	36	43	41	49	56
Total	514	676	703	574	682	694	562	860	744	567	452
Overseas operators											
Disbursements in the United Kingdom	10	14	20	34	44	49	41	58	55	57	63
Total credits	808	1,078	1,257	1,131	1,363	1,339	1,215	1,766	1,616	1,629	1,407
Debits											
Ships owned by UK operators											
Disbursements abroad	113	135	260	237	320	324	272	372	337	483	411
Ships on charter to UK operators											
Charter payments	597	732	716	590	717	727	615	650	546	518	489
Disbursements abroad	106	138	265	259	280	259	208	292	267	227	179
Total	703	870	981	849	997	986	823	942	813	745	668
Overseas operators											
Freight on imports	128	188	196	180	200	170	140	168	97	123	54
Total debits	944	1,193	1,437	1,266	1,517	1,480	1,235	1,482	1,247	1,351	1,133
Balances											
Ships owned by UK operators	+171	+253	+274	+286	+317	+272	+340	+476	+480	+522	+481
Ships on charter to UK operators	−189	−194	−278	−275	−315	−292	−261	−82	−69	−178	−216
Overseas operators	−118	−174	−176	−146	−156	−121	−99	−110	−42	−66	+9
All tankers	−136	−115	−180	−135	−154	−141	−20	+284	+369	+278	+274

Source: Central Statistical Office 1983, table 3.4.

443

Table 10.3 Federal Republic of Germany: sea transport account

in million DM

	1975	1976	1977	1978	1979	1980
Credits						
Total receipts from abroad						
freight on imports, exports, and cross-trades[a]	5,846	5,639	5,878	5,547	6,220	7,013
receipts on port services etc.	1,563	1,603	1,575	1,881	1,987	2,436
passenger revenue	28	27	48	25	35	32
Total	7,437	7,269	7,501	7,452	8,242	9,480
Debits						
Total expenditure abroad						
freight on imports	4,881	5,027	4,705	5,188	6,131	6,173
port charges etc.	2,539	2,748	2,892	2,680	2,934	3,282
charter hire payments	762	634	680	662	821	1,046
Total	8,182	8,409	8,277	8,530	9,887	10,501
Sea transport balance	-744	-1,140	-777	-1,078	-1,644	-1,021
Memorandum item:						
Total receipts of German shipping from international services						
from residents[c]	996	924	1,066	859	987	1,231
from abroad[d]	5,874	5,666	5,926	5,571	6,255	7,045
Total	6,870	6,590	6,992	6,430	7,243	8,276

[a]Including (1) freights on exports (c.i.f.) from German exporters who are compensated by consignees abroad; (2) charter hire receipts from abroad.
[b]Excluding (1) passenger payments which are part of the travel account and cannot be separated; (2) freights on exports (c.i.f.) to foreign shipping which are compensated by respective revenues of German exporters.
[c]Excluded from the balance of payments.
[d]Freight receipts and passenger revenue, i.e. receipts from abroad excluding port charges etc.

Source: Blumenhagen, *Shipping and the Balance of Payments*, table III/1, p. 13.

Despite the international crises from 1977 onwards, the tanker sector actually made a balance of payments surplus of £284 million in 1979, from a deficit of £20 million the previous year, with a record in 1980 of £369 million.[30] However, see Table 10.3 for the West German sea transport account which contrasts to the UK account.

Merchant Shipping and Exchange Control

Because payments for shipping and the related services are always made in foreign currency, shipping tends to be very sensitive to its fluctuations. Such fluctuations can be due to market operations, as in a worldwide recession, or due to deliberate national policies, such as exchange controls.[31] That would be one of the methods by which the monetary authorities can directly influence the balance of payments. Exchange controls or foreign currency restrictions can be applied to the use of foreign exchange for buying goods and services or for transferring capital.[32] If exchange control is in operation the currency is not fully convertible, and the freedom to exchange it into foreign currencies, and pay for shipping services offered by foreign flags, is limited by the requirements laid down by the authorities.[33]

Unfortunately, this restriction is sometimes applied in order to discriminate against imports from particular countries. At other times it is directed against foreign flags. Hence cargo preference and flag discrimination.[34] For example, if dollars are scarce and francs and lira are plentiful the authorities can ration dollars to reduce imports from the USA while leaving citizens free to buy from France or Italy. A balance of payments deficit with one country may thus be corrected without inflicting on third countries, or flags,[35] the difficulties resulting from general measures that do not discriminate between them, such as devaluation, deflation or restrictions on imports. But exchange controls have disadvantages too, both in international shipping and therefore international trade relations.[36]

First, it directly restricts the free choices of countries in which individuals may buy or invest including which flag vessels they may or may not use. Second, it may provoke retaliation by countries discriminated against[37] in the form of countervailing actions, reverse flag discriminations and the imposition of a return exchange control. Usually it creates a 'black market' in the scarce currencies and — particularly in developing nations but also now in the so-called industrialized world — it may lead to corruption of officials.[38] When exchange controls are intended only to restrict movements of capital, some control of the use of foreign exchange for paying shipping companies or buying goods is also necessary, otherwise the regulations can be easily circumvented.[39]

The point to be made here is that exchange control was the precursor to state control and regulation of shipping. We have seen how exchange control was manipulated in order to discriminate against the USA and other national flags.[40] Where multiple exchange rates were in force (as in this case) there was a clear case of discrimination. That notwithstanding, it should be borne in mind that almost any form of trade restriction or exchange control involves some degree of discrimination, even if it is not deliberate but only incidental to some other policy objective.[41] The close association between international trade and the balance of payments, on the one hand, and shipping and international trade on the other enabled the easy application of foreign currency exchange control to shipping discriminations.[42]

When the size of an import or foreign exchange quota, for example, depends upon the recipients' previous imports there is discrimination against new importing firms, or new foreign sources of supply.[43] As we noted earlier this is normally achieved by encouraging importers to use FOB and exporters to use CIF through a combination of incentives and the manipulation of exchange control regulations, the sum total of the policy being to enable domestic exporters and importers to use the national flag and thereby save and earn foreign currency either way.[44] In that situation firms (either at home or abroad), whose costs have fallen to such an extent that they might reasonably have expected to attract to themselves a larger share of the market in the absence of controls, are penalized.[45]

Similarly, the authorities might pride themselves that, although they distinguish between *necessary* and *luxury* imports or even between different types of transactions, they do not discriminate between countries.[46] In practice discrimination on the basis of type of transaction often involves flag or country discrimination and vice-versa. For example, the limitation of tourist expenditure in non-sterling countries by UK residents might affect France and Switzerland more than Argentina and Chile, since few Britons spend their holidays in Latin America.[47] The action would also badly affect Spain, Portugal and Greece where millions of British residents spend their annual summer holidays. It is not only foreign exchange controls that have affected shipping. Another hurdle that has been recently added is restrictive shipping practices.[48]

Restrictive Shipping Practices and the Balance of Payments

In the early post-war years of inconvertible currencies there was a great deal of controversy as to the advisability of a country in serious balance of payments' difficulties *vis-à-vis* a particular country or currency area imposing discriminatory exchange controls[49] on transactions with that country or area while allowing relative freedom in regard to transactions with other countries. Although the detailed analysis of this process is beyond the scope of this study, the gist of the analysis is that countries sought to justify and extend exchange controls to the merchant marine industry.[50] After Keynes' theory of tariff protection and employment in the 1930s, the idea that direct controls should be discriminatory was further developed by Professor Ragnar Frisch in 1947 and 1948. It is probably from the latter's theories that the link between exchange control and flag discrimination was found.[51]

Given the existence of exchange controls, it is arguable that it is better for a deficit country to apply them in a discriminatory manner so that the impact falls upon surplus countries, than apply them indiscriminately to all its trading partners.[52] Similarly cargo preference and flag discrimination, by the emerging maritime nations especially, are aimed at the well established merchant marine fleets of the advanced shipping nations, rather than at those of their fellow developing countries.[53]

If a deficit country attempts to restore a balance of payments equilibrium by non-discriminatory restrictions on countries' exports, those countries in deficit will be driven more deeply into deficit and those which were either in approximate balance or had small surpluses will also find themselves moving into deficit.[54] They, in turn, will feel justified in imposing import controls, again with adverse effects on a wider circle of countries. In fact, taken to their logical conclusion, non-discriminatory controls would multiply until probably only one country would be left not applying restrictions.[55] Accordingly, it would be better for deficit countries as a group to discriminate in favour of one another by imposing restrictions most heavily against strong balance of payments' countries. This is presumably why the emerging maritime nations, jointly or singly, impose cargo preference and flag discrimination against the advanced maritime countries.[56] It is no coincidence that the former have a balance of payments deficit while the latter normally have surpluses.

However, it is not the contention that all developing nations have deficits nor that all balance of payments' surplus countries in the industrialized world are maritime.[57] In fact some rich nations, notably Switzerland, are landlocked and not what would be technically called great shipping nations. Even among the advanced maritime nations the surplus position has started to decline.[58] Take the UK for example: although her overall shipping balance of payments credits were £1,607 billion in 1972 rising to £3,565 billion in 1982, her deficits were nevertheless £1,688 billion and £3,908 billion respectively over the same period.[59] Accordingly, for almost the first time, this once-great shipping nation registered a balance of payments deficit of £81 million in 1972 rising to £343 million in 1982.[60] Curiously though, the pocket surplus of £89 million (1975), £78 million (1976) and £88 million (1977) were characteristically after the 1973 Arab–Israeli war and before the UK's loan from the IMF in 1976.[61]

After another deficit of £13 million in 1978, there followed another brief period of surplus of £127 million (1979) and £141 million (1980). However, the general trend thereafter is of a nation with a fast declining merchant fleet and balance of payments deficits.[62] See Tables 9.7 (p. 409), 9.9 (p. 420) and 9.10 (p. 423) for details. Apart from the general worldwide recession, the fact that many British shipowners have sold off, flagged out and transferred investments to such emerging shipping nations as South Korea, Singapore, the Philippines, Taiwan and Hong-Kong[63] has contributed to the decline of UK shipping. It is probably factors such as these that have put so much pressure on the pound sterling, especially against the dollar, to drop from the ratio of 2.4:1 to 1.3:1. It is not surprising that the UK has recently registered consecutive monthly balance of payments deficits.[64]

Therein lies the link between international trade and the balance of payments, on the one hand, and merchant shipping and both international trade and the balance of payments on the other.[65] The early discussion of this question was largely in terms of the effects of balance of payments discrimination on international trade and shipping relations. The question was whether restrictions applied in a discriminatory manner would restore a balance of payments equilibrium[66] with the minimum reduction in the trade volume of trade generally and ocean-borne trade in particular. Largely due to work of economists such as Fleming and Meade, however, the analysis has been carried forward in welfare terms.[67]

The question now becomes *what is the most effective way of using direct controls for balance of payments purposes in order to secure the minimum reduction in the total volume of world trade after taking into account the contribution of each unit of trade to economic welfare?*[68] In this respect a loss of £1 million of trade to country A might have more adverse welfare consequences than a similar loss to country B. Thus, in his *Trade and Welfare*, Professor Meade has dealt very thoroughly with welfare aspects of discrimination, using the device of apportioning 'welfare weights'[69] to the trade of various participating countries and taking into account also differences in supply elasticities. Meade further develops four *rules* which should be followed if a group of countries is to secure

Table 10.4 UK shipping industry: revenue from international activities: 1974–84

£ million

	1974	1975	1976	1977	1978	1979	1980	1981	1982	1983	1984
Dry cargo and passenger vessels*											
Freight on											
imports	273	305	351	359	309	372	343	256	376	383	442
exports	338	385	445	528	459	461	462	373	428	369	429
cross-trades	439	371	507	558	520	516	616	637	650	539	624
All freight	1,050	1,061	1,303	1,445	1,288	1,349	1,421	1,266	1,453	1,291	1,495
Charter receipts	266	312	384	395	294	300	268	240	172	98	118
Passenger revenue	153	200	224	257	273	311	385	381	510	589	605
Total revenue	1,469	1,573	1,911	2,097	1,855	1,960	2,074	1,887	2,135	1,978	2,218
Tankers											
Freight on											
imports	287	205	217	171	145	172	112	117	87	47	58
exports	19	15	32	37	48	63	84	73	65	79	125
cross-trades	973	834	1,020	1,036	907	1,296	1,160	1,118	653	666	684
All freight	1,279	1,054	1,269	1,244	1,100	1,531	1,356	1,308	805	792	868
Charter receipts	245	248	267	217	219	349	317	382	243	224	118
Total revenue	1,524	1,302	1,536	1,461	1,319	1,880	1,673	1,690	1,048	1,016	985
All vessels											
Freight on											
imports	560	510	568	530	454	544	455	374	462	430	500
exports	357	400	477	565	507	524	546	445	493	449	554
cross-trades	1,412	1,205	1,527	1,594	1,427	1,812	1,776	1,754	1,303	1,205	1,308
All freight	2,329	2,115	2,572	2,689	2,388	2,880	2,777	2,573	2,258	2,084	2,362
Charter receipts	511	560	651	612	513	649	585	623	415	321	236
Passenger revenue	153	200	224	257	273	311	385	381	510	589	605
Total revenue	2,993	2,875	3,447	3,558	3,174	3,840	3,747	3,577	3,183	2,993	3,203

*Includes ferries.

Source: HMSO Department of Transport, *Transport Statistics Great Britain 1974–1984*, table 4.23.

the *ideal* pattern of trade controls. It is impossible here to do more than simply draw attention to the approach.[70]

Meade uses the concept of the protective incidence of an import restriction to draw up various rules which should be followed if the optimum welfare position is to be achieved by countries imposing trade controls such as those applied in shipping.[71] For example, if two countries are restricting imports from each other, they should simultaneously relax their import restrictions on each other's products until one of them has completely removed its restrictions on imports from the other; if there are three countries, they should all relax their restrictions from each other simultaneously[72] (in such a way that each country's balance of payments remains in equilibrium) until one of the countries has completely removed its restrictions on imports from the other two. The idea then is that this liberalization could be extended to ocean-borne trade and then shipping itself.[73]

Meade's rules, however, imply that countries should arrange themselves in a kind of hierarchy in order of balance of payments strength, so that a weaker country is restricting imports from a stronger, and the restrictions which the weakest country imposes on imports from the strongest[74] has a protective incidence equal to the sum of the protective incidences of the restrictions which the weakest country imposes on the intermediate country and which the intermediate country imposes on the strongest country. It would then follow from this reasoning that the emerging shipping countries have a licence to impose cargo preference and flag discrimination restrictions[75] on flags from the advanced maritime nations. But it is impossible to do justice to the Fleming and Meade approach without making this chapter inordinately long. A short cut to discussion on the saving of foreign exchange argument would be acceptable.[76] Otherwise, for the kind of revenue being discussed in shipping and international activities, see Table 10.4.

Savings in the Balance of Payments

The Saving of Foreign Exchange Argument

The central theme of the discussion so far is that the saving of foreign exchange is what makes shipping tick in the minds of many nations. Foreign exchange is, of course, the currency of other countries with whom we deal,[77] and it is required by individuals and institutions to buy goods and services from, and to make gifts or loans to, people in this country. At the same time foreigners will buy our currency to pay for their purchases in or from this country. The two-way nature

450

of these transactions means that as long as relative prices are *right*,[78] most of a country's demands for equivalent demands for the currencies of other countries will be matched, leaving only small differences to be financed by movements of gold or foreign reserves. Most countries tend to hold as reserves only convertible foreign exchange because it will be readily acceptable by almost all countries in payments for goods and services.[79]

Inconvertible currency, on the other hand, may be acceptable only to the country that issued it. Foreign exchange is required in trade because there is no single currency that is accepted by all countries, although many use sterling and others dollars.[80] These have now given way to the SDRs on the IMF. It will be remembered that apart from merchant shipping there are other services that participate in the earning or saving of foreign currency.[81] One such invisible export is financial and allied services. It will be apparent from Table 10.5 that, under this heading, is included such factors as insurance, banking, commodity trading and merchanting of other goods (but not physical commodity exchange which would appear under visible exports).[82]

Also included are solicitors' and arbitrators' services, brokerages, etc. In the case of the UK, these earnings were £529 million in 1972 rising by 75 per cent in ten years to £2,145 billion in 1982. It will be noticed that most (if not all) of these services are related to merchant shipping.[83] Thus, the desire to save foreign exchange may be held to justify the encouragement of the national merchant marine, even when it would be an uneconomic use of the nation's natural resources. If the resources to be used in shipping could be used more productively in another way[84] and a portion of the resulting product exported to yield sufficient foreign exchange to cover the import of shipping services, anti-protectionists would argue that such a policy might be in the best interest of shipping-crazy nations. However, the affected nations would retort that there is no empirical data to back this proposition.[85]

Where, however, a country meets import quotas, tariffs or inconvertible currencies that prevent it from adopting the most economic way of earning or saving foreign exchange, recourse to a second-best solution, the uneconomical use of domestic resources[86] to economize on foreign exchange, becomes an attractive policy. The manifestations of this policy is of course the setting up of national fleets protected by cargo preference, flag discriminations, maritime subsidies, direct state intervention and manipulations of currency regulations.[87] Besides, the idea of *owning* rather than *hiring* merchant marines adds to the national wealth and appeals to nationalism. The extent to which foreign exchange can be saved by

Table 10.5　UK financial services[1] (including allied services)

£ million

	1972	1973	1974	1975	1976	1977	1978	1979	1980	1981	1982
Credits											
Insurance	240	217	251	323	507	599	644	576	447	617	620
Banking[2]	78	107	139	177	243	293	312	344	383	436	520
Commodity trading	90	110	140	209	201	110	163	140	180	160	215
Merchanting of other goods	35	55	80	90	108	120	132	145	160	200	234
Brokerage, etc.	74	99	160	207	215	233	244	331	370	490	481
Solicitors	12	13	15	19	29	36	44	52	61	68	75
Total	529	601	785	1,025	1,303	1,391	1,539	1,588	1,601	1,971	2,145

[1] Financial services are shown as credit entries only.
[2] Excluding the earnings on services rendered to related enterprises overseas by UK banks.

Source:　Central Statistics Office 1983, table 3.8.

the establishment of a national merchant fleet is substantially smaller than the freight cost of imports.[88]

To justify such a claim the yield per unit of investment in shipping should have a larger yield than the equivalent investment in an alternative venture. In addition, the foreign exchange earning or saving capacity of the corresponding investments[89] should likewise be in favour of the merchant marine. Using British figures: for every £100 of freight earnings of British ships, expenditure of foreign exchange was about £40, and this does not appear to vary greatly with changes in the level of freight rates. But this is an example of an advanced self-sustaining maritime nation. No comparable figures are available for a developing nation[90] but, for such a country, which may have to import ships and have repairs carried out abroad, the amortization of the purchase price and expenditures on repairs would absorb a further £15 or so on every £100 of foreign exchange saved.[91]

It may be reckoned, therefore, that for a country which has to import both ships and fuel (as is certainly the case with non-oil-producing emerging shipping nations) the net saving in foreign exchange by establishing its own shipping fleet will probably be less than one-half of the apparent gross or savings.[92] If the country also has to employ skilled foreigners to man the ships (as is again certainly the case with all the DMNs) the net savings or earnings will be further reduced and may be no more than 20 per cent.[93] To save or earn foreign exchange it is therefore necessary to have or create capacity in excess of that currently operated by most emerging shipping nations and then to increase the receipts of that capacity by preferential arrangements to switch cargoes.[94]

Cargo preferences, flag discrimination, maritime subsidies and exchange controls may achieve the same end for tramp ships by reducing costs to the point where national ships can undercut others in world markets.[95] However, at the same time the new national lines will have to spend externally which would doubtless mean spending whatever little foreign exchange they might have earned or saved. It is ironic that on this basis merchant shipping should be cited as a good bet in an effort to reduce external expenditures.[96]

The Reduction of External Expenditures Argument

If we consider a nation which has a significant part of its own foreign trade carried in foreign ships, then, in so far as the freight in either direction is being paid by its own residents, the substitution of national foreign ships must mean a saving of foreign exchange.[97] In so far as the freight earned by the foreign ships is being paid by residents of foreign countries, the earnings of the national ships must mean new

453

foreign exchange earnings. If the substitution takes place in a cross-trade, then, presumably, this second point will apply to the whole of the freight.[98] Precisely the same arguments apply to passenger fares, mail, money and other gross earnings. Thus, the whole of the revenue in both directions, whether or not in a cross-trade adds a gain or savings to the balance of payments.[99]

Any distinction between shipments made FOB or CIF is irrelevant. What is relevant is the freight currently being earned or saved by the foreign ships. If investment in shipping is accompanied by protection — e.g. cargo preference and flag discrimination[100] — which results in higher freight rates in the protected market, it is no longer the earnings of the national flag ships which represent a gain or savings to the balance of payments: it is the earnings of the foreign ships which could replace them without protection and at lower freight rates.[101] This point is equally important in considering the reservation of the coastal trades (cabotage) to the national flag.

Nevertheless, in a world of inconvertible, or only partially convertible currencies, however, it is possible that either the saving or the gains in foreign exchange (or both) may appear in some particularly desirable currency.[102] This possibility depends not on nominal *de jure* but on *de facto* non-convertible currency and the absence of currency leaks. Moreover, if a given currency is especially desirable to one nation, it is probably equally desirable to several others[103] and there may therefore be correspondingly intense competition to enter shipping services in which freight can be received in that currency, thus reducing the profits which are an important component of the net result. Unless they are engaged in purely cabotage trade, the national flag ships will inevitably have expenses outside their own country.[104] Unless their nation is an oil producer they will have to purchase bunkers abroad (indeed, even if it is an oil producer they will normally have to purchase some fuel abroad) and, in any case, they will incur port dues, agents' commissions, cargo handling costs, etc.[105]

In addition there are various other items of which the largest will usually be insurances, repairs, brokerage, repairs and the personal spending of the crew. Thus, a large number of these items involves foreign exchange expenditure incurred as a result of the substitution and must be deducted from the first item.[106] If the ships enter cross-trades they will have almost all of their running expenses (except crews' wages remitted home) in foreign exchange. Thus, for cross-traders this item will be much larger than it would be if a direct out-and-home trade were concerned.[107] Likewise, except where they are fully occupied in cross-trades, their new ships will probably spend large sums in their home territory. This will not enter directly

454

Table 10.6 UK shipping industry: receipts from international services and payments abroad

	1976 Dry cargo £mn	1976 Tanker £mn	1976 Total £mn	1977 Dry cargo £mn	1977 Tanker £mn	1977 Total £mn	1978 Dry cargo £mn	1978 Tanker £mn	1978 Total £mn	1979 Dry cargo £mn	1979 Tanker £mn	1979 Total £mn
RECEIPTS FROM INTERNATIONAL SERVICES												
Freights												
• on UK imports	333	216	549	343	170	513	306	141	447	359	167	526
* on UK exports	445	32	477	528	37	565	459	48	507	461	63	524
* on cross-voyages	507	1,020	1,527	558	1,036	1,594	520	907	1,427	516	1,296	1,812
Total freights	1,285	1,268	2,553	1,429	1,243	2,672	1,285	1,096	2,381	1,336	1,526	2,862
Passenger revenue												
• collected in UK	83	–	83	95	–	95	103	–	103	109	–	109
* collected abroad	141	–	141	162	–	162	170	–	170	202	–	202
Total passenger revenue	224		224	257		257	273		273	311		311
Time charter receipts												
* from abroad	384	267	651	395	217	612	294	219	513	300	349	649
from UK non-shipowners	18	1	19	16	1	17	3	4	7	13	5	18
Total time charter receipts	402	268	670	411	218	629	297	223	520	313	354	667
A Total receipts from international services	1,911	1,536	3,447	2,097	1,461	3,558	1,855	1,319	3,174	1,960	1,880	3,840
PAYMENTS ABROAD												
Disbursements abroad												
bunkers and lubricants	188	333	521	212	340	552	163	278	441	215	359	574
port and other expenditure	550	267	817	637	243	880	599	202	801	572	305	877
Total disbursements abroad	738	600	1,338	849	583	1,432	762	480	1,242	787	664	1,451
Time and voyage charter payments	85	717	802	110	727	837	101	615	716	77	650	727
B Total payments abroad	823	1,317	2,140	959	1,310	2,269	863	1,095	1,958	864	1,314	2,178
A–B Total receipts from international services *less* total payments abroad	1,088	219	1,307	1,138	151	1,289	992	224	1,216	1,096	566	1,662
CONTRIBUTION TO BALANCE OF PAYMENTS												
a credits – receipts from abroad (total of items marked *)	1,477	1,319	2,796	1,643	1,290	2,933	1,443	1,174	2,617	1,479	1,708	3,187
b debits – total payments abroad	823	1,317	2,140	959	1,310	2,269	863	1,095	1,958	864	1,314	2,178
a–b Net contribution to balance of payments	+654	+2	+656	+684	–20	+644	+580	+79	+659	+615	+394	+1,009

Source: General Council of British Shipping, *British Shipping Statistics, 1979/1980*, table 5.2, pp. 90–1.

into the balance of payments, but in so far as they replace the spending on foreign ships which formerly carried the trade, they represent a loss of foreign exchange which would otherwise have been earned.[108]

For much the same reasons as those given above, foreign ships cannot avoid spending large sums in the nations whose ports they visit. In other words, all items of expenditure on current goods and services which do not change the location of the expenditure upon substitution of national flag ships for a foreign one must appear under external and internal expenditures.[109] However, it does not greatly matter which, since both must be deducted from the foreign exchange earned or saved.

In contrast, as the role of merchant marines as earners and savers of foreign exchange dwindles[110] that of civil aviation seems to be on the upsurge. For the UK figures on this point see Table 10.6 where, under the credits, are first earnings from UK airlines. Under this category passenger revenue would be the most obvious[111] and includes expenditure by visitors to the UK and other passengers. Other headings under UK airlines are freight on exports, cross-trades and others. The second item under credits is expenditure by overseas airlines, i.e. their disbursements in the UK.[112] The total credits were £410 million in 1972 rising six times in ten years to £2,471 billion in 1982. Under the debts are, first, expenditures by UK airlines — i.e. their disbursements abroad. Secondly are UK expenditures on overseas airlines — i.e. passenger revenue such as visitors from the UK and other passengers.[113] Also under UK overseas expenditures are those on freight on imports and others. The total debts were £340 million in 1972 rising six times in ten years to £2,080 billion in 1982. The UK's balance of payments surplus was therefore £70 million in 1972 rising by over 500 per cent to £391 million in ten years in 1982.[114] Table 10.6 also shows receipts from international services and payments abroad for the UK shipping industry.

Foreign Exchange and Finance for Vessel Purchase

Thus, the third element which may affect the balance of payments concerns the capital cost of ships. If the investing nation simply purchases them from abroad (which is more often than not the case with the emerging maritime nations) then the immediate result of a decision to substitute national for foreign ships may be the outflow of foreign currency,[115] which is obviously the last thing to be desired. If the ships can be built wholly within the home territory or obtained from abroad as gifts, then this third effect on the balance of payments may be eliminated or minimized.[116] Between these two extremes there is a wide range of possibilities. On the one hand the ships can be purchased abroad on credit terms of varying types and, at the other extreme, the ships may indeed be built at home although only if there is a shipbuilding industry capable of building ships of the appropriate size and types.[117]

Most developing countries do not have any building or ship-repair facilities. Even where such facilities do exist, however, it is probable that some components (e.g. winches, wind glasses, radios and radar equipment, generators, steering gear and, conceivably even the main engine) may have to be imported from abroad.[118] Alternatively, it may be necessary to import specialized technicians, with salaries and expatriation expenses payable in foreign exchange, or to pay licence fees for the manufacture of equipment to foreign designs and patent rights. Such arrangements are quite common[119] even in the highly developed shipbuilding nations within the traditional maritime nations. The first two of these effects on the balance of payments are likely to be roughly constant in real terms over the life of the ship. This would be so except for reductions in earnings.[120]

There may also be higher foreign exchange payments for repairs in the 5th, 9th, 13th and 21st years of the ship's life when the quadrennial surveys (which are of increasing severity) fall due. However, that associated with capital is highly variable[121] and is largely within the control of the investing country. Control can be exercised by obtaining the ships as part of an aid programme, or on credit terms of varying types and at such rates of interest as may be obtainable by negotiations.[122] As yet another alternative the ships can be obtained second-hand, when their operating lives under the new flags would be shorter, the repair costs somewhat higher and the initial cost correspondingly less. It does not, therefore, follow that second-hand ships will necessarily make larger net contributions to the balance of payments.[123]

The Balance of Trade Rationale

Merchant Shipping and the Balance of Trade Argument

The fourth shipping-for-foreign exchange argument concerns expenditures on current goods and services, alternatively known as the balance of trade argument. The balance of trade, or merchandise balance, is the difference between the value of the goods that a nation imports and the value of the goods that it exports.[124] The balance of trade differs from the balance of payments in that it excludes capital transactions, payments for services (e.g. shipping services), and shipments of gold. But the two are interrelated.[125] For, when a country has an export surplus, its balance of payments would be favourable. When it has a deficit balance of trade, its balance of payments would be unfavourable. But shipping and other invisible transactions tend to make the difference between the two balances (trade and payments).[126]

The balance-of-trade concept is losing much of its usefulness because of the growing importance of capital transactions (e.g. capital expenditures on ships as outlined above) and payment for services. For example in every year during the 1980s, the USA enjoyed a balance of trade surplus[127] but suffered an almost uninterrupted succession of balance of payments deficits. The relationship between the balance of payments and merchant shipping has already been described above. International shipping and the balance of trade is related, first, because it is merchant shipping that transports the goods to and from any given country;[128] second, because shipping itself is regarded as the services in the balance of trade equation; and last, because ships can themselves be the subject of international trade. In this latter case they sail themselves rather than being conveyed.[129]

The shipping expenditures on current goods and services can be considered under four major headings. The first is that involving crews' wages. If the crews of the new shipping companies are resident at home, and this was not true of the foreign ships which formerly carried the trade,[130] the place where the crews' wages are paid and spent will change. This might lead to savings in foreign exchange, but not necessarily as the crews do spend half the time abroad incurring expenses in foreign currency. If the new shipping lines enter cross-trades then the crews must be expected to spend more outside their own country.[131]

The second possibility of an item of expenditure on current goods and services appearing under neither of these headings concerns management costs, be they home-based or contracted out.[132] If the management of the new lines (apart from agencies, which are usually enumerated by commissions) is located in the investing country, then the associated costs will be transferred from a foreign country to the home territory.[133] In practice this is very likely, although, as with crew costs, it depends on there being a sufficient number of trained men available.

The third possibility concerns the change in the location of purchases – e.g. of ships' stores – which will arise partly out of convenience and partly out of changes in effective prices; inspection of goods is more expensive at a distance.[134]

The fourth possibility is that, by introducing discriminatory controls, it will be possible to reduce foreign exchange spending by

458

Table 10.7 Sea transport account – balance of payments (UK)

	1976 Dry cargo £mn	1976 Tanker £mn	1976 Total £mn	1977 Dry cargo £mn	1977 Tanker £mn	1977 Total £mn	1978 Dry cargo £mn	1978 Tanker £mn	1978 Total £mn	1979 Dry cargo £mn	1979 Tanker £mn	1979 Total £mn
UK shipping industry contribution to balance of payments	+654	+2	+656	+684	-20	+664	+580	+79	+659	+615	+394	+1,009
of which UK owned ships	+697	+317	+1,014	+752	+272	+1,024	+632	+340	+972	+663	+476	+1,139
Overseas Operators												
Payments to overseas operators by UK residents — freight on imports	765	200	965	860	170	1,030	1,020	140	1,160	1,268	168	1,436
passenger revenue	56	–	56	52	–	52	52	–	52	74	–	74
Total payments to overseas operators by UK residents	821	200	1,021	912	170	1,082	1,072	140	1,212	1,342	168	1,510
Disbursements in UK by overseas operators	369	44	413	429	49	478	485	41	526	506	58	564
Overseas operators net contribution to balance of payments	-452	-156	-608	-483	-121	-604	-587	-99	-686	-836	-110	-946
Sea transport account (net)	+202	-154	+48	+201	-141	+60	-7	-20	-27	-221	-284	+63

Source: General Council of British Shipping, *British Shipping Statistics, 1979/1980*, table 5.3, pp. 92–3.

national flag ships. At first this is an attractive possibility, but as was evident above and in previous chapters, this may not necessarily be so.[135] In this respect, see Table 10.7 for the UK sea transport account — balance of payments — especially that relating to overseas operators. This leads us to our next and fourth argument, that of balancing adverse exchange rates.

The Balancing of Adverse Exchange Rates Argument

The argument that the establishment of own national merchant marine may help to offset adverse exchange rates and, consequently, the balance of payments is sometimes known as compensation for an overvalued exchange rate.[136] Exchange rates are, of course, the rates at which one currency can be exchanged for another. When two countries are on the gold standard, for example, the exchange rate will vary only between very narrow limits. On the other hand, with a system of freely fluctuating exchange rates the rate varies from day to day.[137] Under a system of exchange control, of the restrictions type, there may be an official fixed rate of exchange and two different rates of exchange between the same two currencies according to the purpose for which the foreign currency is required — that is, there may be multiple exchange rates.[138] This happened in Uganda in the early 1980s.

Since Germany first adopted the idea in the mid-1930s, special rates of exchange have been frequently offered to foreign tourists, for example. These and other services do earn or save foreign currency and help the balance of payments,[139] and include commissions, postal services, films and television, royalties, services rendered by enterprises, earnings on construction works overseas, expenditure by overseas students and journalists, overseas governmental and non-governmental bodies, advertising, exploration and exploitation[140] of natural resources, consultancy, research, etc. In the UK, on the credit side, these were £1,094 million in 1972 rising 500 per cent in ten years to £6,564 billion in 1982.[141]

On the debit side the figures were £601 million in 1972 but this time rising only 400 per cent over the same period to £2,861 billion in 1982. Overall, therefore, the balance of payments from this sector was in surplus to the tune of £493 million in 1972[142] rising 600 per cent in the ten years to £2,921 million in 1982. It is these kinds of surpluses that balance the deficits in other services as well as those in the visible trade.

Be that as it may, an aspect of the foreign exchange which may cause a problem is the compensation of shipping companies[143] for the competitive handicap of an overvalued exchange rate. This is simply

460

the removal of an imposed handicap and not part of an attempt to enable national shipping to steal a march on its rivals, although an element of assistance may be contained in an ostensibly compensatory policy.[144]

An undervalued currency, such as the Japanese yen at various periods in the inter-war years and sterling after the 1949 devaluation, is of assistance to shipping but cannot be classified as part of a shipping policy as such.[145] As a service industry, shipping is often adversely affected by policies designed to help sections of the domestic economy. For example, part of the costs of assisting the British cotton industry caused difficulties for British shipping in the Indian trades. Secondly, protection to British agriculture[146] did reduce the cargoes available to British ships seen most clearly in the way in which the beet sugar subsidy reduced trade from the West Indies. Finally, the Imperial Preferences in 1932 reduced the trade from the Argentine and damaged the old established lines in the trade[147] to the disadvantage of the shipping companies handling Commonwealth produce.

When the merchant marine industry suffers from acquired disadvantages arising from the protection of domestic industries, the use of a maritime subsidy to counter this disadvantage represents a movement towards, not away from, the optimum allocation of resources.[148] If at the same time a tariff is imposed on imports, a subsidy is paid to shipping calculated just to offset the increase in wages and other costs caused by the protection of the domestic industry, that subsidy does not harm other maritime nations.[149] Clearly the tariff harms the merchant marine industry and the whole deal can only be prevented from harming world shipping if the protectionist country calculates its subsidy so that its merchant marine fleet is reduced by just that amount by which its demands for shipping services as a whole is reduced by the tariff.[150]

If it did this the subsidy would fail in its compensatory aim. Of the 'services', or invisible trade, the one directly linked to shipping is insurance generally and marine insurance in particular. Table 10.8 shows this among the overseas earnings of UK financial institutions ('The City').[151] It will be apparent that the insurance companies' earnings are made up of underwriting (overseas business written in UK), direct investments (profits from overseas business written outside the UK through subsidiaries, etc.) and portfolio investments.[152] Still on the credit account are earnings by Lloyds which also include underwriting and portfolio investment. Finally are earnings by brokers. The total earnings by this institution was £375 million in 1972 and £1.203 billion in 1982.[153] Against that was the debt account which amounted to a meagre £5 million in 1972

Table 10.8 Overseas earnings of UK financial institutions ('The City')

£ million

	1971	1972	1973	1974	1975	1976	1977	1978	1979	1980	1981
INSURANCE											
Credits											
Companies											
Underwriting (overseas business written in UK)	40	38	34	32	31	44	46	37	22	9	34
Direct investment (profits from overseas business written outside the UK through subsidiaries, etc.)	62	85	76	62	46	190	230	276	256	177	106
Portfolio investment	35	37	47	54	61	73	64	77	95	111	171
Lloyd's											
Underwriting (overseas business written in UK)	141	138	114	127	166	279	334	354	312	188	254
Portfolio investment	16	19	25	37	34	57	48	71	112	153	128
Brokers	55	58	60	84	115	170	205	237	228	238	302
Total	349	375	356	396	453	813	927	1,052	1,025	876	995
Debits											
Direct investment income due to overseas parents of UK branches, etc.	4	5	9	13	5	7	14	13	16	21	21
Net earnings by UK insurance institutions	345	370	347	383	448	806	913	1,039	1,009	855	974
BANKING											
Credits											
Financial (including inter-company) services	71	93	115	150	188	257	300	320	355	388	445
Direct investment income from overseas subsidiaries, branches, etc.	46	70	115	93	118	131	169	190	291	365	504
Portfolio investment income	—	—	—	—	10	10	15	30	40	60	130
Interest and discount on:											
Export credit	68	77	105	132	147	168	172	233	308	359	352
Other lending in sterling	42	57	103	145	159	214	157	198	270	474	872
Balance of interest on borrowing and lending in foreign currencies	16	44	54	151	138	210	107	346	−44	352	1,010
Total	243	341	492	671	760	990	920	1,317	1,220	1,998	3,313

Debits											
Direct investment income due to and services rendered by overseas parents	58	82	97	142	194	257	282	273	293	348	456
Interest on borrowing in sterling	114	137	236	348	354	341	308	343	720	1,203	1,528
Total	172	219	333	490	548	598	590	616	1,013	1,551	1,984
Net earnings by UK banking institutions	71	122	159	181	212	392	330	701	207	447	1,329
COMMODITY TRADING, etc.											
Commodity trading	70	90	110	140	209	201	110	163	140	180	160
Merchanting of other goods	30	35	55	80	90	108	120	132	145	160	200
Total commodity trading, etc.	100	125	165	220	299	309	230	295	285	140	360
INVESTMENT TRUSTS											
Gross income	35	39	47	56	51	58	62	64	70	93	104
Less interest paid abroad on foreign currency borrowing	4	8	14	16	10	11	11	12	12	11	13
Net income of investment trusts	31	31	33	40	41	47	51	52	58	82	91
UNIT TRUSTS (net income)	3	5	6	8	9	11	12	15	22	33	39
PENSION FUNDS (net income)	4	6	9	10	16	14	17	24	46	87	107
SOLICITORS	11	12	13	15	19	29	36	44	52	61	67
BROKERAGE ETC. EARNINGS											
Baltic Exchange	25	35	53	103	146	147	155	153	200	181	285
Stock Exchange	10	15	18	19	18	16	20	21	25	43	35
Lloyd's Register of Shipping	4	6	7	10	14	17	21	20	18	23	28
Other brokerage	18	18	21	28	29	35	37	54	88	123	137
Total brokerage, etc. earnings	57	74	99	160	207	215	233	248	331	370	485
Total net earnings of above institutions	622	745	831	1,017	1,251	1,823	1,822	2,418	2,010	2,275	3,452

Source: Central Statistics Office 1982, table 6.1, p. 35.

and £29 million in 1982, representing a net balance of payments by UK insurance institutions of £370 million and £1.174 billion respectively. It will be remembered that the debt account[154] is represented by direct investments income due to overseas parents of UK branches.

For the first time, the banks are beginning to overtake insurance as the single largest source of foreign currency. This represented net earnings of £122 million in 1972 and £1.656 billion in 1982. The other institutions[155] involved are leasing, commodity trading, investment trusts, unit trusts, pension funds, solicitors and brokerage. Overall, the total net earnings of the above institutions was £745 million in 1972 rising 600 per cent in the ten years to £4.369 billion in 1982.[156]

Guaranteed Trade and Avoidance of Disruptions

The fifth balance of payments argument in favour of merchant shipping is related to protective measures in case of hostilities: to maintain the lifeline in that event. A country dependent on overseas trade may find its shipping withdrawn[157] or becoming very expensive in times of war or international crisis, with serious economic consequences. The establishment and protection of a merchant marine fleet to enable its trade to continue on a regular basis will insulate the economy from these effects,[158] although it may reduce average real income over the long term. The separate experiences of the USA and Australia in the 1914–18 War, in which each suffered from the withdrawal of British ships and from very high freight rates, were important factors leading each country into the establishment of international merchant marine services under their own flags.[159]

The case of the US denial of ships to Japan during the latter's expeditions against China and, later Korea, no doubt influenced the tremendous build-up of Japanese shipping which partly led to Japan becoming the leading shipping nation in the world, apart from the Liberian flags of convenience.[160] Not all that achievement is attributable to her bitter war experience, however. The other factor was the Saudi Arabian actions to stop Arab tanker shipments to the USA and Israel during the 1973 Arab–Israeli War,[161] apparently because of the US support for Israeli against Arab interests. The same Arab–Israeli crisis saw the Liberian government deny her Liberian registered (but US beneficially owned) flag vessels from US use in order to maintain a neutral status.[162]

Many countries' experiences during the Second World War, are all cases in point. The recent Lebanese crisis, the Iran–Iraqi war and the general instability in the oil-rich Middle East has further emphasized the need for each nation to possess its own national fleets.[163] It is for this reason that the USA and her Western allies have in mind a Rapid Deployment Force (RDF) especially for the world's trouble spots. However, of modern examples, that provided by the role of the merchant marine in the 1982 Falklands War[164] remains by far the most outstanding. Thus, many nations would like to avoid that dilemma in the event of future hostilities. The role of merchant shipping in such an event is the proper subject of security and national defence.[165]

It suffices to point out at this stage that the avoidance of disruptions is an excess-capacity position. If only a tramp or tanker fleet is required all that is necessary is to lower costs. Cargo preference, flag discrimination and premium freight rates for government-sponsored cargoes[166] are an alternative to operating subsidies in this instance. A liner fleet is more difficult. Legislation to force liner conferences to accept national merchant marine vessels might have been needed before the UN Code of Conduct for Liner Conferences.[167] Alternatively various forms of cargo preferences, flag discrimination and direct state intervention might serve the same end. The use of preferential arrangements to protect a higher-cost fleet might raise freight rates and possibly reduce trade volumes and exacerbate the problem to which a solution is being sought.[168]

The National Economic Infrastructure

The Development of Shipping-related Infrastructure Argument

The sixth argument in support of state establishment, development and protection (for balance of payments purposes) is that of the possible development of shipping-related infrastructure or industries.[169] Economic infrastructure is the services regarded as the essential basis for creating a modern economy. These are transport, power, education, health services, housing, etc. It is also described as *social* or *public* overhead capital where the emphasis is on the capital assets that provide services[170] such as roads, bridges, railways, houses, schools, reservoirs, etc. The *infrastructure* requires extensive capital for its initial creation but, if it does not attract funds from private enterprise, it may need to be financed by the state, public corporation, local authority or some other public authority.[172]

In the nineteenth century, for example, British private investors financed most of the railway and shipping developments both here and in the former colonies. Roads have seldom been financed by private capital, although they can be paid for by tolls.[173] Mass education usually requires state aid, particularly in the developing nations, but can be financed privately if incomes rise. Investment in social capital thus does not always yield a profit though it may benefit the economy as a whole. For the purposes of this argument the merchant marine industry[174] may be treated as social capital. It may be particularly necessary in initiating the development process in the DMNs where these resources and facilities are still largely under-developed and under utilized.[175]

For example, a road which links the interior of a country to its main seaports will open up possibilities for the production of specialized crops that can be transported to the coast and sold in exchange for goods manufactured in towns or imported[176] from overseas. Therefore, the development of an efficient transport system and means of communication, of which the merchant marine is para-mount, can rapidly extend the potential market for the product and promote further specialization.[177] For most DMNs the creation of the infrastructure is currently best achieved by borrowing from the richer TMNs for two main reasons:[178]

1   income per head is too low to permit much saving; and
2   even when domestic saving is possible the transfer of resources is often blocked by protective commercial and fiscal systems.

Where for political and other reasons the pace of development is forced, or where the political unit is small and its economic future doubtful, or where local laws do not secure security for tenders, private foreign loans may be hard to arrange.[179] Hence the growth in recent years of alternative sources of loans or direct grants such as the IBRD (World Bank), IMF, the UN Special Fund for Economic Development and the governments of the richer industrialized nations.[180]

Some economists have argued that just as the TMNs have advanced by their own efforts, the DMNs would be more firmly based if they did likewise: that is, developing their human as well as their physical resources,[181] creating a framework of laws and institutions in merchant marine banks, insurances, property etc., that encourages efforts and enterprise; and learning from the advanced maritime nations the arts of initiative and the capacity to recognize and provide for risks.[182] These processes take a long time, and the DMNs probably cannot achieve in a decade what took the TMNs centuries to achieve without sacrificing the individual liberty and the initiative that is thought to be at the root of long-term economic development.[183]

The seventh balance of payments argument is that it assists the development of related merchant marine industries. Activities which

466

are closely related to the merchant marine industry and its development and which may contribute to the foreign exchange earnings are:[184] ship-repair, pilotage and touring, ship chartering, the supply of bankers and other services. It is argued that the gradual development of these services will also increase the contribution of the national merchant marine to the balance of payments.[185] The most important, however, remains the coordinated development of the infrastructure in ports, shipbuilding and heavy engineering industry and in land-transport connections in line with the development of foreign trade and the merchant marines, taking into account technological progress.[186]

It is this technological progress that leads to the reduction of unit transport costs in the total transport chain or better quality of services (for example, bigger ships, unitization, etc.).[187] The necessary measures are:

1 Planning of infrastructure development on the basis of pre-investment studies; and
2 Advance initiation of developments in order to avoid congestion in ports and bottlenecks in the inland transport chain.

There are also many other by-products of the merchant marine industry that naturally follow with the establishments of the former.[188]

Supporters of this view, especially the DMNs and other protectionists, argue firstly that foreign currency, which was originally spent on these services abroad, would be saved,[189] and secondly that, when established, these services would in themselves earn foreign currency when they are offered to foreign vessels calling at the country's ports and repair yards. This is probably true, the problem being, however, that they cost foreign exchange to establish in the first place.

The Merchant Shipping Industry's Direct
Contribution to the Balance of Payments

The eighth, and final, argument (with which we should perhaps have started) is the shipping industry's direct contribution to a country's balance of payments. Table 10.9 which dates from the mid-1960s when the going was still favourable, is a much earlier one than the ones used previously herein,[190] and shows that the merchant shipping contribution to the balance of payments was in surplus. Table 10.10 shows a comparison of returns between merchant shipping and other industries. In 1966 the comparison of exports per £100 of annual capital-fixed capital investment was £420 for shipping as against £280

Table 10.9 Direct effect of the UK shipping industry on the current balance of payments: 1966

£ million

	UK-owned ships	Ships' time chartered to UK residents	Total
1 Freight on exports	133	13	146
2 Freight on cross-trades	207	160	367
3 Passenger revenue	52	–	52
4 Time charter hire earned abroad	32	9	41
Gross Foreign Exchange earnings	424	182	606
5 Foreign disbursements including cost of chartering	-241	-240	-481
Net Foreign Exchange earnings	183	-58	125
6 Freight on UK imports paid to overseas shipowners			-223
7 Passage money paid to overseas shipowners			-12
8 Overseas shipowners' disbursements in UK			112
UK balance of payments: shipping account			2
Net Foreign Exchange earnings of UK ships	183		
9 Freight on imports and passenger money paid by UK residents	209		
10 *Estimated* coastal trade earnings by UK-owned ships	31		
	240		
11 *Estimated* extra disbursements in UK by overseas owners, if there were no UK-owned ships	-90		
	150		
12 *Estimated* direct effect on current account of UK balance of payments of operations of UK-owned ships	333		

Notes:
(a) The estimated figure for the direct effect on current account of UK balance of payments of operations of UK-owned ships in 1968 is about £500 million.
(b) Additional information for estimates for items 10 and 11 from the Board of Trade and the Chamber of Shipping.

Source: *The Rochdale Report*, table 19.1, p. 344.

Table 10.10   Comparison of investment return per employee between shipping and manufacturing industry (UK)

	Exports per £100 of annual fixed capital investment (£)	Exports per employee (£)
All manufacturing		
1966	280	466
1967	300	481
UK shipping industry		
1966	420	2,862
1967	350	3,179

Source: *The Rochdale Report*, p. 350.

for the manufacturing sector giving a ratio of 3:2 in favour of shipping. The figures of exports per employee over the same period were £2,862 as against £466 — a ratio of 6:1 in favour of merchant shipping.[191]

This ratio had risen to 9:1 a year later in 1967 — i.e. £3,179 as against £350. Thus, at the time, there was clear-cut evidence to prefer investment in merchant shipping to that in the manufacturing sector. This prompted the then British Chamber of Shipping (now the General Council of British Shipping) and the Department of Economic Affairs to contend in their evidence to the Rochdale Committee[192] that, although an industry's contribution to the balance of payments is not necessarily equal to its value added, in the case of the merchant marine industry, it is. Thereupon the Rochdale Committee reported:

> We have sought to determine whether a given balance of payments benefits is produced significantly more efficiently by devoting national resources to shipping than by devoting them to other activities. This question might be put in another form: what is the cost in domestic resources of producing a given balance of payments returns from shipping operations as compared with the cost of producing the same return from the cost of industry on average and, if possible, compared with a few individual industries which are regarded as good exporters and, or good savers of imports.[193]

As a result, in evidence in support of their views, the then British Chamber of Shipping submitted calculations from which they produced Table 10.10 attempting to compare gross exports per £100 of annual fixed capital investments and estimate export contributions per employee[194] of the UK shipping industry with that for all

469

manufacturing industries. The Chamber therefore claimed that this calculation showed that UK ships were far more effective convertors of domestic resources into foreign currency than the generality of manufacturing industry.[195] The figures given in Table 10.10 do in fact indicate higher exports per £100 (annual) capital investments and much higher exports per employee. These of course were roughly in the ratio of 3:2 and 9:1 respectively in favour of merchant shipping industry.[196]

The simple, but cautious, conclusion to be drawn from this is that, in the case of the UK, the merchant marine industry is both much more efficient in terms of capital investment return and in contributing to the balance of trade and therefore balance of payments[197] than all alternative industries. There is therefore a strong case for more state investment, subsidy and protection of the industry. This state aid would be more necessary, if not urgent, if that industry faced decline[198] presumably due to similar discriminations against it abroad, bearing in mind that its important contribution to the balance of payments extends to its related industries.

Contribution to the Balance of Payments
of the Merchant Marine-related Industries

The development of the merchant marine-related infrastructure was one of the arguments used for state support of the industry. Related to that is the contributions to the balance of payments of these merchant marine-related industries.[199] In this category are these sectors directly aided by, or which could not do without, the merchant marine industry. Among some of these are shipbuilding, fishing, communications equipment, docks and ports, insurance, banking, merchanting, salvage operations, repairs and dry docks, oil and gas industry, etc.,[200] just to mention a few. These maritime-dependent and -related industries not only contribute to the balance of payments but also probably employed over 100,000 people at their peak. It is needless to point out that most are invisible exports without whose contributions the UK balance of payments would be perpetually in the red.[201]

Table 10.11 shows the net invisible earnings, including portfolio investment interest, of the selected few in this category. A large percentage of insurance is marine and aviation both of which are directly related to the merchant marine industry[202] — as are the merchanting and others. In fact were it not for deductions for direct investment income due to overseas parents of UK branches, the insurance figures alone, for instance, would have been £442 million (1975), £797 million (1976), £907 million (1977), £1.015 billion

Table 10.11 Net invisible earnings 1978–82 (£m)

The following table shows the net invisible earnings of the insurance market (companies, Lloyd's and brokers) including portfolio investment interest for 1978–82. The earnings of other UK financial institutions are also shown.

	1978	1979	1980	1981	1982
Insurance	1,039	1,009	848	976	1,174
Banking	701	212	457	1,340	1,656
Commodity trading	295	285	340	360	449
Brokerage	248	331	370	490	481
Other	135	182	277	348	609
Total	2,418	2,019	2,292	3,514	4,369

Source: *Insurance Facts and Figures 1982*, p. 19.

Table 10.12 Overseas earnings of UK insurance market

£ million

	1978	1979	1980	1981	1982
Companies					
Underwriting (overseas business written in UK)	37	22	9	43	25
Direct investment (profits from overseas business written outside the UK through subsidiaries, etc.)	276	256	177	107	77
Portfolio investment	77	95	111	171	264
Total	390	373	297	321	366
Lloyd's					
Underwriting (overseas business written in UK)	354	312	188	254	215
Portfolio investment	71	112	153	128	260
Total	425	424	341	382	475
Brokers	237	228	238	302	362
Total insurance (gross)	1,052	1,025	876	1,005	1,203
Less					
Direct investment income due to overseas parents of UK branches, etc.	13	16	28	29	29
Total net insurance	1,039	1,009	848	976	1,174

Source: *Insurance Facts and Figures 1982*, p. 18.

471

(1978).[203] However, compare Table 10.11 (net) with Table 10.12 which shows gross overseas earnings of the UK insurance market over the same period. This table is also more detailed than Table 10.11.

The exact impact and accurate figures of the contribution, directly and indirectly, might never be known. The total addition of the two is probably within the region of 60–75 per cent of the net invisible earnings to the country. This may be so for two main reasons:[204] first, because the UK is an island country whose livelihood depends on exporting finished manufactured goods and importing mainly raw materials; second, and historically, because the UK had always been a leading maritime power handling over 50 per cent of world merchant shipping tonnage.[205] Currently standing as the sixth or so largest tonnage-owning nation in the world, the above estimation of the merchant marine industry's contribution to the country's balance of payments is probably not an overestimation.[206] See also Table 10.13 for the overall contributions of shipping, insurance and other invisibles in the UK balance of payments.

Table 10.13   Invisibles in the UK balance of payments

				£ million
	1976	1977	1978	1979
Net private invisibles* of which	+4,912	+4,548	+5,142	+4,888
United Kingdom owned ships	+1,014	+1,024	+972	+1,139
Net general government transactions	-2,101	-2,553	-2,976	-3,347
Total net invisibles	+2,811	+1,995	+2,166	+1,541
Total net visible trade balance	-3,927	-2,279	-1,546	-3,404
Current net payments balance	-1,116	-284	+620	-1,863

*Includes private sector and public corporation services, interest profits, dividends and transfers.

Source: General Council of British Shipping, *British Shipping Statistics 1979/1980*, table 5.4.

Notes

1   Ian Atlink, 'Asian Development Bank (ADB) adopting a broader lending policy', *Seatrade*, January 1986, p. 35; J.J. Scott and J. Mazza, 'Trade in services and developing countries', *Journal of World Trade Law*, vol. 20, no. 3, May–June 1986, pp. 253–73.

2 See also P. Enlermann 'Aspects of ship financing in the Federal Republic of Germany', *Current Issues in Shipping Financing*, vol. 1, 1983, pp. 85–121; C.H. Huttman G-S, 'Exchange market intervention and commercial policy', *Journal of World Trade Law*, vol. 20, no. 3, May–June 1986, pp. 287–93.

3 'Financing and insurance. How ship companies must change', *Shipping News International*, December 1985, pp. 75–7; D. Klett, 'The US Tariff Act: Section 337', *Journal of World Trade Law*, vol. 20, no. 3, May–June 1986, pp. 294–312.

4 J.L. Hanson, *A Dictionary of Economics and Commerce*, Macdonald and Evans, London, 1965, pp. 23–4; B. Balasa and C. Michalopoulos, 'Liberalising trade between developed and developing countries', *Journal of World Trade Law*, vol. 20, no. 1, January–February 1986, pp. 1–28.

5 Ibid. (both columns and table on p. 24); OECD, *Maritime Transport*, 1954 on the breakdown of intermediate consumption of national shipping industry for shipping balance of payments; and delimitation of shipping industry and maritime transport section for balance of payments.

6 D. Blumenhagen, *Shipping and the Balance of Payments*, Lectures and Contributions no. 32), Institute of Shipping Economics, Bremen, 1981.

7 Ibid., especially the sections on the shipping contribution to the balance of payments in the Federal Republic of Germany and the United Kingdom.

8 UK Central Statistics Office (CSO), *Annual Report for 1986*; B. Seyoun, 'Export subsidies under the MTN', *Journal of World Trade Law*, vol. 18, no. 6, November–December 1985, pp. 512–41.

9 Ibid., 'Balance of payments'; cf. M.P. Ferreira and P. Rayment, 'Exports of manufactures from South European countries: demands and competitive factors', *Journal of World Trade Law*, vol. 18, no. 3, May–June 1985, pp. 235–51.

10 Ibid., 'Value of the external trade in the balance of payments'; see also H.S. Kibola, 'Stabex and Home III', *Journal of World Trade Law*, vol. 18, no. 1, January–February 1985, pp. 32–51; but see G. Faver, 'The economics of Stabex', *Journal of World Trade Law*, vol. 18, no. 1, January–February 1985, pp. 52–62.

11 *Facts in Issue*, 2nd edn, Penguin Books, Harmondsworth, 1974; M. Rom, 'Export controls in GATT', *Journal of World Trade Law*, vol. 18, no. 2, March–April 1985, pp. 125–54.

12 A. Seldon and F.G. Pennance, *Everyman's Dictionary of Economics*, Dent and Sons, London, 1965, pp. 21–2.

13 See, again, 'Financing and insurance', op.cit.; S. Schultz and D. Schumacher, 'The reliberalization of world trade: some ideas for reducing trade barriers against industrial products from developing countries', *Journal of World Trade Law*, vol. 18, no. 3, May–June 1984, pp. 206–23.

14 UK *Committee of Inquiry into Shipping*, HMSO, London, 1970 (the *Rochdale Report*); M. Pinar *et al.*, 'Transportation cost subsidies: a criterion for policy to promote international trade', *Journal of World Trade Law*, vol. 18, no. 3, May–June 1986, pp. 224–35.

15 The *Rochdale Report*, op.cit.

16 Ibid., Cmnd 4337; G.D.A. MacDougal, 'British and American exports: a study

suggested by the theory of comparative costs, part I', *Economic Journal*, vol. 61, pp. 167–72.

17 Ibid., 'Direct effect of the UK shipping industry on the current balance of payments position as of 1986'; G.D.A. MacDougal, op.cit., reprinted in H.G. Johnson and R.E. Cares (eds), *Readings in International Economics*, Richard D. Irwin Inc., Homewood, Ill., 1958.

18 See also B.R. Mitchell, *European Historical Statistics 1750–1975*, 2nd revised edn, Macmillan Press Ltd, London, 1981.

19 A.J. Hotz, 'The legal dilemmas: the Arab–Israeli conflict', *South Dakota Law Review*, vol. 19, pp. 242–78; R.A. Mundell, 'A geometry of transport costs in international trade theory', *Canadian Journal of Economics and Political Science*, August 1952, pp. 331–48.

20 See also G. Clark, 'What future for shipping in the Gulf?', *Fairplay International Shipping Weekly*, 2 January 1986, p. 19; UNCTAD, *Level and Structure of Freight Rates, Conference Practices and Adequacy of Shipping Services*, UN Doc. no. TD/B/C.4/38, Rev.1, 1969.

21 Robert Asher, *Grants, Loans and Local Currencies*, The Brookings Institution, Washington DC, 1961, p. 16; see also B.R. Mitchell, *European Historical Statistics 1750–1975*, op.cit.; UNCTAD, *Relationships between Changes in Freight Rates and Changes in Costs of Maritime Transport and the Effect on the Export Trade of Developing Countries*, UN Doc. no. TD/B/C.4/112, 1973.

22 Ibid., 'Balance of payments by country'; A.J. Yeats, 'A comparative analysis of the incidence of tariffs and transportation costs on India's exports', *Journal of Development Studies*, vol. 14, October 1977, pp. 97–107. For details on the Gold Standard see R.G. Hawtrey, *The Gold Standard in Theory and Practice*, 5th edn, Longman & Co. Ltd., 1947.

23 The dollar replaced the Gold Standard and now the Special Drawing Rights has replaced the dollar as the international unit of exchange at the World Bank and IMF.

24 The advantages and disadvantages of the barter system are discussed by R.F. Mikesell in the opening remarks to his authoritative book, *Foreign Exchange in the Postwar World*, The Twentieth Century Fund, New York, 1954.

25 Robert Asher, op.cit.; and R.F. Mikesell, ibid.; see also F. Machlup, 'The theory of Foreign Exchange' in Howard S. Ellis and Lloyd A. Metzler, *Readings in the Theory of International Trade*, McGraw-Hill, New York, 1949, chapter 5. See also *British Business*, Weekly News from the Department of Trade and Industry, HMSO, London; G. Simpson *et al.*, 'An evaluation of tariff and transport barriers facing products of export interest to Australia', *Journal of Transport Economics and Policy*, vol. 11, May 1977, pp. 141–54.

26 Mikesell and Machlup, ibid.; see also F. Southard Jr., *Foreign Exchange in Practice and Policy*, McGraw-Hill, New York, 1940, chapters 1–2; J.N. Bhagwati, 'Splintering and disembodiment of services and developing nations', *The World Economy*, June 1984, pp. 133–43.

27 For further information see S. Enke and V. Salera, *International Economics*, Prentice-Hall Inc., Englewood Cliffs, NJ, 1947, chapters 17–18; also for an

excellent discussion of this point see G. Feketekuty, 'Trade in professional services – an overview', processed pp. 2–9.

28 Ibid., 'Sea transport account – balance of payments'; also *Bank of England Quarterly Bulletin*, September 1985, p. 409; see also World Bank, *World Development Report*, 1985, p. 126.

29 Invisibles in the UK balance of payments; World Bank, *Economic Report to the President*, February 1986, pp. 264 and 299. These figures include government.

30 General Council of British Shipping, *British Shipping Statistics 1979/80*, 'Sea transport account – balance of payments'; World Bank, op.cit., pp. 176–9, 214–15.

31 Ibid., 'Invisibles in the UK balance of payments'; cf. G.C. Hufbanner and J.J. Scott, *Trading for Growth: The Next Round of Trade Negotiations*, Institute for International Economics, Washington, 1985, especially chapter 2.

32 Ibid., 'UK-owned ships; receipts from international services and payments abroad', table 5.1, pp. 7–8; IMF, *Balance of Payments Statistics Yearbook*, Part II, 1982, 1985.

33 I. Averim, 'Protectionism may deepen East/West split' [EEC shipping policy effects on Soviet shipping], *Motor Ship*, vol. 66, no. 788, March 1986, p. 78; *IMF Balance of Payments Statistics*, Part 1, vol. 36, 1985.

34 Ibid.; see also D. Serko, 'Protectionism: sentiment is extremely high', *Worldwide Shipping*, vol. 48, no. 7, December–January 1986, pp. 17–20.

35 N. Reynolds, 'Shipping interests must meet fundamental requirements to successfully finance projects', *Fairplay International Shipping Weekly*, 19–26 December 1985, p. 28.

36 See M. Austin, 'Currency features', *Seatrade*, December 1985, pp. 25–8.

37 B. Hogan, 'Protectionism hits bulk trade in Third World', *Lloyd's List*, 20 December 1985, p. 4; UNCTAD, Report by the Secretariat, *Services and the Development Process, Summary and Conclusions*, 2 August 1984, p. 1.

38 D.K. Fleming, 'Safe harbours from high costs, taxes and restrictive regulations in shipping', *Maritime Policy and Management*, vol. 13, no. 1, 1986, pp. 17–25.

39 See I. Middleton and J. McCallum, 'Never mind the politics – what about the economy?', *Seatrade*, February 1986, pp. 4–7; P.N. Batista, Brazilian Ambassador in Geneva, as cited in *New York Times*, 2 October 1985, p. 19.

40 General Council of British Shipping, *British Shipping Statistics 1979/80*, op.cit., 'UK shipping industry: receipts from international services and payments abroad', pp. 90–1.

41 R. Davis, *The Rise of the English Shipping Industry in the Seventeenth and the Eighteenth Centuries*, Macmillan, London, 1962, 'The government and the shipping industry', chapter XIV, pp. 300–315.

42 R.H. Thornton, *British Shipping*, Cambridge University Press, 1939, 'Economic nationalism', chapter VI, pp. 95–114.

43 T. Rinman and R. Linden, *Shipping, How it Works*, Kingsback, 1978, 'The political environment of shipping', pp. 141–8.

44 J. Paul, 'The impact of port charges on shipping freight rates', *Dock and Harbour Authority*, vol. 66, no. 777, March 1986, pp. 256–60.

45 See, generally, J.E. Otterson, *Foreign Trade and Shipping*, 1945; B. Hindley and A. Smith, 'Competitive advantage and trade in services', *The World Economy*, December 1984, p. 389.

46 R. Davis, *The Rise of the English Shipping Industry*, op.cit., 'Shipping and trade', chapter IX, pp. 175–201.

47 General Council of British Shipping, *British Shipping Statistics, 1979/80*, op.cit., 'Sea transport account — balance of payments', table 5.3, pp. 92–4.

48 R.L. Wattenhall, *Aspects of Political Control in Selected Public Transport Corporations*, unpublished PhD thesis, Australia National University, 1961.

49 C. Escarpenter, *The Economics of International Ocean Transport*, The University of Wisconsin Press, Madison and Milwaukee, 1965, 'Balance of international payment and national income in relation to the ocean freight traffic', pp. 106–42.

50 See W.A. Radius, *US Shipping in the Transpacific Trade 1922-1938*, Palo Alto, 1944; A. Sapir and E. Lintz, *Trade in Services: Economic Determinants and Development-Related Issues*, World Bank Staff Working Paper no. 480, Washington DC, 1981, p. 31.

51 General Council of British Shipping, *British Shipping Statistics 1979/80*, op.cit., 'Invisibles in the United Kingdom balance of payments', table 5.4, p. 92.

52 Francis Hyde (with contributions from J.R. Harris and A.M. Bonn), *Shipping Enterprise and Management 1830-1939*, Liverpool University Press, 1967, 'Finance', chapter 6, pp. 98–122.

53 S.G. Sturmey, 'Shipping needs of developing countries', *Shipping Economics, Collected Papers*, Cox and Wyman, London, 1975, pp. 246–55.

54 See, generally, H. Bergman, *Basic Principles of Financing Shipping*; Banco do Brasil SA, *CACEX*, 'Uma opcaco de Creseimento', Information Semanal CACEX, Rio de Janeiro, 5 November 1984.

55 C. O'Loughlin, *The Economics of Sea Transport*, Pergamon Press, London, 1967, 'The theory of international trade and international transport', chapter 2, pp. 13–23.

56 C. O'Loughlin, op.cit., 'International exchange rates', chapter 3, pp. 24–30. This point is treated more extensively in J.F. Radar, 'Advanced technologies and development: are conventional ideas about comparative advantage obsolete?', *Trade and Development*, vol. 5, 1985.

57 C. O'Loughlin, op.cit., 'Shipping and the balance of payments', chapter 4, pp. 31–40. Similar concerns were raised in the UNCTAD Report, *Services and the Development Process*, Geneva, 1984, p. 2.

58 'British and French shipbuilding: the industrial relations of decline', *Industrial Relations Journal*, vol. 16, no. 4, 1985, pp. 7–16.

59 UK Central Statistics Office, *Annual Abstract of Statistics, 1986*, (Balance of Payments: Summary), HMSO, London, 1986; see also B. Hindley, *Economic Analysis and Insurance Policy in the Third World*, Thames Essay no. 22, Trade Policy Research Centre, London, 1982, p. 52.

60 Ibid.; 'Balance of payments: current account'.

61 Ibid.; 'Balance of payments: visible trade'; *UN Statistical Yearbook*, New York, 1985 — summary of balance of payments by country and area and items: UK — imports of merchandise FOB and importations of merchandise FOB.

62 'Recession also hits towing, salvage and heavy lift', *Motor Ship*, vol. 67, no. 789, April 1986, pp. 52-4.

63 UK CSO, op.cit., 'Balance of payments: private sector services: sea transport'; Prem Krimow, Indian Commerce Secretary, as cited in the *New York Times*, 2 October 1985, p. D1.

64 See also D. Stonebridge, 'Impact of the falling dollar on shipping: real costs and revenues highly sensitive to changes in parity', *Asian Shipping*, January 1986, pp. 19-20.

65 See also R. Goss, 'Investment in shipping and the balance of payments: a case study of import substitution policy', *Journal of Industrial Economics*, 1965.

66 See the same article in R.O. Goss, *Studies in Maritime Economics*, Cambridge University Press, 1968, chapter 3, pp. 46-60.

67 An argument developed by Professor Meade in *Trade and Welfare*, Oxford University Press, 1955, chapters 2 and 3; see also UK Central Statistics Office, *Digest of Statistics*, 'External trade: adjustments to visible trade to a balance of payments basis', HMSO, London, 1985.

68 Meade, ibid.; 'External trade, visible trade and balance of payments basis'; see also Bank for International Settlements, *55th Annual Report*, Basle, 1 April 1984-31 March 1985.

69 Meade, ibid.; UK Central Statistics Office, *UK Balance of Payments*, HMSO, London, 1985 edition (the *Pink Book*); World Bank, *World Development Report*, 1985, p. 126.

70 Meade, ibid.; the *Pink Book*, op.cit., 1985, 'Visible trade: adjustments from the overseas trade statistics to balance of payments basis'; US trade representative, *US Statement on GATT Competence*, Geneva, November 1985, processed.

71 Meade, ibid.; 'Volume and unit of indices, analysis by commodity: exports/imports/visible balances'; IBRD, *Report on MIGA: Multilateral Investment Guarantee Policy*, September–October 1985, p. 3.

72 Meade, ibid.; 'Geographical analysis: visible trade on a balance of payments basis'; *Annual Report of the President of the US on the Trade Agreement Programme 1984-85*, February 1986, pp. 88-9.

73 Meade, ibid.; 'Invisible services – services summary: sea transport – dry cargo/tankers/and total credits'. A precedent exists in the collaboration with the International Standards Organization during the negotiation of the GATT Standards Code.

74 Meade, ibid.; 'Sea transport – ships owned by UK operators: freight on exports/freight on cross-trades/charter receipts/and passenger revenue'.

75 A.H. Vanagas, 'Flag discrimination, an economic analysis' in R.O. Goss (ed.), *Advances in Shipping Economics*, Cambridge University Press, 1977, chapter 1, pp. 37-65.

76 B.M. Gardner and P.W. Richardson, 'The fiscal treatment of shipping' in R.O. Goss (ed.), *Advances in Shipping Economics*, op.cit., pp. 65-90.

77 These issues are dealt with fully by Professor F. Machlup in 'Three concepts of the balance of payments and the so-called dollar shortage', *Economic Journal*, vol. IX, 1950, pp. 46-68; see also K. Stuart, 'Transport and finance (deregulation and transport)', *Transport*, December 1985, pp. 12-16; US International Trade Commission, *Review of the Effectiveness of Trade*

Dispute Settlement under the GATT and the Tokyo Round Agreements, USITC Pub. no. 1793, December 1985.

78 F. Machlup, ibid., reproduced in *International Monetary Economics*, London, Allen and Unwin 1968; see also A.E. Branch, *Elements of Shipping*, 5th edn, Chapman and Hall, London, 1981 — see table on invisibles on p. 369; GATT, *International Trade*, 1983–84, table A28.

79 But see again, F. Machlup, 'The theory of Foreign Exchange' op.cit.; see also P.M. Alderton, *Sea Transport: Operation and Economics*, Thomas Reed, London, 1973 — see table on p. 94 for balance of payments.

80 As to the balance of payments within the general framework of economics and political environment see D. Marx, Jr, *International Shipping Cartels: A Study of Industrial Regulation by Shipping Conferences*, Greenwood Press, New York, 1953, pp. 26–45.

81 For shipping see the *Pink Book*, op.cit., 'Ships on charter to UK operators: freight on exports of freights on cross trades/charter receipts'.

82 Ibid., 'Debits: ships owned by UK operators: disbursements abroad'; J.N. Bhagwati, 'GATT and trade in services: how we can resolve the North–South debate', *Financial Times*, 27 November 1985, p. 25.

83 Ibid., 'Ships on charter to UK operators: charter payments/disbursements abroad'; G.C. Hufbanner and J.J. Scott, *Trading for Growth: the Next Round of Trade Negotiations*, op.cit., especially pp. 19–22.

84 Ibid., 'Overseas operators: freight on imports/and passenger revenue'.

85 See S.G. Sturmey, 'The shipping policies of developing countries' in I. Ryden, *Shipping and Ships for the 1990s*, Westbury House, 1981, pp. 71–80; cf. A. Whitley, 'Brazil accuses US of retreat on twin-track talks', *Financial Times*, 23 August 1985, p. 4.

86 Drewery Shipping Consultants Ltd, *Protectionism and the Bulk Shipping Industry*, November, 1985; see again, J.N. Bhagwati, 'GATT and trade in services: how we can resolve the North–South debate', *Financial Times*, November 1985, p. 25.

87 P. Gill, 'Export controls: Export Administration Amendments Act of 1985 (USA)', *World Wide Shipping*, vol. 48, no. 6, October–November 1985, pp. 42–4.

88 See also M.D. Hamilton, 'What is the future of exporting?' in *World Wide Shipping*, op.cit., pp. 15–19; but see W.E. Brock, 'A simple plan for negotiating on trade in services', *The World Economy*, November 1982.

89 F. la Sarponcura, 'Seaports and public intervention', *Maritime Policy and Management*, vol. 13, no. 4, 1986, pp. 139–54; Advisory Committee for Trade Negotiations, *Chairman's Report on a New Round of Multilateral Trade Negotiations*, submitted to the US Trade Representative, 15 May 1985.

90 But see M. Colvin and J. Marks, *British Shipping the Right Course*, Policy Studies no. 67, Centre for Policy Studies, London, 'Role of government', 1984, chapter 8, pp. 36–7.

91 H.L. Beth, 'Fluctuations of exchange rates — their impact on shipping', *Liner Shipping in the Eighties Report of the International Symposium 1979*, Bremen Institute of Shipping Economics, pp. 36–60.

92 Ibid., P.C. Fabre, 'Fleet restructuring in trades with developing countries',

pp. 134–44; *Treasury and Federal Reserve Foreign Exchange Operations*, Federal Reserve Bulletin, November 1985, pp. 850–61.

93 Ibid., Captain J.C. Anand, 'Liner shipping under developing country flags', pp. 314–35; 'Studies of foreign exchange market intervention', IMF *Survey*, 9 May 1983, pp. 137–8.

94 R.O. Goss, 'Seaports should not be subsidized', *Maritime Policy and Management*, vol. 13, no. 2, 1986, pp. 83–104; M. Hutchison, 'US intervention policy', *Weekly Letter*, Federal Reserve Bank of San Francisco, 10 June 1983, pp. 1–3.

95 But see W. Underhill, 'Government rejects aid plea for Swiss shipping', *Lloyd's List*, 7 June 1986, p. 3; for further analysis of the IMF's role in the development of international monetary laws, see J. Gold, 'International law and the IMF', *Finance and Development*, IMF, December 1977, pp. 33–7.

96 A Vegarie, 'State aid for seaports: a Cartesian proposition in the French case', *Maritime Policy and Management*, vol. 13, no. 2, 1986, pp. 127–37.

97 Ibid., S. Farrell, 'The subsidization of seaports: an alternative approach', pp. 177–84; cf. C. Hakkis and J. Whittaker, 'The US dollar — recent developments, outlook, and policy options', *Economic Review*, September–October 1983, pp. 3–15.

98 But see 'Loss of subsidization leave Dutch yards facing a grim future', *Fairplay International Shipping Weekly*, 10 April 1986, pp. 27–9; IMF *Annual Report*, Washington DC, 1985, pp. 44–5.

99 *Trade and Transport Integration, The Global Challenge*, ICHSA 18th Biennial Conference, Brisbane, 11–15 May 1986. The joint communiqué is reprinted in 'Members of Group 5 assess global outlook at meeting in New York', IMF *Survey*, 7 October 1985, p. 296.

100 F. Volckaert, 'Formulation of national maritime policy: the case of Belgium', *Marine Policy*, vol. 10, no. 2, April 1986, pp. 90–101; W.M. Garden, 'Protection, the exchange rates, and macroeconomic policy', *Finance and Development*, June 1985, pp. 17 and 19.

101 D.G. Hebden, 'The role of government in marine salvage: an international perspective', *New Directions in Maritime Law*, 1984, pp. 229–36; J. Bergstrand, 'Bretton Woods revisited', *New England Economic Review*, September–October 1984, pp. 22–33.

102 A.K. Albadawry, *Restructuring of World Shipping Capacity under the Conditions of the UN Code of Conduct*, Michigan University, Ann Arbor, 1980; IMF *Survey*, op.cit., p. 296.

103 Hans Bohme, *Restraint on Competition in World Shipping*, Trade Policy Research Centre, London, 1978, 86p; A. Pine, 'Group of Fives states meeting next week-end', *Wall Street Journal*, 13 January 1986, p. 28.

104 OECD Committee of Experts on Restrictive Business Practices, *Competition Policy in Regulated Sectors with Special Reference to Transport and Banking*, Paris, 1979; Kvasnicka, op.cit.

105 UNCTAD, Report by the Secretariat, *The Impact on World Seaborne Trade of Changes in Shipping Costs*, Doc. no. TD/B/C.4/74, para. 1; 'Report of the Group of 24 calls for basic changes in international system', IMF *Survey*, 26 August 1985, pp. 257 and 269.

106 See UN, *Monthly Bulletin of Statistics*, vol. XXVI, no. 6, June 1972, table 52; for further analysis of the extent of these implications, see J. Kvasnicka, 'Central banks move to halt the dollar rise', *International Letter*, Federal Reserve Bank of Chicago, 8 March 1985, pp. 1-3.

107 IMF/IBRD, *Direction of Trade: Annual 1966-70*, Washington DC, part B, 'World trade', pp. 5-7; see again J. Gold quoted in 'The institutional evolution of the IMF', *Finance and Development*, IMF, September 1984, pp. 7-9.

108 IMF/IBRD, *Direction of Trade*, op.cit., p. 11. According to the IMF the 10 per cent adjustment refers to total trade and not only to seaborne trade.

109 C. O'Loughlin, *The Economics of Sea Transport*, op.cit., pp. 17-18; in addition, a Study Report of the Working Group on Exchange Market Intervention, March 1983 (commissioned by the Seven Industrial Countries) by the Working Group on Exchange Market Intervention, concluded that sterilized intervention alone was not as effective as intervention that had a direct impact on the monetary base.

110 According to the IMF, the estimated weighted average ratio of the value of imports CIF to imports FOB for the advanced maritime nations increased from 1.078 in 1969 to 1.079 in 1970; 'World economic outlook' April 1985, noticed in *Journal of World Trade Law*, no. 5.

111 See IMF, *Balance of Payments Yearbook*, vol. 22, Washington DC, 1965-1969; for a discussion of the IMF balance of payments surveillance problems see IMF, *Annual Report*, op.cit., 1985, pp. 42-3.

112 Committee on Invisible Exports, *World Invisible Trade: An Analysis by the Economists Advisory Group*, London, July 1972; but see C.G. Johnson, 'Enhancing the effectiveness of surveillance', *Finance and Development*, 1985, pp. 2-6.

113 As against the 97 countries included in *World Invisible Trade*, op.cit., see also R. McKinnon, 'Exchange stability, international monetary co-ordination, and the US Federal Reserve System', *How Open is the US Economy?*, 10th Annual Economic Policy Conference, Federal Reserve Bank of St Louis, 11 and 12 October 1985.

114 See Note 21. Also on the basis of the IMF, *Balance of Payments Yearbook*, op.cit.; see also the IMF revised figures reported in *The Economist*, 12-18 October 1985, p. 75.

115 See Note 22. See also UN *Monthly Bulletin of Statistics* which covered 140 countries on territories compared to the 97 above; see A.F. Ewing, *International Capital and Economic Development*, based largely on the World Bank's *World Development Report 1985*, *Journal of World Trade Law*, no. 5.

116 See Note 22. But see IMF/IBRD, *Direction of Trade*, op.cit., '165 countries and territories and its world table', part B; D. Sehydlowsky, *Trade Policies Towards Developing Countries*, AID, Washington DC, 1978, pp. 34-89.

117 See Note 24. Note that in 1970, the FOB value of exports reported in the world invisible trade on the basis of the *Balance of Payments Yearbook* accounted for 86 per cent of the value reported in the *Monthly Bulletin of Statistics and Direction of Trade*.

118 See Note 26. A discussion of some of the limitations of transportation in

the balance of payments are to be found in H.F. Karreman, *Methods for Improving World Transportation Accounts, Applied to 1950-53*, National Bureau of Economic Research (US), Technical Paper 15, Quinn and Boden, New Jersey, 1961.

119 See Note 27. See also S.G. Sturmey, *British Shipping and World Competition*, Athlon Press, London, 1962, pp. 415–18; R. Greenwood, 'The negotiations of a code on subsidies and counterveiling measures: bridging fundamental differences', *Law and Policy in International Business*, vol. 11, 1979, p. 1457.

120 The distinction between freight and port expenditures is not clear-cut, but see IMF *Balance of Payments Manual*, 3rd edn, Washington DC, July 1961, p. 41.

121 But see OECD, *Ocean Freight Rates as Part of the Total Transport Costs*, Publications no. 24283, Paris, October 1968; B. Balassa, *The Newly Industrialised Nations in the World Economy*, Pergamon Press, 1981, p. 135; IMF *Survey*, 22 June 1981, p. 192.

122 Ibid., IMF *Balance of Payments Manual*, op.cit., pp. 71–2; see also K. Vijay, 'Export subsidies and developing countries', *Journal of World Trade Law*, vol. 14, 1980, p. 371; also remarks by J. de Larosiere in *Finance and Development*, June 1982.

123 It should be noted that in the case of imports being reported FOB, the IMF asks that the freight received by domestic carriers on imports be reported as a memorandum item. This information appears not to be included in the *Balance of Payments Yearbook* but is used by the IMF in reconciling FOB and CIF values.

124 Only if all countries reported both imports and exports FOB and the transport was undertaken by third-flag carriers would there be no underestimation of freight costs; *Economic and Policy Weekly of Bombay*, 22 November 1980.

125 For quarterly data on the US balance of payments, for example, see US Department of Commerce, *Survey of Current Business*, which comes out every March, June, September and December. World invisible trade was concerned with the balance of payments and receipts, and not with transport costs or sea transport costs as such. The discussion is therefore in no way a criticism of this report but only an attempt to explain the limitations of such data for our purposes.

126 Ibid. The twelve countries indicated there are Costa Rica, Dominican Republic, Ecuador, Ethiopia, Fiji, Haiti, Honduras, Jamaica, Republic of Korea, Nicaragua, Paraguay and Sierra Leone.

127 See the US Survey, ibid., 1981. See also D. Tresselt, *The Controversy over the Division of Labour in International Seaborne Transport*, Institute of Shipping Research, Bergen, pp. 6 and 24; *Economic and Policy Weekly of Bombay*, 21 February 1981.

128 UNCTAD, Preliminary Report by the Secretariat, *The Estimation of Freight Factors*, UN Doc. no. TD/B/C.4/47; Committee on Appropriations, *US Foreign Assistance and Related Programmes Appropriation Bills*, 95th Congress, 22nd Session, 1 June 1978, pp. 56–7.

129 According to the analysis of the UN *Monthly Bulletin of Statistics*, op.cit.,

the tonnage of seaborne trade from the same source, excluding the average loading/unloading of European countries for consistency, and assuming that 75 per cent of world trade values were seaborne.

130 The limitation due to the nature of the initial sample may here be of particular importance. As was pointed out in UN Doc. no. TD/B/C.4/76 and other UNCTAD Secretariat reports, see also *Congressional Records*, 31 July 1978, H 7548; and IMF *Annual Report*, 1979.

131 Ibid., particularly 'Ocean shipping and freight rates and developing countries', study prepared by the Economist Intelligence Unit, London; but see US *Presidential Commission*, 1980, p. 73; and *Congressional Records*, 23 September 1980, ss. 13202-3.

132 See The Proceedings of UNCTAD, First Session, *Financing and Invisibles: Institutional Arrangements Congressional Records*, vol. V, 23 September 1980, ss. 13203-4.

133 But see UNCTAD, Report by the Secretariat, *Freight Markets and the Level and Structure of Freight Rates*, UN Doc. no. TD/B/C.4/38/Rev.1/Corr.1, Sales no. E.69.11.D.13; see also IMF *Survey*, 22 May 1978; and IMF, EMB/75/181.

134 As pointed out in UN Doc. no. TD/B/C.4/47, op.cit., the statistical interpretation of these concepts may vary somehow, particularly regarding loading expenditures and the possible use of free alongside ship (FAS) instead of FOB; see also IMF, EMB/75/181, op.cit., and IMF, EMB/77/159, p. 15.

135 Reference is made, in this connection, to a quotation from the *Yearbook of International Trade Statistics*, UN Publication, Sales no. E.71.XVII.5, 1969, p. 6; see also *Development Dialogue* 2/1980; IMF *Survey*, September 1979, Supplement, and 8 June 1981.

136 Fearnley and Egers Chartering Co. Ltd, *Trades of World Bulk Carriers*, Oslo, 1970; see also IMF *Survey*, 1 September 1980, p. 273. According to IMF *Survey*, 5 January 1976, over ten years 1965-75, use of Fund resources through the CFF amounted to 9 per cent of Use of Funds Resources through the normal credit.

137 OECD, *Maritime Transport*, Paris, 1970, and a review of the 1960s; C.J. Green, *Insulating Countries' Exports: An Analysis of Compensatory Financing Schemes*, Discussion Paper no. 16, Department of Economics, Manchester Unit, April 1980.

138 UNCTAD, *Freight Markets and the Level and Structure of Freight Rates*, op.cit.; W.L. Hemphill, 'The effect of foreign exchange receipts on imports of less developed countries', IMF *Staff Report*, 1974.

139 Ibid., particularly paras 229-52; IMF *Survey*, June 1981; UNCTAD, *Compensatory Financing: Issues and Proposals for Further Action*, UN Doc. no. TD(229), Suppl. 1, Geneva.

140 Ibid.; see also UNCTAD, Report by the Secretariat, *Shipping in the Seventies*, UN Publication, Sales no. E.72.11.D.15, part one, para. 27; J.G. Borpujary, *Toward a Basic Needs Approach to Economic Development with Financial Stability*; IMF mimeo DM/80/16, 28 March 1980.

141 Institute of Shipping Economics, *Shipping Statistics Yearbook — Facts and Figures about Shipping, Shipbuilding, Seaports and Seaborne Traffic*,

Bremen, 1985; *Hearing on 5970*, 6 February 1980 before the Subcommittee on International Trade, Investment and Monetary Policy, p. 245.

142 Ibid., 'France: shipping payments balance'; G.A. Channary, Statement in *Hearings before the Subcommittee on International Trade, Investment and Monetary Affairs*, House of Representatives, 49th Congress, 2nd Session on HR59 70 to amend the Bretton Woods Agreement Act, 6 February 1980, pp. 105–11.

143 Maritime Institute, *Preinvestment Studies in Maritime Transport*, Proceedings of the Symposium organized by the Maritime Institute at Gdansk and UNCTAD's Shipping Research Branch of the Division of Invisibles in Geneva (26 October 1971), Gdansk – Szczecin, 1972.

144 Prof. M. Krzyzanowski, 'Preinvestment studies in shipping as a form of assistance to developing countries', in ibid.

145 Cf. Prof. Z. Sojka, 'Effectiveness of shipping investments under the conditions of socialist economy' in ibid.; S. Dell, *The Problem of IMF conditionality*, IMF mimeo, 25 March 1980.

146 See also Dr Z. Pelczynski, 'Possibilities to adopt socialist planning methods to the programming of shipping and ports expansion by the developing countries' in Maritime Institute, *Preinvestment Studies in Maritime Transport*, op.cit.

147 But see Dr W.R. Malinowski, 'Changing political climate in which the UNCTAD Committee on Shipping has worked since its formation' in ibid.

148 S.G. Sturmey, 'Main themes of the UNCTAD research studies' in ibid.; T. Connors, *The Apparent Effects of Recent IMF Stabilization Programmes*, Federal Reserve, International Finance Discussion Paper no. 135, Washington DC, 1979.

149 K. Fasvender and W. Wagner, *Shipping Conferences, Rate Policy and Developing Countries: The Argument for Rate Discrimination*, Institut für Wirtschaftsforschung, Hamburg, 1973.

150 T.D. Heaver, *The Structure of Liner Conference Rates*, Occasional Working Paper, Centre for Transportation Studies, University of British Columbia, 1968.

151 IMF, *Balance of Payments Statistics Yearbook*, Washington DC, 1985 – conceptual framework of the balance of payments and its relationship to national accounts by country.

152 Ibid., 'Current account: merchandise/exports FOB/imports FOB; J.D. Arista, 'United States Congressional restraints: the ties that bind 1979' in L.G. France and M. Seiber (eds), *Developing Country Debt*, New York, pp. 215–35.

153 Ibid., 'Shipment: credit vs debt'; J. Gold, *The Legal Character of the Fund's Stand-by Arrangements and Why It Matters*, Pamphlet Series no. 35, Washington DC, 'Gold 1980 A'; cf. M. Idle, 'Guyana – caught in IMF trap', *Caribbean Contact*, October 1978, pp. 12–22.

154 IMF, *Balance of Payments Statistics Yearbook*, op.cit., 'Standard components of the detailed presentation: by category'; see J. Gold, *Financial Assistance by the International Monetary Fund: Law and Practice*, 2nd edn, Pamphlet Series no. 27, Washington DC, 1980, 'Gold 1980 B'.

155 IMF, op.cit., 'Summary of international transactions: merchandise FOB';

T.M. Reichman, 'The Fund's conditional assistance and the problem of adjustment, 1973-1975', *Finance and Development*, December 1978, pp. 38-41.

156 IMF, op.cit., 'Merchandise FOB: debt and credit' and 'Shipment: credit v. debit'.

157 Ibid., 'The inbound/outbound freight rate controversy', Occasional Working Paper, Centre for Transportation Studies, University of British Columbia; J.H. Mensah, 'Some unpleasant truths about debt and development', *Development Dialogue*, 1973, pp. 3-16.

158 *A Theory of Shipping Conferences Pricing and Policy*, Occasional Working Paper, Centre for Transportation Studies, University of British Columbia, 1968; B. Nowzad, *The IMF and its Critics*, Essays in International Finance no. 146, Princeton, 1968.

159 D.V. Harper, *Transportation in America: Users, Carriers, Government*, Prentice-Hall, 1978; cf. Presidential Commission, *Overcoming World Hunger: The Challenge Ahead*, Report of the Presidential Commission on World Hunger, Washington DC, 1980.

160 C.L. Dearing and W. Owen, *National Transportation Policy*, (reprint of 1949 edn), Greenwood 1980; T. Killick, *IMF Stabilization Programmes*, Overseas Development Institute Working Paper no. 6, London, 1981.

161 J. Dunn, *Miles to Go: European and American Transportation Policies*, MIT, 1981; T. Killick, *The Impact of IMF Stabilization Programmes in Developing Countries*, Overseas Development Institute Working Paper no. 7, London, 1982.

162 B. Abrahams, *International Ocean Shipping; Current Concepts and Principles*, Westview Press, 1980; M. Guitran, *Fund Conditionality: Evolution of Principles and Practices*, Fund Pamphlet no. 38, Washington DC, 1981.

163 A. Dixit and V. Norman, *Theory of International Trade*, Cambridge University Press, 1980; O.S.J. Johnson, 'Stabilisation programmes and income distribution', *Finance and Development*, December 1980, pp. 28-31.

164 Cf. B. Gidwitz, *Politics of International Air Transport*, Lexington Books, 1980; W.R. Cline, 'The magnitude and conditions of lending by the International Monetary Fund' in *Hearings* no. 5970, op.cit., pp. 128-44.

165 E. Gold, *Maritime Transport: The Evolution of International Marine Policy and Shipping Law*, Lexington Books, 1981; L. de Silva, *Gold, the International Monetary Fund and the Third World*, IFDA Dossier 5, March 1979, pp. 2-12.

166 A. Altshuler (ed.), *Current Issues in Transportation Policy*, Lexington Books, 1979; T. Harkin, 'The International Monetary Fund, band disclosure and basic human needs' in *Hearings* no. 5970, op.cit., pp. 48-58.

167 J. Bar-Lev, 'UNCTAD Code of Practice for the Regulation of Liner Conferences', *Journal of Maritime Law and Commerce*, vol. 3, 1972, pp. 783-91.

168 A.H. Levine, *National Transportation Policy, a Study of Studies*, Lexington Books, 1978; J. Gold, *The Reform of the Fund*, IMF Pamphlet Series no. 12, pp. 26-32.

484

169 E. Bennethan and A.A. Walters, *Port Pricing and Investment Policies for Developing Countries*, Oxford, 1979; but see J. Nyerere, 'Speech to diplomats on 1 January, 1980', report in *Third World News Forum*, March 1980.

170 M.J. O'Sullivan, *Transportation Policy: An Interdisciplinary Approach*, Barnes and Noble, 1980; A. Jamal, 'Opening Address by the Chairman of the Fund/World Bank Board of Governors', *Third World News Forum*, op.cit.

171 M.J. O'Sullivan, *Transportation Policy: Geographic, Economic and Planning Aspects*, Barnes and Noble, 1980; see also 'Terranova statement on an international monetary system and the Third World', *Development Dialogue*, Uppsala, 1979, which is the outcome of the conference convened in Kingston, Jamaica, 5–7 October 1979.

172 B.W. Hogwood, *Government and Shipbuilding*, Saxon House, 1979; J. Gold, *Conditionality*, IMF Pamphlet Series no. 31, 1979; and J. Gold, *Financial Assistance by the IMF: Law and Practice*, op.cit.; see also the 'Terranova Statement', op.cit.

173 R. Schultz, *Federalism, Bureaucracy and Public Policy: The Politics of Highway Transportation*; J. Gold, 'Aspects of the relations of the IMF with its developing members', *Columbia Journal of Transnational Law*, vol. 10, no. 2, Autumn 1971.

174 R. Pearson and J. Fossey, *World Deep-Sea Container Shipping*, University of Liverpool, 1983; for further comments see S. Mookerjee, 'New guidelines for use of Fund resources follow review of practice of conditionality', *IMF Survey*, vol. 8, 19 March 1979.

175 S. Gilman, *The Competitive Dynamics of Container Shipping*, Gower Publishing House, 1983; for a more detailed study of Decision no. 6056 (for instance) (70–38), see J. Gold, Pamphlet Series no. 31, op.cit.

176 E. Butler and M. Pirie, *Freeports*, Adam Smith Institute, 1983; M. Guritian, 'Fund conditionality and the international adjustment process: the early period, 1950–70', *Finance and Development*, December 1980, p. 24.

177 UK Treasury, *Working Party on Freeports in the United Kingdom*, HMSO, London, 1983; Guritian, op.cit., p. 24; The German Minister (Mattsefer) interview with *Handelsblatt* of 2 April 1980.

178 D.R. Macgregor, *Merchant Sailing Ships 1775–1815*, Model and Allied, 1980; see the German Minister's interview, op.cit. – the French Finance Minister (Manory) struck out in the same direction in the Interim Committee in Hamburg in 1980.

179 I.G. Stewart, *British Gas Carriers and Tankers 1955–79*, IGS, 1979; de Larosiere, Address to the 1980 *Symposium on Monetary Theory and Policy in Africa*, Dakar, January 1980, op.cit.

180 L.A. Sawyer and W.H. Mitchell, *From America to United States. Part II, World Ship Society*, University of Chicago Press, 1981; 'The IMF and the poor', *Economic and Political Weekly of Bombay*, 22 November 1980.

181 Offerspace, *The UK Ocean Freighters*, Offerspace, 1982; G. Helleiner, *World Market Imperfections and the Developing Countries*, Overseas Development Council, Occasional Paper no. 11, May 1978.

182 R.A. Streater and D.G. Greenham, *British Merchant Ships*, Orion, 1983; R.F. Mikeseller, *Foreign Investment in the Petroleum and Mineral Industries*, The Johns Hopkins University Press, Baltimore, 1977.
183 Tames, *Tames Merchant Ships 1982*, Tames, 1982; T. Reichman and R.T. Stillson, 'Experience with programmes of balance of payments adjustments: stand-by arrangements in the higher credit tranches, 1963–1972', IMF *Staff Papers*, June 1978, pp. 293–309.
184 E.C. Talbot-Booth, *Talbot-Booth's Merchant Ships*, vol. 3, Krogan Page, 1979; see also N. Colchester, 'Protection from Chicago', *Financial Times*, 4 February 1983; G. Helleimer, op.cit.
185 P. Plowman, *Passenger Ships of Australia and New Zealand*, vol. 2, '1930–80', Conway, 1981; G. Bird, 'IMF quotas, conditionality and the developing countries', *Overseas Development Institute Review*, no. 2, 1979, p. 67.
186 P. Plowman, op.cit., vol. 1, '1876-1912'; C. Diaz-Alejandro, 'Southern cone stabilization plans', Yale Discussion Paper (stereotype), November 1979, pp. 16–17.
187 B.S. Hoyle and D. Hilling, *Seaport Systems and Spatial Change*, Wiley, 1984; H. Bhagat, 'The mixed blessings of the IMF', *New African*, February 1980; G. Bird, 'The IMF as a source of international finance for developing countries: a critical appraisal', *Indian Journal of Economics*, Allahabad, April 1980, p. 115.
188 H.W. Clayton, *Clayton's Annual Register of Shipping and Port Changes for Great Britain, 1965*, Field and Tuer, 1965; S. Skogstand, 'A note on domestic monetary policy conditions of IMF stand-by assistance', *Indian Journal of Economics*, July 1979, p. 6.
189 J. Horsely, *Tools of the Maritime Trade*, David and Charles, 1980; O. Johnson and J. Salop, 'Distribution aspects of stabilisation programmes in developing countries', IMF *Staff Paper*, no. 27, March 1980.
190 E.A. Branch, *Economics of Shipping Practice and Management*, Chapman and Hall, 1982; J.P. Morgan, 'IMF *Survey* – a modest little bank', *The Economist*, 26 September 1981.
191 N. Bonsor, *North Atlantic Seaway*, vol. 4, Brookside, 1979; see also the *IMF Proceedings of the 2nd International Monetary Conference*, Global Independence Centre, Philadelphia, 16 November 1980, IMF, Washington DC, 1981.
192 The *Rochdale Report*, op.cit., p. 350; there was an attempt at three basic comparisons of shipping and twenty-seven other main industrial sectors using data published in *Economic Trends*, August 1968.
193 G. Alexandersson and G. Norstram, *World Shipping: An Economic Geography of Ports and Seaborne Trade*, Wiley/Almguist and Wiksell, 1973; A.W. Pine, 'Critics change the IMF losses: its rules forcing borrowers to shape up', *Wall Street Journal*, 21 September 1981. Ibid.; see also *The Annual Abstract of Statistics*, 1966, for further comparisons.
194 National Ports Council, *Annual Digest of Port Statistics* (continuation of *Digest and Port Statistics*), 1973; J.H. Reichman, 'The Fund's conditional assistance and the problems of adjustment 1973-75', *Finance and Development*, December 1978. Ibid.; but see data published in the *National Income and Expenditure*, 1968, for a different set of comparative figures.

195 L.M. Bates, *The Merchant Service*, Muller, 1945; *Wall Street Journal*, 21 September 1981, where B. Sprinkel, the US Treasury Under-Secretary of State for Monetary Affairs said, 'For various reasons, there have been [conditionality] shipping in recent years. We want to push the IMF's conditionality back to where it was.'

196 A.G. Course, *The Merchant Navy Today*, Oxford University Press, 1956; T.H. Reichman and R. Stillson, 'Experience with programmes of balance of payments adjustments: stand-by arrangements in the higher credit tranches, 1963–72', IMF *Staff Papers*, vol. 25, no. 2, June 1978.

197 R. Hope, *Introduction to the Merchant Navy*, 3rd edn, Seafarers' Education Service, 1967; W. Beveridge and M. Kelly, 'Fiscal content of financial programmes supported by SBA in the upper credit tranches 1969–78', IMF *Staff Papers*, vol. 27, no. 2, June 1980.

198 Mercantile Marine Service Association, *Ninety-fourth Annual Report of* (with which is amalgamated the Imperial Merchant Service Guild), 1951; see also IMF *Survey*, 7 February 1983.

199 Anglo-American Council of Productivity: *Freight Handling*, Report of a specialist team which visited the USA in 1950; T.A. Connors, *The Apparent Effects of Recent IMF Stabilization Programmes*, International Finance Discussion Papers no. 135, Federal Reserve Board, April 1979.

200 USA Report, ibid.; see also C.H. Nilson, *Guide to the Merchant Navy*, Brown, Low and Ferguson, Glasgow, 1968; M. Kelly, *Analysis Stand-by Programmes During 1971–1980*, IMF *Staff Papers*, vol. 29, no. 4, 1982.

201 National Board for Prices and Incomes, *Pay and Conditions of Merchant Navy Officers*, HMSO Report no. 35, Cmnd 3302; J. de Larosiere, Address to the 1981 *European Management Symposium in Davos*, 'The IMF between Conservatism and Innovation', Davos, 3 February 1981.

202 E.C. Talbot-Booth, *British Merchant Ships*, Rich and Cowan, 1934. Note that US law mandates regular reports by the US Governor to the Fund to Congress on the social, political and economic impact of the Fund's SBAs, entered into in connection with the SFF (Public Law, 96-389, 1980).

203 E.C. Talbot-Booth, *Ships and the Sea*, 7th edn, Sampson Law, 1942; see M. Guritian, 'Fund conditionality and the international adjustment process', *Finance and Development*, December 1980, March 1981 and June 1981.

204 E.C. Talbot-Booth, *His Majesty's Merchant Navy*, 3rd edn; Sampson Law nd; from Cline's Introduction in W. Cline and S. Weinfraub (eds), *Economic Stabilization Programmes in Developing Countries*, Brookings Institution, 1981.

205 J. Woddis, *Under the Red Duster: A Study of Britain's Merchant Navy*, Senior Press Ltd, 1947; since the mid-1970s, private financial institutions – in particular Lazond Frenes, S.G. Warburg and Lenham Bros. have provided technical assistance missions in a number of DMNs to help them restore government finances.

206 OECD, *Statistics of Balance of Payments*, Paris, 1950: 'Trade balance FOB – Countries UK; (a) Merchandise: FOB net, import, exports; (b) transport, debit/credit, shipping'.

PART VI
CONCLUSIONS

11 Conclusions

It is not difficult to understand why there has been a scramble for national fleets. In the first place, water has always been a central feature of man's life. The oceans and the seas cover about 71 per cent of the earth's surface and constitute its most conspicuous feature. Most of the other remaining 29 per cent consists of swamps, deserts, forests and mountains, unsuitable for man's immediate water transport needs. Since time immemorial man has always used the sea for food, recreation, transportation, defence, cleansing and economic livelihood. Equally, from the beginning of recorded history man has used the sea as a means of transport, first for himself, and then as a means of distributing surplus products throughout the world. The bulk of the tonnage of products transported throughout the world today is moved in ocean vessels, ranging from small boats, capable of carrying a few tons, to bulk carriers capable of transporting almost 500,000 tons of oil. The cost of transporting goods on the ocean depends on the type of product, the form of shipment and the type of vessel. Probably the cheapest form of transportation known to man is that of the great oil carriers in which a ton of oil may be shipped, on average, about 100 times cheaper than by land, if the use of pipeline is excluded.

As per capita consumption of material increases, the outlook for marine transport is one of ever-increasing tonnage and size of carrying vessels, not only in conventional vessels but also in ground-effect vessels (already in commercial operation in Europe) and in bulk-carrying submarines to pass beneath the polar ice cap. But that is only the technological side of development. The management and policy aspects of ocean use policy are threatening to disrupt this smooth progress.

With the emergence of sovereign nation-states and international trade, the management of relations between states has changed. First, it gave rise to sovereignty and the national flag, and now it has given way to nationalism and national fleets. Shipping has not escaped the problems arising from recent developments in the international system. The irreconcilable differences of ideologies, perceptions and varying levels of economic developments in different parts of the world have spilled over into the management of national and international shipping. With the emergence from colonial domination of the now developing countries, for instance, the last three decades have witnessed the fragmentation of large shipping multinationals, once serving the colonies, into small national shipping companies serving the needs and aspirations of the now-numerous members of the world community of nations. With this development came restrictive shipping practices *inter alia*. Unless some compromise is reached soon, this trend towards protectionism and other forms of state intervention is bound to have untold repercussions for the future prospects of national and international shipping.

The aim of this book has therefore been to examine the nature of the problem in its past, present and future and to put forward a few ideas for its resolution. Because shipping is probably the most international and most politicized industry, its problems can only, therefore, be appreciated in the context of a multidisciplinary study. This is the approach adopted in this book — an approach which is also in line with the rationale that many nations have given for involvement in shipping. To remind ourselves, these reasons are: economics, politics, finance and security. It goes without saying that what is happening in international shipping is symptomatic of the related developments in international trade relations.

Shipping is both a factor of production and a service industry. As a major component of transportation, it is both vital and also the cheapest form of transportation — cheaper than rail, roads, air, etc. This aspect of shipping includes cargo ships, bulk carriers, tankers, trawlers, cruise ships, ferries and even hydrofoils and hovercraft. We should also include related industries such as marine insurance, shipbuilding, catering, holidays and other invisible services. Equally important is the link between shipping and international trade; not only did shipping develop international commerce, as we know it today, it has continued to sustain it. Shipping as an aspect of transport is crucial for development. A particularly important link between

492

transport and development is in international transactions. That mode of *transportation* is maritime and the *development* is international trade. This is nowhere more pronounced than in the case of the TMNs. Maritime transport is, in general, also crucial to the DMNs that have not yet built important commercial exchanges with their continental neighbours or with the TMNs, and are largely dependent on what is still recognizable as a colonial and semi-colonial pattern of trade with the more or less distant TMNs. However, not all countries have the same social, political and economic systems, nor are they all at the same level of economic development. Certain assumptions have nevertheless been made in order to simplify and clarify this rather complex field, and the use of designations such as TMNs and DMNs can therefore at times be misleading.

No industry is as politicized as shipping. Indeed, almost every maritime literature one encounters these days carries an article or two on the influence of politics. But, again, no industry is as international as maritime transport. Much of the politics involved in shipping owes its roots to the changed world material conditions, especially in the last fifty years. At the end of the Second World War, international shipping was controlled almost exclusively by a few maritime powers (TMNs) which also dominated international trade. For those nations that have emerged from colonial or semi-colonial status since 1945, economic growth is virtually linked with an increasing share of international trade since, in general, a large proportion of their GNP is composed of exports. However, the DMNs have not been so fortunate in their commercial and financial relationships with the outside world. The prices of their major exports, largely primary products, have generally stagnated or declined. Conversely, prices of manufactured goods, which are their main imports, have been rising. The impact of these diverging price trends on the economies of the DMNs has been intensified by an increasing demand for capital goods and industrial imports for the creation of their economic infrastructures, and for agricultural and industrial development. Among the industries they have had to grapple with are airlines, communications, shipping, etc. In this aspect, we are focusing on the interrelationship between maritime transport and the international system.

Quest for National Fleets

As the DMNs discovered, immediately following independence, it was necessary to spend an increasing proportion of their scarce foreign exchange on services from foreign airlines and shipping companies *inter alia*. Most importantly, they neither had shares in, controlled, nor had any other influence upon these companies to enable them to correct the anomaly. It is not surprising, therefore, that in a deteriorating balance of payments' situation, the DMNs became very conscious of the adverse impact on their balance of payments of the outflow of foreign exchange in payment of shipping services and other indivisible transactions provided by foreigners — mainly the TMNs. Hence, the strong link between shipping, the balance of payments and international trade as indicated above. Thus as early as the 1950s, several of the then-newly-independent DMNs began to pay increasing attention to shipping and allied trade problems and evolved their own policies. Shipping problems and policies were also brought up in the Regional Commissions of the UN and especially ECOSOC, ECAFE, ECA and ECLA. But the first global effort to formulate a common approach to shipping and related matters, from the point of view of the DMNs, was not made until UNCTAD I, held in Geneva in 1964. Subsequently, a comprehensive response by these countries to shipping questions, crystallized at the consequent Algiers Conference in 1967 — hitherto these had only existed in large international shipping companies which were in effect national companies of the TMNs. The quest for national fleets by the DMNs had therefore begun in earnest, and brought about the disintegration of these shipping multinationals and, with it, the current problem of national and international shipping today. The assault on the TMNs' dominance of international shipping was in part aided by UNCTAD.

Prior to 1964 the only international organizations dealing with international shipping matters were the ILO and IMCO — later IMO. The former dealt with labour relations, the latter with purely technical issues, apart from the occasional passing reference to economic and political issues. Thus, no international organization had existed that concerned itself with economic, political, financial and other structural aspects of maritime transport. Then came UNCTAD in 1964 which began to change all that. Its significance is that it represents a political, but not necessarily an economic, victory for the DMNs in their efforts to raise capital through increased trade. The TMNs that had resisted UNCTAD's creation as a duplication of GATT's role were consistently out-manoeuvred at the initial session, in 1964, by the DMNs *bloc-caucus* of the Group of 77. Economic gains, however, would depend on whether the TMNs would agree to UNCTAD's objectives of stabilizing commodity prices and extending 'most-favoured-nation' treatment to the DMNs without reciprocity. With regard to UNCTAD's activities in the field of shipping, the formation of the Sub-committee on Shipping (Committee 4 of the

Trade Board) in 1965 was a landmark, and of great significance was the *Memorandum of Understanding on Shipping*. The full discussions of UNCTAD and its implications are nevertheless beyond the scope of this book, but, even if it has not achieved much elsewhere, its highlighting of the plight of the DMNs, through numerous researches and publications, should be commended. As a result, it is not surprising that the TMNs tend to be rather hostile to UNCTAD — it has probably earned its nickname of the 'Poor Man's Club'.

Since its establishment, the UNCTAD Committee on Shipping has discussed a wide variety of subjects, among which are: freight rates; discriminatory practices; improvement of port facilities; and expansion of the merchant marine in the developing countries. This Committee appointed a Working Group on International Shipping Legislation (WGISL) whose first task in 1971 was the examination of the comprehensive report prepared by the Secretariat on bills of lading. After a long discussion, the Working Group submitted to UNCITRAL and invited it to undertake further studies on this subject. The second major task of the Working Group concerned the preparation of the draft Convention on the Code of Conduct for Liner Conferences, which was subsequently adopted on 7 April 1974. Its aims are to facilitate the expansion of seaborne trade and to 'ensure a balance of interests between suppliers and users of liner shipping services'. The Committee went on to work on plans to phase out or reform flags of convenience, culminating in the UN Convention on Registration of 7 February 1986. Other achievements have included the Hamburg Rules 1978; the Convention on Multimodal Transport 1980; and others in progress to deal with internationalization of marine insurance, sharing in bulk trade and combating piracy and fraud. It is not possible to enumerate all the details, but there is no doubt UNCTAD has become the most important centre at which North–South cooperation has been, and will continue to be, demonstrated. No doubt among the shipping circles in the TMNs, UNCTAD is still regarded as a 'dangerous instrument'.

It was only after UNCTAD that it became possible to undertake an interdisciplinary study linking shipping and other aspects of the international system. For it is only in that context that the full extent of its role and function could be best appreciated in international trade relations. Historically, shipping gave birth to exchange and, therefore, international trade as we know it today. In addition, it was the most important single factor that brought the whole world as close as it is now. Was it not shipping that participated in the internationalization of finance capital through the famous triangular trade on the one hand and the flags of convenience on the other?

Equally it was shipping which, as a factor of production, a mode of transport and a servant of commerce, was at the forefront of national and regional economic developments; it also nurtured and sustained international trade. Moreover the fact that the Liner Conference and FOC systems have been sore points in international relations is itself indicative of the role of shipping in international trade relations. No doubt the resolution of these two issues through the Liner and Registration Codes respectively in 1974 and 1986 could not have been possible without international instruments and therefore international cooperation and efforts. It is equally not surprising that one of the ways open to Kuwait to solve a problem caused by the Iran–Iraqi war is by seeking the protection of either the US or USSR flag.

It is also worth repeating that, due to its close proximity to international trade, the industry has not escaped the wave of protectionist and restrictive measures that are currently rampant in this field. In fact shipping responded by developing its own brands of flag discriminations, cargo preferences and maritime subsidies. Likewise shipping's close association with politics has opened it wide to political interventions and regulations as discussed in Chapters 5 and 6 of this book. It has further been pointed out that the industry's economic orientation makes it amenable to the protection and provision of manpower employment, including the employment of national economic resources and the rise of free ports and the manufacturing free trade zones. There could, therefore, be no better summary of the crucial role and pivotal function of, especially, international shipping to international trade relations than in pointing out its priceless influence in international finance — that is, in the saving and earning of foreign exchange and improvement of the nations' balance of payments' positions. Finally, in a world in which the advance in technology has enabled the provision and export of services to gain an upper hand over the traditional heavy manufacturing industry and visible trade, shipping has become even more important. Indeed, it is for this reason that, for the first time, the adverse balance of payments of the UK and other major TMNs are now only offset by export of services and other invisible earnings from principally shipping and its related industries.

ANNEXES

ANNEXES

Annex 1 Text of the Code of Conduct for Liner Conferences

Convention on a Code of Conduct for Liner Conferences[1]

OBJECTIVES AND PRINCIPLES

The Contracting Parties to the present Convention,

Desiring to improve the liner conference system,

Recognizing the need for a universally acceptable code of conduct for liner conferences,

Taking into account the special needs and problems of the developing countries with respect to the activities of liner conferences serving their foreign trade,

Agreeing to reflect in the Code the following fundamental objectives and basic principles:

(a) The objective to facilitate the orderly expansion of world sea-borne trade;

(b) The objective to stimulate the development of regular and efficient liner services adequate to the requirements of the trade concerned;

(c) The objective to ensure a balance of interests between suppliers and users of liner shipping services;

(d) The principle that conference practices should not involve any discrimination against the shipowners, shippers or the foreign trade of any country;

(e) The principle that conferences hold meaningful consultations with shippers' organizations, shippers' representatives and shippers on matters of common interest, with, upon request, the participation of appropriate authorities;

---

1. The text as appears in Appendix I is the Code as adopted in Geneva. Suggested deletions are put in parentheses and proposed amendments are italicized and incorporated in the Code. The rest of the text is accepted without comment.

(f) The principle that conferences should make available to interested parties pertinent information about their activities which are relevant to those parties and should publish meaningful information on their activities,

Have agreed as follows:

PART ONE

Chapter I

DEFINITIONS

Liner conference or conference

A group of two or more vessel-operating carriers which provides international liner services for the carriage of cargo on a particular route or routes (within specified geographical limits) and which has an agreement or arrangement, whatever its nature, within the framework of which they operate under uniform or common freight rates and any other agreed conditions with respect to the provision of liner services.

Liner service

A regular shipping service for the carriage of general cargo on particular routes with fixed schedules and tariffs.

National shipping line

A national shipping line of any given country is a vessel-operating carrier which has its head office of management and its effective control in that country and is recognized as such by an appropriate authority of that country or under the law of that country.

Lines belonging to and operated by a joint venture involving two or more countries and in whose equity the national interests, public and/or private, of those countries have a substantial share and whose head office of management and whose effective control is in one of those countries can be recognized as a national line by the appropriate authorities of those countries.

Third-country shipping line

A vessel-operating carrier in its operations between two countries of which it is not a national shipping line.

Shipper

A person or entity who has entered into, or who demonstrates an intention to enter into, a contractual or other arrangement with a conference or shipping line for the shipment of goods in which he has a beneficial interest.

500

Shipper's organization

An association or equivalent body which promotes, represents and protects the interests of shippers and, if those authorities so desire, is recognized in that capacity by the appropriate authority or authorities of the country whose shippers it represents.

Goods carried by the conference

Cargo transported by shipping lines members of a conference in accordance with the conference agreement.

Appropriate authority

Either a government or a body designated by a government or by national legislation to perform any of the functions ascribed to such authority by the provisions of this Code.

Promotional freight rate

A rate instituted for promoting the carriage of nontraditional exports of the country concerned.

Special freight rate

A preferential freight rate, other than a promotional freight rate, which may be negotiated between the parties concerned.

Chapter II

RELATIONS AMONG MEMBER LINES

Article 1

MEMBERSHIP

1.   Any national shipping line shall have the right to be a full member of a conference which serves the foreign trade of its country, (subject to the criteria set out in article 1, paragraph 2). Shipping lines which are not national lines in any trade of a conference shall have the right to become full members of that conference, (subject to the criteria set out in article 1, paragraphs 2 and 3, and to the provisions regarding the share of trade as set out in article 2 as regards third-country shipping lines.)
2.   A shipping line applying for membership of a conference shall furnish evidence of its ability and intention, which may include the use of *limited* chartered tonnage, provided the criteria of this paragraph are met, to operate a regular, adequate and efficient service on a long-term basis as defined in the conference agreement within the framework of the conference, shall undertake to

abide by all the terms and conditions of the conference agreement, and shall deposit a financial guarantee to cover any outstanding financial obligation in the event of subsequent withdrawal, suspension or expulsion from membership, if so required under the conference agreement.

(3. In considering an application for membership by a shipping line which is not a national line in any trade of the conference concerned, in addition to the provisions of article 1, paragraph 2, the following criteria, inter alia, should be taken into account:

(a) The existing volume of the trade on the route or routes served by the conference and prospects for its growth;

(b) The adequacy of shipping space for the existing and prospective volume of trade on the route or routes served by the conference;

(c) The probable effect of admission of the shipping line to the conference on the efficiency and quality of the conference service;

(d) The current participation of the shipping line in trade on the same route or routes outside the framework of a conference; and

(e) The current participation of the shipping line on the same route or routes within the framework of another conference.

The above criteria shall not be applied so as to subvert the implementation of the provisions relating to participation in trade set out in article 2.)

4. An application for admission or readmission to membership shall be promptly decided upon and the decision communicated by a conference to an applicant promptly, and in no case later than six months from the date of application. When a shipping line is refused admission or readmission the conference shall, at the same time, give in writing the grounds for such refusal.

5. When considering applications for admission, a conference shall take into account the views put forward by shippers and shippers' organizations of the countries whose trade is carried by the conference, as well as the views of appropriate authorities if they so request.

6. In addition to the criteria for admission set out in article 1, paragraph 2, a shipping line applying for readmission shall also give evidence of having fulfilled its obligations in accordance with article 4, paragraphs 1 and 4. The conference may give special scrutiny to the circumstances under which the line left the conference.

Article 2

PARTICIPATION IN TRADE

(1. Any shipping line admitted to membership of a conference shall have sailing and loading rights in the trades covered by that conference.)

2. When a conference operates a pool, all shipping lines members of the conference serving the trade covered by the pool shall have the right to participate in the pool for that trade.

3. For the purpose of determining the share of trade which member lines shall have the right to acquire, the national shipping lines of each country *shall have equal rights to participate in a substantial portion of the trade carried by the conference from their countries* (irrespective of the number of lines, shall be regarded as a single group of shipping lines for that country.)

502

4. Third-country shipping lines, if any, shall have the right to participate in a significant portion of the trade carried by the conference.

(4. When determining a share of trade within a pool of individual member lines and/or groups of national shipping lines in accordance with article 2, paragraph 2, the following principles regarding their right to participation in the trade carried by the conference shall be observed, unless otherwise mutually agreed:

(a) The group of national shipping lines of each of two countries the foreign trade between which is carried by the conference shall have equal rights to participate in the freight and volume of traffic generated by their mutual foreign trade and carried by the conference;

(b) Third-country shipping lines, if any, shall have the right to acquire a significant part, such as 20 per cent, in the freight and volume of traffic generated by that trade.)

(5. If, for any one of the countries whose trade is carried by a conference, there are no national shipping lines participating in the carriage of that trade, the share of the trade to which national shipping lines of that country would be entitled under article 2, paragraph 4 shall be distributed among the individual member lines participating in the trade in proportion to their respective share.)

(6. If the national shipping lines of one country decide not to carry their full share of the trade, that portion of their share of the trade which they do not carry shall be distributed among the individual member lines participating in the trade in proportion to their respective shares.)

(7. If the national shipping lines of the countries concerned do not participate in the trade between those countries covered by a conference, the shares of trade carried by the conference between those countries shall be allocated between the participating member lines of third countries by commercial negotiations between those lines.)

(8. The national shipping lines of a region, members of a conference, at one end of the trade covered by the conference, may redistribute among themselves by mutual agreement the shares in trades allocated to them, in accordance with article 2, paragraphs 4 to 7 inclusive.)

9. Subject to the provisions of article 2, (paragraphs 4 to 8 inclusive) regarding shares of trade among individual shipping lines or groups of shipping lines, pooling or tradesharing agreements shall be reviewed by the conference periodically, at intervals to be stipulated in those agreements and in accordance with criteria to be specified in the conference agreement.

10. The application of the present article shall commence as soon as possible after entry into force of the present Convention and shall be completed within a transition period which in no case shall be longer than two years, taking into account the specific situation in each of the trades concerned.

11. Shipping lines members of a conference shall be entitled to operate *a limited number of* chartered ships to fulfill their conference obligations.

12. The criteria for sharing and the revision of shares as set out in article 2, paragraphs 1 to 11 inclusive shall apply when, in the absence of a pool, there exists berthing, sailing and/or any other form of cargo allocation agreement.

13. Where no pooling, berthing, sailing or other trade participation agreements exist in a conference, either group of national shipping lines, members of the conference, may require that pooling arrangements be introduced, (in respect of

the trade between their countries carried by the conference, in conformity with the provisions of article 2, paragraph 4; or alternatively they may require that the sailings be so adjusted) as to provide an opportunity to these lines to enjoy substantially the (same) rights to participate in the trade between those two countries carried by the conference (as they would have enjoyed under the provisions of article 2, paragraph 4.) Any such request shall be considered and decided by the conference. If there is no agreement to institute such a pool or adjustment of sailings among the members of the conference, the groups of national shipping lines of the countries at both ends of the trade shall have a (majority) *weighted* vote in deciding to establish such a pool or adjustments of sailings. The matter shall be decided upon within a period not exceeding six months from the receipt of the request.

14.   In the event of a disagreement between the national shipping lines of the countries at either end whose trade is served by the conference with regard to whether or not pooling shall be introduced, they may require that within the conference sailings be so adjusted as to provide an opportunity to these lines to enjoy substantially the (same) rights to participate in the trade between those two countries carried by the conference (as they would have enjoyed under the provisions of article 2, paragraph 4.) In the event that there are no national shipping lines in one of the countries whose trade is served by the conference, the national shipping line or lines of the other country may make the same request. The conference shall use its best endeavours to meet this request. If, however, this request is not met, the appropriate authorities of the countries at both ends of the trade may take up the matter if they so wish and make their views known to the parties concerned for their consideration. If no agreement is reached, the dispute shall be dealt with in accordance with the procedures established in this Code.

15.   Other shipping lines, members of a conference, may also request that pooling or sailing agreements be introduced, and the request shall be considered by the conference in accordance with the relevant provisions of this Code.

16.   A conference shall provide for appropriate measures in any conference pooling agreement to cover cases where the cargo has been shut out by a member line for any reason excepting late presentation by the shipper. Such agreement shall provide that a vessel with unbooked space, capable of being used, be allowed to lift the cargo, even in excess of the pool share of the line in the trade, if otherwise the cargo would be shut out and delayed beyond a period set by the conference.

17.   The provisions of article 2, paragraphs 1 to 16 inclusive concern all goods regardless of their origin, their destination or the use for which they are intended, with the exception of military equipment for national defence purposes.

Article 3

DECISION-MAKING PROCEDURES

The decision-making procedures embodied in a conference agreement shall be based on the equality of all the full member lines; these procedures shall ensure that the voting rules do not hinder the proper work of the conference and the service of the trade and shall define the matters on which decisions will be made by unanimity. However, a decision cannot be taken in respect of matters defined in a conference agreement relating to the trade between two countries without the consent of the national shipping lines of those two countries.

Article 4

SANCTIONS

1. A shipping line member of a conference shall be entitled, subject to the provisions regarding withdrawal which are embodied in pool schemes and/or cargo-sharing arrangements, to secure its release, without penalty, from the terms of the conference agreement after giving three months' notice, unless the conference agreement provides for a different time period, although it shall be required to fulfil its obligations as a member of the conference up to the date of its release.

2. A conference may, upon notice to be specified in the conference agreement, suspend or expel a member for significant failure to abide by the terms and conditions of the conference agreement.

3. No expulsion or suspension shall become effective until a statement in writing of the reasons therefor has been given and until any dispute has been settled as provided in chapter VI.

4. Upon withdrawal or expulsion, the line concerned shall be required to pay its share of the outstanding financial obligations of the conference, up to the date of its withdrawal or expulsion. In cases of withdrawal, suspension or expulsion, the line shall not be relieved of its own financial obligations under the conference agreement or of any of its obligations towards shippers.

Article 5

SELF POLICING

1. A conference shall adopt and keep up to date an illustrative list, which shall be as comprehensive as possible, of practices which are regarded as malpractices and/or breaches of the conference agreement and shall provide effective self-policing machinery to deal with them, with specific provisions requiring:

   (a) The fixing of penalties or a range of penalties for malpractices or breaches, to be commensurate with their seriousness;

   (b) The examination and impartial review of an adjudication of complaints, and/or decisions taken on complaints, against malpractices or breaches, by a person or body unconnected with any of the shipping lines members of the conference or their affiliates, on request by the conference or any other party concerned;

   (c) The reporting, on request, on the action taken in connexion with complaints against malpractices and/or breaches, and on a basis of anonymity for the parties concerned, to the appropriate authorities of the countries whose trade is served by the conference and of the countries whose shipping lines are members of the conference.

2. Shipping lines and conferences are entitled to the full cooperation of shippers and shippers' organizations in the endeavour to combat malpractices and breaches.

3. Failure to comply with self-policing decisions will be regarded as a violation of the Code.

Article 6

CONFERENCE AGREEMENTS

1. All conference agreements, pooling, berthing and sailing rights agreements and amendments or other documents directly related to, and which affect, such agreements shall be made available (on request) to the appropriate authorities *and the public* of the countries whose trade is served by the conference and of the countries whose shipping lines are members of the conference.

2. Conference agreements will include obligations to serve the trades adequately.

Chapter III

RELATIONS WITH SHIPPERS

Article 7

LOYALTY ARRANGEMENTS

1. The shipping lines members of a conference are entitled to institute and maintain loyalty arrangements with shippers, the form and terms of which are matters for consultation between the conference and shippers' organizations or representatives of shippers. These loyalty arrangements shall provide safeguards making explicit the rights of shippers and conference members. These arrangements shall be based on the contract system or any other system which is also lawful.

2. Whatever loyalty arrangements are made, the freight rate applicable to loyal shippers shall be determined within a fixed range of percentages of the freight rate applicable to other shippers. Where a change in the differential causes an increase in the rates charged to shippers, the change can be implemented only after (150) *90* days' notice to those shippers or according to regional practice and/or agreement. Disputes in connexion with a change of the differential shall be settled as provided in the loyalty agreement.

3. The terms of loyalty arrangements shall provide safeguards making explicit the rights and obligations of shippers and of shipping lines members of the conference in accordance with the following provisions, inter alia:

(a) The shipper shall be bound in respect of cargo whose shipment is controlled by him or his affiliated or subsidiary company or his forwarding agent in accordance with the contract of sale of the goods concerned, provided that the shipper shall not, by evasion, subterfuge, or intermediary, attempt to divert cargo in violation of his loyalty commitment;

(b) Where there is a loyalty contract, the extent of actual or liquidated damages and/or penalty shall be specified in the contract. The member lines of the conference may, however, decide to assess lower liquidated damages or to waive the claim to liquidated damages. In any event, the liquidated damages under the contract to be paid by the shipper shall not exceed the freight charges on the particular shipment, computed at the rate provided under the contract;

(c) The shipper shall be entitled to resume full loyalty status, subject to the fulfilment of conditions established by the conference which shall be specified in the loyalty arrangement;

(d) The loyalty arrangement shall set out:

    (i) A list of cargo, which may include bulk cargo shipped without mark or count, which is specifically excluded from the scope of the loyalty arrangement;

    (ii) A definition of the circumstances in which cargo other than cargo covered by (i) above is considered to be excluded from the scope of the loyalty arrangement;

    (iii) The method of settlement of disputes arising under the loyalty arrangement;

    (iv) Provision for termination of the loyalty arrangement on request by either a shipper or a conference without penalty, after expiry of a stipulated period of notice, such notice to be given in writing; and

    (v) The terms for granting dispensation.

4. If there is a dispute between a conference and a shippers' organization, representatives of shippers and/or shippers about the form or terms of a proposed loyalty arrangement, either party may refer the matter for resolution under appropriate procedures as set out in this Code.

Article 8

DISPENSATION

1. Conferences shall provide, within the terms of the loyalty arrangements, that requests by shippers for dispensation shall be examined and a decision given quickly and, if requested, the reasons given in writing where dispensation is withheld. Should a conference fail to confirm, within a period specified in the loyalty arrangement, sufficient space to accommodate a shipper's cargo within a period also specified in the loyalty arrangement, the shipper shall have the right, without being penalized, to utilize any vessel for the cargo in question.

2. In ports where conference services are arranged subject to the availability of a specified minimum of cargo (i.e. on inducement), but either the shipping line does not call, despite due notice by shippers, or the shipping line does not reply within an agreed time to the notice given by shippers, shippers shall automatically have the right, without prejudicing their loyalty status, to use any available vessel for the carriage of their cargo.

Article 9

AVAILABILITY OF TARIFFS AND RELATED CONDITIONS AND/OR REGULATIONS

Tariffs, related conditions, regulations, and any amendments thereto shall be made available on request to shippers, shippers' organizations and other parties concerned at reasonable cost, and they shall be available for examination at offices of shipping lines and their agents. They shall spell out all conditions concerning the application of freight rates and the carriage of any cargo covered by them.

Article 10

ANNUAL REPORTS

Conferences shall provide annually to shippers' organizations, or to representatives of shippers, reports on their activities designed to provide general information of interest to them, including relevant information about consultations held with shippers and shippers' organizations, action taken regarding complaints, changes in membership, and significant changes in service, tariffs and conditions of carriage. Such annual reports shall be submitted, on request, to the appropriate authorities of the countries whose trade is served by the conference concerned.

Article 11

CONSULTATION MACHINERY

1. There shall be consultations on matters of common interest between a conference, shippers' organizations, representatives of shippers and, where practicable, shippers, which may be designated for that purpose by the appropriate authority if it so desires. These consultations shall take place whenever requested by any of the above-mentioned parties. Appropriate authorities shall have the right, upon request, to participate fully in the consultations, but this does not mean that they play a decision-making role.

2. The following matters, inter alia, may be the subject of consultation:
    (a) Changes in general tariff conditions and related regulations;
    (b) Changes in the general level of tariff rates and rates for major commodities;
    (c) Promotional and/or special freight rates;
    (d) Imposition of, and related changes in, surcharges;
    (e) Loyalty arrangements, their establishment or changes in their form and general conditions;
    (f) Changes in the tariff classification of ports;
    (g) Procedure for the supply of necessary information by shippers concerning the expected volume and nature of their cargoes; and
    (h) Presentation of cargo for shipment and the requirements regarding notice of cargo availability.

3. To the extent that they fall within the scope of activity of a conference, the following matters may also be the subject of consultation:
    (a) Operation of cargo inspection services;
    (b) Changes in the pattern of services;
    (c) Effects of the introduction of new technology in the carriage of cargo, in particular unitization, with consequent reduction of conventional service or loss of direct services; and
    (d) Adequacy and quality of shipping services, including the impact of

pooling, berthing or sailing arrangements on the availability of shipping services and freight rates at which shipping services are provided; charges in the areas served and in the regularity of calls by conference vessels.

4.   Consultations shall be held before final decisions are taken, unless otherwise provided in this Code. Advance notice shall be given of the intention to take decisions on matters referred to in article 11, paragraphs 2 and 3. Where this is impossible, urgent decisions may be taken pending the holding of consultations.

5.   Consultations shall begin without undue delay and in any event within a maximum period specified in the conference agreement or, in the absence of such a provision in the agreement, not later than 30 days after receipt of the proposal for consultations, unless different periods of time are provided in this Code.

6.   When holding consultations, the parties shall use their best efforts to provide relevant information, to hold timely discussions and to clarify matters for the purpose of seeking solutions of the issues concerned. The parties involved shall take account of each other's views and problems and strive to reach agreement consistent with their commercial viability.

Chapter IV

FREIGHT RATES

Article 12

CRITERIA FOR FREIGHT-RATE DETERMINATION

In arriving at a decision on questions of tariff policy in all cases mentioned in this Code, the following points shall, unless otherwise provided, be taken into account:

(a) Freight rates shall be fixed at as low a level as is feasible from the commercial point of view and shall permit a reasonable profit for shipowners;

(b) The cost of operations of conferences shall, as a rule, be evaluated for the round voyage of ships, with the outward and inward directions considered as a single whole. Where applicable, the outward and inward voyage should be considered separately. The freight rates should take into account, among other factors, the nature of cargoes, the interrelation between weight and cargo measurement, as well as the value of cargoes;

(c) In fixing promotional freight rates and/or special freight rates for specific goods, the conditions of trade for these goods of the countries served by the conference, particularly of developing and land-locked countries, shall be taken into account.

Article 13

CONFERENCE TARIFFS AND CLASSIFICATION OF TARIFF RATES

1.   Conference tariffs shall not unfairly differentiate between shippers similarly situated. Shipping lines members of a conference shall adhere strictly to the rates, rules and terms shown in the tariffs and other currently valid published documents of the conference and to any special arrangements permitted under this Code.

2. Conference tariffs should be drawn up (simply and clearly, containing as few classes/categories as possible, depending on the commodity and, where appropriate, for each class category, they should also indicate, wherever practicable, in order to facilitate statistical compilation and analysis, the corresponding appropriate code number of the item) in accordance with (the Standard International Trade Classification) the Brussels Tariff Nomenclature (or any other nomenclature that may be internationally adopted) the classification of commodities in the tariffs should, as far as practicable, be prepared in co-operation with shippers' organizations and other national and international organizations concerned.

Article 14

GENERAL FREIGHT-RATE INCREASES

1. A conference shall give notice of not less than (150) *90* days, or according to regional practice and/or agreement, to shippers' organizations or representatives of shippers and/or shippers and, where so required, to appropriate authorities of the countries whose trade is served by the conference, of its intention to effect a general increase in freight rates, an indication of its extent, the date of effect and the reasons supporting the proposed increase.

2. At the request of any of the parties prescribed for this purpose in this Code, to be made within an agreed period of time after the receipt of the notice, consultations shall commence, in accordance with the relevant provisions of this Code, within a stipulated period not exceeding 30 days or as previously agreed between the parties concerned; the consultations shall be held in respect of the bases and amounts of the proposed increase and the date from which it is to be given effect.

3. A conference, in an effort to expedite consultations, may or upon the request of any of the parties prescribed in this Code as entitled to participate in consultations on general freight-rate increases shall, where practicable, reasonably before the consultations, submit to the participating parties a report from independent accountants of repute, including, where the requesting parties accept it as one of the bases of consultations, an aggregated analysis of data regarding relevant costs and revenues which in the opinion of the conference necessitate an increase in freight rates.

4. If agreement is reached as a result of the consultations, the freight-rate increase shall take effect from the date indicated in the notice served in accordance with article 14, paragraph 1, unless a later date is agreed upon between the parties concerned.

5. If no agreement is reached within 30 days of the giving of notice in accordance with article 14, paragraph 1, and subject to procedures prescribed in this Code, the matter shall be submitted immediately to *appropriate authorities* (international mandatory conciliation, in accordance with chapter VI). The recommendation of the *appropriate authorities* (conciliators,) if accepted by the parties concerned, shall be binding upon them and shall be implemented, subject to the provisions of article 14, paragraph 9, with effect from the date mentioned in the conciliators' recommendation.

6. Subject to the provisions of article 14, paragraph 9, a general freight rate increase may be implemented by a conference pending the (conciliators') *appropriate authority's* recommendation. When making their recommendation, the (conciliators) *appropriate authority* should take into account the extent of the above-mentioned increase made by the conference and the period for which it has been in force. In the event that the conference rejects the recommendation of the (conciliators') *appropriate authority*, shippers and/or shippers' organizations shall have the right to consider themselves not bound, after appropriate notice, by any arrangement or other contract with that conference which may prevent them from using non-conference shipping lines. Where a loyalty arrangement exists, shippers and/or shippers' organizations shall give notice within a period of 30 days to the effect that they no longer consider themselves bound by that arrangement, which notice shall apply from the date mentioned therein, and a period of not less than 30 days and not more than 90 days shall be provided in the loyalty arrangement for this purpose.

7. A deferred rebate which is due to the shipper and which has already been accumulated by the conference shall not be withheld by, or forfeited to, the conference as a result of action by the shipper under article 14, paragraph 6.

8. If the trade of a country carried by shipping lines members of a conference on a particular route consists largely of one or few basic commodities, any increase in the freight rate on one or more of those commodities shall be treated as a general freight-rate increase, and the appropriate provisions of this Code shall apply.

9. Conferences should institute any general freight-rate increase effective in accordance with this Code for a period of a stated minimum duration, subject always to the rules regarding surcharges and regarding adjustment in freight rates consequent upon fluctuations in foreign exchange rates. The period over which a general freight-rate increase is to apply is an appropriate matter to be considered during consultations conducted in accordance with article 14, paragraph 2, (but unless otherwise agreed between the parties concerned during the consultations, the minimum period of time between the date when one general freight-rate increase becomes effective and the date of notice for the next general freight-rate increase given in accordance with article 14, paragraph 1 shall not be less than 10 months.)

Article 15

PROMOTIONAL FREIGHT RATES

1. Promotional freight rates for non-traditional exports should be instituted by conferences.

2. All necessary and reasonable information justifying the need for a promotional freight rate shall be submitted to a conference by the shippers, shippers' organizations or representatives of shippers concerned.

3. Special procedures shall be instituted providing for a decision within 30 days from the date of receipt of that information, unless mutually agreed otherwise, on applications for promotional freight rates. A clear distinction shall be made between these and general procedures for considering the possibility of reducing freight rates for other commodities or of exempting them from increases.

4. Information regarding the procedures for considering applications for promotional freight rates shall be made available by the conference to shippers and/or shippers' organizations and, on request, to the Governments and/or other appropriate authorities of the countries whose trade is served by the conference.

5. A promotional freight rate shall be established normally for a period of 12 months, unless otherwise mutually agreed between the parties concerned. Prior to the expiry of the period, the promotional freight rate shall be reviewed, on request by the shipper and/or shippers' organization concerned, when it shall be a matter for the shipper and/or shippers' organization, at the request of the conference, to show that the continuation of the rate is justified beyond the initial period.

(6. When examining a request for a promotional freight rate, the conference may take into account that, while the rate should promote the export of the non-traditional product for which it is sought, it is not likely to create substantial competitive distortions in the export of a similar product from another country served by the conference.)

7. Promotional freight rates are not excluded from the imposition of a surcharge or a currency adjustment factor in accordance with articles 16 and 17.

8. Each shipping line member of a conference serving the relevant ports of a conference trade shall accept, and not unreasonably refuse, a fair share of cargo for which a promotional freight rate has been established by the conference.

Article 16

SURCHARGES

1. Surcharges imposed by a conference to cover sudden or extraordinary increases in costs or losses of revenue shall be regarded as temporary. They shall be reduced in accordance with improvements in the situation or circumstances which they were imposed to meet and shall be cancelled, subject to article 16, paragraph 6, as soon as the situation or circumstances which prompted their imposition cease to prevail. This shall be indicated at the moment of their imposition, together, as far as possible, with a description of the change in the situation or circumstances which will bring about their increase, reduction or cancellation.

2. Surcharges imposed on cargo moving to or from a particular port shall likewise be regarded as temporary and likewise shall be increased, reduced or cancelled, subject to article 16, paragraph 6, when the situation in that port changes.

3. Before any surcharge is imposed, whether general or covering only a specific port, notice should be given and there shall be consultation, upon request, in accordance with the procedures of this Code, between the conference concerned and other parties directly affected by the surcharge and prescribed in this Code as entitled to participate in such consultations, save in those exceptional circumstances which warrant immediate imposition of the surcharge. In cases where a surcharge has been imposed without prior consultation, consultations, upon request, shall be held as soon as possible thereafter. Prior to such consultations, conferences shall furnish data which in their opinion justify the imposition of the surcharge.

4. Unless the parties agree otherwise, within a period of 15 days after the receipt of a notice given in accordance with article 16, paragraph 3, if there is no agreement on the question of the surcharge between the parties concerned referred to in that article, the relevant provisions for settlement of disputes provided in this Code shall prevail. Unless the parties concerned agree otherwise, the surcharge may, however, be imposed pending resolution of the dispute, if the dispute still remains unresolved at the end of a period of 30 days after the receipt of the above-mentioned notice.

5. In the event of a surcharge being imposed, in exceptional circumstances, without prior consultation as provided in article 16, paragraph 3, if no agreement is reached through subsequent consultations, the relevant provisions for settlement of disputes provided in this Code shall prevail.

6. Financial loss incurred by the shipping lines members of a conference as a result of any delay on account of consultations and/or other proceedings for resolving disputes regarding imposition of surcharges in accordance with the provisions of this Code, as compared to the date from which the surcharge was to be imposed in terms of the notice given in accordance with article 16, paragraph 3, may be compensated by an equivalent prolongation of the surcharge before its removal. Conversely, for any surcharge imposed by the conference and subsequently determined and agreed to be unjustified or excessive as a result of consultations or other procedures prescribed in this Code, the amounts so collected or the excess thereof as determined hereinabove, unless otherwise agreed, shall be refunded to the parties concerned, if claimed by them, within a period of 30 days of such claim.

Article 17

CURRENCY CHANGES

1. Exchange rate changes, including formal devaluation or revaluation, which leads to changes in the aggregate operational costs and/or revenues of the shipping lines members of a conference relating to their operations within the conference provide a valid reason for the introduction of a currency adjustment factor or for a change in the freight rates. The adjustment or change shall be such that in the aggregate the member lines concerned neither gain nor lose, as far as possible, as a result of the adjustment or change. The adjustment or change may take the form of currency surcharges or discounts or of increases or decreases in the freight rates.

2. Such adjustments or changes shall be subject to notice, which should be arranged in accordance with regional practice, where such practice exists, and there shall be consultations in accordance with the provisions of this Code between the conference concerned and the other parties directly affected and prescribed in this Code as entitled to participate in consultations, save in those exceptional circumstances which warrant immediate imposition of the currency adjustment factor or freight-rate change. In the event that this has been done without prior consultations, consultations shall be held as soon as possible thereafter. The consultations should be on the application, size and date of implementation of the currency adjustment factor or freight-rate change, and the same procedures shall be followed for this purpose as are prescribed in

article 16, paragraphs 4 and 5, in respect of surcharges. Such consultations should take place and be completed within a period not exceeding 15 days from the date when the intention to apply a currency surcharge or to effect a freight-rate change is announced.

3. If no agreement is reached within 15 days through consultations, the relevant provisions for (settlement of disputes provided in this Code) *rate dispute settlements* shall prevail.

4. The provisions of article 16, paragraph 6 shall apply, adapted as necessary to currency adjustment factors and freight-rate changes dealt with in the present article.

Chapter V

OTHER MATTERS

Article 18

FIGHTING SHIPS

Members of a conference shall not use fighting ships in the conference trade for the purpose of excluding, preventing or reducing competition by driving a shipping line not a member of the conference out of the said trade.

Article 19

ADEQUACY OF SERVICE

1. Conferences should take necessary and appropriate measures to ensure that their member lines provide regular, adequate and efficient service of the required frequency on the routes they serve and shall arrange such services so as to avoid as far as possible bunching and gapping of sailings. Conferences should also take into consideration any special measures necessary in arranging services to handle seasonal variations in cargo volumes.

2. Conferences and other parties prescribed in this Code as entitled to participate in consultations, including appropriate authorities if they so desire, should keep under review, and should maintain close co-operation regarding the demand for shipping space, the adequacy and suitability of service, and in particular the possibilities for rationalization and for increasing the efficiency of services. Benefits identified as accruing from rationalization of services shall be fairly reflected in the level of freight rates.

3. In respect of any port for which conference services are supplied only subject to the availability of a specified minimum of cargo, that minimum shall be specified in the tariff. Shippers should give adequate notice of the availability of such cargo.

Article 20

HEAD OFFICE OF A CONFERENCE

A conference shall as a rule establish (its head) *an* office in (a) *each* country whose trade is served by that conference, (unless agreed otherwise by the shipping lines members of that conference.)

Article 21

REPRESENTATION

Conferences shall establish local representation in all countries served, except that where there are practical reasons to the contrary the representation may be on a regional basis. The names and addresses of representatives shall be readily available, and these representatives shall ensure that the views of shippers and conferences are made rapidly known to each other with a view to expediting prompt decisions. When a conference considers it suitable it shall provide for adequate delegation of powers of decision to its representatives.

Article 22

CONTENTS OF CONFERENCE AGREEMENTS, TRADE PARTICIPATION AGREEMENTS AND LOYALTY ARRANGEMENTS

Conference agreements, trade participation agreements and loyalty arrangements shall conform to the applicable requirements of this Code and may include such other provisions as may be agreed which are not inconsistent with this Code.

PART TWO

Chapter VI

PROVISIONS AND MACHINERY FOR SETTLEMENT OF DISPUTES

A. GENERAL PROVISIONS

Article 23

1. The provisions of this chapter shall apply whenever there is a dispute relating to the application or operation of the provisions of this Code between the following parties:
(a) A conference and a shipping line;
(b) The shipping lines members of a conference;
(c) A conference or a shipping line member thereof and a shippers' organization or representatives of shippers or shippers; and
(d) Two or more conferences.
For the purposes of this chapter the term 'party' means the original parties to the dispute as well as third parties which have joined the proceedings in accordance with (a) of article 34.
2. Disputes between shipping lines of the same flag, as well as those between organizations belonging to the same country, shall be settled within the framework of the national jurisdiction of that country, (unless this creates serious difficulties in the fulfillment of the provisions of this Code.)

3. *Disputes between a national line and a conference serving its country shall be settled within the framework of the national jurisdiction of the country of the national line.*

4. *Disputes between a conference and member shipping lines and non-member shipping lines which are third flag carriers shall be settled within the framework of the national jurisdiction of the country in which the conference has its headquarters.*

5. *Disputes between two shipping lines members of a conference from different countries shall be settled within the framework of the national jurisdiction of the country in which the conference has its headquarters.*

6. *Disputes between shippers or shippers' organizations and the conference serving their country's trade shall be settled within the framework of the national jurisdiction of the shippers or shippers' organization.*

7. *Disputes between shippers or shippers' organizations and a shipping line member of a conference shall be settled within the framework of the national jurisdiction of the shippers or shippers' organization.*

8. *Disputes between two conferences shall be settled within the framework of the national jurisdiction of the country where the respondent conference has its headquarters.*

9. (3.) The parties to a dispute shall first attempt to settle it by an exchange of views or direct negotiations with the intention of finding a mutually satisfactory solution.

10. (4.) Disputes between the parties referred to in article 23, paragraph 1 relating to:

(a) Refusal of admission of a national shipping line to a conference serving the foreign trade of the country of that shipping line;

(b) Refusal of admission of a third-country shipping line to a conference;

(c) Expulsion from a conference;

(d) Inconsistency of a conference agreement with this Code;

(e) A general freight-rate increase;

(f) Surcharges;

(g) Changes in freight rates or the imposition of a currency adjustment factor due to exchange rate changes;

(h) Participation in trade; and

(i) The form and terms of proposed loyalty arrangements

which have not been resolved through an exchange of views or direct negotiations shall, at the request of any of the parties to the dispute, be referred to (international mandatory conciliation) *national courts* in accordance with the provisions of this chapter.

Article 24

(1. The conciliation procedure is initiated at the request of one of the parties to the dispute.)

(2. The request shall be made:

(a) In disputes relating to membership of conferences: not later than 60 days from the date of receipt by the applicant of the conference decision, including the reasons therefor, in accordance with article 1, paragraph 4 and article 4, paragraph 3;

(b) In disputes relating to general freight-rate increases: not later than the date of expiry of the period of notice specified in article 14, paragraph 1;

(c) In disputes relating to surcharges: not later than the date of expiry of the 30-day period specified in article 16, paragraph 4 or, where no notice has been given, not later than 15 days from the date when the surcharge was put into effect; and

(d) In disputes relating to changes in freight rates or the imposition of a currency adjustment factor due to exchange rate changes: not later than five days after the date of expiry of the period specified in article 17, paragraph 3.)

(3. The provisions of article 24, paragraph 2 shall not apply to a dispute which is referred to international mandatory conciliation in accordance with article 25, paragraph 3.)

(4. Requests for conciliation in disputes other than those referred to in article 24, paragraph 2, may be made at any time.)

(5. The time-limits specified in article 24, paragraph 2 may be extended by agreement between parties.)

(6. A request for conciliation shall be considered to have been duly made if it is proved that the request has been sent to the other party by registered letter, telegram or teleprinter or has been served on it within the time-limits specified in article 24, paragraphs 2 or 5.)

(7. Where no request has been made within the time-limits specified in article 24, paragraphs 2 or 5, the decision of the conference shall be final and no proceedings under this chapter may be brought by any party to the dispute to challenge that decision.)

Article 25

1.   Where the parties have agreed that disputes referred to in article 23, paragraph 4(a), (b), (c), (d), (h) and (i) shall be resolved through procedures other than those established in that article, or agree on procedures to resolve a particular dispute that has arisen between them, such disputes shall, at the request of any of the parties to the dispute, be resolved as provided for in their agreement.

2.   The provisions of article 25, paragraph 1 apply also to the disputes referred to in article 23, paragraph 4(e), (f) and (g), (unless national legislation, rules or regulations prevent shippers from having this freedom of choice.)

3.   Where conciliation *and/or arbitration* proceedings have been initiated, such proceedings shall have precedence over remedies available under national law. (If a party seeks remedies under national law in respect of a dispute to which this chapter applies without invoking the procedures provided for in this chapter, then, upon the request of a respondent to those proceedings, they shall be stayed and the dispute shall be referred to the procedures defined in this chapter by the court or other authority where the national remedies are sought.)

Article 26

1.   The Contracting Parties shall confer upon conferences and shippers' organizations such capacity as is necessary for the application of the provisions of this chapter. In particular:

(a) A conference or a shippers' organization may institute proceedings as a party or be named as a party to proceedings in its collective capacity;

(b) Any notification to a conference or shippers' organization in its collective capacity shall also constitute a notification to each member of such conference or shippers' organization;

(c) A notification to a conference or shippers' organization shall be transmitted to the address of the head office of the conference or shippers' organization. Each conference or shippers' organization shall register the address of its head office with the (Registrar appointed in accordance with article 46, paragraph 1) *Shipping Committee of UNCTAD.* In the event that a conference or a shippers' organization fails to register or has no head office, a notification to any member in the name of the conference or shippers' organization shall be deemed to be a notification to such conference or organization.

(2. Acceptance or rejection by a conference or shippers' organization of a recommendation by conciliators shall be deemed to be acceptance or rejection of such a recommendation by each member thereof.)

Article 27

(Unless the parties agree otherwise, the conciliators may decide to make a recommendation on the basis of written submissions without oral proceedings.)

B. INTERNATIONAL MANDATORY CONCILIATION

Article 28

(In international mandatory conciliation the appropriate authorities of a Contracting Party shall, if they so request, participate in the conciliation proceedings in support of a party being a national of that Contracting Party, or in support of a party having a dispute arising in the context of the foreign trade of that Contracting Party. The appropriate authority may alternatively act as an observer in such conciliation proceedings.)

Article 29

(1. In international mandatory conciliation the proceedings shall be held in the place unanimously agreed to by the parties or, failing such agreements, in the place decided upon by the conciliators.)

(2. In determining the place of conciliation proceedings the parties and the conciliators shall take into account, inter alia, countries which are closely connected with the dispute, bearing in mind the country of the shipping line concerned and, especially when the dispute is related to cargo, the country where the cargo originates.)

Article 30

(1. For the purposes of this chapter an international panel of conciliators shall be established, consisting of experts of high repute or experience in the fields of law, economics of sea transport, or foreign trade and finance, as determined by the Contracting Parties selecting them, who shall serve in an independent capacity.)

(2. Each Contracting Party may at any time nominate members of the panel up to a total of 12, and shall communicate their names to the Registrar. The nominations shall be for periods of six years each and may be renewed. In the event of the death, incapacity or resignation of a member of the panel, the Contracting Party which nominated such person shall nominate a replacement for the remainder of his term of office. A nomination takes effect from the date on which the communication of the nomination is received by the Registrar.)

(3. The Registrar shall maintain the panel list and shall regularly inform the Contracting Parties of the composition of the panel.

Article 31

(1. The purpose of conciliation is to reach an amicable settlement of the dispute through recommendations formulated by independent conciliators.)

(2. The conciliators shall identify and clarify the issues in dispute, seek for this purpose any information from the parties, and on the basis thereof, submit to the parties a recommendation for the settlement of the dispute.)

(3. The parties shall co-operate in good faith with the conciliators in order to enable them to carry out their functions.)

(4. Subject to the provisions of article 25, paragraph 2, the parties to the dispute may at any time during the conciliation proceedings decide in agreement to have recourse to a different procedure for the settlement of their dispute. The parties to a dispute which has been made subject to proceedings other than those provided for in this chapter may decide by mutual agreement to have recourse to international mandatory conciliation.)

Article 32

(1. The conciliation proceedings shall be conducted either by one conciliator or by an uneven number of conciliators agreed upon or designated by the parties.)

(2. Where the parties cannot agree on the number or the appointment of the conciliators as provided in article 32, paragraph 1, the conciliation proceedings shall be conducted by three conciliators, one appointed by each party in the statement(s) of claim and reply respectively, and the third by the two conciliators thus appointed, who shall act as chairman.)

(3. If the reply does not name a conciliator to be appointed in cases where article 32, paragraph 2 would apply, the second conciliator shall, within 30 days following the receipt of the statement of claim, be chosen by lot by the conciliator appointed in the statement of claim from among the members of the panel nominated by the Contracting Party or Parties of which the respondent(s) is (are) a national(s).)

(4. Where the conciliators appointed in accordance with article 32, paragraphs 2 or 3 cannot agree on the appointment of the third conciliator within 15 days following the date of the appointment of the second conciliator, he shall, within the following 5 days, be chosen by lot by the appointed conciliators. Prior to the drawing by lot:

(a) No member of the panel of conciliators having the same nationality as either of the two appointed conciliators shall be eligible for selection by lot;

(b) Each of the two appointed conciliators may exclude from the list of the panel of conciliators an equal number of them subject to the requirement that at least 30 members of the panel shall remain eligible for selection by lot.)

Article 33

(1. Where several parties request conciliation with the same respondent in respect of the same issue, or of issues which are closely connected, that respondent may request the consolidation of those cases.)

(2. The request for consolidation shall be considered and decided upon by majority vote by the chairmen of the conciliators so far chosen. If such request is allowed, the chairmen will designate the conciliators to consider the consolidated cases from among the conciliators so far appointed or chosen, provided that an uneven number of conciliators is chosen and that the conciliator first appointed by each party shall be one of the conciliators considering the consolidated case.)

Article 34

Any party, (other than an appropriate authority referred to in article 28, if conciliation has been initiated,) may join in the proceedings:
either
(a) As a party, in case of a direct economic interest;
or
(b) As a supporting party to one of the original parties, in case of an indirect economic interest,
(unless either of the original parties objects to such joinder.) *according to the framework of national jurisdiction of the country in which the dispute is resolved.*

Article 35

(1. The recommendations of the conciliators shall be made in accordance with the provisions of this Code.)

2. When the code is silent upon any point, the *courts* (conciliators) shall apply the law which (the parties agree at the time the conciliation proceedings commence or thereafter, but not later than the time of submission of evidence to the conciliators. Failing such agreement, the law which in the opinion of the conciliators) is most closely connected with the dispute (shall be applicable.)

3. The *courts* (conciliators) shall not decide ex aequo et bono upon the dispute (unless the parties so agree after the dispute has arisen.)

4. The *courts* (conciliators) shall not bring a finding of non liquet on the ground of obscurity of the law.

5. The *courts* (conciliators) may *apply* (recommend) those remedies and reliefs which are provided in the law applicable to the dispute.

Article 36

The *decisions* (recommendations) of the *courts* (conciliators) shall include reasons.

Article 37

(1. Unless the parties have agreed before, during or after the conciliation procedure that the recommendation of the conciliators shall be binding, the recommendation shall become binding by acceptance by the parties. A recommendation which has been accepted by some parties to a dispute shall be binding as between those parties only.)

(2. Acceptance of the recommendation must be communicated by the parties to the conciliators, at an address specified by them, not later than 30 days after receipt of the notification of the recommendation; otherwise, it shall be considered that the recommendation has not been accepted.)

(3. Any party which does not accept the recommendation shall notify the conciliators and the other parties, within 30 days following the period specified in article 37, paragraph 2 of its grounds for rejection of the recommendation, comprehensively and in writing.)

(4. When the recommendation has been accepted by the parties, the conciliators shall immediately draw up and sign a record of settlement, at which time the recommendation shall become binding upon those parties. If the recommendation has not been accepted by all parties, the conciliators shall draw up a report with respect to those parties rejecting the recommendation, noting the dispute and the failure of those parties to settle the dispute.)

5. A recommendation which has become binding upon the parties shall be implemented by them immediately or at such later time as is specified in the recommendation.[2]

(6. Any party may make its acceptance conditional upon acceptance by all or any of the other parties to the dispute.)

Article 38

1. A recommendation shall constitute a final determination of a dispute as between the parties (which accept it,) except to the extent that the recommendation is not recognized and enforced in accordance with the provisions of article 39.

2. 'Recommendation' includes an interpretation, clarification or revision of the recommendation made by the conciliators (before the recommendation has been accepted.)

Article 39

1. Each Contracting Party shall recognize a recommendation as binding (between the parties which have accepted it and shall,) subject to the provisions of article 39, paragraphs 2 and 3, enforce, at the request of any such party, all obligations imposed by the recommendation as if it were a final judgement of a court of that Contracting Party.

2. A recommendation shall not be recognized and enforced at the request of a party referred to in article 39, paragraph 1 only if the court or other competent

---

2. Article 37.5 should be replaced and come after article 39.2.

authority of the country where recognition and enforcement is sought is satisfied that:

(a) Any party which accepted the recommendation was, under the law applicable to it, under some legal incapacity at the time of acceptance;

(b) Fraud or coercion has been used in the making of the recommendations;

(c) The recommendation is contrary to public policy (ordre public) in the country of enforement; or

((d) The composition of the conciliators, or the conciliation procedure, was not in accordance with the provisions of this Code.)

3. Any part of the recommendation shall not be enforced and recognized if the court or other competent authority is satisfied that such part comes within any of the subparagraphs of article 39, paragraph 2 and can be separated from other parts of the recommendation. If such part cannot be separated, the entire recommendation shall not be enforced and recognized.

4. *If all parties to a dispute agreed to reject a recommendation, it will not be binding on them and the courts will not enforce it.*

Article 40

1. Where the recommendation has been accepted by all the parties, the recommendation and the reasons therefor may be published with the consent of all the parties.

(2. Where the recommendation has been rejected by one or more of the parties but has been accepted by one or more of the parties:

(a) The party or parties rejecting the recommendation shall publish its or their grounds for rejection, given pursuant to article 37, paragraph 3, and may at the same time publish the recommendation and the reasons therefor;

(b) A party which has accepted the recommendation may publish the recommendation and the reasons therefor; it may also publish the grounds for rejection given by any other party unless such other party has already published its rejection and the grounds therefor in accordance with article 40, paragraph 2(a).)

3. Where the recommendation has not been accepted by any of the parties, each party may publish the recommendation and the reasons therefor and also its own rejection and the grounds therefor.

Article 41

(1. Documents and statements containing factual information supplied by any party to the conciliators shall be made public unless that party or a majority of the conciliators agrees otherwise.)

(2. Such documents and statements supplied by a party may be tendered by that party in support of its case in subsequent proceedings arising from the same dispute and between the same parties.)

Article 42

Where the recommendation has not (become binding upon) *been accepted by the parties,* no views expressed or reasons given by the conciliators, or concessions or offers made by the parties for the purpose of the conciliation procedure, shall affect the legal rights and obligations of any of the parties.

Article 43

1. (a) The costs of the conciliators and all costs of the administration of the conciliation proceedings shall be borne equally by the parties to the proceedings, unless they agree otherwise.

(b) When the conciliation proceedings have been initiated, the conciliators shall be entitled to require an advance or security for the costs referred to in article 43, paragraph 1(a).

2. Each party shall bear all expenses it incurs in connection with the proceedings, unless the parties agree otherwise.

(3. Notwithstanding the provisions of article 43, paragraphs 1 and 2, the conciliators may, having decided unanimously that a party has brought a claim vexatiously or frivolously, assess against that party any or all of the costs of other parties to the proceedings. Such decision shall be final and binding on all the parties.)

Article 44

(1. Failure of a party to appear or to present its case at any stage of the proceedings shall not be deemed an admission of the other party's assertions. In that event, the other party may, at its choice, request the conciliators to close the proceedings or to deal with the questions presented to them and submit a recommendation in accordance with the provisions for making recommendations set out in this Code.)

(2. Before closing the proceedings, the conciliators shall grant the party failing to appear or to present its case a period of grace, not exceeding 10 days, unless they are satisfied that the party does not intend to appear or to present its case.)

(3. Failure to observe procedural time-limits laid down in this Code or determined by the conciliators, in particular time-limits relating to the submission of statements or information, shall be considered a failure to appear in the proceedings.)

(4. Where the proceedings have been closed owing to one party's failure to appear or to present its case, the conciliators shall draw up a report noting that party's failure.)

Article 45

1. The conciliators shall follow the procedures stipulated in this Code.

2. The rules of procedure annexed to the present Convention shall be considered as model rules for the guidance of conciliators. The conciliators may, by mutual consent, use, supplement or amend the rules contained in the annex or formulate their own rules of procedure to the extent that such supplementary, amended or other rules are not consistent with the provisions of this Code.

3. If the parties agree that it may be in the interest of achieving an expeditious and inexpensive solution of the conciliation proceedings, they may

mutually agree to rules of procedure which are not inconsistent with the provisions of this Code.

4. The conciliators shall formulate their recommendation by consensus or failing that shall decide by majority vote.

5. The conciliation proceedings shall finish and the recommendations of the conciliators shall be delivered not later than six months from the date on which the conciliators are appointed, except in the cases *which require expeditious decisions such as those concerning surcharges and currency changes* (referred to in article 23, paragraph 4(e), (f), and (g), for which the time limits in article 14, paragraph 1 and article 16, paragraph 4 shall be valid.) The period of six months may be extended by agreement of the parties.

Article 45A

1. The provisions of the Code shall apply only to conferences sailing from each Contracting Party in the outward direction.

2. Failure to comply with the provisions of the Code is an offence punishable by a fine not exceeding 100,000 U.S. dollars.

C. INSTITUTIONAL MACHINERY

Article 46

(1. Six months before the entry into force of the present Convention, the Secretary-General of the United Nations shall, subject to the approval of the General Assembly of the United Nations, and taking into account the views expressed by the Contracting Parties, appoint a Registrar, who may be assisted by such additional staff as may be necessary for the performance of the functions listed in article 46, paragraph 2. Administrative services for the Registrar and his assistants shall be provided by the United Nations Office at Geneva.)

2. (The Registrar) *The Shipping Committee of UNCTAD* shall perform the following functions in consultation with the Contracting Parties as appropriate:

(a) Maintain the list of conciliators of the international panel of conciliators and regularly inform the Contracting Parties of the composition of the panel;

(b) Provide the names and addresses of the conciliators to the parties concerned on request;

(c) Receive and maintain copies of requests for conciliation, replies recommendation, acceptances, or rejections, including reasons therefor;

(d) Furnish on request, and at their cost, copies of recommendations and reasons for rejection to the shippers' organizations, conferences and Governments, subject to the provisions of article 40;

(e) Make available information of a non-confidential nature on completed conciliation cases, and without attribution to the parties concerned, for the purposes of preparation of material for the Review Conference referred to in article 52; and

(f) (The other functions prescribed for the Registrar in article 26, paragraph 1(c) and article 30, paragraphs 2 and 3.) *Distribute among the Contracting Parties key decisions of national courts in matters concerning this Code.*

Chapter VII

FINAL CLAUSES

Article 47

IMPLEMENTATION

1. (Each Contracting Party shall take such legislative or other measures as may be necessary to implement the present Convention.) *The Contracting Parties shall give effect to this Convention either by giving it the force of law or by including it in their national legislation.*

2. Each Contracting Party shall communicate to the Secretary General of the United Nations, who shall be the depositary, the text of the legislative or other measures which it has taken in order to implement the present Convention.

Article 48

SIGNATURE, RATIFICATION, ACCEPTANCE, APPROVAL AND ACCESSION

1. The present Convention shall remain open for signature as from 1 July 1974 until and including 30 June 1975 at United Nations Headquarters and shall thereafter remain open for accession.

2. All States[3] are entitled to become Contracting Parties to the present Convention by:
(a) Signature subject to and followed by ratification, acceptance or approval; or
(b) Signature without reservation as to ratification, acceptance or approval; or
(c) Accession.

3. Ratification, acceptance, approval or accession shall be effected by the deposit of an instrument to this effect with the depositary.

Article 49

ENTRY INTO FORCE

1. The present Convention shall enter into force six months after the date on which not less than 24 States, the combined tonnage of which amounts to at least 25 per cent of world tonnage, have become Contracting Parties to it in accordance with article 48. For the purpose of the present article the tonnage shall be deemed to be that contained in Lloyd's Register of Shipping — Statistical Tables 1973, table 2 'World Fleets — Analysis by Principal Types,' in respect to general cargo

3. At its 9th plenary meeting on April 6, 1974, the Conference adopted the following understanding recommended by its Third Main Committee:
In accordance with its terms, the present Convention will be open to participation by all States, and the Secretary-General of the United Nations will act as depositary. It is the understanding of the Conference that the Secretary-General, in discharging his functions as depositary of a convention or other multilateral legally binding instrument with an 'All-States' clause, will follow the practice of the General Assembly of the United Nations in implementing such a clause and, whenever advisable, will request the opinion of the General Assembly before receiving a signature or an instrument of ratification, acceptance, approval or accession.

(including passenger/cargo) ships and container (fully cellular) ships, exclusive of the United States reserve fleet and the American and Canadian Great Lakes fleets.[4]

2. For each State which thereafter ratifies, accepts, approves or accedes to it, the present Convention shall come into force six months after deposit by such State of the appropriate instrument.

3. Any State which becomes a Contracting Party to the present Convention after the entry into force of an amendment shall, failing an expression of a different intention by that State:

(a) Be considered as a Party to the present Convention as amended; and

(b) Be considered as a Party to the unamended Convention in relation to any Party to the present Convention not bound by the amendment.

Article 50

DENUNCIATION

1. The present Convention may be denounced by any Contracting Party at any time after the expiration of a period of two years from the date on which the Convention has entered into force.

2. Denunciation shall be notified to the depositary in writing, and shall take effect one year, or such longer period as may be specified in the instrument of denunciation, after the date of receipt by the depositary.

Article 51

AMENDMENTS

1. Any Contracting Party may propose one or more amendments to the present Convention by communicating the amendments to the depositary. The depositary shall circulate such amendments among the Contracting Parties, for their acceptance, and among States entitled to become Contracting Parties to the present Convention which are not Contracting Parties, for their information.

2. Each proposed amendment circulated in accordance with article 51, paragraph 1 shall be deemed to have been accepted if no Contracting Party communicates an objection thereto to the depositary within 12 months following the date of its circulation by the depositary. If a Contracting Party communicates an objection to the proposed amendment, such amendment shall not be considered as accepted and shall not be put into effect.

3. If no objection has been communicated, the amendment shall enter into force for all Contracting Parties six months after the expiry date of the period of 12 months referred to in article 51, paragraph 2.

Article 52

REVIEW CONFERENCES

1. A Review Conference shall be convened by the depositary five years from

---

4. The tonnage requirements for the purposes of article 49, paragraph 1 are set out above in annex 1 to UN Doc. TD/CODE/10.

the date on which the present Convention comes into force to review the working of the Convention, with particular reference to its implementation, and to consider and adopt appropriate amendments.

2. The depositary shall, four years from the date on which the present Convention comes into force, seek the views of all States entitled to attend the Review Conference and shall, on the basis of the views received, prepare and circulate a draft agenda as well as amendments proposed for consideration by the Conference.

3. Further review conferences shall be similarly convened every five years, or at any time after the first Review Conference, at the request of one-third of the Contracting Parties to the present Convention, unless the first Review Conference decides otherwise.

4. Notwithstanding the provisions of article 52, paragraph 1, if the present Convention has not entered into force five years from the date of the adoption of the Final Act of the United Nations Conference of Plenipotentiaries on a Code of Conduct for Liner Conferences, a Review Conference shall, at the request of one-third of the States entitled to become Contracting Parties to the present Convention, be convened by the Secretary-General of the United Nations, subject to the approval of the General Assembly, in order to review the provisions of the Convention and its annex and to consider and adopt appropriate amendments.

Article 53

FUNCTIONS OF THE DEPOSITARY

1. The depositary shall notify the signatory and acceding States of:

(a) Signatures, ratifications, acceptances, approvals and accessions in accordance with article 48;

(b) The date on which the present Convention enters into force in accordance with article 49;

(c) Denunciations of the present Convention in accordance with article 50;

(d) Reservations to the present Convention and the withdrawal of reservations;

(e) The text of the legislative or other measures which each Contracting Party has taken in order to implement the present Convention in accordance with article 47;

(f) Proposed amendments and objections to proposed amendments in accordance with article 51; and

(g) Entry into force of amendments in accordance with article 51, paragraph 3.

2. The depositary shall also undertake such actions as are necessary under article 52.

Article 54

AUTHENTIC TEXTS – DEPOSIT

The original of the present Convention, of which the Chinese, English, French, Russian and Spanish texts are equally authentic, will be deposited with the Secretary-General of the United Nations.

IN WITNESS WHEREOF the undersigned, having been duly authorized to this effect by their respective Governments, have signed the present Convention, on the dates appearing opposite their signatures.

Signatures and ratification of, or accessions to, the Convention on a Code of Conduct for Liner Conferences

The countries, arranged in chronological order, are:

Ghana	24 June 1975	r
Chile	25 June 1975	s
Pakistan	27 June 1975	s
Gambia	30 June 1975	s
Sri Lanka	30 June 1975	s
Venezuela	30 June 1975	s
Bangladesh	24 July 1975	a
Nigeria	10 September 1975	a
Benin	27 October 1975	a
United Republic of Tanzania	3 November 1975	a
Niger	13 January 1976	r
Philippines	2 March 1976	r
Guatemala	3 March 1976	r
Mexico	6 May 1976	a
United Republic of Cameroon	15 June 1976	a
Cuba	23 June 1976	a
Indonesia	11 January 1977	r
Ivory Coast	17 February 1977	r
Central African Republic	13 May 1977	a
Senegal	20 May 1977	r
Zaire	20 July 1977	a
Madagascar	23 December 1977	a
Togo	12 January 1978	r
Cape Verde	13 January 1978	a
India	14 February 1978	r
Kenya	27 February 1978	r
Mali	15 March 1978	a
Sudan	16 March 1978	a
Gabon	5 June 1978	r
Ethiopia	1 September 1978	r
Iraq	25 October 1978	a
Costa Rica	27 October 1978	r
Peru	21 November 1978	a
Egypt	25 January 1979	a
Tunisia	15 March 1979	a
Republic of Korea	11 May 1979	a
Czechoslovakia	4 June 1979	app
Honduras	2 June 1979	a

Union of Soviet Socialist Republics	28 June 1979	acc
German Democratic Republic	9 July 1979	r
Sierra Leone	9 July 1979	a
Uruguay	9 July 1979	a
Bulgaria	12 July 1979	a
Guyana	7 January 1980	a
Morocco	11 February 1980	a
Jordan	11 March 1980	a
Yugoslavia	7 July 1980	r
Guinea	19 August 1980	a
Mauritius	16 September 1980	a
China	23 September 1980	a
Barbados	29 October 1980	a
Romania	7 January 1982	a
Lebanon	30 April 1982	a
Jamaica	20 July 1982	a
Congo	26 July 1982	a
Malaysia	27 August 1982	a
*Federal Republic of Germany	6 April 1983	r
*Netherlands	6 April 1983	a
Trinidad and Tobago	3 August 1983	a

*Also applying the Brussels Package for trade between the EEC–OECD.

Source: Note by UNCTAD Secretariat, Doc. no. TD/B/C.4/INF. 36/Rev.

Notes:

1 As stated in TD/B/C.4/INF.13, the UNCTAD Secretariat will report from time to time on the status of definitive signatures, ratifications or accessions to the Convention on a Code of Conduct for Liner Conferences.
2 By 3 August 1983, 59 countries had made definitive signatures (s) to, approved (app), accepted (acc), ratified (r), or acceded (a) to, the Convention.
3 The 59 countries in Note 2 above owned 20,848,476 grt, or 28.68 per cent of the relevant total referred to in Article 49 of the Convention.

Annex 2 The Brussels Package

COUNCIL REGULATION (EEC) No. 954/79 of 15 May 1979 concerning the ratification by Member States of, or their accession to, the United Nations Convention on a Code of Conduct of Liner Conferences.

THE COUNCIL OF THE EUROPEAN COMMUNITIES

Having regard to the Treaty establishing the European Economic Community, and in particular Article 84(2) thereof, having regard to the draft Regulation submitted by the Commission, having regard to the opinion of the European Parliament, having regard to the opinion of the Economic and Social Committee.

Whereas a Convention on a Code of Conduct for Liner Conferences has been drawn up by a Conference convened under the auspices of the United Nations Conference on Trade and Development and is open for ratification or accession;

Whereas the questions covered by the Code of Conduct are of importance not only to the Member States but also to the Community, in particular from the shipping and trading viewpoints, and it is therefore important that a common position should be adopted in relation to this Code;

Whereas this common position should respect the principles and objectives of the Treaty and make a major contribution to meeting the aspirations of developing countries in the field of shipping while at the same time pursuing the objective of the continuing application in this field of the commercial principles applied by shipping lines of the OECD countries;

Whereas to secure observance of these principles and objectives, since the Code of Conduct contains no provision allowing the accession of the Community as such, it is important that Member States ratify or accede to the arrangements provided for in this Regulation;

Whereas the stabilising role of conferences in ensuring reliable services to shippers is recognised, but it is nevertheless necessary to avoid possible breaches by conferences of the rules of competition laid down in the Treaty; whereas the Commission will accordingly forward to the Council a proposal for a Regulation concerning the application of those rules to sea transport.

HAS ADOPTED THIS REGULATION:

Article 1

1. When ratifying the United Nations Convention on a Code of Conduct for Liner Conferences, or when acceding thereto, Member States shall inform the Secretary-General of the United Nations in writing that such ratification or accession has taken place in accordance with this Regulation.

2. The instrument of ratification or accession shall be accompanied by the reservations set out in Annex 1.

Article 2

1. In the case of an existing conference, each group of shipping lines of the same nationality, which are members thereof shall determine by commercial negotiations with another shipping line of that nationality whether the latter may participate as a national shipping line in the said conference.

If a new conference is created, the shipping lines of the same nationality shall determine by commercial negotiations which of them may participate as a national shipping line in the future conference.

2. Where the negotiations referred to in paragraph 1 fail to result in agreement, each Member State may, at the request of one of the lines concerned and after hearing all of them, take the necessary steps to settle the dispute.

3. Each Member State shall ensure that all vessel-operating shipping lines established on its territory under the Treaty establishing the European Economic Community are treated in the same way as lines which have their management head office on its territory and the effective control of which is exercised there.

Article 3

1. Where a liner conference operates a pool or a berthing, sailing and/or any other form of cargo allocation agreement in accordance with Article 2 of the Code of Conduct, the volume of cargo to which the group of national shipping lines of each Member State participating in that trade or the shipping lines of the Member

States participating in that trade as third-country shipping lines are entitled under the Code shall be redistributed, unless a decision is taken to the contrary by all the lines which are members of the Conference and parties to the present redistribution rules. This redistribution of cargo shares shall be carried out on the basis of a unanimous decision by those shipping lines which are members of the conference and participate in the redistribution, with a view to all those lines carrying a fair share of the conference trade.

2. The share finally allocated to each participant shall be determined by the application of commercial principles, taking account in particular of:

(a) the volume of cargo carried by the conference and generated by the Member States whose trade is served by it;

(b) past performance of the shipping lines in the trade covered by the pool;

(c) the volume of cargo carried by the conference and shipped through the ports of the Member States;

(d) the needs of the shippers whose cargoes are carried by the conference.

3. If no agreement is reached on the redistribution of cargoes referred to in paragraph 1, the matter shall, at the request of one of the parties, be referred to conciliation in accordance with the procedure set out in Annex II. Any dispute not settled by the conciliation procedure may, with the agreement of the parties, be referred to arbitration. In that event, the award of the arbitrator shall be binding.

4. At intervals to be laid down in advance, shares allocated in accordance with paragraphs 1, 2 and 3 shall be regularly reviewed, taking into account the criteria set out in paragraph 2 and in particular from the viewpoint of providing adequate and efficient services to shippers.

Article 4

1. In a conference trade between a Member State of the Community and a State which is a party to the Code of Conduct and not an OECD country, a shipping line of another Member State of the OECD wishing to participate in the redistribution provided for in Article 3 of this Regulation may do so subject to reciprocity defined at governmental or ship-owners' level.

2. Without prejudice to paragraph 3 of this Article, Article 2 of the Code of Conduct shall not be applied in conference trades between Member States or, on a reciprocal basis, between such States and the other OECD countries which are parties to the Code.

3. Paragraph 2 of this Article shall not affect the opportunities for participation as third country shipping lines in such trades, in accordance with the principles reflected in Article 2 of the Code of Conduct, of the shipping lines of a developing country which are recognised as national shipping lines under the Code and which are:

(a) already members of a conference serving these trades; or

(b) admitted to such a conference under Article 1(3) of the Code.

4. Articles 3 and 14(9) of the Code of Conduct shall not be applied in conference trades between Member States or, on a reciprocal basis, between such States and other OECD countries which are parties to the Code.

5. In conference trades between Member States and between these States and other OECD countries which are parties to the Code of Conduct, the shippers and ship-owners of Member States shall not insist on applying the procedures for settling disputes provided for in Chapter VI of the Code in their mutual relationships or, on a reciprocal basis, in relation to shippers and ship-owners of other OECD countries where other procedures for settling disputes have been agreed between them. They shall in particular take full advantage of the possibilities provided by Article 25(1) and (2) of the Code for resolving disputes by means of procedures other than those laid down in Chapter VI of the Code.

Article 5

For adoption of decisions relating to matters defined in the conference agreement concerning the trade of a Member State, other than those referred to in Article 3 of this Regulation, the national shipping lines of such State shall consult all the other Community lines which are members of the conference before giving or withholding their assent.

Article 6

Member States shall, in due course, and after consulting the Commission, adopt the laws, regulations or administrative provisions necessary for the implementation of this Regulation.

This Regulation shall be binding in its entirety and directly applicable to all Member States.

Done at Brussels, 15 May 1979.

For the Council
The President
R. Boulin

ANNEX I

RESERVATIONS

When ratifying the Convention or when acceding thereto, Member States shall enter the following three reservations and interpretative reservation:

1. For the purposes of the Code of Conduct, the term 'national shipping line'

may, in the case of a Member State of the Community, include any vessel-operating shipping line established on the territory of such Member State in accordance with the EEC Treaty.

2. (a) Without prejudice to paragraph (b) of this reservation, Article 2 of the Code of Conduct shall not be applied in conference trades between the Member States of the Community or, on a reciprocal basis, between such States and other OECD countries which are parties to the Code.

(b) Point (a) shall not affect the opportunities for participation as third country shipping lines in such trades, in accordance with the principles reflected in Article 2 of the Code, of the shipping lines of a developing country which are recognised as national shipping lines under the Code and which are:

(i)   already members of a conference serving these trades; or
(ii) admitted to such a conference under Article 1(3) of the Code.

3. Articles 3 and 14(9) of the Code of Conduct shall not be applied in conference trades between the Member States of the Community or, on a reciprocal basis, between such States and the other OECD countries which are parties to the Code.

4. In trades to which Article 3 of the Code of Conduct applies, the last sentence of that Article is interpreted as meaning that:

(a) Without groups of national shipping lines will coordinate their positions before voting on matters concerning the trade between their two countries;

(b) this sentence applies solely to matters which the conference agreement identifies as requiring the assent of both groups of national shipping lines concerned, and not to all matters covered by the conference agreement.

ANNEX II

CONCILIATION REFERRED TO IN ARTICLE 3(3)

The parties to the dispute shall designate one or more conciliators.

Should they fail to agree on the matter, each of the parties to the dispute shall designate a conciliator and the conciliators thus designated shall co-opt another conciliator to act as chairman. Should a party fail to designate a conciliator or the conciliators designated by the parties fail to reach agreement the Chairman the President of the International Chamber of Commerce shall, at the request of one of the parties, make the necessary designations.

The conciliators shall make every endeavour to settle the dispute. They shall decide on the procedure to be followed. Their fees shall be paid by the parties to the dispute.

NON-EEC MEMBERS OF OECD

Australia, Austria, Canada, Finland, Greece, Iceland, Japan, New Zealand, Norway, Portugal, Spain, Sweden, Switzerland, Turkey, United States.

Annex 3   Text of the UN Convention on Conditions for the Registration of Ships, 1986

The States Parties to this Convention,

Recognizing the need to promote the orderly expansion of world shipping as a whole,

Recalling General Assembly resolution 35/56 of 5 December 1980, the annex to which contains the International Development Strategy for the Third United Nations Development Decade, which called, *inter alia*, in paragraph 128, for an increase in the participation by developing countries in world transport of international trade,

Recalling also that according to the 1958 Geneva Convention on the High Seas and the 1982 United Nations Convention on the Law of the Sea there must exist a genuine link between a ship and a flag State and conscious of the duties of the flag State to exercise effectively its jurisdiction and control over ships flying its flag in accordance with the principle of the genuine link,

Believing that to this end a flag State should have a competent and adequate national maritime administration,

Believing also that in order to exercise its control function effectively a flag State should ensure that those who are responsible for the management and operation of a ship on its register are readily identifiable and accountable,

Believing further that measures to make persons responsible for ships more readily identifiable and accountable could assist in the task of combating maritime fraud,

Reaffirming, without prejudice to this Convention, that each State shall fix the conditions for the grant of its nationality to ships, for the registration of ships in its territory and for the right to fly its flag,

Prompted by the desire among sovereign States to resolve in a spirit of mutual understanding and co-operation all issues relating to the conditions for the grant of nationality to, and for the registration of, ships,

Considering that nothing in this Convention shall be deemed to prejudice any provisions in the national laws and regulations of the Contracting Parties to this Convention, which exceed the provisions contained herein,

Recognizing the competences of the specialized agencies and other institutions of the United Nations system as contained in their respective constitutional instruments, taking into account arrangements which may have been concluded between the United Nations and the agencies, and between individual agencies and institutions in specific fields,

have agreed as follows:

Article 1

OBJECTIVES

For the purpose of ensuring or, as the case may be, strengthening the genuine link between a State and ships flying its flag, and in order to exercise effectively its jurisdiction and control over such ships with regard to identification and accountability of shipowners and operators as well as with regard to administrative, technical, economic and social matters, a flag State shall apply the provisions contained in this Convention.

Article 2

DEFINITIONS

For the purposes of this Convention:

'Ship' means any self-propelled sea-going vessel used in international seaborne trade for the transport of goods, passengers, or both with the exception of vessels of less than 500 gross registered tons;

'Flag State' means a State whose flag a ship flies and is entitled to fly;

'Owner' or 'shipowner' means, unless clearly indicated otherwise, any natural or juridical person recorded in the register of ships of the State of registration as an owner of a ship;

'Operator' means the owner or bareboat charterer, or any other natural or juridical person to whom the responsibilities of the owner or bareboat charterer have been formally assigned;

'State of registration' means the State in whose register of ships a ship has been entered;

'Register of ships' means the official register or registers in which particulars referred to in article 11 of this Convention are recorded;

'National maritime administration' means any State authority or agency which is established by the State of registration in accordance with its legislation and which, pursuant to that legislation, is responsible, *inter alia*, for the implementation of international agreements concerning maritime transport and for the application of rules and standards concerning ships under its jurisdiction and control;

'Bareboat charter' means a contract for the lease of a ship, for a stipulated period of time, by virtue of which the lessee has complete possession and control of the ship, including the right to appoint the master and crew of the ship, for the duration of the lease;

'Labour-supplying country' means a country which provides seafarers for service on a ship flying the flag of another country.

Article 3

SCOPE OF APPLICATION

This Convention shall apply to all ships as defined in article 2.

Article 4

GENERAL PROVISIONS

1. Every State, whether coastal or land-locked, has the right to sail ships flying its flag on the high seas.

2. Ships have the nationality of the State whose flag they are entitled to fly.

3. Ships shall sail under the flag of one State only.

4. No ships shall be entered in the registers of ships of two or more States at a time, subject to the provisions of paragraphs 4 and 5 of article 11 and to article 12.

5. A ship may not change its flag during a voyage or while in a port of call, save in the case of a real transfer of ownership or change of registry.

Article 5

NATIONAL MARITIME ADMINISTRATION

1. The flag State shall have a competent and adequate national maritime administration, which shall be subject to its jurisdiction and control.

2. The flag State shall implement applicable international rules and standards concerning, in particular, the safety of ships and persons on board and the prevention of pollution of the marine environment.

3. The maritime administration of the flag State shall ensure:

(a) That ships flying the flag of such State comply with its laws and regulations concerning registration of ships and with applicable international rules and standards concerning, in particular, the safety of ships and persons on board and the prevention of pollution of the marine environment;

(b) That ships flying the flag of such State are periodically surveyed by its authorized surveyors in order to ensure compliance with applicable international rules and standards;

(c) That ships flying the flag of such State carry on board documents, in particular those evidencing the right to fly its flag and other valid relevant documents, including those required by international conventions to which the State of registration is a Party;

(d) That the owners of ships flying the flag of such State comply with the principles of registration of ships in accordance with the laws and regulations of such State and the provisions of this Convention.

4. The State of registration shall require all the appropriate information necessary for full identification and accountability concerning ships flying its flag.

Article 6

IDENTIFICATION AND ACCOUNTABILITY

1. The State of registration shall enter in its register of ships, *inter alia*, information concerning the ship and its owner or owners. Information concerning the operator, when the operator is not the owner, should be included in the register of ships or in the official record of operators to be maintained in the office of the Registrar or be readily accessible to him, in accordance with the laws and regulations of the State of registration. The State of registration shall issue documentation as evidence of the registration of the ship.

2. The State of registration shall take such measures as are necessary to ensure that the owner or owners, the operator or operators, or any other person or persons who can be held accountable for the management and operation of ships flying its flag can be easily identified by persons having a legitimate interest in obtaining such information.

3. Registers of ships should be available to those with a legitimate interest in obtaining information contained therein, in accordance with the laws and regulations of the flag State.

4   A State should ensure that ships flying its flag carry documentation including information about the identity of the owner or owners, the operator or operators

or the person or persons accountable for the operation of such ships, and make available such information to port State authorities.

5. Log-books should be kept on all ships and retained for a reasonable period after the date of the last entry, notwithstanding any change in a ship's name, and should be available for inspection and copying by persons having a legitimate interest in obtaining such information, in accordance with the laws and regulations of the flag State. In the event of a ship being sold and its registration being changed to another State, log-books relating to the period before such sale should be retained and should be available for inspection and copying by persons having a legitimate interest in obtaining such information, in accordance with the laws and regulations of the former flag State.

6. A State shall take necessary measures to ensure that ships it enters in its register of ships have owners or operators who are adequately identifiable for the purpose of ensuring their full accountability.

7. A State should ensure that direct contact between owners of ships flying its flag and its government authorities is not restricted.

Article 7

PARTICIPATION BY NATIONALS IN THE OWNERSHIP AND/OR MANNING OF SHIPS

With respect to the provisions concerning manning and ownership of ships as contained in paragraphs 1 and 2 of article 8 and paragraphs 1 to 3 of article 9, respectively, and without prejudice to the application of any other provisions of this Convention, a State of registration has to comply either with the provisions of paragraphs 1 and 2 of article 8 or with the provisions of paragraphs 1 to 3 of article 9, but may comply with both.

Article 8

OWNERSHIP OF SHIPS

1. Subject to the provisions of article 7, the flag State shall provide in its laws and regulations for the ownership of ships flying its flag.

2. Subject to the provisions of article 7, in such laws and regulations the flag State shall include appropriate provisions for participation by that State or its nationals as owners of ships flying its flag or in the ownership of such ships and for the level of such participation. These laws and regulations should be sufficient to permit the flag State to exercise effectively its jurisdiction and control over ships flying its flag.

Article 9

MANNING OF SHIPS

1. Subject to the provisions of article 7, a State of registration, when implementing this Convention, shall observe the principle that a satisfactory part of the

complement consisting of officers and crew of ships flying its flag be nationals or persons domiciled or lawfully in permanent residence in that State.

2.   Subject to the provisions of article 7 and in pursuance of the goal set out in paragraph 1 of this article, and in taking necessary measures to this end, the State of registration shall have regard to the following:

(a)   the availability of qualified seafarers within the State of registration;

(b)   multilateral or bilateral agreements or other types of arrangements valid and enforceable pursuant to the legislation of the State of registration;

(c)   the sound and economically viable operation of its ships.

3.   The State of registration should implement the provision of paragraph 1 of this article on a ship, company or fleet basis.

4.   The State of registration, in accordance with its laws and regulations, may allow persons of other nationalities to serve on board ships flying its flag in accordance with the relevant provisions of this Convention.

5.   In pursuance of the goal set out in paragraph 1 of this article, the State of registration should, in co-operation with shipowners, promote the education and training of its nationals or persons domiciled or lawfully in permanent residence within its territory.

6   The State of registration shall ensure:

(a)   that the manning of ships flying its flag is of such a level and competence as to ensure compliance with applicable international rules and standards, in particular those regarding safety at sea;

(b)   that the terms and conditions of employment on board ships flying its flag are in conformity with applicable international rules and standards;

(c)   that adequate legal procedures exist for the settlement of civil disputes between seafarers employed on ships flying its flag and their employers;

(d)   that nationals and foreign seafarers have equal access to appropriate legal processes to secure their contractual rights in their relations with their employers.

Article 10

ROLE OF FLAG STATES IN RESPECT OF THE MANAGEMENT OF SHIPOWNING COMPANIES AND SHIPS

1.   The State of registration, before entering a ship in its register of ships, shall ensure that the shipowning company or a subsidiary shipowning company is established and/or has its principal place of business within its territory in accordance with its laws and regulations.

2.   Where the shipowning company or a subsidiary shipowning company or the

541

principal place of business of the shipowning company is not established in the flag State, the latter shall ensure, before entering a ship in its register of ships, that there is a representative or management person who shall be a national of the flag State, or be domiciled therein. Such a representative or management person may be a natural or juridical person who is duly established or incorporated in the flag State, as the case may be, in accordance with its laws and regulations, and duly empowered to act on the shipowner's behalf and account. In particular, this representative or management person should be available for any legal process and to meet the shipowner's responsibilities in accordance with the laws and regulations of the State of registration.

3. The State of registration should ensure that the person or persons accountable for the management and operation of a ship flying its flag are in a position to meet the financial obligations that may arise from the operation of such a ship to cover risks which are normally insured in international maritime transportation in respect of damage to third parties. To this end the State of registration should ensure that ships flying its flag are in a position to provide at all times documents evidencing that an adequate guarantee, such as appropriate insurance or any other equivalent means, has been arranged. Furthermore, the State of registration should ensure that an appropriate mechanism, such as a maritime lien, mutual fund, wage insurance, social security scheme, or any governmental guarantee provided by an appropriate agency of the State of the accountable person, whether that person is an owner or operator, exists to cover wages and related monies owed to seafarers employed on ships flying its flag in the event of default of payment by their employers. The State of registration may also provide for any other appropriate mechanism to that effect in its laws and regulations.

Article 11

REGISTER OF SHIPS

1. A State of registration shall establish a register of ships flying its flag, which register shall be maintained in a manner determined by that State and in conformity with the relevant provisions of this Convention. Ships entitled by the laws and regulations of a State to fly its flag shall be entered in this register in the name of the owner or owners or, where national laws and regulations so provide, the bareboat charterer.

2. Such register shall, *inter alia*, record the following:

(a) the name of the ship and the previous name and registry if any;

(b) The place or port of registration or home port and the official number or mark of identification of the ship;

(c) the international call sign of the ship, if assigned;

(d) the name of the builders, place of build and year of building of the ship;

(e) the description of the main technical characteristics of the ship;

(f) the name, address and, as appropriate, the nationality of the owner or of each of the owners;

and, unless recorded in another public document readily accessible to the Registrar in the flag State:

(g) the date of deletion or suspension of the previous registration of the ship;

(h) the name, address and, as appropriate, the nationality of the bareboat charterer, where national laws and regulations provide for the registration of ships bareboat chartered-in;

(i) the particulars of any mortgages or other similar charges upon the ship as stipulated by national laws and regulations;

3. Furthermore, such register should also record:

(a) if there is more than one owner, the proportion of the ship owned by each;

(b) the name, address and, as appropriate, the nationality of the operator, when the operator is not the owner or the bareboat charterer.

4. Before entering a ship in its register of ships a State should assure itself that the previous registration, if any, is deleted.

5. In the case of a ship bareboat chartered-in a State should assure itself that right to fly the flag of the former flag State is suspended. Such registration shall be effected on production of evidence, indicating suspension of previous registration as regards the nationality of the ship under the former flag State and indicating particulars of any registered encumbrances.

Article 12

BAREBOAT CHARTER

1. Subject to the provisions of article 11 and in accordance with its laws and regulations a State may grant registration and the right to fly its flag to a ship bareboat chartered-in by a charterer in that State, for the period of that charter.

2. When shipowners or charterers in States Parties to this Convention enter into such bareboat charter activities, the conditions of registration contained in this Convention should be fully complied with.

3. To achieve the goal of compliance and for the purpose of applying the requirements of this Convention in the case of a ship so bareboat chartered-in the charterer will be considered to be the owner. This Convention, however, does not have the effect of providing for any ownership rights in the chartered ship other than those stipulated in the particular bareboat charter contract.

4. A State should ensure that a ship bareboat chartered-in and flying its flag, pursuant to paragraphs 1 to 3 of this article, will be subject to its full jurisdiction and control.

5. The State where the bareboat chartered-in ship is registered shall ensure that the former flag State is notified of the deletion of the registration of the bareboat chartered ship.

6. All terms and conditions, other than those specified in this article, relating to the relationship of the parties to a bareboat charter are left to the contractual disposal of those parties.

Article 13

JOINT VENTURES

1. Contracting Parties to this Convention, in conformity with their national policies, legislation and the conditions for registration of ships contained in this Convention, should promote joint ventures between shipowners of different countries, and should, to this end, adopt appropriate arrangements, *inter alia*, by safeguarding the contractual rights of the parties to joint ventures, to further the establishment of such joint ventures in order to develop the national shipping industry.

2. Regional and international financial institutions and aid agencies should be invited to contribute, as appropriate, to the establishment and/or strengthening of joint ventures in the shipping industry of developing countries, particularly in the least developed among them.

Article 14

MEASURES TO PROTECT THE INTERESTS OF LABOUR-SUPPLYING COUNTRIES

1. For the purpose of safeguarding the interests of labour-supplying countries and of minimizing labour displacement and consequent economic dislocation, if any, within these countries, particularly developing countries, as a result of the adoption of this Convention, urgency should be given to the implementation, *inter alia*, of the measures as contained in Resolution 1 annexed to this Convention.

2. In order to create favourable conditions for any contract or arrangement that may be entered into by shipowners or operators and the trade unions of seamen or other representative seamen bodies, bilateral agreements may be concluded between flag States and labour-supplying countries concerning the employment of seafarers of those labour-supplying countries.

Article 15

MEASURES TO MINIMIZE ADVERSE ECONOMIC EFFECTS

For the purpose of minimizing adverse economic effects that might occur within developing countries, in the process of adapting and implementing conditions to meet the requirements established by this Convention, urgency should be given to the implementation, *inter alia*, of the measures as contained in Resolution 2 annexed to this Convention.

Article 16

DEPOSITARY

The Secretary-General of the United Nations shall be the depositary of this Convention.

Article 17

IMPLEMENTATION

1.   Contracting Parties shall take any legislative or other measures necessary to implement this Convention.

2.   Each Contracting Party shall, at appropriate times, communicate to the depositary the texts of any legislative or other measures which it has taken in order to implement this Convention.

3.   The depositary shall transmit upon request to Contracting Parties the texts of the legislative or other measures which have been communicated to him pursuant to paragraph 2 of this article.

Article 18

SIGNATURE, RATIFICATION, ACCEPTANCE, APPROVAL AND ACCESSION

1.   All States are entitled to become Contracting Parties to this Convention by:

   (a) signature not subject to ratification, acceptance or approval; or

   (b) signature subject to and followed by ratification, acceptance or approval;
or

   (c) accession.

2.   This Convention shall be open for signature from 1 May 1986 to and including 30 April 1987, at the Headquarters of the United Nations in New York and shall thereafter remain open for accession.

3.   Instruments of ratification, acceptance, approval or accession shall be deposited with the depositary.

Article 19

ENTRY INTO FORCE

1.   This Convention shall enter into force 12 months after the date on which not less than 40 States, the combined tonnage of which amounts to at least 25 per cent of world tonnage, have become Contracting Parties to it in accordance with article 18. For the purpose of this article the tonnage shall be deemed to be that contained in annex III to this Convention.

2.   For each State which becomes a Contracting Party to this Convention after

the conditions for entry into force under paragraph 1 of this article have been met, the Convention shall enter into force for that State 12 months after the State has become a Contracting Party.

Article 20

REVIEW AND AMENDMENTS

1.   After the expiry of a period of eight years from the date of entry into force of this Convention, a Contracting Party may, by written communication addressed to the Secretary-General of the United Nations, propose specific amendments to this Convention and request the convening of a review conference to consider such proposed amendments. The Secretary-General shall circulate such communication to all Contracting Parties. If, within 12 months from the date of the circulation of the communication, not less than two-fifths of the Contracting Parties reply favourably to the request, the Secretary-General shall convene the Review Conference.

2.   The Secretary-General of the United Nations shall circulate to all Contracting Parties the texts of any proposals for, or views regarding, amendments, at least six months before the opening date of the Review Conference.

Article 21

EFFECT OF AMENDMENTS

1.   The decisions of a review conference regarding amendments shall be taken by consensus or, upon request, by a vote of a two-thirds majority of the Contracting Parties present and voting. Amendments adopted by such a conference shall be communicated by the Secretary-General of the United Nations to all the Contracting Parties for ratification, acceptance, or approval and to all the States signatories of the Convention for information.

2.   Ratification, acceptance or approval of amendments adopted by a review conference shall be effected by the deposit of a formal instrument to that effect with the depositary.

3.   Any amendment adopted by a review conference shall enter into force only for those Contracting Parties which have ratified, accepted or approved it, on the first day of the month following one year after its ratification, acceptance or approval by two-thirds of the Contracting Parties. For any State ratifying, accepting or approving an amendment after it has been ratified, accepted or approved by two-thirds of the Contracting Parties, the amendment shall enter into force one year after its ratification, acceptance or approval by that State.

4.   Any State which becomes a Contracting Party to this Convention after the entry into force of an amendment shall, failing an expression of a different intention by that State:

(a) Be considered as a Party to this Convention as amended; and

(b) Be considered as a Party to the unamended Convention in relation to any Contracting Party not bound by the amendment.

Article 22

DENUNCIATION

1. Any Contracting Party may denounce this Convention at any time by means of a notification in writing to this effect addressed to the depositary.

2. Such denunciation shall take effect on the expiration of one year after the notification is received by the depositary, unless a longer period has been specified in the notification.

IN WITNESS WHEREOF the undersigned, being duly authorized thereto, have affixed their signatures hereunder on the dates indicated.

DONE at Geneva on 7 February 1986 in one original in the Arabic, Chinese, English, French, Russian and Spanish languages, all texts being equally authentic.

Annex I

Resolution 1

Measures to protect the interests of labour-supplying countries

The United Nations Conference on Conditions for Registration of Ships,

Having adopted the United Nations Convention on Conditions for Registration of Ships,

Recommends as follows: —

1. Labour-supplying countries should regulate the activities of the agencies within their jurisdiction that supply seafarers for ships flying the flag of another country in order to ensure that the contractual terms offered by those agencies will prevent abuses and contribute to the welfare of seafarers. For the protection of their seafarers, labour-supplying countries may require, *inter alia*, suitable security of the type mentioned in article 10 from the owners or operators of ships employing such seafarers or from other appropriate bodies;

2. Labour-supplying developing countries may consult each other in order to harmonize as much as possible their policies concerning the conditions upon which they will supply labour in accordance with these principles and may, if necessary, harmonize their legislation in this respect;

3. The United Nations Conference on Trade and Development, the United Nations Development Programme and other appropriate international bodies should upon request provide assistance to labour-supplying developing countries for establishing appropriate legislation for registration of ships and attracting ships to their registers, taking into account this Convention;

4. The International Labour Organisation should upon request provide assistance to labour-supplying countries for the adoption of measures in order to minimize labour displacement and consequent economic dislocation, if any, within labour-supplying countries which might result from the adoption of this Convention;

5. Appropriate international organizations within the United Nations system should upon request provide assistance to labour-supplying countries for the education and training of their seafarers, including the provision of training and equipment facilities.

Annex II

Resolution 2

Measures to minimize adverse economic effects

The United Nations Conference on Conditions for Registration of Ships,

Having adopted the United Nations Convention on Conditions for Registration of Ships,

Recommends as follows: —

1. The United Nations Conference on Trade and Development, the United Nations Development Programme and the International Maritime Organization and other appropriate international bodies should provide, upon request, technical and financial assistance to those countries which may be affected by this Convention in order to formulate and implement modern and effective legislation for the development of their fleet in accordance with the provisions of this Convention;

2. The International Labour Organisation and other appropriate international organizations should also provide, upon request, assistance to those countries for the preparation and implementation of educational and training programmes for their seafarers as may be necessary;

3. The United Nations Development Programme, the World Bank and other appropriate international organizations should provide to those countries, upon request, technical and financial assistance for the implementation of alternative national development plans, programmes and projects to overcome economic dislocation which might result from the adoption of this Convention.

Annex III

Merchant fleets of the world

Ships of 500 grt and above as at 1 July 1985

	Gross registered tons (grt)
Albania	52,698
Algeria	1,332,863
Angola	71,581
Argentina	2,227,252
Australia	1,877,560
Austria	134,225
Bahamas	3,852,385
Bahrain	26,646
Bangladesh	300,151
Barbados	4,034
Belgium	2,247,571
Benin	2,999
Bolivia	14,913
Brazil	5,935,899
Bulgaria	1,191,419
Burma	94,380
Cameroon	67,057
Canada	841,048
Cape Verde	8,765
Chile	371,468
China	10,167,450
Colombia	357,668
Comoros	649
Costa Rica	12,616
Côte d'Ivoire	124,706
Cuba	784,664
Cyprus	8,134,083
Czechoslovakia	184,299
Democratic Kampuchea	998
Democratic Yemen	4,229
Denmark	4,677,360
Djibouti	2,066
Dominica	500
Dominican Republic	35,667
Ecuador	417,372
Egypt	835,995
Equatorial Guinea	6,412
Ethiopia	54,499

Merchant fleets of the world (cont.)

Ships of 500 grt and above as at 1 July 1985

	Gross registered tons (grt)
Faeroe Islands	39,333
Fiji	20,145
Finland	1,894,485
France	7,864,931
Gabon	92,687
Gambia	1,597
German Democratic Republic	1,235,840
Germany, Federal Republic of	5,717,767
Ghana	99,637
Greece	30,751,092
Guatemala	15,569
Guinea	598
Guyana	3,888
Honduras	301,786
Hungary	77,182
Iceland	69,460
India	6,324,145
Indonesia	1,604,427
Iran (Islamic Republic of)	2,172,401
Iraq	882,715
Ireland	161,304
Israel	541,035
Italy	8,530,108
Jamaica	7,473
Japan	37,189,376
Jordan	47,628
Kenya	1,168
Kiribati	1,480
Korea, Democratic People's Republic of	470,592
Korea, Republic of	6,621,898
Kuwait	2,311,813
Lebanon	461,525
Liberia	57,985,747
Libyan Arab Jamahiriya	832,450
Madagascar	63,115
Malaysia	1,708,599
Maldives	125,958
Malta	1,836,948
Mauritania	1,581
Mauritius	32,968
Mexico	1,282,048

Ships of 500 grt and above as at 1 July 1985

	Gross registered tons (grt)
Monaco	3,268
Morocco	377,702
Mozambique	17,013
Nauru	64,829
Netherlands	3,628,871
New Zealand	266,285
Nicaragua	15,869
Nigeria	396,525
Norway	14,567,326
Oman	10,939
Pakistan	429,973
Panama	39,366,187
Papua New Guinea	10,671
Paraguay	38,440
Peru	640,968
Philippines	4,462,291
Poland	2,966,534
Portugal	1,280,065
Qatar	339,725
Romania	2,769,937
Saint Vincent and the Grenadines	220,490
Samoa	25,644
Saudi Arabia	2,868,689
Senegal	19,426
Singapore	6,385,919
Solomon Islands	1,018
Somalia	22,802
South Africa	501,386
Spain	5,650,470
Sri Lanka	617,628
Sudan	92,700
Surinam	11,181
Sweden	2,951,227
Switzerland	341,972
Syrian Arab Republic	40,506
Tanzania, United Republic of	43,471
Thailand	550,585
Togo	52,677
Tonga	13,381
Trinidad and Tobago	9,370
Tunisia	274,170

Merchant fleets of the world (cont.)

Ships of 500 grt and above as at 1 July 1985

	Gross registered tons (grt)
Turkey	3,532,350
Uganda	3,394
Union of Soviet Socialist Republics	16,767,526
United Arab Emirates	805,318
United Kingdom of Great Britain and Northern Ireland	13,260,290
Bermuda	969,081
British Virgin Islands	1,939
Cayman Islands	313,755
Gibraltar	568,247
Hong Kong	6,820,100
Montserrat	711
Saint Helena	3,150
Turks and Caicos Islands	513
Total	21,937,786
United States of America	13,922,244
Uruguay	144,907
Vanuatu	132,979
Venezuela	900,305
Vietnam	277,486
Yugoslavia	2,648,415
Zaire	70,127
Unallocated	4,201,669
World total	383,533,282

Source: Compiled on the basis of data supplied by Lloyd's Shipping Information Services (London).

Notes:

(i) Types of ship included:
Oil tankers
Oil/chemical tankers
Chemical tankers
Miscellaneous tankers (trading)
Liquefied gas carriers
Bulk/oil carriers (including ore/oil)
Ore and bulk carriers
General cargo ships
Containerships (fully cellular and lighter carriers)
Vehicle carriers
Ferries and passenger ships and passenger/cargo ships
Livestock carriers

(ii) Excluding the reserve fleet of the United States of America and the United States and Canadian Great Lakes Fleets.

The Final Act of the Conference was signed by representatives of the following states (as at 14 February 1986):

Algeria
Angola
Argentina
Australia
Austria
Bahamas
Bangladesh
Belgium
Benin
Brazil
Bulgaria
Byelorussian Soviet
    Socialist Republic
Cameroon
Canada
Cape Verde
Chile
China
Colombia
Côte d'Ivoire
Cyprus
Czechoslovakia
Denmark
Ecuador
Egypt
Ethiopia
Finland
France
Gabon
German Democratic
    Republic
Germany, Federal
    Republic of

Ghana
Greece
Hungary
India
Indonesia
Iran (Islamic Republic
    of)
Iraq
Israel
Italy
Japan
Jordan
Kenya
Korea, Republic of
Kuwait
Lebanon
Liberia
Libyan Arab
    Jamahiriya
Madagascar
Malaysia
Mauritania
Mexico
Morocco
Netherlands
New Zealand
Nicaragua
Nigeria
Norway
Oman
Pakistan
Panama
Peru

Philippines
Poland
Qatar
San Marino
Saudi Arabia
Senegal
Singapore
Spain
Sri Lanka
Sweden
Switzerland
Thailand
Trinidad and
    Tobago
Tunisia
Turkey
Ukranian Soviet
    Socialist
    Republic
Union of Soviet
    Socialist
    Republics
United Arab
    Emirates
United Kingdom of
    Great Britain and
    Northern Ireland
United States of
    America
Uruguay
Venezuela
Yugoslavia
Zaire

Total: 85

About the author

Dr Ademuni-Odeke, who lives and works in the United Kingdom, was born in the eastern Ugandan town of Tororo. He was educated there and at King's College Budo and Makerere University, Kampala, before being forced into exile, by the former Amin dictatorship. He lived briefly in East and Central Africa and obtained a Bachelor's Degree in Law (LLB) with honours in Legal Aspects of International Trade and Investments, International Law, and International Relations from the Faculty of Law, University of Dar es Salaam–Tanzania. He later obtained a Master's degree (LLM) in Maritime Law from the Faculty of Law of Southampton University, and a Doctorate (PhD) in International Shipping at the Institute of Maritime Law of the same university. Professionally, he is a full Corporate Member of the British Institute of Management (MBIM); a Companion of the Nautical Institute; a Member of the Institute of Export (MIEx); and an Associate of the Chartered Insurance Institute (ACII) (Marine and Aviation).

He has had a varied career ranging from a mining engineer (trainee) at a copper mining concern, in Uganda, to a National Organizing Secretary of an International Charity and Coordinator of the World Council of Churches' (WCC) Economic Feasibility Studies of the Anglican Provinces of the Churches of Uganda, Ruanda, Burundi and Zaïre. He later became a State Attorney at the Ministry of Justice and Attorney General's Chamber, United Republic of Tanzania; Legal/Deputy Corporation Secretary of an International Investment

Bank in the same country; Administrative Officer (Legal), East African Harbours' Corporation (EAHC); and Executive Officer (Legal), Eastern African National Shipping Line (EANSL) of the former East African Community (EAC). In this latter aspect Dr Ademuni-Odeke's experience involved handling the purchase of second-hand ships for the defunct Eastern African National Shipping Line.

After several years at the Institute of Maritime Law, Southampton University, he spent some time on consultancy at Southampton with the Transport Commission of the International Chamber of Commerce Project, looking into possibilities of joint shipping ventures between the advanced and developing countries. He is currently a Lecturer in Maritime Law and Legal Aspects of International Trade, with the School of Law of the University of Buckingham and Visiting Professor, in Maritime Law and Policy, at the (UN/IMO) World Maritime University, Malmo, Sweden, *inter alia* as well as being on the list of experts with the UNCTAD Shipping Committee, the International Maritime Organization (IMO), Commonwealth Development Corporation, International Labour Organization (ILO), and the United Nations Development Programme (UNDP). He is also a consultant with the United Kingdom Trade Agency for Developing Countries (UKTDG) at the London Chamber of Commerce; an Associate of the London School of Foreign Trade; International Relations, African Studies and the Centre for Defence Studies (Aberdeen).

His research and publication interests are in the legal, economic and political aspects of international shipping — especially the New International Maritime Order, developing country shipping, flag discriminations, flag preferences, cargo reservations, cabotage restrictions, state interventions, maritime subsidies, bilateralism, and other restrictive shipping practices. He has written on the UN Code of Conduct for Liner Conferences. He is the author of *Protectionism and the Future of International Shipping*, Martinus Nijhoff, Dordrecht, The Netherlands, 1984; *National Defence, Global Security and the Geopolitical Role of Merchant Shipping*, Lexington, Mass., USA, 1988; *Demurrage*, Collins, London, 1987; and *The Political Economy of International Shipping*, 1988. He is a member of several professional and international maritime organizations including: the International Society of African Lawyers; the Society of Public Law Teachers; The International Bar Association; Third World Foundation (founder member); the National Maritime Economists' Conferences; the Export Group of the Southampton Chamber of Commerce; the British Institute of International and Comparative Law; the Maritime

Economists' Discussion Group (London), *inter alia*. He has written and lectured extensively on maritime law and policy and international trade law, in the UK, North America and the Scandinavian countries.

He is also the Managing Director of the A-O Associates (Maritime Consultants), Southampton.

Bibliography

Abrahamson, B.J. (1980), *International Ocean Shipping: Current Concepts and Principles*, Westview Press.

Abrahamson, B.J. and Singer, M.A. (1972), 'A shipping research program with particular reference to smaller nations', *Journal of Israel Shipping*, April.

Ackley, G. (1961), *Macro-Economic Theory*, New York: Macmillan, pp. 485–93, 518–29.

Ademuni-Odeke (1983), 'Differences which set the US apart', *Lloyd's List*, no. 52434, 5 August, p. 4.

Ademuni-Odeke (1983), 'How the Brussels Package will effectively undermine the Liner Code', *Lloyd's List*, no. 52434, 5 August, p. 4.

Ademuni-Odeke (1983), 'Joint ventures could become more attractive', *Lloyd's List*, no. 52434, 5 August, p. 4.

Ademuni-Odeke (1984), 'Implementing the UNCTAD Code of Conduct – the UK Merchant Shipping (Liner Conferences) Act 1982', *Marine Policy*, vol. 6, no. 1, January, pp. 56–64.

Ademuni-Odeke (1984), *Protectionism and the Future of International Shipping*, Dordrecht: Martinus Nijhoff.

Afro Asian Corporation (1967), *Shipping Report of the Fleet Committee*, Cairo, 8–11 May.

Agirotto, E. (1974), 'Flags of convenience and sub-standard vessels: a Review of ILO's approach to the problem', *International Labour Review*, vol. 110.

Agman, R.S. (1976), 'Competition, rationalisation and the US shipping policy', *Journal of Maritime Law and Commerce*, vol. 7, no. 1, October, pp. 1–50.

Albadawry, A.K. (1980), *Restructuring of World Shipping Capacity under the Conditions of the UN Code of Conduct*, Ann Arbor: Michigan University Press.

Alderton, P.M. (1973), *Sea Transport: Operation and Economics*, London: Thomas Reed.

Alexander, L.M. (1980), 'The Law of the Sea Conference: issues in current negotiations' in R.B. Lillich and J.N. Moore, *Readings in International Law*, Newport, pp. 188–98.

Alexander, Y. and Kittrie, N.N. (eds) (1973), *Crescent and Star: Arab–Israel Perspectives on the Middle East Conflict*, Toronto: AMS Press.

Alexandersson, G. and Norstram, G. (1973), *World Shipping: An Economic Geography of Ports and Seaborne Trade*, Wikesell: Wiley and Almguist.

Alisa, F. (1986), 'Troon Uard to close by end of year', *The Times*, 15 May, p. 1d.

Altshuler, A. (ed.) (1979), *Current Issues in Transportation Policy*, Lexington Books.

American Bureau of Shipping (1967), *Surveyor*, August, pp. 15–20.

American Legion (1958), *Merchant Marine Bulletin*, March, p. 4.

Anderson, D.R. (1964), 'Reservations to multilateral conventions: a re-examination', *International and Comparative Law Quarterly*, vol. 13, pp. 450–81.

Anderson, R.E. (1945), *The Merchant Marine and World Frontiers*, CIO Maritime Postwar Programme Series, New York: Cornell Maritime Press. Reprint, Greenwood, Westpoint, Connecticut, 1978.

Anglo-American Council of Productivity (1950), *Freight Handling*, report of a specialist team which visited the US in 1950.

Anon (1972), 'Tariff surcharges and Article II of GATT', *New York University Journal of International Law and Politics*, vol. 5, pp. 341–56.

Apter, J. (1986), 'France bids to stem flow to foreign flags', *Lloyd's List*, no. 53274, 8 May, p. 1.

Apter, J. (1986), 'Action by unions on Dreyfus register bid', *Lloyd's List*, no. 53380, 11 September, p. 1.

Arista, J.D. (1979), 'United States Congressional restraints: the ties that bind 1979' in L.G. France and M. Seiber (eds), *Developing Country Debt*, New York, pp. 215–35.

Arosemera, C. (1984), 'The enrolment of vessels under the flag of the Republic of Panama and the registration of mortgages thereon' and 'Remedies available for creditors of ships enrolled under the

Panama Flag', *Current Issues in International Ship Finance*, pp. 149–75 and 177–206.

Atlink, I. (1986), 'Asian Development Bank (ADB) adopting a broader lending policy', *Seatrade*, January, p. 35.

Austin, M. (1985), 'Currency features', *Seatrade*, December, pp. 25–8.

Australian Bureau for Transport Economics (1983), *Marine Oil Spill Risk in Australia*, Report no. 53, Canberra.

Averim, I. (1986), 'Protectionism may deepen East/West split: EEC shipping policy effects on Soviet shipping', *Motor Shipping*, vol. 66, no. 788, March, p. 78.

B.J. (1980), 'The IMF and the poor', *Economic and Political Weekly of Bombay*, 22 November.

Bakke, K.E. (1977), 'US regulation of intermodal ocean cargo movements', *International Container Industry Conference Proceedings*, November, pp. 23–7.

Balassa, B. and Michalopoulos, C. (1980), 'Liberalising trade between developed and developing countries', *Journal of World Trade Law*, vol. 20, no. 1, January–February, pp. 1–28.

Balassa, B. (1981), *The Newly Industrialised Nations in the World Economy*, Pergamon Press.

Banco do Brasil, SA, CACEX (1984), 'Uma opcaco de Creseimento', *Information Semanal CACEX*, Rio de Janeiro, 5 November.

Bank for International Settlement (1985), 55th Annual Report, Basle, 1 April.

Bank, G. (1979), *Finance for Ship Purchasing*, Bangor: University of Wales.

Bank of England (1985), *Quarterly Bulletin*, September.

Bank of Israel, Research Department (1962), *The Israel Merchant Marine, An Economic Appraisal*, Jerusalem.

Banks, A.S. (ed.) (1978), *Political Handbook of the World, 1977*, New York: McGraw-Hill.

Banks, J.S. (1979), 'Scandinavian liner companies — maintaining a bold front with a massive investment in ro-ro', *Cargo Systems International*, vol. 6, no. 2, February, pp. 28–31.

Banquet, M.R. (1959), *No Gallant Ship: Studies in Maritime Local History*, London: Halis and Couter.

Barber, M. (1986), 'Irish line set to transfer to new register', *Lloyd's List*, no. 53392, 25 September, p. 1.

Barraclough, R.N. and Crampton, W.G. (1978), *Flags of the World*, New York: Frederick Warne.

Barry, M. (1979), *Occupational Health and Safety of Seafarers: Survey of Statistics: Preliminary Report*, Sealife Programme.

Bassis, M.S., 'Ship contingencies and nautical education. A problem of level and scope of certification', *Maritime Policy and Management*, vol. 2, no. 3, pp. 154–64.

Bates, L.M. (1981), 'The merchant service', *Wall Street Journal*, 2 September.

Batista, P.N. (1985), Brazilian Ambassador in Geneva as cited in the *New York Times*, 2 October, p. D.19.

Bayley, G. (1978), 'Problems ahead with Soviet tanker surplus', *Fairplay International Shipping Weekly*, vol. 265, no. 4927, 9 February, pp. 7–8.

Bellagazu (1981), 'Statistische Beihefte zu den monatsberichten der Deutschen Bundesbank', Reihe 3, *Zalhungsbilanzstatistik*, no. 7, July, p. 41, footnote 8.

Benham, A.Y. (1974), 'A study of the value of national fleets and shipping policies in developing countries', unpublished Master's thesis, Cardiff: UWIST.

Bennethan, E. and Walters, A.A. (1979), *Port Pricing and Investment Policies for Developing Countries*, Oxford: Oxford University Press.

Bergin, A. (1986), 'Australian ocean policy: the need for review', *Marine Policy*, vol. 10, pp. 155–8.

Bergstrand, J. (1984), 'Bretton Woods revisited', *New England Economic Review*, September–October, pp. 22–3.

Bergstrand, S. and Doganis, R. (1985), 'The impact of flags of convenience' in W.E. Butler (ed.), *The Law of the Sea and International Shipping*, New York.

Berguido, C. *et al.* (1957), *Manual for Masters and Seamen on Ships under the Panamanian Flag*, Philadelphia.

Bertran, S. (1969), 'The internationality of shipping', *The Institute of Transport Journal*, May, pp. 140–7.

Bess, D. (1979), 'The maritime academics are all wet', *US Naval Institute Proceedings*, October, pp. 70–6.

Beth, H.L. (1978), 'Restructuring of European industries and shipbuilding', *European Shipping and Shipbuilding* (Conference Proceedings), pp. 96–116.

Beth, H.L. (1979), *Fluctuations of Exchange Rates — Their Impact on Shipping*, Lectures and Contributions, no. 26, Bremen: Institute of Shipping Economics.

Betham (1976), 'Political factors and the evolution of national fleets in developing countries', *Maritime Studies and Management*, vol. 3, p. 131.

Beveridge, Lord W.W. (1931), *Full Employment in a Free Society: A Postscript*, London: Longmans.

Beveridge, Lord W.W. (1980), 'Fiscal content of financial programmes supported by SBA in the upper credit tranches 1969-1978', *IMF Staff Paper*, vol. 27, no. 2, June.

Bhagat, H. (1980), 'The mixed blessings of the IMF', *New African*, February.

Bhagwati, J.N. (1984), 'Splintering and disembodiment of services and developing nations', *The World Economy*, June, pp. 133-43.

Bhagwati, J.N. (1985), 'GATT and trade in services: how can we solve the North-South debate?', *Financial Times*, 27 November, p. 25.

Bierman, H. (1959), *Managerial Accounting Introduction*, New York: Macmillan.

Bird, G. (1979), 'IMF quotas, conditionality and the developing countries', *Overseas Development Institute Review*, no. 2, p. 67.

Bird, G. (1979), 'The IMF as a source of international finance for developing countries: a critical appraisal', *Indian Journal of Economics*, Allahabad, April, p. 115.

Birinie, P. (1980), 'Contemporary maritime legal problems', *Maritime Dimension*, p. 169.

Bishop, V. (1980), 'HK hints at rethink on taxes for new registries', *Lloyd's List*, no. 53431, 10 November, p. 3.

Bishop, V. (1986), 'Dual Hong Kong register set to start in 1991', *Lloyd's List*, no. 53409, 15 October, p. 1.

Bishop, V. (1986), 'Taxation plans threaten proposed Hong Kong register', *Lloyd's List*, no. 53429, 7 November, p. 2.

Bishop, V. (1986), 'Manila to act over vogue crew agencies', *Lloyd's List*, no. 53437, 17 November, p. 1.

Bishop, W.W. (1971), *International Law Cases and Materials*, 3rd edn, Boston: Little Brothers.

Bixler, R.W. (1957), *The Foreign Policy of the United States in Liberia 1819-1955*, New York: Pageant Press.

Black (1968), *Law Dictionary*, revised edn, p. 1542.

Black, R.A. (1977), 'The Australian shipper — his shipping needs', *Australian Symposium on Shipping and Management*, November, vol. 1, pp. 17-22; vol. II, pp. 1-2.

Blackwell, R.J. (1974), 'Implementation of the Merchant Marine Act 1970', *Journal of Maritime Law and Commerce*, vol. 5, no. 2, January, pp. 167-81.

Blake, G. (1985), 'Maritime policy issues for Turkey', *Maritime Policy Reports*, vol. 7, no. 4, p. 6.

Blumenhagen, D. (1981), *Shipping and the Balance of Payments*, Lectures and Contributions, no. 32, Bremen: Institute of Shipping Economics.

Bohme, H. (1978), *Restraint on Competition in World Shipping*, Trade Policy Research Centre, p. 86.

Bohme, H. (1979), 'Die deutsche Seeschiffahrt im Strukfurwandel der Weltwirtschaft. Weltbewerbsgrundlagen — Anpassungs-erfordenisse–Entwicklungsmoglichkeiten', *Weltwirtschaft*, no. 1, pp. 159-95.

Bolan, M. (1967), *The Shipping Industry in India: Strategic Factors in Industrial Relations Systems*, Institute for Labour Studies.

Bonn, A.M. (1967), *Shipping Enterprises and Management 1930-1939*, Liverpool University Press.

Bonsor, N. (1979), *North Atlantic Seaway*, vol. 4, Brookside.

Borpujary, J.G. (1980), *Towards a Basic Needs Approach to Economic Development with Financial Stability*, IMF mimeo DM/SO/16, 28 March.

Bors (1977), 'Regulatory and political restraints and their efforts on international shipping', International Container Industry Conference Proceedings, November, pp. 17-22.

Boszeck, B.A. (1962), *Flags of Convenience, An International Legal Study*, Cambridge, Mass: Harvard University Press.

Boyes, J.R.C. (1981), 'No quick fix for US maritime industry', *Containerisation International*, vol. 15, 6 June, pp. 32-6.

Brajkovik, V. and Pallua, E. (1960), 'Lien substantiel et la nationalité des navires', *Jugoslovenska revija za medunaroduo pravo*.

Branch, E.A. (1981), *Elements of Shipping*, 5th edn, London: Chapman and Hall.

Branch, E.A. (1982), *Economics of Shipping Practice and Management*, Chapman and Hall.

Branch, E.A. (1982), *Dictionary of Shipping, International Trade Terms and Abbreviations*, 2nd edn, Witherby.

Breedmas, A.E. (1981), 'The common shipping policy of the EEC', *Common Market Law Review*, vol. 18, pp. 9-32.

Bremen Institute of Shipping Economics (1985), *Monthly Figures of Shipping, Freight Markets, Seatrade, Ports and Sea Canals*.

Bremen Institute of Shipping Economics (1985), *Shipping Statistics Yearbook — Facts and Figures about Shipping, Shipbuilding, Seaports and Seaborne Traffic*.

Brewer, J. (1983), 'West Germany in dramatic move over the Liner Code', *Lloyd's List*, no. 52318, 18 March, front page.

Briss, W.D. (1969), 'The basic international structure of LAFTA and the proposals for its modifications: internationalism v. regionalism', *Case Western Journal of International Law*, vol. 2, pp. 34-57.

British Petroleum Ltd (1965), *Statistical Review of the World Oil Industry*.

Britt, S.H. (1960), *The Spenders*, New York: McGraw-Hill Book Co.

Brock, W.E. (1982), 'A simple plan for negotiating on trade in services', *The World Economy*, November.

Brower, C.N. and Tepe, J.B. (1975), 'The Charter of Economic Rights and Duties of States', *International Lawyer*, vol. 9, pp 295-318.

Brown, B. (1966), *Human Factors in Australian Shipping*, Bedford Park, South Australia: National Institute of Labour Studies, Flinders University.

Brown-Hume, C. (1986), 'Widespread backing for ship identity number plans', *Lloyd's List*, no. 53382, 13 September, p. 3.

Brown, E.D. (1968), 'The lessons of the Torrey Canyon: international law aspects', *Current Legal Problems*, p. 113.

Brown, R.B. (1966), *Transport and the Economic Integration of Latin America*, Washington DC: Brookings Institution.

Brown, V.M. (1984), 'Legislacion y jurisprodencia Holandesa en 1981', *Anuario de Deredo Maritimo*, pp. 329-40.

Brownlie (1973), *Principles of Public International Law*.

Buchanan, N. and Ellis, H.S. (1955), *Approaches to Economic Development*, New York: The Twentieth Century Fund, chapter 16.

Buckingham, L. (1983), 'Owners view EEC competition moves as threat to conferences', *Lloyd's List*, no. 52535, 2 December, p. 4.

Buckingham, L. (1983), 'Wrangles open Soviet-British shipping talks', *Lloyd's List*, no. 52540, 8 December, Headlines.

Buckingham, L. (1986), 'Shell to switch entire UK fleet to IOM register', *Lloyd's List*, no. 53338, 23 July, p. 1.

Buckingham, L. (1986), 'Luxemburg in move to start vessel register', *Lloyd's List*, no. 53431, 10 November, p. 1.

Buckingham, L. (1986), 'Flag rights in wartime confirmed by Liberia', *Lloyd's List*, no. 53447, 28 November, p. 3.

Burwash, D. (1947), *English Merchant Shipping 1460-1564*, University of Toronto Press.

Bush, W.L. (1972), 'Steamship Conference Contract rate agreement and the dual rate system', *ICC Practitioner's Journal*, November-December.

Butler, E. and Pirie, M. (1983), *Freeports*, Adam Smith Institute.

Butler, W.E. (ed.) (1985), *The Law of the Sea and International Shipping: Anglo-Soviet Post UNCLOS Perspective*, New York.

Buzan, B. (1981), 'Negotiating by consensus: developments in technique at the United Nations Conference on the Law of the Sea', *American Journal of International Law*, vol. 75, pp. 324-48.

Cadwallader, F.J.J. (1976), 'Flag discrimination or something more?', *Current Legal Problems*, pp. 99-111.

Calisle, R. (1980), 'The American century implemented: Stettinus and the Liberian flag of convenience', *Business History Review*, vol. 54, pp. 175-91.

Calisle, R. (1981), *Sovereignty for Sale: The Origins and Evolution of the Panamanian and Liberian Flags of Convenience*, Annapolis, Maryland: Naval Institute Press.

Campbell, G. and Evans, I.O. (1975), *The Book of Flags*, 7th edn, Oxford University Press.

Canadian Transport Commission (1977), *Report of Conference Agreements Filed With*, December.

Canadian Transport Commission (1979), *Cargo Reservation and Liner Conference Shipping Servicing Canada: An Analysis Related to the UNCTAD Code of Conduct*, Ottawa.

Caran, E. (1968), *Oil and Water: The Torrey Canyon Disaster*, New York: Lippincott.

Carlson, V. (1962), *Economic Security in the US*, New York: McGraw-Hill.

Carrell, W.P. (1962), *A Study of American Owned Vessels Under the Flags of Panama, Honduras and Costa Rica*, unpublished Masters thesis, Charlottesville: University of Virginia.

Casanova, M. (1964), 'Requisite di naxionlita e dismission di bandieva (Conditions for granting of nationality and change of flag) Studi in onori di Berlingeri', *Diritto Maritimo*, pp. 137-53.

Casas, J. (1981), *Shipping Costs and Revenues*, Lectures and Contributions no. 31, Bremen: Institute of Shipping Economics.

Cassing, J.A. (1979), 'Trade pattern production and resource allocation in a model with jointly supplied international transport services', *Transportation Economics*, vol. 6, no. 3, December, pp. 293-309.

Ceres, A.F. (1927), *Merchant Marine: National Necessity*, US Naval Institute Proceedings, vol. 53.

Chalmers, H. (1953), *World Trade Policies*, Berkley, California: University of California Press.

Chambers (1977), *Twentieth Century Dictionary*.

Chandrahasan, N. (1984), 'The Indian Ocean peace zone proposal: is it valid today?', *Journal of the Indian Ocean Law Institute*, vol. 26, pp. 543-55.

Chang, M. (1985), *The UNCTAD Model Marine Hull and Cargo Insurance Clauses: Recent Developments in Marine Insurance Law from Korean Perspective*, unpublished LLM thesis, Dalhousie University.

Channary, G.A. (1980), *Statements in Hearings before the Sub-Committee on International Trade, Investment and Monetary Affairs*, House of Representatives, 49th Congress, 2nd Session on Hearings no. 5970 to Amend the Bretton Woods Agreement Act, 6 February 1980.

Chenery, H.B. (1961), 'Comparative advantage and development policy', *American Economic Review*, March.

Chiavbas, J. (1979), 'Murphy's second law' (US Maritime Proposals), *Seatrade*, vol. 9, no. 7, July, pp. 3–5.

Chrzanowski, E. (1978), 'Current aspects of international shipping policy', *Maritime Policy and Management*, vol. 5, p. 289.

Church, A.J., Jr (1980), *Flags of Convenience or Flags of Necessity?*, US Naval Institute Proceedings, vol. 106, no. 6.

Clark, G. (1986), 'What future for shipping in the Gulf?', *Fairplay International Shipping Weekly*, 21 January, p. 19.

Clark, G. (1986), 'Owners consider doubtful future now that the euphoria is over', *Fairplay International Shipping Weekly*, 9 October, pp. 16–21.

Clark, G. (1986), 'Positive government attitude bodes well for Cypriot fleet', *Fairplay International Shipping Weekly*, 13 November, pp. 36–9.

Clark, J.M. (1964), 'Business acceleration and the laws of demand: the technical factor in economic cycles', reprinted in *Readings in Business Cycle Theory*, New York: McGraw-Hill.

Clawson, M. and Held, B. (1957), *The Federal Lands: Their Use and Management*, Baltimore: The John Hopkins Press.

Clayton, H.W. (1965), *Clayton's Annual Register of Shipping and Port Charges for Great Britain 1965*, Field and Turner.

Clement, A.G.A. (1979), 'A promising future for owners and builders', *Latin American Shipping*, p. 13.

Clincop, A. (1980), 'The Libyan Malta continental shelf', *International Insights*, vol. 2, pp. 43–9.

Cline, W.R. (1980), 'The magnitude and conditions of lending by the International Monetary Fund', *Hearings*, no. 5970, 6 February, pp. 128–44.

Cline, W.R. and Weinfraub, S. (eds) (1980), *Economic Stabilization Programmes in Developing Countries*, Brookings Institution.

Colchester, N. (1983), 'Protection from Chicago', *Financial Times*, 4 February.

Coleman, T. (1976), *The Liners: A History of the North Atlantic Crossing*, London: Allen Lane.

Colombos (1967), *International Law of the Sea*, 6th edn.

Comité des Armateurs de France (1967), *Effects de l'investissement maritime sur la balance des paiements*, Paris.

Committee of the American Economic Association (1980), *Readings in the Theory of International Trade*.

Committee on Invisible Exports (1972), *World Invisible Trade: An Analysis by the Economists Advisory Group*, London, July.

Connors, T.A. (1979), *The Apparent Effects of Recent IMF Stabilization Programmes*, Discussion Paper no. 135, Washington DC: Federal Reserve, International Finance.

Conrad, J. (1959), *An Introduction to the Theory of Interest*, Berkley, California: University of California Press.

Couper, A.D. (1972), *The Geography of Sea Transport*, London: Hutchison.

Course, A.G. (1956), *The Merchant Navy Today*, Oxford University Press.

Cufley, C.F.H. (1967), 'The bulk carrier revolution', text of the lecture given at Thurrock Technical College, Grays, Essex, England, 15 February 1967, p. 9.

Cufley, C.F.H. (1974), *Ocean Freight and Chartering*, Reprint.

Cummins, P. (1978), 'Oil tanker pollution control: design criteria v. effective liability assessment', *Journal of Maritime Law and Commerce*, vol. 7, p. 169.

Currie, D.P. (1963), 'Flags of convenience, American labour and the conflicts of law', *Supreme Court Review*, p. 34.

Dalton, G. (1965), 'History, politics and economic development in Liberia', *Journal of Economic History*, vol. 25, p. 569.

David, P. (1986), 'The politically unsafe ports', *Lloyd's Maritime and Commercial Law Quarterly*, February, pp. 112–28.

Davies, J.C. II (1970), *The Politics of Pollution*, New York: Pegasus.

Davis, R. (1962), *The Rise of the English Shipping Industry in the Seventeenth and Eighteenth Centuries*, London: Macmillan.

Dawson, F.G. (1975), 'Towards a New International Economic Order', *Virginia Journal of International Law*, vol. 76, pp. 297–353.

Dearing, C.L. and Owen, W. (1980), *National Transportation Policy* (reprint of 1949 edn), Greenwood.

Deck, H. (1953), *Foreign Commerce*, New York: McGraw-Hill.

Dell, S. (1980), *The Problems of IMF Conditionality*, IMF mimeo, 25 March.

Deutsche Bundesbank (n.d.), *Die Zahlungsbilanz der Bundesrepublik Deutschland 1977 bis 1980 nach Regionen*.

Devamney, J.W. (1971), *Marine Decisions under Uncertainty*, Cambridge, Maryland: Cornell Maritime Press.

Diaz-Alejandro, C. (1979), 'Southern cone stabilization plans', *Yale Discussion Paper* (stereotype), November, pp. 16–17.

Dimock, M. (1951), *Free Enterprise and the Administrative State*, University of Alabama Press.

Dixit, A. and Norman, V. (1980), *Theory of International Trade*, Cambridge University Press.

Dobler, J.P. (1981), 'Restructuring French shipbuilding industry offers high technology', *Norwegian News International*, vol. 37, no. 6, May, pp. 87–90.

Doganis, R.S. (1976), *Flags of Convenience*, Research Paper no. 8, Transport Studies Group, Polytechnic of Central London, November.

Doganis, R.S. (1983), *Buy the Flag: Developments in the Open Registry Debate*, Research Paper no. 13, Transport Studies Group, Polytechnic of Central London, August, p. 2.

Doganis, R.S. and Metaxas, B.N. (1976), *The Impact of the Flags of Convenience*, Research Paper no. 3, Transport Studies Group, Polytechnic of Central London.

Donelan, E.J. (1983), 'Offshore exploration and exploitation: the legal regime of the United Kingdom and the Republic of Ireland', *New Law Journal*, vol. 133, pp. 461-4.

Dorsey, J.F. (1977), 'Preferential treatment: a new standard for international economic relations', *Harvard International Law Journal*, vol. 18, pp. 109-35.

Drewery, H.P. (1973), *US Oil Imports, 1971-1985: Repercussions on the World Tanker and Oil Industries*, London.

Drewery, H.P. (1976), *The Involvement of Oil-Exporting Countries in International Shipping*, London.

Drewery, H.P. (1978), 'World shipping under flags of convenience: maritime safety aspects', *International Regulation of Maritime Transport*, New York, pp. 231-40.

Drewery, H.P. (1978), *The Emergence of Third World Shipping*, Publication no. 6.

Drewery, H.P. (1981), *Shipping Statistics and Economics*, no. 125, March.

Drewery, H.P. (1982), *The Impact of Inflationary Cost Tendencies on Dry Cargo Shipping Operation*, Survey no. 25, London.

Drewery, H.P. (1983), *Shipping Statistics and Economics*, no. 154, August.

Drewery, H.P. (1985), *Protectionism and the Bulk Shipping Industry*, November.

Dryden, M.M. (1964), 'Capital budgeting: treatment of uncertainty and investment criteria', *Scottish Journal of Political Economy*, Edinburgh, November.

Duff, E.A. (1957), *The United Fruit Company and the Political Affairs of Guatemala 1944-1954*, Masters thesis, Charlottesville: University of Virginia.

Duff, P. and Anderson, C. (1949), *British Ships and Shipping*, London: George G. Harrap & Co. Ltd, pp. 137-8.

Dunn, J. (1981), *Miles to Go: European and American Transportation Policies*, Boston: MIT Press.

Durairaj, G. (1982), 'Evergreen to transfer ships to Malaysian flag', *Lloyd's List*, no. 53411, 17 October, p. 2.

Ealy, L. (1970), *The Republic of Panama in World Affairs 1903-1950*, Pennsylvania State University Press, 1951: Reprint, Westport Connecticut: Greenwood.

Economist Intelligence Unit (1979), *The Open Registry Shipping*, London.

Economist Intelligence Unit (1980), *Ocean Shipping and Freight Rates and Developing Countries*, London.

ECOSOC-(UN), *Main Issues in Transport for Developing Countries during the 3rd UN Development Decade 1981-1990*, Doc. no. ST/ESA/177, New York.

EEC (1962), *Council Regulation*, 17/62.

EEC (1962), *Council Regulation*, 141/62.

EEC (1968), *Council Regulation*, 1017/68.

EEC Economic and Social Committee (1979), *EEC Shipping Policy: Flags of Convenience Option*, Brussels.

Ehlermann, P. (1983), 'Aspects of ship financing in the FRG', *Current Issues in Shipping Financing*, vol. 1, pp. 85–121.

Ellis, H.S. and Metzler, L.A. (1949), *Readings in The Theory of International Trade*, New York: McGraw-Hill.

Ellsworth, P.T. (1958), *The International Economy*, New York: Macmillan.

Emery, S.W. (1970), 'The effective United States Control Fleet', *US Naval Institute Proceedings*, vol. 96, p. 160.

Engle, W.P. (1952), *Economic Stabilization*, New Jersey: Princeton University Press, pp. 75–6.

Engler, R. (1961), *The Politics of Oil*, New York: Macmillan.

Engler, R. (1970), *Brotherhood of Oil*, Chicago: Chicago University Press.

Environmental Resources Ltd (1982), *The Law and Practice Relating to Pollution Control in the Netherlands*, 2nd edn, London: Graham and Trotman.

ESCAPE (1968), *Regional Economic Co-operation in Asia and the Far East*, Report of ESCAPE Working Party on Shipping and Ocean Freight Rates and Related Papers, Regional Economic Cooperation Series, no. 5, New York: UN.

Escarpenter, C. (1965), *The Economics of International Ocean Transport*, Madison, Milwaukee: The University of Wisconsin Press.

Eversheim, F. (1958), *Effects of Shipping Subsidization*, Bremen: Institute of Shipping Economics.

Ewing, K. (1980), 'Union action against flags of convenience: the legal position in Great Britain', *Journal of Maritime Law and Commerce*, vol. II, no. 4, pp. 503–8.

Fabrega, J. (1951), *Consular Traffic of Panama*: Decree 41 of 1935, Panama City.

Fair, M.L. and Williams, E.W. (1973), *Economics of Transportation and Logistics*, Dallas: Business Publications.

Farrell, S. (1984), 'The use of flags of convenience by Latin American shipping', *Maritime Policy and Management*, vol. 11, no. 1, pp. 15–20.

Farrell, S. (1984), 'The use of flags of convenience by Latin American countries', *Maritime Policy and Management*, vol. 11, pp. 15–20.

Farrell, S. (1986), 'The subsidization of seaports: an alternative approach', *Maritime Policy and Management*, vol. 13, no. 2, pp. 177–84.

Farudan, R. (1986), 'UK flag-out shipping set to top domestic tonnage', *Lloyd's List*, no. 53424, 1 November, pp. 1. and 2.

Fasvender, K. and Wagner, W. (1973), *Shipping Conferences, Rate Policy and Developing Countries: The Argument for Rate Discrimination*, Hamburg: Institut für Wirtschaftsforschung.

Faver, G. (1985), 'The economics of Stabex', *Journal of World Trade Law*, vol. 18, no. 1, January–February, pp. 52–62.

Fayle, C.E. (1981), *A Short History of the World's Shipping Industry*, London: Allen and Unwin.

Fearnley (1981), *Fearnley's Review 1980*, Oslo.

Featherstone, J.M. (1978), 'Through transport and the total export concept', *Conference on Maritime Commercial Practices*, November, pp. 1–8.

Ferguson, A.R. (1961), *The Economic Value of the US Merchant Marine*, Illinois: Transport Centre, Northwest University.

Ferreira, M.P. and Rayment, P. (1985), 'Exports of manufactures from South European countries: demands and competitive factors', *Journal of World Trade Law*, vol. 18, no. 3, May–June, pp. 235–51.

Finger, J.M. (1976), 'Effective protection by transportation costs and tariffs: a comparison of magnitudes', *Quarterly Journal of Economics*, vol. 90, February, pp. 169–76.

Finney, H.A. and Miller, H.E. (1957), *Principles of Accounting*, 5th edn, Englewood Cliffs, NJ: Prentice-Hall Inc.

Fisher, F.M. (1957), *Tramp Shipping*, Bremen.

Fitzpatrick (1974), 'Soviet-American trade 1972–74: a summary', *Virginia Journal of International Law*, vol. 15, p. 39.

Fleming, D.K. (1986), 'Safe harbours from high costs, taxes and restrictive regulations in shipping', *Maritime Policy and Management*, vol. 13, no. 1, pp. 17–25.

Flourney, R.W.R. Jr (1929), *A Collection of Nationality Laws of Various Countries as Contained in Constitutions, Statutes and Treaties*, Oxford: Oxford University Press.

Foighel, I. (1970), 'Aid to developing countries — a legal analysis', *Nordisk Tid. Int. Ref.*, vol. 40, pp. 87–175.

Forde, F. (1981), *The Long Watch: The History of the Irish Mercantile Marine since World War II*, Dublin and New York: Grill and Macmillan.

Forrester, E. (1981), *Sale and Purchase Report*, October.

France, L.G. and Seiber, M. (eds) (1979), *Developing Country Debt*, New York, pp. 215–35.

Frank, T.M. and Chesler, E.R. (1974–75), 'At arm's length: the coming law of collective bargaining in international relations between equilibriated states', *Virginia Journal of International Law*, vol. 15, pp. 179–609.

Frankel, E.G. (1972), *Ocean Transportation*, Cambridge, Mass: MIT Press.

Frankel, E.G. (1982), *Regulation and Policies of American Shipping*, Boston, Mass: Aubrun House Publishing Co.

Frankel, E.G. (1985), 'Global economics — commodity, trade and shipping development', *Bulk Handling of Transport*, vol. 5 (Conf.), pp. 13–16.

Frankel, E.G., Arnold, J. and Read, P. (1981), 'Impact of cargo sharing on US liner traders', *Marine Policy*, vol. 5, pp. 23–39.

French, C. (1979), 'Poor nations may rock the boat at Manila Conference', *Global Mail*, Toronto, 22 March, p. 1310.

Friedman, W. (1964), *The Changing Structure of International Law*, New York: Petter and Simons.

Gal-Edd, I. (1969), 'Israeli foreign trade', *Journal of World Trade Law*, vol. 3, no. 1, January–February, p. 1.

Gamble, J.K. Jr (1980), 'Post World War II multilateral treaty making: the task of the Third United Nations Law of the Sea Conference in perspective', *San Diego Law Review*, vol. 17, pp. 527–56.

Gamble, J.K. Jr (1979), *Law of the Sea, Neglected Issues*, Honolulu: University of Hawaii.

Gandhi, D.S. (1977), 'Shipowners, mariners and the new Law of the Sea: the effect of technical, legal and political constraints upon the traditional users of the world's oceans', *Fairplay International Shipping Weekly*, p. 38.

Garcia, A.F.V. (1967), 'Institutional and economic perspectives on Latin American integration', *Proceedings of American Society of International Law*, vol. 61, pp. 167–86.

Garden, W.M. (1985), 'Protection, the exchange rates, and macroeconomic policy', *Finance and Development*, June, pp. 17 and 19.

Gardner, B.M. and Richardson, P.W. (1977), 'The fiscal treatment of shipping' in R.O. Goss (ed.), *Advances in Shipping Economics*, Cambridge University Press.

Garoche, P. (1968), 'The effects of handling charges on ships' operations costs', *UN Transport Communications Review*, vol. 3, April–June.

Garvey, A.J. (1970), *Garvey and Garveyism*, New York: Macmillan.

Gatewood, R.D. (1927), 'Seapower and American policy', *US*

Naval Institute Proceedings, vol. 53, October, p. 1070.

GATT (n.d.), *International Trade 1983–84*.

General Council of British Shipping (1980), *British Shipping Statistics 1979/80*.

General Council of British Shipping (1986), *British Shipping Statistics 1986*.

Georgandopolous (1978), *Shipping in Developing Countries – Problems and Prospects*, Lectures and Contributions no. 20, Bremen: Institute of Shipping Economics.

Gidwitz, B. (1980), *Politics of International Air Transport*, Lexington Books.

Gilberman, R.M. (1976), 'Cargo preferences: the United States and the future regulation of international shipping', *Virginia Journal of International Law*, vol. 16, pp. 865–901.

Giles, P.A. (1983), 'Registration of a British flag vessel in the Port of Hong Kong and registration of mortgages', *Current Issues in International Ship Financing*, vol. 1, p. 191.

Gill, E.W.S. (1985), 'Export controls: Export Administration Amendment Act 1985 (USA)', *Worldwise*, vol. 48, no. 6, October–November, pp. 42–4.

Gill, E.W.S. (1985), 'Containerisation: a seaman's viewpoint', *Asian Shipping*, December, pp. 29–32.

Gilman, S. (1983), *The Competitive Dynamics of Container Shipping*, Gower Publishing House.

Gold, E. (1960), 'The rise of the coastal state in the Law of the Sea', in *Maritime Policy and the Coastal Community*, London, pp. 13ff.

Gold, E. (1978), 'Flags of convenience', *New Directions in Maritime Law*, pp. 100–2.

Gold, E. (1981), *Maritime Transport: The Evolution of International Marine Policy and Shipping Law*, Lexington Books.

Gold, J. (n.d.), *The Reform of the Fund*, IMF Pamphlet Series no. 12, pp. 26–32.

Gold, J. (1971), 'Aspects of the relationship of the IMF with its developing country members', *Columbia Journal of Transnational Law*, vol. 10, no. 2, Autumn.

Gold, J. (1977), 'International law and the IMF', *Finance and Development*, IMF, December, pp. 33–7.

Gold, J. (1979), *Conditionality*, IMF Pamphlet Series no. 31.

Gold, J. (1980), *The Legal Character of the Fund's Standby Arrangements and Why It Matters*, IMF Pamphlet Series no. 35.

Gold, J. (1980), *Financial Assistance by International Monetary Fund: Law and Practice*, IMF Pamphlet Series no. 27, 2nd edn, p. 20.

Gold, J. (1984), 'The institutional evolution of the IMF', *Finance and Development*, IMF, September, pp. 7–9.

Goldie, L.F.E. (1963), 'Recognition and dual nationality: a problem of the flags of convenience', *British Yearbook of International Law*, p. 200.

Goldie, L.F.E. (1970), 'International principles of responsibility for pollution', *Columbia Journal of Transnational Law*, Autumn.

Goldie, L.F.E. (1975), 'Liability for oil pollution disasters: international law and the delimitation of competencies in federal policy', *Journal of Maritime Law and Commerce*, vol. 6, p. 303.

Gomer, H. (1977), 'Tanker scrapping – a small contribution to a big problem', *Seatrade*, vol. 17, no. 12, December, pp. 41–3.

Gorter, W. (1955), *United States Merchant Marine Policies: Some International Economic Implications*, Essays in International Finance, Princeton, New Jersey: Princeton University Press.

Gorter, W. (1956), *United States Shipping Policy*, for Council of Foreign Relations, New York: Harper & Bros.

Gosele, W. (1979), 'Grandzug des Europaischen Warhrungssystems', *Kredit und Capital*, no. 12. (Summary in English.)

Gosovic (1972), *UNCTAD: Conflict and Compromise*, Leiden: Sithhoff.

Goss, R.O. (1965), 'Investment in shipping and the balance of payments. A case study of import substitution policy', *Journal of Industrial Economics*, March.

Goss, R.O. (1979), *Advances in Maritime Economics*, Cambridge University Press.

Goss, R.O. (1986), 'Some economic aspects of flag discrimination', *Marine Policy and Management*, vol. 13, no. 3, pp. 245–50.

Goss, R.O. (1986), 'Seaports should not be subsidized', *Maritime Policy and Management*, vol. 13, no. 2, pp. 83–104.

Goy, R. (1981), 'Shipping and the European Community' in M.B.F. Ranken (ed.), *Greenwich Forum: World Shipping in the 1990s*, Guildford.

Grant, E. and Horton, P. Jr (1949), *Depreciation*, New York: The Ronald Press Co.

Gray, M. (1979), 'United States: the building of a maritime policy', *Fairplay International Shipping Weekly*, vol. 272, no. 4015, 11 October, pp. 6–11.

Green, C.J. (1980), *Insulating Countries' Exports: An Analysis of Compensatory Financing Schemes*, Discussion Paper no. 16, Department of Economics, Manchester University, April.

Green, P. (1986), 'Growing pressure against switch to Dutch Antilles (Holland flagging out)', *Lloyd's List*, no. 53446, 27 November, p. 3.

Greenwood, R. (1979), 'The negotiations of a code on subsidies and counterveiling measures: bridging fundamental differences',

Law and Policy in International Business, vol. 11, p. 1457.

Greiger, R. (1974), 'The unilateral change of economic development agreements', *International and Comparative Law Quarterly*, vol. 23, pp. 73-104.

Grodan, B.A. (1985), *Africa's Share of Water Resources: Legal and Institutional Aspects*, Boulder and London: Frances Pinter.

Grossman, W.L. (1950), *Ocean Freight Rates*, Cambridge Md.: Cornell Maritime Press.

Grundey, K. (1979), 'Research into flags of convenience at the PLC', *Pynder Leader*, Winter, pp. 21-4.

Guest, A.G. (1974), *Benjamin's Sale of Goods*, 1st edn.

Guitran, M. (1981), *Fund Conditionality: Evolution of Principles and Practices*, Washington DC: IMF Fund Pamphlet no. 38.

Guitran, M. (1980-81), 'Fund conditionality and the international adjustment process', *Finance and Development*, December, March and June.

Hackworth (1943), *International Law*, vol. 5.

Hagberg, L. (ed.) (1983), *Handbook on Maritime Law*: vol. III-A: *Registration of Vessels: Mortgages on Vessels: Argentina–Norway*, written by Members of the Committee on Maritime and Transport Law of the Section on Business Law of the International Bar Association, Kluwer.

Haji, I. (1972), 'UNCTAD and shipping', *Journal of World Trade Law*, vol. 6, p. 58.

Hakkis, C. and Whittaker, J. (1983), 'The US dollar — recent developments, outlook and policy options', *Economic Review*, September–October, pp. 3-15.

Hallberg, C.R. (1978), 'Shipping under flags of convenience: maritime safety aspects', *International Regulation of Maritime Transport*, New York, pp. 231-40.

Hamburg, D. and Schultze, C.L. (1961), 'Autonomous investment v. induced investment', *Economic Journal*, London: Royal Economic Society, March.

Hamilton, M.D. (1985), 'What is the future of exporting?', *Worldwide Shipping*, vol. 48, no. 6, October–November, pp. 42-4.

Hansen, A.H. (1941), *Fiscal Policy and Business Cycles*, New York: W.W. Norton & Co. Inc.

Hansen, A.H. (1947), *Economic Policy and Full Employment*, New York: McGraw-Hill.

Hanson, E.P. (1970), 'Soviet Union and world shipping', *Journal of Soviet Studies*, July.

Hanson, E.P. (1974), *United States Invades Africa*, Harpers, February.

Hanson, J.L. (1977), *A Dictionary of Economics and Commerce*, 5th edn, Macdonald and Evans.

Harberler, S. (1950), *Theory of International Trade with its Application on Commercial Policy*, New York.

Harbride House (1968), *The Balance of Payments and the US Merchant Marine*, Boston.

Hardy, M. (1963), 'The UN and general multilateral treaties concluded under the auspices of the League of Nations', *British Yearbook of International Law*, vol. 39, pp. 425–40.

Harkin, T. (1980), 'International Monetary Fund, band disclosure and basic human needs' in *Hearings* no. 5970, 6 February, pp. 48–58.

Harolds, L.R. (1959), 'Some legal problems arising out of foreign flag operations', *Fordham Law Review*, vol. 28, p. 295.

Harper, D.V. (1978), *Transportation in America: Users, Carriers and Governments*, Prentice Hall.

Harris, J.R. (1967), *Shipping Enterprises and Management 1830–1939*, Liverpool University Press.

Harris, S.E. (1949), *Economic Planning*, New York: Alfred A. Knopf Inc.

Harrods, Sir Roy (1952), *Life of John Maynard Keynes*, London: Macmillan.

Hathron, M.L. (1982), 'The Vessel Documentation Act of 1980', *Maritime Lawyer*, vol. 7, pp. 303–17.

Hattori, K. (1985), 'Analytical review of overtonnaging of large tankers', *Tanuri Report*, no. 10, July.

van Hayek, E.A. (1944), *The Road to Serfdom*, Chicago: The University of Chicago Press.

Hayman, C. (1978), 'Canadian shipowners make their feelings known', *Seatrade*, vol. 8, no. 7, July, p. 15.

Hazard, J.L. (1977), *Transportation Management Economics Policy*, Cambridge, Maryland: Cornell Maritime Press.

Heaton, P.M. (1979), 'In eastern waters', *Sea Breezes*, vol. 53, no. 408, December, pp. 761–5.

Hebden, D.G. (1984), 'The role of government in marine salvage: an international perspective', *New Directions in Maritime Law*, pp. 229–36.

Heine *et al.* (1962), *An Analysis of the Participation of US and Foreign Flags in the Oceanborne Foreign Trade of the US 1928, 1937, 1951-60*, Washington DC: GPO.

Heine *et al.* (1962), *An Analysis of the Ships under Effective US Control, and their Employment in the US Foreign Trade During 1960*, Washington DC: Maritime Administration.

Heine *et al.* (1970), *Effective US Control of Merchant Ships: A Statistical Survey*, Washington DC: GPO.

Helleiner, G. (1978), *World Market Imperfections and the Developing Countries*, Occasional Paper no. 11, Overseas Development Council, May.

Hemphill, W.L. (1974), 'The effect of foreign exchange receipts on imports of less developed countries', *IMF Staff Report*.

Henkin, L. *et al.* (1971), 'The social scientist looks at international law of conflict management', *Proceedings of American Society of International Law*, vol. 65, pp. 1400–15.

Herman, L.L. (1978), 'Flags of convenience — new dimensions to an old problem', *McGill Law Journal*, vol. 24, pp. 1–28.

Hernandez, Y.S. (1960), *Pabellones de Conveniencia* (Flags of Convenience), Barcelona: Canite de Derecho Maritimo.

Hill, J.J.M. (1972), *The Seafaring Career*, London: The Tavistock Institute of Human Relations.

Hindley, B. (1982), *Economic Analysis and Insurance Policy in the Third World*, Thames Essay no. 22, London: Trade Policy Research Centre.

Hindley, B. and Smith, A. (1984), 'Competitive advantage and trade in services', *The World Economy*, December, p. 389.

Hirschman, A.O. (1958), *The Strategy of Economic Development*, New Haven: Yale University Press.

Hlophe, S. (1977), 'A class analysis of the politics of ethnicity of the Tubman and Tolbert administrations in Liberia', paper presented at Liberia Studies Association, Macomb III, 2 April.

Hogan, B. (1983), 'Protectionism talks break up', *Lloyd's List*, no. 52326, 28 March, front page.

Hogan, B. (1983), 'US–Europe deadlock over liner trades', *Lloyd's List*, no. 52328, 30 March, front page.

Hogan, B. (1983), 'MARAD warns of Liner Code repercussions', *Lloyd's List*, no. 52322, 6 April, front page.

Hogan, B. (1983), 'West German ratification of the Liner Code may fuel talks', *Lloyd's List*, no. 52334, 11 April, front page.

Hogan, B. (1985), 'Boat people at the mercy of pirates', *Lloyd's List*, 10 May, p. 4.

Hogan, B. (1985), 'Protectionism hits bulk trade in Third World', *Lloyd's List*, 20 December, p. 4.

Hogan, B. (1986), 'Seafarers seek support for co-ops: lawyer close to first deal in plan for networks of co-operative shipping lines', *Lloyd's List*, 10 January, p. 4.

Hogan, B. (1986), 'Ship registration treaty expected', *Lloyd's List*, 20 January, p. 1.

Hogan, B. (1986), 'UNCTAD close to a treaty on registration', *Lloyd's List*, no. 53193, 30 January, p. 1.

Hogan, B. (1986), 'EEC intervention delays flag treaty', *Lloyd's List*, no. 53197, 4 February, p. 3.

Hogan, B. (1986), 'Numast unhappy about UN registration talks', *Lloyd's List*, no. 53198, 5 February, p. 3.

Hogan, B. (1986), 'Progress on UN ship register treaty', *Lloyd's List*, no. 53199, 6 February, p. 1.

Hogan, B. (1986), 'Ship registration treaty is uncertain of support', *Lloyd's List*, no. 53200, 7 February, p. 1.

Hogan, B. (1986), 'How the UN reached a ship registration treaty', *Lloyd's List*, no. 53202, 10 February, p. 3.

Hogan, B. (1986), 'Owners urged to ignore captive open registries', *Lloyd's List*, no. 53393, 26 September, p. 3.

Hogan, B. (1986), 'Christian Haaland announces reflagging', *Lloyd's List*, no. 53398, 2 October, p. 7.

Hogan, B. (1986), 'Shipping contribution to Danish Exchequer falls', *Lloyd's List*, no. 53419, 27 October, p. 3.

Hogan, B. (1986), 'Radical shipping industry plan to be put to UNCTAD', *Lloyd's List*, no. 53420, 28 October, p. 1.

Hogan, B. (1986), 'Pledge on Liberian register standards', *Lloyd's List*, no. 53436, 15 November, p. 3.

Hogwood, B.W. (1979), *Government and Shipbuilding*, Saxon House.

Hoorn, H., Peet, G. and Wieriks, K. (1985), 'Harmonising North Sea policy in the Netherlands', *Marine Policy*, no. 9, pp. 53–61.

Hope, R. (1967), *Introduction to the Merchant Navy*, 3rd edn, Seafarers' Education Service.

Hope, R. (1976), 'The political economy of marine transportation', *Marine Policy and the Coastal Community*, London: Croom Helm, p. 103.

Hornick, R.N. (1976), *Indonesian Maritime Law*, vol. 8, no. 1, October, pp. 73–85.

Horsely, J. (1980), *Tools of the Maritime Trade*, David and Charles.

Horstmann, H. (1971), *Vor — Und Fruhgeschichte des europaischen Flaggensvessens*, Bremen: Jchunemann.

Hotz, A.J. (1974), 'Legal dilemmas: the Arab–Israel conflict', *South Dakota Law Review*, vol. 19, p. 242.

House of Commons, *Hansard*, vol. 23, col. 726 and vol. 21, col. 708.

House of Lords (1982), *Hansard*, 29 June, cols 163–66.

House of Lords (1983), 'Select Committee Report on the European Communities', HMSO, 12 July.

Hoyle, B.S. and Hilling, D. (1984), *Seaport Systems and Spatial Change*, Wiley.

Hudec, R.E. (1975), *The GATT Legal System and World Diplomacy*, New York.

Hufbanner, G.C. (1980), 'The GATT codes and unconditional MFN et al.: principle', Symposium on Multilateral Trade Agreements, *International Law Journal of Washington University*, vol. 12, no. 1, pp. 59–95.

Hufbanner, G.C. and Scott, J.J. (1980), *Trading for Growth: The*

Next Round of Trade Negotiations, Washington DC: Institute for International Economics.

Hughes, G.R. (1986), 'Nautical institutes' response to economic and social pressures arising from shipping: The President's Address to the 1986 AGM', *Seaways*, July, pp. 3–5.

Humphrey, R.A. 'The open registry phenomena: some economic and political aspects' in *New Trends in Maritime Navigation — The Future of the Law of the Sea and Economy*, pp. 57, 58.

Hunter, A. (1967), 'Some notes on national shipping lines: the Australian case', Leaflet extract from the *Economic Record*, Australia, March.

Hurn (1969), 'Nationalism and internationalism in shipping', *Journal of Transportation Economics and Policy*, vol. 3, no. 5.

Hutchison, M. (1983), 'US intervention policy', *Weekly Letter*, Federal Reserve Bank of San Francisco, 10 June, pp. 1–3.

Huttman, C.H. (1986), 'Exchange market intervention and commercial policy', *Journal of World Trade Law*, vol. 20, no. 3, May–June, pp. 287–93.

Hyde, F. (1967), *Shipping Enterprise and Management, 1830–1939*, Liverpool University Press.

Hyde, J.N. (1962), 'Economic development agreements', *Hague Recueil*, vol. 105, pp. 267–74.

ICHSA (1985), 'Members of Group 5 assess global outlook at meeting in New York', *Joint Communiqué of ICHSA*, Brisbane Biennial Conference, IMF Survey, 7 October, p. 296.

ICHSA (1986), *Trade and Transport Integration*, The Global Challenge, ICHSA 18th Biennial Conference, Brisbane, 11–15 May.

Idle, M. (1978), 'Guyana — caught in IMF trap', *Caribbean Contact*, October.

Indian Department of Transport (1951), *Indian Shipping*, vol. III, no. 4, Bombay, April.

Indian Department of Transport (1980), *Economic and Political Weekly of Bombay*, 22 November.

Indian Department of Transport (1981), *Economic and Political Weekly of Bombay*, 21 February.

Industrial Bank of Japan (1970), 'The economics of shipping', *Survey of Japanese Finance and Industry*, p. 13.

Instituto de Estudios de la Marine Mercante (1961), *Law Marina Mercante Argentina*, Buenos Aires, p. 31.

International Bank for Reconstruction and Development (1967), *IBRD/IDA Annual Report, 1966–67*, pp. 66, 67.

International Bank for Reconstruction and Development (1967), 'Direction of trade', *Annual Report 1966–70*, part B, pp. 5–7.

International Bank for Reconstruction and Development (1981), *Annual Report*, p. 21.

International Bank for Reconstruction and Development (1985), *World Development Report*, p. 126.

International Bank for Reconstruction and Development (1985), *The World Bank, IFC, and IDA Policies and Operations*, April.

International Bank for Reconstruction and Development (1985), *Report on MIGA: Multilateral Investment Guarantee Policy*, September–October.

International Bank for Reconstruction and Development (1986), *Economic Report to the President*, February.

International Chamber of Shipping (1974), *Third UN Conference on the Law of the Sea – Caracas 1974: The Shipping Issues*, London: ICS.

International Court of Justice, *Constitution of the Maritime Safety Committee of the Inter-Governmental Maritime Consultative Organisation 1960*, ICJ Rep. 150.

International Development Agency (1967), *Seventh Annual Report, 1966*, Washington DC.

International Labour Conference (1976), *Report of the Director General* (first item on the agenda) Report no. 1, 62 (maritime) session, Geneva.

International Labour (office) Organization (1926), 'Seamen's Articles of Agreement', *ILO Convention*, no. 22, UNITS vol. 38, p. 295.

International Labour (office) Organization (1946), 'Mandatory Medical Examination (Seafarers)', *ILO Convention 1946*, p. 214; UNITS p. 233.

International Labour (office) Organization (1951), *Conditions in Ships Flying the Panama Flag: Report of the Committee of Enquiry of the International Labour Organization (ILO)*, London, May–November 1949.

International Labour (office) Organization (1956), 'Hours of Work (Industry), ILO Convention 1919', *Conventions and Recommendations*, p. 1.

International Labour (office) Organization (1983), *Conventions des recommendations sur le travail maritime*, Geneva.

International Labour Organization (n.d.), 'Multilateral Convention (no. 9) for Establishing Facilities for Finding Employment for Seamen'; 'Convention Concerning Continuity of Employment' (Convention no. 145 of 1976); 'Recommendation Concerning Continuity of Employment of Seafarers' (Recommendation 154 of 1976).

International Labour Organization (1976), 'ILO Convention and Recommendation concerning Minimum Standards in Merchant Ships', *International Legal Materials*, vol. 15, p. 1288.

International Maritime Associates (1979), *Economic Impact of Open Registry Shipping*, Washington DC.

International Maritime Associates (1979), *Economic Impact of Open Registry Shipping*, Commissioned by the Bureau of Maritime Studies, Ministry of Finance, Republic of Liberia.

International Monetary Fund (n.d.), *International Financial Statistics*, Annual.

International Monetary Fund (1961), *Balance of Payments Manual*, 3rd edn, July, Washington DC.

International Monetary Fund (1980), *World Economic Outlook*, Washington DC, May.

International Monetary Fund (1980), *Balance of Payments Yearbook*, vols 13 and 31, December.

International Monetary Fund (1981), *IMF Survey*, 22 June.

International Monetary Fund (1981), *Annual Report on Exchange Arrangements and Exchange Restrictions*, Washington DC.

International Monetary Fund (1981), *Proceedings of the 2nd International Monetary Conference*, Global Independence Centre, Philadelphia, 16 November 1980, Washington DC: IMF.

International Monetary Fund (1983), 'Studies of foreign exchange market intervention', *IMF Survey*, 9 May, pp. 137-8.

International Monetary Fund (1983), *Balance of Payments Statistics Yearbook*, vol. 34, part 2, Washington DC.

International Monetary Fund (1985), *Balance of Payments Statistics Yearbook*, parts I and II.

Ion, E. (1986), 'How South Africa has coped with the oil embargo', *Lloyd's List*, no. 53385, 17 September, p. 3.

Ion, E. (1986), 'Five of OSA's vessels to switch flag', *Lloyd's List*, no. 53407, 13 October, p. 1.

Jagota, S.P. (1984), 'India and the Law of the Sea', *Archive des Valkerrechts*, vol. 22, pp. 29-68.

Jamal, A. (1980), 'Opening Address by the Chairman of the Fund — World Bank Board of Governors', *Third World News Forum*, March.

Jantscher, G. (1975), *Bread Upon the Waters: Federal Aid to Maritime Industries*, Washington DC: The Brookings Institution.

Japanese Shipowners' Association (1970), *Review of Japanese Shipping 1970*.

Jenks, C.W. (1937), 'Nationality, the flag and registration: criteria for demarcating the scope of maritime conventions', *Journal of Comparative Legislation and International Law*, vol. 19, 3rd series, p. 245.

Jenks, C.W. (1937), 'The significance of the international tripartite character of the International Labour Organisation', *Transactions of the Grotius Society*, vol. 22, p. 45.

Johnson, D.H.N. (1959), 'The nationality of ships', *Indian Yearbook of International Law*, vol. 8, p. 3.

Johnson, H.G. (1985), 'Enhancing the effectiveness of surveillance', *Finance and Development*, pp. 2–6.

Johnson, H.G. and Cares, R.E. (eds) (1958), *Readings in International Economics*, Homewood, Ill.: Richard D. Irwin.

Johnson, O.S.J. (1980), 'Stabilisation programmes and income distribution', *Finance and Development*, December, pp. 28–31.

Johnson, O.S.J. and Salop, J. (1980), 'Distribution aspects of stabilization programmes in developing countries', *IMF Staff Paper*, no. 27, March.

Jones, C. (1922), *British Merchant Shipping*, London: Edward Arnold & Co.

Joyner, C.C. (1974), 'Latin America's communal response to energy crisis', The Latin American Energy Organisation (OLADE), *Lawyer of Americas*, vol. 6, pp. 637–61.

Juda, L. (1981), 'World shipping, UNCTAD, and the New International Economic Order', *International Organization*, vol. 35, pp. 493, 494.

Kadoi, T. (1980), 'Shipbuilding under reduced facilities', *Zosen*, vol. 24, no. 11, February, pp. 17–19.

Kahn, H. (1960), *Personal Deductions in the Federal Income Tax*, National Bureau of Economic Research Inc. New Jersey: Princeton University Press.

Karmel, R.S. (1961), 'Labour law, international law and the Panlibho fleet', *New York University Law Review*, vol. 3, 1961, p. 1342.

Karreman, H.F. (1958), *Review of Economics and Statistics*, February (supplement).

Karreman, H.F. (1961), 'Methods of improving world transport accounts applied 1950–53', *Technical Paper 15*, USA: National Bureau of Economic Research.

Keezer, D.M. (1969), *New Forces in American Business*, New York: McGraw-Hill.

Kelly, M. (1980), 'Fiscal content of financial programmes supported by SBA in the upper credit tranches, 1969–1978', *IMF Staff Paper*, vol. 27, no. 2, June.

Kelso, L. and Adler, M.J. (1958), *The Capitalist Manifesto*, New York: Random House.

Kendall, L.C. (1974), *The Business of Shipping*, Cambridge, Maryland: Cornell Maritime Press.

Kendall, L.C. (1979), 'The modern American merchant marine', *US Naval Institute Proceedings*, October, pp. 70–6.

Kennedy, J.O.S. (1986), 'Australian fisheries management: industrial transferable quotas for southern blue fin tuna', *Marine Policy Reports*, vol. 8, no. 4, p. 6.

Keynes, J.M. (1923), 'Free trade and underemployment', *Nation and Athenaeum*, November.

Keynes, J.M. (1926), *The End of Laissez-Faire*, London: L. & V. Wolf.

Keynes, J.M. (n.d.), *Treatise on Money*, London: Macmillan, vol. 1.

Keynes, J.M. (1931), 'Proposals for a revenue tariff', *New Statesman and Nation*, London, 7 March.

Keynes, J.M. (1931), 'Letter to the *Times*', 29 September.

Keynes, J.M. (1936), *General Theory of Employment, Interest and Money*.

Kibola, H.S. (1985), 'Stabex and Home Ill', *Journal of World Trade Law*, vol. 18, no. 1, January–February, pp. 32-51.

Kilgour, J.G. (1975), 'Double subsidy issue in shipping', *Journal of Maritime Law and Commerce*, vol. 4, no. 6, pp. 395-407.

Kilgour, J.G. (1976), 'The Energy Transportation Security Act 1974', *Journal of Maritime Law and Commerce*, vol. 7, p. 557.

Kilgour, J.G. (1977), 'Effective United States control', *Journal of Maritime Law and Commerce*, vol. 8, p. 377.

Killick, T. (1981), *IMF Stabilization Programmes*, Working Paper no. 6, London: Overseas Development Institute.

Killick, T. (1982), *The Impact of IMF Stabilization Programmes in Developing Countries*, Working Paper no. 7, London: Overseas Development Institute.

Kincaid, C. (1986), 'Wallsend site to be closed by end of year', *The Times*, 15 May, p. 11.

Kindleberger, C.P. (1958), *International Economics*, New York: Macmillan.

Klett, D. (1986), 'The US Tariff Act: Section 337', *Journal of World Trade Law*, vol. 20, no. 3, May-June, pp. 294-312.

Knudsen, O. (1973), *The Politics of International Shipping*, New York: Lexington Books.

Kreimin, M.E. and Finger, J.M. (1976), 'A critical survey of the New International Economic Order', *Journal of World Trade Law*, vol. 10, pp. 493-572.

Kreussler, H. (1978), 'Auslvirkungen der Dollar Kursverluste auf die deutsche Seeschiffahrt', *Hansa*, no. 19, pp. 1588-91.

Krimow, P. (1985), *New York Times*, 2 October, p. D1.

Krzeezkowaski, E. (1966), 'Sraveniia natsional nogo dokhoda PNR i nekotorykh evropeiskikh stran' (Comparisons of national incomes of PPR and certain European countries), *Vestnik Statistik*, no. 2, Moscow, p. 37.

Krzyzanowski, Prof. M. (1972), 'Preinvestment studies in shipping as a form of assistance to developing countries', *Preinvestment Studies in Maritime Studies*, Southampton Institute of Maritime Law.

Kurani, P. (ed.) (1983), *Bombay: Shipping Handbook*, Bombay Shipping and Allied Services.

Kust, M.J. (1964), *Foreign Enterprise in India: Law and Policies*, Chapel Hill: University of Carolina Press.

Kvasnicka, J. (1985), 'Central banks move to halt the dollar rise', *International Letter*, Federal Reserve Bank of Chicago, 8 March, pp. 1-3.

Kwik, K.H. (1986), 'Collision rates as a danger criterion for marine traffic', *Journal of Navigation*, vol. 39, May, pp. 203-12.

Laishley, R. and Bruley, T. (1980), 'What future for flags of convenience?', *African Business*, March, pp. 13-14.

Landauer, C. (1947), *The Theory of National Economic Planning*, 2nd edn, Berkley, California: University of California Press.

Lansing, J. (1966), *Transportation and Economic Policy*, New York: Free Press.

Lansing, R. (1921), *Notes on Sovereignty from the Standpoint of the State and the World*, Washington DC: Carnegie Endowment for International Peace.

de Larosiere, J. (1980), Address to the 1980 Symposium on *Monetary Theory and Policy in Africa*, Dakar, January.

de Larosiere, J. (1982), 'Export subsidies and developing countries', *Finance and Development*.

Larsen, B. and Vetterick, V. (1981), 'The UNCTAD Code for Liner Conferences — reservations, reactions and US alternatives', *Law and Policy in International Business*, vol. 13, pp. 223-80.

Latin American Free Trade Association (1966), 'Convenion de Transporte por Agna de la Associacion Latinamericana de libre Comercio' (Convention on Transport by Water), drawn up at Montevideo, 30 September 1966.

Lawistoski, J. (1985), 'Limitation of liability for stevedores and terminal operators under the Carriers' Bill of Lading and Carriage of Goods by Sea', *Journal of Maritime Law and Commerce*, vol. 16, pp. 3377-8.

Lawrence, S.A. (1966), *United States Merchant Shipping Politics and Policies*, Washington DC: Brookings Institution.

Lawrence, S.A. (1972), *US Merchant Shipping Policy and Politics*, Washington DC: Brookings Institution.

Lawrence, S.A. (1972), *International Sea Transport: The Years Ahead*, Lexington Books.

League of Nations (1931), 'The comparative study of national laws concerning the granting of the right to fly the merchant flag', *League of Nations Official Journal*, vol. 12, p. 1631.

Learner, A.P. (1951), *Economics of Employment*, New York: McGraw-Hill.

Lebuhn, J. (1981), 'Practising CIF and FOB today', *European Transportation Law*, vol. 16, no. 1, pp. 24–36.

Lec, S.H. (1986), 'Distant water nations' response to extended fisheries jursidiction: the case of South Korea', *Maritime Policy Reports*, vol. 6, no. 5, p. 6.

Legion, R. (1980), 'Shipping and the EEC', *Seaways*, October, pp. 13–16.

Levin, A.H. (1980), *National Transportation Policy, a Study of Studies*, Lexington Books.

Levy, H. (1977), 'US liner shipping policy', *International Container Industry Conference Proceedings*, November, pp. 17–22; 80–81.

Lewis, B.W. (1951), 'The nationalisation of British industry', *Law and Contemporary Problems*, Durham: Duke University School of Law, Autumn.

Lewis, W.A. (1955), *The Theory of Economic Growth*, London: Allen and Unwin.

Liberian Shipping Corporation (1984), 'Is the Convention on Registration really necessary?', *UNCTAD Registration of Ships Conference*.

Lillich, R.B. and Moore, J.N. (1980), *Readings in International Law*, Newport.

Lloyd, I.S. (1961), *The Times*, 5 and 6 July.

Lloyds of London (1979), *Lloyd's Nautical Yearbook 1979*.

Lloyds of London (n.d.), *Calendar and National Yearbook*, Annual, London: Lloyds of London Press.

Lloyds of London Press (1987), 'Survey 1986', *Lloyds Ship Manager*.

Lloyd's Register of Shipping (n.d.) *Annual Register of Shipping Statistics*.

Lloyd's Register of Shipping (1973), *Shipping Statistical Tables*.

Lloyd's Register of Shipping (1985), *Annual Report*.

Lopez, N.J. (1985), 'A training treaty to tame the laws (Convention on standards of training, certification and watch keeping for seafarers)', *Asian Shipping*, December, pp. 19–22.

Lopez, N.J. (1986), 'Mariner's view (crewing, manning, certification)', *Asian Shipping*, January, pp. 19–20.

Lopez, N.J. (1986), 'The Hong Kong Register of Shipping – general principles examined', *Asian Shipping*, November, pp. 21–5.

Macgregor, D.R. (1980), *Merchant Sailing Ships 1775-1815*, Model and Allied.

MacGuire, C.J. and McDaniel, R.E. (1981), 'Conquering the maze: a proposed reorganisation of the US shipping laws', *Proceedings of the Maritime Safety Council*, vol. 38, no. 4, pp. 93–9.

Machlup, F. (1949), 'The theory of foreign exchanges' in E.H. Ellis and L.A. Metzler, *Readings in the Theory of International Trade*, New York: McGraw-Hill.

Madigan, R.E. (1982), *Taxation of the Shipping Industry*, Cornell Maritime Press.

Makarcyzyk, J. (ed.) (1984), *Essays in International Law in Honour of Judge Manfred Lachs*, The Hague.

Malinowski, W.R. (1972), 'Towards a change in international distribution of shipping', *International Conciliation*, no. 582, March.

Malinowski, W.R. (1972), 'Changing political climate in which the UNCTAD Committee on Shipping has worked since its formation', *Preinvestment Studies in Maritime Transport*, Southampton Institute of Maritime Law.

Mangrove, G.J. (1977), *Marine Policy for America*, Lexington Books.

Mankabady, S. (1973), 'Rights and immunities of the carrier's servants or agents', *Journal of Maritime Law and Commerce*, vol. 5, p. 111.

Manning, H.J. (1967), 'Liberia exploits the flags of convenience practice', *Bulletin of the African Institute of South Africa*, vol. 15, nos 5-6, pp. 186-90.

Marens, H.S. (1972), *Ocean Transportation*, Cambridge, Mass.: MIT Press.

Marshall, A. (1986), 'Owners welcome new Norwegian register plan', *Lloyd's List*, no. 53304, 13 June, p. 3.

Marston, G. (1986), 'The UN Convention on Registration of Ships', *Journal of World Trade Law*, vol. 20, no. 5, October–November, pp. 573-8.

Maruno, Y.O. (1978), *Practice and Law of International Ship Finance*, unpublished PhD thesis, Southampton University.

Marx, D. (1953), *International Shipping Cartels: A Study of Industrial Regulation by Shipping Conferences*, New York: Greenwood Press.

Mason, G.W. (1975), 'Regulation of public policy and efficient provision of freight transportation', *Transport Journal*, Autumn.

Mayer, C. (1986), 'Liberia makes cuts in ship register fees', *Lloyd's List*, no. 53372, 4 September, p. 1.

Mayer, C. (1986), 'Sea docks registry may collapse', *Lloyd's List*, no. 53437, 17 November, p. 1.

McCallum, J. and Middleton, I. (1986), 'Never mind the politics — what about the economy?', *Seatrade*, February, pp. 4-7.

McCarnell, M.L. (1985), 'Darkening confusion mounted upon darkenin confusion: the search for the elusive genuine link', *Journal of Maritime Law and Commerce*, vol. 16, pp. 365-96.

McConnell, J.M.L. (1985), 'UN Conference on the Convention for Registration of Ships', *Journal of Maritime Law and Commerce*, vol. 16, no. 3, p. 10.

McConville, J. (1977), *The Shipping Industry in the United Kingdom*, Research Series no. 26, International Institute for Labour Studies.

McDougal, M.S., Burke and Vlasic (1960), 'The maintenance of public order at sea and the nationality of ships', *American Journal of International Law*, pp. 25, 104.

McDougal, M.S. and Burke (1962), *The Public Order of the Oceans*.

McDowell, C.E. and Gibbs, H.B. (1954), *Ocean Transportation*, New York: McGraw-Hill.

McKinnon, R. (1985), *Exchange Stability, International Monetary Co-ordination, and the US Federal Reserve System*.

McKinnon, R. (1985), 'How open is the US economy?', *10th Annual Economic Policy Conference*, Federal Reserve Bank of St Louis, 11–12 October.

McLachlan, D.L. (1963), 'The price policy of liner conferences', *Scottish Journal of Political Economy*, vol. 10, November.

McWhinney, E. (1976), 'The international law making process and the New International Economic Order', *Canadian Yearbook of International Law*, vol. 14, pp. 57–72.

Meade, J.E. (1955), *Trade and Welfare*, Oxford University Press.

Meade, J.E. (1958), *Planning and the Price Mechanism: The Liberal-Socialist Solution*, New York: Macmillan.

Meir, G. (1964), *Leading Issues in Development Economics*, Oxford University Press.

Mendoza, R.G. (1979), 'Currency fluctuations in the shipping industry — banker's view', *Money and Ships, 1979*, transcript, London.

Mensah, J.H. (1973), 'Some unpleasant truths about debt and development', *Development Dialogue*, pp. 3–16.

Mercantile Marine Service Association (1951), *Ninety-Fourth Annual Report*.

Merchant, A.J. and Sykes (1963), *The Finance and Analysis of Capital Projects*, London: Longmans.

Mervis, C.D. (1976), 'The United Nations Seventh Special Session: Proposals for a New World Economic Order', *The Vanderbilt Journal of Transnational Law*, vol. 9, pp. 601–39.

Metaxas, B.N. (1971), *Economics of Tramp Shipping*.

Metaxas, B.N. (1973), 'OECD study of the flags of convenience', *Journal of Maritime Law and Commerce*, vol. 4, pp. 231–54.

Metaxas, B.N. (1978), 'Notes on the internalization process in the maritime sectors', *Maritime Policy and Management*, January.

Metaxas, B.N. (1978), *Flags of Convenience*, Discussion Paper no. 8, Transport Studies Group, Polytechnic of Central London, November.

Metaxas, B.N. (1983), *Buy the Flag: Developments in the Open Registry Debate*, Discussion Paper no. 13, Transport Studies Group, Polytechnic of Central London, August.

Middleton, I. and Renouf, A. (1979), 'Washington doors close', *Seatrade*, vol. 10, no. 10, November, pp. 691–701.

Mikesell, R.F. (1954), *Foreign Exchange in the Postwar World*, New York: The Twentieth Century Fund.

Min, B.K. and West, J.M. (1985), 'Limitation of shipowners' liability under the commercial code of Korea', *Journal of Maritime Law and Commerce*, col. 16, pp. 21–37.

van Misco, L. (1936), *Socialism and Economic and Social Analysis*, New York: Macmillan.

Mitchell, B.R. (1981), *European Historical Statistics 1750–1975*, 2nd revised edn, Macmillan.

Mogridge, B., 'Labour relations and labour costs' in S.G. Sturmey (ed.), *British Shipping and World Competition*, The Athlen Press, University of London, pp. 283–321.

Mookerjee, S. (1979), 'New guidelines for use of fund resources — following review of practice of conditionality', *IMF Survey*, vol. 8, 19 March.

Moore, J.N. (1979), 'Flags of convenience', *New Trends in Maritime Navigation*, Proceedings of the 4th International Ocean Symposium, Ocean Association of Japan 1979, pp. 69, 70, 71.

Moore, K.A. (1980), 'Development of USSR and CMEA shipping', *GREENWICH FORM VI World Shipping in the 1990s*, Records of a Conference at the Royal Naval College, Greenwich, 23–25 April 1980, Westbury House, Guildford.

Morgan, J.P. (1981), 'IMF Survey — a modest little bank', *The Economist*, 26 September.

Morris, M.A. (1979), *International Politics and the Sea*, Boulder, Colorado: Westview Press.

Morris, M.A. (1986), *The Law of Seamen*, 4th edn, Rochester, San Francisco: Lawyers' Co-operative Publication, Bancroft — Whitney.

Moses, E. (1983), 'The UNCTAD 40:40:20 Convention. Should Israel join or not?', *Sapanut*, vol. 13, no. 1, Summer, pp. 1–5.

Mott, D. (1983), 'UNCTAD Code will lead to trade war', *Lloyd's List*, no. 52373, 25 May, p. 3.

Mott, D. (1985), 'New navy transfer scheme to be launched for merchant navy officers', *Lloyd's List*, 17 December, p. 2.

Mott, D. (1986), 'Norwegian seamen plan attack on UN ship treaty', *Lloyd's List*, no. 53205, 13 February, p. 1.

Mott, D. (1986), 'Ten man crew is proposed by Norway owner', *Lloyd's List*, 17 February, p. 1.

Mott, D. (1986), 'Register plan may be advanced: warning of RCCL reflagging', *Lloyd's List*, no. 53446, 27 November, p. 1.

Mott, D. (1986), 'UK owner warns over the rate of flagging out', *Lloyd's List*, no. 53422, 22 December, p. 1.

Moyer, C.N.A. (1974), 'A critique of the rationales for present US maritime programmes', *Transportation Journal*, Winter.

Muller, M. (1986), 'Strikes: strikes of crew members supported by the ITF held unlawful by Dutch Court applying Philippine law: "The Saudi Independence"', *Journal of Maritime Law and Commerce*, vol. 16, pp. 423-6.

Munby, D. (1968), *Transportation: Selected Readings*, Baltimore: Penguin Books.

Mundell, R.A. (1952), 'A geometry of transport costs in international trade theory', *Canadian Journal of Economics and Political Science*, August, pp. 331-48.

Murase, S. (1976), 'The MFN in Japan treaty practice during the period 1854-1905', *American Journal of International Law*, vol. 70, pp. 273-987.

Musgrave, R.A.A. (1959), *A Theory of Public Finance*, New York: McGraw-Hill.

Myles, J. *et al.* (1962), *The Political Order of the Oceans*, Yale University Press.

Naess, E.D. (1972), *The Great Panlibho Controversy — The Fight over Flags of Convenience*, Gower Press.

Nakamura, G. (1980), 'Diversification in Japanese shipbuilding industries', *Zosen*, vol. 24, no. 11, February, pp. 84-7.

Napier, D. *et al.* (1982), *Multinational Transport in Canadian International Trade*, Research Branch, Transport Industries Analysis, Canadian Transport Commission.

National Board for Prices and Incomes (1967), *Pay and Conditions of Merchant Navy Officers presented to (HE) Parliament by the First Secretary of State and Secretary of State for Economic Affairs and the Minister for Labour*, report no. 35, London: HMSO, June.

National Board for Prices and Incomes (n.d.), *Pay and Conditions of Merchant Navy Officers*, Cmnd 3302, report no. 35, London: HMSO.

National Dock Labour Board (1964), *The Place of the Shipping Industry in the National Economy*, Derek Bibby.

National Dock Labour Board (1967), *The Dock Worker Employment Scheme*.

National Dock Labour Board (1975), *Annual Report and Accounts 1975*.

'National Income', *Polish Perspectives*, Warsaw, February 1967, p. 50.

National Maritime Board (1964), *Yearbook 1964*.

National Maritime Board (1978), *Yearbook 1976-7* (Summary of Agreements).

National Ports Council (1973), *Annual Digest of Port Statistics*.

National Union of Seamen (1981), *Flags of Convenience: The Unacceptable Face of Shipping*, London.

Nautical Institute (1979), *Conference on International Shipping*, London.

Neubecker, O. and Wappenbilder, W.R. (1974), *Lexikon*, Munich: Battenberg.

Nilson, C.H. (1968), *Guide to the Merchant Navy*, Glasgow: Brown, Low and Ferguson.

Norman, D.R. (1984), 'Has something been lost? An analysis of a seldom utilised concept in maritime law', *Loyola Law Review*, vol. 30, pp. 875-900.

North, H.R. (1986), 'Norway's shipowners in call for dual register', *Lloyd's List*, no. 53304, 13 June, p. 3.

North, H.R. (1986), 'Norwegian flagging out approval likely', *Lloyd's List*, no. 53308, 18 June, p. 1.

North, H.R. (1986), 'Norway owners applaud move on flagging out', *Lloyd's List*, no. 53384, 16 September, p. 1.

North, H.R. (1986), 'Exodus of ships from Norwegian flag', *Lloyd's List*, no. 53419, 27 October, p. 3.

North, H.R. and Watt, D. (1986), 'Ten man crew is proposed by Norway owner', *Lloyd's List*, 17 February, p. 1.

Northrup, H.R. and Rowan, R.L. (1983), *The International Transport Workers Federation and the Flags of Convenience*, Philadelphia: Shipping Industrial Research Unit, Wharton School, University of Pennsylvania.

Norton, H.S. (1971), *Modern Transportation Economics*, 2nd edn, Columbus, Ohio: Charles E. Merrill Publishing Co.

Nyerere, J.K. (1980), 'Speech to diplomats on 1 January 1980', *Third World News Forum*, March.

O'Connell, D.P. (1969-70), 'The Federal problem concerning the maritime domain in Commonwealth countries', *Journal of Maritime Law and Commerce*, vol. 1, no. 1, October, pp. 441-2.

Odier, F. (1979), 'La Code de Condiute des Conferences Maritimes', *Française de Droit International*, pp. 686-92.

OECD (n.d.), *Maritime Transport*, Annual Reports.

OECD (1950), *Statistics of Balance of Payments*, Paris.

OECD (1968), *Ocean Freight Rates as Part of the Total Transport Costs*, Doc. no. MT (68), 7 May.

OECD (1979), *Committee of Exports on Restrictive Business Practices, Competition Policy in Regulated Sectors with Special Reference to Transport and Banking*, Paris.

OEEC (1958), *Study on the Expansion of the Flags of Convenience*

Fleets and Various Aspects Thereof, Doc. no. C (57) 246, 28 January.

OEEC (1961), *Maritime Transport*, Annual Report 1953–1961.

Olof, H. (1956), *Flag Discriminations, Purposes, Motives, and Economic Consequences*, Publication no. 3, Swedish School of Economics.

O'Loughlin, C. (1967), *Economics of Sea Transport*, 1st edn, Oxford: Pergamon Press.

Oribe-Stemmer, J.E. (1978), 'Flag preference in Latin America', *Journal of Maritime Law and Commerce*, vol. 10, October, pp. 123–34.

O'Sullivan (1980), *Transportation Policy: An Interdisciplinary Approach*, Barnes and Nobles.

O'Sullivan (1980), *Transportation Policy: Geographic, Economic and Planning Aspects*, Barnes and Nobles.

Otterson, J.E. (1945), *Foreign Trade and Shipping*.

Pallua, E. (1983), 'The nationality of ships in Yugoslavia law with reference to the present international developments', *Essays on International and Comparative Law in Honour of Judge Erades*, The Hague, pp. 123–33.

Parton, D. (1980), 'Swedish yards on the brink — but where there is life . . . ', *Seatrade*, vol. 10, no. 2, February, pp. 65–7.

Paul, J. (1986), 'The impact of port changes on shipping freight rates', *Dock and Harbour Authority*, vol. 66, no. 777, March, pp. 256–60.

Pawson, W.R. (1970), 'Resource allocation and integration in the Central American common market', *New York University Journal of International Law and Politics*, vol. 3, pp. 107–35.

Pearson, C.S. (1975), *International Marine Environment Policy: The Economic Dimension*, Baltimore: Johns Hopkins University Press.

Pearson, J. (1981), 'Shipping and the EEC', *Seaways*, July, pp. 11–15.

Pearson, R. and Fossey, J. (1983), *World Deep-Sea Container Shipping*, University of Liverpool Press.

Pedersen, C. (1971), *The International Flag Book in Colour*, New York: Morrow.

Pedohl, A. (1950), *Verkehrspolitik*, Gottingen.

Pegrum, D.F. (1973), *Transportation: Economics and Public Policy*, 3rd edn, Homewood, Ill.: R.D. Irwin.

Pelczynski, Dr Z. (1972), 'Possibilities to adopt Socialist planning methods to the programming of shipping and ports expansion by the developing countries', *Pre-investment Studies in Maritime Transport*, Southampton Institute of Maritime Law.

Perry, M.W. (1976), 'US foreign policy and emerging legal policy issues of technology transfer', *Proceedings of the American Society of International Law*, vol. 70, pp. 1–10.

Phillips, A. (ed.) (1975), *Promoting Competition in Regulated Markets*, Washington DC: Brookings Institution.

Phillips, F. (1980), 'The innovative line', *Containerisation*, vol. 14, no. 3, March, pp. 26–30.

Piffer, L. (1951), *The Closing of the Public Domain*, Stanford, California: Stanford University Press.

Pigou, A.C. (1937), *Socialism and Capitalism*, London: Macmillan.

Pinar, M. (1986), 'Transportation cost subsidies: a criterion for policy to promote international trade', *Journal of World Trade Law*, vol. 18, no. 3, May–June, pp. 224–35.

Pine, A.W. (1986), 'Group of five states meeting next weekend', *Wall Street Journal*, 13 January, p. 28.

Pine, A.W. (1986), 'Cities change the IMF losses: its rules forcing borrowers to shape up', *Wall Street Journal*, 21 September.

Plowman, P. (1981), *Passenger Ships of Australia and New Zealand*, vols 1 and 2, 1930–1980, Conway.

Plymouth Polytechnic, Learning Resources Centre (n.d.), *Maritime Studies, Current Awareness Bulletin* (fortnightly).

Polonska, P. (1978), *Ocean Politics in South-East Asia*, Singapore Institute of South East Asian Studies.

Powell, R.A. (1978), 'New developments in taxation of shipping under flags of convenience', *International Regulation of Maritime Transportation*, New York, pp. 211–29.

Pratt, E.E. (1956), *Modern International Commerce*, Boston: Allyn and Bascon Inc.

Pratt, E.E. (1965), *Modern International Commerce*, reprint, Boston: Allyn and Bascon Inc.

Pratt, F. (1934), 'Commerce destruction, past, present and future', *US Naval Institute Proceedings*, vol. 54, p. 1513.

Prescott, J.R.V. (1985), *Australia's Maritime Boundaries*, Canberra: Australia National University, Department of International Relations.

Press, J. (1979), 'The collapse of the contributory pension scheme', *Transportation History*, vol. 5, no. 2, September, pp. 91–115.

Price, D.E. (1986), 'Sanctions on South Africa, implications for shipping', *Asian Shipping*, September, pp. 43–4.

Puri, R. (1985), *India and National Jurisdiction in the Sea*, New Delhi: ABC Publications House.

Puty, J. (1979), 'To scrap or not to scrap?', *Nautical Review*, vol. 3, no. 3, March, pp. 5–7.

Quandt, R.E. (1959), *The New Inflation*, New York: McGraw Hill Book Co.

Radius, W.A. (1944), *US Shipping in the Transpacific Trade, 1922–1938*, Palo Alto.

Rajwar, L.M.S. (1971), *Shipping and Developing Countries*, International Conciliation no. 582, Carnegie Endowment for International Peace.

Rakowski, M. (1966), *Efficiency of Investment in a Socialist Economy*, London and Warsaw: Pergamon Press.

Ramsay, R.A. (1978), 'Organisation of shipping', *Ocean Yearbook I*, Chicago, p. 211 ff.

Ramsay, R.A. (1980), 'World trade versus the supply of shipping and ships', *Marine Policy*, vol. 4, no. 1, January, pp. 63–7.

Randall, H. (1947), *Keynesian Commercial Policy*, London: Dobson.

Ranis, G. and Fei, J.C.H. (1964), *Development of the Labour Surplus: Theory and Policy*, Homewood, Ill.: R.D. Irwin.

Ranken, M.B.F. (ed.) (1980), *Greenwich Forum VI: World Shipping in the 1990s*, Guildford.

Rather, D. (1975), 'The best congress money can buy', *CBS News Reports*, 31 January.

Raymond, F.M. (1954), *Foreign Exchange in the Postwar World*, New York: Twentieth Century Fund.

Reichman, T.M. (1978), 'The Fund's conditional assistance and problems of adjustment 1973–1975', *Finance and Development*, December, pp. 38–41.

Reichman, T.M. and Stillson, R.T. (1978), 'Experience with programmes of balance of payments adjustments: stand-by arrangements in higher credit tranches, 1963–1972', *IMF Staff Papers*, June, pp. 293–309.

Reitze, I.F. (1980), *Wahrungszuschlage in der Schiffahrt und ihre Auswirkungen auf die Exportwirtschaft Forschungsinstitut für Wirtschaftspolitik an der Universität Mainz*.

Renouf, A. (1978), 'Under-rated dollar — over-rated problems', *Seatrade*, September, pp. 3–4.

Republic of Liberia (1957), *Liberia Code of Laws of 1956 Adopted by the Legislature of the Republic of Liberia, 22 March 1956*, New York: Ithaca/Cornell Maritime Press.

Republic of Liberia (1972), *Liberia — 25 Years as a Maritime Nation*, Monrovia: International Trust Company.

Revel, M.D. (1979), 'Financial needs and trends of international shipping', *Maritime Management*, vol. 2, no. 2, March, pp. 7–10.

Reynolds, N. (1985), 'Shipping interests must meet fundamental requirements to successfully finance projects', *Fairplay International Shipping Weekly*, 19–26 December, p. 28.

Ricardo, D. (1917), *Principles of Political Economy and Taxation*, New York: Everyman's Library.

Rich, G. (1978), 'The Plymouth experience', *European Shipping and Shipbuilding* (Conference Proceedings), pp. 51-74.

Richardson, H.J. (1960), *The Economics and Financial Aspects of Social Security*, University of Toronto Press.

Rienow, R. (1937), *The Test of the Nationality of a Merchant Vessel*, New York: Columbia University Press.

Rinman, T. and Linden, R. (1978), 'The political environment in shipping', *Shipping, How it Works*, Kingsbackar: Elanders Boktryckeri AB, pp. 141-8.

Robertson, D.W. (1985), 'Current problems in seamen's remedies: seamen's status, relationship between Jones Act and LHWCA, and unseamanworthiness actions by workers not covered by LHWCA', *Louisiana Law Review*, vol. 45, pp. 875-906.

Robinson, M.A. and Lawson, R. (1986), 'Some reflections on aid to fisheries in West Africa', *Marine Policy*, vol. 10, pp. 101-10.

Rohreke, H.G. (1961), *The Formula and Material Concept of Flag*, Bergen: Institute of Shipping Economics.

Rom, M. (1985), 'Export controls in GATT', *Journal of World Trade Law*, vol. 18, no. 2, March-April, pp. 125-54.

Romans, T.J. (1963), 'The American merchant marine — flags of convenience and international law', *Virginia Journal of International Law*, vol. 3, p. 121.

Rose, F.D. (1982), 'Merchant Shipping (Liner Conferences) Act 1982 — annotated', *Current Law Statutes* Annotated 1982, Sweet and Maxwell.

Rosenstein, P.N. (1943), 'Problems of industrialisation of Eastern and South-Eastern Europe', *The Economic Journal*, June.

Rosenthal, A. (1975), 'The Charter of Economic Rights and Duties of States and the New International Economic Order', *Virginia Journal of International Law*, vol. 16, pp. 309-53.

Rowlinson, M. (1985), 'Flags of convenience: the UNCTAD case', *Maritime Policy and Management*, vol. 12, pp. 241-4.

Rubenowitz, S. (1977), *The Shipping Industry in Sweden*, Strategic Factors in Industrial Relations Systems, Research Series no. 25, Geneva: International Institute for Labour Studies.

Rubin, A.P. (1977), 'The international legal aspects of unilateral declarations', *American Journal of International Law*, vol. 71, pp. 1-30.

Rubin, S.J. (1966), *The Conscience of the Rich Nations, The Development Assistance Committee and the Common Aids Efforts*, New York: Harper and Row.

Rubin, S.J. (1975), 'The Charter of Economic Rights and Duties of States', *Proceedings of the American Society of International Law*, vol. 69, pp. 225-46.

Sager, K.H. (1978), 'Russia has signed the UNCTAD (Liner) Code, but will she ratify?', *Norwegian News*, no. 17, 1 September, pp. 8–11.

Sampson, R.J. (ed.) (1968), *Proceedings on the Colloquium Series on Transportation 1967-68*, Winnipeg: Centre for Transportation Studies, University of Manitoba.

Samuelson, P.A. (1961), *Economics*, 5th edn, New York: McGraw-Hill.

Sanklecha, S.N. (1967), 'Development of Indian shipping and foreign exchange earnings', *Foreign Trade Review*, New Delhi: Indian Institute of Foreign Trade, July–September.

Santoro, F. (1983), 'The EEC and the transportation market', *International Journal of Transport Economics*, vol. 10, nos 1–2, April–August, pp. 67–79.

Sapir, A. and Lintz, E. (1981), *Trade in Services: Economic Determinants and Development — Related Issues*, World Bank Staff Working Paper no. 480, Washington DC, p. 31.

la Sarponcura, F. (1986), 'Seaports and public intervention', *Maritime Policy and Management*, vol. 13, no. 4, pp. 134–44.

Sasaki, H. (1977), *The Shipping Industry in Japan*, Strategic Factors in Industrial Relations System Research Series no. 3, Geneva: International Institute for Labour Studies.

Sasoon, D.M. (1983), *FOB and CIF: British Shipping Laws*, 3rd edn, vol. 5.

Sawyer, L.A. and Mitchell, W.H. (1981), *From America to the United States, Part II*, World Ship Society.

Scermi, M. (1963), 'La Nationalita delle navi cane oggetto delle marne internazionale' (Nationality of ships as an object of international rules), *Communitaxionie Studi*, pp. 87–111.

Schmidt, W. (1979), 'No reduction in Danish fleet', *Norwegian News*, no. 5, 9 March, pp. 5–7.

Schultz, S. and Schumacer, D. (1984), 'The liberalisation of world trade: some ideas for reducing trade barriers against industrial products from developing countries', *Journal of World Trade Law*, vol. 18, no. 3, May–June, pp. 206–23.

Schumpter, J.A. (1942), *Capitalism, Socialism and Democracy*, New York: Harper and Row.

Schwarzenberger, G. (1971), 'Equality and discrimination in international economic law', *Yearbook of World Affairs*, vol. 25, pp. 163–81.

Scitorsky, S. (1959), 'Growth — balanced and unbalanced' in M. Abramovitz *et al.*, *The Allocation of Economic Resources*, Stanford University Press.

Scott, J.J. and Mazza, J. (1980), 'Trade in services and developing countries', *Journal of World Trade Law*, vol. 20, no. 3, May–June, pp. 253–73.

Scott, R. (1986), 'South Korean shipping', *Fairplay International Shipping Weekly*, vol. 298, June, pp. 27–30.

Scott, R. (1986), 'Bermuda faces US tax setback', *Lloyd's List*, no. 53432, 11 November, p. 1.

Scrivastava, C.P. (1977), 'International shipping law and developing countries', *Maxims*, no. 21, Oslo: Nordik Institute for Research.

Sealife Programme (1975), *Report on an Examination of the Validity of the Flanesburg Project Data with respect to its Applicability to the UK Merchant Marine*, Sealife Project 1, Report no. 11, London Sealife Project Office.

Sealife Programme (1978), *Central Manpower Supply to the Merchant Navy:* Second Report and Recommendations, London Sealife Project Office.

Sehydlowsky, D. (1978), *Trade Policies Towards Developing Countries*, Washington DC: AID.

Seldon, A. and Pennance, F.G. (1965), *Everyman's Dictionary of Economics*, London: Dent and Sons.

Seltzer, L.H. (1959), *The Place of the Personal Exemptions in the Present Day Income Tax*, vol. 1, New York: Taxation Revision Compendium, Tax Foundation.

Serko, D. (1986), 'Protectionism: sentiments are quite high', *Worldwide Shipping*, vol. 48, no. 7, December–January, pp. 17–20.

Seyoun, B. (1985), 'Export subsidies under the MTN', *Journal of World Trade Law*, vol. 18, no. 6, November–December, pp. 512–41.

Shah, M.J. (1977), 'The implementation of the UN Convention on a Code of Conduct for Liner Conferences', *Journal of Maritime Law and Commerce*, vol. 9, October, p. 79.

Shaw, J. (1981), 'Empressor Maritimas Lineas, Argentinas S.A.', *Asian Shipping*, May, p. 709.

Shearer, I.A. (1986), 'Australia and the International Law of the Sea', *Archiv des Volkerrechts*, pp. 22–40.

Shootwell, J. (ed.) (1934), *The Origins of the International Labour Organisation*.

Shutz (1964), 'Industrial unrest in the nation's maritime industry', *Labour Law Journal*, vol. 15, p. 337.

Silto, R. (1963), 'Depreciation: a special report', *Journal of Taxation*, May.

de Silva, L. (1979), 'Gold, the International Monetary Fund and the Third World', *IFDA Dossier*, 5 March, pp. 2–12.

Simmonds, K.R. (1967), 'The Central American common market: an experiment in regional integration', *International and Comparative Law Quarterly*, vol. 16, pp. 911–45.

Simon, E. (1986), 'Exodus from West German flag gains momentum', *Lloyd's List*, no. 53414, 21 October, p. 3.

Simon, E. (1986), 'West German flag loses 60 vessels', *Lloyd's List*, no. 53455, 8 December, p. 3.

Simons, H.C. (1948), 'A positive programme for laissez-faire', *Economic Policy for a Free Society*, Chicago: The University of Chicago Press.

Simpson, G. (1977), 'An evaluation of tariff and transport barriers facing products of export interests to Australia', *Journal of Transport Economics and Policy*, vol. II, May, pp. 141–54.

Sinan, I.M. (1984), 'UNCTAD and the flags of convenience', *Journal of World Trade Law*, vol. 18, pp. 95–109.

Singh, N. (n.d.), *International Maritime Law Conventions*, vols 2 and 3, London: Stevens.

Singh, N. (1984), 'Maritime flags and state responsibility', *Essays in International Law in Honour of Judge Manfred Lachs*, The Hague, pp. 657–69.

Skogstand, S. (1979), 'A note on domestic monetary policy conditions of IMF stand-by assistance', *Indian Journal of Economics*, July, p. 6.

Slichter, S.H. (1958), *Reconciling Expansion with a Stable Price Level: Problems of the US Economic Development Committee for Economic Development*, vol. 1, New York.

Smith, A. (1937), *The Wealth of Nations*, New York: Random House, Inc.

Smith, A.M. (1979), 'Taiwan restraint is unleashed', *Containerisation International*, vol. 13, no. 5, May, pp. 17–20.

Smith, A.M. (1981), 'Korean mixes its Pacific presence', *Containerisation*, vol. 15, no. 6, June, pp. 32–6.

Smith, H. (1983), 'EEC moves to prevent independent operators', *Lloyd's List*, 24 May, front page.

Smith, H. (1983), 'Call for EEC shipping policy', *Lloyd's List*, no. 52383, 7 June, p. 2.

Smith, J.R. (1906), 'Ocean freight rates', *Political Science Quarterly*, no. 2.

Smith, J.R. (1919), *Influence of the Great War upon Shipping*, New York.

Smith, J.S. (1945), *Foreign Commerce Weekly*, Washington DC, 22 September.

Smith, W. (1965), *The Bibliography of Flags of Foreign Nations*, Boston: G.K. Hall.

Smith, W. (1980), *Flags and Arms Across the World*, London: Cassell Ltd, pp. 5–8.

Soerensen, P.H. (1986), *Proceedings of the Institute of Mechanical Engineers, Part B: Management and Engineering Manufacture*, 200 no. B2.

Sojka, Prof. Z. (1972), 'Effectiveness of shipping investments under the conditions of socialist economy', *Preinvestment in Maritime Transport*, Southampton Institute of Maritime Law.

Sonderstein, B. (1980), *International Economics*, 2nd edn.

Sorrell, L.C. (1939), *Government Ownership and Operations of Railways for the United States*, Englewood Cliffs, NJ: Prentice-Hall, Inc.

Spasiamo, E. (1967), 'Le discrimminaxioni di bandiera' (flag discrimination), *Rivista di Diritto della Navigaxioni*, pp. 85ss.

Spurrier, A. (1986), 'Fourteen French ships in Kerguelen flag switch', *Lloyd's List*, no. 53398, 2 October, p. 1.

Spurrier, A. (1986), 'Kerguelen transfer rise', *Lloyd's List*, no. 53455, 8 December, p. 3.

Standard, W.L. (1979), *Merchant Seamen: A Short History of their Struggles*, Coleman, Stanferdille.

Stanstad, J.E. (1932), *Shipping and Shipbuilding Subsidies*, Washington DC: US Department of Commerce.

Starring, G. (1985), Meting out misfortunes: how the courts are allotting the costs of maritime injury in the eighties', *Louisiana Law Review*, vol. 45, pp. 907-26.

Stonebridge, D. (1986), 'Impact of the falling dollar on shipping: real costs and revenues highly sensitive to changes in parity', *Asian Shipping*, January, pp. 9-10.

Streater, R.A. and Greenham, D.G. (1983), *British Merchant Ships*, Orion.

Streeten, P. (1959), *Unbalanced Growth*, Oxford: Oxford Economic Papers, June.

Stuart, K. (1985), 'Transport and finance (deregulation and transport), *Transport*, December, pp. 12-16.

Sturmey, S.G. (1962), *British Shipping and World Competition*, London: Athlen Press.

Sturmey, S.G. (1972), 'Main themes of the UNCTAD research studies', *Pre-investment Studies in Maritime Transport*, Southampton Institute of Maritime Law.

Sturmey, S.G. (1975), *Shipping Economics, Collected Papers*, London: Cox and Wyman.

Sturmey, S.G. (1979), 'The development of the Code of Conduct for Liner Code Conferences', *Maritime Policy and Management*, vol. 3, no. 2, April, pp. 133-48.

Sturmey, S.G. (1985), 'CONVENIENCE — food for thought', *Motor Ship*, vol. 65, no. 776, March, p. 90.

Svendsen, A. (1958), *Sea Transport and Shipping Economics*, Bremen.

Swanstran, E.E. (1938), *The Waterfront Problems of Labour*, New York: Fordham University Press.

Sweeny, P.M. (1949), *Socialism*, New York: McGraw-Hill.

Symmens, C.R. and Gardiner, P. (1983), 'Marine scientific research in offshore areas: Ireland and the Law of the Sea Convention', *Marine Policy*, vol. 7, pp. 291–301.

Talbot-Booth, E.C. (n.d.), *His Majesty's Navy*, 3rd edn, Sampson and Law.

Talbot-Booth, E.C. (1934), *British Merchant Ships*, Rich and Coran.

Talbot-Booth, E.C. (1942), *Ships and the Sea*, 7th edn, Sampson and Law.

Talbot-Booth, E.C. (1979), *Talbot-Booth's Merchant Ships*, vol. 3, Krogan Page.

Tames (1982), *Tames Merchant Ships*, Tames.

Tanesco, G.F. (1978), 'The ambitious achievements and developments of the Philippine shipping industry', *Seatrade, Hong Kong Conference*, November, pp. 31–41.

Taylor, P.S. (1923), *Sailors Union of the Pacific*, New York: Ronald Press.

Terborgh, H. (1954), *Realistic Depreciation Policy*, Washington DC: Machinery and Allied Products Institute.

Third World Quarterly (1984), 'Conference on Conditions for Registration of Ships, Geneva, 16 July–4 August 1984' (North–South Monitor), *Third World Foundation for Social and Economic Studies*, vol. 7, no. 1, pp. 147–8.

Third World Quarterly (1985), 'UN Conference on Conditions for Registration of Ships, Third Session, Geneva, July 8–9, 1985', (North–South Monitor), *Third World Foundation for Social and Economic Studies*, vol. 8, no. 1, January, pp. 280–1.

Third World Quarterly (1986), 'UN Conference on Conditions for Registration of Ships, Fourth Session, Geneva, 20 January–7 February 1986' (North–South Monitor), *Third World Foundation for Social and Economic Studies*, vol. 8, no. 3, July, pp. 1032–3.

Thomas, M. (1982), *Hawaiian Inter-Island Vessels and Hawaiian Registered Vessels*, Santa Barbara: Seacost Press.

Thompson, D. (1978), 'The competition policy of the European Community', *Journal of World Trade Law*, vol. 12, no. 3, May–June, p. 249.

Thorburn, T. (1960), *The Supply and Demand of Water Transport*, Stockholm School of Economics.

Thornton, R.H. (1939), 'Watchkeepers', *British Shipping*, Cambridge University Press, pp. 229–46.

Thorpe, W.L. (1959), *The New Inflation*, New York: McGraw-Hill.

Thwaites, R.M. (1959), 'The economics of shiptime', *Transaction of the North East Institution of Engineers and Shipbuilders*, vol. 75, part I, 3 January.

Tiewul, S.A. (1975), 'The United Nations Charter of Economic Rights and Duties of States', *Journal of International Law and Economics*, vol. 10, 1975, pp. 645–88.

Timberg, J. *et al.* (1962), *Shaping the World Economy*, New York: Twentieth Century Fund.

Timberg, J. *et al.* (1975), 'Control of international restrictive business practices', *Proceedings of American Society of International Law*, vol. 69, pp. 170–92.

Tinsley, D. (1979), 'Seeking greater freedom La France Libre', *Fairplay International Shipping Weekly*, vol. 269, no. 4985, 18 March, pp. 7–10.

Tinsley, D. (1979), 'Knowing where one's strength lies', *Fairplay International Shipping Weekly*, pp. 13–15.

Tolofari, S.R., Button, K.J. and Pitfield, D.E. (1986), 'Shipping costs and the controversy over open registry', *Journal of Industrial Economics*, vol. 34, no. 4, pp. 409–22.

de Tony J. (1980), 'Netherlands maritime industries', *Fairplay International Shipping Weekly*, vol. 276, no. 5076, 11 November, pp. 27–33.

Totland, T. (1980), 'Protectionism in international shipping and some economic effects', *Maritime Policy and Management*, vol. 7, no. 2, pp. 103–14.

Transport Canada (1979), *Shipping Policy for Canada*, Ottawa.

Triffin, R. (1966), *The World Money Maze: National Currencies in International Payments*, New Haven: Yale University Press.

Uder, G. (1969), *British Ships and Seamen*, Book II, London, Macmillan.

UK Central Statistics Office (n.d.), *Annual Abstracts of Statistics*, London: HMSO.

UK Central Statistics Office (1961), *Output–Input Tables for the UK 1954 Board of Trade*, London: HMSO.

UK Central Statistics Office (1981), *Monthly Digest of Statistics*, no. 429, HMSO, September.

UK Central Statistics Office (1986), *Annual Report*, London: HMSO.

UK Chamber of Shipping (1968), *Annual Report 1966–67*, London: Witherby and Co. Ltd.

UK Department of Employment (1976), *British Labour Statistics Yearbook 1976*, London: HMSO.

UK Department of Trade and Industry (1931), *Addendum 1 of the Report of Committee on Finance and Industry*, (Macmillan Report), London: HMSO.

UK Department of Trade and Industry (1944), *Employment Policy*, White Paper, London: HMSO.

UK Department of Trade and Industry (1963), *Growth of the United Kingdom Economy to 1966*, London: HMSO.

UK Department of Trade and Industry (1966), *Investment Incentives*, Cmnd 2874, London: HMSO, January.

UK Department of Trade and Industry (1966), *Report of the Shipbuilding Inquiry Committee 1965-66* (Geddes Report), Cmnd 2937, London: HMSO, March.

UK Department of Trade and Industry (1966), *ECGD Services*, London: Export Credits Guarantee Department and Central Office of Information.

UK Department of Trade and Industry (1967), *Nationalised Industries: A Review of Economic and Financial Objectives 1967*, Cmnd 3437, London: HMSO.

UK Department of Trade and Industry (1968), *Report of the Committee of Inquiry into the Major Ports of Great Britain*, Cmnd 1824, London: HMSO, September.

UK Department of Trade and Industry (1972), *Steering Committee on the Safety of Merchant Seamen at Work*, London: HMSO.

UK Department of Trade and Industry (1972), *Census of Seamen as of April 26, 1971 Vessels Registered in the UK*, London: HMSO.

UK Department of Trade and Industry (1986), 'Examination for the Certificate of Competency in the Merchant Navy', *Annual Report*, London: HMSO.

UK Department of Trade and Industry (n.d.), *British Business*, weekly news from the Department of Trade and Industry, London: HMSO.

UK Department of Transport (1918), *Report of the German Control Stations and the Atlantic Emigration Traffic, November 1916*, Cmnd 9092.

UK Department of Transport (1978), *Working Group on the Employment of Non-domiciled Seafarers*, London: HMSO.

UK Department of Transport (1982), *Transport Statistics Great Britain 1971-81*, London: HMSO.

UK Treasury (1983), *Working Party on Freeports in the United Kingdom*, London: HMSO.

UNCTAD (1969), *Establishment and Expansion of Merchant Marines in Developing Countries*.

UNCTAD (1969), *Report by the Secretariat of*, Doc. no. TD/B/C.4/46, 6 January, part D, paras 27-9, pp. 11-12.

UNCTAD (1969), *International Transoceanic Transport and Economic Development*, Doc. no. TD/B/C.4/46, 6 January, pp. 3-5.

UNCTAD (1969), *Official Records of the Trade and Development Board*, 3rd Session, Geneva, 9 April 1969, Item II.

UNCTAD (1969), *Level and Structure of Freight Rates, Conference actices and Adequacy of Shipping Services*, Doc. no. TD/B/C.4/3/Rev.1.

CTAD (1970), *Review of Maritime Transport*, Tables 13 and 15.

CTAD (1972), *Third Session, Report and Annexes*, Santiago de Chile, vol. 1.

NCTAD (1973), *Relationship between Changes in Freight Rates and Changes in Costs of Maritime Transport and the Effect on the Export Trade of Developing Countries*, Doc. no. TD/B/C.4/112.

UNCTAD (1976), *Fourth Session, Reports and Annexes*, Nairobi.

UNCTAD (1977), *Economic Consequences of the Existence or Lack of a Genuine Link between Vessel and Flag of Registry*, Doc. no. TD/B/C.4/168/Add.1, December, p. 9.

UNCTAD (1978), *Report of the First Session*, 6–10 February 1978.

UNCTAD (1979), *Beneficial Ownership of Open Registry Fleets*, Doc. no. TD/B/C.4/216.

UNCTAD (1979), *The Proceedings of the Fifth Session of the United Nations Conference on Trade and Developments*, Manila, 7 May–3 June 1979, Doc. no. TD/269, vol.1, Report and Annexes.

UNCTAD (1979), *Proceedings of the United Nations Conference on Trade and Development*, Manila, 1979, 5th Session, vol. 1.78, para. 195.

UNCTAD (1980), *Beneficial Ownership of Open Registry Fleets*, Doc. no. TD/B/C.4/218.

UNCTAD (1980), *Report of the Second Session of the United Nations Conference on Conditions for Registration of Ships*, 14–22 January 1980.

UNCTAD (1980), *Review of Maritime Transport*, p. 12.

UNCTAD (1981), *Report of the Group of Experts on Problems Faced by the Developing Countries in the Carriage of Bulk Cargoes on its Second Session*, Doc. no. TD/B/C.4/234, Geneva.

UNCTAD (1981), *Action on the Question of Open Registry*, Doc. no. TD/B/C.4/220, March, p. 11.

UNCTAD (1981), *Beneficial Ownership of Open Registry Fleets*, Doc. no. TD/B/C.4/231.

UNCTAD (1982), *Beneficial Ownership of Open Registry Fleets*, Doc. no. TD/B/C.4/255.

UNCTAD (1982), *Report of the Intergovernmental Preparatory Group on Conditions for Registration of Ships on its Second Session*, 8–26 November 1982, Doc. no. TD/B/935.

UNCTAD (1982), *Note by the Secretariat*, Doc. no. TD/B/AC.34/2, 22 January.

UNCTAD (1983), *Review of Maritime Transport*, Doc. no. TD/B/C.4/266, table 22.

UNCTAD (1983), *Beneficial Ownership of Open Registry Fleets*, Doc. no. TD/B/C/C.4/261.

UNCTAD (1983), *Report of the Preparatory Committee for the United Nations Conference on Conditions for Registration of ships*, Palais des Nations, Geneva, 7–18 November 1983, Doc. no. TD/RS/CONF/3.

UNCTAD (1983), *Handbook of International Trade and Development Statistics*.

UNCTAD (1984), *Report by the Chairman of the Committee in Pre-Conference Meeting of Senior Officials*, Palais des Nations, Geneva, 12–13 July 1984, Doc. no. TD/RS/CONF/6.

UNCTAD (1984), *Press Release* TAD/INF/1534, 1 February.

UNCTAD (1984), *Press Release* TAD/INF/1538, 8 February.

UNCTAD (1984), *Press Release* TAD/INF/1542, 13 February.

UNCTAD (1984), *Bulletin*, no. 199, February.

UNCTAD (1984), *Report of the Group of Experts on International Sea Transport of Liquid Hydrocarbons in Bulk* (2nd Session), Doc. no. TD/B/C.4/263, Geneva.

UNCTAD (1984), *Report of the United Nations Conference on Conditions for Registration of Ships on the first part of its session*, Palais des Nations, Geneva, 16 July–3 August 1984, Doc. no. TD/RS/CONF/10/Add.2/Annex V, p. 3.

UNCTAD (1984), *Shipping in the Context of Services and the Development Process*, Doc. no. TD/B/1013, 9 November, p. 5.

UNCTAD (1986), *Final Act of the United Nations Conference on Conditions for Registration of Ships*, Doc. no. TD/RS/CONF/22, 7 February.

UNCTAD (n.d.), *Working Paper by the President of the Conference*, Doc. no. TD/RS/CONF/CRP1.

UNCTAD (n.d.), *Draft Resolution Submitted by the President of the Conference on the Conditions for Registration of Vessels*, Doc. no. TD/RS/CONF/L.3.

UNCTAD (n.d.), *Report of the Intergovernmental Preparatory Group on Conditions for Registration of Ships*, Doc. no. TD/B/904.

UNCTAD (n.d.), *Communication Received from the Government of the Union of Soviet Socialist Republic*, Doc. no. TD/B/AC.34/3.

UNCTAD (n.d.), *The Third Special Session of the Committee on Shipping*, Doc. no. TD/B/C.4/227.

UNCTAD (n.d.), *Official Records of the Trade and Development Board, Twenty-third Session*, Doc. no. TD/BB/855.

UNCTAD (n.d.), *Repercussions of Phasing Out Open Registry*, Doc. no. TD/B/C.4/AC.1/5.

UNCTAD (n.d.), *Official Records of the Trade and Development Board at its Fourteenth Session*, Supp. 2, Doc. no. TD/B/C.4/123.

UNCTAD (n.d.), *Report of the Committee on Shipping on its Sixth Session*, Doc. no. TD/B/521.

UNCTAD (n.d.), *Rules of Procedure of the United Nations Conference on Conditions for Registration of Ships*, Doc. no. TD/RS/CONF/8.

UNCTAD (n.d.), *Report of the Conference of Plenipotentiaries*, vol. II, Doc. no. TD/CODE/13/Add.1.

UNCTAD (n.d.), *Draft Report of the First Committee of the Conference on Registration of Ships*, Doc. no. TD/RS/CONF/C.1/L.1, pp. 48–54.

UNCTAD (n.d.), *United Nations Conference on Conditions of Registration of Ships*, Doc. no. TD/RS/CONF/G/L.2.

UNCTAD (n.d.), *Ad Hoc Intergovernmental Group on Economic Consequences of the Existence or Lack of Genuine Link between Vessels and Flag Registry*, Doc. no. TD/B/C.4/Ac.

UNCTAD (n.d.), *Report of the Preparatory Committee for the Conference on Conditions for Registration of Ships*, Doc. no. TD/RS/CONF/PC/4.

UNCTAD (n.d.), *Second Communication Received from the International Chamber of Shipping*, Doc. no. TD/RS/CONF/NGO/2.

UNCTAD (n.d.), *First Communication Received from the International Association of Independent Tanker Owners* (Intertanko), Doc. no. TD/RS/CONF/NGO/13.

UNCTAD (n.d.), *Second Communication Received from the International Association of Independent Tanker Owners* (Intertanko), Doc. no. TD/RS/CONF/NGO/4.

UNCTAD (n.d.), *Communication Received from the International Shipping Federation* (IFS), Doc. no. TD/RS/CONF/NGO/5.

UNCTAD (n.d.), *Checklist of Documents*, Doc. no. TD/RS/CONF/Mis.I.

UNCTAD (n.d.), *Checklist of Documents*, Doc. no. TD/RS/CONF/Mis.II, Rev.1 (in English only).

UNCTAD (n.d.), *Conference Report*, Doc. no. TD/RS/CONF/19/Add.1/Cov.1.

UNCTAD (n.d.), *First Provisional List of Participants*, Doc. no. TD/RS/CONF/Misc.1.

UNCTAD (n.d.), *Second Provisional List of Participants*, Doc. no. TD/RS/CONF/Misc.2/Add.1–2.

UNCTAD (n.d.), *The Final List of Participants*, Doc. no. TD/RS/CONF/INF/1.

UNCTAD (n.d.), *First Communication Received from the International Chamber of Shipping*, Doc. no. TD/RS/CONF/NGO/1.

UNCTAD (n.d.), *Statements of Administrative and Financial*

Implications Submitted by the UNCTAD Secretariat, Doc. no. TD/RS/CONF/L.3/Add.1/Item 8.

UNCTAD (n.d.), *Report of the First Committee of the United Nations Conference on Conditions for Registration of Ships*, Doc. no. TD/RS/CONF/L.4.

UNCTAD (n.d.), *Text Transmitted by the Drafting Committee to the Conference*, Doc. no. TD/RS/CONF/L.5.

UNCTAD (n.d.), *Report of the United Nations Conference on the Convention for Registration of Ships*, Doc. no. TD/B/C.4/L.152.

UNCTAD (n.d.), *A Set of Basic Principles Concerning the Conditions upon which Vessels should be Accepted on National Shipping Registers*, Doc. no. TD/RS/CONF/PC/2, PC/3/Add.1-3.

UNCTAD (n.d.), *Beneficial Ownership of Open Registry Fleets*, Doc. no. TD/222/Supp.1.

UNCTAD (n.d.), *Communications Received from the Government of Liberia*, Doc. no. TD/B/AC.34/7.

UNCTAD (n.d.), *Practices in Relation to Recording of Operators, the Use of Bearer Shares and Bareboat Charter*, Doc. no. TD/B/AC.34/6.

UNCTAD (n.d.), *Trade Routes of Open Registry Vessels*, Doc. no. TD/B/222 Supp.5.

UNCTAD (n.d.), *Report of the Conference on Conditions for Registration of Vessels*, Doc. no. TD/RS/CONF.15.

UNCTAD (n.d.), *Text Transmitted to the Drafting Committee by the First Committee of the Conference on Conditions for the Registration of Ships*, Doc. no. TD/RS/CONF/C.1/CRP.1 (Identification and Accountability) Agenda Item no. 8.

UNCTAD (n.d.), *The Draft Report of the Second Committee of the Conference on the Conditions for the Registration of Vessels*, Doc. no. TD/RS/CONF/C.2/L.2.

UNCTAD (n.d.), *An Addition to the Draft Report of the Second Committee of the Conference*, Doc. no. TD/RS/C.2/L.2/Corr.1 Agenda Item no. 8.

UNCTAD (n.d.), *Conference Report*, Doc. no. TD/RS/CONF/15/Add.1/Corr.1.

UNCTAD (n.d.), *Draft Provisional Rules of Procedure*, Doc. no. TD/RS/CONF/12/Corr.1 Agenda Item 3.

UNCTAD (n.d.), *Draft Final Provisions for an International Agreement on Conditions for Registration of Ships*, Doc. no. TD/RS/CONF/4/Corr.1.

UNCTAD (n.d.), *Communication Received at the Secretariat from the United Kingdom Submitting a Proposal on Behalf of Group B*, Doc. no. TD/RS/CONF/5/Corr.1.

UNCTAD (n.d.), *Draft Texts for Consideration by the Second Committee*, Doc. no. TD/RS/CONF/C.2/L.1, Agenda Item no. 8.

UNCTAD (n.d.), *The Proposal by the Chairman of the Second Committee*, Doc. no. TD/RS/CONF/C.2/CRP.1.

UNCTAD (n.d.), *Text Transmitted to the Drafting Committee by the First Committee*, Doc. no. TD/RS/CONF/C.1/CRP.2, Agenda Item no. 8.

UNCTAD (n.d.), *Report of the Conference on Conditions for the Registration of Vessels*, Doc. no. TD/RS/CONF/19.

UNCTAD (n.d.), *Merchant Fleet Development*, Doc. no. TD/222.

UNCTAD (n.d.), *Maritime Transport of Hydro-Carbons*, Doc. no. TD/222 Supp.3.

UNCTAD (n.d.), *Legal Mechanisms for Regulating the Operations of Open Registry Fleets during the Phasing Out Period*, Doc. no. TD/B/C.4/AC.1/6.

UNCTAD (n.d.), *Report of the Ad Hoc Intergovernmental Working Group on the Economic Consequences of the Existence or Lack of a Genuine Link between Vessel and Flag of Registry*, Doc. no. TD/B/C.4/191.

UNCTAD (n.d.), *Report of the Ad Hoc Intergovernmental Working Group on the Economic Consequences of the Existence or Lack of a Genuine Link between Vessel and Flag of Registry*, Doc. no. TD/B/C.4/AC.1/8.

UNCTAD (n.d.), *Report of the Ad Hoc Intergovernmental Working Group on the Economic Consequences of the Existence or Lack of a Genuine Link between Vessel and Flag of Registry*, Doc. no. TD/B/C.4/650.

UNCTAD (n.d.), *Report of the Ad Hoc Intergovernmental Working Group on the Economic Consequences of the Existence or Lack of a Genuine Link between Vessel and Flag of Registry*, Doc. no. TD/B/C.4/168.

UNCTAD (n.d.), *Report of the Ad Hoc Intergovernmental Working Group on the Economic Consequences of the Existence or Lack of a Genuine Link between Vessel and Flag of Registry*, Doc. no. TD/B/C.4/177.

UNCTAD (n.d.), *Guidelines for the Study of the Transfer of Technology to Developing Countries*, Doc. no. E.72:11:D:19.

UNCTAD (n.d.), *Shipping Policies for the Implementation of the Strategy for the Third UN Development Decade*, UN Publication Sales no. E.72.11.D.15, chapter 1.

UNCTAD (n.d.), *Final Reports of the Group of Experts on Model Rules for Multimodal Container Tariffs*, Doc. no. TD/B/C.4/AC.1/5/7.

UNCTAD (n.d.), *Guidelines on the Introduction of Containerisation and Multimodal Transport and the Modernization and Improvements of the Infrastructure of Developing Countries*, Doc. no. TD/B/C.4/238 and Supp. 1–4.

UNCTAD (n.d.), *Following Report on the Aspect of Economic and Social Implications of International Multimodal Transport in Developing Countries*, Doc. no. TD/B/C/4/181.

UNCTAD (n.d.), *Report of the Group of Experts on Problems Faced by Developing Countries in the Carriage of Bulk Cargoes in its Second Session*, Doc. no. TD/B/C.4/234.

UNCTAD (n.d.), *Activities in the Field of Shipping*, Doc. no. TD/278, Corr.1.

UNCTAD (n.d.), *Monthly Commodity Bulletin*, December (yearly).

UNCTAD (n.d.), *The Liner Conference System*, Doc. no. TD/B/C/C.4/62.

UNCTAD (n.d.), *Protection of Shippers' Interests*, Doc. no. TD/B/C.4/176.

UNCTAD (n.d.), *Adequacy of Services and Level and Structure of Freight Rates*, Doc. no. TD/B/C.4/62/Rev.1.

UNCTAD (n.d.), *Consultation in Shipping*, UN Publication Sales no. 68.11.D.1.

UNCTAD (n.d.), *Freight Markets and the Level and Structure of Freight Rates*, Doc. no. TD/B/C.4/38, chapter VII.

UNCTAD (n.d.), *Development of Ports*, Doc. no. TD/B/C.4/42.

UNCTAD (n.d.), *The Economic Position of Landlocked Developing Countries*, Doc. no. TD/B/C.4/206.

UNCTAD (n.d.), *Services and the Development Process*, Doc. no. TD/B/1008 and Corr.1.

UNCTAD (n.d.), *Shipping in the Seventies*, Doc. no. TD/177.

UNCTAD (n.d.), *Establishment or Expansion of Merchant Marines in Developing Countries*, Doc. no. TD/26/Rev.1, p. 31.

UNCTAD (n.d.), *Proceedings of UNCTAD*, vol. 1, Final Act and Report, UN Publications Sales no. 64.11.B.11, Annex A.IV.22, p. 54.

UNCTAD (n.d.), *Official Records of the Trade and Development Board*, 5th Session, Supp.2, p. 26.

UNCTAD (n.d.), *Review of Developments in Shipping*, Doc. no. TD/B/4/25 and Corr.1 and 2, paras 8–11.

UNCTAD (n.d.), *The Impact on World Seaborne Trade on Changes in Shipping Costs*, Doc. no. TD/B/C.4/74, para. 1.

UNCTAD (n.d.), *The Estimation of Freight Factors*, Doc. no. TD/B/C.4/47.

UNCTAD (n.d.), *Terms of Reference of the Committee on Shipping Regarding Multimodal Transport*, Doc. no. TD/B/740.

UNCTAD (n.d.), *Services and the Development Process*, Doc. no. TD/B/301, Annex II.

UNCTAD (n.d.), *Compensatory Financing: Issues and Proposals for Further Action*, Doc. no. TD/229, Supp.1.

Underhill, W. (1986), 'Government rejects aid plea for Swiss Shipping', *Lloyd's List*, 7 June, p. 3.

United Nations (n.d.), *Main Issues in Transport for Developing Countries During the 3rd UN Development Decade 1981–1990*, New York, Doc. no. ST/ESA/177.

United Nations (n.d.), *United Nations Conference on the Law of the Sea*, Geneva, vol. IV, 2nd Committee, A/Conf.13/40.

United Nations (n.d.), *Publications*, Sales nos E.70.11.D.7; E.70.11.D.9; E.69.11.D.1; E/F.83.11.D.2; E.64.11.D.1; E.79.11.D.3.

United Nations (1958), *Geneva Convention on the Law of the Sea*.

United Nations (1969), *Yearbook of International Trade Statistics*, Publication Sales no. E.71.XVII.5.

United Nations (1972), *Monthly Bulletin of Statistics*, vol. XXVI, no. 6, June.

United Nations (1980), *Development Dialogue*, 2.

United Nations (1982), *Action on the Question of Open Registries*, Report by the UNCTAD Secretariat, UN Doc. no. Ref A/Conf.62/122 of 7 October.

United Nations (1982), *General Assembly Resolution 37/209* of 20 December.

United Nations (1983), *United Nations Convention on the Law of the Sea 1982*, with Index and Final Act, UN Publications Sales no. E.83.V.S., UN, New York.

United Nations (1985), *Statistical Yearbook*, New York.

UN Economic and Social Council (n.d.), *Resolution 1372 (XLV)* concerning activities of the UN system of organisations in the transport field.

UN Economic and Social Council (1967), *Monthly Bulletin of Statistics*, January.

UN Economic and Social Council (1970), *International Trade Statistics — Concepts and Definitions*, Series M, no. 52, New York.

UN Economic and Social Council (1970), *Resolution 1556 (XLIX)*, 31 July.

UN Economic and Social Council (1981), *Monthly Bulletin of Statistics*, vol. XXXCV, no. 6, June.

UN General Assembly (1961), *Declaration of the First United Nations Development Decade*, G.A. Res. 1710 (XVI), 19 December.

UN General Assembly (1961), *Resolution 1715 (XX)*, 19 December.

UN General Assembly (1965), *Resolution 2084 (XX)*, 20 December.

UN General Assembly (1966), *Declaration on Permanent Sovereignty over Natural Resources*, G.A. Res. 1803 (S-VII), 14 December.

UN General Assembly (1966), *International Covenant on Economic, Social and Cultural Rights*, 16 December.

UN General Assembly (1966), *International Covenant on Civil and Political Rights*, 16 December.

UN General Assembly (1970), *Declaration of the Second United Nations Development Decade* and *The International Development Strategy for the Second United Nations Development Decade*, G.A. Res. 2626 (XXV), 24 October.

UN General Assembly (1973), *The First Biennial Over-all Review and Appraisal of Progress in the Implementation of the International Development Strategy for the Second United Nations Development Decade*, G.A. Res. 3176 (XXVIII), 17 December.

UN General Assembly (1974), *The Programme of Action for the Establishment of a New International Economic Order*, G.A. Res. 3202 (S-VI), 1 May.

UN General Assembly (1974), *Declaration on the Establishment of a New International Economic Order*, G.A. Res. 3201 (S-VI), 1 May.

UN General Assembly (1974), *Charter of Rights and Duties of States*, G.A. Res. 3281 (XXIX), 12 December.

UN General Assembly (1975), *Mid-Term Review and Appraisal of Progress in the Implementation of the International Development Strategy for the Second United Nations Development Decade*, G.A. Res. 3577 (XXX), 15 December.

UN General Assembly (1979), *High Level Intergovernmental Group of Officials to Consider the Review and Appraisal of the International Development Strategy for the Third United Nations Development Decade*, Draft Report, UN Doc. no. A/AC/196/L.3, 12 April.

UN General Assembly (1979), *High Level Intergovernmental Group of Officials to Consider the Review and Appraisal of the International Development Strategy for the Third United Nations Development Decade*: UN Doc. no. A/AC/196, 29 September.

UN General Assembly (1979), *Declaration of the Third United Nations Development Decade*, G.A. Res. 33/197.

UN General Assembly (1980), *Consensus Text for the International Development Strategy for the Third United Nations Development Decade*, UN Doc. no. A/35/64, 15 September.

UN General Assembly (1980), *International Reform Aspect of the International Development Strategy for the Third United Nations Development Decade*, UN Doc. no. A/35/465, 4 October.

UN General Assembly (1980), *Progressive Development of the Principles and Means of International Economic Law Relating to the*

Legal Aspects of the New International Economic Order, UN Doc. no. A/35/466, 10 October.

UN General Assembly (1980), *International Development Strategy for the Third United Nations Development Decade*, UN Doc. no. 1/35/464, 23 October.

UN General Assembly (1980), *International Monetary Reform Aspects (Shipping and Invisibles) of the International Development Strategy for the Third United Nations Development Decade*, UN Doc. no. A/35/465/Add.1, 27 October.

US Chamber of Commerce (1962), *An Introduction to Doing Import and Export Business*, Washington DC.

US Congress (n.d.), *Hearings on Operation and Administration of Cargo Preference Act before the House on Merchant Marine and Fisheries*, H.R. Rep. no. 1818.

US Congress (n.d.), *Senate Committee on Agriculture and Forestry*, Amendments to Public Law 480, 83rd Congress, Senate Report no. 2290.

US Congress Committee on Merchant Marine and Fisheries (1954), *Defence Department Directive on Mutual Defence Shipments*, Senate Hearings.

US Congress Committee on Merchant Marine and Fisheries (1956), 'Cargo preference and its relation to the farm surplus disposal program', *House Hearings*, Report no. 1818, 84th Congress, 2nd Session, 6.

US Congress Committee on Merchant Marine and Fisheries (1962), *The Ocean Freight Industry*, House Report no. 1419, 87th Congress, 2nd Session, GPO, Washington DC.

US Congress Joint Economic Committee (1955), *Study of the Operations of MARAD and FMB*, Hearings before the Committee on Merchant Marines and Fisheries, 84th Congress, 1st Session, Washington DC: GPO.

US Congress Joint Economic Committee (1960), *Subsidy and Subsidy-like Programme of the US Government*, Washington DC: GPO.

US Congress Joint Economic Committee (1965), *Discriminatory Ocean Freight Rates and the Balance of Payments*, 89th Congress, 1st Session, 6 January.

US Congress Joint Economic Committee (1965), Hearings before the Sub-Committee on Federal Procurement and Regulation, *Discriminatory Ocean Freight Rates and the Balance of Payments*, Part I, Washington DC: GPO, April.

US Congress Joint Economic Committee (Science and Transportation) (1977), *Illegal Rebating in the US Ocean Commerce*, Hearings before the Subcommittee on Merchant Marine and

Tourism, 95th Congress, 1st Session, Serial no. 95-13.

US Congress Presidential Commission (1980), *Overcoming World Hunger: The Challenge Ahead*, Washington DC.

US Congress Senate Committee (1965), *Rates and the Balance of Payments*.

US Congress Senate Committee on Appropriations (1978), *US Foreign Assistance and Related Programmes Appropriation Bills*, 95th Congress, 22nd Session, 1 June.

US Congress Senate Committee (1978), *Congressional Records*, 31 July, H.7548.

US Congress Senate Committee (1980), *Investment and Monetary Policy*, Hearings before the Subcommittee on International Trade, Hearing no. 5970, 6 February.

US Congress Senate Committee (1980), *Congressional Records*, 23 September, ss. 13202-4.

US Department of Agriculture (1959), *Export Credit Program for Financing Dollar Sales of US Agricultural Commodities*.

US Department of Commerce, MARAD (n.d.), *Maritime Subsidies*, Annual Report.

US Department of Commerce, MARAD (1937), Federal Maritime Commission, *Economic Survey of the American Merchant Marine* (Kennedy Report).

US Department of Commerce, MARAD (1953), *Review of Essential US Foreign Trade Routes*, Washington DC: GPO.

US Department of Commerce, MARAD (1953), *US Oceanborne Foreign Trade Route Traffic Carried by Dry Cargo Ships 1948, 1950, and 1953*, Washington DC: GPO.

US Department of Commerce, MARAD (1953), *Review of Essential Foreign Trade Routes*, Washington DC: GPO.

US Department of Commerce, MARAD (1955), Bureau of Census, *US Waterborne Trade*, Washington DC: GPO, 24 June.

US Department of Commerce, MARAD (1965), *Assistance to Maritime Industries in the Western Hemisphere Nations*, Washington DC.

US Department of Commerce, MARAD (1967), 'North Atlantic-Mediterranean Freight Conferences — Rates on Household Goods', *Federal Maritime Commission Docket* no. 65-49, Washington DC: GPO, November.

US Department of Commerce, MARAD (1968), *Ships Registered under the Liberian, Panamanian and Honduran Flags Deemed by the Navy Department to be under the United States Effective Control*, Washington DC.

US Department of Commerce, MARAD (1972), *The Annual Report of MARAD. Fiscal Year 1972*, Washington DC: GPO.

US Department of Commerce, MARAD (1975), *Foreign Flag Merchant Ships Owned by US Parent Companies as of June 30*, Washington DC: GPO.

US Department of Commerce, MARAD (1976), *Foreign Flag Merchant Ships Owned by US Parent Companies, as of December 31*, Washington DC: GPO.

US Department of Commerce, MARAD (1977), *Seafaring, Longshore and Shipyard Employment as of April 1977*, Manpower Report, Report no. MAR 4055, Washington DC.

US Department of Justice, Antitrust Division (1977), *The Regulated Ocean Shipping Industry*, Report, Stock no. 027-000-0047-1.

US Department of State (n.d.), *Treaty of Friendship, Commerce and Navigation between the US and West Germany*, Article IV (1), TIAS, no. 3593.

US Department of State (n.d.), *US–Belgium Treaty of Friendship, Commerce and Navigation*, Article XII, 1875 (19, St.628, 1 Mallay Treaties 90).

US Department of State (1954), *US–Spanish Agreement*, 30 July 1954, para. 2(9(ii), 1954 UST & DIA 2328; TIAS, no. 3094.

US Department of State (1957), *US–UK Agreement*, 13 May 1957, para. 3, 1957. (8 UST & DIA 835; TIAS, no. 3843).

US Department of State (1957), *US–Italy Agreement*, 22 June 1957 (8 UST & DIA 881; TIAS, no. 3850).

US Department of State (1957), *Commission for Education and Exchange Agreement between the US and Paraguay*, 12 April 1957, (1957 8 UST & DIA 946; TIAS, no. 3856).

US Department of State (1966), 'Diplomatic adjustments by the maritime nations', *Bulletin*, 17 January.

US Department of State (1972), *Agreement Regarding Trade Act*, 18 October 1972, Treaty no. 595.

US Department of State (1975), *Agreement Regarding Certain Marine Matters*, Bulletin no. 661, 1972, Annex III(1)(c)(iii), 29 December.

US Department of State (1976), *Agreement Regarding Certain Maritime Matters*, 29 December 1975, Bulletin no. 96.

US Department of Trade (1965), *Memorandum Submitted to the President's Advisory Committee*, August.

US Department of Transportation (1968), 'Report on United States Department of Transportation Research Study', *Lloyd's List and Shipping Gazette*, London, 20 August.

Usher, J.A. (1983), 'Injunction to prevent breach of EEC competition rules', *Journal of Business Law*, November, pp. 494–5.

US International Cooperation Administration (1957), *Investment Guarantee Handbook 1957*, Washington DC: GPO.

US International Trade Commission (1985), *Review of the Effectiveness of Trade Dispute Settlement under the GATT and the Tokyo Round Agreements*, USITC Publications, no. 1793, December.

US National Association of Manufacturers, Economic Principles Commission (1946), *The American Individual Enterprise System*, New York: McGraw-Hill.

US Office of Technology Assessment (1985), *Alternative Approach to Cargo Policy: A Supplement to an Assessment of Maritime Trade and Technology*, Washington DC.

US Seamens' Union (1973), *Proceedings of the Convention of the International Seamens' Union of America*, Washington DC, February.

US Senate (1980), Merchant Marine Study and Investigation: *Government Aid to Shipping*, Washington DC: GPO.

US Senate (1980), *Report to the President on Foreign Economic Policies*, Washington DC: GPO.

US Treasury Department (1953), *Scope and Effects of Tax Benefits Provided to the Maritime Industry*, Communication from the President, Washington DC: GPO.

US Treasury Department (1985), 'Treasury and federal reserve foreign exchange operations', *Federal Reserve Bulletin*, November.

Vamberg, R.G. (1974), 'Nationalism in shipping', *Maritime Studies and Management*, vol. 1, p. 243.

Vanagas, A.H. (1977), 'Flag discrimination: an economic analysis' in R.O. Goss, *Advances in Maritime Economics*, London: CUP, pp. 37–64.

Vanzant, J.C. (1974), 'The Charter of Economic Rights and Duties of States: solution to the development aid problem?', *Georgia Journal of International and Comparative Law*, vol. 4, pp. 414–62.

Vegarie, A. (1986), 'State aid for seaports: a Cartesian proposition in the French case', *Maritime Policy and Management*, vol. 13, no. 2, pp. 127–37.

Venhausser, C.W. (1980), 'The US merchant marine at the crossroads', *Port Baltimore Bulletin*, November, p. 22.

Verbit, G.P. (1969), *Trade Agreements for Developing Countries*, New York.

Vidal, A. (1958), 'El abanderamiento de buques extranjeros en Espana' (Registry of Foreign Ships in Spain), Barcelona, Ponencias odel v Congresso. *International de Derecho Comparado*, pp. 335–41.

Vijay, K. (1980), 'Export subsidies and developing countries', *Journal of World Trade Law*, vol. 14, p. 371.

Vinci, J. (1951), *International Economics*, Glencoe, New York: The Free Press.

Vinci, J. (1964), *Leading Issues in Development Economics*, Oxford University Press.

Viner, J. and Meir, C. (1964), *The Theory of Economic Growth*, London: Allen and Unwin.

Volekaert, F. (1986), 'Formulation of national maritime policy: the case of Belgium', *Marine Policy*, vol. 10, no. 2, April, pp. 90–101.

Wade, S. (1986), 'Anti-FOC lobby marshalls forces at the ILO (Port State Control)', *Fairplay International Shipping Weekly*, vol. 147, pp. 12–15.

Wade, S. (1986), 'US shipping policy in the melting pot', *Fairplay International Shipping Weekly*, vol. 279, no. 6105, 2 July, p. 47.

Waitehouse (1978), 'Maritime spring clean', *Seatrade*, vol. 8, no. 5, May, pp. 3–4.

Walker, V. (1986), 'Owners threaten to pull down the flag', *Shipbroker*, March, pp. 7–9.

Wallace, A. (1978), 'Denmark', *Fairplay International Shipping Weekly*, vol. 266, no. 4941, 11 May, pp. 8–10.

Wallin, B. (1978), 'Sweden, one of the world's great carrying nations', *Shipbroker*, vol. 4, no. 2, March, pp. 21–9.

Wasserman, U. (1976), 'Key issues in developments: interview with UNCTAD Secretary General', *Journal of World Trade Law*, vol. 10, no. 1, January–February, p. 17.

Watt, D.C. (1980), 'Integrated policy for the oceans – teaching in the university world', *Marine Policy*, vol. 4, no. 1, January, pp. 67–9.

Wattenhall, R.L. (1961), *Aspects of Political Control in Selected Public Transport Corporations*, unpublished thesis, Australia National University.

Wellington, M.D. (1970): 'The better part of valour – applicability of the Jones Act to the flags of convenience fleet', *San Diego Law Review*, vol. 7, pp. 674–83.

Wells, J.M. (1981), 'Vessel registration in selected open registries', *Maritime Lawyer*, vol. 6, pp. 221–45.

Westinform (1973), *Manning the Merchant Fleets of the World*, Westinform Shipping Reports, no. 299, Westinform Services.

Wettery, D. (1980), 'High speed surface craft', *International Shipping Weekly*, vol. 19, nos 9–10, June–July, p. 24.

Whiteman (1965), *Digest of International Law*, vol. 4.

Whitfield, M. (1980), 'Yugoslavia may open flag to foreign owners', *Lloyd's List*, no. 53435, 14 November, p. 1.

Whitfield, M. (1985), 'Norway to review its policy of flagging out', *Lloyd's List*, 28 December 1985, p. 1.

Whitfield, M. (1986), 'BP shipping to end direct employment', *Lloyd's List*, no. 53205, 9 January, p. 1.

Whitfield, M. (1986), 'Crewing terms in British Petroleum switch shock unions', *Lloyd's List*, 14 January, p. 1.

Whitfield, M. (1986), 'Sealink men want guarantees: five week "sit in" at Harwich over job security', *Lloyd's List*, 16 January, p. 3.

Whitfield, M. (1986), 'Japan's seamen seek more free flag jobs', *Lloyd's List*, no. 53213, 6 March, p. 1.

Whitfield, M. (1986), 'CP to transfer tankers to IOM register', *Lloyd's List*, no. 53320, 2 July, p. 1.

Whitfield, M. (1986), 'Unions will not allow IOM free flag register', *Lloyd's List*, no. 53340, 25 July, p. 3.

Whitfield, M. (1986), 'Free flag growth attacked by the ITF', *Lloyd's List*, no. 53317, 28 June, p. 3.

Whitfield, M. (1986), 'IOM register is expected to double in size' and 'Manpol adoption sets the stage for major Manx register growth (IOM)', *Lloyd's List*, no. 53318, 30 June, pp. 1 and 3.

Whitfield, M. (1986), 'Furness Withy to switch vessels to HK', *Lloyd's List*, no. 534232, 11 November, p. 1.

Whitfield, M. (1986), 'Aland register proposed for Finnish fleet', *Lloyd's List*, no. 53433, 12 November, p. 1.

Whitfield, M. (1986), 'Kloster Cruise to flag out eight ships: transfer will save at least US $25m a year', *Lloyd's List*, no. 53438, 18 November.

Whitfield, M. (1986), 'Panamanian labour law ruling', *Lloyd's List*, no. 53455, 8 December, p. 3.

Whitley, A. (1985), 'Brazil accuses US of retreat on twin-track talks', *Financial Times*, 23 August, p. 4.

Whittaker, G. (1986), 'Vanuatu appoints a Piraeus agent', *Lloyd's List*, no. 53308, 28 June, p. 5.

Whittaker, G. (1986), 'Greek register's future hangs in the balance', *Lloyd's List*, no. 53419, 27 October, p. 1.

Whittaker, G. (1986), 'Crewing moves to halt Greek flag exodus', *Lloyd's List*, no. 53447, 28 November, p. 1.

Wijkman, M. (1980), 'Effects of cargo reservation: a review of UNCTAD's Code of Conduct for Liner Conferences', *Marine Policy*, vol. 4, pp. 271–89.

Wilhelm, B. (1974), *Rantzmann Wappenbilder Lexikon*, Munich: Battenberger.

Williams, H. (1983), 'Owners in US plea on UNCTAD position', *Lloyd's List*, no. 25310, 9 March, p. 3.

Williams, H. (1983), 'EEC lashed over transport policy failure', *Lloyd's List*, no. 52312, 11 March, front page.

Williams, H. (1983), 'US prepares to adopt Northern shipping rules', *Lloyd's List*, no. 52324, 24 March, p. 3.

Williams, H. (1986), 'Senate studies US register plan for foreign ships', *Lloyd's List*, no. 53299, 7 June, p. 1.

Williams, H. (1986), 'Reagan vetoes US-flag ship loan pledges', *Lloyd's List*, no. 53423, 31 October, p. 1.

Wilson, A. (1979), *The Aegean Dispute*, Adelphi Papers no. 155, London: International Institute for Strategic Studies.

Wilson, B. (1986), 'How Stena made major reductions in fleet costs', *Lloyd's List*, no. 53308, 18 June, p. 4.

Witherspoon, K.A. (1985), 'Watch out watchmen! Congress has excluded security employees from maritime employment coverage under the Longshore and Harbour Workers' Compensation Act Amendments of 1984', *San Diego Law Review*, vol. 22, pp. 941-62.

Witiig, E.A. (1979), 'Tanker fleets and flags of convenience', *Texas International Law Journal*, vol. 14, pp. 115-38.

Witiig, E.A. (1979), 'Tanker fleets and flags of convenience, advantages, problems and dangers', *Texas International Law Journal*, Winter.

Woddis, J. (1947), *Under the Red Duster: A Study of Britain's Merchant Navy*, Senior Press Ltd.

Wolfgang, F.S. and Samuelson, P.A. (1941), 'Protection and real wages', *Review of Economic Studies*, p. 100.

Wood, S. (1986), 'Wallen to transfer office to Isle of Man', *Lloyd's List*, no. 5338, 12 September, p. 1.

Working Group on Exchange Market Intervention (1983), *Study Report*, March.

Yeats, A.J. (1977), 'A comparative analysis of the incidence of tariffs and transportation costs on India's exports', *Journal of Development Studies*, vol. 14, October, pp. 97-107.

Yolland, B. (1982), 'Crew costs and international shipping', *Lloyd's World of Shipping Conferences in Hong Kong 12-16 October 1981*, Lloyds of London Press Ltd.

Young, R.T. (1980), 'The United States and international shipping: the economic future', *Lloyd's Shipping Economist*, pp. 1-5.

Zahiriou, G.A. (1976), 'The UN Economic Charter and US investment policy', *Merchant Law Review*, vol. 27, pp. 749-80.

Zannetos, Z.S. (1967), *The Theory of Oil Tank Ship Routes*, Cambridge, Mass: MIT Press.

Zannetos, Z.S. (1973), 'Persistent economic misconceptions in the transportation of oil by sea', *Maritime Studies and Management*, vol. 1, no. 1.

Author index

623

Subject index